DENMARK

DENMARK

Compiled by the Editors of the Danish
National Encyclopedia

The Royal Danish Ministry of Foreign Affairs

Denmark
Published by the Royal Danish Ministry of Foreign Affairs,
Department of Information,
Asiatisk Plads 2, DK-1448 Copenhagen K

Editors of 2nd edition: Henrik Sebro and Judy Skov Larsen (Gyldendal Leksikon)
Co-editors: Flemming Axmark
(The Royal Danish Ministry of Foreign Affairs)

Graphic edition: Bodil Hammer (Gyldendal Leksikon)
Production: John Jensen (Gyldendal Leksikon)

Translation: W. Glyn Jones, Malene Madsen and Judy Skov Larsen

Graphic design: Finn Evald
Reprographic work: Nordisk Bogproduktion, Haslev

Type-set in Zapf Book and Frutiger

Printing and binding: narayana press

2nd edition, 1st impression
© by the Royal Danish Ministry of Foreign Affairs and
Gyldendal Leksikon, 2002
Printed in Denmark 2002

ISBN 87-7964-214-4

Cover:
Karl Isakson (1878-1922): *View over Gudhjem* (Udsigt over Gudhjem), 1921 (76 x 92 cm).
The Art Mueum of Bornholm

Preface

This book is based on the article on Denmark published in the Danish National Encyclopedia (volume 4, 1996). However, some paragraphs have been rewritten to make the book accessible to foreign readers, and the illustrations have been modified considerably compared to the original article.

The first edition of *Denmark* was published in an English version in 1996 and subsequently, a German version was published in 1998, a French in 1999 and a Spanish in 2001. In comparison to the previous editions of the book, the paragraphs and figures of the present edition have been updated and revised to the extent considered necessary. Furthermore, some newly written paragraphs have been added.

This edition closed for contributions in February 2002.

Copenhagen, March 2002
Gyldendal Leksikon

Contents

Introduction

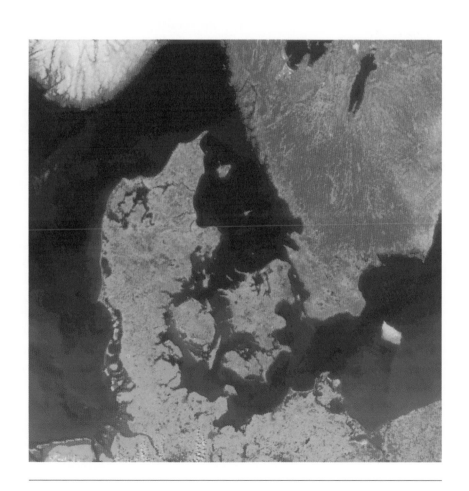

Introduction

Denmark lies between 54° and 58° of latitude north and 8° and 15° of longitude east. In addition to Denmark itself, the kingdom also includes the Faeroe Islands and Greenland.

Denmark consists of the peninsula of Jutland and c. 406 islands, of which c. 78 are inhabited (2001). Of these, the largest and most densely populated are Zealand on which the capital of Copenhagen is situated, Funen and the north Jutland island. The North Sea defines Denmark to the west, while the islands divide the Baltic from the Kattegat. The Danish islands are thus on the sea lane from the Baltic to the main oceans of the world and at the same time on the trade route from the Nordic countries to central Europe. Throughout the history of the country, this position has been influential on the circumstances governing developments in trade and on political and military strategy.

Administratively, the country is divided into 14 counties (*amter*) and 275 local authorities (*kommuner*), two of which (Copenhagen and Frederiksberg) are not included in the counties.

Towards the end of the 10th century, Denmark was united into a single kingdom. It has been an independent country ever since, and is thus one of the oldest states in Europe.

The form of government is a parliamentary democracy with a royal head of state. The system of production is capitalist (economic liberalism) with private ownership of businesses and production. The state and other public authorities, however, exercise a considerable regulatory control and provide comprehensive services for the citizens.

Denmark is a developed industrialised country. By international standards, the standard of living is high, and the differences between rich and poor are smaller than in many of the countries with which Denmark is traditionally compared.

Denmark is a member of the European Union. The proximity of Germany has traditionally orientated the country south in an economic and political sense, but close co-operation with Sweden, Norway, Finland and Iceland, with which Denmark enjoys a passport union, also ties Denmark to the North.

The country has a coastline totalling c. 7,300 km in all and a 68-km-long frontier with Germany. It is a distinctly low-lying country, the highest point being only 173 metres above sea level, but the landscape is undulating and varied; only occasionally is it possible to find undisturbed nature, and the view everywhere shows signs of human activity. Only on the island of Bornholm do we find bedrock, and otherwise the land is characterised by fertile clayish or sandy moraine landscapes.

Denmark is poor in mineral deposits. However, chalk for the production of cement is found in considerable quantities, and more oil and gas

is extracted from the North Sea than is needed for home consumption.

Most of the country, c. 64%, is under cultivation. 12% is covered by deciduous or coniferous forest, while meadow, heath, marshland, bogs, sandhills and lakes constitute c. 10%. Built-up areas and traffic areas make up the remaining c. 13%. The climate is temperate, and precipitation is sufficient to provide all the water needed.

The population stands at c. 5.37 million, and the population density is c. 125 per square kilometre. Foreign immigrants and their descendants amount to c. 395,000, 165,000 of whom come from Europe; in addition there is a small German minority in southern Jutland. The language is everywhere Danish, and the vast majority of the population has been baptised into the established protestant church. Denmark is therefore nationally and culturally very homogeneous.

85% of the population lives in towns. Greater Copenhagen accounts for c. 1.08 million inhabitants. The second city is Århus (218,000 inhabitants). In addition the entire country is otherwise covered by a network of medium-sized towns.

Danish agriculture is highly developed, producing a considerable surplus of manufactured foods which are exported to other countries. Industrial production is very varied in relation to the size of the country. Among the commodities that have made Denmark known abroad are, in addition to agricultural produce, beer, medicines, furniture, shipping, wind turbines and products of the advanced metal industries.

Both agriculture and industry are highly effective. Agriculture and fisheries employ only 4%, and industry and construction 23% of the population. The remaining 73% are employed in the service sector, 35% in public and personal services and 38% in private business, including financial activities and the traditional shipping trade.

Denmark is well provided with traffic systems. The road network is good everywhere in the country; railways and air links provide quick transport, and the islands are connected by ferries and a large number of bridges. Kastrup near Copenhagen is the largest international airport in the country and is at the same time a crossroads for air traffic to and from the other Scandinavian countries.

Denmark has an open economy, and trade with the rest of the world is of great importance. Imports and exports of goods and services thus represent, respectively, c. 33% and 36% of the country's GDP (2000). Around 2/3 of foreign trade is with the other countries in the EU; the remainder is divided among a very large number of trading partners, of which Norway and the USA are the most important.

Bue Nielsen

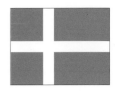

The Kingdom of Denmark
Form of government: Constitutional Monarchy
Area: 43,094 sq. km
Population: 5,368,354 (as per 1 January 2002)
Capital: Copenhagen (1,081,673 inhab. in the metropolitan area)
Currency: Danish Krone (DKK)

Official Denmark

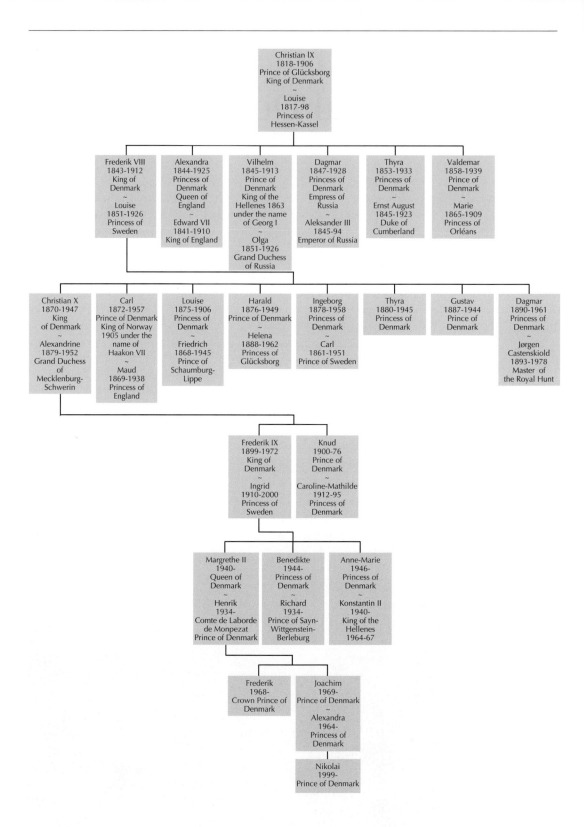

The Royal House

By a Royal House, we understand in a broad sense the reigning monarch's family and relations, and in a narrower sense the circle of closely related royal persons who are subject to special rules. In the case of Denmark in 2002, this circle includes, in addition to Queen Margrethe II, the Royal Consort Prince Henrik, Crown Prince Frederik, Prince Joachim, his spouse Princess Alexandra and their son Prince Nikolai, as well as all the other princes and princesses in line of succession to the throne, together with their spouses. These persons may not travel abroad or - enter into marriage without the permission of the Queen (the monarch).

From Elective to Hereditary Monarchy

The Danish Royal House can be traced back to Gorm the Old (buried 958 in Jelling in Jutland) and his son Harald I Bluetooth, who moved the royal residence to Zealand. These are the first two kings who with any certainty can be dated and located in connection with the unification of

Denmark. The monarchy was an elective monarchy limited to the royal house, but not to the male line. Thus Svend II Estridsen, the nephew of Knud II (Canute II) the Great, was the son of Knud's sister. The royal house culminated with the Valdemars, whose influence extended over most of the Baltic area, and again later with Queen Margrete I, who united Scandinavia in the Kalmar Union.

After the direct lines died out, Count Christian of Oldenborg was in 1448 elected Danish King under the name of Christian I; in addition he was elected Duke of Schleswig and Count of Holsten. He was descended over six generations, three of them on the distaff side, from the royal house. His direct successors, the House of Oldenborg adopted alternately the names of Frederik and Christian from the election in 1523 of Frederik I until Frederik VII died without issue in 1863. The elective monarchy existed until 1660/61, when Frederik III introduced a hereditary, absolutist monarchy for Denmark

Every year on her birthday on 16 April, Queen Margrethe receives the cheers of the crowd from the balcony of Amalienborg Palace. From the left: Crown Prince Frederik, Princess Alexandra, Prince Joachim, Queen Margrethe and Prince Henrik.

Christian IX has been called the father-in-law of Europe, as he was related through his children to many branches of European royal and princely houses. The 1880s saw great gatherings of royal families, known as the Fredensborg Days. In the summers children, children-in-law and grandchildren as well as guests from other princely houses came to the royal family's summer residence in Fredensborg to spend their holidays; Christian IX is said to have forbidden all political discussion. In 1882, the Royal Family commissioned the young Danish painter Laurits Tuxen to do a painting of the family gathering, which is here seen in one of the garden rooms at Fredensborg. The work was finished in 1886 and hangs today in Christiansborg.

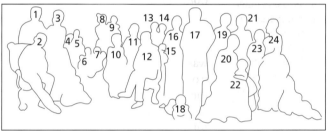

1 Albert, Prince of Wales, **2** Prince Edward, later Edward VII of England, **3** Princess Alexandra, **4** Princess Ingeborg of Denmark, **5** Prince Harald of Denmark, **6** Prince George of Cumberland, **7** Princess Marie Louise of Cumberland, **8** The Duchess Thyra of Cumberland, **9** Princess Alix of Cumberland, **10** Queen Louise of Denmark, **11** Prince Valdemar of Denmark, **12** King Christian IX of Denmark, **13** Prince Christian of Denmark, **14** Grand Duke Nicholas, later Emperor Nicholas II of Russia, **15** Grand Duke Michael of Russia, **16** Empress Dagmar of Russia, **17** Emperor Alexander III of Russia, **18**, Grand Duchess Olga of Russia, **19** Crown Prince Frederik, the later Frederik VIII of Denmark, **20** Crown Princess Louise of Denmark, **21** King Georg I of the Hellenes, **22** Princess Thyra of Denmark, **23** Princess Alexandra of Greece, **24** Queen Olga of Greece.

The Queen's New Year message is transmitted live on radio and television and is one of the occasions on which Queen Margrethe addresses her people directly. In her speeches, which are often very personal, she comments for instance on social trends, and she expresses her views on controversial subjects such as the immigrant question. Her messages thus give rise to discussion among the general populace.

and Norway. Among other things, the Royal Law of 1665 laid down the conditions pertaining to the royal house, and these paragraphs remained in force after the introduction of a constitutional monarchy by Frederik VII under the terms of the Constitution of 5 June 1849.

Constitutional Monarchy

Prince Christian of Glücksborg, who was descended in direct male line from the royal house, acceded to the throne as Christian IX on the death of Frederik VII in 1863. The throne thus passed to the House of Glücksborg.

Christian IX became known as the

In Denmark members of the royal house can appear in public without special security arrangements need to be made. The Queen and Prince Henrik are here riding through the streets of Copenhagen in an open carriage on the Queen's 60th birthday on 16 April 2000.

father-in-law of Europe, his daughter Alexandra being married to King Edward VII of Great Britain, his daughter Dagmar to Czar Alexander III of Russia, and his daughter Thyra to Duke Ernst August of Cumberland. When Christian IX's son Vilhelm had become King of the Hellenes in 1863 under the name of George I, a large proportion of the European royal houses could meet in Fredensborg Palace for family gatherings in the home of Christian IX. In 1905 his grandson Carl became King of Norway under the name of Haakon VII.

In 1906 Frederik VIII succeeded his father, but only reigned for a short time, dying in 1912. His eldest son, Christian X, reigned until 1947 and inscribed himself in history as the king who rode across the border into Southern Jutland in 1920, when Denmark recovered this territory lost in 1864, and who became the focus of national sentiment during the German occupation 1940-1945.

In 1935, his eldest son, the later Frederik IX, married Princess Ingrid of Sweden, the daughter of King Gustav VI Adolf. He succeeded to the throne in 1947 and his activities as king strengthened the constitutional monarchy, as he accepted that the king had no political power. As head of state, the monarch takes part in the formation of new governments, stands formally at the head of the government and represents Denmark abroad. The royal house's understanding of these circumstances and the family's close contact with the general population has meant that its position is firmly based and not a matter of discussion at a time when royal houses in other countries have caused a debate on the justification for a monarchy.

In the Act of Succession of 27 March 1953 the House of Glücksborg's right of succession was confirmed, and according to this the throne passes to the successors of Christian X. According to the Act, sons have precedence over daughters, but if there are no sons, the throne is inherited by the eldest daughter. So after her father's death in 1972, Princess Margrethe could succeed to the throne as Margrethe II, the first female monarch since the death of Margrete I in 1412.

Queen Margrethe II, who on 10 June 1967 married Henrik, Prince of Denmark, born Henri-Marie-Jean-

In 1986, on his 18th birthday, the Crown Prince was given a seat in the Council of State and since then, being successor to the throne, his has often represented the royal house on official occasions. Before embarking on a wide-ranging study of economics and political science in 1989, he had received a military education in the military's three forces, subsequently, supplemented by a demanding course with the navy's elite Diving Corps. In the photo, the Crown Price is wearing the Navy uniform during a visit to the Hungarian army's exercise camp in Szolnok in 1998.

André, Comte de Laborde de Monpezat in France, succeeded to the throne on 14 January 1972. The royal couple have two sons, Crown Prince Frederik and Prince Joachim. In

Princess Alexandra and Prince Joachim with their son, Prince Nikolai. The couple was married in November 1995, and Prince Nikolai, born on 28 August 1999, is the royal couple's first grandchild.

Margrethe II, Margrethe Alexandrine Þorhildur Ingrid, b. 16.4.1940, Queen of Denmark since 1972, daughter of King Frederik IX and Queen Ingrid. Margrethe was born at Amalienborg Palace and, being a woman, she was not heir to the throne. The new Law of Succession adopted in 1953 along with a revision of the Constitution opened the way for female succession. Thus, on her 18th birthday in 1958 Margrethe took her place in the State Council as heir to the throne. Crown Princess Margrethe took her matriculation examination in 1959 and the same year completed training as a squad leader in the Women's Flying Corps. In 1960-1965 she studied at the universities of Copenhagen, Cambridge, Århus, the Sorbonne and London, focusing on political science and archaeology. In 1967 she married the French diplomat, Comte Henri de Laborde de Monpezat, Prince Henrik, and together the couple had two sons, Frederik (b. 1968) and Joachim (b. 1969). On the death of Frederik IX on 14 January 1972, Margrethe II ascended the throne.

The Queen has engaged in translation work and made her mark artistically in several genres. As a textile artist she has created episcopal copes for Viborg Diocese and Elsinore Diocese (1986 and 1989) and chasubles for Fredensborg Castle Church (1976) and other churches. As a graphic artist Queen Margrethe has illustrated several books, and she designed the costumes for TV Theatre's performance of *The Shepherdess and the Chimney Sweep* (1987). One of her major works was the set design for the ballet *A Folk Tale* (1991).

Queen Margrethe has made a point of knowing and reaching out to all parts of the realm, and the Faeroe Islands and Greenland are favorite destinations. The Queen has also succeeded in giving her traditional New Year message a strongly personal touch, which has helped to consolidate her popularity.

Amalienborg Palace in Copenhagen is the royal residence, but one of the functions of Marselisborg Castle near Århus is to be a summer residence. Fredensborg Castle in North Zealand is used in spring and autumn. Queen Margrethe and Prince Henrik also acquired a more private abode in 1974, when they purchased the Château de Caïx in Cahors, where the Queen can devote herself to her painting and other pursuits. Since 1988, her works have been displayed at several exhibitions.

Lorenz Rerup,
Knud J.V. Jespersen

God's Help –
the People's Love –
Denmark's Strength

Henrik, b. 1934, Prince of Denmark, Prince Consort, until 1967 Comte Henri de Laborde de Monpezat, married on 10 June 1967 to the heir to the throne Princess Margrethe (II), with whom he has the sons Frederik (born 1968) and Joachim (born 1969); son of Comte André de Laborde de Monpezat. Henrik spent his early childhood in Indo-China, but grew up at his parents' château Le Cayrou near Cahors. In 1952 he matriculated in Hanoi and after studying in Paris he gained a master's degree in literature and oriental languages in 1957. In 1962 he entered the French foreign service and while stationed in London he met the Danish heir to the throne in 1964; they became engaged in 1966.

The Prince's published works include a collection of poems, a memoir and several translations of French works into Danish (translated jointly with the Queen). He is also heavily involved in the winegrowing at Château de Caïx in the

Cahors district, which the royal couple acquired in 1974.

Knud J.V. Jespersen

1995 Prince Joachim married Princess Alexandra, born Alexandra Christina Manley, and together they have a son, Nikolai William Alexander Frederik.

The Queen has two sisters, Princess Benedikte, who is married to Richard, Prinz zu Sayn-Wittgenstein-Berleburg in Germany, and ex-queen Anne-Marie, married to ex-king Constantine of Greece.

Hans H. Worsøe

The National Flag

The name of the Danish flag, the *Dannebrog*, meaning 'the flag of the Danes' or 'the red flag', is first encountered in a Danish text from 1478 and in a Netherlandish text from 100 years before that.

In a Netherlandish armorial (Gelre) from 1370-1386 a red banner with a white cross is annexed to the coat of arms of Valdemar IV Atterdag.

According to legend, the Dannebrog fell from heaven during a battle in Estonia; this legend is mentioned in Christiern Pedersen's Danish Chronicle from the beginning of the 1520s and by the Franciscan monk Peder Olsen c. 1527. This latter relates the event to a battle in 1219, and tradition has maintained that the flag appeared at Lyndanisse on 15 June 1219. The legend presumably came into being around 1500 on the basis of the idea that the royal banner which King Hans lost at his defeat in the Ditmarshes in Northern Germany in 1500 was the Dannebrog that had fallen from heaven. In 1559 Frederik II recaptured the banner and had it hung in Schleswig Cathedral in present-day northern Germany. In a song from the campaign of 1500 the banner charged with the cross is associated with the Roman Emperor Constantine's dream of the cross in 312 before the battle in which he became absolute monarch in the Roman Empire and according to tradition was converted to Christianity.

The Southern Jutland artist C.A. Lorentzen's 1809 painting of the Dannebrog falling from heaven during the Battle of Lyndanisse, 15 June 1219. With the burgeoning national feeling of the Romantic age the Dannebrog was given a special place in the hearts of the people and inspired painters and poets. The painting is in The Danish National Gallery.

This vision of the cross, to which are linked the words *in hoc signo vinces* ('under this sign you shall be victorious') is the prototype of the miracles in the shape of crosses in the sky, which particularly in the Iberian Peninsula were connected with battles between Christians and infidels.

A white cross formy with a red bordure was used by the Portuguese Order of Christ that was founded in 1318 during a crusade against the Moors. The Portuguese gold coin, the *portugalese* or *português*, reproduced the Cross of Christ and the words *in hoc signo vinces*. From 1591 Christian IV struck Danish coins with a similar cross which quickly became associated with the cross of the Dannebrog. 1603 saw the addition of Constantine's apophthegm, which Arild Huitfeldt had quoted in his Chronicle where Constantine's vision and the legend of the Dannebrog falling from heaven are also compared.

Use

During military actions in Sweden in the 15th century, the Dannebrog was the principal banner. After 1625 military colours displayed a Dannebrog in the canton, and during the 17th century this also appeared with a cross formy. The most distinguished military units carried the Dannebrog alone. Since 1842 all military units have used the Dannebrog with a cross formy as distinct from the cross in the national flag and the naval flag, where it has continued to have straight sides. A naval ensign showing the coat of arms of Erik VII of Pomerania with a white Dannebrog cross was one of the spoils of war in 1427 and was hung in the Maria Church in Lübeck in northern Germany. At sea it can be said with certainty that the Dannebrog has been flown since the 1580s.

Valdemar IV Atterday's coat of arms in Gelre's armorial from 1370-1386. It is the oldest known coloured reproduction of the Danish flag. Valdemar Atterdag was probably also the first Danish king to use the Dannebrog. While growing up at the imperial court he might have seen the red banner of the Holy Roman Empire with its white cross; shortly before 1200 it had developed from the originally completely red flag of the realm, on which the Emperor placed a white cross when he embarked on crusades.

From a decree of 1630 it can be seen that the swallow-tailed flag was reserved for the navy, and in 1635 it was emphasised that merchantmen were not allowed to fly a swallow-tailed flag. In 1696 the proportions of the Dannebrog were determined, and they are largely unchanged today. It became customary for the State also to fly the swallow-tailed flag ashore. In 1748 it was definitely decided that as a merchant flag the Dannebrog is square, without a cleft end. As a rule, the swallow-tailed flag is reserved for the royal house and the state, whereas private individuals must use the square flag. Since 1731 the royal standard has had the royal coat of arms in a central field, and later similar special flags have been introduced for other members of the royal family. With the royal family's flags as a distinguishing mark the navy and air force indicate that a member of the royal family is on board. There are flags for Prince Henrik, the Crown Prince and the members of the royal house in general. These flags, like the royal standard and that of the regent, can be flown where those concerned are in residence. The royal standard, the regent's standard, a special standard for the Minister of Defence (actually the Minister for the Navy) and admirals' standards are flown as marks of command on warships with the chief concerned on board. Over the years, special emblems or letters representing certain service branches have been added in the red canton of the Dannebrog. Certain private institutions use the Dannebrog similarly marked and in some cases fly the swallow-tailed flag.

The naval ensign is deep or dark red, the national flag bright red.

In 1833 private citizens were for-

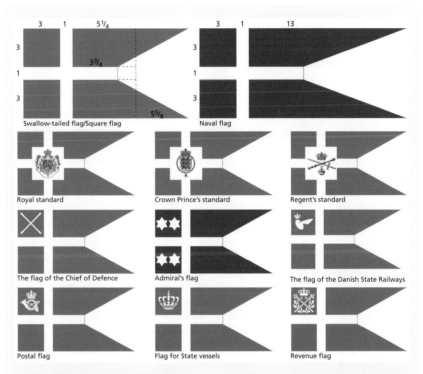

Swallow-tailed flag/Square flag

Naval flag

Royal standard

Crown Prince's standard

Regent's standard

The flag of the Chief of Defence

Admiral's flag

The flag of the Danish State Railways

Postal flag

Flag for State vessels

Revenue flag

The proportions of the Dannebrog.
On the left the swallow-tailed flag in its present form, established in 1856, with the outside fields and the cleft ends foreshortened, and the square flag (indicated with dotted lines) in the extended form that was sanctioned in 1893. On the right the naval flag that was established in 1696. The basis for the proportions is the width of the cross, which is 1/7 of the height of the flag.

Below these are examples of special flags as used today. The royal standard, Queen Margrethe II's standard, has since 1731 had the royal coat of arms in the central field. The Crown Prince's standard was introduced in 1914 and has in its central field the small national arms surrounded by the collar of the Order of the Elephant. The Regent's standard was introduced in 1914 and has the regalia in the central field; it is used by the member of the royal family acting as regent. Then come the flag for the Chief of Defence, which has two crossed batons in the sheet, and the admiral's flag; a vice-admiral has three stars, a rear-admiral two and a flotilla admiral one. The flag for the State Railways was introduced in 1887 and changed in 1999. The present Post Office flag dates from 1898; this had contained a horn since 1793. Flags for State vessels were introduced after 1927 and finally a revenue flag was introduced in 1986; however, there has been a revenue flag bearing special marks since 1743.

bidden to fly flags, and the prohibition was not annulled until 1854. Meanwhile, between 1848 and 1850, a time of national fervour, the population regularly flew the Dannebrog. The Danes still fly the flag at their homes and, for instance, in private allotment gardens on festive occasions of both family and official nature, and they decorate their Christmas trees with small Dannebrog flags.

Nils G. Bartholdy

Festive occasions, for instance weddings, anniversaries and birthdays, are traditionally marked with the national flag; thus, a birthday cake can well be decorated with small paper flags.

Days on which Flags are to be Flown
There are certain days on which it is traditional for both public authorities and private individuals to hoist flags. In 1886, the Ministry of War introduced the rule that flags should be flown from military establishments on the birthdays of 13 specified members of the royal family, on the anniversary of the signing of the Constitutional Act of 5 June 1849 and on 7 anniversaries of military battles. In 1913, the Ministry of Naval Affairs produced its own list of flag flying days applicable to the navy. In addition to regulations concerning members of the royal family and a number of naval battles, this regulation required that flags should be flown on religious holidays. In 1922-1923 the two ministries supplemented their lists with dates including 15 June, Valdemar Day. At intervals, the Court publishes lists of the members of the royal family for whom flags are to be flown. In time, many private individuals began to observe the military flag flying days. Apart from the military occasions it is formally only royal birthdays on which flags are required to be flown by all public authorities, as no regulations have ever been published concerning other days on which flags are flown, e.g. 9 April and 5 May. Despite the formal basis, days for hoisting flags are observed by the public authorities and by many private citizens.

Royal Family birthdays (applicable to public authorities)

16 April	Queen Margrethe II
29 April	Princess Benedikte
26 May	Crown Prince Frederik
7 June	Prince Joachim
11 June	Prince Henrik
30 June	Princess Alexandra

Religious holidays (applicable to defence authorities)
New Year's Day
Good Friday (flags at half mast)
Easter Day
Ascension Day
Whit Sunday
Christmas Day

National days (observed informally by both public authorities, private institutions and ordinary citizens)

9 April	Occupation of Denmark 1940 (flags at half mast until 12.00 and then at full)
5 May	Liberation of Denmark 1945
5 June	Constitution Day
15 June	Valdemar Day commemorating the Dannebrog (1219) and reunification with Southern Jutland 1920

In addition there is a number of special military flag flying days which apply to the defence authorities.

National and Royal Arms

There are two versions of the Danish coat of arms, the small one now called the National Coat of Arms and the large one now called the Royal Coat of Arms. The two coats of arms are used by the royal house and state authorities as a national symbol denoting sovereignty. The National Arms are in principle the coat of arms known from the time of the Valdemars, three lions surrounded by hearts. The Royal Arms with quarterings in one shield held by savages in a pavilion and surrounded by collars of orders of chivalry, has been altered on various occasions, most recently by a royal decree in 1972. In 1959 it was decided that the Royal Arms are used by the monarch, the royal house and the court, and by the Life Guards, while other authorities are to use the National Arms. The Danish coat of arms are ensigned by a crown which was originally open, but since 1624 has been reproduced with arches and an orb with a cross above. The crown symbolises both the royal and national authority. With reproductions of the national arms in seals and on coins, and in connection with the exercise of authority, rights of succession are asserted and sovereignty of the monarch and the state as well.

The national arms and the crown are legally protected against misuse. When the designation is indicated, a purveyor to the Royal Court is allowed to use the crown and a Royal Court purveyor the royal coat of arms or the crown alone.

The Development of the Royal Arms

The contents of the monarch's coat of arms have varied over the years. The escutcheon originally contained quarterings for areas over which the king actually reigned at various periods or to which he laid claim. In the Middle Ages the king's younger sons bore one or two lions to denote their status as vassals. The two Schleswig lions are known from 1245 and in 1460 became part of the king's coat of arms together with the Holstein nettle leaf, which was originally the family coat of arms of the Schauenburgers. In the 13th century, the Counts of Halland, one of the bastard lines of the royal family, bore a lion above a number of hearts. In 1449 Christian I added a lion surmounting nine hearts to his coat of arms for the title of 'the Goths', presumably as part of his efforts to dominate Sweden where the patriotic myth of the Swedes as the descendants of the victorious Goths greatly contributed to a sense of national

The State arms, designed for official use by Aage Wulff, 1991. The colours in the escutcheon are documented from c. 1270. The lions have been crowned since the 13th century. In the 16th century the number of hearts was fixed at nine.

The royal coat of arms, designed by Claus Achton Friis, 1972. In the escutcheon, which is held by two 'savages' and surrounded by the collars of the Orders of the Elephant and the Dannebrog, can be seen the cross of the Dannebrog, the Danish lions and hearts, the two lions of Southern Jutland, the three crowns of the Kalmar Union, the Faeroese ram, the Greenlandic bear and the Oldenborg fesses. The Oldenborg colours, yellow and red, are seen again in the royal livery and are used by the Post Office.

understanding. In 1440, the dragon-like wyvern representing the title of 'the Wends' was added; it can symbolise heathendom and thus refer to the earlier victory over the heathen Wends. The two Oldenborg bars were introduced by Christian I, and in the king's coat of arms from the time of Frederik I we find the Delmenhorst cross. The swan of Stormarn with a coronet around its neck is known from 1476. The Dannebrog cross was incorporated into the king's coat of arms from the time of Erik VII of Pomerania, as were the axe-bearing lion of Norway and the Swedish coats of arms. The three crowns were actually the coat of arms of Sweden, but became a symbol of the Kalmar Union's three Scandinavian realms. After the break-up of the Union Christian III, from 1546, used the three crowns as arms of pretence, and in this way Danish-Norwegian kings betokened a political will also to rule Sweden.

The use of the three crowns was opposed by Sweden, especially in the 16th century. Quarterings for Bavaria and Pomerania were found under the kings who hailed from those countries. The conquest of the Ditmarshes in 1559 was marked by a quartering with a horseman. From the 16th century Iceland was represented by a crowned stockfish, but from 1903 by a falcon. The ancient arms of the Faeroe Islands, the ram, were from 1668 combined with that of the king, and the Greenlandic bear is known from 1665. In 1819 a horse's head was added for Lauenburg. Furthermore, the following arms have been used: the Agnus Dei of Gotland, the eagle of Oesel, the crown of Femern and the dragon of Bornholm. Buffalo horns, sometimes clad in ermine, with peacock feathers, was the royal crest from the end of the 13th century to the 1420s.

Nils G. Bartholdy

The reverse of Knud VI's seal from c. 1194. Three lions are seen in an escutcheon surrounded by heart-like figures. With the adoption of the figure of a lion, the Danish king marked his independence from the Holy Roman Emperor, whose emblem was an eagle.

Erik VII of Pomerania's seal from 1398. After the formation of the Kalmar Union the actual Danish coat of arms was incorporated into an escutcheon composed of fields representing the areas which the kings ruled over or claimed. Here can be seen in the quartered principal escutcheon the three Danish lions surrounded by hearts, the three crowns, which like the Folkung lion over three narrow bends denotes Sweden, and the Pomeranian griffin; in the small escutcheon on the cross we see Norway's axe-bearing lion. The Swedish triple-crown coat of arms, which Queen Margrete had assumed after 1389, became ambiguous because it could stand for both Sweden and the union of the three Scandinavian kingdoms.

Crown Jewels

The Order of the Dannebrog is a Danish order of chivalry, which may be awarded to Danes and foreign citizens for meritorious civil or military service, for a particular contribution to the arts, sciences or business life or for working for Danish interests. The reigning monarch heads the Order. In its present form the Order of the Dannebrog has six grades: Grand Commander (only representatives of the royal family), the Grand Cross, Commander First Class, Commander, Knight First Class, Knight. In addition there is the Cross of Honour of the Dannebrog; this can be awarded to Danish citizens who have already been decorated with the Order and is also worn by individual members of the royal family. On the death of the holder, the insignia must be returned to the Chapter of the Royal Orders.

The Danish crown jewels, the symbols of the monarchy, consist of the crown, the sceptre (symbolising supreme authority), the orb (vault of heaven and earth), the sword of state and the ampulla. The oldest of these is Christian III's sword of state from 1551. Further elements in the regalia are the chains and insignia of the Order of the Elephant and the Order of Dannebrog, which the monarch wears on special occasions. Since c. 1680 the crown jewels have been kept in Rosenborg Castle in Copenhagen.

The regalia were worn at the coronation of the elective monarchs, when the clergy and nobility placed the crown on the king's head. After the introduction of absolutism in 1660 the crowning of the king was replaced by anointment, for which the king arrived in the church wearing the crown and was consecrated to his calling by being anointed with oil. For the anointing of Christian V, a new crown was made along with a throne of narwhal teeth (the unicorn's horn) and three silver lions. With the 1849 Constitution anointing was discontinued and since then the crown jewels have only been used on the occasion of the monarch's castrum doloris when the crown is placed on the coffin and the other regalia laid at its foot, guarded by the three lions.

Jørgen Hein

The Order of the Elephant is Denmark's oldest and most distinguished order of chivalry. The elephant is used for religious reasons, as this exotic animal symbolises chastity and purity, and an elephant carrying a tower is associated with the Virgin Mary. The reigning monarch heads the Order, which is awarded to members of the Danish royal family, foreign royal houses and heads of state. In recent times only an extremely small number of people outside this circle have been awarded the Order of the Elephant: Niels Bohr, Montgomery, Eisenhower, Churchill and Mærsk Mc-Kinney Møller. Since 1958 women have also been eligible for admission to the order; since 1892 Danish queens have worn the insignia. The Order of the Elephant has a single class, Knight; the members of the royal family and a few others wear it in a collar.

Frederik III's sceptre, orb and sword, used at his coronation in 1648 and at the anointing of the absolute monarchs. The sceptre was made in Copenhagen, the orb in Hamburg, both by unknown goldsmiths. The sword is the work of Lucas Schaller of Hamburg and was originally a wedding present from Christian IV to Frederik III in 1643. On the scabbard can be seen the arms of the land areas where the king's word was law.

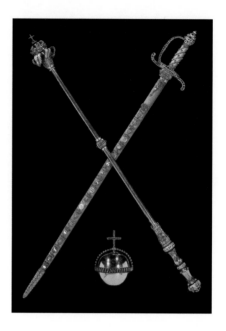

Christian IV's crown of gold, enamel, diamonds and pearls, created 1595-1596 by Dirich Fyring in Odense. The large figures represent the king's virtues; for instance, the woman suckling symbolises his love of God and the people. On the inside of the points of the crown we see coats of arms representing the king's realms and possessions.

Christian V's crown, created 1670-1671 by Paul Kurtz in Copenhagen after a French model. At the front of the crown's ring there is the large, costly sapphire, the family treasure of the royal family and presumably a gift to Christian I from the Duke of Milan in 1474. At the sides are fixed two garnets and at the top of the cross a corundum refracting in red and blue, perhaps a stone from a medieval ring.

Frederik III's ampulla, made by an unknown Copenhagen goldsmith and used at the coronation in 1648 and at the anointing of the absolute monarchs. The ampulla contained a salving oil to which had been added sweet-smelling essences. The ampulla is 4.9 cm high.

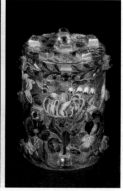

The National Anthems

Denmark has two officially recognised national anthems. Royal House red-letter days are marked by *Kong Christian stod ved højen mast* (King Christian stood by lofty mast), which sings the praises of warrior heroes of former times; the text is by Johannes Ewald, 1779, the melody by an unknown composer. The oldest known version of the melody is anonymous and is found under the title of *Aria* in 'Basts Violinbog' from the second half of the 18th century; the melody has been ascribed on to Ditlev Ludvig Rogert (regional judge in Bornholm, 1742-1813) and wrongly to Johann Ernst Hartmann; it received its final shape from Daniel Friedrich Rudolf Kuhlau, who wrote a set of piano variations on it (opus 16 from c. 1817) and used it in the overture to *Elverhøi* (Elfin Mound) from 1828. To mark national events use is made of *Der er et yndigt land* (There is a lovely land), praising the country's gentle character; the text is by Adam Oehlenschläger, c. 1819, the melody by Hans Ernst Krøyer, c. 1835.

Peter Ryom

There is a lovely land
that proudly spreads her beeches
beside the Baltic strand,
a land that curves in hill and dale,
that men have named Old Denmark;
and this is Freys' hall.

Coinage

Under the terms of the Constitution, the production of coinage in Denmark is a royal prerogative. Since 1975 the administration of the Royal Mint has been assigned to the National Bank of Denmark, which is responsible for providing the country with money.

Sven I Forkbeard's *penning* in c. 995 was the first coin with the name of the King and the country to be struck, and by the Middle Ages certain types must already have been struck in millions. In 1541 the coins were furnished with an indication of value, *marks* at 16 *skilling* at 3 *hvid* at 4 *pennings*. The *daler* was 3, later 4, and finally 6 *marks*. The krone or 4 marks was assigned a place in the coinage in 1625. Banknotes, which were issued by the *Kurantbank*, came into permanent use in 1737. After the so-called State Bankruptcy in 1813 the coinage was reformed, and 1818 saw the establishment of the National Bank, which issued the banknotes. In 1873 a change was made to *krone* and *øre*, and the silver standard was replaced by the gold standard, which meanwhile was abandoned in 1931. Since 1920 almost all coins have been struck in copper and nickel alloys. On account of inflation there is now a tendency to mint coins with increasing face values (5 kr. in 1960, 10 kr. 1979, 20 kr. 1990), while the smaller coins (1, 2, 5 and 10 øre) have disappeared. The use of banknotes is limited to a small number of values, especially 100 *kroner* and – since 1997 – 200 *kroner*. Generally speaking Denmark's coinage must be said to be characterised by stability and by a certain inflation.

In daily life, cash has long played a secondary role. Payment by cheque dominated until the 1980s, but has now been mostly replaced by electronic payment transfers, including the *Dankort* issued by the banks. Corresponding coin cards issued on a private, commercial basis have a certain significance for smaller payments.

Jørgen Steen Jensen

The coins are, from the left: 1) Svend Forkbeard's penning from c. 995. The motif is a close copy of the English King Ethelred II's coins from c. 991-997. 2) The first Danish skilling was struck under Christoffer of Bavaria in the 1440s. The obverse has three Danish lions, the reverse the king's own coat of arms. 3) The first Danish mark with indications of both value and date was struck under Christian III, 1541. 4) On the 1873 transition to krone and øre and to the gold standard, the 20 krone became the largest coin, with the portrait of Christian IX on the obverse and symbols of the national branches of agriculture and shipping on the reverse. 5) The latest version of the present 20 krone came into circulation in 2001. The obverse has the portrait of Margrethe II, and the reverse has the Danish coats of arms and ornaments which are inspired by Bronze Age designs.

Population

It is possible to follow demographic developments in the Danish population back to 1735 on the basis of censuses and statistics of births and deaths. The population then was roughly 718,000. The first census took place in 1769, when the population was estimated at c. 798,000. After 1840 censuses were held in Denmark every 5 or 10 years, most recently in 1970. Since that date administrative registers have been used to calculate the size of the population. On 1 January 2002 the number stood at c. 5,368,354.

The geographical area used as the basis for censuses has twice been altered: in 1864, when the duchies of Schleswig and Holstein were ceded to Prussia after the defeat of that year, and in 1920, when Southern Jutland (North Schleswig) was reunited with Denmark. In 1900 the population in Southern Jutland was c. 148,000.

Population Growth

The size and growth of the population is the result of the interplay of mortality, fertility and migration. Danish demographical statistics provide a unique possibility for tracing the development since the 18th century, four periods reflecting the different population trends.

1735-1780

Both the crude death and birth rates (i.e. the number of deaths or births per 1,000 inhabitants) were high at this time; the mean life expectancy for a newly born infant was probably 35-40 years, and infant mortality stood at about 20%. Mortality and fertility were at about the same level, so that the natural rate of growth was low and in certain years actually negative. This is typical of a pre-industrial society in which modern social and medical progress has not yet begun. The high mortality rate, which rose dramatically in these years, was linked to epidemics, for instance resulting from wars. In earlier periods the epidemics were even more terrible, for instance it is thought that in the 1650s the Danish population declined by 25-30% as a consequence of the Thirty Years War and a number of wars between Denmark and Sweden.

1780-1890

This period was characterised by a noticeable fall in mortality, while fertility remained at the same level as in the previous period. The fall in mortality is striking, in that no pioneering medicines had been invented apart from smallpox vaccination, which was introduced into Denmark already at the beginning of the 19th century; current medical practice included blood-letting, while admission to hospital was associated with great risks of infection. It must be assumed that the fall in mortality rates resulted from better food, a greater understanding of hygiene and better living conditions. Midwife services were also improved during this period. From about the middle of the 1850s improvements were made in the sewerage system when on the basis of British experience the authorities realised the causes of cholera. The decrease in mortality rates was meanwhile interrupted about 1830 by a serious epidemic of malaria in Zealand and Lolland. Malaria was epidemic in Denmark until the beginning of the 20th century.

The constant high fertility rate along with the falling mortality rate

Altogether over a quarter of a million Danes emigrated in the second half of the 19th century, mainly to America. The leave-taking with their native land in Copenhagen Harbour is portrayed here by Edvard Petersen in his *Emigrants at Larsens Plads* (1890).

meant an accelerating growth in population. In the 1860s population growth was 1.37% a year, the highest ever recorded in Denmark. During this period emigration from Denmark increased, mainly to the USA, which can be interpreted as a reaction to population pressures. Between 1869 and 1914 altogether 285,000 Danes emigrated, 255,000 of them to the USA.

1890-1966

In the first half of the 20th century both fertility and mortality rates declined, which led to a slowing down in the growth of population. The decline in fertility rates from about 1890 was due to changed family circumstances, particularly for women, resulting from the development of an industrialised society. In the agricultural society there was a tradition of having large numbers of children; for one thing, they were a valuable source of labour, taking part in the family's work of running the farm. The movement to an industrialised society and paid work brought about a distinction between home and place of work, and children could no longer in the same way enter natu-rally into a commonalty of family work. This made it more difficult to have many children, both from a financial and a practical point of view. The average size of a family was consequently significantly reduced over a number of years, remarkably enough since there was no access to modern methods of birth control. Around 1900 women had about 4 children on average, whereas in the mid-1960s the number stood at 1.7. Years with large numbers of births were characteristic of the 1940s and the beginning of the 1960s, while the birth rate was particularly low in the 1930s. A comprehensive improvement in the state of health of the population extended the average life expectancy for a newly born infant from 52.9 years for men and 56.2 for women in the period 1901-1905, and to 70.3 and 74.5 respectively in the period 1961-1965.

Post 1967

The last 30 years of the 20th century showed a far-reaching change in the demographical characteristics of the Danish population. The decline in fertility accelerated from 1967, and the lowest level so far was reached in

1983 when the average number of children born per woman was 1.4. As c. 2.1 births per woman are necessary to avoid a fall in the size of the population, fertility rates are thus below the level needed for reproduction. Corresponding declines have been noted in most western European countries, in North America, Australia and Japan. The reasons for the fall in fertility are thought to be many, but as before, they are rooted in changed social and economic conditions. Women have increased their participation in training and work, which has necessitated predominantly paid child care, typically in institutions for small children. It has become more difficult for both practical and financial reasons to have many children, and today women are generally older when they have children than were the women of the 1960s. A contributory cause of easier family planning was the introduction in 1973 of free abortion before the 12th week of pregnancy, and the development and distribution of contraceptives such as the pill and the coil. The number of legal abortions in relation to the birth rate is much higher in Denmark than in the rest of Western Europe, but it was nevertheless declining until the mid-1990's. In 1996 there were c. 18,000 legal abortions and c. 70,000 births. Since 1973 sterilisation has been available to all over 25 years of age. The declining fertility rate has meant that population growth has become very slow and in certain years (1981-1984) actually ne-

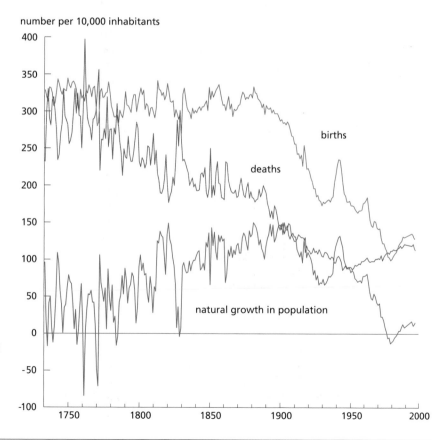

number per 10,000 inhabitants

births

deaths

natural growth in population

Number of births and deaths per 10,000 inhabitants and the natural growth in population 1735-2000.

gative. From 1983 fertility began to increase again, principally among slightly older women. The average life expectancy rose over this period, and in 1998 it was 73.7 years for men and 78.6 for women. However, it is notable that there has not been the same rise in life expectancy in Denmark as in the countries with which Denmark is normally compared (the OECD countries). This stagnation applies particularly to women. Immigration to and emigration from Denmark have undergone changes during this period. Migration between Denmark and the European countries that resemble Denmark socially and economically has throughout the period been the most important, and the numbers of immigrants to Denmark from these countries has more or less corresponded to the number of emigrants to them. On the other hand there has been an increasing number of immigrants from countries with different backgrounds, in particular from Turkey, former Yugoslavia and Asia, especially from Pakistan. Thus for virtually the entire period immigration has been greater than emigration. In 1999 foreign citizens represented 4.8% of the population as against e.g.

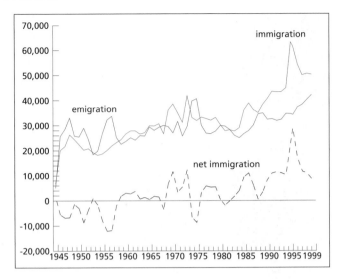

Population movements 1945-1999

2% in 1984. More than half of the foreign nationals live in the metropolitan area, and more than a quarter of them come from either Scandinavian or other EU countries.

Age Structure

The far-reaching demographical changes that have occurred in Denmark over the last couple of hundred years have altered the age structure of the population. Thus the population was noticeably younger in 1901 than in 1997. In 1901 34.3% were under 15 years of age, while

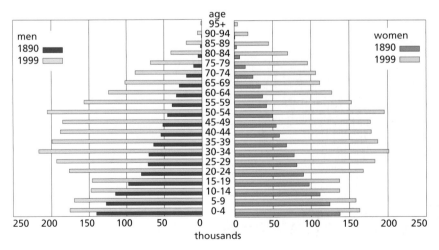

The age distribution of the population in 1890 and 1999.

only 6.6% were over 65. In 1997 the numbers were 18.8% and 15.0%. This represents noticeably more old people in Denmark in 1997 than a hundred years ago: in 1901 0.2% of the population was over 85; in 1997 it was 1.7%. There are twice as many women as men over 80.

Otto Andersen

Language

The language of Denmark is Danish. It is the native language of pretty well the entire population and is the sole language for official purposes. Of c. 20,000 pro-German Danish citizens in Southern Jutland, about two thirds speak Danish at home, even though this minority cultivates German to reflect its identity. Neither foreign citizens resident in Denmark nor immigrants who have obtained Danish citizenship have so far had any demonstrable influence on the Danish language.

Under the terms of the home rule acts, Danish enjoys equality with Faeroese and Greenlandic in the Faeroe Islands and Greenland respectively, and Danish is a compulsory school subject. In Icelandic schools, too, Danish was the first foreign language to be learned until the late 1990's and Danish still serves as a means of communication with the other Nordic countries. In addition, Danish is the mother tongue or the language of culture for c. 50,000 pro-Danish German citizens in South Schleswig (Germany), and is to a certain extent maintained by Danish immigrants in America and Australia. On an international level, Danish has been an official EU language since 1973.

General Linguistic Situation

Within the Indo-European family of languages Danish belongs to the North Germanic (or Nordic) group together with Icelandic, Faeroese, Norwegian and Swedish. The relationship with Norwegian and Swedish is so close that the three languages are to a large extent mutually intelligible. While written Danish is characterised by a very strict norm, the spoken language may vary considerably in pronunciation, although few people actually speak dialect. The vast majority speak either standard Danish or more often a regional and/or social variation of it. However, the concept of standard Danish implies constant and clearly generation-determined changes in pronunciation which tend to have their source in Copenhagen.

The Written Language

Danish is written in the Roman alphabet, expanded with the umlaut letters æ and ø and, since 1948 with å, which before that was written aa, representing vocalic sounds similar to those in e.g. Eng. *call* and *hop*. The letters *c, q, w, x* and *z* are only used in certain loanwords, for instance *check, quiz, weekend, fax*. The orthography is principally conservative and only partly conforms to present-day pronunciation. In for instance *ligge* (to lie), *skylle* (to rinse), *mund* (mouth), the *i, y* and *u* represent a sound corresponding to *e, ø, å*, while the same vowel sign in *kigge* (to look), *skylde* (to owe), *hund* (dog) is pronounced as it is written. The sequence *eg* indicates a long vowel plus a consonant in e.g. *veg* (weak, indulgent), but in *leg* (game, play) it represents a diphthong like in Eng. *lie*, and the same diphthong may also be written *ej* as in *vej* (road, way). From the spelling *hul* it is impossible to see whether the vowel is long or short; in fact, *hul* is one of two different words, either an adjective meaning 'hollow' with a close long vowel, or a noun meaning 'hole' with an open short vowel. But in *hule* (to hollow; cave) and *hulle* (to make holes), a single consonant indicates a preceding long vowel, while a double consonant indicates a short vowel. The written sequences *ld* and *nd*, in which *d* can be silent, always indicate a preceding short vowel as for instance in *huld* (benevolent), *bold* (ball; bold), *vind* (wind), *bande* (gang; to swear). Loanwords, however, often reflect their foreign origin; thus, for instance, *cykel* (bicycle), *etape* (stage), *kapitel* (chapter) are spelt with a single consonant after a short vowel.

Pronunciation

Danish is unusually rich in vowels. The 9 vowel letters represent 16 different vocalic sounds; for instance, in *sal* (hall), *salt* (salt) and *saks* (scissors), the letter *a* stands for three different pronunciations. In addition there are several diphthongs, e.g. one similar to Eng. *I, eye* as in *leje* (to hire) and *lege* (to play), and one comparable to (though not identical with) Eng. *owe* as in *skov* (forest) and *sogn* (parish). Of 21 consonants few are voiced; even *b, d* and *g* are unvoiced, and the articulation of the fricatives corresponding to *d* and *g* is slack (though the fricative *d* is resemblant to Eng. *th* in *with*), as is also the case with the postvocalic *r*, which is changed into an å-like vowel (compare Eng. *hop*). When this is combined with the typical weak vowel (similar to Eng. -er in e.g. *undertaker*) in flectional endings such as -*er*, -*ede*, -*ene*, etc., the pronunciation becomes somewhat indistinct. Moreover, the particular sound of Danish is partly due to the *stød*, a near-closing of the vocal chords which occurs regularly in specific word types, for instance in monosyllables like *tab* (loss), *fugl* (bird), *hånd* (hand) and in the present form *læser* (read(s)) as opposed to the noun *læser* (reader). This peculiar feature has no representation in writing.

Inflections

Within the Germanic languages there are two grammatical traits that are peculiar to the Nordic languages, namely the enclitic definite article, e.g. *dag-en* (the day), *år-et* (the year), *dage-ne* (the days), *år-ene* (the years), and the passive form of the verbs, e.g. *føl-es* (is/are felt), *følt-es* (was/were felt). When combined with an adjective in the definite form the article is an independent word placed in front: *den lang-e dag* (the long day), *det ny-e år* (the new year), *de kær-e børn* (the dear children).

Nouns are classified as either common gender, e.g. *en dag, dagen* (a day, the day), or neuter, *et år, året* (a year, the year); and adjectives and pronouns are inflected according to gender, *stor, stor-t* (big), *nogen* (some(one)), *noget* (some(thing)). The plural of nouns is expressed in four different ways: *dag-e* (days), *uge-r* (weeks), *måned-er* (months), *år* (with zero ending) (years). In a few nouns, the plural ending is combined with vowel mutation, e.g. *fod – fødder* (foot – feet), *mand – mænd* (man – men). In the plural, adjectives and pronouns add -*e*, *stor- e* (big), *min-e* (my, mine). Nouns have two cases, nominative and genitive, *gæst-s* (guest's), *gæst-er-s* (guests'), *gæst-en-s* (the guest's), *gæst-er-ne-s* (the guests'). In addition, seven personal pronouns have accusative forms, e.g. *hun – hende – hende-s* (she – her – her/hers). Adjectives can be compared, *dyb – dyb-ere – dyb-est* (deep – deeper – deepest).

Verbs are inflected in two tenses, present and past. The present tense is formed by adding -*er* or -*r*, *elsk-er* (love(s)), *stå-r* (stand(s)). In the past tense a distinction is made between weak and strong verbs. The weak inflection includes two types, *elsk-ede* (loved), *føl-te* (felt). The strong inflection is characterised by a zero ending or -*t*, often combined with vowel shift (ablaut), e.g. *skyd-er – skød* (shoot(s) – shot), *find-er – fand-t* (find(s) – found), *fald-er – fald-t* (fall(s) – fell). The corresponding participles are *elsk-et* (loved), *føl-t* (felt), *skud-t* (shot), *fund-et* (found), *fald-et* (fallen). The optative, which exists only in the present, has the same form as the infinitive, *Brude-parret lev-e!* (Long live the newlywed couple!) *Pokker stå i det!* (Confound it!). The imperative is identical to the root of the verb, *lev* (live), *stå* (stand).

Sentence Structure

In Danish as in Norwegian and Swedish, a main clause is clearly different from a subordinate clause. In the main clause, the subject, object and certain adverbial elements can be freely interchanged: *Men jeg læste ikke avisen i går / Men avisen læste jeg ikke i går / Men i går læste jeg ikke avisen* (But I did not read the newspaper yesterday). On the other hand, the position of the elements in a subordinate clause is fixed: *da jeg ikke læste avisen i går* (because I did not read the newspaper yesterday); note the insertion of the sentence adverb *ikke* (not) between the subject and the verb.

Vocabulary

The vocabulary of the Danish language is in principle unlimited, as new words can freely be formed by means of compounding or deriving, e.g. *lang-tids-planlægge* (plan long-term), *tvær-faglig-hed* (interdisciplinarity), *op-bak-ning* (backing up), *i-værk-sætter* (person who carries out, entrepreneur) (the hyphens are not in keeping with Danish orthography). The largest Danish dictionaries contain over 200,000 words.

Rasmus Kristian Rask, 1787-1832. Partly as the result of a stay in Iceland 1813-1815, the linguist Rasmus Rask completed a seminal study of the origins of the Scandinavian languages and the connections between them. During a prolonged journey 1816-1823 through Sweden, Finland and Russia to the Caucasus, India and Ceylon, he became familiar with a large number of European and Asian languages, so that in a study entitled *Om Zendsproget* (1826, On the Zend Language) he was able to define the Indo-European family of languages and distinguish it from for instance Finnish, Hungarian and Tamil. Rask created a new basis for comparative linguistics by investigating not only the languages' vocabularies, but also their phonetical and grammatical idiosyncrasies. One of the results was that he discovered the Germanic sound shift before J. Grimm, to whom the honour has otherwise always been ascribed. From the long journey home, Rask brought home with him a large number of ancient Iranian and Singhalese manuscripts which he had collected, and which have since made the Copenhagen Royal Library a centre for the study of comparative philology for many scholars in Rask's tradition.

Olaf Pedersen

The History of the Language

Historically speaking, Danish is a dialect of a common Nordic language which is known from c. 200 AD. Only towards 1200 AD does a split become obvious; the many Viking loanwords in English, *law, window, ill, loose, die, take, both, they*, etc., are Nordic rather than Danish. Characteristic Danish changes in pronunciation in the 12th century are the reduction of *a, i, u* to the weak vowel written *e* in unstressed syllables, e.g. *kaste, time, morgen* from the common Nordic *kasta, timi, morgunn*, cf. the Swedish *kasta, timme, morgon*; the reduction of i.a. the fricative *g* by disappearance as in *tie* (be silent), *flue* (fly), or by diphthongisation as in

Vilhelm Thomsen, 1842-1927. Vilhelm Thomsen was the last important linguist in the Rasmus Rask tradition and like Rask he was eager to use philology as a tool for the historian. In 1876 he gained international attention with a series of lectures at Oxford in which he examined the connections between ancient Russia and Scandinavia and demonstrated the role played by the Scandinavians in fashioning the first Russian states. 20 years later he founded modern turkology by interpreting the Asian Orkhon inscriptions and demonstrating that they were written in an ancient Turkish dialect.

Olaf Pedersen

øje (eye), *skov* (forest), cf. the plosive g in Modern Swedish *tiga, fluga, öga, skog,* and the change of post-vocalic *p* to *b,* and of *t* and *k* to the corresponding fricative sounds, for instance in *reb* (rope), *uden* (without), *kage* (cake), cf. Modern Swedish *rep, utan, kaka.*

Over the centuries Danish has adopted thousands of words from foreign languages, especially from Low German in the Middle Ages, e.g. *krig* (war), *smuk* (beautiful), *håbe*

Louis Hjelmslev, 1899-1965. While Danish linguistics had concentrated on the development of languages over time, Hjelmslev broke new ground by putting aside the historical approach to the advantage of a synchronous study of language as a system, 'the language itself'. His essay *Omkring Sprogteoriens Grundlæggelse* (1943, On the Foundation of the Language Theory) is one of the seminal works of modern linguistics and one of the few that have persuaded foreign scholars to learn Danish.

Olaf Pedersen

(hope) and derivative elements such as *be-, bi-, -agtig, -bar, -hed, -inde, -mager, -eri.* Examples of words adopted from High German after the Reformation (1536) are *gevær* (gun), *munter* (cheerful), *anstrenge* (to strain), *omsonst* (in vain); since the 17th century a considerable number of loanwords have been taken from French, e.g. *affære* (affair), *nervøs* (nervous), *genere* (to bother, to annoy), *partout* (by all means); words from English have been loaned especially in the 20th century, e.g. *klub, smart, skippe, okay.* Throughout the entire period loanwords have been taken from Latin and Greek, e.g. *præst* (priest), *motor, telefon, krise* (crisis), *immun* (immune), *senil* (senile), *vital, skrive* (to write), *imponere* (to impress), *cirka, ekstra.* As can be seen from the examples, the great majority of foreign elements have been adapted to the Danish sound and inflection systems.

The historical changes in the vocabulary were to a large extent brought about by external factors such as Christian missionaries in the Viking Age, trade links with Hanseatic merchants, immigration by north

German artisans and noble families in the Middle Ages, the Lutheran Reformation in the 16th century, and since then a broad cultural contact with the modern international prestige languages, first German and French and from the end of the 19th century mainly with English; and the whole of this western European cultural milieu has constantly adopted words from the 'dead' languages, Latin and Greek. Under the same external influences, Danish, Norwegian and Swedish have in all essential respects undergone a parallel development.

Allan Karker

Constitution

The cornerstone of the Danish constitution is *Danmarks Riges Grundlov* (The Constitutional Act of the Kingdom of Denmark) of 5 June 1953. This is the result of developments in constitutional law that began in 1849 with the introduction of a bicameral parliament and with human rights guaranteed by the Constitution. Today Denmark has a unicameral system, a system of parliamentary government and a queen who has only formal and ceremonial functions. The Constitution has not been changed since 1953, but by way of legislation and treaties far-reaching changes have been made in the constitutional legal structure, not least as a result of Danish membership of the EU.

The Government until 1849

The Constitution of 1849 brought an end to the system of government that had obtained since the introduction of absolutism in 1660-1661. Under the absolute monarchy, the king had an unusually powerful position according to European reckoning. Not only did he head the government and administration, but he also formally held the presidency of the country's highest court, the Supreme Court, which was established in 1661. Neither the nobility, clergy or citizenry had any formal check on the king's power.

During the 18th century profound changes took place in the organisation of the state. Under the influence of French political philosophy the independence of the courts in relation to the king and the rest of the executive power was acknowledged; the king did not take part in the work of the Supreme Court; the nobility and the citizens took part in the administration of the state.

The first steps towards a democratic representation were taken 1834, when the king established the Advisory Provincial Assemblies. Discussion here acted as a preparation for the constitutional system that was introduced 1848-1849 by the National Constitutional Assembly. The fact that on 5 June 1849 Denmark was given a new Constitution replacing the absolute monarchical system was due in part to contemporary developments in Europe and in part to internal problems in the Danish monarchy.

The Constitution

The Constitution of 1849 is based on the principle of distribution of power, putting the legislative power in the joint hands of the king and Parliament, and the judicial power with the independent courts. The Parliament (the *Rigsdag*) consisted of two chambers, the *Landsting* and the *Folketing*. Every man of 30 and above had the right to vote in elections to the Folketing; exceptions were servants, those in receipt of charitable relief, those with criminal convictions and bankrupts. Although suffrage was universal according to the standards of that time, only about 13-14% of the adult population were in fact entitled to vote. All those with a right to vote in Folketing elections could also vote in Landsting elections, but the election of members of the Landsting was carried out indirectly, by electors, and eligibility was restricted to those aged 40 or more with a sizeable income.

In stipulating that anyone arrested should be brought before a judge within 24 hours, the 1849 Constitution established the right to freedom of the individual; it also ensured the inviolability of one's dwelling and the right of property. At the same time freedom of expression, freedom to form associations, and freedom of assembly were guaranteed. The Constitution ensured everyone the right to public assistance and free schooling.

The king's powers were strictly limited, but the monarchy retained certain prerogatives. The royal assent was necessary for bills passed by both chambers of the Rigsdag. The king himself chose his ministers, and he represented the nation in relation to other countries.

The courts achieved independence in their functions, but the judges were still appointed by the king. The Constitution promised the introduction of juries in major criminal and political cases, a promise that was not fulfilled until the 1916 Administration of Justice Act.

Changes to the Constitution 1866-1953

Denmark's relations with its southern neigbours, particularly Prussia, has played a decisive role for constitutional developments. In 1866 a new Constitution was adopted for the radically reduced area of Denmark left after the Danish defeat at the hands of Prussia in 1864. The 1866 Constitution included strict limits on the almost universal male suffrage that had been recognised by the 1849 Constitution.

In 1915, during the First World War, broad agreement was reached on constitutional reform. Universal suffrage was introduced, so that women and servants were also given the right to vote. While since 1849 there had been elections by majority vote in single constituencies, in 1918 an electoral system was introduced combining proportional representation with elections in individual cons-

On 5 June 1915, about 15,000 women marched through Copenhagen to Amalienborg Palace Square to celebrate the coming into force of the Constitution giving them full political rights. A deputation presented an address to the King and the Parliament. In this the women expressed their joy at the new constitution and their hope that women's participation in politics would be to the benefit of the country and the people. At the front in the middle of the deputation we see Jutta Bojsen-Møller of *Dansk Kvindesamfund* (Danish Women's Society).

King Frederik IX signs the new constitution, the Constitution of 5 June 1953. The Prime Minister Erik Eriksen was present. The voters' interest in reform was muted, but the associated Act of Succession, which ensured Princess Margrethe the right of accession, led to the then necessary 45% of voters turning out and voting in favour.

tituencies. Although since the beginning of the century there had been a desire to introduce referenda, partly by the Social Democrats and partly the Social Liberals, which were in power during the war, the 1915 Constitution only contained provision for referenda in connection with constitutional change.

A constitutional reform in 1920 adapted the 1915 Constitution to the expanded Danish territory following the return of Southern Jutland to Denmark.

In 1939 the Rigsdag passed a new Constitution, but it did not receive sufficient support in the referendum, and the 1915/20 Constitution thus remained in force during the Second World War. During the German occupation considerable departures from the provisions of the Constitution were necessary; thus decrees replaced certain laws after the resignation of the government on 29 August 1943. These decrees were issued by the civil servant heads of departments.

The Constitution of 1953

After the end of the Second World War work began on reforming the Constitution, but only in 1953 was a result achieved that could gain suffi-

cient political support. The Constitution of 5 June 1953 abolished the Landsting and confirmed the parliamentary principle for the composition of the government. Since 1901 the Danish king had accepted that he could not appoint a government that would lack the confidence of the majority in the Folketing; however, it was only in the 1953 Constitution that it was expressly stated that the Folketing can declare its lack of confidence in a government, which in that case must either resign or call an election.

The 1953 Constitution maintains and expands the protection of human rights. Defence of personal freedom was extended to intensified control by the courts of administrative deprival of freedom, e.g. in the case of insanity. And the experiences of the war formed the background of an express prohibition of deprivation of freedom on account of descent, religious or political convictions.

The 1953 Constitution applies also to the Faeroe Islands and Greenland. On the basis of special legislation these two areas have achieved a relatively high degree of self-government, the so-called home rule government (the Faeroe Islands in 1948, Greenland in 1979).

Linked to the Constitution of 1953 there is a special Act of Succession, according to which women also have the right of succession to the Danish throne, but only secondarily. On the death of King Frederik IX in 1972 his eldest daughter acceded to the throne as Queen Margrethe II. As head of state the Queen represents Denmark abroad and heads the government, but has no political power.

The Folketing and the Government

The most important political organs are the Folketing and the Government.

The Folketing

The Folketing consists of 179 members, two of whom are elected in Greenland and two in the Faeroe Islands. The remaining 175 members are elected in Denmark. The nominated candidates are elected on the basis of proportional representation, but the candidates run in individual single constituencies, and so most of those elected have a local connection reminiscent of those elected by majority voting in individual constituencies. 135 of the 175 members of the Folketing are elected on the basis of the votes cast for them in the local constituencies, while the remaining 40 members are chosen with a view to ensuring an overall proportional representation of the parties to which the candidates are linked. It is possible to run without belonging to the political parties, but only in once instance (1994) has a candidate succeeded in gaining election in this manner.

The voting age is not specified in the Constitution, but is decided in a special Act that must be approved by referendum. The voting age since 1978 has been 18. Immigrants without Danish nationality do not have the right to vote for the Folketing, but since 1989 they have been able to vote and had the right of election in local elections.

The Government

The Government is appointed by the Queen and consists of the Prime Minister and the other ministers each with their own Department; individual ministers can be without a specific Department (i.e. without portfolio). The choice of Prime Minister and other ministers is determined by the party composition in the Folketing. The government appointed may not have a majority of the Folketing against it. A newly appointed govern-

The chamber of the Folketing in Christiansborg Palace.

ment begins working without necessarily having achieved a positive vote of confidence from the Folketing.

Legislation

The Folketing and the government co-operate in legislation. Bills are laid before the Folketing, where they are read three times. Bills contain not only the proposed legal text, but also the proposer's motives for the proposal. These motives, together with minutes of discussions in the Folketing and its committees can be of significance in a subsequent interpretation of the act when passed.

When a bill has been passed by the Folketing it must be approved by the Queen and the government. The Queen does not adopt an independent stance, but follows the advice of the government.

Elections

Elections to the Folketing take place at least every four years, but the Prime Minister has the right to dissolve the Folketing and thus force an election. This right plays an important part, as the Prime Minister

Traditionally, the level of voter participation in elections is very high, especially in general elections. On 20 November 2001 elections to the Folketing, to the municipal and county councils were held at the same time. 87.1% of the registered voters participated in the election to the Folketing and a little fewer in the elections to the municipal and county councils.

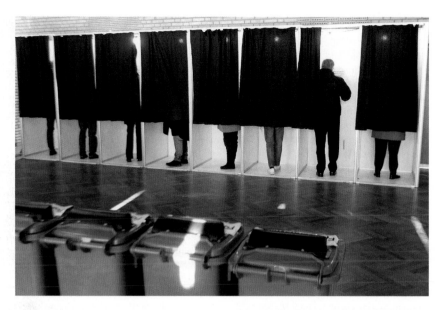

and the Government have, over the years, often been in a weak position in relation to the Folketing. Most governments since the Second World War have been minority governments without any firm agreements on Co-operation, and the government has therefore had to carry out its programme by means of compromise from one matter to another with parties outside the government. The threat of a dissolution of the Folketing has occasionally motivated parties that could foresee a poor election result to enter into a compromise with the government.

The government has a number of other powers that are directly provided for in the Constitution. It is thus the Government that leads the country's foreign policy, but the Folketing controls the government's activities. In major foreign policy decisions the government must consult a special parliamentary committee, the Foreign Policy Committee. Before entering into treaties, the approval of the Folketing can be legally necessary.

Of particular significance is the co-operation developing within the EU. In accordance with the Constitution, accession to the EU (then the EC) took place on the basis of section 20 of the Constitution, which deals with co-operation in the field of foreign policy implying the surrender of constitutional powers to so-called supranational organisations. According to section 20 the establishment of this intense kind of international co-operation demands that there must be a majority in the Folketing of at least 5/6 of the members; if this is not the case a referendum must be held. Such a referendum was held in October 1972, demonstrating that a significant majority of the people was in favour of Denmark's joining the EC. Furthermore, the co-operation within the EU has led to five referenda: in 1986 on the Single European Act, in 1992 on the Maastricht Treaty, in 1993 on the Edinburgh Agreement, in 1998 on the Amsterdam Treaty, and in 2000 on Denmark's joining the Single European Currency, the euro. When the Folketing has passed a bill, a minority of 1/3 of the members can demand a referendum according to the terms of section 42 of the Consti-

Together with Great Britain, Norway and Ireland, Denmark applied for membership of the EC in 1961 and 1967, but on each occasion de Gaulle vetoed British membership, and Denmark did not wish to enter the Community without Great Britain. Negotiations for admission were resumed after the summit meeting in the Hague in 1969, and from 1 January 1973 Denmark became a member together with Ireland and Great Britain. This was preceded by a binding referendum in which 63.3% voted in favour and 36.7% against membership.

In the Council of Ministers, the decisions are normally passed by simple majority, but certain matters demand a qualified majority with weighted voting. Denmark has 3 votes out of 87. Of the Commission's 20 members, Denmark has 1 Commissioner, currently Poul Nielson with responsibility for development and humanitarian aid. The EU Parliament has 626 members, of whom 16 are Danes, and is elected for periods of 5 years. The first direct election was in 1979, and the numbers voting in European elections in Denmark have varied between 46% and 53% of the electorate.

Since 1973 more areas of policy have been brought under the influence of the Community, and six new countries have been admitted (Greece, Portugal, Spain, Sweden, Finland and Austria).

Denmark has held several referenda on EU policy: In 1986 56.2% voted for and 43.8% against the Single European Act. In 1992 49.3% voted for and 50.7% against the Maastricht Treaty. In 1993 56.8% voted in favour and 43.2% against the Maastricht Treaty with the opt-outs agreed in Edinburgh. The opt-outs encompassed defence policy, the third phase of EMU and a common currency, union citizenship, the judicial field and finally stipulated that the objectives of the Union should not apply to these four areas. In 1998 55.1% voted for and 44.9% against the Amsterdam Treaty, and in 2000 53.1% voted against and 46.9% for Denmark's joining the Single European Currency, the euro.

Denmark's attitude to membership changed character in the mid-1980s. In the first period EU policy was strongly influenced by the fact that the Social Democrats were divided on the issue, and for this reason special emphasis was placed on furthering economic and monetary co-operation. Since the 1986 referendum, which marked the culmination of domestic political disagreements, Denmark has been more active, for instance seeking to improve environmental policy in order to create greater openness in the EU and to encourage a broad intake of East European countries. There is, however, still widespread scepticism in the population as regards integration and the further renunciation of sovereignty.

Mogens Rüdiger

tution. A minority in the Folketing thus has the possibility of ensuring that the majority that has just passed a bill also has a corresponding majority of the people behind it. If it emerges in the referendum that this is not the case, the bill is lost.

The state administration is in the hands of the individual ministers who in accordance with the law issue orders more closely regulating individual areas. Part of the state administration is accorded functional independence of the government and the individual minister. This applies in particular to committees re-

quiring special expert knowledge or with representatives of organisations or political groupings as members.

Public administration is not the province solely of the state. Local authority independence is established in section 82 of the Constitution, and many of the administrative powers are delegated to the 14 counties and the 275 local authorities into which Denmark is divided (2002).

The passing of the Constitution of 1953 allowed for the introduction of a special check on the administration, the Folketing Ombudsman, who took up his duties in 1954. The

Ombudsman is chosen by the Folketing and on the basis of complaints or on his own initiative he examines questions of mistakes or negligence in the public administration.

Courts

The independent courts constitute part of the distribution of power. Cases are generally dealt with in the first instance by a local or city court, and appeals against the judgements of the city courts can be made to one of the two High Courts. A few big cases and cases touching on administrative matters and certain other categories are dealt with by one of the two High Courts in the first instance. The highest court is the Supreme Court (*Højesteret*), which only deals with cases that have already been dealt with by one of the two High Courts. In the Danish court system there is no provision for special procedures or court organisation for administrative cases. These are dealt with by the ordinary courts. Nor is there a constitutional court. Constitutional questions must be decided by the court that is otherwise dealing with the case, and in the final instance the question can be decided by the Supreme Court. Danish courts have been very reluctant to have recourse to the Constitution, and it was not until 1999 that the Supreme Court rejected a politically important Act as being contrary to the Constitution.

The independence of the judges in carrying out their duties is ensured by section 64 of the Constitution, according to which in the performance of their duties judges shall be governed solely by the law. In contrast to other state appointed employees, judges cannot be dismissed administratively; they can only be dismissed by a court judgement. In 1999 the administration of the courts was transferred to an independent state institution, the Court Administration. An independent comittee has been established which recommends the Ministry of Justice to appoint judges. These recommendations have so far been complied with. The courts have an essential function in protecting the human rights enshrined in the Constitution. To a great extent the central element in this protection consists in access to checks by the courts. The checks can be obligatory as with arrest of over 24 hours (cf. section 71 of the Constitution), or they can result from informal applications on the part of interested parties as in the case of checks on administrative imprisonment according to section 71, subsection 6, introduced in 1953. Court supervision can also be precursive as with checks on searches and breaches of the secrecy of communications (section 72).

Political freedom encompasses especially the freedom of expression, section 77, freedom of assembly, section 79, and the freedom to form associations, section 78. These provisions, however, are not limited to political expressions, assemblies and associations, but also apply to financial, cultural, religious and other activities.

Constitutional Changes

It is difficult to change the Constitution. The procedure is spelt out in section 88 of the Constitution. A change or addition to the Constitution must first be passed by the Folketing; this approval must then be repeated after a general election; there is the further demand that a referendum shall be held on the constitutional proposal in which a majority of the votes cast must be in favour of the proposal, and this majority shall be of at least 40% of all those entitled to vote. It is especially this last condition which might be difficult to fulfil.

Denmark's membership of the EU since 1973 has radically changed the conditions for parliamentary supervision of the production of regulations. A significant proportion of the regulations obtaining in Denmark have come from EU institutions or have been approved at national level for implementing EU directives. To strengthen parliamentary control a special Folketing committee has been established, the European Committee, chosen by and from the members of the Folketing. The Government consults the committee, which authorises the Government to assert its various standpoints. The European Committee has therefore a basis to exert a very tight control of the Government. The enormous volume of matters to be dealt with, however, makes it difficult to exercise the controls effectively, and preparation in the European Committee does not ensure a public discussion of the matters under review. A Danish Supreme Court judgement confirmed in 1998 that Denmark's membership of EU as regulated by the Maastricht Treaty is not a contravention of the Danish Constitution.

Consideration is regularly given to the question of whether the 1953 Constitution ought to be revised. Some politicians, for instance, would like to strengthen the Folketing by limiting the Government's right to dissolve it and call an election, and by making possible an independent judicial assessment of bills. Other politicians see a great need to strengthen the government, which, for instance in a minority situation, is often in a weak position.

The European Convention on Human Rights

In 1953 Denmark ratified the European Convention on Human Rights. Before ratification certain minor changes were carried out in Danish law, so that Danish law was assumed to be in agreement with the Convention. The Convention's provisions could not be directly applicable to Danish law, because it would be necessary to start from the dualistic concept of the relationship between Danish law and international law as two separate judicial areas. With the expansive interpretation which the Court of Human Rights practises, it was a problem that the Convention does not constitute part of Danish law, and in an Act from 1992 it was determined that the Convention is to be considered part of Danish law. The Convention's protection of human rights applies, however, only as a parliamentary act and is not at a level with the protection of human rights contained in the Constitution. Nevertheless, the courts have used the Convention more than the Constitution as the basis for criticising legislation.

Henrik Zahle

Political System

After the passing of the Constitutional Act in 1849 a number of loose political groupings emerged in the newly-established parliament, the Rigsdag. These crystallised into three main groups: *Venstre* (Left), *Højre* (Right) and *Centrum* (Centre). Although parties are not mentioned in the Constitution, they were soon performing a key role in the political process. During the 1870s and 1880s mass membership parties were formed with their own organisations, and soon after the turn of the century the classical Danish four-party system had developed: *Højre*, from 1915 called *Det Konservative Folkeparti* (The Conservative People's Party), supported by townspeople, independent tradesmen, and larger farmers, *Venstre* (The Liberal Party), with its roots in *Det forenede Venstre* (The United Left) from 1870, with its main support in the farming community, *Det Radikale Venstre* (The Social Liberal Party, formed 1905), supported by smallholders and radi-

cal intellectuals in the cities, and *Socialdemokratiet* (The Social Democratic Party) (founded 1871), the workers' party. The four-party system remained largely intact until 1960. Of smaller parties, the Danish Communist Party had a certain backing between 1945 and 1957, but was excluded from influence. Facist and Nazi parties have never achieved much support or influence. *Danmarks Retsforbund* (The Single Tax Party), based on the principles of Henry George, had a certain significance between 1947 and 1960 and was in the government coalition from 1957-1960. Industrialisation and the development of the public sector made the party divisions more complicated. After the 1960 election, *Socialistisk Folkeparti* (The Socialist People's Party) drew electors standing to the left of the Social Democrats, and in what was known as the landslide election in 1973 three new parties came into the Folketing: the centre parties *Kristeligt Folkeparti* (The

Grassroots movements in the 1970s gained increasing political significance. Especially visible was the Organisation for Information on Atomic Power formed in 1974 and argued against the introduction of atomic power to Denmark. Thanks to campaigns and demonstrations – as seen here in Copenhagen in 1977 – the movement was in 1980 able to exert its influence and put a stop to plans for building atomic power stations. The movement also protested against the recently built Swedish Barsebäck atomic power station only 23 km from Copenhagen.

Christian People's Party) and *Centrum-Demokraterne* (The Centre Democrats) and also *Fremskridtspartiet* (The Progress Party) which started as a protest party, from which *Dansk Folkeparti* (The Danish People's Party) split in 1995.

In 1989 a number of smaller Socialist parties and groups were gathered into *Enhedslisten* (Unity List), including the *DKP* (Danish Communist Party) and *VS* (Left Socialists). At the 1994 election the Unity List polled enough votes to be represented in Parliament.

As well as electors, non-governmental organisations have considerable influence. Until 1995-1996 the trades unions were closely connected with the Social Democratic Party, while to a certain extent the major trade organisations co-operate with the two main non-socialist parties, The Conservative People's Party and The Liberal Party; the powerful agricultural organisations work especially with The Liberal Party. In addition representatives of trades unions and trade organisations are used by governments in connection with tribunals and committees, commissions and fact-finding exercises.

Since about 1960, grass-roots movements have gathered supporters around single policy issues. For instance the Campaign against Nuclear Weapons, the Popular Movement Against the EC, the women's movement, Danish Nature Conservancy Association, the peace movement and the environmental group NOAH have been successful in influencing policy. In the 1970s the Organisation for Information on Atomic Power was instrumental in ensuring that no atomic power stations were built in Denmark.

Danish governments have usually been minority governments. So Danish politics have been characterised

by compromises among the parties. If the Folketing passes a vote of no confidence, the government must resign unless it calls an election. It can choose to resign and/or call an election if it finds itself in a minority on issues which it itself considers important. The government can also call an election without resigning or it can resign without calling an election. Under the terms of the Constitution, however, elections must be held at least every four years.

If the distribution of seats after an election points unambiguously to a specific government, this is appointed by the monarch on the advice of the retiring prime minister. If, on the

Having won the general election of 20 November 2001, the new Prime Minister, Anders Fogh Rasmussen, from the Liberal Party presented his government to Queen Margrethe on 27 November. The photo shows him on Amalienborg Palace Square after his visit to the Queen, followed by Conservative Bendt Bendtsen, Minister of Economic and Business Affairs.

other hand, there is uncertainty, the Queen initiates a meeting (sometimes a series of meetings) at which representatives of each of the elected parties tender their advice to her.

On this basis, the Queen appoints a royal investigator to chair negotiations between the parties concerning the formation of a government. At the end of these, the result is announced at yet another meeting with the Queen, after which the Queen appoints the new prime minister. It is crucial to the formation of any government that there should not beforehand have been revealed a majority against the new government.

Lorenz Rerup, Niels Finn
Christiansen

The Legal System

In the Middle Ages Denmark was divided into three areas of jurisdiction, Jutland, Zealand and Scania. The oldest written sources of law are the so-called provincial laws (*landskabslove*) from the end of the 12th century, the most famous of which is the Jutlandic Law from 1241. The provincial laws applied until a unified legal system was achieved in 1683 by the establishment of Christian V's Danish Law (*Danske Lov*), which was one of the first reforms introduced under the absolute monarchy. A number of provisions from the provincial laws were incorporated into the Danish Law. Only a small number of these provisions apply today, but the fundamental principles in Danish law can be traced back to the Middle Ages. This does not mean that Danish law has not been influenced by foreign law. Especially in the 18th and 19th centuries the influence from natural law and later especially from German jurispru-

dence was considerable. One particular feature of Danish law is moreover that there are not, as for instance in France and Germany, civil codes, but that the civil law rules are found in specific legislation or are established by practice. Finally, Nordic co-operation since the end of the last century has played an important part in the development of Danish law.

Branches of Law

Danish jurisprudence operates on the basis of a division into *public law* and *civil law*.

The borderline is not easy to define, and the basis for this division is much debated. It is characteristic of public law that it is often about taking care of general social interests, and that state organs other than the courts play the major role in applying the legal regulations. Public law is divided into *constitutional law*, which concerns the provisions gov-

The courtroom of the Supreme Court in Christiansborg Palace was designed by the architect Thorvald Jørgensen and taken into use on 1 October 1919. The arrangement corresponds in the main to that in courtrooms used by the Supreme Court since 1670. Only the form of the bench has been altered in the course of time. Since the court was taken into use in 1919 it has been in the shape of a semi-circle with room for 15 judges; in 1937 the judges' seats were placed on a platform corresponding to a tradition followed in other countries and deriving from the antique model. The courtroom is used for the Court's First Division of the court.

With the growing acceptance of the right of grown people to arrange their lives as they wish, came the demand that homosexual couples should be allowed to have their relationships legitimised and recognised. It was not only a question of acceptance, but also of practical matters such as taxation, pensions and rights of inheritance, in which cohabiting homosexuals felt that they were being discriminated against in relation to their fellow citizens. The question was solved by an 1989 Act allowing homosexuals to have a registered partnership which in general carries with it the duties and rights that accompany marriage. Here a couple is being registered in Copenhagen Town Hall.

erning the supreme state organs, *international law* which regulates relations between states, *administrative law*, i.e. the legal rules applying to or used by local authority and state administration, *criminal law*, which contains the rules for what actions are punishable by law, and the *law of procedure*, the rules concerning the handling of cases by the courts.

Civil law regulates reciprocal relations between citizens and between natural persons and legal persons, e.g. companies and institutions. The rules must weigh and protect the interests of the individual parties. Important areas in civil law are *the law of contracts and torts, the law of property* and *the law of capacity, family law* and *the law of wills and succession*. In contrast to German and French law, commercial law in the Danish legal system is not distinct as a special area of jurisprudence, but trade is regulated by e.g. the Sale of Goods Act and the Consumer Contracts Act, which require greater responsibility and care from traders than from private individuals, and similarly offer protection to consumers.

Sources of Law

At the top of the legal hierarchy stands the Constitutional Act, which regulates the relations between the highest state organs and provides for civil liberties (Human Rights); it can only be changed by special procedure.

The citizens' liberty of action can only be restrained by law or by legal precedent. The Constitution determines the conditions under which Acts are valid. After being passed by the Folketing and having recieved the Royal Assent, Acts must be published in the official journal *Lovtidende*. They come into effect one week after publication if no other date is specifically fixed in the Act concerned. Many Acts are given the form of framework laws containing general guidelines and leaving it to the minister concerned to provide more precise regulations. Regulations determined administratively within the framework of an Act, and containing rules of general applicability, are called *anordninger* (regulations), *bekendtgørelser* (orders) or in certain areas *reglementer* (regulations) or *vedtægter* (statutory instruments). Such provisions are often supplemented by government circulars, i.e. rules directed solely at the authorities.

An Act is amended or repealed by a new Act being passed. As a result of developments in computerisation, consolidation Acts, called *lovbekendtgørelser* have become quite common. They consist of up-dated law texts consisting of the relevant parts of the original Act supplemented with changes to it.

From ancient times the contents of the law have moreover been determined by the courts by means of case law in areas where there is no legislation, and this still occurs, for instance especially in the law of compensation. In other legal systems, especially in countries with legal systems inspired by Anglo-Saxon law, *common law*, the courts have, however, a far greater law-creating function than in Denmark

Customary law are also sources of law. A legal custom arises when a specific manner of behaviour has been followed *generally, constantly and over a long period of time*, because the persons concerned were convinced that they were legally obliged to do so. Such legal customs are deemed part of the law of the land. They can be set aside by legislation, or the courts can overrule them as unreasonable.

Danish Law and International Law

The legal norms that govern the relationship between states are called international law. In Denmark the government has the authority to act on behalf of the country in international legal matters, including the authority to enter into internationally binding agreements by treaty. However, the approval of the Folketing and in certain circumstances a referendum is required for arrangements of major significance.

A treaty obligation containing the demand for a change of Danish legislation is fulfilled through incorporation, whereby the treaty is made part of Danish legislation. Before incorporation the provisions of the treaty cannot be applied without further ado by the Danish authorities, and consequently a conflict can emerge between Denmark's obligations in international law and under Danish legislation. The courts will then seek to interpret the legislation in accordance with international law. For instance, the European Convention on Human Rights, to which Denmark acceded by ratification in 1953, was applied by the courts as a contribution to the interpretation of legislation before the treaty was incorporated in 1992.

Danish Law and EU Law

Through Denmark's membership of the EU since 1973, the rules in the EU have become part of Danish law.

The EU legal acts, which are called *forordninger* (regulations), are directly applicable to Danish citizens when they have been published in Danish in the Official Journal of the European Union. EU directives on the other hand do not bind Danish citizens before they have been given legal force in Denmark, e.g. by legislation.

The Courts

The ordinary courts that can deal with all kinds of cases, i.e. both civil cases and criminal cases, are divided on hierarchical lines. At the bottom there are city courts, which are to be found in each of the country's 82 circuits; then High Courts, the Western High Court (*Vestre Landsret*) and the Eastern High Court (*Østre Landsret*), and finally the highest court in the country, the Supreme Court (*Højesteret*). Special courts with the right of conviction are not allowed in Denmark. On the other hand special courts, so-called *undersøgelsesretter* (investigative courts), can be established to determine a course of events. In addition to the ordinary courts there are courts which on a permanent basis deal with special areas of law, for instance the Maritime and Commercial Court. There is in Denmark no separate constitutional court as in Germany, France and Spain. Nor is there a separate administrative court as in Germany and France or special divisions of the courts as in Spain. Such cases are dealt with by the ordinary courts. Laymen have from ancient times taken part in the administration of justice in Denmark. In maritime and commercial cases specialist assistant judges take part, and in criminal cases lay assessors usually play a role, while serious criminal cases are normally decided with the help of a jury.

Courtroom E, the courtroom used for cases tried by jury, in the principal building of the Western High Court in Viborg. The construction of the court building did not quite reach completion in time for the coming into force of the Administration of Justice Act on 1 October 1919. The courtroom for jury cases was the first to be taken into use in 1920, and it stands today largely unchanged. The tapestries by Nanna Hertoft from 1971 hang on the wall on the right.

The Administration

Public administration has many tasks, but three predominate. The administration makes grants and services available for the citizens; it raises taxes and duties, and it takes part in the comprehensive and detailed legal control of virtually all areas of life characteristic of Danish society; in particular it ensures that the general rules are observed and that specific permission is given for activities which otherwise transgress them. The legal rules governing the administration are as in other western European countries characterised by traditional ideals of law and order. The Administrative Procedure Act ensures citizens free access to being heard or otherwise to participate in cases concerning them, and there is often access to administrative review by a superior administrative authority, or possibly an administrative tribunal. In addition the Folketing Ombudsman has a supervisory power over the administration and can criticise faults or negligence. The Ombudsman's statements have no legal force for the administration, but they are normally complied with.

Elisabeth Thuesen, Ditlev Tamm,
Tom Latrup-Pedersen, Bent
Christensen

Public Administration

Public administration in Denmark is a vast field, providing work for 1/3 of the labour force, and it is rather amorphous and difficult to delimit vis-à-vis the rest of society.

The Organisation of the Administration

At its heart are the state public administration and municipal administration. The most important areas of *state administration* are the central administration and the local administration. The central administration is divided into a number of ministries each with its special area; of these, most consist of a department and one or more directorates. The departments are headed by a minister, that is to say a politician. The directorates have civil service heads. A feature of the departments is that they must serve the minister. Their

most important duties are therefore tasks directed at the Folketing, e.g. drafting bills, answering questions from the Folketing, considering applications for appropriations from the Folketing or issuing statutory instruments. In addition to the departments and directorates there is in the central administration a large number of organs with several members, allowing the involvement of specialists and representatives of interest groups. Such councils and committees are usually advisory, but there are also some committees which can decide on complaints or distribute sums of money.

The local state administration consists of some national branches of administration, such as the police, the prison service, the post office and factory inspection authorities and some institutions or bodies that

The central administration is located at the seat of power on Slotsholmen in Copenhagen. Christiansborg Palace is at the centre, containing i.a. the Folketing and the Prime Minister's Office. Most ministerial departments are housed on or near Slotsholmen.

Esbjerg Town Hall was designed by the architect Jens Sottrup-Jensen and built in 1970 to replace the old town hall from 1891, which for many years had been too small for all the municipal administration. The sculpture on the right, *Large Wave*, was done by Bent Sørensen and erected in 1978.

provide services in different parts of the country, e.g. universities, regional archives, the lifeboat service, etc.

Municipal Administration

Local authority administration, which since 1970 has grown even more rapidly than state administration, is under political control to a greater extent than the state administration; there are some 5,000 members of local governments, but only about 20 ministers. The areas of competence of municipal administrations include a very large part of the specialist areas in which the public administration is in any way involved. Municipal administration is limited geographically rather than according to specialist areas.

The municipal authorities consist of 14 county councils (*amtskommuner*) and 275 city or district councils (*primærkommuner*), including the two metropolitan areas of Copenhagen and Frederiksberg. The highest authority in each municipality is a popularly elected council, and the form of management is arranged in such a way that all political groupings are able to exert influence on the administration. The distinction between government and opposition, which is a feature of state government, is only found in a watered-down version in the local authorities.

Around the nucleus represented by the public state or municipal administration, there is a large number of different kinds of institutions bordering on the private sector. It is typical that they carry out the same or similar functions as the state and municipal administrations; and these have indeed more influence here than they have on activities in the private sector. Examples of this can be self-governing institutions within the social and education sectors, private nurseries and schools, vocational colleges, incinerator plants used by more than one local authority, or state-run companies.

The Administration in the State Apparatus

Numerically, the administration is by far the greatest part of the Danish state apparatus. Its relationship to other state organs is therefore of the greatest importance for an understanding of the administration and of the state governmental apparatus as a whole.

The relationship of the administration to the Folketing, the dominant element in the legislature, is clear: According to the Constitution the administration is 'the executive power'. The administration is to be dependent on the Folketing and to have no independent legal authority of its own in relation to it. The entire administration, including ministers and members of municipal councils, is to observe the rules that the Folketing establishes as laws or as the basis for statutory instruments. It is also the administration's duty to seek to put into effect the intentions of the Folketing.

The relationship between the government, whose legitimacy is dependent on its having sufficient support in the Folketing, and the remainder of the administration is less clear. Historically the starting point has been that within his own purview each minister was empowered to control all the organs of administration. This no longer applies. The minister can only control municipal administration, councils, committees, or institutions, bodies, etc. bordering on the private sector, insofar as he has specific authority to do so. And even within the state administration, where the minister's power to manage is the general rule, there is a tendency for at least some organs of administration to be given considerable independence within the economic frameworks and objectives on which a political decision has been made. Similar tendencies characterise the relationship between local councils and parts of the rest of municipal administration.

Supervision of the Administration
It is the administration that makes the services of the welfare state available to the citizens, levies taxes and duties, and is responsible for the detailed legal regulation that is a mark of Danish society. When the ideological point of departure is that the administration is not to be independent, its activities derived from the Folketing, it is obvious that the

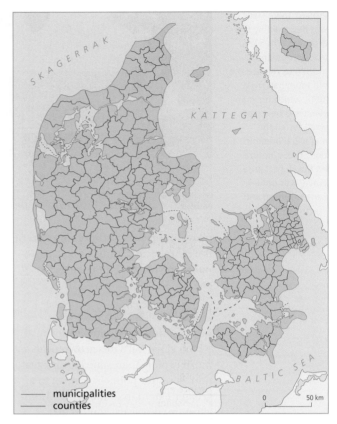

municipalities
counties

administration will be subject to close control. An essential part of this control is aimed to ensure the individual citizen's rights. Citizens have extensive opportunities to complain about one organ of administration to another, although this facility has been restricted in recent years. It frequently occurs that the complaint can be directed to boards of appeal or administrative tribunals that can offer particular procedural safeguards. Municipal administration is subject to special supervision which in the wake of complaints or of its own accord can take action to correct clear breaches of the law. And the Folketing Ombudsman can, following complaints or on his own initiative, carry out examinations to discover whether the administration has transgressed current law or in any other way been guilty of faults or

The administrative division of Denmark into counties and municipalities.

Several of the buildings under the central administration are to be found in Slotsholmsgade in Copenhagen. The Ministry of Finance and the Ministry of the Interior are at Christiansborg Slotsplads 1 in the Chancellery building, otherwise known as 'The Red Building', with the large semicircular pediment; it was built 1716-1721 by the architect J.C. Ernst for Frederik IV. The long building behind the trees on the left, Lerches Palæ from the 1740s was taken over by the State in 1805 and contains the Ministry of Justice and the Ministry of Food, Agriculture and Fisheries.

negligence. Finally, section 63 of the Constitution gives the independent courts the right to decide whether the administration has acted in accordance with current law.

Alongside these controls, which are mainly based on consideration for the individual citizen, the administration is subject to other equally important checks. The administration's use of its considerable financial resources is subject to independent scrutiny. The mass media keep a close watch on the activities of the administration, and this is strengthened by the quite extensive access to the documents of the administration provided for by the Access to Public Administration Files Act. Finally, through questions to ministers and through its standing committees, the Folketing keeps a check on the administration, a check which since the middle of the 1970s has been considerably intensified.

Bent Christensen

Defence and Military

In May 1945, after the liberation from the German Second World War occupation, Danish defence had to start rebuilding the various services almost from scratch. In 1950, the USA embarked on its military assistance programme to countries including Denmark, and a thorough reorganisation of the military and political control of defence was carried out that same year. Only then did the various services gradually attain force levels and a state of readiness approaching the official force levels regularly prescribed by NATO. However, throughout the Cold War, the strength of Danish military forces was on the low side compared to the common goals of the alliance. A broad majority in the Folketing has traditionally supported the defence arrangements which provide the financial and political basis for the work of the defence forces.

Poul Villaume

Danish defence is (2001) being realigned after the break-up of the Soviet Union and the Warsaw Pact. The removal of an immediate threat of invasion to Denmark has made it possible to use resources to support international efforts to limit and prevent conflicts in and outside Europe. The new situation was clearly reflected in a 1993 Act establishing that on receipt of a mandate from the UN or the OSCE the defence forces shall contribute i.a. to operations aimed at maintaining peace or seeking to prevent conflict or establish peace. These new duties are a supplement to the defence of Denmark and the surrounding areas within the framework of NATO. But the new situation is underlined also with regard to Denmark's contribution to NATO.

The Danish defence forces are empowered to take part in the alliance's crisis control in distant parts with forces sufficient to demonstrate the solidarity of alliance members through their presence in a country under threat.

Command
The higher levels of command in the defence forces are organised in such a way that in peacetime the Chief of Defence, responsible to the Minister of Defence, has command of the army, navy and air force. The Defence Staff assists the Chief of Defence in carrying out this task, and the Chief of Defence Staff is the deputy to the Chief of Defence Forces. Together the Chief of Defence and the Defence Staff make up the supreme command of defence forces. In wartime the combat troops are directed by the Commander Operational Forces of the Defence, who is also NATO Chief.

Security Policy
The new situation obtaining in the field of security policy has furthermore led to the Danish defence forces having a role in the military stabilisation of the part of the area immediately to the southeast of Denmark, from which the threat to Denmark formerly came. The role of the defence forces is carried out by means of bilateral co-operation agreements with Poland, the three Baltic countries and Russia. However, the defence forces also have a defence role within the area of Nordic co-operation and in the NATO Partnership for Peace (PfP), which also includes Finland and Sweden.

The situation of the defence forces is influenced partly by international developments, and partly by the need for most of the equipment to be replaced, which will presumably be done between 2000 and 2010. The armed forces took delivery of most of their equipment in the 1960s and 1970s, and then, on account of the need to economise, second-hand equipment was bought in subsequent years, while existing equipment has been modernised or given an extended life.

Military resources 2000

Army
1 divisional and 7 military region headquarters.
4 brigades and 3 battle groups of brigade size.
281 tanks.
786 other armoured vehicles.
8 Multiple Launch Rocket System launchers.
467 pieces of artillery.
12 anti-tank and 13 other helicopters.
13,000 complement including 4,400 conscripts and 460 women.

Air Force
C. 69 warplanes.
3 fighter/fighter bomber squadrons.
In addition 8 ground-to-air rocket squadrons.
C. 5,000 complement of which 125 are conscripts and 300 women.

Navy
3 corvettes.
4 inspection vessels.
3 submarines.
8 smaller vessels.
14 vessels which by means of modules can be equipped for various duties.
6 minelayers and mine cleaning vehicles, 2 mobile missile batteries and 8 helicopters.
4,060 complement including 496 conscripts and 200 women.

Home Guard
Army Home Guard: 49,000 complement.
Naval Home Guard: 4,400 complement.
Air Force Home Guard: 5,700 complement.
Joint Service Corps: 3,000.
The Naval Home Guard has 40 vessels at its disposal.

Defence budget 2000:
    1.36% of GDP.

Force Numbers
Since 1975 the defence forces have consisted partly of personnel appointed on contract, and partly of conscripts. On an annual basis c. 6,000 are conscripted, corresponding to c. 20% of a given year. National service, which only applies to men, entails 4-12 months' service, depending on the duties to which the conscript is assigned. For certain medical duties there is a four-month service, for ordinary military service the period is 8-9 months, whereas infantry soldiers serve for 10 months; the Royal Lifeguard and the Household Mounted Squadron serve for 12 months. Women can undertake voluntary military service on a contractual basis or under conditions similar to those applying to men doing their compulsory military service.

The Army
The defence forces on full mobilisation number c. 46,000 men. The army's peacetime size is c. 13,000, civilians included. Its operations are directed by The Army Operative Command in Karup and the Army Material Command in Hjørring. The army consists of 15 regiments drawn from the different service branches (battle troops, artillery, etc.) which train the troops up to subdivision level (company, etc.). After this, the companies are given training in mutual co-operation by the larger unit (brigade, military region, etc.) to which they are assigned. Of such larger units, three armoured brigades make up the Danish Division. A fourth is deployed as the Danish International Brigade (DIB). This brigade consists of 4,500 serving and reserve personnel. C. 1/3 of these could be sent at any given time within the framework of the UN or OSCE. This number corresponds ap-

The Danish defence forces also maintain sovereignty over Greenland and the Greenland waters. The fleet patrols the waters with small vessels and inspection ships equipped with helicopters. Here we see two naval cutters in a west Greenland fjord.

proximately to the number of personnel sent by Denmark in mid-1995, primarily within the framework of the UN. DIB forms part of NATO's rapid reaction force.

The Navy

After mobilisation the wartime strength of the navy is c. 7,300. In peacetime the navy accounts for c. 4,060, civilians included. Its operations are led by respectively the headquarters of Admiral Danish Fleet in Århus, the Greenland Command and the Faeroe Islands Command and in overall logistical terms by the Naval Material Command in Copenhagen. The principal naval bases are at Korsør and Frederikshavn.

Daily operations are centred on the squadrons, which in principle consist of ships each serving the same purpose. These squadrons encompass submarines, inspection vessels, corvettes, missile boats, minelayers and various smaller vessels. In addition the navy has mobile missile batteries on shore. A number of the smaller vessels belong to the modular-constructed STANDARD FLEX 300 class. Depending on armament and the training of the crew, these can be used as surveillance vessels, combat vessels or mine-laying or mine-hunting vessels. In addition to their support functions, the bases are in charge of supervising shipping lanes, a task that is divided among three naval districts, and also of training facilities ashore. The navy has permanently stationed units engaged on fisheries inspection and the maintenance of sovereignty off Greenland and the Faeroe Islands. The navy regularly has a corvette on loan to NATO to take part in peace-support operations and it also mans ice-breakers and environmental protection vessels.

The Air Force

The wartime strength of the air force after mobilisation is c. 11,600. Its peacetime strength is c. 5,000, civilians included. Its operations are directed by, respectively, Tactical Air Command Denmark in Karup and Air Material Command in Værløse. Units engaged on flying operations are distributed among the combat

Helicopters pass tanks in the military exercise area near Oksbøl in West Jutland. In modern warfare helicopters play an increasingly important role as close tactical air support and transport for land forces.

squadrons with F-16 fighters at the air force stations of Skrydstrup and Ålborg and among the transport squadrons with C-130 Hercules and Gulfstream-III as well as S-61 helicopters at Karup. The radar stations of the Surveillance and Early Warning group keep a constant watch on Danish air space and can immediately launch fighters in defence and repulse operations, in wartime also using anti-aircraft missiles on orders from the Tactical Air Command, Denmark.

Home Guard

A volunteer force of c. 62,000 constitutes the Home Defence forces, which in peacetime are under the command of the Home Guard Command. The force includes the military home defence forces, organised in territorially defined home defence companies which in wartime form part of the forces of the military regions, and the naval home defence force, which supports the navy, and

Home Guard exercise 1997. The Danish Home Guard is both a force for local defence and a popular movement. Members spend part of their free time in military training. With the terrorist attack on the USA on 11 September 2001 and the focus on international terrorism that followed, interest in the Home Guard increased considerably.

The National Rescue Preparedness Corps

The Danish Emergency Management Agency (DEMA) is responsible for the national rescue preparedness in Denmark. DEMA is an agency under the Ministry of the Interior and Health.

The Preparedness Act is the statutory basis of the activities of DEMA and the national rescue preparedness. Pursuant to section 1 of the Preparedness Act, the principal objective of the national rescue preparedness is to prevent, reduce and remedy injuries to persons and damage to property and the environment in case of accidents and disasters, including war or the imminent danger thereof.

The national rescue preparedness in Denmark comprises the regional divisions of the National Rescue Preparedness Corps. These divisions, stationed at six of seven rescue centres (one centre does not perform conventional rescue preparedness tasks), assist the municipal rescue service and other preparedness services upon request. The principal tasks of the rescue centres are each year to train con-scripts (900 conscripts, who serve for three months and 500 conscripts, who serve for six months) for rescue preparedness and to handle the State's operative regional tasks as part of the overall rescue preparedness. The overall rescue preparedness in Denmark is designed with the aim of being a single-strand, flexible preparedness, operational at three levels. The three-level preparedness is intended for responding to accidents and disasters occurring without prior warning.

DEMA also performs a series of internationally oriented tasks presupposing co-operation across national borders. A fully equipped operational taskforce designed according to the specific type of disasters can be deployed within 12 hours. The national rescue preparedness personnel has been brought into action in connection with earthquake disasters, floods, forest fires, refugee crises, etc. DEMA also takes part in a number of international exercises and discussions as well as close co-operation within the framework of the EU, NATO the UN and the OECD.   DEMA

finally include the air force home defence force supporting the air force Surveillance and Early Warning group by monitoring low-altitude air space, assisting with surveillance tasks, etc.

Michael H. Clemmensen

Church and Religion

Ecclesiastical and religious matters in Denmark are subject to the Constitution, the main principles being established by the stipulation that the *Evangelical Lutheran Church* – as the established Church of Denmark – shall be supported by the State, and also by provisions on freedom of religion, speech and assembly. State support is partly moral and political (Sunday observance legislation and legislation on church matters), partly financial and administrative (contributions to clergy salaries and pensions, the collection of church taxes, the maintenance of the national church governance by means of a Ministry of Ecclesiastical Affairs and diocesan administration, supervision, advisory services, etc.).

Of religious communities, the established church is by far the largest (encompassing 85.4% of the population in 1998). Alongside the established church various other *Christian churches* are represented in Denmark and have been accorded the status of officially recognised religious communities. These are (in order of size) the Roman Catholic Church with c. 35,000 members, the

Danish Baptist Church with c. 5,500 adult members and the Pentecostal churches with c. 5,000 members; of communities with 3,000 members and under mention should be made of the Seventh Day Adventists, the Catholic Apostolic Church, the Reformed Churches in Fredericia and Copenhagen, the Salvation Army, the Methodist Church, the Anglican Church and the Russian Orthodox Church in Copenhagen. In addition, with a rather more distant relationship to Christianity, there are Jehovah's Witnesses with c. 15,000 members and the Church of Jesus Christ of the Latter-Day Saints (Mormons) with c. 4,500 members. Outside the National Church there are nine other independent recognised Lutheran congregations of Grundtvigian origin. (The Grundtvigian and other elective congregations form part of the National Church) The German minority in Southern Jutland has its own parishes within the National Church, with its own clergy in the four southern Jutland towns of Haderslev, Aabenraa, Sønderborg and Tønder, in addition to which they have six independent Lutheran congregations outside the National Church.

Among the numerically smaller, but characteristically Christian congregations mention must finally be made of the Moravian Brethren in Christiansfeld and the Unitarian Church in Copenhagen (The Free Church Congregation), which in 1907 was expelled from the National Church on account of its denial of certain central Christian doctrines. The oldest of the *non-Christian* communities in Denmark is the Jewish Community, recognised in 1814, with c. 3,100 members and with a synagogue in Copenhagen. During the last decades of the 20th century, the largest of the non-Christian communities has been dominated by Muslim immigrants; on the basis of the number of immigrants from Muslim countries now resident in Denmark, the number is estimated to be c. 150,000 (2000), made up of a number of mutually independent Islamic communities. Official recognition has been given to a number of communities, enabling them to offer religious support to foreign Christians living in Denmark. This applies to the Norwegian, Swedish and German congregations in Copenhagen, all of them Lutheran, the Anglican community in Copenhagen, the German and French Reformed communities in Copenhagen and Fredericia and the Russian-Orthodox Church in Copenhagen. Greek Orthodox services are only occasionally held in Denmark. Icelandic and Finnish Lutherans are offered religious support through the Icelandic community in Copenhagen and the Finnish Church in Denmark. The Roman Catholic Church in Denmark offers Roman Catholics from all parts of the world who are resident in Denmark the support of its churches, which are found throughout the country.

The form of recognition (before 1969) enjoyed by the Norwegian, Swedish and English communities in Copenhagen, the Roman Catholic, Russian Orthodox and Danish Reformed communities, the Baptist Community and the Methodist Church as well as the Jewish Community, allows them to keep legal registers and to issue legally valid personal documents (certificates of marriage and baptism). This is to be seen in the light of the fact that primary civil registration (registration for the central personal register) of all citizens in Denmark is otherwise undertaken by the National Church clergy and church offices; similarly funerals are carried out with the National Church clergy acting as the authority.

With the 1969 Matrimonial Act, state recognition ceased to have such widespread implications. Since 1969, the Danish State has permitted the clerics of all other recognised communities, both Christian and Non-Christian, to perform legally va-

During service in the Danish National Church, the priest distributes Holy Communion in both kinds to each individual communicant. Farum Church, northwest of Copenhagen, was built in the 12th century; the chancel is so narrow that fewer than ten communicants at a time can kneel at the altar-rail. The lower part of the altarpiece in this church, which dates from 1599, consists of panels containing the words of consecration written in Latin and Danish.

On 2 April 1995, Lise-Lotte Rebel was installed as Denmark's first woman bishop. She is seen here after the consecration in St Olai Church in Elsinore together with the bishop of Copenhagen, Erik Norman Svendsen, the bishop of Greenland, Kristian Mørch, who is walking behind her. The cope she is wearing was designed and embroidered by Queen Margrethe II in 1986. On 28 May 1995, Kristian Mørch was succeeded by Sofie Petersen, who thereby became the second woman bishop in the national church.

lid wedding ceremonies, though they have a duty to report them to the civil authorities and they do not have the right to keep legal church registers. Both forms of state recognition give tax benefits in the form of the right to receive regular tax-deductible financial contributions from private individuals. However, such recognition is only granted when a number of more precisely defined organisational and theological/ideological requirements are fulfilled; for instance, the Church of Scientology has failed in its application for this kind of recognition.

In addition, there is a number of small organised religious communities (e.g. the Bahais and a number of Buddhist centres), which like the other recognised religious communities have the right to perform marriage ceremonies with civil validity and to receive tax-deductible gifts from private individuals.

Alongside the recognised religious communities, the provisions in the Constitution concerning the freedom of belief and association provide for the possibility of establishing individual religious associations. A number of such associations are often described as 'new religious groups', but on account of their private nature it has been impossible to register them statistically, and they often seem to represent religious and philosophical trends rather than constituting organised religious communities or denominations which can be registered as such. At all events, the borderlines between such groups and religious communities proper are difficult to define, and members of these groups will often fail to de-register from the National Church.

In church matters, the Kingdom of Denmark is divided into 12 dioceses, including those of Greenland and the Faeroe Islands. In the 10 Danish dioceses the National Church offers its members the services of just under 2,000 clergy; the country is divided into 2,176 parishes, which are again combined into 1,366 livings and 111 deaneries. The National Church is governed with the Folketing as the legislative body and the government (The Ministry of Ecclesiastical Affairs) as the supreme administrative body. Otherwise, however, the National Church is run on democratic principles on the basis of specially elected ecclesiastical bodies in collaboration with the clergy: in the individual parishes there is an elected parish council, in which the clergy are ex officio members, but where the other members are elected directly from and by the members of the national church in that parish. (Participation in elections is very low indeed, and in many places there are uncontested elections or agreed elections with only one list). The parish councils exercise a decisive influence on the choice of clergy in the individual livings, and the diocesan bishops are chosen by the diocesan council and the clergy together. The bishops manage the diocesan administration and – with the support of the deans and the deanery committees – ensure that the various duties of the national church in individual parishes and livings are properly carried out; the administration of the National Church in individual parishes is the responsibility of the parish councils, which under supervision are responsible for finances and fabric maintenance. Church services and religious advice are the responsibility of the clergy (with the assistance of other church representatives, e.g. organists and vergers) who at the same time, assisted by parish clerks and the church offices, keep the church registers and act as funeral authorities. The clergy of the National Church are university trained at the state-run theological faculties in Copenhagen and Århus, which also offer an academic theological training to all, irrespective of ecclesiastical or confessional affiliation.

Jørgen Stenbæk

Church History

By about 700 AD, Willibrord, the 'apostle of the Netherlands' was already carrying out missionary work among the Danes, but it was only with the missionary activities of Ansgar, from 826, that Christianity gained a foothold in Denmark. As Archbishop of Hamburg-Bremen in present-day northern Germany, Ansgar was able to ensure that churches were built in the trading centres of Hedeby (Schleswig) and Ribe. The first document from the Papal See in Rome to a Danish king dates from 864. Christianity became the religion of the king when Harald Bluetooth allowed himself to be baptised by the priest Poppo c. 950. Scandinavian heathendom, however, died hard, and the words on the large Jelling stone to the effect that King Harald 'made the Danes Christian' must be taken with a pinch of salt.

In the Dano-English kingdom at the beginning of the 11th century, Danish church life came under English influence. The Archbishop of Hamburg-Bremen, however, was able to maintain his authority over the Danish church until the founding of the Danish (Nordic) archbishopric in Lund (in present-day Sweden) in 1104. In one area after another, relations between the Church and society were organised according to the wishes of the Holy See. The years from c. 1100 to the mid-13th century are the great age of church building in Denmark; churches were now made of stone (brick from the middle of the 12th century), and throughout the Middle Ages many churches were decorated with frescoes. In addition, a large number of monasteries and convents were founded in the 12th and 13th centuries. The most important Danish theologian of the Middle Ages was Anders Sunesen (d. 1228). The harmony

The late 16th-century predella for the altarpiece in Tinglev church in Southern Jutland. With the Reformation the sermon in the vernacular became the centrepiece of church services. In good Lutheran manner, the preacher is pointing to the crucified Christ as the focal point for those meeting for divine service. The women in the congregation are sitting on the right, the men standing on the left.

existing in the 13th century between Church and Crown – reflected in Jutlandic Law, 1241 – was replaced in the course of the following century by a series of conflicts between the king and the archbishop. After the middle of the 14th century, King Valdemar Atterdag started moving towards a national or even state church, and this was an important condition for the Reformation in the 16th century.

The Reformation
In the 1520s the Lutheran Reformation movement spread throughout Germany, via Holstein and Schleswig to Viborg, Malmö and Funen. The first evangelical hymn book in the vernacular was printed in Malmö (in present-day Sweden) in 1528, and in Copenhagen the evangelical preachers proclaimed their beliefs in *Confessio Hafniensis*, The Copenhagen Confession. Hans Tausen was the most outstanding evangelical preacher in the Reformation struggle, which lasted until 1536, when the Lutheran Christian III and the nobility had overcome the peasantry and burghers in the civil war known as the Count's War. The Catholic bishops were imprisoned and dismissed, and at the meeting of the national assembly in Copenhagen in October 1536, the power of the Catholic bishops was finally eradicated, and Church property was taken over by

the Crown, which thereby trebled its possessions. With the Reformation, the church became a Lutheran church owing allegiance to the Crown, and Lutheranism the only permitted religion; the university, schools, welfare and hospitals were reorganised, though they went through a prolonged period of straitened circumstances. The place of the former Catholic bishops was taken by seven Lutheran 'superintendents', who were consecrated in 1537 and soon again called bishops. As its most important religious reform, the *Church Ordinance* (1537-1539) introduced the divine service in the vernacular, with emphasis on the sermon and the congregation's singing. Christian III's Danish Bible from 1550, the main literary achievement of the century, must be seen in the same perspective. In 1569 came the first authorised Danish hymn book, 'Hans Thomesen's Hymn Book'. Until his death in 1560, Peder Palladius, the Bishop of Zealand, led the way in building up the Lutheran church and the people's Lutheran education. Niels Hemmingsen, a pupil of Melanchthon, was one of the most learned theologians in Protestant Europe in the second half of the 16th century, and during this same period Hans Christensen Sthen wrote his hymns.

Nikolai Frederik Severin Grundtvig, 1783-1872, was a Danish author for almost 75 years. Most of his many works have not been read by great numbers either in his own day or subsequently. His ideas and attitudes are more important than the individual titles.

Grundtvig broke through the framework of the literary institutions and encompassed the entire population with his projects. His thoughts were first disseminated through his highly singable poetry, and then the teachers at the *folk high schools*; these taught according to no syllabus and led to no examinations, and on the basis of Grundtvig's loosely formulated plans they arose in various parts of the country, starting with Rødding in 1844, but in particular experienced rapid growth after the defeat in the 1864 war. Academic and narrow vocational training was here replaced by a general preparation for everyday life as a Danish citizen.

As a rule, Grundtvig's patriotic songs combined a national historical stance with a Christian view of mankind, and especially after the loss of the fleet in 1807 and of Norway in 1814 this played an important part in building up a new Danish identity based on a straightforward, energetic, active role in society. In his many original and translated hymns, which were mainly published in his *Sang-Værk*, 1-5 (1837-1881), he brought renewal to the National Church of Denmark by imparting a living, homely character to the great Christian festivals. Even today, his hymns dominate the authorised hymn book, so much so that even non-churchgoing Danes can scarcely imagine Christmas, Easter and Whitsuntide, weddings or funerals without the inclusion of some verses by Grundtvig.

Grundtvig's work as a theologian, scholar, poet and popular educator was epoch-making. In *Nordens Mytologi* (1808, The Mythology of the North), he was the first to see an inner cohesion in the pagan myths, and in a greatly expanded, revised edition in 1832 he was able to turn them into the paradigm of a modern Nordic view of life. In practice, his theology concentrated on the experience of baptism and holy communion, both proclaimed by words from the lips of Christ. From the 1830s, on the background of a Christian faith brought to life in this way, he placed increasing emphasis on conditions of life on earth, keeping a suitable pace with the slow political developments in Denmark towards democracy. He advocated a freedom that ensured the individual citizen the same potential for life and action in everyday life as that citizen would wish for his neighbours. By happiness, he understood the right undisturbedly to be oneself, without an eye to greatness and honour. He discovered the untapped abilities in the rural population corresponding to the distribution of population: he was talking about the majority of Danes. At a time which cultivated an intellectual and artistic elite, he adopted the ordinary man's – and woman's – point of view, for in the Danes he saw a loving people with a patient female character that endures through some inner strength and finally conquers.

Despite stormy transitions from one phase to another in the course of his own life, he taught himself and others to look forward to a gentle growth in nature's divinely created order. The way of the world he saw as an enigma that would be made clear at the end of time. On the basis of a kind of family feeling with everything human, he thought in terms of comprehensive fellowships: that of the congregation stretching all the way back to Christ, that of the history of the world stretching all the way back to Paradise, that of the history of Denmark going all the way back to King Dan. He saw every form of compulsion in intellectual and spiritual life as being perverse. His great argument was for choice cutting through congealed institutions and lifeless writing. He advocated oral formulation, whether spoken or sung, and he made conversation with a lively exchange of views between the parties into his main educational tool. He stressed the significance of a native language that had been handed down in its purest form by women and unlearned peasants. As a poet he often combined content and form in potent images, the intent and meaning of which were prophetically obscure, and at other times he was able as no one else in his day to speak simply and comprehensibly on the most elevated subjects. As a member of parliament during the first decade of Danish democracy he could be extremely realistic, always giving voice to an anti-authoritarian attitude; he supported peaceful change rather than revolution. With Grundtvig, compromise became a way of life in Danish politics and society. He left behind him religious and popular movements which in the folk high schools, the church, the parliament and in the public at large are still influential in Danish society.

Flemming Lundgreen-Nielsen

Orthodoxy and Pietism

State control of the church was tightened in the hundred years from the death of Christian III to the introduction of absolutism in 1660, and like the most authoritative theologians, for instance Bishop Jesper Brochmand, changing governments were on the look-out for any deviation from the true faith (i.e. Lutheran orthodoxy). The King's Law of 1665 established that the king was to make all decisions concerning the church, and Danish Law of 1683 defined 'the King's religion', i.e. the State Church, as being in conformity with the Bible, the three Creeds of the ancient Church, the Augsburg Confession and Luther's Little Catechism. In 1699 an official hymn book was published, the second of its kind, which was quickly given the name of 'Kingo's Hymn Book' after the Bishop of Odense, Thomas Kingo, the greatest hymn-writer of Danish Baroque at the transition from orthodoxy to 18th-century pietism. Halle Pietism, so called after the German city of Halle, which in the 1730s was raised to the status of 'court religion' under Christian VI, made its impact in missionary initiatives (e.g. the mission to Tranquebar and Hans Egede's mission to Greenland) and an extensive reform of the laws governing church discipline, confirmation and schooling. The Moravian Brethren also made their entry into Denmark, working quietly in the background until the Brethren established their community in Christiansfeld in 1773. The great hymn writer of pietism was Hans Adolph Brorson.

The National Church and its Breadth

The Enlightenment in the second half of the 18th century led to a sharp criticism of the church and dogma, but also to an ecclesiastically rationalist theology, against which both the Romantic and evangelical movements reacted. The evangelical movement, which was partly rooted in the agricultural reforms in the 1780s and the School Act of 1814, was to have a decisive impact on church life in the 19th century. The movement split during the century; the fact that its main ideas led to 'movements within the church' is a result of the abolition of absolutism in 1848, the Constitution of 1849 and not least the influence of N.F.S. Grundtvig. The Constitution introduced the principle of religious freedom, but not of religious equality, as the state was given responsibility for supporting the *Evangelical Lutheran Church* as the Danish *National Church*. The dogmatic foundation of the church was unchanged. The Constitution promised a representative, synodal church constitution, though the 'promise' has never been fulfilled. The second half of the 19th century saw a number of Acts seeking to accommodate the Grundtvigian wish for independence: the compulsion to attend the local parish church was abolished in 1855, compulsory baptism was abandoned in 1857, permission was granted for elective congregations in 1868 and in 1872 permission was given to those refusing to attend services conducted by their parish priest to bring in a pastor from outside. Grundtvig's 'view on the Church' – first expressed in 1825 and leading to a grandiose renewal of the Danish hymn tradition – emphasises the living word of God, orally proclaimed in baptism and holy communion in the presence of the congregation as what creates and sustains the Church.

A contrast to the views of Grundtvig and his followers was represented by the call for repentance and conversion and the view of the Bible as the word of God in the evangelical

Søren Kierkegaard, 1813-1855. 'Geniuses are like thunderstorms – they go against the wind, terrify people, cleanse the air'. Thus wrote Søren Kierkegaard in 1849. He saw himself as a genius and related his intellectual brilliance to 'being in the minority'. He always went against the wind, against prevailing movements and systems, and he did so because he believed that 'truth is always only to be found in the minority'. In opposition to the majority, the abstract, he posited the concrete, 'the single individual'.

Søren Kierkegaard lived all his life in his native city of Copenhagen. His peculiar childhood in his home on Nytorv bore the stamp of his father's pietism and melancholy. He studied theology at the University of Copenhagen 1830-1840; for a considerable period, however, theology played a secondary role and was replaced by literature, theatre, politics and philosophy – and a dissolute life that was partly fashioned as a challenge to the strict and sombre Christian views that characterised his home. But after a religious awakening in 1838 and his father's death that same year, he once more set about studying theology and graduated in that subject in July 1840.

Two months later, Kierkegaard became engaged to the nine-years-younger Regine Olsen. But since 'in a religious sense', he had 'from childhood been promised' to God, he could not marry Regine. After thirteen intense months, he broke off the engagement in October 1841. The unhappy love affair made a deep impression on him for the rest of his life, and set him going as the author of *Either/Or* and *Two Edifying Discourses*, which were published on the same day in 1843.

However, as early as 1838 Kierkegaard had published his first book, *From the Papers of One Still Living*, a critical analysis of Hans Christian Andersen's novel *Only a Fiddler*, and in 1841 he had defended his doctoral dissertation, *On the Concept of Irony*. His philosophical, psychological, religious and Christian publications, which make up some 40 titles, fall into two phases: 1843-1846 and 1847-1851. In addition to *Either/Or* and a number of edifying discourses, the first phase includes titles such as *Fear and Trembling*, *The Concept of Anxiety*, *Philosophical Fragments* and *Concluding Unscientific Postscript*, this latter representing the transition between the two phases. The second, Christian, phase, consists of books such as *Works of Love*, *Christian Discourses*, *The Sickness unto Death* and *Practice in Christianity*. In addition there are the journals, some 64 notebooks and diaries which Kierkegaard kept from 1833 to 1855, and which give an insight into his way of working, into his 'back-stage rehearsals'.

In his work, Søren Kierkegaard describes the various possibilities of existence, especially its three principal stages, which he calls 'spheres of existence': the aesthetical, the ethical and the religious, demonstrating their inadequacy in relation to the truly Christian. Man only becomes an authentic self by relating himself to God who created him. And he can only become a true self by professing his faith in Christ and having his sins forgiven by Him. But 'in addition to professing Christ, there is also the demand to act as a Christian'.

Therefore truth is always a truth in action, just as faith is always a faith in works. Kierkegaard saw himself as a religious author with the task of 'presenting Christianity'. He wanted to 'clear the air', to have all sense illusions and all hypocrisy scraped off and to find his way back to 'the Christianity of the New Testament'.

On this background, he embarked during his last years on an attack on the church authorities and the Christianity they officially preached. He started his 'battle with the Church' at the end of 1854 with a series of newspaper articles and continued it with great astuteness, radical views and journalistic flair in the pamphlets he called *The Moment* 1-9.

In October 1855 he collapsed in the street, ill and burned out; he was taken to hospital where he died five weeks later.

Through German translations, Søren Kierkegaard's fame became established outside Denmark about the turn of the century, and his work achieved great international significance after the First World War. For instance, he became the great source of inspiration for dialectical theology, for existential philosophy, the philosophy of dialogue and for existential theology. From the 1960s to the middle of the 1980s he fell into neglect, but since then his work has undergone a dramatic renaissance, not only among scholars, but also in the broader public, both nationally and internationally – not least in the countries that have been fashioned by marxist thoughts and views of life. In addition, he has been discovered by fresh disciplines such as philosophy of language, phenomenology and literary theory.

The renewed interest in Kierkegaard is partly connected with the longing for an overall understanding of life on both a scientific and philosophical level and also an ethical and existential level. And likewise, it is linked to a renewed search for answers to the fundamental questions on the meaning of the individual, the foundations for ethics and the relationship between religion/Christianity and society.

'There are two kinds of geniuses. The characteristic of the one is roaring, but the lightning is meager and rarely strikes; the other kind is characterized by reflection by which it constrains itself or restrains the roaring. But the lightning is all the more intensive; with the speed and sureness of lightning, it hits the selected particular points – and is fatal.' Søren Kierkegaard belonged to this latter kind of genius.

Niels Jørgen Cappelørn

Home Mission, founded in 1853 and from 1861 under the firm leadership of Vilhelm Beck. The rationalist criticism of revelation dating from the Enlightenment was behind the debate on biblical views, and that debate is still not concluded at the end of the 20th century.

Like Grundtvig, Søren Kierkegaard also countered the challenge from the age of Enlightenment with his idiosyncratic philosophical and theological writings; they were produced in confrontation with German idealist philosophy (G.W.F. Hegel). Kierkegaard and Grundtvig acted as counterweights to German influence in university theology, and they have been crucially important for the teaching of the National Church long after their own day.

Alongside ecclesiastical Grundtvigianism, in which it was the clergy who held sway, there was also a popular Grundtvigian wing related to the folk high school movement, influencing the development of society through their educational work and their establishment of associations. As for Home Mission, the 'rural' movement clashed to some extent with its 'urban' counterpart in the Copenhagen Home Mission that was founded in 1865, which believed that preaching to effect conversion should be accompanied by welfare work in the city conditions resulting from industrialisation.

Partly on the English pattern, the 19th century in Denmark was the great age of religious associations and foundations; the Danish Bible Society was founded in 1814, Danish Missionary Association in 1821, and from the end of the century the Copenhagen Church Foundation (1896, from 1974 known as the Church Foundation), which was behind the building of a number of the architecturally interesting Copenhagen churches. The 19th century was also the age of great church figures; men like the bishops J.P. Mynster and H.L. Martensen were at the same time prominent in social and cultural life. Søren Kierkegaard fought their kind of churchmanship, his protest culminating in his one-man 'church battle' in the last year of his life, 1855.

The Twentieth Century
1903 saw the Parish Council Act, heralding a process of democratisation that has continued ever since; thus, for instance, the participation of the national church in ecumenical work, enacted by law in 1989, was given a democratic structure. This development has been of significance for the social status of the clergy. Since 1947 women have been able to apply for posts as priests and it looks as though they will finally represent a majority of the clergy. In 1995, the first female bishop was elected. During the 20th century, all formal connection between school and church has ceased; however, Christianity still has a place as a subject in school timetables. Theologically speaking, the most important new departure of the 20th century was the periodical 'Tidehverv' (from 1926), representing an independent Danish dialectical theology which in addition to Luther and Kierkegaard based itself on Otto Møller and Jakob Knudsen. However, none of the century's main currents (liberal theology, Karl Barth's theology, Tidehverv, existential theology, creation theology, political theology, feminist theology, etc.) have established themselves in the popular mind. In particular, three theologians have been of significance for the position of the church and Christianity in the political and cultural landscape of the 20th century, i.e. Hal Koch, P.G. Lindhardt and K.E. Løgstrup. In political and cultural life, it appears to be accepted that the National Church is to be left untouched, and after a fall in the 1960s and 1970s, the growing number of baptisms and other church ceremonies in the last two decades of the century suggest that the (national) church has by no means lost its place in people's consciousness.

Steffen Kjeldgaard-Pedersen

International Relations

The global economic, political and cultural internationalisation of the post war years has, especially along with the economic integration of Europe made its mark on Danish foreign policy and Danish participation in international co-operation.

Foreign Policy

Danish foreign policy aims to ensure Danish security by establishing the greatest possible economic well-being and promoting Danish standards of right and wrong. Denmark's international relations can be seen on the basis of three contexts. A global circle characterised by co-operation in the UN, links with the Third World and by global economic integration; an Atlantic circle governed by a close relationship to the USA in security policy; a European circle determined by developments within the EU; and finally a local circle determined by developments within the Baltic states and relationships with the Nordic countries.

During the Cold War an attempt was made to create a balance in Danish foreign policy between relations with the USA via NATO, membership of the EC, now the EU, and active participation in the UN and international co-operation in assistance to under-developed countries. There were four principle cornerstones to Danish foreign policy: NATO, Europe, the UN and the Nordic countries. This policy of maintaining a balance has since been replaced by one based on the EU. However, Denmark has increasingly become an active minor state taking its own initiatives, especially outside the EU.

EU

The most important element in Danish foreign policy is the EU. The end of the Cold War and the unification of Germany has reinforced this trend. At the same time Germany has become a central foreign-policy partner. The immediate security threat to Danish territory has disappeared. Instead, Denmark's position as a neighbour to the new Baltic states and Poland and to both Scandinavian and European countries has given rise to an active Danish policy aimed at the admission of the Baltic countries into the EU and NATO. Considerable popular resistance to

Denmark has been the principal supplier of soldiers for the UN's peace-keeping operations. Most actions have been peaceful, but in Bosnia in 1994 and 1995 Danish UN troops were drawn into the war, and several were killed. The Danish UN soldiers are part of the 4,500-man Danish international brigade established in 1992, which must be capable of turning out at short notice to undertake duties for the UN and NATO. Thus, Denmark took part in NATO's military action in Kosovo in 1999. Denmark cannot participate in EU-actions.

further integration into the EU has led to Danish opt-outs from some areas of EU co-operation.

The North

The North has been and is still an important ideological partner for co-operation, as is seen especially in the work of the Nordic Council and the Baltic Council. The broad community of cultural interests, the Nordic passport union and the free internal labour market have created close ties between Denmark and the other Nordic countries. One of the great challenges for Denmark is to combine this community with its European policy. The Nordic countries' EU policies differ increasingly. Finland joined the euro from the beginning while the Danes voted against joining the euro in a referendum in 2000. At the same time Norway, Iceland, Greenland and the Faeroe Islands are outside the EU.

NATO

Denmark has worked to maintain NATO as the central institution for political security in Europe, and it has been important to Denmark that the USA has continued as an active participant in NATO. In security policy Denmark has positioned herself close to the USA. Thus, Denmark took part in the American attacks on Afghanistan in response to the terrorism attacks on the USA on 11 September. From 2002 Danish assistance aims at providing assistance to Afghanistan and combating terrorism.

In addition, like the other European countries, Denmark is a member of the Organisation for Security and Co-operation in Europe, OSCE.

UN

The UN has always enjoyed strong support from Denmark, both econo-

Since 1985 the organisation known as Operation Day's Work has organised an annual day of work. Students from grades 9-12 participate. The object is to collect funds for some assistance project. The pupils cut lawns, weed gardens, clean windows, etc. In 2001 Operation Day's Work produced 5.7 million kroner.

mically and politically. Denmark participated in its establishment in 1945 and has taken part in over half of the UN peace-keeping operations. Denmark has also actively sought to ensure that the UN acts as the central agency for aid to the Third World. The UN's work on human rights, the environment, social developments, common security and democracy, has been fully backed by Denmark. From 1995, Denmark has embarked on a more critical policy and called for reforms of the UN system. Furthermore Denmark has taken the initiative for the establishment of a standby multinational brigade capable of rapid UN deployment.

Danish Assistance Policy

Denmark is one of the few countries in the world to donate 1% of its gross national income to the work of international development. The business community and popular movements over the years have been actively involved in developing an assistance policy, partly by participating in a special council and agency for that purpose. Non-governmental organi-

Women in Bangladesh learn about hygiene and how to remove arsenic from drinking water as part of a project receiving Danish assistance. Bangladesh is one of Danida's (Danish International Development Assistance) 15 programme co-operation countries.

sations (NGOs) take care of significant areas of bilateral assistance. Almost half the Danish assistance is given through international organisations. In bilateral co-operation, Denmark seeks to support the poorest population groups in the 15 Third World countries with which Denmark principally co-operates. Having revised and reduced the assistance in 2002, Denmark focuses on the combating of poverty, the development of trade and industry and good governance.

In addition there is emphasis on the furtherance of economic growth in the Third World, protection of the environment, respect for human rights and the role of women in the developmental process. Almost half the direct assistance goes to Africa. Since 1999 initiatives aimed at preventing conflicts are supported by a special section in the Ministry of Foreign Affairs.

Hans-Henrik Holm

Production and Communications

The Economy

The Danish economy is small and open, very dependent on trade with other countries and without any possibility of influencing international trading conditions or central economic factors, e.g. interest rates. The value of both exports and imports constitutes c. 1/3 of GDP. About 2/3 of foreign trade is with other EU countries. Germany is clearly the most important bilateral trading partner, but Sweden and Great Britain, are also of significance. Outside the EU, Denmark trades especially with Norway, the USA and Japan.

On account of the great importance of foreign trade for the domestic economy, Denmark is very keen to deal freely in goods and services with other countries. Consequently, Denmark has joined collaborative organisations such as the EU, OECD and GATT (known as WTO from 1995) and within the framework of these has striven actively to remove obstacles to free trade.

Since the Second World War, the composition of exports has undergone a great change. Industrial exports are greater than agricultural exports and play an ever-increasing role in the export of Danish products. The export of agricultural products used to dominate. Thus, in the late 1990s, industrial exports made up almost 80% of total export values, while the share of agricultural exports was just under 11%. Rather more than 26% of industrial exports consist of machines and instruments, while chemical products and industrially manufactured agricultural products, including tinned meat, account for c. 12% and 4% respectively. After a considerable growth in the 1970s and 1980s, the export of services stagnated in the 1990s, and in 1999 it accounted for c. 22% of total exports.

Industry's import of raw materials and half-finished products, including energy, and of machines and other capital equipment accounts for c. 70% of total imports. In the 1980s, Danish oil production rose considerably, and this has effected a steep fall in energy imports. The remaining just under 30% of imports generally speaking encompass consumer products, including cars. Denmark also has a considerable import of foreign services.

Economic Policy

Denmark seeks as far as possible to regulate economic activity and inflation through fiscal policy. Monetary policy has to an increasing extent been aimed at supporting exchange rate policy, the object of which is to ensure a stable exchange rate for the Danish krone. Since the Second World War, Denmark has taken part in a number of international pro-

Although originally developed for the domestic market, Danish windmills have become a major export product. Here we see part of a windmill farm in the state of Tamil Nadu in India, containing altogether 10 mills from Vestas Wind Systems A/S; each mill can produce 500,000 kW. With support from the Ministry of Foreign Affairs (Danida) a local windmill industry is being developed in India, which is the fastest growing market in the world for windmills.

grammes of exchange rate co-operation: the Bretton Woods Agreement from its start in 1948 to its breakdown in 1971; since then the purely European exchange rate agreements: from 1972 to 1979 the 'snake' and then the European Monetary System (EMS), which was developed into an Economic and Monetary Union (EMU) in 1999. However, Denmark has chosen to stay outside the EMU, but participates in the ERM2 with a central parity at DKK 7.46 per euro and a fluctuation band of +/- 2,25%.

The level of Danish interest rates is closely linked to developments in international interest rates. From the beginning of the 1960s to about 1990 a higher Danish interest rate was needed to ensure a sufficient inflow of capital to finance the deficit on the balance of payments current account. The liberalisation of capital movements in the 1980s, however, has meant that the Danish interest level increasingly reflects the credibility of the krone rate. In principle, the Danish bond interest rate should be equal to that in Germany, fixed with a premium for the expected percentual change in the exchange rate against the euro. Expectations for exchange rate developments will normally be determined by historical changes in exchange rates and by conditions such as inflation trends, budgetary developments and the balance of payments. A favourable economic climate in Denmark compared with the euro area will reduce the risk of a reduction in the value of the krone and thus, everything else being equal, lead to a narrowing of the interest rate difference between Denmark and the euro area.

Main Lines in Economic Developments from 1960

Throughout the 1960s and until the first oil crisis in 1973, Denmark, like the rest of Europe, experienced a period of high growth in which the average growth in GDP was more than 4.5%. This high growth rate meant an increased demand for labour, which among other things was met by increased participation on the part of women. During this period there was almost full employment. This affected wage developments, which showed significant growth in the 1960s. In the 1970s, when there were strong price rises internationally, the rate of wage increases rose accordingly.

The 1973 oil crisis led to a significant international recession which also had a negative influence on Danish production and employment, and again an attempt was made to counteract this by means of change in fiscal policy on the part of both the liberal government in 1974 and the new Social Democratic government in 1975. Thus, for instance, VAT was lowered from 15 to 9.25% for a time in 1975-1976, but an improvement in international trade conditions remained elusive, and the result was a further deterioration in the balance of payments, which had shown a deficit since 1963. This led to a new change in economic policy. Financial policy

GDP at fixed prices of 1995
billion kroner

Balance of payments as a percentage of GDP

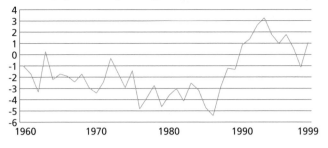

Average unemployment rate

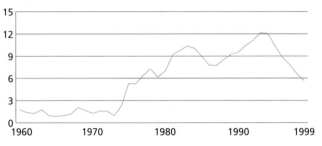

Inflation rates

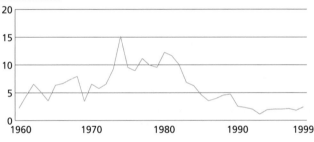

Average bond yields

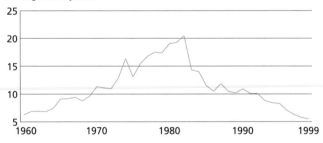

Denmark's foreign debt as a percentage of GDP

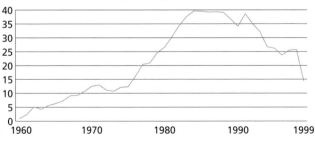

was tightened a little, while demand was made favourable to imports by measures such as energy savings in the building sector and increased public service, which brought about a strong growth in employment, but a corresponding deterioration in public finances.

The second oil crisis arose in 1979, some of the consequences being rising inflation and interest rates. The balance of payments deficit grew further and employment fell, which brought about a change in exchange policy. Consequently, the krone was devalued twice in the autumn of 1979 within the framework of the EMS, but despite this, economic activity fell in both 1980 and 1981. The decade from 1973 to 1982, known as the period of stagflation was thus characterised by low economic growth averaging less than 2% a year and by a relatively high wage inflation of over 13% a year on average.

When interest rates rose to over 20% at the beginning of the 1980s, the national debt grew drastically. In the light of the poor economic progress the Social Democratic government resigned in September 1982 and was followed by a coalition led by the Conservatives, known as the four-leaf clover government. This government initiated a tight incomes policy which included the suspension of indexation of pay and benefits, i.e. automatic compensation to wage and salary earners for price rises. Legislation was introduced in 1986 finally abolishing this indexation. Furthermore, public expenditure policy was further tightened, and a firm policy on exchange rates introduced, according to which the krone was tied to the ECU and the German mark. The economic and political measures together with a liberalisation of capital movement between Denmark and abroad led to a strong fall in Danish interest rates, which therefore approached those of Germany in the mid-1980s. The lower interest rate led to rises in property prices, increased private expenditure and not least greater investment until 1986.

From 1983 to 1986 annual economic growth averaged over 3.5%, and unemployment fell to below 8% in 1987, the second-lowest in the EU. The favourable economic development meant further that for the first time since 1975, the national budget deficit was transformed into a surplus in 1986 and 1987.

This rise did not result in new inflationary pressures. On the contrary the rate of increase in consumer prices fell from over 12% at the beginning of the 1980s to under 3% in 1990. This development is due to the greater wages restrained and currency stability of the period as well as to lower overseas inflation. In an economy as open as the Danish about 1/3 of total price inflation can be ascribed to development in import prices.

The strong rise in activity and deterioration of competitiveness on the other hand led to record deficits on the balance of payments and a surge in overseas debt, which in 1986 amounted to about 260 billion kroner, or almost 40% of the GDP. Against this background and for the sake of the economy, the government put through a number of indirect and direct tax rises (nicknamed the potato cure), including a tax on consumer loans, and a tax reform the main aim of which was to promote personal savings. At the same time an attempt was made by way of indirect tax policy to promote competitiveness. The attempt was successful. The growth in private consumption and investments was re-

duced and even fell for a couple of years, which led to a noticeable drop in imports. With exports growing at the same time, the result was such a strong improvement in the trade balance that in 1990 the balance of payments showed a surplus for the first time in almost thirty years. With this, Denmark was able to start reducing its foreign debts, which by this time had reached over 320 billion kroner.

The package of indirect taxes and the tax reform, however, did not solve the problems of balance at home. Property prices fell, and unemployment rose appreciably. The recession was worsened by an international slow-down at the beginning of the 1990s, which diminished export potential in some of Denmark's principal markets, Great Britain and Sweden. However, this was partly compensated for in 1990-1991 by an export boom to a reunited Germany, though the German market was also hit by stagnation 1993-1994. Economic growth in the period from 1987 to 1993 was on average under 1% a year.

An investigation leading to criticism of the administration in certain refugee cases brought about the resignation of the non-socialist government in January 1993. It was replaced by a coalition led by the Social-Democrats which tried to stimulate production and employment by relaxing fiscal policy, partly through a tax reform and the abolition of various measures from the potato cure which had been intended to limit consumption. The government also managed to pass a number of measures in employment policy, including enhanced provision for training and parental leave. As part of the tax reform the government furthermore moved a larger part of the income basis from direct

Promotion of Foreign Direct Investments

Denmark is located in Europe's most prosperous region from which trade to the Nordic countries, Western and Central Europe as well as the expanding economies in Eastern Europe evolves. Furthermore, Denmark's membership in the European Union provides unlimited access to a total EU market of 350 million people and a further 200 million to the east.

Denmark has one of the strongest economies in Europe, characterised by a balanced state budget, stable currency and low interest rates as well as low inflation. The attractiveness of the Danish business environment has been consistently documented in the *World Competitiveness Report* published by the IMD/World Economic Forum. According to this and other research institutions, Denmark is perceived as one of the top ten trading and economic countries in the world.

Businesses investing in Denmark do not only profit from an attractive macroeconomic climate, but also from competitive conditions concerning taxation and total labour costs. Investors in Denmark are offered a number of important tax advantages, but first of all it is worth taking note of the fact that the Danish legislation is to be regarded as a straightforward system. In addition, companies in Denmark benefit from favorable rules on depreciation.

Denmark also offers competitive labour costs when both direct and indirect wages are taken into consideration. This is due to the employer's low cost burden in terms of social security, labour taxes, etc. Competitive labour costs and high productivity levels combine to make Denmark's work force one of the most efficient in Europe. Rules governing the labour market in Denmark also mean that adjustments to the size of the labour force are significantly easier than is the case elsewhere in Europe.

Invest in Denmark is the national investment promotion organisation established in 1989 in order to market Denmark abroad and attract potential foreign investors and companies. The organisation assists foreign companies in identifying and analysing business opportunities when establishing business activities in Denmark.

Typical services provided confidentially and free of charge to potential foreign investors and companies by Invest in Denmark are:

– Provision of market studies, background material and information
– Preparation of information on business and trade conditions in Denmark
– Advice on business opportunities in Denmark
– Preparation of investment proposals
– Arrangement of visit programmes
– Identification of potential co-operation partners
– Information on finance possibilities
– Establishment of contact between potential investors and possible Danish partners
– Identification of building sites and leaseholds
– Establishment of contact to public authorities and regional institutions working in the fields of investment promotion and research

Invest in Denmark is an organisation under Denmark's Export Advice within the Ministry of Foreign Affairs. The headquarters is located in Copenhagen but the organisation is also represented in Europe, Asia and the USA. Further information on Invest in Denmark is available on www.investindk.com or by contacting info@investindk.com.

Ministry of Economic and Business Affairs

to indirect taxes, including the so-called green taxes, which also aim to reduce the consumption of scarce resources and materials causing environmental pollution. A considerable fall in interest rates in the second half of 1993 produced a wave of conversions of mortgages formerly at high rates of interest, and this together with increasing activity abroad and the more relaxed financial policy resulted in a consumer-led rise in economic growth. In 1994-1996 economic growth averaged 3.4%. The increase in activity, along with a widespread use of the leave schemes, led to a big fall in unemployment, which at the end of 1997 was just below 7% as against nearly 12% in the winter of 1993-1994.

The following years economic growth continued, reinforced by a worldwide drop in interest rates. Unemployment fell and the balance of payments once again showed a deficit. To counter overheating of the economy the government felt obliged to promote private saving and tighten economic policy. The 'Whitsun package' was passed in 1998 with the support of the left wing in the Folketing. The Whitsun package included a reduction of the taxable value of interest relief from around 46% to 32% in 2001, increased pension contributions, heavier property taxation and more 'green taxes'. The tightening of economic policy combined with rising interest rates led to the desired decline in activity in 1999. The average GDP growth fell to c. 2.5% after having shown an annual growth of 3% in 1997-1998, but in 2000 GDP increased again to 3.6%.

The balance of payments was in surplus again in both 1999 and 2000. However, as the labour market reacts slowly to changes, unemploy-

ment continued to fall throughout 1999 to c. 5% in late 1999. In late 2001 the unemployment rate had been reduced to 4.5%. Reinforced by rocketing oil prices, inflation increased in 1999 reaching the highest level of the 1990s with an annual average of 2.5%. Inflation continued to increase in 2000 reaching 2.9%, but throughout 2001 inflation fell to an annual average of 2.4%.

Kristian Hjulsager, Helge Pedersen

CHL, Chr. Hansen's Laboratorium, is known for high quality food ingredients such as animal rennet, bacterial culture, natural colours and flavours, supplied to the dairy industry world-wide.

Trends in Employment and Trades

Denmark possesses limited natural resources. They consist principally of agricultural land which over a long period of time has been vastly improved through human action. On the other hand, the amount of materials that could form the basis for mining and industry is very modest and mainly limited to clay, stone, gravel, chalk, lime, peat and lignite. This dearth of many important minerals has meant that there have never been natural conditions for heavy industry in Denmark, though the present-day Danish community has tried to make up for this through a foreign trade which in relation to the size of the country has been very extensive indeed.

Agricultural Community

The first people came to Denmark after the last Ice Age, living on hunting and fishing and gathering berries and wild plants. From about 4000 BC a gradual transition ensued to agriculture, and over the next 6,000 years this became the principal occupation. Even in the middle of the 19th century over half the population was employed in agriculture, and before that the proportion had been considerably greater. This had been necessary in order to produce sufficient food; only with the agricultural reforms after the middle of the 18th century, it was possible to achieve a production surplus which on the one hand could provide food for a growing urban population and on the other could be exported. A minority of the population earned its livelihood from other occupations, e.g. as smiths, wheelwrights, weavers or building workers, and gradually it became possible to add business people and seafarers to this list. With the developing social organisation, administrative functions also emerged, including service in the royal court or in state institutions, the military and the church.

Some trades utilised the natural resources of the country, for inst-

The Danish population distributed according to occupation (1787)
in percentages

	Copen-hagen	Provincial towns	Coun-try districts
Agriculture	–	–	52
Crafts and industry	25	30	10
Trade and transport	6	12	3
Public employees	8	8	2
Military	25	10	–
Servant and day-labourers	18	20	26
Other occupations	8	8	1
No occupation	10	12	6

The Danish population distributed according to occupation (1845-1950)
in percentages

	1845	1901	1950
Agriculture	55	40	24
Crafts and industry	25	29	35
Trade and business	4	10	13
Administration, Professions, etc.	6	5	8
Other occupations	3	7	9
No occupation	7	9	11

ance bog iron ore, which over a long period was used in the production of iron, and chalk and lime, where these raw materials were found sufficiently close to the surface, for instance in chalk cliffs. Other trades were based on the use of cultured plants and on the processing of animal products, but as stated above, even at an early stage, Denmark stood in need of foreign trade because of a lack of important raw materials.

At the end of the 18th century, about a fifth of the population lived in the towns, where artisan trades were the principal occupation, though about a quarter of Copenhagen's c. 90,000 inhabitants consisted of members of the army and navy with their families. Most craft undertakings were small, and the shoemakers constituted the largest group. In Copenhagen and a few provincial towns, however, there were established state-subsidised manufactories, i.e. large-scale businesses, especially within the textile industry, employing artisan labour; they each provided employment for a fairly large number of workers. Another kind of large-scale undertaking was represented by cottage industries in which merchants or shopkeepers provided people with raw materials

in their home and took back the finished goods from them.

Industrialisation

As a result of the economic crisis in the years following 1814, state support was discontinued, and most factories were closed. Other businesses stagnated, too, for a number of years, and not until about the middle of the 19th century did the urban trades start providing employment for a growing proportion of the population.

With a background in the agricultural reforms at the end of the 18th century, corn production was increased, so that it became possible to export surplus produce to England at profitable prices after the repeal of the British Corn Laws. Danish agriculture could increasingly concentrate on seriously producing foodstuffs for sale instead of merely cultivating for domestic use. So it was possible to buy a variety of goods, which created a larger market for the products of urban trades; this in its turn was able to form the basis for an expansion of business activities and thus support an increase in the urban population. At the same time forms of production in the urban trades underwent a change as real industrial undertakings were established with

Percentage distribution of total employment for the main areas of trade 1840-1990.

- Agriculture, etc.
- Crafts and industry
- Trade, etc.
- Transport and communication
- Professions
- Public services
- Other

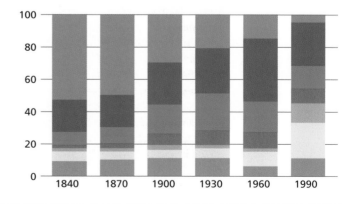

	Occupation	GVG
Agriculture, market gardening and forestry	3.4	2.3
Fisheries, etc.	0.2	0.2
Extraction of raw materials	0.1	3.1
Manufacturing		
Food, beverages and tobacco industry	2.8	2.5
Textiles, clothing and leather industry	0.5	0.4
Wood, paper and graphic industries	2.5	2.4
Mineral oil, chemical products and plastics industries	1.8	3.3
Stone, clay and glass industry	0.8	0.7
Iron and metal industry	6.7	6.4
Other industries	1.2	0.8
Energy and water supply	0.5	2.2
Building and construction	6.1	4.9
Trade, hotels and restaurants	19.3	14.2
Transport, postal services and telecommunications	6.6	8.6
Financial services, business services, etc.	12.2	22.7
Public and private services		
Public administration, etc.	7.4	6.8
Teaching	7.2	5.0
Health services, etc.	5.6	4.1
Social institutions, etc.	10.4	5.7
Other services	4.8	4.0
Total	100.0	100.0

Source: Statistics Denmark

large-scale production based partly on new foreign inventions, first the steam engine and then other forms of motive power, followed by various other machines. Industrial undertakings were earliest developed within the textile and engineering - industries.

The change to a more industrialised and urbanised society did not take place at a steady pace from the middle of the 19th century to the middle of the 20th. Until 1914 it was especially in boom years that many workers moved to the towns and found employment in newly-established undertakings.

A rapid early development took place in the 1850s and 1860s, a period which saw not only growing investments in industry, but also the establishment of a transport system with the opening of railways and telegraph communications, at the same time as shipping connections between the various parts of the country were improved, and the first major commercial banks founded.

In the 1870s, too, there was strong growth in urban undertakings with the founding of a large number of new industrial enterprises and several large banks and shipping companies; the years from 1890 to 1914 represented a new era of considerable progress.

The period after the First World War was characterised by crises and uneven growth, but the beginning of the 1930s saw an extensive programme to protect urban business undertakings against foreign competition, and industrial production again grew quickly and absorbed labour from the crisis-ridden agricultural sector. The result was that during the 1930s trade and industry came to provide employment for a greater proportion of the population than agriculture, and this trend continued until the years immediately following the Second World War. Right until the end of the 1950s, however, Danish agriculture continued to employ a large section of the population and to account for a large proportion of production when compared with the rest of the western world. This was because a significant part of agricultural production had long gone to exports, first in the form of corn products, and later, after the reorganisation of agriculture in the second half of the 19th century resulting from competition from cheap foreign corn products, in the form of meat, butter and eggs, still with Great Britain as its principal market.

The 40 leading firms in Denmark (2000)

Ranking Company	Turnover in millions of kroner	Numbers employed
1. A.P. Møller Gruppen	84,301	60,000*
2. TDC	44,552	28,643
3. Arla Foods	37,800	18,600
4. Danish Crown	36,896	19,449
5. Carlsberg	34,918	23,641
6. FDB Koncernen	29,508	19,502
7. ISS	28,719	253,200
8. Borealis	27,996	5,306
9. Danisco	27,829	17,712
10. Novo Nordisk	20,811	12,698
11. Statoil Danmark	20,139	2,488
12. Dansk Supermarked	19,575	6,784
13. J. Lauritzen Holding	19,466	10,900
14. FLS Industries	19,205	14,641
15. Group 4 Falck	18,210	111,325
16. Maersk	17,932	10,477
17. Skandinavisk Holding	16,842	7,644
18. Danfoss	14,797	16,665
19. Danske Trælast	13,139	6,772
20. SAS Danmark	11,987	8,840
21. Dagrofa	11,741	1,340
22. DONG	11,673	610
23. Post Danmark	10,936	24,867
24. DLG	10,214	2,094
25. Dansk Shell	9,903	1,461
26. KFK	9,780	2,074
27. Lego Gruppen	9,467	7,669
28. IBM Danmark	8,790	4,518
29. Egmont Fonden	8,574	1,076
30. Føtex	8,208	5,222
31. Velux Industri	8,138	7,596
32. Bilka Lavprisvarehus	8,103	4,352
33. Odense Staalskibsværft	7,906	8,498
34. DSB	7,866	9,705
35. O.W. Bunker Holding	7,786	375
36. ØK	7,768	6,244
37. Rockwool International	7,621	7,458
38. Akzo Nobel	7,256	4,460
39. GN Store Nord	7,003	5,162
40. DaimlerChrysler Skandinavien Holding	6,612	1,130

* Estimate

The Service Society

In the 1960s urban industry once more experienced a boom, while the agriculture's potential for selling its produce abroad was weakened by growing state subsidies for their own farmers on the part of the EEC and other countries. Consequently, great structural changes took place during this decade, bringing about the industrialisation of many rural areas, and resulting in industry taking over the role as the most important export sector. In the first half of the decade, industry further increased its share of total employment, while agriculture declined. After the middle of the 1960s, growth in industrial production certainly continued, but it was now achieved by extensive investments in modern machinery, and the increase in the number of employees could instead mainly be seen in the service industries; in particular, the public sector grew rapidly in step with developments in education and the health and social services areas.

After 1973, several branches of business in the private sector fell into difficulties due to structural problems as business life had to adapt to higher energy prices. Meanwhile, growth continued within the public sector as well as in a variety of public service areas, for instance banks and insurance companies. In the 2000s, Danish business structure is thus very different from that existing shortly after the end of the Second World War, and Denmark is marked by a transition from an industrialised society to a service society.

Where the production facilities in the form of business buildings, machines and transport facilities, etc. played a relatively small part in the Danish society of former times, the investments of the last century have transformed the means of production into a very important prerequisite for carrying out the rational and increasingly mechanised production of consumer goods and investment products and thus for ensuring a high living standard for the citizens.

As for developments in the structure of the economy, these are shown in increased production per employee, and although the increase in productivity has not been the same in all areas, the trend in the contribution made by individual trades to Danish overall production was the same throughout the 20th century, i.e. a development from an agricultural society via an industrial society to a service society, as is shown by employment figures.

The part played by agriculture in the national economy has been very sharply reduced despite a continued high share of the export market, whereas public sector services make up the largest occupational sector.

Hans Chr. Johansen

Agriculture

Danish agriculture produces food-stuffs sufficient for c. 15 million people, which is three times the population of Denmark. Although the part played by agriculture in the Danish economy overall has steadily fallen in step with industrialisation and economic developments as a whole, it is still an essential occupation by dint of its net foreign currency earning capacity, its effect on employment and its importance in supplying everyday foodstuffs. As farming accounts for almost 2/3 of the total area of the country, the industry also plays an important part for its impact on both the cultural and the scenic landscapes.

Area Devoted to Agriculture

In 2000, the area of Denmark devoted to agriculture constituted c. 2,659 million hectares, including 0.2 million hectares set aside or used for non-food crops in accordance with the EU set-aside rules. Topographically this area is well suited to cultivation, and plant production benefits from a normally good climate and precipitation evenly spread over the year. The area devoted to agriculture peaked in the 1930s with 3,270 million hectares under cultivation. A reduction in the area has occurred as agricultural land has been given over to urban development and re-

Collecting wild oat-grass in wheat fields. The collection and destruction of wild oat-grass are required by law, as it can reduce harvest yields in wheat fields. This is an example of a job that has to be done by hand.

Post-1988 trends in agricultural areas devoted to organic farming. Arrangements for controls and support for organic farming were introduced the year before, which made statistical comparisons and statistics possible.

Numbers of farms

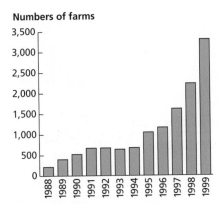

creational activities, especially since 1960. At the same time profound changes have taken place in farm structures.

Farm Structures

In the first half of the 20th century there were about 200,000 farms with an average area of c. 16 hectares, but after 1950 numbers began to decline slowly. From 1960 this trend accelerated, and during the 1960s an average of 5,000 farms disappeared each year. In the 1970s and 1980s the decline levelled off to 2,600 holdings a year, and in the 1990s to 2,300 so that in 2000 the number of holdings had

fallen to 53,000 with an average area of 50 hectares. The drop has been most pronounced among farms offering full-time family employment, and in 2000 only c. 20,000 farms provided full-time employment, each with an average area of c. 100 hectares. At the same time changes have taken place in methods of working; farmers are to an increasing extent concentrating their efforts on one sole branch of farming, and specialisation in animal production has led to fewer types, but larger numbers, of livestock. Between 1973 and 2000 there was an annual production increase of 2.8 %. The background to the changes in both the farm structures and methods of working were the demands for a steady improvement in productivity to compensate for deteriorating terms of trade and profitability trends.

Since 1995 the number of organic farms has risen steadily. In 2000 Denmark counted about 3,500 organic farms, representing c. 6.6% of the total number of farms, and organic land area amounted to about 165,000 hectares, corresponding to 6.2% of the total agricultural land area. As to the distribution of organic farm types, 25% of organic farmers are cattle farmers, 14% are pig farmers c. 20% are crop farmers

Numbers Employed

In 2000, primary agriculture, including fur farming and horticulture, employed 84,000 people, or 3% of the country's workforce; in western parts of the country, employment in agriculture can account for as much as 5-7% of the workforce. Half of the 12,200 who are occupied in the horticulture sector are paid employees as opposed to 1/3% in agriculture, which is dominated by family-owned farms. About one farm in four employs one or more permanent hel-

A successful calving. A milking cow has on average one calf a year. 85% of all fertilisation of Danish cows is achieved by artificial insemination; 500-600 bulls produce semen for 1 million inseminations.

Nykøbing Falster Sugar Factory. In the course of three months, from October to December, sugar is extracted from c. 124,000 tonnes of sugar beet, which is about 26% of the total Danish harvest.

pers. In manufacturing concerns relating to agriculture – i.e. dairies, abattoirs, etc. – there were 52,000 employees in 2000. In addition a further 64,000 were in supply, transport and other service activities. Thus, directly and indirectly, agricultural production provided work for altogether 200,000 people, corresponding to approximately 8% of all those in full-time employment.

Most Danish farms are freehold, 91% of them being family-run farms in individual ownership, 8% run by companies of various kinds, and the rest owned by the State, local authorities, foundations, etc. In 2000 areas in leasehold make up 26.5% of the agricultural area and principally represent land leased out to supplement existing holdings.

Production

The annual harvest yield in plant production varies between 160 and 170 million crop units, of which c. 60% are cereal crops. Over 90% of plant production is used as animal feed, primarily for pigs and cattle.

From the beginning of the 1980s the production of pork has risen by almost 50% to c. 1.8 million tonnes in 2000. Over the same period milk production fell by 15% to 4.7 million tonnes, partly as a result of the EU's introduction of milk quotas. The popu-

Feeding of organic outdoor pigs. Organic farming is in a strong position in Denmark and not least on the domestic market, sale of different organic farming products has been a success.

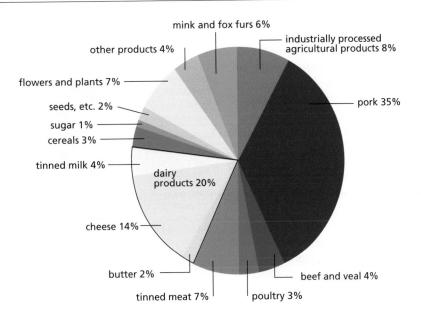

The average composition of annual Danish agricultural exports in the 1990s.

mink and fox furs 6%

industrially processed agricultural products 8%

other products 4%

flowers and plants 7%

pork 35%

seeds, etc. 2%

sugar 1%

cereals 3%

tinned milk 4%

dairy products 20%

cheese 14%

butter 2%

beef and veal 4%

tinned meat 7%

poultry 3%

lation of cows was reduced by 33%, but a rise in milk yield per cow (to over 7,500 kg milk per year) compensated for the decline.

In 2000 the net value of Danish agricultural production in the home and export markets was 71.6 billion kroner a year, including funds from the EU agricultural support arrangements. In 2000 these funds amounted to 6.1 billion kroner. C. 20 billion of the production came from primary agriculture and c. 45 billion from manufacturing and processing. C. 64% of agricultural production goes to export, which in 2000 brought in 42.1 billion kroner.

Agricultural Policy

Danish agriculture is to a great extent governed by the agricultural policies laid down by the EU, the agricultural products of whose member countries are guaranteed a sale price above that of the world market, irrespective of whether sales are to the domestic market, the EU or to markets outside the EU. Economically, Danish agriculture has benefit-

ted greatly from the EU agricultural policy, which in 1992 meant a profit of c. 19 billion kroner measured according to the OECD's unit of measurement PSE (Producer Subsidy Equivalent), which is a quantitative measurement of the effects of the various support arrangements.

With the 1992 EU reform a gradual adjustment of earlier support arrangements was set in motion with a view to reducing both agricultural production and support, partly through set-aside and area subsidies rather than product subsidies. With the 1993 GATT agreement, and later, in 1995 when GATT was replaced with WTO (World Trade Organization), the international framework for EU agricultural policy up to the year 2000 was further determined. The aim of the agreements gradually to introduce unsupported world market prices for agricultural products is judged to imply a considerable advantage for the export-oriented Danish agriculture.

Kai Skriver

Horticulture

Danish horticulture includes fruit and berry cultivation, vegetable growing and nurseries, with a total area of 18,645 hectares distributed among about 4,500 concerns (1999). In addition there is mushroom production and the production of flowers and vegetables in hothouses with a total area of c. 500 hectares distributed among 700 concerns. In 2000 total exports of potted plants amounted to 2.5 billion, the most important export market for potted plants being Germany, which took 33% in 2000, followed by Sweden with 21%.

The industry has developed from nurseries in the gardens of country houses through mixed market gardening for a local market to highly specialised mass export production by ever fewer but larger firms. In geographical terms, open-air horticulture is evenly distributed in contrast to the area occupied by greenhouses, of which 53% is found in Funen, 14% in Århus county, 10% in the remainder of Jutland, and 23% in Zealand and the eastern islands.

Aage Søgaard Andersen

Horticulture
Production values and exports in 2000

(millon kroner)	Value	Exports
Hothouses		
Potted plants, etc.	2,602	2,496
Vegetables	340	0
Open air		
Vegetables	503	45
Nurseries	553	132
Fruit and berries	261	26
Mushrooms	112	0
Total	4,371	2,699

Source: Dansk Erhvervsgartneriforening

In market gardens the plant growth is accelerated partly by increasing the hours of light, and during the winter and at night many greenhouses are lit up. The photosynthesis mechanism of the plants is particularly sensitive to the red and blue areas of the visible light spectrum.

Forestry

C. 10% of Denmark is covered by forest, altogether 4,500 square kilometres. It is expected that this proportion will continue to increase, as the Folketing has set the goal of doubling the area of woodland in the course of a tree generation (80-100 years). The most important reasons for this are agricultural over-production, leaving areas free for adaptation to forestry, and the environmental and recreational values of forests. The greater part of the forested area of Denmark is strictly designated as forest reserve under the Forestry Act. The forests are owned by c. 20,000 private individuals as well as institutional and public bodies. The largest owner of forested areas is the state through the Danish Forest and Nature Agency which owns and manages c. 1/3 of the forested area and also administers the Forestry Act.

About 2 million cubic metres of wood are produced in Danish forests each year, at a value of c. 800 million kroner; this production covers only 1/4 of the wood used in Den-

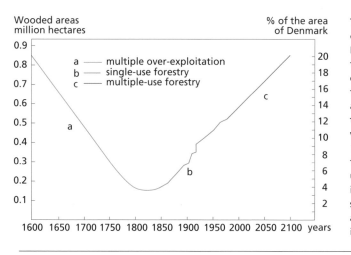

Wooded areas million hectares / % of the area of Denmark

a — multiple over-exploitation
b — single-use forestry
c — multiple-use forestry

The area devoted to forests and the development of forestry from 1600 to 2100: From a multiple over-exploitation of the forests (for wood, grazing, hunting and clearing for agriculture) to single-use forestry with the principal aim of managing and restoring the forests so as sustainably to be able to meet society's demand for wood products. From the Forestry Act of 1989 it is a demand that in the future forests must be managed for multiple values, i.e. with a view both to increasing and improving the production of trees and the social values of forest recreation, landscape amenity, biological diversity, cultural heritage and environmental protection.

mark. The wood increases 5-6 times in value in the Danish wood industry. About 300,000 cubic metres of wood are used as fuel by private individuals, and c. 200,000 cubic metres are used in wood-chip-fired district heating stations. More than 700 million kroner's worth of greenery for decoration is produced (Christmas trees and cuttings from trees), and of this the greater part is exported. Denmark is Europe's leading exporter of Christmas trees.

Primary forestry occupies c. 2,500 employees, and forestry forms the basis for most of the work for c. 36,000 employees in the wood manufacturing industry. Forestry makes only little use of raw and auxiliary materials, and the industry is thus not dependent to any significant extent on imported goods and services.

There are certain social benefits of forested areas to which a price can only be attached with difficulty; benefits such as e.g. outdoor recreation, plant and animal life, landscape aesthetics and protection of the ground water are presumably of even greater value than the produc-

Marking Christmas trees (Nordmann firs) for felling. About 7 million Christmas trees are felled each year, some 80% of them for export. Denmark is Europe's leading exporter of Christmas trees. The Nordmann fir is by far the most important species used for Christmas trees, after which come nobilis and Norway spruce.

tion of wood and decorative greenery. In a social perspective it is particularly valuable that the material production can proceed at the same time as the non-material values of the forests are taken into consideration. It is called 'multiple-use forestry' and is a demand in the Forestry Act of 1989 (amended 1996).

Niels Elers Koch

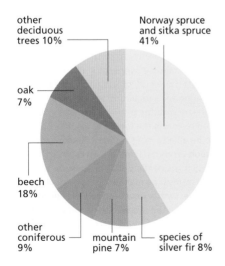

other deciduous trees 10%

Norway spruce and sitka spruce 41%

oak 7%

beech 18%

other coniferous 9%

mountain pine 7%

species of silver fir 8%

The wooded area of Denmark (417,000 hectares) divided according to tree species (1990). 64% is made up of conifers. Of these, most (81%) are in Jutland, especially deriving from the planting of poor soils. Most of the deciduous trees (57%) are on the islands. As new forests are planted, deciduous trees are being used to an increasing extent.

Fisheries

Fish has been caught in Denmark from the very earliest times, and right from the start the implements used were fundamentally the same as are used today: nets, traps and hooks. For centuries fishing was seasonal and those who engaged in it had other work as smallholders, day labourers, etc. The fishing was done in fresh water or close to the coast, though fresh water fishing has never been particularly significant. The first full-time fishermen are known from the 17th century, in the Limfjord area and elsewhere. The fish was normally salted or dried; fresh fish was the preserve of the coastal population.

The development of the railway system at the end of the 19th century and the installation of motors in boats around 1900 led to a tremendous increase in off-shore fishing. The fresh fish could now be transported over great distances. The boats were able to go further out to sea, and bigger, more efficient equipment, for instance the Danish seine, was taken into use. Fishing was now a real industry, and the numbers employed in it grew rapidly. In 1913 there were about 12,000 full-time fishermen, a number that remained constant for many years, still standing at about 11,000 in 1982. From the start of the 1980s the numbers fell as a result of the crisis in the fishing industry, so that in 2000 there were only about 4,500 full-time registered fishermen in Denmark. The crisis resulted from a combination of reduced stocks and over-capacity in the fishing fleet. It became necessary to reduce the numbers of boats, and this was done with the help of various

Large-toothed, double-row harpoon of reindeer antler from the Early Stone Age found at Skaftelev near Sorø.

Trawling for herring in the Baltic. In weight, herring is the most important Danish fish caught for immediate consumption. It is caught with trawl and net in all Danish waters. Practically speaking the entire catch is processed for various fish products.

support arrangements, including grants towards the cost of laying up the ships. Since 1900 enormous improvements have been made in ships, equipment, engines and electronic equipment; the 12,000 fishermen in 1913 caught c. 66,000 tonnes, while the 4,500 in 2000 caught 1.5 million tonnes. This puts Denmark among the world's 10-15 top fishing nations.

Fresh-water catches in the 1990s account for only a few hundred tonnes, mainly eel, perch and pike-perch plus certain species used as industrial fish. C. 35,000 tonnes of rainbow trout are produced in marine and freshwater farms.

Off-Shore Fishing

The Danish off-shore fishing industry can be divided into industrial fishing and fishing for human consumption.

Industrial fishing means catching fish for industrial use, i.e. for producing fish meal and fish oil. Industrial fishing began in the North Sea at the end of the 1940s with herring fishing. Later, species such as sand eel, Norway pout and sprat were added to these. The ratio of species was altered, and by 1998 sand eel accounted for 60%. Industrial fishing has for a number of years been by far the most important branch of fishing with a total catch in 2000 of 1.1 million tonnes. Sand eel is thus the most common species of fish in the Danish fishing industry; in terms of cash value, however, it is surpassed by cod. Industrial fishing is done employing trawls of various types.

The most important species of fish caught for immediate human consumption are cod, plaice and herring; furthermore species such as hake, Dover sole and turbot. Fishing for Norway lobster, deep water prawn and common mussels is also of importance. If all fish landed are listed in order of value, the order

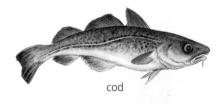

plaice

cod

sand eel

herring

Plaice – one of the commonest of Danish fish. It is caught from the North Sea to Bornholm with net and trawl.

Cod – economically the most important fish in Denmark. It is caught with trawl and net from the North Sea to far into the Baltic.

Sand eel – by weight the most important fish in Danish fishery. Caught in the North Sea by large industry trawlers and used for the production of fish meal and fish oil.

Herring – very common in Danish fishing. Its economic significance has been considerable, especially at an earlier period. Herring is a Danish gastronomic speciality and may be prepared in many ways.

80% of the catches come from the North Sea and the Skagerrak. In 2000 fish catches' contribution to gross value added was some 3 billion kroner, of which the North Sea was responsible for about 50%. By far the greater part of Danish fish catches are exported either fresh or processed. In 2000 the export value was c. 14 billion kroner, corresponding to some 3.5% of Denmark's total exports.

Fishery Regulations

Fishing in EU waters is managed on the basis of an annual EU regulation which fixes the total allowable catch per fish stock and divides the quotas among the individual member countries. The regulation is based i.a. on biological advice on fisheries and prognoses for the development of fish stocks. The biological advice is administered by the International Council for Exploitation of the Sea (ICES) in Copenhagen in conjunction with the marine research institutes of the individual countries.

Erik Hoffmann

Modern Danish stern trawler of medium size. The trawl drums and wires are fixed aft in the boat, which makes them easier to work with. In addition, more deck room is achieved by placing the wheelhouse in the prow. The boat can be used for fishing for herring, cod, flatfish and Norway lobster.

runs as follows: cod, sand eel, plaice, herring and Norway lobster. Eel used also to be important, but after a serious diminution of stocks in the 1970s it has been of less importance. Fish for immediate human consumption is caught by means of stationary or dredging gear. Gillnets and poundnets, traps and hooks belong to the former, trawls and Danish seine to the latter. Special dredgers are used for catching mussels.

In 2000 the most important fishing ports are Esbjerg, Thyborøn, Hanstholm, Hirtshals and Skagen. Over

Manufacturing

The manufacturing sector in Denmark is varied and produces a large number of goods, both for export and for domestic consumption. Bacon factories, dairies, corn mills and breweries are among the most important sectors of the food, beverages and tobacco industries. Petrol, insulin and plastic goods are counted among the sales successes in the chemical industry. From the mechanical engineering industry come motors, agricultural machines, pumps, thermostats, refrigerators, telecommunications equipment and shipping. Finally, furniture, clothing, toys and newspapers are among the Danish industrial products sold in the greatest numbers.

Between 1990 and 1999, production in constant prices in the manufacturing sector rose by c. 22%, while employment fell by c. 32,000, corresponding to almost 7%. In 2000 real growth reached 6.3% despite slightly falling employment. This development hides a very steep increase in productivity.

Behind developments in production and employment within the manufacturing sector in general lie quite extensive structural changes among the different areas of trade. The manufacture of mechanical engineering products, which also include electronic goods, represents a growing proportion of the sector's productive value. The same applies to the chemical industry. Since 1990, the food, beverage and tobacco industries have had a more or less constant share of production, whereas the textile, clothing and leather industry has had a clearly declining proportion. This latter trend results from the increased competition on wages from third-world countries and, more recently, the countries of central and eastern Europe.

Employment

The general fall in employment has particularly hit textiles and clothing, which was reduced by some 13,000 employees between 1990 and 1999. In the same period employment in mechanical engineering fell slightly, however, on account of the decline in employment over all, it brought the share of employment in the manufacturing industries up to c. 40%. A relatively very steep increase in the share of employment in the chemical industry corresponds to an absolute rise of 7,000 employees.

The manufacturing sector is marked by the fact that more than 80% of employment is concentrated in four of the seven main areas. Nevertheless, this sector is differentiated with regard to both the distribution of areas of trade and company sizes. It is for example characterised by a large number of small and medium-sized enterprises. Thus only just under 4% of all firms in the manufacturing sector had more than 100 full-time employees in 1999, but this accounted for more than 50% of all the full-time employed in

The brew-house of the Carlsberg breweries as it was in 1901. With its headquarters in Valby, Copenhagen, the Carlsberg group is one of the giants in Danish trade. Among its products are Carlsberg and Tuborg beers and a large number of non-alcoholic drinks. The company includes about 100 subsidiaries of which most are outside Denmark.

The Danish pharmaceutical industry's long-standing concentration on research into and development of enzymes for industrial use and insulin for diabetics has given the pharmaceutical industry a prominent place in the international market. In order to make self-injection easier for diabetes patients, Novo Nordisk has developed the injection pens NovoPen and Novolet.

this sector. Conversely, over half the places of work had fewer than 5 employees, but these accounted for less than 4% of total employment. It is in mechanical engineering works and in the iron, steel and metal industries that we find the relatively greatest number of large businesses, but the chemical industry and the food, beverages and tobacco industries also have relatively large businesses.

Exports

A very large proportion (45%) of manufacturing industry's total production goes to export, corresponding to 75% of total exports.

Exports are largely based on the processing of imported raw materials and semi-manufactured pro-

ducts. Because it derives a large proportion of its supplies from agriculture and fishing, the food, beverages and tobacco industries require only a small proportion of imports, but in general the lack of raw materials leads to a relatively large amount of direct imports.

The export surplus (exports minus imports) for the manufacturing sector as a whole is just under 24% of the total production value. The food, beverages and tobacco industries have a high net export percentage of just under 40% on account of the low import content, while mechanical engineering, which accounts for almost 1/3 of all manufacturing exports, has an export surplus of just under 23%.

Kristian Hjulsager

The Lego brick was launched in 1958 and has since grown to be loved by children the world over because of the infinite number of construction possibilities on which the only limits are those of the imagination. The Lego company's products for the youngest children, consisting of larger bricks, carry the name of DUPLO. For bigger children with a greater technological interest the company has developed LEGO Technic.

The Building and Construction Industry

The activities in the building and construction industry comprise construction, repairs and maintenance of houses, offices and industrial buildings, and the establishment and maintenance of roads, harbours and airports, bridges and tunnels and sewerage systems. The drastic fall in house building throughout the 1970s and 1980s has reduced production and employment in this sector considerably. In the late 1990s the sector experienced an increase in production and employment. In 2000 production value of this sector constituted nearly 5% of the total gross factor income as against 12% in 1972 when the sector's activities reached a peak. Since then almost 43,000 jobs have been lost in this sector, so that employment in 2000 was down to c. 166,000, corresponding to c. 6% of total employment.

The building and construction industry is mainly made up of small companies in which independent and assisting spouses constitute a relatively large proportion of those employed.

The rapid decline in this sector in Denmark has in the first half of the 1990s led to the industry being more export-oriented, partly through Danish firms with their employees being increasingly active in the German market. However, since 1996 the domestic market has grown constantly.

Kristian Hjulsager

In the summer of 2000, drilling in connection with the first phase of the Copenhagen Metro was finished. In the photo, drilling under the streets of Copenhagen has just been finished. The first phase is due for completion by late 2002. 3 phases have been planned so far, providing Copenhagen with 23 metro stations, 9 of which will be underground.

Exploitation of Raw Materials

The most important raw materials found in Denmark are oil and gas together with clay, silt, sand, gravel and stone. In addition limestone and chalk, salt and groundwater are also among the most important raw materials. A number of others such as mo-clay, plastic clay, bentonite, peat, granite, gneiss, sandstone, phosphorite, glauconite and heavy minerals are extracted to a lesser extent or are being examined with a view to extraction. Brown coal, flint, marl and iron ore have formerly been extracted.

Sand, gravel and stone are extracted both at sea and on land, and production, mainly stemming from Ice Age deposits, is primarily used for cement and concrete products, road and bridge construction, landfills, coastal defences and harbour construction. Refined special products (glass sand, moulding sand, polishes, etc.) are manufactured i.a. from quartz sand from central Jutland and Bornholm.

Clay is extracted in particular in southern Jutland and Funen for the manufacture of red and yellow-fired bricks and other brick products. Super-light, insulating and absorbent bricks are made of mo-clay (diatomite) from the Limfjord area. Pressure resisting, insulating granulates are made by firing plastic clay (sand-free clay).

Limestone and chalk are extracted especially in Himmerland, Thy and Zealand. They are used for the production of cement, by heavy goods manufacturers for ground chalk and for various other purposes, e.g. as filler in the manufacture of paper. Denmark has a comprehensive export of both cement and chalk products.

Salt is found in considerable quantities in the deep underground. Exploitation is on the basis of solution mining of rock salt (halite, sodium chloride) from a salt dome southwest of Hobro in Jutland. Potassic

Aalborg Portland Cement Factory is one of the few major Danish companies whose products are entirely based on domestic raw materials: limestone and clay. Production, which commenced in 1889, is c. 2 million tonnes annually. The extensive expertise in this area has also resulted in a considerable export of Danish cement producing plants, not least to developing countries.

salt (sylvite, potash chloride), which among other things can be used in fertilisers, has been found in several Jutlandic salt domes.

The heavy minerals ilmenite, rutile and zircon have been identified in Miocene strata in Jutland and in the sand on the shores of many Danish coastal stretches. These minerals can be used to manufacture e.g. pigments, strong light metals and advanced technical ceramics.

Bentonite (expanding clay), which is used for many purposes including waterproof membranes, has been found in considerable quantities in Jutland and Lolland. *Glauconite*, which is used among other things for ion exchange and water purification, has been identified in large concentrations in Zealand and Jutland.

Ground water can be extracted almost everywhere in the country from sand and chalk strata. The ground water is of a generally higher quality than in other industrialised and agricultural countries, so it can still be used direct or after minimum treatment (aeration).

Jens Morten Hansen

Bornholm granite has been quarried for hundreds of years, an operation which in places has left deep scars in the landscape, as here in a granite quarry near Rønne. By far the greater part used to be quarried for cobblestones and used for cobbling the streets and roads in the country.

Quarrying for raw materials completely changes the character of the landscape. The photography shows a quarry for raw materials in Thy, where a bank of gravel is being dug out, transforming an undulating landscape into flat terrain.

Since the Second World War granite cobbled streets have almost everywhere been replaced with asphalt, cement and flagstones, but the old cobblestone trade is still kept alive for when a beautiful and striking cobbled surface is needed.

Energy

Denmark's energy production is mainly based on oil and natural gas from the Danish sector of the North Sea, imported coal and wind energy. In addition there are straw and other biological fuels, solar energy and geothermal energy, which together constitute a small proportion. This is, however, increasing with technological developments.

Coal is the most important fuel for the production of electricity. The coal is imported in particular from countries outside Europe, as the cost of mining and the combustion characteristics are more important than transport costs.

In the Danish sector of the North Sea *oil and natural gas* are produced in considerably larger quantities than are needed for domestic con-

sumption. The oil and gas are taken ashore, distributed and exported via pipelines. The gas is exported to Sweden and Germany, while the surplus oil is mainly sold in the spot market. Denmark is the third largest oil producer in Western Europe, after Norway and Britain, and together with gas production, oil is an important reason why Denmark has had a balance of payments surplus since the beginning of the 1990s.

Production comes exclusively from production rigs in a geological structure called the Central Trough in the North Sea. Present production is mainly based on A.P. Møller's monopoly on nine geographical blocks, usually referred to as 'the contiguous area'. The licensee is Dansk Undergrunds Consortium (DUC),

The Tyra East gas rig in the Danish sector of the North Sea. As it is extracted, the gas is pumped by pipeline to the Nybro factory near Varde. From here the purified gas is distributed to the rest of the country, Germany and Sweden through a network of

pipelines that is still being extended and which will finally reach many individual users. Meanwhile, periodical gas surpluses from the North Sea are stored in suitable subterranean formations such as sandstone layers and salt domes.

The Ensted power station near the Åbenrå Fjord in Southern Jutland has the largest coal harbour in northern Europe. Coal from different parts of the world is brought to the Ensted power station on large coal transporters, some of it then being taken by barge to other power stations in Jutland and Funen. Most Danish electricity production is based on coal-fired stations.

owned jointly by A.P. Møller, Shell and Texaco. The monopoly must be liquidated by 2012. In the remaining Danish sector of the North Sea other companies have made a number of discoveries, and several have been put into production by the Norwegian company Statoil and the Danish state-owned company Dansk Olie og Naturgas (DONG), among others. On land and in coastal waters no commercially viable finds have yet been made despite a considerable amount of prospecting.

Most of the oil and gas produced is taken ashore in pipelines north of Esbjerg. Most of the oil products for Danish consumption are refined in oil refineries at Stigsnæs and Fredericia.

The gas is taken for processing in the Nybro factory, 9 km northeast of Varde, from where main pipelines are taken north through Jutland, south to Germany and east across Funen and Zealand, and under the Sound to Sweden. Large underground storage facilities for natural gas to offset seasonal variations in use have been established in sandstone strata in Zealand and in a salt

dome in Himmerland. The raw energy products are mainly used in the production of electricity and heating, and for transport.

Electricity is mainly produced in regional power stations by burning coal supplemented with natural gas, oil, biological fuel and waste products. Natural gas plays an increasingly important role, while the use of oil is decreasing. The regional power stations supply is distributed throughout the country by two electricity companies: Elkraft (Zealand, Falster and Lolland) and Elsam (Jutland and Funen).

Heating is mainly decentralised, being produced in the home, but the number of district heating stations is increasing. Installations in homes (and offices) for decentralised heating include oil and gas boilers, biological fuel burners (i.e. straw and wood), solar, ground heat and geothermal heating systems. Centralised producers include combined power and heating plant stations (heating as a bi-product of electricity production) and solely heating stations. Oil-fired boilers in individual homes is the traditional Danish form of heat-

Energy saving measures and alternative energy such as wind power, solar energy and geothermal heat are increasingly being taken into use for both economical and environmental reasons. These dome houses are located in the eco-village Øko-samfundet Dyssekilde in North Zealand. The south facing glass areas of the big houses ensure an optimum exploitation of solar heat.

ing, but numbers are falling, and domestic heating is being replaced by district heating or natural gas. Only in rural districts outside the supply networks are oil-fired boilers included in plans for heating in the future. In the second half of the 1980s and the beginning of the 1990s natural gas pipes have been taken to most homes in the towns and to villages in the more densely populated areas. There is no obligation to be connected to the pipelines.

Industrial consumption of energy per head of population is lower in Denmark than in most industrialised countries. Particularly high in energy

Wind power is increasingly being used in Denmark, where the wind almost always blows, and Danish industry is assuming a prominent place in the development of large, efficient windmills. The photo shows the world's largest offshore wind farm located on the shallow area of Middelgrunden near Copenhagen.

consumption are e.g. the cement works in Aalborg and steel production in Frederiksværk.

Energy-Saving Measures
Conservation of energy plays an important part in energy planning. After the energy crisis of 1973 a num-

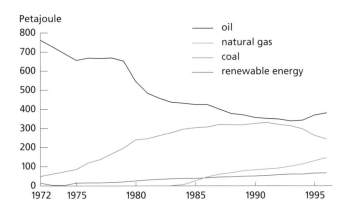

Petajoule

—— oil
—— natural gas
—— coal
—— renewable energy

The consumption of energy has changed considerably since the oil crisis of 1973-1974. Before 1972 Denmark was almost totally dependent on imported fuel, but in the mid-1990s Denmark had become self-sufficient with regard to three quarters of its fuel consumption. These remarkable changes are the result of the conversion of power plants from oil to coal burning, the extraction of oil and gas in the North Sea, the establishment of a natural gas network and the construction of combined power and heat plants. The total fuel consumption remained almost unchanged in the period in question, although GDP increased by 50%. Thus, Denmark's energy efficiency has increased considerably.

ber of grant facilities were introduced for insulating homes. Practically speaking all homes have been insulated with i.a. mineral wool under roofs or in lofts, and outer walls have been provided with cavity insulation. Thermostatic valves, insulation of radiator pipes and electronic heating control systems are standard in new buildings and have been introduced into most older ones. A heating inspection report is usually required when houses are sold. In addition users are encouraged by information campaigns and grants to economise in the use of energy. Altogether, campaigns for saving energy have had the effect that Denmark has generally speaking been able to maintain its use of energy at the same level for a considerable number of years.

Jens Morten Hansen

Private Services

The private service sector encompasses trade, business and household services, private education and health services, hotels and restaurants as well as amusements and cultural activities. In addition, the financial sector, and transport and communications are counted as being in the service sector.

Since 1970, private services as a whole have represented a gradually increasing proportion of all economic activity, but there has been a wide divergence in the ways in which the individual groups have developed.

Trade

The wholesale and retail trades, which from the point of view of employment constitute the major element in the private service sector, have both undergone changes since the 1970s. This is partly because the traditional distinctions between the part sectors in a great many cases have been erased by an integration of retail, wholesale and in certain cases producer sectors (vertical integration). Moreover, both areas have been marked by mergers within the sector (horizontal integration).

Wholesale Trade

The wholesale trade accounts for c. 63% of overall turnover in the trade sector (1999). This share has been growing for a number of years, which is linked to the continued specialisation in the manufacturing sector, which brings with it more trade between the firms and thus greater activity in the wholesale trade. The increase in activity has moreover resulted in a small growth in employment since the middle of the 1980s.

Since the middle of the 1980s, the wholesale trade has undergone a major restructuring in which a number of retail chains i.a. have established their own purchasing organisations or, like for instance Dansk Supermarked (consisting of Føtex, Bilka and Netto) and the FDB

During the 1960s rationalisation in the retail trade meant that shops were built bigger and bigger. This led to the demand for more customers and easier access, and many shops were built in malls away from the town centres, to which they provided a considerable competition. The photo shows the interior of the shopping centre Fisketorvet housing more than 100 retail shops, 15 restaurants and 10 cinemas. The centre was opened in 2000 and is located right on the waterfront south of the centre of Copenhagen.

(Co-operative Wholesale Society) group, have engaged in international co-operation. At the same time the major shopping chains increasingly buy direct from the producers. Turnover in the wholesale trade is completely dominated by the major firms in the sector. Thus, 2% of firms accounted for c. 70% of the total turnover in 1999. In sharp contrast to this, almost half of the VAT-registered entities were small one-man businesses, which together accounted for less than 1% of total turnover.

Retail Trade
Despite a strong rise in turnover, employment in the retail trade fell since the 1980s, mainly, because the retail trade concentrated into far fewer but larger entities. In all important respects decisions regarding product ranges still rest with the individual retailer, but with the increased integration with the wholesale trade, the wholesale sector has achieved greater influence. Changes in product ranges are seen partly in the shape of new goods, but also in shops in one sector taking over the range of goods sold by other sectors; this is known as compound trading. New types of shops have appeared in the form of supermarkets, low-price warehouses and discount stores, while the self-service system dominates entirely. Moreover a number of part functions have to a certain extent been taken over either by other areas in the turnover chain or by the consumers. As the result of an increasing proportion of turnover being made up of nation-wide branded goods, a good deal of – for instance – advertising is now in the hands of the producers.

To this must be added a new location pattern: In the older, central town areas and in the rural districts a large number of retail shops have been closed, while new shops have been collected in centres on the outskirts of the towns. From c. 1970 to the beginning of the 1990s, this trend has among other things resulted in a reduction in the number of shops selling everyday goods to 60%.

Although the structural changes in the retail trade have thus led to a concentration of turnover – 3% of the shops accounted for just over 70% of total turnover in 1999 – there is still a large number of small shops; thus about 2/3 of shops together accounted for only 6% of total retail turnover in 1999. Three out of four retail shops are one-man businesses, while the remainder are mainly limited companies or co-operative undertakings.

Kristian Hjulsager

Business Services
Employment in private services has seen the largest growth in the group of business services, which at the beginning of the 1990s employed more than twice as many as in 1970. Business services comprise three sectors: *professional services*, e.g. accountants, solicitors and advertising agencies, *technical services* such as engineering consultants, architects and surveyors, and *operational services* including the hiring of computer and office equipment, temporary employment agencies and security companies. The customers consist mainly of Danish businesses; only about 5% of production goes to private individuals; approximately a further 5% is exported. The export share, however, varies greatly between the different areas. Thus, engineering consultants export over 30% of their production, while the percentage for architects and solicitors is under 5%.

To the tourist, the table by the roadside displaying fruit, vegetable or eggs alongside an open till is a sight emphasising the relaxed charm of Danish life. For the Danes it is a normal part of the summer's trade pattern, deriving partly from the belief that the goods are probably a little fresher than in the supermarket. They are moreover cheaper; the supplier saves the cost of a middleman and now and again perhaps also the trouble of having to tell the taxation authorities about his income.

Domestic Services

This group of undertakings includes a large number of specialised businesses in the fields of e.g. motorcar repairs, cleaning services, laundries and dry cleaners, hairdressers, photography businesses and refuse collection. By far the largest group is made up of motorcar repairers. Then comes cleaning, with a large number of part-time workers.

In contrast to the other main groups, employment in domestic services has been declining since 1970. This is due partly to an increasing amount of moonlighting and do-it-yourself work, while the increase in the numbers of women going out to work and the increasing number of senior citizens have deflected demand from private services to the public welfare services. Domestic services are clearly not export oriented, and they are used in business and by private individuals in roughly equal proportions.

Private Tuition and Health Services

Most posts in this group are attached to private health services; only 5% are employed in private tuition. The total number employed in the sector rose by c. 50% between 1970 and 1993.

Private tuition includes all teaching offered at market rates, e.g. tuition in driving, languages and music. Most of the activities are controlled or financed, however, by the public sector, and private tuition only accounts for c. 1% of jobs in the teaching sector as a whole.

Private health services are represented mainly by general practitioners and dentists. In addition, the group includes e.g dental technicians, veterinary surgeons and chiropractors. Private health services provide employment for about 1/4 of all employees in the health sector as a whole. As expenditure by the National Health Insurance Service on private health services is considered to be public procurement, the public sector buys almost 2/3 of the production value of the private health services.

Hotel and Restaurant Services

This group's proportion of total employment has remained largely unchanged since 1970; about half of those employed in it are part-time workers.

The restaurant trade, which accounts for the largest proportion of jobs, includes, in addition to restaurants proper, takeaways, hot dog stands, catering businesses and catering services, also public houses, discotheques and nightclubs. The fast food area is experiencing particularly rapid growth.

The hotel trade comprises hotels, motels, youth hostels, campsites and provisions for residential courses. As a whole, this trade has been characterised by a growing demand for overnight accommodation since the end of the 1980s. In 1999 hotels had c. 13 million overnight guests, campsites had almost 11 million , while youth hostels had about 1 million. Foreign visitors remain relatively stable, accounting for about half of all overnight stays in hotels and youth hostels, and for about 1/3 of overnight stays on campsites. Most foreign visitors come from Germany and Sweden. Although there has been a general rise in the number of overnight stays, the use of capacity is relatively low, c. 53% in hotels and c. 21% on campsites (1999).

Amusements and Cultural Activities

Overall employment in this group rose by about 50% between 1970 and 1990. Among its main groups this sector includes film and video, radio and television, other forms of entertainment such as amusement parks, museums and zoos, dance schools and sports instruction as well as lottery and other gambling activities. About 75% of the production in this sector goes on private consumption, the remainder being used by business; only about 2% goes to export.

Karsten Stetkær

The Financial Sector

The financial sector encompasses financial institutions, mortgage lenders, insurance companies and pension funds, etc. From the 1960s to the end of the 1980s, this sector was marked by strong growth, employment in it rising from just under 34,000 in 1960 to c. 88,000 in 1989, and thus, during this period, this sector's share of total employment rose from 1.6% to about 3%. Since then, there has been an appreciable reduction in the numbers employed, which in 1999 totalled 73,000 which is equivalent to about 2.5% of total employment.

The high economic growth until the first oil crisis brought about a sizeable increase in activity in the financial sector, while liberalisation of the financial markets and the significance of technological developments for the supply of financial products created fertile ground for a particularly strong increase in employment in the second half of the 1980s.

The end of the 1980s was characterised by a clear tendency towards concentration in Danish business life in the form of takeovers and mergers, which for their part created a need for larger and financially stronger Danish financial institutions. So during these years the financial sector experienced a period of amalgamations which, broadly speaking, halved the number of financial institutions and saw the establishment of the two major banks, Den Danske Bank and Unibank.

In common with the international trend, compound trading had started in Denmark leading in the direction of so-called financial supermarkets, which were able to offer all forms of financial services. Thus both Danske Bank and Unibank built up their own mortgage lending institutions and pension funds at the beginning of the 1990s, while existing mortgage lenders and insurance companies on the other hand began to offer traditional banking services, e.g. borrowing and lending.

Internationalisation had moreover meant that Danish financial companies had already established themselves abroad in the 1980s with representative offices, branches or subsidiaries. On the other hand, they experienced increasing foreign competition in the domestic market.

The generally sharper competition together with unfavourable market conditions from 1987 to 1993 led to losses amounting to billions of kroner in the financial sector. The resulting losses and debt provisions amounted to c. 2.5% of total outstanding loans and guarantees 1992- 1993, which was high, though not without precedence. This was gradually improved, following the economic upswing which began around 1993. In 2000, losses and debt provisions amounted to less than 0.3% of total loans and guarantees.

Financial Institutions

The potential for rationalisation in the wake of the period of amalgamations, together with deteriorating results in the sector, led to a considerable adjustment of the financial institutions' balances and operations between 1992 and 1993. Among other things, this has resulted in a better balance between deposits and loans, a reduction in the number of domestic branches by a third, and a reduction in the number of employees by 25% between 1989 and 2000. Although this has considerably reduced total costs, the Danish banking sector continues to be too labour intensive in an international perspective. An attempt has been made to improve profits in the financial institutions through greater use of bank charges. Furthermore, the financial institutions have benefited from the technological development and the concept of e-banking has expanded substantially since the late 1990s.

The creation of the EMU in 1999 caused a new wave of European mergers which did not spare Denmark. Unibank decided to take part in a Nordic co-operation, while Danske Bank merged with Danish institutions. Thus, Unibank merged with the Swedish-Finnish Bank MeritaNordbanken in March 2000, and in November that same year the Norwegian bank Christiania Bank og Kreditkasse joined the group which changed its name to Nordea shortly after. Nordea is clearly the leading financial institution in the Nordic countries. In October 2000 Danske Bank merged with RealDanmark (BG Bank and Realkredit Danmark) to form the largest Danish financial institution.

Mortgages
The mortgage lending institutions suffered very substantial losses during these years as a result of the downward trend in the property market. Between 1986 and 1990 house prices fell by roughly a third, and the number of compulsory sales rose from a good 8,000 a year to more than 20,000. The high rate of compulsory sales was maintained until 1993, when trading conditions improved. A significant fall in interest rates had made way for a massive conversion of householders' bond loans at a high rate of interest to loans at a low rate of interest. A change in legislation had opened up the possibility of an extension of the loan period.

The generally improved economic situation from 1993-1994 has been very important for developments in operating results in the financial and mortgage institutions, which in 1995 again began to show a profit.

The improvement in the economic situation in Denmark has reduced the number of compulsory sales to just under 2,400 in 1999 and 2000.

Insurance
At the beginning of the 1990s, the insurance sector was exposed to an aggressive buying policy that helped to bring about a series of bankruptcies in the sector. Thus both Hafnia and Baltica saw their net capital disappear. Hafnia was taken over by the biggest Danish insurance company, Codan, which is owned by the British insurance company Sun Alliance. The life insurance sector together with part of the general insurance sector in Baltica was amalgamated with Danica, which forms

The Financial Sector has since the 1980s been characterised by growing internationalisation and the use of new technology.

The photo shows the busy securities department of Danske Bank, the day when a referendum was held on Danish participation in the single European currency, the euro.

The 6 leading financial institutions in Denmark (2001)

Ranking	Company	Balance in millions of kroner	Numbers employed
1	Nordea	1,798,060	22,700
2	Danske Bank	1,539,000	17,564
3	Jyske Bank	133,156	3,328
4	Sydbank	66,048	1,897
5	Nykredit Bank	63,473	299
6	Spar Nord	28,990	1,110

Source: Børsen Research

part of the Danske Bank group, while the main part of the general insurance sector in Baltica was amalgamated with Tryg Forsikring to form Tryg-Baltica Forsikring. In 1999 Tryg-Baltica merged with the Unibank group.

Pensions

The pension fund system in Denmark is undergoing a change, so that it will become more like the system in other countries. The most important change is the emphasis in the system being gradually moved from social security pensions to labour market pensions. However, this will take a great deal of time, as 40-50 years normally elapse from someone's entering the labour market to the person's taking up a pension. Labour market pensions are managed partly by commercial and partly by non-commercial undertakings. The commercial managers are financial institutions and life insurance and pension funds. The non-commercial ones are company pension funds and joint pension funds. Finally, the public funds, ATP (*Arbejdsmarkedets Tillægspension* – The Danish Labour Market Supplementary Pension) and LD (*Lønmodtagernes Dyrtidsfond* – The Employees' Capital Pension Fund) are in charge of considerable pension funds.

At the end of 1999, life and pension insurance companies and joint pension funds administered 65% of pension funds, financial institutions 14%, ATP 17% and LD 4%. In 1999 the total amount under administration was 1.378 billion kroner, equivalent to 118% of GDP.

Helge Pedersen

Transport and Communications

Transport is one of Denmark's most important sectors. In 2000, it accounted for almost 10% of Denmark's total production value and nearly 7% of total employment. The sector is extremely varied with regard to the size of the individual undertakings. On the one hand there is a very small number of large public or private undertakings in the field of public transport, shipping and aviation. On the other hand, there is a considerable

The Danish merchant fleet of a little over 6.5 million GT is mainly engaged in the foreign trade; the greater part of domestic trade is transported by rail and road. The tradition-rich Greenland trade, which for centuries was the purview of the Royal Greenland Trade, has since 1 January 1993 been the responsibility of Royal Arctic Line, which sails the route with modern container ships. Here we see the M/S Arina Arctica on its way from Ålborg to Nuuk.

number of smaller firms concerned with both the transport of goods (haulage contractors) and personal transport (taxi companies).

Production

Activity in the transport sector as a whole has risen steadily since the 1980s and more than in society as a whole. Thus, production value in the sector rose by 88% between 1986 and 2000, when the total growth in the economy was c. 70%.

Overland transport accounts for just under half of the total production in this sector, while the remaining production value is divided among auxiliary undertakings for the transport sector (22%), shipping (22%) and aviation (8%). Especially transport by sea has experienced strong growth on account of increased specialisation in high-technology vessels such as liners and gas and chemical tankers. On the other hand, because of the general stagnation in the economy between 1987 and 1993 growth in road transport has been more modest which has changed afterwards owing to the higher economic activity. Rail transport experienced a rising level of activity through most of the 1990s. However, passenger rail transport posted a small decline of 0.1% in 1998-1999 while freight rail

transport declined by 6% between 1998 and 1999. This decline is probably due to the opening of the road bridge of the Great Belt Fixed Link.

After a considerable growth in the 1980s, air traffic experienced a decline at the beginning of the 1990s, and since then international air traffic has increased significantly, the number of departures and arrivals of 1999 being almost 17% higher than the level of 1996. During this same period domestic air traffic declined by about 30%, measured against the number of departures and arrivals. This decline is, once again, the result of the Great Belt Fixed Link.

Business Structures

The transport sector is dominated by a number of large limited companies such as A.P. Møller (Maersk) and DSB (Danish State Railways). Altogether there were some 16,000 VAT-registered firms within the field in 1998, to which could be added some 3000 businesses exclusively concerned with passenger transport, most of which are not subject to VAT. The great majority of these firms are small individual undertakings offering transport by road. The other companies are dominated by partnerships and company-owned undertakings and are primarily concerned with transport by sea and activities as forwarding agents.

Freight Transport

For moving freight inland, road is the most commonly used form of transport. Thus 80% of tonnage was carried by road in 1999, 8% by sea and the remainder mainly by train. Transport by sea dominated Denmark's international freight traffic. C. 70% of freight was sent by sea, just under 25% by road and the remainder mainly by rail.

Passenger Traffic

Overall passenger traffic in Denmark has multiplied more than fivefold since 1950. This corresponds to every Dane travelling on average 15,100 km in 1999 as against 2,300 in 1950. A significant part of this rise is due to the fact that the distance between home and place of work or education during the same period has increased considerably. The average Dane's means of transport in 1999 could be reckoned at 7,500 km by car as the driver, 2,450 km by car as a passenger, 1,900 km by bus or train, and 500 km by bicycle. In the period 1990-1999, bus transport was the means of transport which experienced the largest increase in percentages.

Communications

The real production value within postal and telecommunication services and telecommunications rose by more than 80% between 1990 and 2000. The growth is mainly due to the technological advances in the fields of computing and data transmission, which has produced a marked increase in new telecommunication activities. On account of technological innovations the developments in activity have taken place without a corresponding increase in employment. Thus the numbers employed within the sector in 2000 was about 52,000 which was the same level as in 1990.

Kristian Hjulsager

The average Dane travels this far each year (1999):

by own car: 7,500 km

passenger in car: 2,450 km

by bus or train: 1,900 km

by bicycle: 500 km

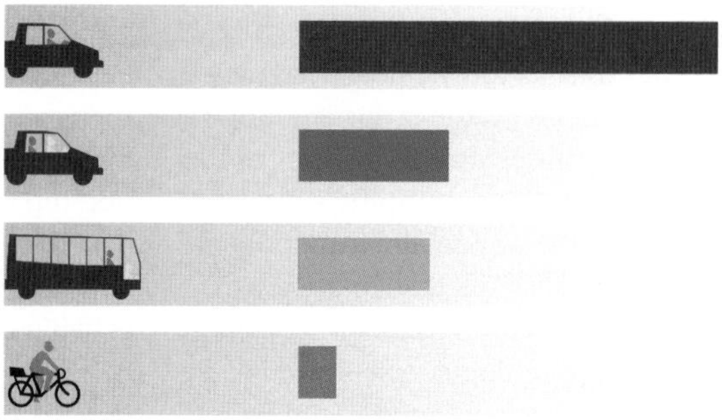

Tourism in Denmark

Each year almost 7 million people spend their holidays in Denmark, corresponding to about 43 million bednights in Danish hotels, youth hostels, campsites and holiday cottages. Danish resident visitors to Denmark and German visitors are the two most dominant nationalities of visitors to Denmark, accounting each for 40% of total bednights, followed by visitors from Sweden, Norway, the Netherlands and England.

German tourists prefer to stay in holiday cottages along the Jutland West Coast. The Danish beaches and pure nature attract, in particular, German families with children. The Danish nature and the relaxed lifestyle appeal to Norwegians and Swedes while Americans and Japanese are attracted by Danish history and culture and by 'fairy-tale attractions' like the Royal House, Tivoli, Hans Christian Andersen and Danish design.

Third largest industry

Tourism is the third largest industry in Denmark, following agriculture and the manufacturing industry. It has a turnover of 43 billion kroner a year – the 30 billion kroner being in foreign exchange – and provides jobs for 72,000 Danes.

The Danish Tourist Board (established in 1967) is a governmental agency working under the Ministry of Economic and Business Affairs and it is the national marketing organisation whose task is to promote Denmark as a tourism destination on both domestic and foreign markets. The Danish Tourist Board works in close co-operation with the Danish tourist industry. It has 10 foreign offices and promotes Denmark on both traditional neighbouring markets and new markets, such as South East Asia and Eastern Europe.

Global competition

During the decade between the early 1980s and the early 1990s Danish tourism grew considerably, but has, however, stagnated in recent years, especially on the German market, when counting the number og bednights.

This stagnation is the result of the stiff global competition faced by the Danish tourist industry in present

With over 3.5 million visitors in 1999, Copenhagen's Tivoli is Denmark's greatest tourist attraction. Among the favourite attractions in the old pleasure park are the Tivoli Guard, established in 1844, and the Pantomime Theatre. The theatre was built in 1874 and rebuilt after 1945 with a colourful peacock curtain that opens when the performances with Pierrot, Columbine and Harlequin in the main roles are about to start.

years. To be competitive, the Danish Tourist Board has, in co-operation with the Danish tourist industry, taken the initiative to create a strong brand emphasising Denmark's characteristics. This brand presents Denmark as an oasis in a hectic and harassed world offering the tourist the opportunity to relax in a well-organised society. Denmark needs this brand in order to attract the tourists' attention in the myriad of different offers that tourists receive from all around the world.

Extention of the season

The tourist industry is also faced with the challenge of extending the season to be able to attract tourists all year round. New offers include e.g. city breaks, cultural tourism and various forms of activity holidays (golfing, fishing, etc.). Another priority of the Danish tourist industry is reaching the business tourism. Business tourism includes e.g. conferences, meetings, field trips and incentive travels to reward skilled employees.

Danish Tourist Board

Since the 1980s, increasing numbers of Danes and foreign tourists have chosen to use the bicycle as their holiday transport. The counties provide special cycling maps showing 3,300 km of national cycle routes and more regional ones. The longest of these routes, along the east coast of Jutland is 600 km, the shortest, round Bornholm, 100 km.

Public Services

Especially since the Second World War, the government sector has grown significantly, as through its activities it has become more concerned with both regulatory activities and welfare. If we ignore the general rise in incomes and prices, the government sector in 2000 used c. 4.5 times as much as in 1950, which is also reflected in the growth in the number of governmental employees from c. 7% of all those in work in 1950 to 29% in 2000.

Between 1950 and 2000, an increasing proportion of overall Danish consumption has been accounted for by public services. Public services or non-market services are services, which are either actively controlled by public authorities or

are made available to the general public, free of charge. The majority of authorities and institutions producing public services are public.

Especially between 1960 and 1970, those available grew at an almost explosive rate corresponding to a doubling within c. 12 years. The present Danish welfare state was founded during this period: institutional buildings such as schools, social service offices and hospitals grew to a hitherto unknown extent. For example, the number of day nurseries, nursery schools and recreation centres trebled in the period 1960-1970; there was a corresponding increase in the number of study places in the universities. This is explained by the large birthrate from the middle of

Governmental services in Denmark Government expenditure and revenue 1950-2000; in percentage of GDP						
	1950	1960	1970	1980	1990	2000*
Governmental expenditure	**23**	**25**	**43**	**57**	**57**	**53**
Distributed in economic terms:						
Government consumption	11	14	21	27	26	25
Current transfer (transfer income)	5	6	11	16	18	17
Other expenditure	7	7	12	13	13	11
Distributed according to objective:						
General services	3	3	4	5	4	4
Defence	2	2	3	2	2	2
Education	3	3	7	7	7	8
Social services	6	7	14	20	23	23
Health	3	3	6	6	5	5
Other objectives	6	7	9	14	16	11
Taxes and duties (tax burden)	**21**	**26**	**40**	**44**	**47**	**48**
Taxes on income and wealth	9	12	21	25	28	29
Taxes on production and import	10	13	17	18	17	17
Other taxes	2	1	2	1	2	3
Government sector employment in relation to total employment	**7**	**8**	**16**	**26**	**28**	**29**

*provisional figures

Source: Statistics Denmark

Most basic and advanced courses of education are publicly funded. Students in festive mood are here celebrating their high school leaving examination with a dance on the town square.

the 1940s until the beginning of the 1950s, which created an enormous need for care and training facilities at the beginning of the 1960s, while women were entering the labour market in large numbers. With this, tasks that had previously been the responsibility of the family, became in part a responsibility of the public authorities.

The use of government funds in relation to the gross domestic product (GDP) rose year by year, but in 1982 it peaked and was turned into a decline. The proportion used by public authorities in relation to GDP was thus less in 1990 than in 1980, but in the 1990s again started to increase, implying that governmental expenditure in 1996 reached the same level as that of 1982. Payment of public debt explains partly why the relatively declining governmental expenditure 1990-2000 has not resulted in an equivalent tax reduction.

Governmental expenditure has not gone exclusively on public consumption. The welfare society has very largely been characterised by a very considerable growth in transfer payments, i.e. expenditure on pensions,

support for education and training, child benefits, unemployment benefit, etc. This amount has risen from 5% of GDP in 1950 to 17% in 2000. The economic prosperity – and falling unemployment – of the mid-1990s altered the development in the government sector's expenditure on transfer payments. Between 1990 and 2000 this amount fell from 18 to 17% of GDP.

The marked increase in governmental sector activities has had an effect on taxation, which has provided the means for financing the public services. There has been an almost constant rise in the tax burden, from 21% in 1950 to 48% in 2000. Tax revenue alone has not been able to finance government sector activities. It has been necessary to borrow money, and since the 1970s servicing the interest on the growing debt has helped to shelve other governmental activities.

In an international perspective, the government sector in Denmark went through a remarkable period of development between 1950 and 2000. In 1950, the government sector in Denmark accounted for less than in the countries with which Denmark is traditionally compared (the OECD countries). This very modest position held until the beginning of the 1960s. Since the 1970s, Denmark, along with Sweden and Holland, has taken the lead in government sector expenditure. Sweden and Denmark differ from Holland by mainly channelling their expenditure via public consumption, while Holland gives greater priority to transfer payments.

Preben Etwil

The Co-operative Movement

The Danish co-operative movement (*andelsbevægelsen*) has its roots and major significance in the rural population. The object has always been the purely financial one of buying and selling agricultural products through co-operative undertakings and providing agriculture and the rural community with goods for its use and its production. Hand in hand with increased urbanisation since the 1950s, the consumer co-operative movement, the co-operative wholesale society stores, have established themselves in towns, while the production co-operative movement continues to be linked to agriculture and related trades such as market gardening and fishing.

Linked to the workers' movement another co-operative movement (*kooperationen*) emerged about the turn of the century, encompassing both trades and producers, but now consisting mainly of non-profitmaking housing associations. In agriculture's co-operative movement and in the co-operative (wholesale) stores the members have always been single individuals, while in the workers' co-operative movement it has been the trade unions. In Danish the word 'kooperation' is used of undertakings which historically have been linked to the workers' movement, whereas 'andelsbevægelsen' is associated with the rural community.

For more than a century the co-

Vorbasse Co-operative Society near Billund, a typical rural store around 1914. The piece goods on the shelves behind the manager (right) were the only area on which women had any direct influence, as some wives of members of the management committee were in charge of the purchases of drapery. Not until the 1950s did it become common for women to be eligible for election to co-op management committees.

Membership democracy continues to form the basis of the cooperative movement in Denmark. In the undertakings where there is a personal membership, voting is on the basis of one man, one vote. Women are playing an increasing role in the decision-making organs, as is the case here at the meeting of the Cooperative Wholesale Society (FDB) in 1994.

operative movement has played a considerable part in Danish economic life, and in important sectors such as the food industry, co-operative undertakings play a leading role, with more than 90% of milk and pork production going through co-operative dairies and bacon factories. In the retail trade co-operative stores are responsible for an estimated 35% of the total turnover in every-day goods.

The first co-operative store was established in Thisted in 1866, but it was the first co-operative dairy in Hjedding in West Jutland (founded 1882) that heralded the start of the agricultural co-operative movement which by the time of the First World War had expanded to its fullest extent with production facilities (co-operative dairies and bacon factories), marketing undertakings (co-operative egg and butter exports) and purchasing organisations (co-operative heavy goods undertakings). An important precondition for this development was the fact that Danish farmers and smallholders owned their own land, for which reason the co-operative undertakings could be financed by joint liability on the part of the members. Within the co-operative movement the fundamental principle has been

one man, one vote (vote entitlement was not decided by the number of cattle owned).

Even in the middle of the 20th century, the co-operative movement in Denmark consisted of a large number of quite small local undertakings, but since then an extensive process of rationalisation has taken place, resulting in fewer but by Danish standards often very large countrywide undertakings. This applies for instance to the Dansk Landbrugs Grovvareselskab (DLG – Danish Agricultural Feeding-stuffs and Fertilisers Company), founded 1969 and MD Foods, established 1970. In 1999 MD Foods merged with the Swedish co-operative dairy ARLA. At the same time the co-operative stores played an important part in modernising trade in every-day goods on the American pattern, not least in the in-town stores that gradually came to dominate the movement.

There is no special legislation in Denmark governing the co-operative movement, but from its early days in the 1880s and right up to the present, the movement has developed on the basis of members' needs and the constant practical adaptation of the movement's fundamental principles to the demands of the day. Apart from the principle of one man, one vote, which applies in primary production activities, i.e. where there is a question of personal membership, other characteristics of the movement are the open membership and the distribution of profit in relation to the individual member's volume of business with the undertaking. Most co-operative undertakings used to be based on joint responsibility, but now by far the greater number of co-operative undertakings are co-operative societies with limited liability.

Feta cheese production at Rødkærsbro Dairy, an undertaking that is part of ARLA Foods. Cheese overtook butter in the Danish dairy industry long ago, but the aim, as it was in the 1880s, is still to produce goods for export. The production of feta cheese is a result of continued specialisation and adaptation to changed market conditions.

Internally and externally, co-operative undertakings today look like any other business venture, and on a secondary level there is often co-operation between co-operative and non-co-operative concerns. The process of rationalisation has still not been completed in several sectors, for instance in the field of co-operative bacon factories. With the development of the EU, the largest agricultural co-operative undertakings are faced with new challenges which promise co-operation beyond the Danish borders, as is already the case in the dairy sector.

The co-operative movement in Denmark is felt to be an integral part of the community and business, which many Danes encounter as consumers (co-operative stores) or as producers (agriculture, market gardening and fishing). Only to a limited extent is there any question of ideological attitudes, but co-operative undertakings have for generations been seen as practical instruments for protecting of financial interests.

Claus Bjørn

The Labour Market and Employment

Of the Danish population of 5.4 million (2002), the labour force, i.e. those in employment and the unemployed, constitutes c. 2.9 million. Of the remaining 2.5 million Danes, just under half are children and students without work, and over 40% are pensioners and those taking early retirement. The remaining 10% consists i.a. of husbands or wives at home and those receiving state support but unconnected with the labour market.

Between 1940 and 2002, the population in Denmark rose by c. 1.5 million, while the labour force rose by c. 1 million during the same period. The labour force's proportion of the population has thus increased during this period from 51% to 55%. This is partly because a larger proportion of the population is of working age (16-66), and partly because more people in this age group are active in the labour market.

Rate of Economic Activity

Of the population group of working age, the labour force makes up 78%. This rate of economic activity is one of the highest in the world, which is due to the very high proportion of economically active women in Denmark. Thus 74% of women in this age group go out to work (2001), a figure only exceeded in Sweden.

The growth of the labour force 1940-2002 is divided among 0.3 million men and 0.7 million women. The male increase in the labour force was concentrated in the period 1940-1960, resulting from the growth

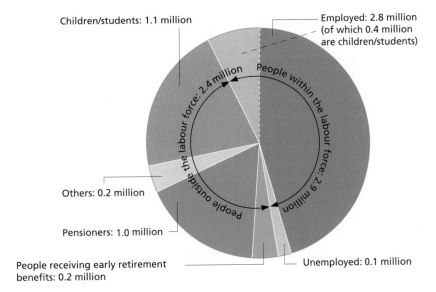

Children/students: 1.1 million

Employed: 2.8 million (of which 0.4 million are children/students)

People within the labour force: 2.9 million

People outside the labour force: 2.4 million

Others: 0.2 million

Pensioners: 1.0 million

People receiving early retirement benefits: 0.2 million

Unemployed: 0.1 million

Denmark's labour force accounts for a little over half the population (2002). Outside the labour force, just under half receive early retirement benefits or pensions, and a similar number is made up of children and students without jobs. The remainder (the rest on the graph) consists partly of husbands and wives at home, though this labour force reserve is very small compared with the situation in most other countries.

in population, whereas the increase on the part of women was only started around 1960 and derived especially from changes in the pattern of the roles of the sexes and in living arrangements. Trends in the 1990s suggest that the rate of economic activity of women of all age groups will end up being only a couple of percentages below that of men. A particular Danish (and in part Nordic) characteristic is that women retain their links with the labour market after having children.

A more recent tendency is for a decline in the participation in the labour market of the younger and older age groups, both men and women. In the youngest age groups the reason is a longer period of education for a large proportion of the group. In the older age groups the reason is earlier withdrawal from the labour market, due to pensions and early retirement benefits.

Working Hours
Although the work force has grown by almost 50% since 1940, the number of hours worked has not increased correspondingly. Holiday entitlement has been extended from three to five weeks a year, and the working week has dropped from 48 to 37 hours. Many groups employed in the private sector have had their holiday entitlement extended to six weeks. Finally, the proportion of part-time employees has grown, although the trend has been reversed in recent years. With this, the overall number of hours worked in 2001 has recorded a real decline of 10% as compared to 1940.

Educational Status and Industry
The level of education of the work force has risen between 1940 and 2001, as is seen partly in the fact that the proportion of salaried employees

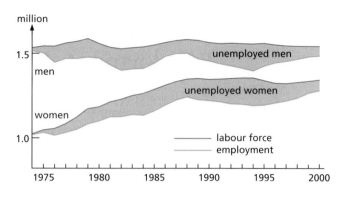

and skilled workers has risen at the cost of self-employed persons and unskilled workers. This in its turn is also connected with recent years' shift in employment in different industries. Since the 1970s, the number of people in work has grown by 7% primarily on account of increased employment in the public sector. On the other hand, employment in agriculture and manufacturing has fallen. For the remaining industries taken together, employment has been unchanged.

Unemployment
While unemployment in the 1960s and early 1970s was under 3%, which in practice meant there was full employment, it has since 1973 risen considerably; it peaked in 1993 at 11% for men and 14% for women. In 2001 it had fallen to 5% for men, and 6% for women. Measured in terms of the average unemployment rate on a monthly basis, this meant just under 150,000 unemployed. At the same time it meant that just under 550,000 – or one in five of the labour force – was unemployed for a shorter or longer period in any one year. (For unemployment on a regional basis, see below on the regional distribution of occupations and population since 1945).

The growing rate of unemployment at the beginning of the 1970s

The number of women in the labour force grew by a third (c. 321,000) from 1974 to 2000, while the number of men with an increase of c. 8,000 was almost unchanged. During the same period the number of unemployed women rose by 57,000 and the number of unemployed men by 38,000. Therefore, the total numbers employed rose by c. 234,000, but in such a way that this represented a fall of just under 30,000 for men and an increase of c. 264,000 for women.

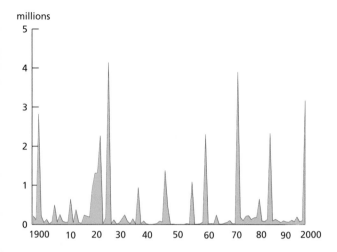

millions

Industrial action in Denmark 1897-1998. The graph shows the number of lost working days in millions. From 1947 only industrial action leading to the loss of more than 100 working days is included. The labour market in the 1920s was affected by a general strike and lock-outs; 1925 was the year with the largest number of lost working days. Since then the labour market has experienced major conflicts with an interval of 10-12 years, the latest taking place in 1998. In general major conflicts in Denmark do not last long and in most places the loss of production is soon recovered.

was seen as a passing phase that would be solved by ensuring that the unemployed did not suffer financially until they could find work again. At the same time the economy was being stimulated through a financial policy aimed at creating more jobs. At the end of the 1970s an attempt was made to reduce the rate of unemployment by limiting the labour force by encouraging older members to leave the labour market and take early retirement benefits or pensions. At the same time emphasis was placed on a more active labour market policy (training and job offers), in which the qualifications of the unemployed should be maintained or improved. In 1994 these efforts were intensified by the passing of a labour market reform at the same time as leave arrangements were introduced partly to give employed persons or unemployed a period of freedom from the labour market to be used for further training or looking after their own children, and in part to create vacancies enabling others to get into the labour market as a result of the jobs thus falling vacant. In 1999 the aim of the labour market policy changed again. According to population projections, the work force will decline and as a consequence, the conditions permitting early withdrawal from the labour market and early retirement benefits have been tightened.

The Industrial Court

The Industrial Court is a court of law concerned with disputes about the collective agreements in the labour market. It deals with cases concerning breaches of agreements, the legality of conflicts, strike notices and the validity of agreements. Finally, the court decides on cases concerning the jurisdiction of the Conciliation Board. The Industrial Court is the only court in its field, and appeals against its judgements can thus not be made to the ordinary courts.

In the composition of the Industrial Court an attempt has been made to ensure that it enjoys the confidence of the various organisations in the labour market. The Bench consists partly of a number of lay assessors, of whom half are selected by workers' organisations, and half by employers' organisations, and partly by a presidium of professional judges who are selected by the lay assessors. The presidium is traditionally chosen from among the judges in the Supreme Court.

It is only the workers' or employers' organisations that can take a case to the Industrial Court. Individual employees and employers cannot themselves take legal action except in the case of employers who do not belong to the employers' association but have themselves accepted an agreement.

If the Industrial Court finds a breach of agreement it can impose a financial sanction, a fine, on those responsible. If the breach of an agreement consists of an illegal strike, the employees taking part have, however, fines imposed on them according to a system of fixed rates per strike hour.

Per Jacobsen

Organisations

In contrast to the labour markets in most other European countries, where essential conditions are regulated by legislation, those in the Danish labour market are mainly founded on agreements between the employers' and employees' organisations. They encompass basic areas such as minimum wages, the right to strike and hours of work. In more recent times, however, it has happened that the organisations have not been able to agree despite help from the conciliation board. In these cases the Folketing has typically legislated to give legal force to a compromise proposal put forward by the conciliation officer.

On the part of the employees, membership of unions in Denmark is very high, around 80%. Far fewer employers belong to an employers' organisation, but employers outside the organisations usually come to an agreement with their employees based on the conditions worked out between the employees' and employers' organisations.

Vøgg Løwe Nielsen

Regional Distribution of Occupations and Population since 1945

Post-war developments in trades and occupations have changed the geographical distribution of occupations and population in Denmark.

Industry

In the 1950s the distribution of industry throughout the country was very uneven indeed. At that time over half of jobs in industry were in Copenhagen and the remainder of north-east Zealand; in the 1990s the figure had fallen to only a quarter. On the other hand industry has undergone an appreciable growth in Jutland. West Jutland, which until 1965 was the least industrialised area in the country, has today more industrial jobs per 1000 inhabitants than any other region.

In the 1960s a partial reason for the growth of industry in Jutland was that firms were moving there from Copenhagen. However, since 1970 redistribution has resulted particularly from the establishment of a far greater number of new undertakings in Jutland than in the Copenhagen area.

In Jutland, industry has grown especially in the smaller and medium-sized towns in west, central and southern Jutland; in several of the old industrial towns on the east coast employment has stagnated. The most rapidly expanding industrial towns tend to be dominated by a single large firm. Examples of this are Danfoss in Nordborg, Lego in Billund and Grundfos in Bjerringbro.

Not all industry has disappeared from the Copenhagen area. High technology, for example the pharmaceutical industry, which is based on research and employs a highly paid work force, has remained in north-east Zealand. The greater the proportion of low-paid and unskilled workers employed by a branch of industry, the greater is the share of the western areas in this branch.

Service Industries

In terms of employment, agriculture and industry have been overtaken by business and the service industries. By the end of the 1960s these had risen so far as to account for half of all those in employment, and their share had grown to 73% in 2000.

Regional trends 1961-1998 in the number of industrial jobs.

Legend:
- Metropolitan region
- Central Denmark
- North, West and South Jutland

North, West and South Jutland chart (1961 1970 1980 1990 1998): 67,900 / 96,700 / 115,900 / 137,800 / 158,000

Metropolitan region chart (1961 1970 1980 1990 1998): 197,100 / 170,800 / 118,800 / 101,100 / 95,400

Central Denmark chart (1961 1970 1980 1990 1998): 128,600 / 158,100 / 149,600 / 154,100 / 163,800

Production of television sets at Bang & Olufsen. In the 1950s, Denmark had several radio and television factories. Only one, Bang & Olufsen in Struer, western Jutland, is left. It has survived by aiming at an international market with its emphasis on exclusive design. The factory's products are regularly awarded international prizes for art and design.

It is especially in the public service sector that the growth has been strong – the numbers employed doubled from 1970 to 1985 and subsequently growth stagnated – and it has been strongest in many rural districts and small towns where until 1970 it had been modest in extent. Business services (banks, insurance, advertising, electronic data processing, etc.) also grew in the 1970s, but here growth continued throughout the 1980s and the 1990s. Unlike the public service sector, these are clearly city establishments; about a quarter of the jobs are in the municipality of Copenhagen and a further quarter in the remainder of the metropolitan area. Thus, in the 1980s these expanding areas provided the cities with an increase in jobs to replace those branches of industry that were lost during the same years.

Unemployment

Seen from a structural point of view, unemployment in the 1950s was associated with the rural population and the moves to increase agricultural efficiency. Pools of unemployment were reduced during the prosperous years from 1958 to 1973. The start of the 1974 economic crisis meant that unemployment returned in the entire country. In the late 1990s unemployment declined sharply.

Generally speaking, unemployment is highest in the islands outside the metropolitan area and in northeastern Jutland. In the remainder of Jutland and in the metropolitan area unemployment is by and large near or below the national average.

In the metropolitan area there are clear local differences in the unemployment rate. In the city of Copenhagen it is above average, while in the counties of Frederiksborg and Roskilde it is low. Similar differences between the urban centres and outlying areas in the same geographical labour market are also found in other parts of the country.

The highest rate of unemployment today is found in areas where industrialisation occurred before the Second World War, and results from the changes taking place in industrialised society. Unemployment is moreover higher in some rural areas, especially in the islands in the South of the country.

The unemployment rate is generally higher among women than men. In particular there is a large percentage of unemployed women in the smaller urban communities, whereas unemployment is virtually the same for the two sexes in the more adaptable Copenhagen labour market.

Geographical Division of Labour
Occupational trends since the Second World War have geographically speaking divided Denmark into three principal types of area:

Western, central and southern Jutland are distinguished by relatively new industry employing a large number of unskilled workers. There is a larger percentage of self-employed in most occupations than in the rest of Denmark.

The metropolitan area and the Århus area are characterised by service industries, in particular business service and major public institutions. State employees are concentrated in the metropolitan area, salaried workers forming the majority, and incomes are higher than in the remainder of the country, the city of Copenhagen being the notable exception.

In *the remainder of the country*, i.e. northern Jutland, parts of eastern Jutland and the islands outside the metropolitan area there is a greater proportion of older industry than elsewhere in the country. These are relatively labour-intensive, often employing skilled workers, and the rate of unemployment is higher than in other parts of the country.

There is thus a certain division of labour between the various regions in the country. Some areas specialise in agriculture and industry, while others offer financial and major public and private services.

In general the service sectors, both the public and the private ones, are most strongly represented in the islands, especially in the metropolitan area, and in Århus, whereas manufacturing sectors dominate the rest of Jutland, especially central and western Jutland.

Population
Until 1970 the population was concentrated in the larger towns and cities. There was a movement of population especially from the rural areas. However, many smaller towns also experienced stagnating populations in the 1950s and 1960s.

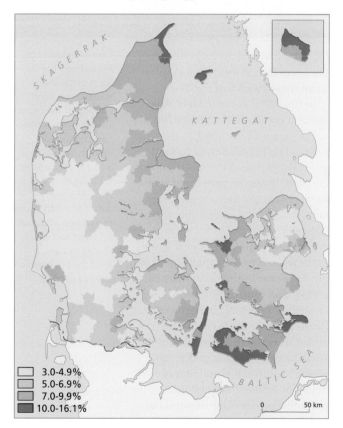

3.0-4.9%
5.0-6.9%
7.0-9.9%
10.0-16.1%

Regional distribution of unemployment in 1998.

The rationalisation of agriculture meant that the number of employees declined noticeably in the 1950s and that the number of farms began to fall from 1960. Together with the expansion of industry and the service sector, this meant a change in the geographical distribution of the population.

In the 1950s the towns, especially the larger cities, experienced a period of strong growth. On the other hand, the population in many rural districts declined, though the birth rate there was higher than in the towns.

In the 1960s some of those moving away from agriculture found employment locally thanks to the expansion of industry in the smaller and medium-sized towns. On the other hand, the service sector continued to grow strongly in the major cities, and here the population continued to increase more rapidly than the national average, despite the reduction in industrial employment these cities had to offer.

In the 1970s the pattern of development reversed, resulting in an increase in numbers living in the small towns. The population of Jutland grew, while that in the metropolitan area fell. However, purely rural districts continued to decline in numbers, though at a slower rate than hitherto.

The new population trend in the 1970s related to the expansion of the public sector in the new enlarged county and municipal authorities created in the local government reforms in 1970. To this could be added the growth of industry in the small towns. Housing policy, too, which favoured the building of detached houses, created the potential for a greater dispersal of family housing.

Since 1980 population numbers

Central Jutland's textile industry has its roots in the sheep farming and hand knitting of the heathland farmers of the past. The textile industry continues as a highly competitive trade by aiming at a high degree of automatisation, niche production of special products and sophisticated designs. A large part of production is exported.

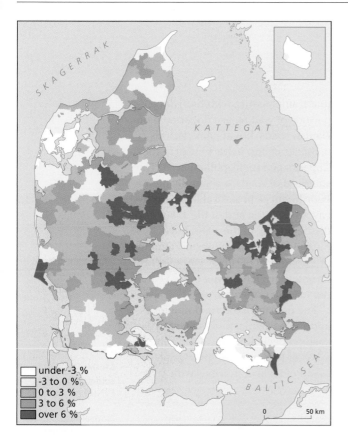

under -3 %
-3 to 0 %
0 to 3 %
3 to 6 %
over 6 %

Growth of population by region 1990-1999.

The modest decline in population in the metropolitan area continued into the 1980s, and in the 1990s it was replaced by a moderate increase. It is in particular neighbouring towns such as Holbæk and Ringsted that have experienced an influx of newcomers from Copenhagen, though to a great extent these new arrivals work in the capital.

The Århus area also underwent noticeable growth in the 1980s and 1990s, especially as a result of the expansion of the public and private service sectors. In the 1980s and 1990s the major provincial cities saw a certain growth in population numbers; changes in taxation policy and new housing in the inner areas have again made the towns more attractive as places to live in.

On the other hand, towns and rural districts in Lolland, Falster, Bornholm and the smaller islands, as well as in northwest Jutland have seen a decline in population numbers. This results from the continued rationalisation of agriculture, fishing and traditional industry.

Bue Nielsen

have been fairly stable, and there have only been minor changes in the geographical distribution of the population.

Transport

Denmark has a well-developed infrastructure. The railway system serves almost all towns with over 10,000 inhabitants and has a significant unused capacity. The airline network is one of the densest in the world, and few countries have more traffic harbours in relation to the length of coastline than Denmark. The road network is fine-meshed and generally of a high standard, and similarly the capacity is large in relation to the density of traffic. The great majority of residences and firms have direct access to the road network. Even in rural areas the distance to the nearest road is usually very modest. Thus the infrastructure gives excellent possibilities for the transport sector effectively to serve both companies and private individuals in Denmark.

Roads

Towards the end of the 19th century the main network of highroads was established and cobbled. Together with the secondary roads, the Danish road network had a high density compared with the rest of contemporary Europe. Later the network was further consolidated, drained and asphalted and supplemented with motorways and new main roads as well as many new local roads, in particular during the 1960s and 1970s, to keep pace with demand in the expanding urban areas. In 2000 Denmark had c. 71,500 km of road, 910 km being motorways. With 1.65 km of public roadways per square kilometre, Denmark, then, has a road density that is among the highest in the world, and with a general excess capacity. Ac-

tual traffic queues with hour-long periods of waiting are not known on Danish roads, but at peak periods tailbacks occur, in particular in the Copenhagen metropolitan area. The standard of roads is generally high. Poor finances in several local authority areas at the end of the 1980s and the beginning of the 1990s have meanwhile led to the postponement of a good deal of repair work, so that the standard fell during these years, not least in Copenhagen.

The density of the road network and the particularly high standard of roads especially in thinly populated areas of Denmark are primarily the result of local authorities with large

Motorways and ferry routes 2002.

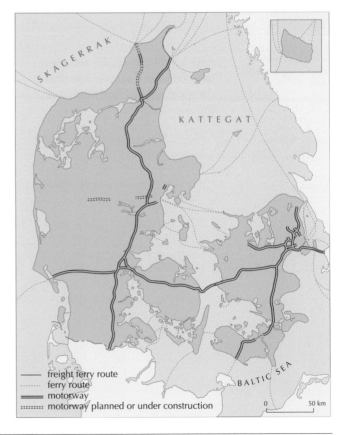

SKAGERRAK

KATTEGAT

BALTIC SEA

—— freight ferry route
······ ferry route
══ motorway
▓▓▓▓ motorway planned or under construction

0   50 km

numbers of unemployed over long periods being able to reduce their expenditure on social relief by starting road works, for which the State then paid the greater part. The development of the motorway network on stretches with very limited traffic density (for instance in the northernmost part of Denmark) is likewise especially the result of local political interests: the state covers all expenses, while the construction work brings employment to the area, and the new road relieves the locally-financed local road network. Today, the total length of roads in a local authority area is included in the basis for calculating the equalisation of expenditure between local authorities. This especially favours thinly populated and less affluent local authority areas.

Railways 1928 and 2002.

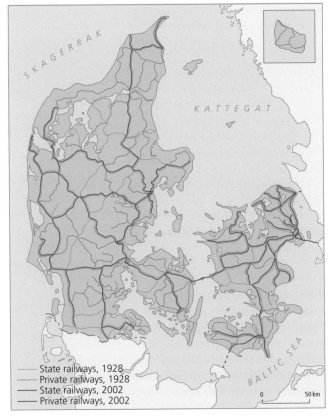

State railways, 1928
Private railways, 1928
State railways, 2002
Private railways, 2002

0   50 km

Railways

The first stretch of railway in Denmark was opened to traffic in 1844, running between Altona and Kiel (in present-day Germany). Three years later, on 26 June 1847, the line between Copenhagen and Roskilde was inaugurated. But it was not until after 1864 that the building of railways took off, and the most important stretches were constructed in the years up to 1880. In 1888, with 92 km of railway per 100,000 inhabitants, Denmark was only surpassed as regards railway density by Sweden and Switzerland. In the country that pioneered railways, England, there was, by way of comparison, 78 km per 100,000 inhabitants. The development of the network continued until the 1920s, especially with the building of local lines and often to the accompaniment of vehement parliamentary and popular debate about the route taken by the lines, etc.

In the period leading up to the 1940s the railway network was linked up by the building of the bridges across Lillebælt (1935) and Storstrømmen (1937) at the same time as stretches carrying the least volume of traffic began to close. This meant that many new stretches of railway only survived for a very short time.

Since then, the network has been reduced from a total rail length of c. 5,000 km (about half of which was accounted for by private railways) to c. 2,800 km in 2000 (of which 17% was private railways). Although the present railway network is only just over half the size of what it was at its peak, Denmark still has a relatively extensive railway network, the maintenance of which is dependent on significant annual state subsidies.

The linking of the Danish railway network has been completed with the opening of the fixed link across

Storebælt, between Halsskov and Knudshoved (1997) and the Øresund Link between Copenhagen and Malmö (2000).

Environmental considerations and problems of capacity on the roads of Europe throughout the 1990s led to increased interest in rail transport of passengers and goods – not least in Denmark. This has resulted in fresh investment in developing railway installations and goods terminals with equipment for the fast transfer between road and rail transport and the establishment of new stretches of railway for especially passenger traffic, for instance to Copenhagen Airport in Kastrup. Similarly, the railborne local traffic has been expanded in Århus and the metropolitan area of Copenhagen, where the gradual expansion of the S train network of metropolitan and suburban trains to Hillerød, Farum, Frederikssund, Høje-Tåstrup and Køge is supplemented with the Copenhagen Metro, a light railway – partly in tunnels – between Frederiksberg and Amager (the metro), expected to be inaugurated in late 2002.

The railway network accounts for about 6% of passenger transport (though some 20% in the Copenhagen area) and about 7% of goods traffic in Denmark (1995) after a continuous decline over the previous 40 years.

In 2001 a new chapter in the history of Danish railways was opened when rail traffic (but not the tracks) on some rail lines in Central and West Jutland was put out to tender. A private company, British Arriva, won the contract and will begin operating these rail lines in 2003.

Ports

Of the more than 100 commercial ports in Denmark, 90 are traffic ports, of which many are served by the 75-80 ferry lines in the country.

The ports handle c. 3/4 (by volume) of the total Danish foreign trade. In addition there is c. 9 million tonnes of internal traffic, especially coal moving through ports serving power stations. While the competition between the commercial ports leads to considerable over-capacity there has been an unsatisfied demand for investment in marinas, which among other things can attract tourists.

Airports

Of Denmark's c. 25 serviced airports, 7 are part of the national network of domestic routes, all of them having their point of departure in Copenhagen Airport in Kastrup. 80% of all air transport in Denmark goes through Kastrup (1999). A few provincial airports (especially Billund) have established routes abroad, and most of the state-owned provincial airports cater for a certain amount of military traffic.

Peter Maskell

Telecommunications

Compared to other countries, Denmark's public tele-network is modern and according to OECD figures, its tariffs are among the lowest. PSTN and ISDN are provided nationwide and by mid-2002, 95% of Danish households were able to access

Especially after the Second World War many lengths of railway lines were closed; at the same time the main lines were modernised. A few stretches have been electrified and are being prepared for high speed trains.

Denmark consists of a peninsula and 78 populated islands. Especially in the 20th century, more and more parts of the country have been linked by means of a large number of bridges, but travel by ferry is still part of everyday life in Denmark. In this photo cyclists are waiting to embark the ferry 'Thor Sydfyen' sailing between Fynshav and Bøjden.

broadband services via ADSL. By mid-2001, Denmark numbered 72 subscriber lines, 70 mobile telephone subscribers and 40 Internet subscribers per 100 inhabitants.

The Danish telecommunications sector was completely liberalised in 1996 and Denmark is considered to have one of the most open markets offering the keenest competition in Western Europe. The former incumbent operator, TDC A/S, has been privatised, and in 1997 the Danish State sold the rest of its shares to the American telecommunication company SBC.

The entire fixed network is digitalised and the transmission network is based on the optical fibre technology. Denmark is a hub for international submarine cables, having e.g. cable connections to North America, Great Britain and Russia. Many foreign telecommunication companies use these cable connections to transit traffic, but they are also used by many companies to provide access to international telephone and data services in Denmark. Like the other Nordic countries, Denmark has been a pioneer in the field of mobile telephone services and by late 2001 the number of mobile telephone subscribers exceeded the number of fixed telephone lines.

Four GSM-nets are competing against each other, and they are also used by several independent service providers. In 2001 four licenses were awarded for the nationwide UMTS-net. Cable television covers about 50% of Danish households and the two dominating companies provide access to the Internet via cable modems.

Mogens Ritsholm

Information Technology

The use of computers is more widespread in Denmark than in most other countries. Leaving general factors such as high education level out of account, two main reasons explain this situation. Firstly, competition has traditionally been keen on the consumer electronic market in Denmark, resulting in low prices and broad access to computers and computer equipments. Secondly, the public authorities have focused on the dissemination of information technology (IT) since the mid-1980s.

By late 2001 60% of the Danes between 16 and 74 years of age had access to the Internet at home; 74% had access either at home, at work or at an educational institution. 40% of the population used the Internet daily. The dissemination of the Internet in businesses was coming close to reaching a saturation point in 1999. 80% of all businesses with more than 5 employees had access to the Internet. In 2000 Danish businesses had a turnover of c. 12 billion kroner on the Internet, just under 1% of their total turnover. However, only 12% of Danish businesses offered online sales, and these Internet sales accounted on average for 7% of their total turnover.

Successive governments' support of the dissemination of information technology has resulted in specific initiatives such as Digital Denmark, a committee set up by The Ministry of Science, Technology and Innovation (the former Ministry of Research and Information Technology) for the purpose of recommending the Danish government's future IT policy strategy. Examples of major IT initiatives include compulsory IT training of teachers and students, an action plan for electronic trading and the establishment in Northern Jutland and in Ørestaden of two IT lighthouses, that is, geographic areas promoting IT development. Moreover, many public institutions have used information technology as a means of creating greater openness in the administration, for instance through websites offering information on local authorities and giving direct access to different services such as application for home care and changes to the income tax return.

The focus on IT qualifications and knowledge has brought increased attention to IT training in Danish elementary and junior secondary schools. It is compulsory to integrate IT in most subjects, even in the youngest classes. While local authorities procure educational material, the Danish State, that is the Ministry of Education, aims at supporting the development of IT material appropriate for students.

Focus on IT training do not only concern elementary and junior secondary schools. In 1999 the Danish State took the initiative to establish the IT University of Copenhagen (IT-C), which offers a range of courses in IT, most of them leading to master's or higher degrees. In 2002 the IT University numbered more than 1,000 students.

Cliff Thaudahl Hansen

The Øresund Region

The idea of the establishment of an 'Ørestad' was conceived as early as in the 1950s. This 'Ørestad' would consist of the Copenhagen area and North Zealand in Denmark and of the coast on the other side of Øresund (the Sound) with the Swedish towns Malmö, Lund, Landskrona and Helsingborg. The crisis of the 1970s put a damper on these plans, but with the discussions concerning the construction of the Øresund link in the late 1980s, the idea of creating a joint metropolitan area across the sound, arose again, now designated the Øresund region.

The Øresund region is the largest metropolitan area in the Nordic countries. This region, situated within a distance of 50 km from the centre of Copenhagen, counts 2,540,000 inhabitants (2001) of which 735,000 live in Sweden.

The Øresund is only 4 km wide between Elsinore and Helsingborg, and 14 km between Dragør and Limhamn. Thus, the Øresund region is situated were the distance between Scandinavia and the Continent is shortest, a fact that partly explains why the Øresund fixed link was constructed.

In 1999 the ferries operating between the two coasts transported 19 million passengers, many being Swedes shopping in Denmark. On average they carried 8,600 cars a day, 7,200 being passenger cars. For the Øresund fixed link to be profitable, c. 10,000 cars must cross the bridge each day; in 2001 the figure was 8,100 cars per day. As to international air traffic, Copenhagen Airport in Kastrup serves most of the Øresund region.

Trade across the Øresund is relatively modest. On both sides of the Øresund, business activities are directed towards the domestic market. Copenhagen is characterised by private and public services having customers in most parts of Denmark but only a few in Scania. Many branches of large Swedish industrial groups are situated in Malmö and Helsingborg and consequently companies in Scania have 10-15 times as much contact with Stockholm as with Copenhagen, e.g. as to trade, telephone conversations and business trips. These branches choose Swedish suppliers, though a Danish supplier is often situated closer to the Swedish branch. The Øresund fixed link will not, in itself, change this trade pattern which depends on property conditions, product standards and knowledge of the market. Although differences in language and traditions may moderate purchases, competition is expected to increase for businesses operating mainly on the local market of the Øresund region, such as the building sector and parts of the retail trade.

6,900 Swedes live in the Danish part of this large city and 7,300 Danes in the Swedish part (2001). About 4,000 people live in one country and work in the other. The main incentive to do this is that income taxes are low in Sweden and gross wages and salaries are high in Denmark. Thus, the number of commuters crossing the Øresund is expected to increase in future, depending on toll prices and differences in tax legislation.

Several networks have been established across the Øresund. Copenhagen and Scania are both strong within pharmaceutical industry and manufacture of medical equipment. The regional organisation Medicon Valley Academy unifies the interests of private companies, universities and some hospital authorities for the purpose of developing this sector. The numerous universities and university colleges of the Øresund region, the universities of Copenhagen and Lund being the largest, co-operate on education and research through the Øresund University. The Danish counties located east of the Great Belt, Copenhagen, Frederiksberg, Scania and the four Scanian municipalities located by the Øresund are all members of a joint Øresund Committee whose task is to market the strong points of the entire Øresund region.

Various efforts have been made within culture and the media to stimulate a common, regional identity. A Danish-Swedish media co-operation has e.g. been established between the television stations *Lorry* and *Sydnytt*, between the regional radio stations *Københavns Radio* and *Radio Malmöhus* and between the newspapers *Berlingske Tidende* and *Sydsvenska Dagbladet*. Plans also calls for Danish-Swedish arts festivals to be held biennially. The initial 'cultural bridge', *Kulturbro 2000,* opened on 15 September 2000.

Such networks usually expect to create economic growth and common identity, but it is impossible to predict if these expectations will be fulfilled as to the Øresund region.

Bue Nielsen

The Major Bridges

Building bridges across the Danish straits such as Lillebælt (Little Belt) and Storstrømmen had been discussed for fifty years or so before the opening of the
first of them in the 1930s: the bridge across Lillebælt
in 1935 and the one across Storstrømmen in 1937.
The 1930s was a great era of bridge-building in Denmark, as a major bridge was finished on average
once a year. At the end of the 1930s, the country was
largely collected in two units as far as land traffic was
concerned: Jutland-Funen on the one hand and
Zealand-Lolland-Falster on the other.

The Danish bridges from the 1930s were also internationally speaking of a high standard, a position that
was maintained after the Second World War with for
instance a new bridge across Lillebælt: the Lillebælt
Suspension Bridge, and with the Vejle Fjord Bridge and
the Farø Bridges. It is moreover noticeable that after
the Second World War several of the bridges from the
1930s were duplicated before the decision was taken
to establish a fixed link across Storebælt (Great Belt).

The Storebælt Link

After several false starts, the final step was taken in
1987 with the passing of an Act providing for the construction and for the formation of the state-owned
company A/S Storebæltsforbindelsen. The link was to
be established in two stages, with the railway link first
and then the motorway link. It was the result of a
political compromise between the desire to promote
public transport and the wish to establish a link that
would unify both the railway and the road networks
on either side of the Belt. Therefore the link across the
East Channel in Storebælt was to be separated into a
tunnel for the railway and a bridge for the motorway,
whereas it was possible to build the link across the
West Channel as a combined road and railway bridge.

The 8 km-long bored railway tunnel, the East Tunnel, between Zealand and Sprogø was inaugurated in
1997 and is the second-longest under-water railway
tunnel in Europe, only surpassed by the one under the
English Channel. The railway link was designed as two
tubular tunnels each with an internal diameter of 7.7
m and at a distance of 25 m centre to centre. Between
the two tubes there are cross passages every 250 m

partly for technical installations and partly to facilitate
an evacuation in the case of an accident.

The West Bridge, between Sprogø and Funen was
built between 1989 and 1993 as a low-level bridge in
pre-stressed concrete consisting of a large number of
identical spans with lengths of 110 m. With its length
of 6.6 km it was the longest bridge in Europe on completion.

The third major structure, the East Bridge, between
Zealand and Sprogø, a 6.8 km long motorway bridge,
was started in 1991. It is built as a suspension bridge
across the fairway through the East Channel allowing
passage up to 65 m in height and with a span of 1624
m; for far into the future this will be the longest single
span in Europe, in a world-wide context only surpassed
by the Akashi Kaikyo Bridge in Japan.

The roadway part of the East and West Bridges was
opened in 1998. Apart from the three main components, the East Tunnel, West Bridge and East Bridge,
the Storebælt Link also comprises considerable reclamation works around Sprogø, which after the building
of the bridge and tunnel ramps has found its area
quadrupled.

The fixed Storebælt Link, at a total price of c. 25 billion kroner, has cost more than all the earlier Danish
bridges together, and it has reduced journey times
between east and west Denmark by over an hour.

The major bridges. From the left: the Lillebælt Suspension Bridge (1970), the Storebælt Link (1998) and
the Øresund Link (2000).

The Øresund Link

Once construction of the Storebælt Link had started, the way was open for a Danish decision on the next major fixed link – across Øresund (the Sound) – as it had always been a Danish wish that the country should be joined by a fixed link across Storebælt before Zealand was linked to Sweden.

Preparations for a fixed link across the Øresund reached the construction stage in 1995 after long and careful studies, not least of its environmental impact. Like the Storebælt Link, the Øresund Link consists of both a motorway and railway. And similarly, there are both tunnel and bridge links, but in a different combination than in the case of Storebælt.

At the Øresund, the main fairway through Drogden between Amager and Saltholm is traversed in a submerged tunnel for both road and railway, while the Flinterende Channel between Saltholm and Scania is crossed by a high bridge on two levels with the motorway on the top deck and the railway lines on the lower deck.

From coast to coast the Øresund Link is 15.9 km long, including a 430 m-long artificial peninsula off Amager. The submerged tunnel with a length of 3,750 m is the world's longest combined road and rail submerged tunnel and the eastern high bridge with its length of 7,840 m is 1 km longer than the East Bridge across Storebælt.

Across the Flinterende Channel a cable-stayed bridge is being built with a main span of 490 m, the longest in the world for cable-stayed bridges carrying both road and rail.

The Øresund Link, inaugurated in July 2000, was constructed so that trains can cross at a speed of 200 km/h.

Conditions of Life

The Scandinavian Welfare Model

The Scandinavian welfare model is often used as a general term for the way in which Denmark, Sweden and Norway have chosen to organise and finance their social security systems, health services and education. The Scandinavian countries are clearly distinguished from other European countries in these areas.

History

Germany was the first country in the world in which the State engaged in the social insurance of its citizens. This took place in 1883 with the introduction of a public health insurance. The other countries in Europe – including the Scandinavian countries – were not unaware when the German initiative forced the question of the State and social insurance higher up on the political agenda. In the succeeding years many countries in Europe set up arrangements for insuring their citizens in cases of accidents, illness, old age and unemployment – what we know as the essential welfare state benefits.

Although the development of welfare arrangements took place in the individual countries, certain countries may have common features in their systems justifying our talking of an actual *welfare model*. The European countries can be divided up according to four welfare models: *The Scandinavian model*, in which social benefits are the same for everyone. This model is also referred to as the Nordic model, the Social Democratic model or the institutional model. *The Beveridge model*, thus called after the British civil servant who led the work of devising the principle on which this model is based, offers social benefits only to those in greatest need. It is also called the Anglo-Saxon model, the liberal model or the residual welfare model. *The Bismarck model* is called after the German Chancellor, the man who provided the ideas behind the first laws on social insurance. Here the social benefits are only given to those who have been on the labour market. This model is also known as the Central European, the conservative or the achievement-oriented model. *The Subsidiarity model*, in which social responsibilities are to be solved within the family, or as close to the family as possible, is also called the Southern European or Catholic model.

General Description

The principle behind the Scandinavian welfare model is that benefits should be given to all citizens who fulfil the conditions, without regard to employment or family situation. The system covers everyone; it is universal. And the benefits are given to the individual, so that e.g. married women have rights independently of their husbands. In the fields of sickness and unemployment the right to benefit is, however, always dependent on former employment and at times also on membership of a trade union and the payment of contributions; however the largest share of the financial burden is still carried by the State and financed from general taxation, not in the main from earmarked contributions.

In the Scandinavian countries the State is involved in financing and organising the welfare benefits available to the citizens to a far greater extent than in other European countries. For that reason the welfare model is accompanied by a

Welfare is also reflected in the fact that handicapped people can live a relatively normal life on equal terms with non-handicapped people. Public support is granted to design special residences enabling e.g. wheelchair users to be less dependent on other people's help in everyday life.

taxation system which has both a broad basis of taxation and a high taxation burden. The benefits given are more generous than is the case in the British Beveridge model – and in combination with the taxation system this brings about a greater redistribution than is the case in the Bismarck model, which is aimed rather at maintaining the present status. The Scandinavian pattern of organisation is also far simpler and immediately comprehensible than is the case in the other European countries. In the Scandinavian countries most of the social welfare tasks are undertaken by the State or local au-

thorities, and only to a limited extent by individuals, families, churches or national welfare organisations.

A further characteristic of the Scandinavian welfare model is the fact that rather than cash benefits, citizens are entitled to a wide range of service benefits provided by the authorities; these are often either free or subsidised. Both the health service and education are free. In the social field the organisation and financing of both transfer payments and service benefits take place within the same unified system.

Since the Second World War it has been a politically important part of

The need for community and proximity is the basis of article 68 of the Social Security Act, which deals with the establishment of shared living accommodation for people with severe physical or mental handicaps. Shared living accommodation does not constitute an institution, but consists of small collective residences, which are the residents' own home, where it is possible to feel secure and find support through living close to others in the same situation. Shared living accommodation projects receive practical and pedagogical support from home counsellors employed by the municipality, aimed at providing for the needs of the individual handicapped person.

the Scandinavian welfare model to seek to ensure full employment for all citizens. However, this has not been possible in Denmark since the middle of the 1970s; since then unemployment has become an urgent problem in Sweden and Norway, too. The Scandinavian countries are nevertheless the countries with the highest participation rate in the world, partly because women are engaged in active employment almost as much as men. At the beginning of the new millenium, unemployment had been reduced markedly.

The Scandinavian welfare model acts within a controlled capitalist market economy in which inequalities in income distribution and the concentration of wealth and power are allowed less free play. In political terms, there is in all the Scandinavian countries a parliamentary democracy with close relations between the organisations representing the interests of both employers and employees and the political system. The relaxed attitude of the population towards both the central government and the other public authorities is a fundamental characteristic of the political system.

Discussion of the organisation and development of the welfare state also forms part of the political debate in the Scandinavian countries. To call the Scandinavian welfare model 'the Social Democratic model' – as is

sometimes done – is, however, misleading. Generally speaking, all political parties in the Scandinavian countries have contributed to the development of the welfare state over the last 100 years. This applies to all the parties that have been in government without exception, and all the Scandinavian countries have had non-socialist governments or non-socialist participation in government for a large part of this time. Thus, the welfare state does not represent a common Social Democratic ideology, but a national political compromise on how to organise and finance the social, health and educational benefits on which a political decision has been taken to provide for the population. The Social Democratic parties have thus not invented the Scandinavian welfare state, but in comparison with other parties they have shown the greatest initiative. At the same time there has been far greater agreement on the development of the welfare state between the political wings in the Scandinavian countries than has been the case in other European countries. The difference in points of view has been less, and the coincidence of interests greater. Consequently, a welfare system has been established which is more harmonious and in many areas more comprehensive than in most other countries in the world.

Crisis in the Welfare State

However, the welfare state has never been an unchallenged system, either in Scandinavia or elsewhere, and in recent years the crisis in the welfare state has been high on the political agenda both in the Scandinavian countries and elsewhere. The crisis consist many individual elements and is partly due to the fact that the present welfare arrangements originated and developed in the 1960s and 1970s at a time of high economic growth and low unemployment. It has never been the intention either with unemployment, sickness benefits or with cash benefits that so many people should receive them or that they should receive them for so long as has been the case in recent years. The financing of the welfare state has thus become a problem, which, on the long view, could re-present a threat to the welfare systems.

The question is therefore whether the national compromise can be maintained in the future. Generally speaking, the changes and cuts which have been made in the welfare systems in the Scandinavian countries in recent years – and there are actually many – betoken an ongoing adaptation of the systems to the present economic situation. This does not mean that changes are being contemplated in the concept of the welfare state, i.e. that it is the intention to adopt another welfare model. However, there is already now much to suggest that a more fragmented welfare system is slowly but surely emerging in the Scandinavian countries.

In all the Scandinavian countries a supplementary welfare system has developed in recent years, giving greater benefits to those who are in the labour market. This is a clear

In Denmark it is no longer a family responsibility to take care of the old. It has become a duty of society, and many people spend their last years in a nursing home. Here, a friendly staff do what they can to make the nursing home into a real home for the residents, so in the midst of all the activity, there must also be time for a little chat.

deviation from the equality principle which is at the heart of the Scandinavian welfare model. The breach has occurred partly because better arrangements have been reached relating to maternity leave, sickness and pensions through the free collective agreements between employers and employees that regulate conditions in the labour markets in all the Scandinavian countries. That is to say benefits that are paid out to the vast majority of employees in the Scandinavian labour markets, who are included in such an agreement – but not to all citizens.

Niels Ploug

Social Security

Danish citizens are to a considerable extent insured financially against, for instance, illness, unemployment and the needs of old age, to which can be added supplementary aid schemes for i.a. the cost of housing and expenditure in connection with children. In addition there are a great number of highly developed services in the form of day-care institutions, health service, home help, etc.

Developments in Social Policy

Until the end of the 19th century social policy measures were virtually synonymous with poor relief, and only in the 1708 Poor Relief Act did help to the poor assume a relatively organised form; before this, the help offered consisted mainly of building poorhouses for those incapable of work and giving the poor permission to beg in their own parish. The Poor Relief Act of 1708 meant that each individual parish was given the responsibility of ensuring food, etc. for the poor of the parish who were incapable of work. The poor who were capable of work were sent to forced labour in, for instance, workhouses. From 1803 a tax was introduced to cover parishes' expenditure on poor relief. Recipients of poor relief had, after the introduction of a free constitution in 1849 no right to vote, and neither were they permitted to marry. An act of 1856 established the Fund for the Poor, which relied entirely on private donations, e.g. from church collection boxes; the Fund was aimed at giving relief before the poor were obliged to resort to the general system of poor relief and thereby lose their civil rights.

In 1891 the Act on Support in Old Age was passed, together with a revised Law on Poor Relief; this ensured, for instance, public aid for medical care, midwifery services and burial. The introduction of support in old age was epoch-making. Those above 60 years of age were given the status of deserving poor, i.e. they were given relief without losing their right to vote, a break with the previous practice governing poor relief, which smacked of alms-giving. In addition, it was no longer only the parishes that bore the financial burden, but the State now also made its contribution.

In 1892 an Act on Health Insurance Societies was passed, encompassing a private, voluntary insurance principle with payment of contributions, but with a state subsidy. The idea of sickness benefit institutions built on a number of older, completely private health insurance societies which provided members with various kinds of help during illness. Just prior to the passing of the Health Insurance Act, there were around 1,000 private health insurance societies with altogether over 100,000 members.

An Act on Insurance against Accident came into force in 1898. From 1907 the State began to subsidise the unemployment benefit funds without implying the loss of civil rights for anyone receiving help. Similarly, in 1921, a compulsory Act on Disablement Benefits was introduced, ensuring the disabled help without the loss of civil rights.

The many individual acts that had been passed in the period from about 1890 to 1930 were combined and simplified through the great Social Reform Act of 1933. It was now generally established that financial aid to citizens as a result of some unforeseen occurrence should not limit civil rights; however, limitations were not completely abolished until the Public Assistance Act of 1961.

After the Second World War social legislation reflected a constant development in the welfare state; a number of acts were introduced covering special cases of need, including one for the deaf (1950), the blind (1956) and the mentally deficient (1959). In 1956, on the basis of an agreement with the two sides in the labour market, a sick pay scheme was established. In 1958 arrangements for home help were established, replacing the previous arrangement for mother's helps.

A new Act on National Pensions and Disablement Pensions (1956) introduced the principle that everyone had the right to a pension irrespective of capital and income, and independently of former employment and income. Everyone over 69 was thus given entitlement to a minimum national pension. In 1964 the Supplementary Pension Fund was introduced, a compulsory arrangement for employees, in which the pension depends on the contributions paid.

In 1973 a compulsory health insurance programme was introduced, funded from general taxation, and replacing the sickness benefit funds, and at the same time a reform of daily cash benefits was introduced, ensuring everyone against loss of income resulting from illness.

In 1976 the Social Assistance Act came into force. This introduced a single, unified structure, implying that the social assistance office in the local authority area must deal with the problems, irrespective of the reasons for social need. With this act, a principle of discretion was introduced, i.e. that support should be given from an overall evaluation of the client's situation. Since then a large number of changes have been made to the Social Assistance Act. Of central importance is that in 1987 the principle of discretion was changed to a principle of entitlement, which meant fixed rates for most forms of help. With effect from 1 July 1998, the Danish parliament has passed new Social Welfare legislation covering legal safeguards, social service, and active social policy.

An anticipatory pension scheme was introduced in 1979, making it possible for 60-66-year-old members of an unemployment benefit scheme to withdraw from the labour market before reaching pensionable age. This benefit, like subsequent arrangements for leave and activation was established largely with a view to reducing unemployment.

Administration, Finance and Overall Expenditure

The State has the supreme responsibility for social legislation and planning, while the local authorities in almost all areas are responsible for the administration vis-à-vis the citizens; exceptions from this are the hospitals, which are administered by the counties, daily cash benefits which are administered by the unemployment agencies, and compensation for injuries in the workplace, which are the responsibility of insurance societies and the Agency for Injuries in the Workplace. In comparison with most other EU countries, it is characteristic of Denmark that only to a small extent are social benefits based on employers' contributions and direct contributions from the insured, and that the right to financial assistance is only partly dependent on earlier employment. About 2/3 of total social expenditure in Denmark is financed by the State via

It is the wish in Denmark that elderly people should stay in their own homes for as long as possible. A condition for achieving this is extensive social service provisions, with meals on wheels, home helps to take care of cleaning, washing and shopping and, where necessary, regular visits from a district nurse to tend to the frailties of old age.

taxes and duties as against 1/3 for the EU countries on average (1998), which has meant that of the EU countries Denmark has one of the heaviest tax and duty burdens.

Social expenditure in 2000 accounted for 40% of all day-to-day State expenditure and 28% of GDP. At constant prices and in kroner per head of population, this expenditure has remained constant in recent years, increasing by only 1% in the period 1995-2000. A slightly falling proportion of the benefits takes the form of cash benefits (62% in 2000), and in the period 1995-2000, there has been a particularly large fall in expenditure on unemployment benefit and a considerable growth in expenditure on activation programmes. Benefits linked to old age, sickness and families make up over 70% of all social expenditure. Alongside the public arrangements there are several hundred voluntary church and humanitarian organisations, crisis centres, arrangements for voluntary visits, places where those in need can contact others or find drop-in centres, etc.; the amount of voluntary social work has increased in recent years.

The Family
Women, both employees and self-employed, are entitled to *maternity leave* from four weeks before the birth to 14 weeks after, and during this period the father is entitled to two weeks' leave; in addition there

are a further ten weeks leave which the father and mother can share between them as they see fit. During this leave they receive a per diem payment corresponding to unemployment benefit, but on the basis of agreements with their employers, many employees have the right to their full salary. The maternity leave will be changed and extended in 2002.

All families with children under 18 receive, irrespective of income, *family allowances* as a regular, tax-free amount per child, with a higher rate for children under seven years of age; bread-winners who are single parents or pensioners can in addition receive *child allowances*. Benefits for children are relatively high in Denmark. Families with children are entitled to free *home help* if the person who has the responsibility for the home and the children cannot manage it on account of, for instance, illness or confinement. Among other things, families living in rented accommodation can, depending on family income and the size of the rent, receive *housing benefit* (174,000 recipients in December 2000).

The publicly supported *day-care institutions* for children include creches (0-2-year-olds), nursery schools (3-5-year-olds), after-school recreation centres (6-10-year-olds) and out-of-school arrangements for pupils at the *folkeskole* (state primary and lower secondary school). In addition there is local authority day care, in which children are looked after in private homes; parental contributions make up a maximum of 30% of the costs, and for financial or social reasons places can be partly or completely free. A constantly increasing proportion of children attend some kind of day-care institution; in 2000 this included 56% of the 0-2-year-olds and 92% of the 3-5-year-olds.

Outdoor life is wonderful in all weathers and throughout the year if you are wearing clothes that are suited to the weather. In Denmark there is a tradition for day-care centres to organise excursions when the children take packed lunches with them and spend many hours in the forest or on the beach. Outdoor life gives children plenty of opportunity to explore and experiment. Out in the open, there is room for all, and children and adults discover new sides of each other. There are a number of outlying kindergartens and woodland kindergartens, in which most activities are based on outdoor life.

According to need, the local authority has the duty to provide practical, educational and financial advice and support for families with small or teenage children. If the child cannot stay in its own home, the local authority – with or without the approval of the parents – can place it elsewhere, for instance in family care or in a residential institution; compulsory removal can take place when there is a clear risk that the child's health or general development will otherwise suffer. At the end of 2000, 13,600 children were placed outside their own home, 1,300 of whom had been compulsorily removed.

Unemployment and Social Security

Employees and the self-employed have the right to *unemployment benefit* after a minimum of a year's membership of an unemployment insurance fund and a minimum of 52 weeks' work within the last three years; the newly qualified have the right to daily cash benefits (82% of the full benefit) a month after the end of their training; the period during which this benefit can be given is five years, split into a period with daily cash benefit (the first two years) and an active period (the last three years); during the active period the unemployed person has the right and duty to receive job training and education. Young unemployed under 25 have the right and duty to receive job training and education after only 6 months on daily cash benefit. The daily cash benefit constitutes at most 90% of previous income, subject to a maximum figure; on average the daily cash benefit constitutes 65% of previous income. Measured in full time equivalents about 150,000 persons were unemployed in 2000 against 350,000 in 1994. These figures include both insured and uninsured unemployed. Uninsured unemployed can, depending on their position as breadwinners and the overall financial position of the family, receive cash benefits under the Social Assistance Act (from 1998 Act on Active Social Policies). Measured in full time equivalents 86,000 people received subsistence grants in 2000. This figure includes both uninsured unemployed and those receiving subsistence grants for social reasons, not being able to seek employment on ordinary terms.

The social policy strategy of the 1990s prioritises *activating provision* for the unemployed and to a certain extent the obligation to accept such offers as the condition for continued financial support. With a reform of the labour market in 1994 a number of new arrangements were introduced covering both insured and uninsured unemployed: concerning *subsidised work* (job training, wage-subsidised jobs, the setting up and launching of own businesses), *leave opportunities* (child care, training, sabbaticals) and *training opportunities* with financial support. *Anticipatory pensions* and *transitional financial support* are arrangements to enable older employees to leave the labour market, which among other things should stimulate employment for younger people. People aged 60-66 are eligible for anticipatory pension. Under the anticipatory pension scheme which came into force on 1 July 1999, people have to pay a monthly anticipatory pension contribution together with their unemployment fund contribution for at least 25 years to qualify for anticipatory pension (with a transitional arrangement for persons aged 35 or more). The anticipatory pension benefit amounts to a maximum of 91% of the unemployment benefit and other pension schemes result in deductions from the anticipatory pension benefit. Premiums are awarded to those who postpone their anticipatory pension from 60 to 62.

Correspondingly, employees aged between 50 and 59 are entitled to a transitional benefit (at a lower rate), this scheme ceased on 1.1.1996, although existing participants continue until they become eligible for anticipatory pension. In 2000 the numbers covered by these activation and retirement provisions were equivalent to about 290,500 full-time participants.

Sickness

All those engaged in active employment who suffer a loss of income on account of illness or injury have the right to *sickness benefit* from the first day of absence; however, this only applies to the self-employed after three weeks unless they have taken out a special insurance.

The official *health insurance* covers all expenses for general and specialist medical care, part expenses for treatment by dentists, chiropractors, etc. and for medicine. General practitioners provide treatment or refer patients to a specialist or hospital. The hospital system is run by the counties. Hospital treatment is free and, since 1993, patients have had free choice of hospital. After a reference from a doctor, free *home nursing care* is available so that patients can stay in their own homes during illness. The local authority dental care for children and young people is free.

Old Age and Disablement

For those employed in the public sector, the maximum pensionable age is 70. There is no general pensionable age for those in private employment, but there are usually locally established regulations governing pension conditions and pensionable age. In practice the pattern of retirement is strongly influenced by current legislation on the possibility of transferring to the national pension, the early retirement pensions or anticipatory pension arrangements, etc. The average age

Poverty in the Welfare State

Poverty in a modern society is not only the need to survive but also the need to be able to take part in life in society. In other words, poverty is not only about economic needs but also about social and cultural needs.

In Denmark, like in other European countries, no official poverty limit has been set, but inequalities do exist in Denmark, too, even in some important areas such as education, unemployment, housing, health and social contact. About 5% of a youth cohort never enter an education giving access to the labour market. 75% of the Danes are never unemployed, but the 10% most affected by unemployment account for 17% of total unemployment. Almost all Danes have a good residence but 2,500 Danes live in a reception centre and an unknown number of Danes spend the night in a lodging house. As to inequalities in health and social contact, it appears that those badly off, in general, also suffer from poor health and lack contact with society.

In Denmark poor people are not financially poor in the traditional sense of the term but pile up bad conditions of life, making them unable to achieve the lifestyle prevailing in Danish society. Thus, even in a well-developed welfare state, people fall through the social safety net, however, being few in number, they are difficult to perceive.

Niels Ploug

for retirement is generally falling; in 2000 c. 71% of 60-66- year-olds were in receipt of an early pension, anticipatory pension or other forms of salary replacement. Those of 67 years and above have the right to a *national pension*, which is financed from taxation and independent of former income. From 1 July 2004 the retirement age will be lowered to 65 years. Denmark is one of the countries in which the national pension (together with early pensions and anticipatory pensions) has the highest contribution ratio (pension in relation to former income) for low-income families. Altogether 706,000 Danes are in receipt of a national pension (2001). In addition, employees on pension receive a graduated pension (ATP), a compulsory scheme for employees aged between 16 and 66, in which the pension is dependent on contributions from employers (2/3) and employees (1/3). In addition there are many *contractual pension arrangements* and supplementary *private pensions* (annuities, etc.), which altogether mean that many employees have greater cover than the national pension alone.

People aged between 18 and 67 can on application transfer to an early retirement pension when their ability to work has been permanently reduced by at least 50% on account of physical or psychological disablement. Those between 50 and 67 with a permanent need of care are in addition entitled to (normal) *early retirement pensions* when health and/or special circumstances justify it. Depending on the degree of disability, they qualify for normal, medium or maximum early retirement pensions (altogether 262,000 in 2001).

Dependent on financial circumstances, both national and early retirement pensions can be supplemented in various ways, for instance by personal supplements, heating supplements and grants towards expenses on medicine. In addition, those receiving national or early retirement pensions, who rent property, are members of a co-operative housing association or live in their own houses, depending on income and expenditure on housing, are entitled to a *rent allowance* according to rules that are more advantageous than the rules for housing benefits applying to non-pensioners.

The proportion of elderly living in *residential homes* has been falling noticeably in recent years; traditional residential homes are generally speaking no longer being built, as for a number of years it has been the aim that as many elderly people as possible should remain in their own homes. In 1982 16% of those over 75 were living in residential accommodation, as against 6% in 2000. Along with this development an increasing number of *dwellings for the elderly* have been built with special facilities and a varying degree of services attached. In 2000 11% of those aged over 75 lived in such dwellings. At the same time more and more are in receipt of home help and services for the elderly (free), which is linked to the fact that more elderly people are living longer and staying in their own homes.

It is similarly the aim that the handicapped should stay in their own homes for as long as possible; irrespective of income, the necessary aids are placed at their disposal, and help is given to equip the home and for extra expense as a result of the disability; in addition, the local authority is responsible for rehabilitation, re-training and offers of employment. For the handicapped who cannot live in their own homes there has for a number of years been a process of reorganisation from large institutions to small communities or individual residences with common facilities and services.

Carsten Torpe

The nuclear family with one or two children is the typical Danish family group, but about a quarter of children at home do not live with both their biological parents.

The Family

The average family size in 2002 is 2.2 persons. Throughout the 20th century a significant drop has occurred, the average in 1901 having been 4.3 persons. This is due to a decrease in the number of families with children, especially a decrease in the number of large families, and a growth in the number of one- or two-person households.

Since the 1960s living arrangements have undergone a change: the number of marriages has declined steeply, the number of divorces has risen, as has the number of people cohabiting. In addition, marriages generally take place later in life; the average age of marriage in 2000 was thus 36 for men and 33 for women. Just over 1/5 of all couples living together in 2002 were unmarried – an arrangement particularly popular among young couples without children. A large proportion of these relationships are formalised by marriage, however, when the couples have children. Since 1989 two per-

sons of the same sex may have their partnership registered. On 1 January 2002 more than 2,000 partnerships had been registered. Despite the radical changes in the pattern of living arrangements, 3/4 of all children under 18 were living at home with both their biological parents in 2002. There is, however, a tendency for the number of children living with single parents to increase.

The number of children in day-care centres or private day care con-

The average age at which people marry in Denmark is rising; they often wait to formalise their relationships until they have had children. In 2000 the average age for a bride was 33 and for a bridegroom 36 years.

The Danish family has taken to the computer, and soon every other home will have a PC that is regularly used both for work and play. For some it is merely an efficient typewriter, but for the more advanced it is a window on the wide world via the Internet. In schools, electronic data processing has been integrated into the teaching.

tinues to increase; more than 90% of 3-5-year-olds were registered in 2000 as opposed to 75% ten years earlier. This must be seen in relation to a steep increase in the proportion of working mothers with small children. The role of housewife looking after children at home has almost disappeared.

The division of work in the home has become more equal, especially in families with small children, where the woman is younger, goes out to work and has a higher education. But it is still the women who do most of the domestic work. When both parents go out to work, there is in families with children less time for contact between parents and children, and a greater need for having the children looked after. But with families based on couples living together it is precisely in those with children and more particularly those with small children that the adults spend more time on work and training. In general, despite reduced hours of work and a greater amount of unemployment, adults have less free time than used to be the case, which is due to the significantly increased participation of women in work.

Carsten Torpe

Families distributed by family types as per 1.1.2002. The total number of Danish families was 2.9 million.
Source: Statistics Denmark.

Family types

- singles without children (49,4%)
- married couples without children (21,1%)
- other couples without children (6,1%)
- singles with children (4,3%)
- married couples with children (14,4%)
- other couples with children (4.1%)
- children under 18 living away from their parents (0,6%)

A cosy get-together organised by the Pensioners' Association, one of several Danish non-government organisations taking care of the interests of the elderly vis-à-vis the politicians. Through courses and periods in folk high schools the elderly are themselves encouraged to seek to achieve influence on such things as their living conditions by taking part in municipal senior citizen councils.

Private Finances

Although transfer incomes and direct taxation to a certain extent even out differences in income, there is still a good deal of inequality in the distribution of disposable income: in 2000, the 20% of the families with the lowest incomes accounted for 6% of the total income, while on the other hand the 20% of families with the highest incomes accounted for 40% of the total. During the 1990s income distribution was relatively stable. Income varies according to job and type of family. In real terms, the wages of privately employed workers and wage earners increased by more than 15% during the period 1975-1995, while they remained almost constant for public employees.

If the major groups of earners are compared, it emerges that during this period there has been a narrowing of income differentials. Since 1984, families with children have had a relatively favourable income trend thanks to transfer payments, i.e. child allowances that are not dependent on income.

The distribution of capital is far more uneven than the distribution of income. Over a long period a certain levelling out has taken place, but from the mid-1980s to the mid-1990s there has been a trend towards increasing inequality. The self-employed have a larger share of their capital invested in their own companies, while in the case of wage-earners it is invested in their houses.

Carsten Torpe

Benefits for children are relatively high in Denmark.

Housing

A typical Danish district of small detached houses, as they were built in the 1960s and beginning of the 1970s. The houses are uniform, but as the gardens have become established they have gradually assumed a more individual aspect. About 2/3 of Danes live in single-family houses, and these are especially popular among families with children.

In a world-wide context, Denmark, together with Sweden, has the largest and best provision of housing in relation to the size of population. About 62% of the population lives in individual houses (2001), which is a proportion twice as high as 45 years previously. Conversely, the proportion living in flats has been reduced from 50% to 30% in the same period. It is especially single people without children who live in flats, and couples with children who live in individual houses. In contrast to many other countries, there is little publicly owned housing in Denmark. One-family houses have almost always been individually owned, but they are sometimes rented out. In 2001, 53% of households lived in privately owned houses as against 43% in 1955; the proportion has, however, been constant since 1980. The rise in household incomes as a result of women's increased partici-

Living Conditions Types of accommodation as per 1.1.2001	numbers	%
(in thousands)		
Owner-occupied:		
Detached houses	925	38.6
Terraced houses, etc.	119	5.0
Farmhouses	108	4.5
Owner-occupied flats	124	5.2
Business residences, etc.	4	0.2
Owner-occupied in all:	1,280	53.4
Privately owned rented accommodation:		
Detached houses	53	2.2
Terraced houses, etc.	35	1.3
Farmhouses	14	0.6
Private flats	313	13.1
Business residences, etc.	6	0.3
Private accommodation in all	421	17.6
Non-profitmaking rented accommodation	473	19.7
Private co-operative flats	159	6.6
Student residences	29	1.2
Publicly owned residences	35	1.5
Actual residences in all	2,398	100.0
Communal residences	18	
Weekend cottages	217	

Source: Statistics Denmark.

Especially since the 1960s, many attractive coastal areas have had weekend or holiday cottages built on them; thus, in 2000 there were some 200,000 holiday cottages in Denmark. Holidays in such cottages are greatly favoured by families with children, but in the high season the Danish holiday cottage areas also attract many German and Dutch tourists who rent summer cottages, especially on the west coast of Jutland.

pation in employment can be related to the growth in the number of one-family houses and the proportion of people living in them.

The proportion of subsidised housing and owner-occupied houses in relation to rented property has increased considerably since the Second World War as a result of new building and the transformation of rented flats to owner-occupied flats.

From c. 1980 terraced houses and cluster houses in the form of co-operative or other housing associations made up a large part of the residential property construction, while there has been a fall in the number of individual houses being built.

On account of the building of larger homes and a fall in the average size of households the standard of homes has noticeably improved in

Just under a fifth of Danish housing consists of social housing. Since the 1980s, facilities for collective use have been incorporated into several new social housing developments, as here in Blangstedgård near Odense, designed and built in 1988 by the architects Boje Lundgaard and Lene Trandberg. The collective buildings contain various facilities for general use, for instance party rooms, conference rooms, laundry and other activity rooms that are of importance for the well-being of the residents.

A typical block of flats in a city, in this case in Copenhagen, designed by Edvard Thomsen and built in 1931 for Copenhagen Municipality. The relatively anonymous block with the plastered facade overlooks the canal in the popular Christianshavn district.

the second half of the 20th century; thus, in 1955, 45% of the population lived in dwellings with less than 1 room per inhabitant, while the percentage in 2000 had fallen to 11%. The average living area is now 109 square metres, so that every Dane on average has at his disposal a living area of 52 square metres (2001). Moreover, the facilities in the homes have been improved. In 1970 almost

1/3 of houses and flats were without either their own toilet or bath or central heating (or more than one); in 2001 the proportion had fallen to 7%, and it is in particular baths that are lacking. Houses and flats lacking installations are especially inhabited by single people, which reflects that to a large extent they are pensioners.

By far the greatest proportion of all modern residences are heated by central heating (oil, natural gas) or district heating, while a modest proportion are still heated by oil, paraffin or solid fuel stoves. Since 1985 there has been an appreciable rise in the number of dwellings heated by district heating or natural gas. In 2001 the proportions were 59% and 13% respectively, as against 38% and 1% in 1985.

Carsten Torpe

Danes spend much time in their private residence and therefore they put much effort in designing the interior of their home. Although it is popular to frequent restaurants and cafes, Danes very often invite friends and family to their home, decorated for the occasion with candlelight to make it cosy.

Personal Safety

Along with a rapid increase in the density of traffic and the number of cars on the roads, safety on the roads has also improved considerably. The number of people killed or severely injured in traffic accidents each year more than halved between 1970 and 2000. Far more men than women are injured in traffic accidents (in 2000 almost 2/3 more), and especially the group aged between 15 and 19 is at a high risk.

Theft and vandalism have become more widespread in the period 1980-2000. The number of reported offences, mainly offences against property, rose by 24%, corresponding to 9 reports annually per 100 inhabitants in 2000.

The number of reported violent crimes stood at 15,200 in 2000, showing a rise of over 40% in ten years. This type of crime is particularly common in urban areas, and it is in particular the rate of less serious violent crimes that has increased, while the rate of the most serious ones such as murder (or attempted murder) has fallen.

Carsten Torpe

A room in Horserød Open Prison. Sentences are served in open prisons unless the length of the punishment and the gravity of the crime or the danger of abscondence makes it inadvisable. There are normally no fences to open prisons. Several open prisons have public roads through them, and there are few security measures. The prisoner, as it were, deprives himself of his own freedom. Each prisoner has his own room, which he can equip with radio, television, telephone and other private possessions. In 1998 there were 1,339 places in open institutions, 754 places in the five closed prisons and 1,619 places in the Copenhagen Prisons and the 38 local prisons used for remand prisoners or those serving sentences of up to a month.

Health

Danes have for decades lived with the notion that their state of health was one of the best in the world, as the average life expectancy around 1960 was only surpassed by Sweden, Norway and Holland. By 1990, Denmark had been overtaken by all the countries in the EU with the exception of Ireland and Portugal, while e.g. Japan and Cuba could also both boast of a higher life expectancy than Denmark. Between 1965 and 1997 the average life span in Denmark rose from 72 to 75 years (men: 73, women: 78), while broadly speaking all other countries have experienced a greater rise, with the former Communist countries in eastern Europe as the most important exceptions. However, in recent years the average life span has risen considerably and more than in most European countries. In 2000 it was 74.3 years for men and 79,0 for women. The calculation of average life span is strongly influenced by infant mortality in the first year of life; it has fallen through the 20th century, but the decline has been replaced by stagnation in relation to the countries with which we most often compare ourselves, all other Scandinavian countries having

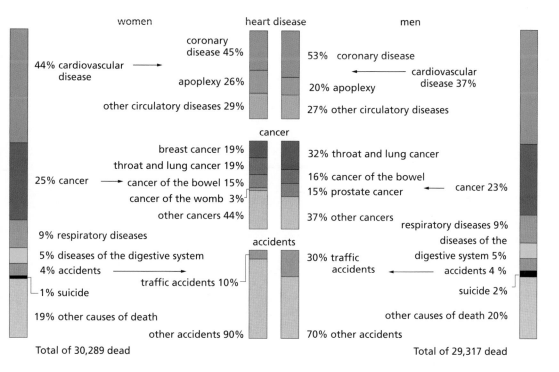

women

heart disease

men

coronary disease 45%

53% coronary disease

44% cardiovascular disease ⟶

cardiovascular disease 37%

apoplexy 26%

20% apoplexy

other circulatory diseases 29%

27% other circulatory diseases

cancer

breast cancer 19%
throat and lung cancer 19%
25% cancer ⟶ cancer of the bowel 15%
cancer of the womb 3%
other cancers 44%

32% throat and lung cancer
16% cancer of the bowel
15% prostate cancer ⟵ cancer 23%
37% other cancers

respiratory diseases 9%

9% respiratory diseases
5% diseases of the digestive system
4% accidents ⟶
traffic accidents 10%
1% suicide

accidents

diseases of the digestive system 5%
30% traffic accidents ⟵ accidents 4 %
suicide 2%

19% other causes of death

other causes of death 20%

other accidents 90%

70% other accidents

Total of 30,289 dead

Total of 29,317 dead

A total of 59,606 deaths were recorded in Denmark in 1997. Heart disease and cancer account for 2/3 of these deaths. Heart disease is the most common cause of death for both men and women, and coronary diseases causes by hardening of the arteries leading to blood clots in the heart account for the greatest number of deaths. The next most common cause of death is cancer. In the case of women, this generally means breast cancer which is becoming increasingly common. Lung cancer is the most common form of the disease found in men. As the number of women who smoke is currently rising, it is thought that lung cancer will become increasingly more common among the female population. The increase in lung cancer is thought to be the single most important reason for the current stagnation in the development of the mean life expectancy in Denmark.

Infant mortality per 1,000 liveborn

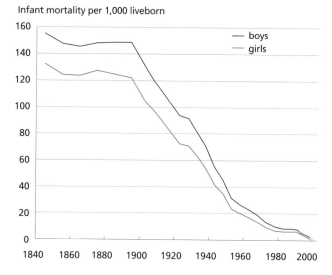

Mean life expectancy for women

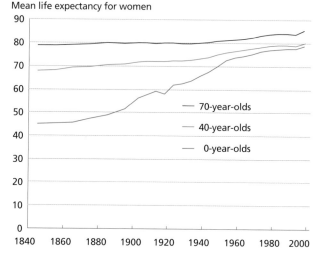

Mean life expectancy for men

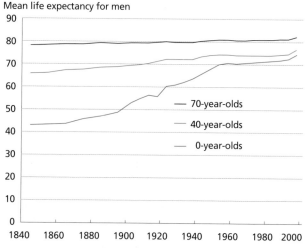

The diagram at the top shows the develop-ment in the infant mortality rate (i.e. the number of deaths in infants under 1 year of age) in Denmark during the last 150 years. There has been a marked decrease since 1900 and numbers seem to have levelled out from around 1960 onwards. The decrease must be attributed primarily to the rise in the standard of living including improvements in nutrition and housing along with better hygiene. Medical advances are of no real significance until the end of the period. The small break in the curve around 1920 shows the rise in infant mortality associated with the Spanish flu.

The two diagrams at the bottom show the mean life expectancy for men and women in a number of age groups. The mean life expectancy is generally defined as the statistical remaining life-time for a 0-year-old; this is strongly influenced by the infant mortality rate. The curves for 40-year-olds and 70-year-olds show the age which these groups are expected to attain. The marked difference in the mean life expectancy for a 0-year-old and a 40-year-old levels out around 1960 in line with the fall in the infant mortality rate. The rise in the number of elderly people in Denmark at the end of the 1900s is principally a result of the fall in the infant mortality rate and the large numbers of children born in the early years of the century.

a lower rate of infant mortality than that in Denmark, which is 4.2 per 1,000 live births (1999).

Mortality from various diseases is not the best way to measure a population's state of health, but the trend in death rates provides some important information. Since 1980, cardiovascular disease has become a less frequent cause of death and in 1997 accounted for 25% of all deaths. Deaths resulting from coronary disease amounted to c. 18% of all deaths in 1997, which is a drop of one third since 1981. The number of deaths resulting from cancer continues to rise and constitutes 25.6% (1997). The increase in the number of cases of lung cancer in women is one of the greatest in the world, while a gradual decline has occurred in the case of

men. The incidence of breast cancer in women is one of the highest in Europe. Compared with the other western European countries, the number of suicides registered is high but has nevertheless shown a decline in recent years. The number of deaths resulting from accidents at work or in traffic is low, and in the case of traffic accidents has been halved in the period 1975-2000. However, a good half of all male deaths in the age group 15 to 24 results from accidents. The number of deaths from accidents at home is still on the increase, especially those resulting from complications in connection with fractures of the neck of the femur in very old people.

Chronic diseases, the extent of which is not reflected in the mortali-

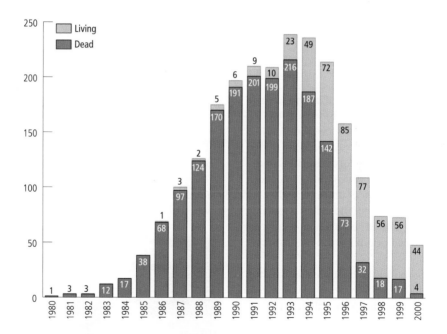

The columns show the total number of people who have been diagnosed as having AIDS during the relevant year in Denmark. The number of deaths, marked in red on the column, shows the number of people who had died at the time of this survey (2000); the rest are marked in grey. The figures do not include those who have tested

HIV-positive without showing any sign of AIDS. The AIDS epidemic in Denmark seems to have peaked around 1993. At the time of the survey, a total of 2,311 people have been diagnosed as having AIDS; of these, 1,813 had died whilst the remaining 498 were still alive.

ty statistics, is the cause of much suffering and expense to society and the individual. In addition to psychological illnesses, this also applies to diseases of the joints and muscles which can be caused by hard physical work. More than 10% of the population report that they have had difficulties in coping with everyday life in their own homes; the percentage rises with increasing age.

The average state of health in Denmark, judged for instance on the basis of mortality, extends over significant variations, although these are not so great as in many other parts of the world. In Copenhagen, the mean life expectancy is a couple of years less than the national average, which is also reflected in the fact that mortality in the age group 30 – 50 is twice the national average. Certain occupational groups, e.g. seamen and restaurant staff, have a mortality rate twice the average.

Health Services

The tasks carried out by the Danish health services, which are determined by law, have predominantly been made the responsibility of the counties and local authorities and consist of the prevention, detection and treatment of illness together with the care of the sick. To these can be added research and the training of personnel in the health services.

Some 100,000 persons (calculated as full-time employment) work in the Danish health sector, the cost of which accounts for c. 68 billion kroner, corresponding to c. 8.4% of GDP (1999). The individual's direct contributions towards health benefits make up c. 15 billion kroner, or c. 19% of total health expenditures (1999) and mainly cover own payments towards the cost of medicines and dental treatment, but considerable sums are also spent on herbal medicines and other alternative treatments.

The health services are mainly administered through the county councils. Together with the municipalities of Copenhagen and Frederiksberg these have the duty via the public health insurance to finance the essential areas of primary health care (doctors in general practice, dentists, physiotherapists, etc.) and provide subsidies for medicines. Similarly they have the task of maintaining hospital services (secondary health services). As from 1995 the Copenhagen and Frederiksberg hospitals and the State University Hospital (*Rigshospitalet*) are operated by a public trust, the *Copenhagen Hospital Corporation*. The responsibilities of the local authorities include the provision of funding for home nursing, health visitors and dental care for children and young people. Providing help for the elderly and handicapped in their own homes and establishing and running nursing homes and other types of home for the elderly is mainly a local authority responsibility.

In the primary health care sector 3,700 general practitioners, 900 specialists and 3,700 dentists have contracts with the health service. More

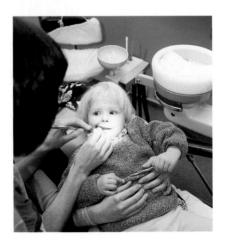

Children's dental care in Denmark is carried out by regular dental checks in municipal clinics, which are usually situated in the schools. Treatment is free for children and young people under 18. Treatment is mainly aimed at caries (cavities in the teeth) and gum disease, and in addition 25% of children have orthodontic treatment.

The health visitor comes to the home and weighs the baby on the classical steelyard. The parents are offered 4-5 visits during the child's first year, and in the case of a first child 7-8 visits, during which they are given advice on diet and care of the child. In addition, the health visitor might have made an introductory visit a couple of months before the birth.

than 5,000 nurses, 1,100 dentists and other groups of personnel are appointed under local authority health care arrangements. A characteristic of the primary medical service is the fact that c. 98% of the population choose to have their own doctor. On average, a Dane pays six visits a year to his doctor, who in c. 90% of cases can complete the treatment himself.

Hospital services employ 9,000 doctors, 26,000 nurses and c. 16,000 other staff. There are 1.1 million hospitalisations annually and 4.3 million out-patient treatments, which is a notable increase in activity, especially when seen in conjunction with a reduction of over 35% in the number of beds in the period after 1978 to 23,000 in 2000.

Nils Rosdahl

History

The State's interest in the health of the population goes back to new political ideas in the middle of the 18th century, seeing a large and healthy population as a prerequisite for the wealth of the nation. A few hospitals of between 10 and 20 beds were established by counties and towns for the care of the poor, servants and others who could not be treated in the home. The State appointed district surgeons whose task it was to treat the sick with no financial means of their own, to make sure that food was not a danger to health and to take part in combating infectious diseases. The treatment of illnesses requiring surgery was undertaken by barber-trained surgeons who also received some theoretical training, while the considerably smaller number of medically trained doctors had a theoretical university training which was only supplemented with practical, clinical training in 1757 with the establishment of the 300-bed Royal Frederik's Hospital in Copenhagen. In 1838 the two forms of training were amalgamated.

In the second half of the 18th century a school for midwives was established in the Maternity Hospital (*Fødselsstiftelsen*) with the aim of reducing infant mortality, and the State also provided support for the treatment of infectious and venereal diseases.

The Royal College of Health was established in 1803 with the task of supervising health service, which was developed during the 19th century; midwives were appointed throughout the country, and vaccination against smallpox was introduced. The number of general practitioners grew, and in the second half of the 19th century hospitals had been established in most Danish towns. The State ran four large mental hospitals: Sankt Hans Hospital in Roskilde was built by the city of Copenhagen.

From about 1850 health insurance societies were formed in which by paying a weekly subscription the less prosperous could insure themselves against financial consequences of illness. The health insurance societies were given statutory form in 1892 and thereafter received a state subsidy intended to provide help supplementary to one's own efforts, this being the guiding principle behind the policy towards the poor at that time. The doctors supported the idea of creating health insurance societies, which assured them of an income also from the poorer strata of society. This was a contributory factor in the increase in the number of general practitioners. Until the 1930s, these constituted the majority of doctors in the country. The agreements between the local health insurance societies and the doctors were centralised and finally put on a nation-wide footing. In 1973 the tasks of the health insurance societies were replaced by provisions under the county councils and financed from taxes. The number of general practitioners had been almost constant since 1950, but now it again increased.

In the 19th century the prevention of disease had been directed towards providing sewerage, water services, food inspection, and education in hygienic habits. This work continued and in the 1930s and 1940s it was supplemented with publicly financed health checks; thus a system of health visitors for infants was introduced in 1937, medical health checks for children in 1946, school health services in 1946, various infant vaccinations from 1943 and ante-natal care in 1945.

Until the 1930s, the hospitals, which had grown steadily in numbers from the middle of the 19th century, were mainly what were known as general hospitals without specialised departments. Patients were treated by a small number of doctors; the number of hospitals later declined at the same time as there was an increase in specialisation and a rise in the numbers of wards in the individual hospitals and, furthermore, the number of doctors and nurses increased considerably. At the same time there

Niels Ryberg Finsen, 1860-1904, Danish physician. As a young man, Finsen already suffered from a serious heart condition, which meant that he had to give up any thought of practising after qualifying in 1890. He was appointed assistant lecturer in anatomy at Copenhagen University, where he started some highly successful research into the effect of light on certain skin diseases. In 1893 he attracted attention in Denmark with a dissertation on red light and its beneficial effect on smallpox. Two years later, Finsen made the great breakthrough that established his international reputation by introducing the revolutionary carbon arc treatment (Finsen's Therapy) of lupus (*lupus vulgaris*). The following year he established a light institute, subsequently The Finsen Institute, in Copenhagen. In 1898 he became a titular professor. Finsen was the first Danish doctor to receive the Nobel Prize for Physiology/Medicine, in 1903, for his unique research into treatment with ultraviolet rays.

Johannes Brix

The Municipal Hospital in Copenhagen was taken into use in 1863. Its construction had been preceded by a lengthy study by a commission set up after a cholera epidemic in 1853 had revealed the provision of hospital facilities in Copenhagen was quite insufficient. When completed, the hospital was of the highest international standard, and its plan arrangement was so advanced that with few changes it is able to serve as a modern hospital even as late as 1999. This contemporary illustration is the work of the architect Christian B. Nielsen.

was an increase in the number of specialist fields. New groups of staff were introduced, especially in the 1950s: physiotherapists, nursing auxiliaries, laboratory technicians, medical secretaries, etc.

Before 1930 the average length of a stay in hospital was approximately a month; this has gradually fallen to 6 days in 1999. The number of admissions to somatic hospitals per 1,000 inhabitants has risen from 40 in 1918 to 205 in 1999. Although the proportion of the elderly in the population is rising, which results in an increase in the need for treatment, the number of patient days per 1,000 inhabitants has been reduced. Since the 1980s the number of hospital beds has also fallen to c. 20,000, i.e. from 6 beds per 1,000 inhabitants to 3.8 in 1999.

The drop in the number of hospital beds is most pronounced in the case of the psychiatric hospitals, which in 1998 accounted for some 4,200 beds. The administration of psychiatric hospitals was in 1976 transferred from the State to the counties. The establishment of district psychiatric centres has led to a larger proportion of patients being treated as out-patients.

Sickness rates in the country were not well documented in the period before the introduction of fuller medical statistics at the beginning of the 20th century; only deaths had been registered since the middle of the 17th century. However, although it is impossible to produce actual figures, the major epidemics left their mark, with the Black Death in the 14th century, the plague in 1711, cholera in 1853 and Spanish Flu in 1918. Malaria and smallpox made regular appearances until the middle of the 19th century. From more recent times there is the polio epidemic of 1952.

The most striking change in the general state of health is the decline in infant mortality since the end of the 19th century. This decline is mainly due to the fact that infectious diseases have increasingly been prevented through better care of infants, water hygiene, food and better living conditions. Along with this decline, cardiovascular diseases and cancer have become more common as causes of death.

Signild Vallgårda

Health Expenditures since 1980

The health services consist of three sectors: the hospital services, the general practice sector and the local authority sector providing for children's dental care, prevention and home nursing. Of these, the hospital services dominate, accounting for 70% of the total public expenditure on the health services (1999).

In the period 1980-1987 the hospital services were characterised by growth in real term expenditures and activities, but from 1988 to 1991 there was a slight decline in real expenditure and a slower but positive growth in activities. From 1992 to 1999 expenditures increased annually by c. 3% in real terms. In the period 1988-1999, public health care expenditure accounted for an initially falling but then increasing proportion of total public operating and capital expenditures. In 1999 the percentage was 9.9% – the same level as in 1988.

The annual number of discharges have risen by about 0.6% annually from 1988 to 1999. In the same period the number of patient days fell by c. 1.8% a year, while out-patient treatment 1980-1987 rose by c. 1% a year, in the period 1987-1992 by c. 3% a year, and from 1993 to 1999 by about 5% a year.

Between 1980 and 1999 Danish hospitals have improved their productivity through a radical reorganisation that has made possible a continuous fall in the average length of stay. This must be viewed in connection with the fact that during this same period the less serious cases have been transferred to the increasingly important out-patient clinics and intensive use of day surgery.

August Krogh, 1874-1949, Danish physiologist, graduate in zoology 1899, Professor of Animal Physiology at the University of Copenhagen 1916-1945. At an early stage, Krogh became a pupil of the respiratory physiologist Christian Bohr, who became an important influence in his subsequent research. The special character of this research was determined by Krogh's great understanding of physics and chemistry and also by his unusual skill in constructing scientific apparatus. Krogh's *metabolism apparatus*, which could measure oxygen consumption, was still being used in hospitals in the 1980s to measure metabolism. His principal contribution was in circulation physiology, as he was able to explain the control of the capillaries, which regulate the flow of blood as needed. This gave him the Nobel Prize for Physiology/Medicine in 1920. In collaboration with H.C. Hagedorn, he introduced insulin treatment in Denmark in 1922; together, they started the production of insulin which has since given Denmark a leading position in this field.

Nils Engelbrecht

Johannes Fibiger, 1867-1928, Danish physician, bacteriologist and pathologist. In 1902 he demonstrated that bovine tuberculosis can be transmitted to humans. Fibiger was the first person to produce experimental proof of the possibility of cancer being caused by external influence. 1907-1913 he proved that rats fed on cockroaches hosting a roundworm (*Spiroptera neoplastica*), developed cancer of the stomach, spreading to the lymph glands and lungs. This observation introduced a new epoch in cancer research, and provided inspiration for studies of, for instance, the carcinogenic effects of tars. Fibiger was awarded several honorary doctorates, and in 1926 he became the first cancer researcher to receive a Nobel Prize for Physiology/Medicine.

Jørgen Rygaard

In the same period the lengthening waiting times for surgical treatment have attracted attention. The increase in productivity in this area has failed to keep up with an increase in need for treatment.

Financial Management of the Health Services

The county councils and the municipalities of Copenhagen and Frederiksberg have both operational and financial responsibility for the health services and health insurance.

Roughly 70% of the county councils' total operating expenditure goes to the health services. The financial resources for the health services have in the period after 1980 been placed under constraint mainly stemming from the overall condition and development of the Danish economy. During the same period, by means of clearly defined frame budgets, the counties have introduced a tight expenditure control of hospitals. Provided they keep within the expenditure constraints which they are obliged to observe, the hospitals have a large measure of freedom to apply their resources as they wish,

but with gradually clearer indications of productivity goals. Staying within the budgets has had a high priority. At the beginning of the 1990s, several authorities introduced so-called contracts which are precise, specific agreements between the country health committees and the individual hospitals as to how much the hospitals are to achieve and how large the budget for this is to be. This has increased the interest in and need for prioritising between the various patient groups. In 2000-2001 hospital reimbursement by means of diagnosis related groups, DRG, has been introduced in some areas, e.g. for patients choosing hospital treatment away from their home county.

The potential for exercising expenditure control in the field of primary health care, e.g. general practice, practising specialists, dentists and medicines, is limited because practising specialists are paid per treatment, whereas general practitioners are paid by a combination of a regular payment per registered patient (per capita) and fee-for-service. These expenditures are fully tax-financed as are hospital expenditures. This limited potential for control, which also applies to subsidies for medicines, doubtless provides the main explanation as to why growth in primary health expenditures has been greater than in the hospital services, namely c. 3% per year from 1988 to 1999. In the practice sector the expenditure trends reflect demand much more closely, while it is artificially kept down in the hospital services, partly through waiting lists. To this can be added the fact that since the 1970s there has been a systematic attempt to move treatment from the hospitals to the practice sector. How much this has meant for the increase in expenditure in the practice sector cannot be calculated precisely.

International Comparison of Health Expenditure

Together with Sweden, Denmark differs from general trends in the western world. In all other countries the proportion of GDP accounted for by health expenditure has been on the rise, but for Denmark the proportion fell from 8.5% to 8.4% between 1990 and 1999, and the Swedish proportion went down from 8.5% to 7.9%. In the same period the Norwegian proportion rose from 7.8% to 9.3%. There are many explanations for the Danish trend, but the two most important are doubtless the strict control on the part of the State and the fact that on account of their general financial and operational responsibility the counties have been able to manage very effectively, especially in the hospital field.

Kjeld Møller Pedersen

Jens Christian Skou, born 1918, Danish physician and physiologist. After graduating from medical school at the University of Copenhagen in 1944, Skou was appointed to the Institute of Physiology at Aarhus University in 1947. In 1957, while investigating the active mechanism of local anaesthetic drugs, he discovered that the nerve cell membranes of crabs contain an enzyme, sodium potassium ATPase, which in the form of the sodium potassium pump helps to maintain the salt balance between the cells and the tissue fluid by pumping sodium ions out of the cells and potassium ions into the cells. 1963-1978 Skou held the chair of Physiology in Aarhus, and 1978-1988 the chair of Biophysics, also in Aarhus; in 1997 Skou shared the Nobel Prize for Chemistry with the Briton John Walker and the American Paul Boyer.

Nils Engelbrecht

Niels K. Jerne, 1911-1994, Danish physician and immunologist. After occupying professorial chairs in Switzerland, USA and Germany he headed the independent Basel Institute for Immunology in Switzerland 1969-1980, an institution with no commercial obligations, established especially for him by the pharmaceutical company Hoffmann-La Roche. During his time of office the Institute became the international centre for immunological research. Jerne finished his career as professor at the Institut Pasteur in Paris (1981-1982). He formulated several new theories on the way in which white blood corpuscles form antibodies, thus overturning accepted assumptions. According to the final theory he formulated, the network theory (1973), the organism forms antibodies combatting its own antibodies in such a way that a kind of immunological balance and an exchange of information is established in the immune system in the same way as in the central nervous system. Together with Georges Köhler and César Milstein, Jerne was awarded the Nobel Prize for Physiology/Medicine in 1984.

Nils Engelbrecht

Education and Training

The concept of education and training denotes formalised learning. In Danish tradition an education leading to formal qualifications is often supplemented with adult classes and popular education not ending in exams. The dividing line between the two is not easy to define: professional training develops the personality, and education with personal development as its aim contributes at the same time to practical proficiency.

There are some 3,000 schools and other educational establishments in Denmark. Of these, the *folkeskole* (state primary and lower secondary school) accounts for c. 1,700, private primary schools c. 400 and *gymnasier* (upper secondary schools) and *HF-courses* (Higher Preparatory Examination courses) rather more than 150. The figures also include c. 225 *efterskoler* (continuation schools), c. 100 folk high schools, just over 100 vocational schools and about 225 further and higher educational establishments. The Ministry of Education is the supreme supervisory authority. Expenditure on education has grown rapidly since the 1950s, from just over 2% of GDP to just under 7% in 1995. In 1998 total public expenditure on education and training was c. 88 billion kroner (state education grants and loans included), corresponding to c. 13.5% of all public expenditure.

Of a year group in the folkeskole (1998), c. 95% continue in the education system, c. 53% in general and vocational upper secondary school type education and c. 41% in vocational training (EUD). C. 77% of a year group gain practical qualifications through basic vocational education or various kinds of advanced post-compulsory education.

Educational Principles

In Denmark there is compulsory education: the obligation to ensure teaching for your child, but not compulsory school attendance. This is the result of historical conflicts between parents, State and Church. After the Reformation in 1536 teaching was primarily the Church's task, and it was closely linked to upbringing in the home and the parish. In the towns instruction in reading and writing was provided in schools, and in rural areas by the priest or the parish clerk giving instruction in the catechism once or twice a week.

For reasons both ideological and practical, State interest in children's education grew in the 18th century. The 1708 Poor Law requirement for schools in rural areas, the establishment of 240 so-called *rytterskoler* on the royal estates in the 1720s, the introduction of church confirmation in 1736 and legislation providing for the establishment of schools in country parishes for all children from the age of 5-6 (1739) were all expressions of State and Church interest in educating children and servants with the object of turning them into God-fearing and literate Christians.

Nevertheless, the creation of the general elementary school is normally not reckoned to have taken place until 1814 when the principle of compulsory education from the age of 6-7 until confirmation was introduced. The primary school was funded locally, i.e. by all the inhabitants of the parish (though with a state subsidy from 1856), and governed in each parish by a school commission with the parish priest at its head. Until 1958 different rules governed the folkeskole in village and town schools, the former having fewer classes, and the pupils only attending school every other day.

From the end of the 18th century there were separate private schools for boys and girls in the towns, and tuition in the home was not unusual. After the middle of the 19th century small, private 'free' schools arose in the rural areas, established by groups of parents who wished to have their children brought up according to their own principles. Rooted in the demands for freedom in church and school advanced by N.F.S. Grundtvig and Christen Kold, the right to provide for a child's education without first having to have the approval of the authorities was established by law in 1855 and given constitutional force in 1915. From 1899 the free schools received state subsidies. *Educational freedom* has since also been utilised by other educational interests: Catholic schools, the German minority schools in North Schleswig after 1920, progressive free schools in the 1960s, Steiner schools, schools for immigrants, etc.

With the 1903 school reform which had as its objective the democratisation of the higher levels of school

Graphic presentation of the structure of the public educational system.

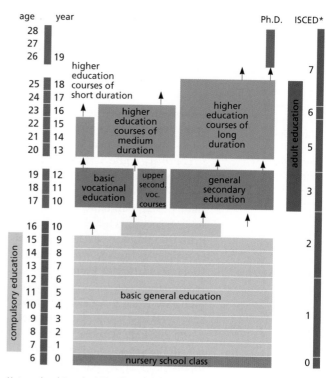

*International Standard Classification of Education

education, a four-year middle school was introduced leading either into a one-year secondary school course or a three-year grammar school course. From the 1950s the educational sector expanded, partly as a result of society's demands for technological progress. In the following decades education was an almost constant source of discussion. More educational establishments were built, from central schools to universities. In the political vision of the 1960s educational progress was synonymous with investment in the future.

Until 1933 the primary school was under Church supervision, and until 1975 it had the duty of promoting a Christian view of life. Since then it has only been linked to the demand for comprehensiveness and democracy. Little by little a *unified school* has been established by scrapping the middle school in 1958 and the one-year secondary classes in 1975 and then in 1980 by integrating children with special educational needs. In 1972 the period of compulsory education was extended from seven to nine years.

Interior from a West Jutland school, painted in 1900 by Hans Smidth. Until far into the 20th century, schooling in West Jutland was characterised by poverty and long journeys to school. Special 'provisions for schools in West Jutland', introduced in 1818, did not come to an end until 1958. According to these arrangements, the older children scarcely went to school in the summer because the boys were needed as cowherds and the girls to tend the geese; to compensate for this, they went to school more often in the winter, every day in some places.

Basic Education

The basic education is provided either by the local authority *folkeskole* or the private elementary schools, which have the same structure, and which are also known as 'free elementary schools'. The present law on primary education (1993) obliges schools among other things to 'familiarise pupils with Danish culture and contribute to their understanding of other cultures and of mankind's interaction with nature'. The cost of teaching is met by the local authorities. Private schools are obliged to provide teaching that is comparable with that in the folkeskole.

The folkeskole comprises a one-year nursery class, a nine-year basic school and a one-year 10th class. The nursery class and the 10th class are not covered by the compulsory education requirement, but almost all children attend nursery classes, and about half of all pupils in the 9th class go on into the 10th.

The folkeskole is a unified school in which there is no streaming at any level. The curriculum is determined by the Primary Education Act, while regulations concerning the aims of

the different subjects, etc. are drawn up by the Minister in accordance with the law. On completing the 9th and 10th classes the pupils can, if they so wish, take the final folkeskole examination.

The local authorities have the ultimate responsibility for the folkeskole, including appointments, financial frameworks and curricula. Every school has a board of governors in which parent representatives are in the majority. The board of governors determines the principles for the school's activities, draws up proposals for curricula and approves teaching materials that are made available to the pupils without payment. The head teacher has the educational and administrative responsibility for the school, while the teachers enjoy a considerable degree of freedom concerning contents and teaching methods. Since 1791 teachers have been trained in training colleges, originally state-run and since 1860 also in some cases privately run. There are at present 18 training colleges. Teachers' in-service and further training takes place primarily in the Royal Danish School of Educational Studies, which also offers graduate courses.

The private elementary schools teach c. 13.5% of all children (1998). The State and local authorities cover about 75-80% of the expenditure of private schools.

As an alternative to the top classes of the folkeskole pupils can choose to go to *efterskoler* (continuation schools), which are private boarding schools for 14-18-year-olds. In 1998, these schools were catering for 28% of pupils in the top two classes. As a supplement to the folkeskole pupils in this age group can also attend local authority day continuation schools for a general training with its emphasis on practical and social subjects.

Vocational training includes both theory and practice. Holbæk Technical School. Department of Motorcar Engineering.

Post-Compulsory Education

Post-compulsory education can be either general or vocationally oriented, and pupils are normally aged 16-19.

General upper secondary education can comprise three years at a *gymnasium* (upper secondary school) or two or three years attending a further education course leading to the *Studentereksamen* (upper secondary school leaving examination) or a two-year course leading to the *Højere Forberedelseseksamen* (HF – Higher Preparatory Examination). They do not provide vocational qualifications, but they qualify for further training. The *Studentereksamen* was introduced by the University of Copenhagen around 1630 and in 1850 was delegated to the individual grammar schools. In 1871, the increasing number of subjects brought about a division into a mathematical-scientific side and a language side, which in 1903 was divided into a classical language side and a modern language side. From 1875 girls were allowed to take the Studentereksamen. In 1958 the middle school section of the grammar schools was abolished, and the three-year upper secondary school was supplemented with a division into different 'lines' in the second and third years. The increase in numbers of pupils was followed by an upper secondary school building programme throughout the country and the introduction of HF in 1967. In the school reform of 1987 'lines' were replaced by a system of optional subjects within a language or mathematical side.

Post-compulsory education also includes 2-3-year *vocational training at upper secondary school level*: *Højere handelseksamen* (HHX – Higher Commercial Examination) and *Højere teknisk eksamen* (HTX – Higher Technical Examination), which normally presuppose a one-year vocational training or a completed apprenticeship. These examinations qualify for both the labour market and further training.

Vocational education and training (EUD), which is of 3-4 years' duration, prepare students through alternating school tuition and practical training for skilled work in the labour market. There are about 100 individual courses covering some 200 special subjects; in 1991 they replaced both the older basic vocational training courses (EFG), which were introduced in 1978, and traditional apprenticeships. The new structure, which among other things contains rules for credit transfer, covers e.g. business and clerical training, trades and agriculture. In 1956 business schools and technical schools, which had so far all been evening schools, were turned into day schools. A new type of youth training is the two-year vocational basic training introduced in August 1993 and designed specially for the individual. 1995 saw the introduction of the two-year free individually organised youth education, which is composed by the young person con-

Danish universities are characterised by offering research-based teaching. The Technical University of Denmark and the University of Copenhagen were both strongly involved in the development of the first Danish satellite, Ørsted, launched in 1999. This photo shows a test of the satellite carried out at the Technical University of Denmark.

cerned from a minimum of three different elements in established or new courses of training and education.

Further and Higher Education

These branches of education are divided into short, medium and long-term courses of further and higher education, lasting for up to 3 years, 3-4 years and more than 4 years respectively.

The *short duration further education courses* include such things as training as laboratory technicians, training in market economy and as computer specialists. Entrance requirements are schooling up to upper secondary school level or vocational training.

The *medium duration further education courses*, which in most cases presuppose an upper secondary level education, include training as journalists, teachers in the folkeskole, educationalists, librarians and nurses. The universities' 3-year bachelor courses (B.A. and B.Sc.) are included in this group. Most of the short and medium-term further and higher education courses were established in the 20th century.

Long higher education courses, which include courses leading to the degree of *kandidat* (roughly equivalent to M.A or M.Sc.) in i.a. arts, social studies, science, medicine, food sciences, technology, theology and business economics, are taken in universities and other institutions of higher education. As a supplement to the courses leading to the degree of *kandidat*, there is now a three-year research training leading to an academic degree; from the 1960s this was the degree of Licentiate, but since 1992 it has been the Ph.D. degree. The courses leading to the *kandidat* degree are traditional courses. Oldest among them, dating from

1629 is the examination in theology; this was followed by that in law from 1736 and medicine from 1788.

In the case of both youth and further and higher education courses there is provision for scholarships and study loans from the State Education Grant and Loan Scheme (SU). Students are entitled to support when they have reached the age of 18, are of Danish nationality and are actively engaged in studies. In 1998 the State granted SU to just over 285,000 persons, amounting to a total of about 8.4 billion kroner.

Adult Education and Continuing Training

Since the 1990s adult education courses have been an expanding field offering a range of possibilities. *Arbejdsmarkedsuddannelser* (AMU – Labour market courses) are vocationally oriented short courses designed jointly by the State and the parties in the labour market with a view to improving labour force qualifications. The training courses, which date back to 1960, are taken in AMU centres and vocational schools and are available both to those in work and to the unemployed.

Vocational courses for adults have since 1992 enabled adults engaged in special educational courses and with credit transfers from earlier vocational experience to achieve vocational qualifications corresponding to the youth EUD, and since 2000 also qualifications corresponding to further adult education and diploma and master's courses.

Open education is organised by vocational schools, universities, educational institutions, etc. and is available both to those in work and to the unemployed, with both full-time and part-time courses on offer.

Almen voksenuddannelse (AVU – general adult education) was the subject of special legislation in 1989. In county training centres, courses and tests are offered in general individual subjects on the levels of the folkeskole final examination, HF and grammar school. The object of these courses is to supplement basic schooling or to prepare or improve examination results giving access to further or higher education.

Folk High Schools

Folk high schools are 'free boarding schools', offering teaching in general subjects for adults. There are no examinations in these schools, which decide the intellectual or practical contents of their subjects for themselves. Like free schools and continuation schools, the folk high schools are part of the tradition of popular education going back to N.F.S. Grundtvig. Some of them have promoted ideas and initiatives that have had a profound effect on local cultural and vocational life. The first folk high school was established in 1844.

Part of the tradition in popular education is represented by *non-formal adult educational courses* run by adult education associations, evening schools and university extension courses. The first adult education association was the Workers' Educational Association (AOF), founded in 1925. Later this was followed by others, including the FOF (Popular Educational Association) and LOF (Liberal Educational Association). In the university extension courses, founded in 1898, teachers who themselves are active researchers pass on scholarly working methods and results; the teaching takes place not only in the five university towns, but also locally through a network of some 150 local committees. The day high schools, which came into existence in the beginning of the 1980s, offer folk high school teaching, but are not boarding schools.

There are some 1.5 million participants each year in vocationally-oriented or general adult education courses. This is achieved with support from a number of different support schemes, of which the most important is AMU reimbursement, paid leave, adult education support and the adult educational fund.

Vagn Skovgaard-Petersen

Research

Danish research has grown out of public and private initiatives in a line of development stretching back more than 500 years. It has been supported by three pillars: the universities and other institutes of higher education, other public research institutes and research undertaken by private firms.

The total expenditure on Danish research in 1999 amounted to 25.3 billion kroner. Of this, universities, etc. were responsible for c. 5.2 billion, and the other public research institutes a further 4.0 billion, while the expenditure on research by private firms amount to a good 16 billion kroner. Denmark spends c. 2% of GDP on research initiatives and thereby occupies a relatively low position in relation to the countries with which it is normally compared (the OECD countries).

When the University of Copenhagen was founded in 1479 the aim was not to create a research institution. The university was to provide tuition within the scholastic tradition that was the mark of all mediaeval universities. Only during the 18th-century Enlightenment, but realized in the university reforms of 1788, did independent and general research achieve a distinct place among the responsibilities of the university. In the 19th century this was supplemented by other seats of higher learning such as the Technical University of Denmark (1829), the College of Pharmacy (1857) and the Royal Veterinary and Agricultural College (1858). In the 20th century four universities (Århus, Southern Denmark, Roskilde and Aalborg) and two schools of economics and business administration (Copenhagen and Århus) have been established. Final-ly, the Danish University of Education has developed into an institute of higher education, so that in 2000 there are 11 universities or university-type institutions, all of which will be called universities below.

Universities

A common feature of the universities is that via the annual budget they receive basic funding for research. The use of these funds is determined by decisions reached by the university authorities. To this can be added funding from other sources for financing special research programmes, research contracts or participation in research co-operation with Danish or foreign partners.

In 1998 direct grants from the budget amounted to 2.4 billion kroner, while those from other sources amounted to c. 1.7 billion.

The universities have the main responsibility for Danish basic research. While various other countries have chosen to let academies or similar national research institutes take care of basic research, the Danish research system is founded on the ideals which Wilhelm von Humboldt developed at the beginning of the 19th century in Prussia, and which maintain a close link between higher education and independent research.

The most important elements in university research are the institutes in each individual university, and the researchers appointed by the universities are free to choose their own research subjects.

Research Institutes

Outside the university world there is a number of research institutes aiming at furthering specific objec-

Tycho Brahe, 1546-1601. With his discovery of 'the new star' in 1572, Tycho Brahe became famous as an astronomer throughout Europe. To secure him for Denmark, Frederik II endowed him in 1576 with the island of Ven, where he gradually built up a research institution of an entirely new kind. This comprised the extensive castle of Uranienborg, the observatory of Stjerneborg, a paper mill and printing press, and a workshop for making instruments, by means of which Tycho Brahe gradually increased the accuracy of his observations to the limits of what the naked eye could see. He rejected all previous observations as dubious, and aimed to 'reconstruct astronomy' by personally surveying all heavenly phenomena from scratch. This work continued until 1597, when after a quarrel with Christian IV Tycho Brahe left Denmark. He took all his equipment with him and ended his days as a 'mathematician' at the court of the Emperor Rudolph II of Vienna.

Among Tycho Brahe's many results was the demonstration in 1577 that a comet was a heavenly body and not an atmospheric phenomenon as previously assumed. In addition came the discovery of two hitherto unknown 'anomalies' in the movements of the moon and a catalogue containing the positions of 1,000 fixed stars. He himself did not manage to utilize his many planetary observations, but in 1600 he handed a series of observations of Mars to Johannes Kepler, who used them in deriving his three fundamental laws for the movement of the planets in general. Tycho Brahe's cosmology with the Earth at the centre of a system, circled by the Sun, around which the other planets rotate, was widely used in the 17th century as an alternative to the Copernican system condemned by the Church.

Olaf Pedersen

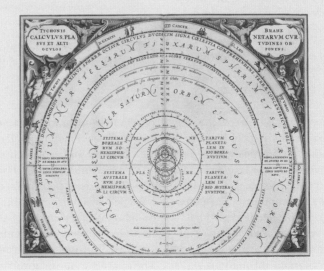

Niels Stensen (Nicolaus Steno), 1638-1686. In 1660, after spending three years studying medicine in Copenhagen, Stensen went to Amsterdam, where he made his first anatomical discovery: the duct between the parotid gland and the oral cavity (*ductus parotideus stenonis*). In succeeding years in Leiden he explained the principal features of the physiology of the glands, at the same time as his contributions to embryology and comparative anatomy made him a researcher of European standing. Most discussed was his demonstration that the heart is neither more nor less than a muscle.

After failing to be appointed professor in Copenhagen in 1664, he spent a year in Paris, where in a famous lecture on the anatomy of the brain in 1665 he demonstrated the incorrect anatomical basis of cartesianism. In his study of muscular physiology he was the first to argue that a mathematical description is also necessary in biology. After being employed at the Medici court in Florence, he converted to Catholicism in 1667. He continued his scientific work with outstanding results, summing them up in his dissertation *Prodomus* (1669, English translation 1671), in which he laid the foundations of three new sciences. *Palaeontology* was given a solid foundation with the demonstration that fossils were petrified remains of living creatures. As fossilised shark's teeth were found in mountains, these must once have been covered by the sea, so that the earth's crust must have undergone profound changes over the ages. By means of field work Stensen succeeded in demonstrating and interpreting the geological stratification of Tuscany, whereby the principles of *histori-cal geology* were established. Finally, *crystallography* was given a scientific foundation through Stensen's demonstration that crystals grow when materials are deposited on their outer surfaces, the mutual angles of which remain constant during this process.

In 1672 Stensen returned to Copenhagen to a newly-established post as Royal Anatomist; he attracted many students from the university, which on several occasions invited him to carry out public dissections, but bypassed him in 1674 and appointed the 19-year-old Caspar Bartholin to a vacant Chair of Anatomy. This was partly responsible for Stensen's decision to return to Florence, where he was ordained priest in 1675 in order to devote the rest of his life to the service of the Church. In 1677 he was consecrated bishop in Rome, after which he worked for the rest of his life among the widely dispersed Catholics of northern Germany and as a consequence of his vow of poverty came to live in extreme need. After an unheeded visit to Copenhagen in 1685 he died the following year in Schwerin, from where his body was transported to Florence to be buried in the Medici church of San Lorenzo. He was beatified by Pope John Paul II in 1986.

Olaf Pedersen

tives. The emphasis is predominantly on applied research, including advice to public authorities. This type of institution also has a long tradition. It is worth emphasising that Frederik II gave massive support to the astronomer Tycho Brahe between 1580 and 1597 when he was running one of Europe's most distinguished research institutions through his observatory of Uranienborg on the island of Ven. From the end of the 19th century, but especially since 1945, government research institutes with research as their main task, have been established within all the main areas of research, to which can be added 17 research-oriented archives, libraries and museums. The characteristic of government research is that its choice of subject, in contrast to that of the universities, is governed by the needs formulated by society via the ministries and their advisory bodies.

Also part of the picture of publicly financed research is that carried out in the more than 100 hospitals throughout the country. The basic expenses for this are covered mainly by the counties, although Rigshospitalet (the State University Hospital) and a few others receive budgetary grants.

The administration of the public research system is in the care of different ministries. The Ministry of Science, Technology and Innovation grant is the largest, accounting for just under 70% of the total, because the basic grants to the universities are derived from this source. A nucleus of the Ministry is the state research councils and the Council on Research Policy. The research councils have as their task to advise public authorities on the development of research and to support Danish research. The councils were established by a Folketing Act in 1972, though the Technical and Scientific Research Council was formed as early as 1946. The Research Planning Council, established in parallel with this (since 1988 called the Council for Research Policy) advises the government and the Folketing on overriding questions of research policy. In 1991 the Danish Fund for Basic Research was founded, which with a start capital of 2 billion kroner is to support outstanding Danish research on an international level.

The total publicly financed research system has as one of its aims to Co-operate with private companies to further technological developments. A technological service system incorporating the Danish Technological Institute, technologi-cal information centres and a number of institutes under the Academy for Technical Sciences (ATV) are at the disposal of business as vehicles for new knowledge.

Business Research

Danish businesses use less on research and development than the European average. The reason must be sought in the limited number of very large concerns. A pioneer in the efforts to use research in the service of industry was the founder of the Carlsberg Breweries, J.C. Jacobsen. From his youth he was preoccupied with science, and in 1875 he founded his own brewery. In 1876 he established the Carlsberg Foundation, which became the owner of Carlsberg and thereby a significant source of finance for Danish research. The executive board of the Carlsberg Foundation is appointed by members of the Royal Danish Academy of Sciences and Letters. It is presumably unique that five people whose most important qualifications are to be researchers thus constitute the management committee of a large industrial enterprise. Almost equally unique is the fact that since its formation, the Carlsberg Laboratory has been a laboratory for basic research, the results of which are available to the public.

In the 2000s, the sector of Danish industry with the greatest research requirements is in particular the pharmaceutical industry and the electronics and measuring instrument industry. The research departments co-operate closely with Danish and foreign university institutes, and an increasing tendency can be observed for Danish businesses like, for instance, the pharmaceutical firm Novo Nordisk, to establish their own laboratories outside Denmark.

Ole Rømer, 1644-1710. As a student living in Rasmus Bartholin's house, Rømer was given the task of preparing an edition of Tycho Brahe's works, for which reason he accompanied the French astronomer Jean Picard to Paris in 1672. Here, in 1676, he demonstrated that certain irregularities in the timing of the eclipses of the moons of Jupiter could be explained as the result of light's 'hesitation' or its finite velocity, which has since emerged as the most fundamental natural constant in physics. After his return to Denmark in 1681 he reorganised the observatory in the Round Tower at the same time as undertaking various public duties which included surveying the Danish road network, establishing a unified system of weights and measures, and introducing the Gregorian calendar in 1700. Long before Celcius, Rømer was using the freezing and boiling points of water as natural fixed points on thermometers. In his private observatories, Rømer first developed the transit instrument and then the meridian circle, which 100 years later became astronomy's most accurate instrument for measuring position. Apart from a notebook called Adversaria and three days' observations from 1706, all Rømer's scientific notes were lost in the Fire of Copenhagen in 1728.

Olaf Pedersen

Both private and public research in Denmark are dependent on international co-operation. Of particular significance is Danish participation in EU research programmes, the aim of which is to improve the scientific and technological foundations for European business, and in EUREKA co-operation, the programmes of which are to stimulate the competitive ability of individual businesses.

In financial terms, international programmes and funds contributed c. 775 million kroner to the Danish research budget in 1997. However, to this can be added the great significance of Danish researchers' co-operation with colleagues from other countries in international networks.

Central Research Areas

At the end of the 20th century, Danish research occupies a strong position in various areas. In the humanities, archaeology and comparative linguistics are important disciplines with their roots in Danish university and museum traditions. With Niels Bohr as the great international name, physics is still an area of strength, while marine biology has achieved a powerful research base in this century. Danish agriculture has been able to build up powerful research areas both in the government research and university research systems, and research in health has a strong position in international research co-operation.

In order to further Danish research in selected areas, a number of special research programmes have been undertaken in the 1980s and 1990s in areas such as materials technology, biotechnology, food technology and energy and environmental research. The aim of these contributions is to develop new areas in which the research can further the competitive ability of Danish business and win prominence in the world of international research.

Knud Larsen

The History of Research

Scientific activities as such in Denmark arose in the 12th century under the influence of the Paris schools. Bishop Anders Sunesen's great theological didactic poem *Hexaëmeron* continued an old European tradition, while Saxo Grammaticus' *Gesta Danorum*, written in ornate Latin depicted the history of Denmark until 1185. The vernacular was used in the 13th century in the codification of the Danish regional laws as well as in a medical herbal. In 1274 systematic astronomical observations were made in Roskilde, and this was also the home of Peder Nattergal (Petrus Philomena), who became known throughout Europe as a mathematici-

an, a constructor of instruments for making astronomical calculations, and the author of an extremely widely read calendar for the period 1292-1368. In Paris, Boëthius de Dacia and other Danish philosophers and language theorists were active. In the late Middle Ages a large collection of proverbs appeared as well as an lengthy textbook of medicine and astrology and the first map of the Scandinavian countries by Claudius Clavus Schwartz (c. 1425).

In 1479 *the University of Copenhagen* was founded, after the 1536 Reformation becoming to all intents and purposes a Lutheran seminary, and only the theologian Niels Hemmingsen played any part in a European context. Outside the university the court doctor Peder Sørensen became widely known for his Paracelsian nature philosophy; the first major history of Denmark in Danish was written about 1600; and Anders

Hans Christian Ørsted, 1777-1851. Ørsted was the son of an apothecary and himself a trained pharmacist. His first publication, in 1797, was a treatise on amniotic fluid, and two years later he was awarded a doctorate for a dissertation on Kant's philosophy. After 1800 he studied the new galvanism, spending 1801-1804 in Germany, where he worked with J.W. Ritter and was fascinated both by J.J. Winterl's remarkable chemical philosophy and by Fichte's ideas on universal reason and the unity of natural forces. On the other hand he was put off by French mathematical physics. In 1806 he was the first to be appointed Professor of Physics in Copenhagen since 1732, and from 1815 to his death he was Secretary to the Royal Danish Academy of Sciences and Letters. His discovery of the magnetic effect of electrical currents in 1820 was immediately recognised as an epoch making advance, although he left further work on electromagnetism to others. He himself studied the compressibility of

water and also succeeded in producing pure aluminium. After 1820 he was the determining influence on research policy in Denmark. In 1824 he founded the popular Society for the Propagation of the Natural Doctrine, and in 1829 he was the initiator behind the establishment of the Technical University of Denmark, where engineering received a scientific foundation.

Olaf Pedersen

Christian Jürgensen Thomsen, 1788-1865. Without any academic training, Thomsen became head of the Collection of Northern Antiquities in 1816, which he began to reorganise in the church loft of Trinitatis Church in 1818. Here he rejected the former random arrangement of antiquities in favour of a new, strictly chronological arrangement. It was here he first used the designations Stone Age, Bronze Age and Iron Age, which he explained in his *Ledetraad til nordisk Oldkyndighed* (Guidelines on Nordic Antiquarianism) from 1836. The terms were in time accepted in archaeology throughout Europe. Thomsen's collections were moved in the 1850s to Prinsens Palæ, which in 1892 was reorganised into the present National Museum.

Olaf Pedersen

Sørensen Vedel collected historical source materials and published the first collection of ballads. Of particular significance was the astronomer Tycho Brahe, who founded modern astronomy by making observations of the heavens from his richly equipped observatory on the island of Ven with a precision never seen before.

The foundations of the Danish museum were laid in the 17th century with a collection of natural history and archaeology, and with the Royal Cabinet of Curiosities. The University of Copenhagen established itself more firmly from this century with a new observatory on the Round Tower in Copenhagen, a new university library and an 'anatomy theatre and museum'. Caspar Bartholin was known over all Europe for his anatomical textbook; his son Thomas Bartholin identified the lymph glands and published the country's first scientific journal, Acta Medica (1673-1680), while another son, Rasmus Bartholin, produced the first account of the double refraction of light in Icelandic calcite crystals. Of fundamental significance for physics was Ole Rømer's demonstration in

1676 of the 'hesitation' or definitive speed of light. Meanwhile, the nepotism of the Bartholin family kept many away from the university. The mathematician Georg Mohr worked abroad, as did Niels Stensen, who in addition to making outstanding anatomical discoveries is remembered as the founder of historical geology, palaeontology and crystallography.

To reinforce specific subjects, new university regulations in 1732 forbade professors to change subjects; with this the age of the polymath was passed. Ten years later *the Royal Danish Academy of Sciences and Letters* was founded with the historian Hans Gram, known throughout Europe, as its driving force. A great deal of work was put into the study of the natural history and culture of the country. Large collections of words were made, which have been used in all subsequent Danish dictionaries. Important sources for older history were published in *Scriptores Rerum Danicarum*, which was started by Jacob Langebek in 1772, while Peter Frederik Suhm wrote a 14-volume history of Denmark, covering the period up to 1400. The country's topography was described in

Danske Atlas (Danish Atlas) by Erik Pontoppidan; the waters around the country were surveyed; and a large geodetic survey carried out between 1760 and 1820 by Thomas Bugge resulted in the first accurate maps of Denmark. Modern Newtonian physics was neglected in the university, but it received a splendid account in the important work entitled *Forelæsninger over Mekanik* (Lectures on Mechanics) (1763) by Professor Jens Kraft at Sorø Academy. Natural history was studied, and a comprehensive survey of all the fauna of Scandinavia was written. Distant lands were also explored by major expeditions to Egypt 1737-1738 and to Arabia, Persia and India 1761-1767; Carsten Niebuhr brought back i.a. precise copies of Persian inscriptions in cuneiform. In Rome Georg Zoëga was active as an egyptologist and as one of the founders of modern archaeology.

Research on an International Level

After this, developments accelerated with the establishment of ever more research areas at a growing number of educational institutions and specialised institutes. In the following, mention will be made of areas in which Danish learning has had international significance. This was the case with philology, in which Rasmus Kristian Rask founded *comparative philology* and from a journey to the East in 1816-1823 brought home large collections of manuscripts. Among other things, these formed the basis of a major, as yet unfinished, dictionary of Pali, the sacred language of Buddhism. Important philological works were also published by Karl Verner, Vilhelm Thomsen and Otto Jespersen. In the field of classical philology Johan Nicolai Madvig was a leading figure, while Johan Ludvig Heiberg produced the critical editions of Euclid, Archimedes and Ptolemy that are still used throughout the world.

In *archaeology and prehistory*, Christian Jürgensen Thomsen established the now commonly used division into Stone, Bronze and Iron Ages. Of great significance in this field was at the same time the discovery of the kitchen middens. Subsequently, large numbers of excavations in the Near East have established Danish archaeology on an international level, including the discovery of the ancient culture of Bahrain by P.V. Glob.

The Light Hall in the Finsen Institute was painted by P.S. Krøyer in 1903, the year when Niels Finsen received the Nobel Prize. Finsen (with arms crossed) founded the institute in 1896 with the objective of treating skin diseases, especially lupus, with light from a carbon arc lamp. The four red curtains each hide an arc lamp, from which the light is conducted to the patients through tubes.

Physics was given a new direction with Hans Christian Ørsted's discovery of electro-magnetism in 1820, while Ludvig August Colding's establishment of the principle of energy remained unnoticed. Mathematical physics were also ignored until it was introduced at the end of the 19th century. This created the prerequisite for Niels Bohr, who in 1913 became world-famous for his application of quantum mechanics to the hydrogen atom and for his explanation of the periodic system of elements which brought him the Nobel Prize in 1922. The Niels Bohr Institute for Theoretical Physics (1920, since 1965 known as the Institute) has since been a centre of international research. It was here the element hafnium was discovered in 1923, while Christian Møller became known for his work on the theory of relativity. A Nobel Prize awarded in 1975 to Aage Bohr and Ben Mottelson demonstrated the dynamism in this

Niels Henrik David Bohr, 1885-1962. Niels Bohr was the son of the physiologist Christian Bohr, in whose private laboratory he carried out his first and only experimental work on surface tension, which brought him the gold medal of the University of Copenhagen. His doctoral dissertation from 1911, on the other hand, was purely theoretical. Co-operation with Rutherford in Manchester was the start of an unusually fruitful process, which over the years produced four fundamental contributions to scientific knowledge, all of which concerned quantum mechanics and its application to atomic and nuclear phenomena. In 1913 Bohr explained the structure of the hydrogen atom and the circumstances relating to the emission and absorption of light. Further studies led to an explanation of the periodic system of elements, for which he was awarded the Nobel Prize in 1922. After this he started on the formulation of general quantum mechanics together with Heisenberg, Pauli and others. In the 1930s there followed important works on the interaction of atomic particles and matter, followed by the 'liquid drop model' for the nucleus of an atom and a theory on the fission process of uranium. In 1943, during the German occupation of Denmark, Bohr went via Sweden to England and the USA, where he worked together with the physicists creating the atomic bomb. Bohr's eye for the general consequences of atomic power persuaded him to turn to Roosevelt and Churchill, but without success; and in 1950 he published an 'Open Letter to the United Nations', in which the idea of an 'open world' with the free exchange of knowledge was propounded as a necessary condition for peace. Bohr's status as one of the unchallenged pioneers of physics led already in 1920 to the establishment of the Copenhagen University's Institute for Theoretical Physics (since 1965 known as the Niels Bohr Institute), which attracted researchers from all over the world. Bohr's own understanding of quantum mechanics became known as the Copenhagen Interpretation, and his thoughts on 'complementarity' between apparent opposites (first used on waves and particles) has since been used as a philosophical tool far beyond the field of physics.

Olaf Pedersen

Niels Bohr and his son Aage Bohr in 1957 discussing a still unsolved problem concerning the superconductivity of metals; at the bottom of the picture Bohr's grandson, Tomas Bohr, can be seen

school to which the very versatile theoretician Jens Lindhard also belongs.

In *astronomy*, Heinrich Louis d'Arrest undertook pioneering observations of nebulae, while Ejnar Hertzsprung, working abroad, became one of the pioneers in astro-physics, to which Bengt Strömgren also made crucial contributions.

Marine research has benefitted from Danish circumnavigations of the globe, beginning with the *Galathea* expedition 1845-1847, which among other things brought back large palaeontological collections from Brazil; later followed i.a. the three Dana expeditions 1920-1930 and finally a new circumnavigation of the globe by the *Galathea 2* in

1950-1952, producing a wealth of oceanographic and natural history information. Mention must also be made of the ethnographical journeys to the Arctic, especially the exploration of Greenland, in the first half of the 20th century, and to Central Asia, which brought back a wealth of ethnographical collections and manuscripts.

In the field of *biology and medicine* Hans Christian Gram became famous for his method of colouring bacteria (1884). In 1903, Niels Ryberg Finsen was the first Dane to receive the Nobel Prize for Medicine for his light treatment of lupus. In 1920 another Nobel Prize was awarded, this time to August Krogh for his work on the physiology of respiration. Nobel Prizes were also given to Johannes Fibiger in 1927 (for 1926) for his cancer research, to the biochemist Henrik Dam in 1943 for the discovery of vitamin K., and to Niels K. Jerne in 1984 for his research in immunology. Of crucial importance for later generations were the studies in genetics by W.L. Johannsen, which betokened the start of genetic research, and for Peter Boysen Jensen's discovery of plant growth hormones.

In 1997 the Nobel Prize for Chemistry was shared by the British researcher John Walker, the American researcher Paul Boyer, and the Danish physician Jens Christian Skou for pioneer research in elucidating the enzymes which play a part

Bengt Strömgren, 1908-1987. Bengt Strömgren was the child prodigy of Danish science, who even while no more than a boy published articles on classical astronomy, and was awarded a doctorate before reaching the age of 21. He then turned to the new experiments in astrophysics aimed at applying quantum mechanics to the structure of the stars. This led to his epoch-making works on the atmospheres of the stars and their chemical constitutions and on hydrogen in the space between them. In 1950 Strömgren left his professorial chair in Copenhagen to work for the next 17 years in the USA as Director of the Yerkes Observatory and later as researcher at the Institute for Advanced Study in Princeton. His main interest was now to study the structure and development of our galaxy by using the ever-increasing amount of data concerning the movements, ages and chemical compositions of the stars. Strömgren was not only a leading figure in astrophysics, but he also made important contributions to practical astronomy, including the calculation of mirrors and object lenses. In addition he was one of the first to attempt photoelectric registration of stars, a principle which is now used to perfection in the Carlsberg meridian circle on La Palma. The joint European observatory in La Silla in the southern hemisphere benefited from his initiatives in its early years.

Olaf Pedersen

in the transfer of adenosine triphosphate, ATP. Skou's contribution was the discovery of the pump which helps to maintain the sodium potassium ion balance between the cells and the tissue fluid of an organism by pumping sodium ions out of the cells and potassium ions into the cells.

Olaf Pedersen, Nils Engelbrecht

The interior of the Black Diamond.

Libraries

The Royal Library dates from 1906 and in 1999 it was extended. The large new extension, the Black Diamond, has greatly increased and differentiated the library's study facilities and furthermore, it is a significant architectural element of the Copenhagen waterfront: the bright, black façade of the building contrasts with its light interior. Research institutions are located in the lower building to the right, closeness to the library offering great practical advantages for them.

In Denmark there are both general public libraries and research libraries that are freely accessible to anyone.

Research Libraries

Denmark's national library is the Royal Library (*Det Kongelige Bibliotek*), founded c. 1653 by Frederik III. Since 1697 it has been a copyright deposit library, entitled to receive copies of any book printed in Denmark, and in 1793 it was opened for general use. It possesses large collections of manuscripts, music, maps and pictures, and it is an important centre for Oriental, Jewish and

Hebrew studies. Containing the largest collection of foreign literature in the country, the Royal Library acts as a library for Copenhagen University and was in 1990 combined with the arts department of the University Library. Total holdings are 4.6 million volumes.

The University Library (*Universitetsbiblioteket*), founded 1482, the oldest collections of which burned in 1728, was in 1938 divided into arts and science departments, the latter under the name of the Danish Library for the Natural and Medical Sciences (*Danmarks Natur- og Lægevidenskabelige Bibliotek*). Possessing

The law stipulates that every public library must have a section with children's literature. In this picture, paperbacks and books for reading aloud to the smallest children and reading books, cartoon books, etc. for bigger children are being loaned out.

1.6 million volumes, it is the main library for these subjects with the exception of botany, which is provided for by the Central Library for Botanical Studies (*Botanisk Central-bibliotek*), founded 1752 and containing 144,000 volumes. The National Library (*Statsbiblioteket*) in Århus, founded 1902, also has nation-wide responsibilities; it is the central agency for the inter-library loan service, and it houses the National Media Archives. Originally intended as a superstructure above the local libraries, it also became the library for University of Aarhus in 1935. (Holdings comprise 3.2 million volumes, and the library is a deposit library). Of the remaining university libraries in Denmark, that in Odense (founded 1965, 1.3 million volumes) is the most comprehensive, having acquired several large old collecti-

ons. The libraries belonging to major teaching institutions are at the same time the main subject libraries in their fields, e.g. the library of the Academy of Fine Arts (founded 1754, 163,000 volumes), the Danish Library of Veterinary and Agricultural Sciences (*Danmarks Veterinær- og Jordbrugsbibliotek*) (founded 1773, 586,000 volumes), the Danish Library of Educational Studies (*Danmarks Pædagogiske Bibliotek*) (founded 1887, 932,000 volumes), the Copenhagen Business School Library (*Handelshøjskolens Bibliotek*) (Copenhagen, founded 1922, 292,000 volumes) and the Technical Knowledge Centre & Library of Denmark (*Danmarks Tekniske Videncenter & Bibliotek*) (founded 1942, 782,000 volumes).

Public Libraries
The Danish public libraries can trace

Although not all public libraries are as roomy as this one in the affluent municipality of Hørsholm, just to the north of Copenhagen, well-built, comprehensive public libraries are obligatory in all municipalities in the country. Effective cooperation between the many libraries ensures that literature and information material is easily available even in the less favoured parts of the country.

their ancestry back to the end of the 18th century, but as in the other Scandinavian countries, the encounter with especially the American public library system was of decisive importance for the development of the educational and philanthropic provisions into a service agency for the whole population. Fundamental was the 1920 Act, according to which the State was by law to provide subsidies for the initiatives of local authorities and associations. In 1984 the direct, earmarked state subsidy was abolished, and the local authorities can now make their own dispositions, although they are still under the obligation to maintain a library service.

The Danish National Library Authority (*Biblioteksstyrelsen*), an independent agency under the Ministry of Culture, is the central advisory and coordinating body for both research and public libraries. The public libraries are today an important social and cultural entity, in many local authority areas the most important. In 1999 the Danish public libraries had a total holding of c. 29 million volumes and lent a total of c. 58 million. The total lending of other media (audio books, music, audio visual materials and multimedia) amounted to c. 14 million items. This equals on average 14 items per citizen.

Torben Nielsen

Associations

Together with the rest of Scandinavia, Denmark is one of the countries in the world where the population has the highest proportion of association membership; only just under 10% of the population does not belong to any organisation, and more than 73% are members of more than one. Danish society is an association-loving society in which the many non-governmental organisations are integral parts of both public administration and the political system. Danish political democracy's relatively harmonious development and stable position must in part be seen in relation to the development of a broad, locally based network of voluntary associations based on common interests.

The First Associations

As a non-government organisation, the association is a product of the second half of the 19th century, when new social classes – farmers and workers – and the movements representing them developed it into a tool for taking care of their own interests. At the same time, their organisations enabled the new classes to become integrated in the democracy that was developing.

In Denmark, this process was seen first and most comprehensively among the farming population. With the agricultural reforms from the end of the 18th century and good agricultural conditions lasting up to the last quarter of the 19th century, agriculture became the principal occupation in the process of economic modernisation, and the foundation for the nascent industrialisation. The process meant the emergence of a relatively affluent farming class. The introduction of a constitutional

bourgeois democracy resulting from the 1849 Constitution and, at local level, the introduction in 1841 of local government and its radical expansion in 1867, created the potential for people to influence their own situation and to take care of their own interests.

The result was a widespread formation of associations built up and fashioned on the basis of local initiatives, the association being used to solve virtually all religious, cultural, economic, social and political questions. The creation of associations encompassed large sections of the rural population, but it was the farmer classes that took the initiative and occupied the leading positions.

A number of diffuse revivalist movements produced the two great popular religious movements – Home Mission (*Indre Mission*) and Grundtvigianism – both of which led to a large number of local associations: rifle associations, gymnastic

It is said that where three Danes meet with some interest in common, they immediately form an association. There is indeed an enormous number of associations in Denmark, and their aims, sizes, ages, organisation, etc. vary greatly. So every major municipal library has in its reading room a couple of dozens of metres of shelving dedicated to publications by these associations.

associations, lecture associations, youth associations, folk high school associations, free schools and independent church congregations, YMCA and YWCA, Sunday schools and the Blue Cross temperance society, and in order to house these many activities meeting houses and so-called mission houses were built in parish after parish.

The switch in Danish agricultural production to predominantly animal husbandry from the 1880s was also largely achieved through the farmers' own organisations, one of which, the co-operative movement, brought with it the co-operative dairies and co-operative slaughterhouses. On a political level, electors' associations were formed, and on a social level people insured themselves through sickness benefit associations, relief funds, savings banks and funeral associations.

The first popular movements in rural society were followed by popular movements among the lower social groups in the towns and country districts.

Trade Organisations

With the establishment of the International Workers' Association for Denmark in 1871 the socialist workers' movement was founded as a united trade and political movement drawn from organisations according to trade. Later, with the formation of the Social Democratic Union in 1878, a formal distinction was made between trade and political work. The workers' movement developed a wide network of associations not only in the form of local electors' associations and trade unions, but also of youth organisations, and associations for support, financial help, funeral expenses, co-operatives, meeting houses, sports associations, music and singing clubs, etc.

While the breakthrough of the popular movements was characterised by locally based organisations, the years around the turn of the century were marked by the transformation of these movements into actual non-governmental organisations through the merging of the local associations into national associations.

The breakthrough of national and federal organisations as pressure and interest groups came during the First World War, when the government involved the organisations in organising the strictly regulated wartime economy. The crises of the inter-war years and the resulting commercial arrangements and other forms of crisis measures helped establish the importance of the non-governmental organisations as part of public administration and the political decision-making process.

Twentieth-Century Developments

Alongside and under the large major organisations there flourished a vibrant locally based association life. In 1896, the Danish Sports Association was established as an umbrella organisation for the new sports movement, and in the following years cycling, cricket, football and handball clubs as well as athletics associations arose all over the country.

With the emergence of the welfare state and the youth rebellion in the 1960s and 1970s, members began to desert the traditional associations. Among the many reasons for this were partly the new potential for using free time (e.g. television viewing), partly the fact that the strongly hierarchical and centralised organisations were seen by many as being far removed from the individual and outside his or her immediate influence. New extra-parliamentary groupings began to emerge. The first example was the Campaign Against Atomic Weapons, which was founded in 1960. The campaign came to form the pattern for a number of movements in these years like, for instance, the Vietnam movement, the Women's Movement, the Popular Movement Against the EC, and the environmental movement. Characteristic of these grass-roots organisations was a flat and informal organisational structure. In the long run, however, it has turned out to be difficult for the grass roots organisations to achieve real influence, and today a number of the more established, for instance parts of the Women's Movement, the Popular Movement Against the EC, the environmental movement and others have developed into more formal associations. While the political parties today have a declining membership, there is on the other hand considerable backing for associations with more limited objectives such as the Red Cross, the Nature Conservancy Association, Help the Aged and local citizens' associations, local historical associations, etc.

Inge Bundsgaard

Body Culture and Sport

Sport is not just sport in Denmark. Sport is 'idræt', though 'idræt' is not always sport. Like their Scandinavian neighbours, the Danes hesitate between this Old Scandinavian word and the international term 'sport' when talking about one of the most important phenomena of the modern age. Though the two words are often mixed in everyday language, the difference is not merely cosmetic. 'Idræt' is used as a rule about a large range of body culture activities in which the aim can be well-being, exercise, fun, a sense of community or personal development, and all sports organisations have adopted the term 'idræt'. 'Sport' is seen only as one part of this multiple body culture, a part where the Olympic spirit with its quest for results and achievements prevails, and the mass media use the term sport. For practical reasons, we shall use 'sport' as synonymous with 'idræt' in this text. Similarly, clubs are not just clubs. Clubs are associations, but associations are not always clubs. To form a club is to join with others in some activity; to form an association – a 'forening' – is furthermore to join in a binding, democratic community that has a number of historical values and cultural connotations.

When body culture is occasionally called 'the greatest popular movement in Denmark', this is mainly because of the number of active participants in such activities. Almost every other Dane goes in for one or other form of body culture, and only the State Church can boast of a greater membership than the sports organisations. However, the nickname is also due to the fact that since 1861 body culture in Denmark has been organised in clubs/associations. Rifle associations, gymnastics associations and sports associations made up an important part of the popular movements that helped build up Danish democracy in the years around 1900. Strongest was the link between body culture and nation-

Danish Gymnastics and Sports Associations (DGI) have a national meeting every fourth year, one of the biggest sports events in the world. The 1998 event in Silkeborg brought in 45,000 participants for three days of demonstrations, competitions, meetings and parties. Half the participants were gymnasts, the others team members for ball games and other sportspeople.

The Fyn Rundt long distance race of 137 nautical miles has been sailed since 1934. Fyn Rundt, Fyn Cup and Sjælland Rundt are Denmark's three major popular sailing races in which thousands of sailors, both amateur and professional, compete. The record number of participants was in 1986 when about 2,200 boats entered for Sjælland Rundt.

al politics in the liberal farmers' movement in which gymnastics was thought to be a valuable means of liberating the individual, both physically and mentally. One's posture and one's attitude to life were indissolubly linked. Furthermore, to practice shooting and gymnastics allowed people to manifest their sentiment of Danish nationality because the fight to recover North Schleswig was one of the movement's high objectives. The workers' movement and the urban middle classes also appreciated the democratic schooling in associations and the social and cultural value of sports.

Although the number of joggers, body-builders, surfers and others taking part in sports, whether attending private institutes or pursuing their interest on their own, has risen significantly since the 1970s, the association is still the preferred organisational form. In 1998, almost every third Dane was a member of a sports association, and around 200,000 adult Danes hold voluntary, unpaid office in sports associations.

The Youth and Adult Education Act provides for financial support and premises for association activities. Since the first Leisure Time Act of 1968, local authority grants to sport have grown significantly and in 2001 accounted for c. 2.5 billion kroner. Among other things, this has been reflected in the Danish landscape, where sports and swimming halls have sprouted, so that the village church is no longer the only landmark. Denmark holds the European and probably the world record for the number of sports halls per head of population. In 1996 there were c. 1,550 sports halls, 300 swimming halls, 5,000 football stadia, 2,400 gymnastics halls and a large number of association premises and other kinds of sports facilities.

Development

At the beginning of the 20th century, gymnastics were the preferred sports of the rural population, while at the same time English sports – ball games and competitive sports – were gaining a foothold in the towns. After the Second World War migration from agriculture in the countryside to industry in the cities speeded up and this distinction was removed, and sports occupied a dominant position for a number of years. Since then, the picture of sports has again changed, partly because since the 1960s large groups of children and the middle-aged have taken part in sport, which used to be mainly an activity for the young. An increasing number of women are also taking an active part. A number of new activities and concepts have appeared; for instance, from the USA fitness activities such as body-building and aerobics, and from the East yoga and the Asian martial arts.

The interest in nature and the environment can be seen in the increase in leisure time activities such as jogging, golf, surfing, canoeing, kayaking, while the desire to remain active throughout life can among other things be seen in the interest in bowling, pétanque and other activities suitable for the family and older people. The traditional forms of sport still occupy centre stage, but there is a tendency for popular sports such as badminton, football and handball to stagnate or even fall in popularity.

Elite Sports

While gymnastics account for by far the largest number of participants both in and out of the associations, football is the national sport for spectators. The national football team regularly attracts a couple of million Danes to the television screen, and so far, the high point in the national euphoria has been the Gold Medal in the 1992 European Championship in Sweden.

The Danish countryside offers excellent facilities for sailing, swimming, canoeing and kayaking, rowing and cycling, and Denmark is able to hold its own in these branches of sport also in an international context. The yachtsman Paul Elvstrøm (b. 1928), who in 1996 was chosen as Danish Sportsman of the Century, is the only man in the world to have won a gold medal at four consecutive Olympic Games (1948-1960). He also won 13 World Championships, and at the age of 60 competed in his ninth – and so far last – Olympic Games in 1988.

The victory of cyclist Bjarne Riis in the 1996 Tour de France is considered one of the best individual performances of any Danish sportsman despite cycling's notorious reputation for resorting to doping. Handball, which is partly accounted a Danish invention, enjoys special popularity; among notable achievements of the Danish women's team are the Olympic Gold in 1996 and 2000, the World Championship in 1997, and the European Championship in 1994. In badminton Danish players have since the Second World War been among the international elite. In recent years Danish golf players have entered the top of the world's ranking lists with Thomas Bjørn as the leading figure. Furthermore, a natualised dane, the Kenyan-born 800 m runner Wilson Kipketer, has brought his new country the long-missed international medals and world records in track and field.

The growing significance of sport as a branch of the entertainment industry has, also in Denmark,

The Wonderful Copenhagen Marathon is run every year in May. About 6,000 men and women start from Vester Voldgade by Copenhagen Town Hall Square. In participant numbers, however, it is exceeded by the Marselisborg Run, near Århus, and the Eremitage Race that takes place in the Dyrehave north of Copenhagen.

In the mid 1980s the All-Denmark football team decisively entered the world scene. Since the European Championships of 1984, Denmark has participated in most European Championships and World Cup finals, and Danish football players have proved to be a solid export success. The photo shows Ebbe Sand, German league top scorer 2000-2001, scoring the second goal in the 6-0 match against Iceland on 6 October 2001.

resulted in large sums of money being at stake for those taking part, their trainers, their sponsors, the mass media and the whole of the organisational machinery. To raise the level of Danish elite sports and to make provisions for the elite sportsmen and women socially, the Folketing decided in 1984 to establish the Institution for the Promotion of Danish Elite Sports, in everyday language Team Denmark. This independent organisation carries out its many duties in co-operation with the individual federations within the National Olympic Committee and Sports Confederation of Denmark. Team Denmark supports selected sportsmen and sportswomen by covering many of the expenses connected with training and participation in competitions, and the institute advises them in the use of sports medicine and in long-term planning of their education and working career.

Sports for the Disabled

Denmark is one of the very few countries in the world to have a single sports organisation covering several types of disability. Since 1971 the Danish Association of Sports for the Disabled has worked to promote exercise and competition sports among the deaf, the blind, the physically disabled and the mentally handicapped. Although the association's 23,000 members only constitute a small proportion of the total number of handicapped, it is when seen through international eyes a high degree of organisation. On the elite level, Denmark is one of the leading countries, especially in swimming, riding, athletics and shooting. The main task has in recent times changed from adapting normal sports to different kinds of disability, towards developing physical activities in which the disabled can have great sports experiences on their own terms.

Organisation

Association sports have several national organisations which, like Team Denmark, benefit from increasing public support. The organisations receive a fixed share of the profit from the Danish Pools Organisation (41% after 2000), which has a nationwide monopoly of competitions with cash prizes. Since the introduction of the Lottery in 1989 the income for sport trebled in five years. In 1999 the Pools Organisation distributed nearly 500 million kroner among Team Denmark, the Sports Confederation of Denmark, the Danish Gymnastics and Sports Associations and the Danish Association of Company Sports. The four organisations regularly consult each other in the Joint Sports Council, partly with a view to adopting a common policy on general questions of sports policy.

There is a tradition for the public authorities to respect the independence and autonomy of sport, both locally and nationally. Sport and association life belong respectively under the Ministry of Culture and the Ministry of Education, but the Ministers do not normally interfere in the way in which the grants are used. However, during the 1990s, rising pools and lottery income has prompted the State and the public to show more active interest in how the sports organisations handle their social and cultural tasks.

The sports organisations are agreed in defending the independence of sport, but among themselves they disagree as to whether sports best serves its interests through one or several organisations.

Jens Sejer Andersen

Danish pentathlon competitor Jakob Mathiasen throwing a pentathlon javelin world record at the Para Olympic Games in Sydney 2000. During the 1970s public financial support for sport increased, which benefited the Danish Association of Sports for the Disabled (founded 1971); the association has about 23,000 members.

The Danish Cuisine

The Danish cuisine still contains elements harking back to the time before industrialisation, i.e. the time before c. 1860, the age of storage housekeeping with a cuisine based on beer and rye bread, salted pork and saltet herrings. Among the dishes from those days which are still eaten today are *øllebrød* (a dish made of rye bread, sugar and non-alcoholic beer), *vandgrød* (porridge, usually barley porridge, made with water), *gule ærter* (split pea soup), *æbleflæsk* (slices of pork with apples fried in the fat), *klipfisk* (dried cod), *blodpølse* (black pudding), *finker* (an approximation to haggis) and *grønlangkål* (thickened stewed kale).

In the second half of the 19th century, i.e. the age of the co-operative movement, milk and potatoes played a prominent part, and the stove, the mincer and the developing retail trade provided new possibilities for dishes such as roast pork and gravy, boiled cod with mustard sauce, consommé with meat, bread or flour

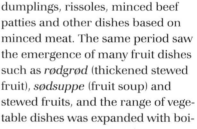

Danish pastry is in Danish called Wienerbrød, Viennese bread, though it is completely unknown in Vienna. In Denmark, it has been known since 1840 and is said to have been created by immigrant bakers from Vienna, perhaps strike breakers. It is made from bread dough rolled out several times in layers with butter between (like puff pastry) and filled with various confectionaries and other sweet things. The spandauer in the picture is very popular; it is filled with confectionary cream or jam and decorated with split almonds and iced. All kinds of Danish wienerbrød have established names with a long tradition behind them.

dumplings, rissoles, minced beef patties and other dishes based on minced meat. The same period saw the emergence of many fruit dishes such as *rødgrød* (thickened stewed fruit), *sødsuppe* (fruit soup) and stewed fruits, and the range of vegetable dishes was expanded with boi-

The island of Bornholm is so famous for its smoked herring that a 'bornholmer' in everyday speech is more likely to mean a smoked herring than someone from the island. The herrings are hot-smoked over elm and then cleaned, but with the head, skin and bones left on. They are usually eaten filleted with chives and radish – and on special occasions with a raw egg yoke. Then they are referred to as *Sol over Gudhjem* (Sun over Gudhjem) (after a fishing village on the east coast of Bornholm).

The sausage stall with its gas-fired water-bath, frying pans and gridirons is a popular element in the Danish urban landscape. As a predecessor of fast food restaurants it has created a culture of its own.

led cabbage in white sauce, red cabbage, pickled beetroot, cucumber salad, and peas and carrots in white sauce.

Great changes and increased choices appeared in the Danish cuisine in the 1960s as a result of increased affluence, internationalisation, the advent of self-service in the retail trade, the use of electricity in the kitchen, refrigerators and freezers, and also of the increasing number of women going out to work. American influence is obvious with such dishes as salads, pasta, baked potatoes, barbecue, turkey and ready-to-eat chicken dishes. Italian cuisine has also established itself with for instance pizzas, pasta and a widespread use of tomatoes. Meat consumption has risen dramatically, still with pork as the most common kind of meat. The tendency is towards steaks and to minced meat. Gravy and potato dishes still maintain their place, so that sausages and rissoles are the dishes most frequently seen on Danish dinner tables.

The packed lunch is still the most common way of taking lunch. For this purpose, open sandwiches with sausage, cut meat, sliced cheese, etc. are most suitable, although the individual pieces are separated by a sheets of greaseproof paper. Open sandwiches such as herring, salads in mayonaise and trimmings such as pickled cucumber or beetroot are not suitable for lunch boxes, but ought to be eaten as soon as prepared.

Provision of Raw Materials

Thanks to industrial methods, produce and dishes that were once the preserves of the upper classes have become commonplace. This applies for instance to mushrooms, chicken, caviar (in Denmark usually synonymous with lumpfish roe), smoked salmon and duck as well as mayonnaise and other cold sauces. Imports and new technology have evened out seasonal differences, so that most foodstuffs are on offer all the year round. At the same time exotic foods such as aubergine, avocado, fresh pineapple, baby maize, Barbary duck breast, courgettes, Chinese prawns, kiwi fruit and peppers have become everyday sights on the Danish table. In the 1980s, meanwhile, a reaction set in against industrialisation, the levelling off of seasonal dishes and the influence of the foreign fast food concept: chefs like Erwin Lauterbach and Jan Hurtigkarl have created an original Danish cuisine based on the vegetables and fish that thrive best beneath Danish skies.

Eating Patterns

The pattern of meal times has changed from the five meals a day of pre-industrialised society to the three that are common now. Most people have their midday meal away from home in the form of a packed lunch or a canteen meal. Hot food is eaten in the evening, and most people only have a single course on weekdays. First courses consisting of gruel, fruit soup or porridge are nowadays only eaten by older people. The individualisation of meals, such as is known in the USA, has only caught on in Denmark with respect to breakfast; at the evening meal families make an effort to arrange for a family meal prepared at home. Ready-to-eat dishes are mainly used by single people.

Danish Specialities

Smørrebrød (open sandwiches) consisting of rye bread, buttered and covered with sliced meat, cheese, etc. has long been known, whereas the more elaborate open sandwiches used on festive occasions only appeared in the decades around 1900. Among the best-known of these are open sandwiches with shrimps, smoked salmon, marinated herring, smoked herring and egg yolk, radishes and chives, smoked eel with scrambled egg, pork with red cabbage, apples and prunes, and liver paste with pickled cucumber or gherkins. Otherwise, Denmark has made few original contributions to gastronomy. Among those to be mentioned are *wienerbrød* (Danish

Open sandwiches, one of Denmark's contributions to international gastronomy, are here portrayed by the painter Fritz Syberg (1906): egg and herring, roast meat, rolled meat sausage and cheese make up the four pieces.

Rødgrød med fløde. The fruit dish the name of which is a test in pronunciation for all non-Danes. The stew is made of for instance redcurrants, raspberries and blackcurrants, which are boiled until soft. The juice is sweetened and thickened, and the dish is then served with cream or milk.

pastry) and *kransekage* (almond cake rings), *æblekage* (apple charlotte) with fried breadcrumbs and fruit preserves, and then hot dishes such as boiled cod with mustard sauce, melted butter, chopped hard-boiled egg, horse-radish and boiled potatoes, and roast duck, goose or pork with apples, prunes, caramelised potatoes, red cabbage and brown gravy.

Else-Marie Boyhus

Culture

Museums

In Denmark there are several hundred large and, more particularly, small museums, owned by the state, local authorities and private institutions and individuals. Key concepts in their activities, all of which are object-oriented, are collection, registration, conservation, research and information.

Museums of Cultural History

All the large state-owned museums in Copenhagen have their roots in the Royal Collection or private 17th-century collections such as *Museum Wormianum* (Ole Worm's Museum). This applies to the collections that today make up the National Museum, the *Tøjhusmuseum* (The Danish Defence Museum), the *Rosenborgsamling* (Rosenborg Collection) and *Statens Museum for Kunst* (The Danish National Gallery). The history of the *Orlogsmuseum* (the Naval Museum) goes back to 1670 when the collection of the ships models belonging to the navy was established in the Royal Dockyard in Copenhagen. The first provincial museums were established about 1850, but the great majority of the museums in the country date from after 1900. A special position is occupied by the *National History Museum at Frederiksborg Castle* in Hillerød, which J.C. Jacobsen, the brewer, founded in 1878.

The new social organisation replacing absolutism in 1849 provided the impetus for enterprising citizens to try to break the capital's monopoly of culture. The large towns and cities (Ribe, Odense, Viborg, Århus, Aalborg, etc.) established museums with the educational aim of as far as possible covering the same themes as the major collections in Copenhagen: prehistory, history, numismatics, ethnography, natural history and art.

In addition to archaeology the cultural historical museums were until the end of the 19th century particularly concerned with the history of the bourgeoisie. Thanks to the

The permanent exhibition in the Bornholm Museum in Rønne is typical of the way in which Danish museums are arranged today. The original objects are displayed in exhibition cases; small modules make it possible to illustrate many different themes. The often short texts are supplemented by maps and enlarged photographs. The exhibition shows Bornholm earth finds from 600-700 AD, including a find of Roman denars.

Grundtvigian movement and the folk high schools, this interest was extended to peasant culture, which this ideology saw as the bearer of national culture. Several museums with rural foundations were established: *Dansk Folkemuseum* (The Danish Folk Museum) (1885), which, however, was soon to collect bourgeois exhibits from more modern times, followed by an innovation: the open air museum: *Frilandsmuseet* (1897) and later *Hjerl Hedes Frilandsmuseum* (Hjerl Hede Open Air Museum) (1928) and *Den Fynske Landsby* (The Funen Village) (1946). This kind of museum exhibited entire farms and interiors. Rural culture 'came in from the cold', and the old museums now also began to collect rural exhibits.

This last type of museum expressed a wish to save the material remnants of a culture and a way of life that were disintegrating; *Dansk Folkemuseum* was thus established when the old peasant culture was undergoing a rapid transformation resulting from the change in agricultural production methods and increased industrialisation; similarly, *Det Danske Kunstindustrimuseum* (The Danish Museum of Decorative Art) was founded (in 1890) when the old crafts were under threat from industrial mass production, and in 1914, when industrialisation had changed both artisan life and urban ways, came *Den Gamle By, Danmarks Købstadmuseum* (The Old Town, The National Open Air Museum of Urban History and Culture) in Århus. As the latest museums in this category for the time being we can see the *Arbejdermuseum* (Workers' Museum) in Copenhagen (1983) and *Danmarks Grafiske Museum* (Denmark's Graphical Museum) in Odense (1983).

The 20th century saw the establishment of a number of specialised museums and trade and service museums, for instance several agricultural museums, the *Handels- og Søfartsmuseum* (Trade and Shipping Museum) in Kronborg in Elsinore, and the *Jernbanemuseum* (Railway Museum) in Odense, in addition to numerous local historical museums. For many people the reorganisation of local authorities in 1970 produced an increased local awareness, leading to the establishment of new small local museums.

The museums which are not state owned have only at a relatively late date been able to appoint keepers, i.e. university-trained archaeologists, historians, ethnologists; only with the museum acts of 1958 and 1976 were the financial and legal frameworks created for the appointment of professionally trained, academic staff. At the end of the 20th century, Denmark possesses an unusually fine-meshed network of professionally manned local museums. It is a typically Danish phenomenon that the archaeological surveillance of the country should be in their hands.

Birgitte Kjær

Art Museums

Around 40 museums in Denmark have as their principal task the collection, preservation and promotion of visual art. It is a special feature of the country that the art museums are placed at a distance of 30-50 km from each other. Each art museum has its own special area, and together they form a network constituting a large, decentralised presentation of Danish art.

The first Danish art museum was *Thorvaldsens Museum* in Copenhagen, which opened in 1848 to exhibit the sculptor's works and collections. In 1896 the largest art museum in the country opened, *Statens Museum*

Since its opening in 1958, Louisiana Museum of Modern Art in Humlebæk has been extended in several stages. The south wing was built for the Museum's own collection and was finished in 1982 along with this corridor linking it to the older buildings in the museum. The paintings by Richard Mortensen receive light both from above and from the large windows overlooking the park.

for Kunst (The Danish National Gallery), also in Copenhagen and based on the Royal Collection of Paintings. In late 1998 a new wing of the museum was opened. The new spear shaped building will make room for the growing collections as well for a Children's Art Museum. The first provincial art museum, *Aarhus Kunstmuseum*, opened in 1859, and later a number of provincial museums opened in which fine art collections constituted part of a cultural historical whole. In time these collections have gained the status of independent museums of fine arts, and since 1964 the art museums have been entitled to state support on a par with museums of cultural history. After the reunion with Southern Jutland in 1920, museums with departments of fine arts were established in Tønder, Sønderborg and Aabenraa.

A number of museums of fine arts were created on the basis of donations from private collectors: the *Ny Carlsberg Glyptotek, Den Hirschsprungske Samling* (The Hirschsprung Collection), *Davids Samling* (The David Collection), *Ordrup-gaardsamlingen* (The Ordrupgaard Collection) (all in Copenhagen), *Nivaagaards Malerisamling* (The Picture Gallery of Nivaagaard) (30 km north of Copenhagen) and the *J.F. Willumsen Museum* (Frederikssund). The sculptors Niels Hansen Jacobsen and Rudolph Tegner each had a museum built for their own works in Vejen and North Zealand respectively. The Skovgaard family of painters has its museum in Viborg, and in Skagen and Faaborg there are museums for the Skagen painters and the Funen painters respectively, both created on the basis of local initiative in collaboration with the artists themselves. *Silkeborg Kunstmuseum* houses many of Asger Jorn's works and his collection of Danish and foreign works of art, and in Herning there is the museum for Else Alfelt and Carl-Henning Pedersen.

In 1958 the *Louisiana Museum for Moderne Kunst* (Louisiana Museum of Modern Art) opened in Humlebæk, founded by private initiative with a large collection of Danish and international 20th-century art, and mounting a large number of visiting exhibitions. It was installed in new buildings constructed for the purpose, as was *Nordjyllands Kunstmuseum* (The North Jutland Museum of Fine Arts) in Aalborg (1972). At the same time important museums of fine arts were opened in Herning and Holstebro. The *Køge Skitsesamling* (Køge Sketch Collection) (1977) is concerned with the artistic work process and contains sketches and preparatory work as its particular field of interest. The newest art museum is *Arken Museum of Modern Art* in Ishøj south of Copenhagen (1996). In 1996 a new wing containing fine furniture opened at *Trapholt Museum* in Kolding. A new art museum in Århus will open in 2003.

Nina Damsgaard

Natural History Museums

The three oldest and most important natural history museums are the Zoological, Geological and Botanical museums belonging under Copenhagen University, all of which play a part in undergraduate teaching. The first two have a mixed 200-300-year history and originated through an amalgamation of the university collections and various private collections. A few exhibits have survived from Ole Worm's Museum and the Royal Collection from the mid-17th century. By dint of their age and a comprehensive input from expeditions dating from the 1760s to the present, all three museums contain scientific collections of international standing, for example 2.3 million herbarium specimens in the Botanical Museum.

The principal museum outside Copenhagen is the *Naturhistorisk Museum* (Natural History Museum) in Århus (1921), with its main scientific emphasis on Danish fauna. Other natural history museums are the state-owned *Jagt- og Skovbrugsmuseum* (Museum of Hunting and Forestry) in Hørsholm (1942), the local authority *Zoologisk Museum* (Zoological Museum) in Svendborg (1935) and the geological museums of Gram, Fur and Fakse.

Other Scientific Collections

Copenhagen's *Zoologisk Have* (Zoological Garden) opened in 1859 and has an international reputation for its breeding results, its animal friendly design, the children's zoo, services to schools, and behavioural studies; the zoological gardens in Odense (1930) and Aalborg (1934) are also of a high standard. At Knuthenborg on Lolland and Givskud in Jutland there are large safari parks. *Danmarks Akvarium* (The Danish Aquarium) in Charlottenlund is the oldest aquarium in the country (1939), followed by the saltwater aquaria in Esbjerg (together with the *Fiskeri- og Søfartsmuseet* – the Fisher-

The largest mussel in the world, *Sphenoceramus steenstrupi*, discovered in a c. 80 million-year-old layer from the Cretaceous Period at Nuussuaq, West Greenland. The mussel's length is 187 cm. It is on view in the Geological Museum in Copenhagen.

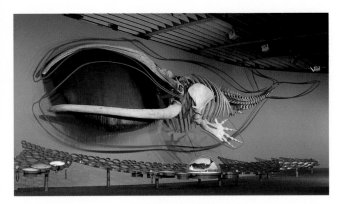

Skeleton of a 20-metre long Greenland whale in the Zoological Museum in Copenhagen. This section of the museum consists of a large blue hall in which the skeletons of sperm whale and Greenland whale together with a giant squid, a thresher and a sunfish are hung on the walls. A large engraved wall provides an account of plankton and the food chains in the oceans. In the adjoining theme room there is an account of the biology of marine animals and life in the depths of the sea.

ies and Maritime Museum) and Hirtshals (together with the *Nord-sømuseum* – North Sea Museum), and most recently the *Kattegat Centre* in Grenå; *AQUA* in Silkeborg exhibits fresh-water fauna.

Copenhagen University's botanical garden was established in 1600. Other botanical gardens are found at *Den Kongelige Veterinær- og Landbohøjskole* (The Royal Veterinary and Agricultural University), in Århus (under the University) and in Kolding. The arboretum in Hørsholm contains trees and tree-like plants.

The university's *Medicinsk-Histo-risk Museum* (Museum of Medical History) in Copenhagen was established in 1906. The *Steno Museum* (1994) under Aarhus University contains a collection built around the history of medicine and the history of science.

The *Ole Rømer Museum* at Tåstrup specialises in astronomy and discoveries made from Rømer's terrestrial observatory. *Danmarks Tekniske Museum* (National Museum of Science and Technology) encompasses both the Teknisk Museum (Museum of Technology) and the *Trafikmuseum* (Transport Museum) in Elsinore and the *Kommunikationsmuseum* (Museum of Communications) in Aalborg. The *Elmuseum* (Electricity Museum) is at the Gudenaa Centre in Bjerringbro, the biggest working hydro-electric works in Denmark. The *Eksperimentarium* at Tuborg in Hellerup is a major centre for science and technology.

Torben Wolff

Architecture

Danish building in the early Middle Ages was based on wood, a perishable material which has left little evidence of the buildings of the period.

The Viking Age

The Vikings built military encampments which are known through excavations at Trelleborg, Aggersborg and Fyrkat, all dating back to about 1000 AD; they were built within circular earthen ramparts. The complexes were built with great precision on the basis of a cross-shaped, symmetrical network of streets, the main axes of which cut through and divided up the entire complex into smaller units. The large houses with curved walls, 32.5 m long in Aggersborg, were built within these areas in regular squares of four that enclosed an inner square courtyard. Aggersborg, which measured c. 240 m in diameter comprised 12 such groups, 48 houses in all, while the smaller Trelleborg with a diameter of 134 m contained four squares.

The Middle Ages

The art of building with wood was thus a well-established tradition in Denmark when about 960 the country was converted to Christianity, and a new building culture, church building, arose. The oldest of the wooden churches known today through excavations is King Harald's church in Jelling to the west of Vejle, dating from precisely this time. The prevailing shape of the buildings for the new religion was the simple hall church consisting of a rectangular nave and a choir to the east. The wooden churches were small in comparison with the succeeding stone-built churches; for instance, the mid-11th century Hørning church, north of Århus, measured c. 9.5 x 4.5 m. From Hørning stems one of the quite small number of extant fragments of buildings from the period, a part of a hammer brace whose delicately carved interlaced serpents suggest that other churches can have boasted similar rich decorative work. Only after almost another century was a serious start made to building churches of stone. The earliest stone church which is known from written records is Estrid's church in Roskilde, built already about 1026 as a replacement for an earlier wooden church. Like most of the early stone churches, it was built of easily worked travertine.

Romanesque Architecture

The Romanesque period, which was heralded by the stone churches, encompassed both large cathedrals and smaller village churches. The structures were based on a more rigorous, regular ground plan, the heavy walls being articulated through the rhythmical sequence of pillars and recesses; the rounded arch became the dominant form, and selected elements in the buildings could be furnished with rich sculptural adornment. In a group of churches in the Randers area, the ornamental tradition represented by the interlaced serpents tracery on the Hørning plank was transferred to limestone in the form of gently rounded looped motifs. A prerequisite for developing a local tradition in this way was, however, the Danish artisans' familiarity with the techniques of stonemasonry, a stage that must be assumed only to have been reached after a certain time.

The cathedral in the Swedish (at

that time Danish) city of Lund was started soon after the establishment of the archbishopric in 1103; it was the first of the three great Romanesque cathedrals, all in the shape of a three-aisled basilica with transepts. The cathedral in Lund seems – like the radically restored cathedral in Viborg – especially to have been related to earlier German buildings, though there are also traces of Anglo-Norman and Lombard influences. Ribe, which followed with its great cathedral in the middle of the century, had close contacts via trade and shipping with the Rhine area of Germany, and both the materials and the models were taken from there.

Seen as a whole, the village churches are built to the same pattern. They were single-aisled churches with a choir, built in the 12th and 13th centuries, possibly with an apse and in certain cases a tower to the west. Regional characteristics could also assert themselves, possibly through defensive structures as in the Bornholm round churches, but especially due to available building materials, so that the walls of the Jutland churches, made of large, dressed ashlars stand in contrast to the churches on the islands, which are built of undressed or partly dressed granite boulders.

Gothic

Around 1160, a new and more easily handled building material, the brick, was introduced, presumably through links with northern Italy. After this the use of natural stone gradually ceased. Roskilde Cathedral, started in the 1170s, is built almost entirely of brick; likewise, especially monasteries and convents made use of bricks, for instance the Cistercian church in Sorø and the Benedictine Saint Bendt's (Benedict's) Church in Ringsted. Roskilde Cathedral moreover

reveals the earliest influence of French Gothic, for during the long building phase the plans for the church were changed in favour of the new style. Saint Knud's Church in Odense occupies a special position as a building that despite a very protracted building process – it was completed at the end of the 15th century – is built consistently in the spirit of High Gothic. Like the many market town churches of the time, Saint Knud's is dominated by the soaring lines of Gothic, the pointed arch, the buttresses, the ribbed vaulting, the greater access of light and the spatial combination of nave and chancel. The details of Danish brick Gothic are strongly influenced by the north German variety. From Germany came the hall church which was principally used by the monastic orders, for instance the Bridgettine church in Maribo (now Maribo Cathedral).

In the rural parishes Gothic showed itself mainly in alterations and extensions to the Romanesque churches, which were provided with sacristies, chapels, bell towers, extensions to the east and west – often accompanied by vaulting above the naves – and not least, larger windows with pointed arches in accordance with the Gothic's demand for light-filled space. Externally, the new sections of the buildings were often dominated by the characteristic stepped gables of the time, which were supplemented by richly decorated blind arcades.

In the secular field, ordinary buildings continued to be built of wood and half-timbered construction, but here, too, in some cases stone-built houses were erected, for instance Næstved Town Hall from c. 1450. Major castles like those in Vordingborg, Kalundborg and Hammershus were supplemented by the late-mediaeval castles, including Gjorslev on Stevns and Spøttrup in Salling, both built for bishops at the beginning of the 15th century. While Gjorslev lies as a compact series of buildings to a cruciform plan with a tower at the centre, Spøttrup is a three-winged complex closed off by a solid barrier wall containing a tower. A simpler form was given to the rectangular and, from a defensive point of view, well-equipped Glimmingehus, which Jens Holgersen Ulfstand built in 1499 in Skåne, now part of Sweden.

The Renaissance

Under Christian III, work on the defence of the kingdom was intensified, and included the castles of Nyborg and Sønderborg. The latter was transformed into a cohesive but irregular four-winged complex by Hercules von Oberberg. Defence was now concentrated in prominent gun emplacements. The building of mansions was the dominant influence in determining the profile of the architecture of the following period. To a certain, symbolical extent, the mansions continued the defence structures of the bishops' castles. Villestrup in Jutland from 1538-1542 and the almost contemporary Rygård on Funen are both enclosed, four-winged buildings which have retained something of the character of castles. The individual house, the single wing, which was the most common mansion type throughout the 16th century, was less well fortified. The Funen buildings around the middle of the century, such as Hesselagergård and Nakkebølle, are distinguished by corbels between the different floors and flanking towers. A corresponding construction is found in the contemporary Egeskov on Funen. This belongs to the double house type, where two parallel wings share a common centre wall, though

Bishop Oluf Mortensen's porch at Roskilde Cathedral was built about 1450. The stepped gable of the porch is adorned with a profusion of recess decorations and pinnacles. The building is distinguished by the fine brickwork and the remarkable composition of the facade, which is at once asymmetrical and well-balanced. Survey drawing from 1961.

each has its independent gable end and pitched roof.

While stone buildings thus became more and more common, farms continued to be built in the half-timbered manner, sometimes in conjunction with a single stone house. The ordinary people lived as before in half-timbered and bole houses.

In mansion building, the trend towards the end of the century was towards less fortified castles, and the individual house lost its defensive towers. In the last part of the century complexes with several wings became more common, and not least in royal buildings. Kronborg, started in 1574 by Hans van Paeschen and completed in 1585 by Antonis van Opbergen, was built as a four-winged complex. The model was the three-winged French castle, with a fourth wing only consisting of a low terrace wing. However, the plans were chan-

Hover Church near Ringkøbing represents the simply Romanesque village church consisting only of a chancel and a nave, and with small windows placed high in the walls. Typically of the Jutlandic churches, it is built of large, rough-hewn granite ashlars. The porch is an addition from c. 1550.

ged in the process, and Kronborg was completed as a full four-winged building. On the other hand, what had not been achieved in Kronborg, Hans van Steenwinckel the Elder managed in Christian IV's Frederiksborg Castle in Hillerød (1602-1620), which was built as a three-winged complex with a low terrace wing around a *cour d'honneur*. Thus, the building adhered to the French pattern, but in both Kronborg and Frederiksborg the architectural expression, the decorative finish, was in the Dutch Renaissance style. The new foreign architectural ideals were already fully developed in Hesselagergård in Funen. The building was adorned with Venetian gables presumably brought to Denmark via Germany. Rustic work wall surfaces like those at Holckenhaven near Nyborg (c. 1580) were also popular. Nevertheless, the native and mediaeval stepped blind gables maintained their popularity, as for instance is demonstrated by Egeskov. A similar situation arose in church building. After the Reformation in 1536, which led to the formation of protestant churches, ecclesiastical building was marked by a period of stagnation, after which new churches often preserved features from mediaeval tradition.

From the 1570s the new Dutch Renaissance tendencies really established themselves in Danish architecture, as is seen in both Kronborg and Frederiksborg castles. Red bricks form the background of extravagant, lavish sandstone ornamentations of the portals and windows and especially in the sweeping Italianate gables, characteristics that similarly dominate in the royal palace of Rosenborg in Copenhagen (1613-1634). The ideals in the royal buildings were, whenever possible, taken over by the burghers and transformed into expensive and richly decorated stone buildings, for instance Mathias Hansen's House from 1616 on Amager Torv in Copenhagen and Jens Bang's House (1623-1624) in Aalborg.

Under Christian IV many buildings

St Knud's Church in Odense, which was completed at the end of the 15th century, is a fine example of Danish High Gothic. The huge nave is dominated by soaring lines, pointed profiles in arcades, openings for galleries and clerestory windows and the bunches of slender mouldings on the columns, meeting in the star vaults.

Kronborg Castle was built in the reign of Frederik II as a regular four-winged complex to the French pattern, but the decorations were done in the Dutch Renaissance style. The gable end of the chapel wing from c. 1578 is one of the finest examples of the sweeping Italianate gable ends and rich ornamentation, which untypically is here executed in pale sandstone.

Jens Bang's House in Aalborg was built 1623-1624 for the merchant Jens Bang. The rich sandstone ornamentation of the Renaissance building rises over a base of red brick, and in addition to its own actual gable ends it was provided with three decorative gables looking towards the street, which provided the potential for lavish decoration.

of various kinds were erected, from Børsen (the Stock Exchange) (1619-1640) and Rundetårn (The Round Tower) (1637-1642), both in Copenhagen, to the construction of towns and districts like Kristianstad in Sweden (1614) and Christianshavn (1618) and Nyboder (started 1631) in Copenhagen. When it came to ecclesiastical buildings *Holmens Kirke* (the Naval Church) in Copenhagen followed the new ideals of a centralised ground plan when in 1642 the anchor smithy was rebuilt here as a cruciform church.

The Baroque

The almost hectic building activity that took place under Christian IV disappeared with him. The country's economy was weakened, and for a time it did not allow of any major building enterprises. When building was resumed, the architectural ideals might well be imported from Italy and France, but it was Holland that had the surest grip on Danish Baroque. Regularity became the order of the day. The dominant lines were to harmonise with strict symmetry, clear proportions and regularity. The perpendicular division of the facade became common and pilasters in the colossal order were highly rated. In the field of royal buildings, an important undertaking was the royal palace, which after the introduction of absolutism in 1660 was no longer in keeping with the times or a worthy setting for the absolute monarch. Lampert van Haven was entrusted with the task, and he proposed a four-winged complex. However, this project was completely eclipsed by another proposal – which was not realised, either – by the Swedish architect Nicodemus Tessin the Younger. Despite this setback, van Haven remained the leading architect in the first phase of Danish Baroque. His greatest work was *Vor Frelsers Kirke* (Our Saviour's Church) in Copenhagen (1682-1696). Van Haven has, as has also Ewert Janssen, been named as a possible originator of another of the main works of the period, Charlottenborg in Kongens Nytorv in Copenhagen, which was started in 1672. Charlottenborg is French in its plan, but Dutch in idiom.

Although the architectural creations of the age were thus mainly concentrated in private building undertakings in Copenhagen, for instance Niels Juels Palæ near Kongens Nytorv (1696), building work was still going on in other parts of the country. By 1673 Jens Lauridsen had built the mansion of Nysø near Præstø, where the entire complex was based on strict axiality. In Clausholm (1693-1694) near Randers, the architect Ernst Brandenburger planned the building on the basis of the predilection of the period for enfilade, i.e. aligned doors providing a vista down through all the rooms.

About the turn of the century an Italian wind blew through Danish architecture. In the *Staldmestergård* (1706) in Copenhagen, W.F. von Platen and Christof Marselis abandoned the Dutch style in favour of the Italian. Frederik IV, too, on his travels abroad had expressed great admiration for Italian architecture, and in the same spirit, in 1708-1709, he had J.C. Ernst extend Frederiksberg Castle in Copenhagen, which consequently was given its present aspect overlooking the park.

Fredensborg Palace near Copenhagen was another of Frederik IV's building projects. This hunting lodge was completed in 1722 under the direction of J.C. Krieger, who was the most important figure in the Danish architecture of the 1720s, and as such responsible for most of the royal building projects of the period. In addition, Krieger distinguished himself as a landscape gardener and in the 1720s designed the palace gardens at Fredensborg and Frederiksborg.

Frederik IV had chosen to have Copenhagen Castle rebuilt by Krieger and Ernst. Christian VI had it demolished and handed the task of building a new royal residence to the German architect E.D. Häusser, who thereby introduced South German-Austrian architecture into Denmark. Of the Christiansborg that arose in

Charlottenborg in Kongens Nytorv was built 1672-1683 as an elegant Baroque mansion for the viceregent in Norway, Ulrik Frederik Gyldenløve, the son of Frederik III; the builder was probably Ewert Janssen. Survey drawing from 1929.

Niels (Nikolai) Eigtved, 1701-1754, was the most outstanding Danish Rococo architect in the 18th century. He became acquainted with the light, elegant, Rococo style with its stress on surface in Germany and Poland, after which he returned to Copenhagen in 1735. Thanks to his knowledge of this most recent architectural fashion he was immediately appointed court architect to Christian VI. Eigtved's first task was to design a number of Rococo interiors (1737-1742) in the first Christiansborg Palace. The still existing entrance to the palace near the Marble Bridge is also Eigtved's work, as is Prinsens Palæ opposite, (1743-1744), now the National Museum. Meanwhile, Eigtved's greatest achievement was the grandiose plan for a new district of Copenhagen to be called Frederiksstaden (started 1749). Here, Eigtved was responsible for the overall design, planned around an octagonal central piazza, but he was also the architect behind several of the houses in this part of the city, including the four identical mansions constituting the Royal Palace of Amalienborg, a major achievement in European Rococo architecture.

Elisabeth Buchwald

the years after 1730, the royal mews, *Ridebanen,* still exist. It was, however, less Häusser than the leading architects of the following generation, Lauritz de Thurah and Niels Eigtved, who made their mark on the interiors of the palace. Throughout his life, Thurah retained the powerful style of late Baroque, for instance in the Eremitage Palace in *Dyrehaven* near Copenhagen (1734) and in the Ledreborg complex near Roskilde, which in the 1740s he succeeded in unifying into a well balanced and cohesive Baroque structure. What Thurah had started in Ledreborg found a serene expression in the mansion of Lerchenborg near Kalundborg, which from 1742 arose as a clearly designed structure built around a deep main axis running through farm buildings and stables, the main building and into the park. In 1749-1750 Thurah gave Our Saviour's Church in Copenhagen its idiosyncratic spiral tower.

The Amalienborg mansions in Copenhagen were built to designs by the court architect Niels Eigtved. Moltkes Palæ (Christian VII's Palæ) was finished in 1754 and was the only one of the four mansions in which Eigtved himself – together with the sculptor L.A. Le Clerc – could oversee the internal decorations. The picture shows the Great Hall, which has panelled walls with gentle, intertwined rocaille shapes in the panelling.

Ordinary buildings were still half-timbered. However, brick-built buildings began to appear, and after the 1728 Copenhagen fire attempts were made, without success, to prohibit half-timbering in buildings facing the street. Town houses were in particular of two types, gable attic houses and pediment houses.

Rococo

Alongside Lauritz de Thurah, his colleague and rival, Niels Eigtved, was the spokesman for the latest ideas of French Rococo. Inspired by the Parisian *hôtel* he built *Prinsens Palæ* (now the National Museum) 1743-1744 in Copenhagen, while the French country residence, the *maison de plaisance* was the more direct model for his design of Frederiksdal near the Furesø Lake (1744-1745). As court architect, Eigtved left his greatest memorial in the planning of Frederiksstaden in Copenhagen 1749. This part of the city, which was planned around the octagonal square containing the four Amalienborg Palaces, was at first left to Eigtved. He decided on the rules for the facades, and for the town houses he produced type designs in a

discreet pilaster strip and recessed style with delicate relief effects. In 1752 he started building *Frederiks Hospital* (now the Danish Museum of Decorative Art), also in Copenhagen. The pavilions facing the street are, however, the work of Thurah. Eigtved's death in 1754 brought Thurah back as the leading architect, and he attempted unsuccessfully to take over Eigtved's task of completing the principal building in Frederiksstaden, *Frederikskirken*, now known as *Marmorkirken* (The Marble Church).

Neo-Classicism

It was the French architect Nicolas-Henri Jardin who as the representative of the entirely new style, Neo-Classicism, came to continue the work on *Frederikskirken*. His first project in 1756 was dominated by a certain antique, almost Piranesian architectural style, which he reluctantly had to adapt to a more traditional manner. Under Jardin's direction the walls of Frederikskirken only managed to rise 9 metres above ground level before the expensive marble structure was stopped in 1770. In addition Jardin was in charge of both parks and other building projects, for instance the Bernstorff Palace in Gentofte and Marienlyst in Elsinore, both started 1759. Of Copenhagen town houses, which otherwise conformed to the lines laid down by Eigtved, Jardin built *Det Gule Palæ* in Amaliegade (1764). His town houses had their successors, but especially the *Bernstorff Slot*, thanks to its *maison de plaisance* form seems to have set the tone, for instance for Glorup in Funen, built by C.J. Zuber (c. 1765).

Among Jardin's pupils the most important was C.F. Harsdorff, who had also studied at J.F. Blondel's school in Paris. Thus trained in the idiom of Neo-Classicism, he became the leading architect of his day both as court architect and as a professor in the newly-created Academy of Fine Arts. In Frederik V's chapel in Roskilde Cathedral (1774-1778) a small number of terse forms with their background in classical architecture were fused together in a monumental design. 1779-1780 he built the large town house beside Charlottenborg, Kongens Nytorv 3-5. With his simple idiom, well-balanced proportions and a facade design with accentuated lateral bays and an accentuated, pilastered central section, he introduced a new norm for the Copenhagen town house. In the provincial towns they followed the developments, but half-timbering still survived, not least in buildings away from the street. In mansions, Neo-Classicism also asserted itself, for instance Hagenskov (Frederiksgave) near Assens (1774-1776) by Jardin's pupil G.E. Rosenberg, and

the nearby Krengerup (1770s), where the architect, presumably Hans Næss has combined characteristics from both Jardin and Harsdorff.

Greek Antique architecture was the object of considerable interest at this time, and it left its traces for instance in Harsdorff's colonnade (1794) between two of the Amalienborg palaces. In church building there was especially one task that demanded attention, the completion of Frederikskirken. In Harsdorff it seemed that the right man with the necessary artistic talent to take up the inheritance of Eigtved and Jardin had been found, but this time, too, work was stopped with the architect's death in 1799.

The Nineteenth Century

Of C.F. Harsdorff's pupils, both Peter Meyn and Andreas Kirkerup made names for themselves, but the most important one was C.F. Hansen who

C.F. Hansen, 1756-1845, is one of the most important neo-classical architects in Denmark. His severe and simple, but very powerful style, inspired partly by ancient Roman architecture and Italian Renaissance building, found its expression already in his earliest work – a row of houses for wealthy citizens in Altona near Hamburg, built in the years after C.F. Hansen's appointment as regional architect in the Duchy of Holstein in 1784. Several of the most striking and monumental buildings in Copenhagen are likewise the work of C.F. Hansen, who at the beginning of the 19th century was called to Copenhagen to take part in the huge work of reconstruction after the great fire of 1795 and the British bombardment of the city in 1807. Thus both the City Hall and the Courthouse on Nytorv (1805-1815) and Copenhagen Cathedral, *Vor Frue Kirke* (1811-1829), were designed by C.F. Hansen. He was moreover also entrusted with the rebuilding of the partially burned down royal palace of Christans-

borg (1803-1833), where he skilfully and by simple means transformed the smoke-blackened Baroque ruin into a grandiose, neo-classical palace complex. The palace burned down again in 1884, but the domed palace church belonging to it (1829) still stands.

Elisabeth Buchwald

In 1779-1780, the architect C.F. Harsdorff built himself a house in Kongens Nytorv that was to serve as a pattern for the correct form for town houses at that time. The facade with emphasis on the lateral sections was frequently used in new buildings in Copenhagen erected after the 1795 fire.

from 1784 occupied the post of regional architect in Holstein, now part of northern Germany. Among other things, he built a number of striking houses in Altona. His ideal was a stricter classical style dominated by pure, simple forms and large unbroken expanses. His starting point was Antique architecture, and his expression was monumental. From 1800 he was placed in charge of all major works in the rebuilding of Copenhagen after the great fires in 1794 and 1795, and the bombardment of the city by the English fleet in 1807. On the ruins of Christiansborg, which burnt down in 1794, he built a new palace of which only the *Slotskirke* (Palace Church) from 1829 still stands; the remaining, unfinished palace buildings burned down in 1884. C.F. Hansen was also the architect of the City Hall and Courthouse on Nytorv (1805-1815) and the rebuilt *Vor Frue Kirke* (Copenhagen Cathedral) (1811-1829).

Even before C.F. Hansen's death in 1845 new fashions had begun to replace his ideals. For Neo-Classicism, the Antiquity was still a neces-

Of C.F. Hansen's many undertakings in Copenhagen, the greatest was the rebuilding of Christiansborg Palace, which had burned to the ground in 1794. He was given with the task in 1800, and the main body of the building was finished by 1822; his drawing of the facade facing Slotspladsen was done in 1804 (the Royal Danish Academy of Fine Arts). The outer walls of the old palace were still standing and were as far as possible to be incorporated in the new structure. With this clearly defined task, Hansen made the palace arise again as a new building in his own neo-classical idiom. It burned down again in 1884, and yet another palace was built on the basis of the old walls.

Ferdinand Jensen's Apartment Block in Bredgade in Copenhagen, built 1886-1887. The artistry is mainly in the facade, which in keeping with the international outlook at the time is designed in authentic Renaissance style.

sary foundation, but the massive structures favoured by Hansen gave way to a more delicate, decorative style. G.F. Hetsch, together with N.S. Nebelong and H.C. Stilling represented a new generation indebted to the German architect K.F. Schinkel. It was in Schinkel's spirit that in his main work, the Synagogue in Krystalgade in Copenhagen (1831-1833), Hetsch sought to give the building a character in keeping with its muse. In the Catholic Saint Ansgar Church in Bredgade in Copenhagen (1841-1842), he introduced brick architecture with patterned walls. Late Classicism's more liberal view of historical styles after that of Antiquity, not least Gothic, found its expression in the mansions built in the 1830s and 1840s, for instance the rebuilding of Basnæs to the south east of Skælskør in 1846. The tendency towards Gothic is also seen in Peder Malling's University building (1831-1836) at Frue

Plads in Copenhagen, where it stands opposite the Cathedral as a representative of the new age.

With Gottlieb Bindesbøll, Neo-Classicism seemed to crumble. The polychrome Thorvaldsen's Museum in Copenhagen (1839-1847) and the neo-Gothic Hobro Church (1850-1852) reflect the great range of his free, personal interpretations of historical styles. In continuation of this, Christian Hansen built the Copenhagen General Hospital, *Kommunehospitalet* (1859-1863) with a Byzantine touch; in addition he was responsible for buildings in Athens, together with his brother, Theophilus Hansen, who later practised in Vienna. An architectural style of a more dispassionate and utilitarian nature is found in Bindesbøll's work with social architecture in *Lægeforeningens Boliger* (The Medical Association Dwellings) in Østerbro, built after

In 1855-1861, J.D. Herholdt built the University Library beside the main building of Copenhagen University in Vor Frue Plads. The building is the principal work of the national current in historicism. The interior bearing constructions were made of cast iron, at that time a new material.

the cholera epidemic in Copenhagen in 1853.

Historicism

The second half of the 19th century was the age of historicism. Historical styles, Romanesque art, Gothic, Renaissance and Baroque among others, constituted the sources of inspiration which were eagerly drawn on, often in an eclectic manner. Two main currents could be distinguished, a national and an international. The national tendency was represented especially by J.D. Herholdt. In his principal work, the University Library in Fiolstræde in Copenhagen (1855-1861), he worked with a Dano-Italian architectural style. His idiom bore the stamp especially of north Italian motifs, which he combined with native materials. The brick in an unadorned wall and its material qualities were decisive. The bricks for the wall, like all the materials used, were meticulously finished to a high, professional standard. The genuine quality and honesty of the materials were important factors. In Herholdt's National Bank in Copenhagen (1866-1870 – now demolished) there was inspiration from the Florentine Renaissance palace, while

the wooden chapel in the New Roskilde Cemetery (1883-1885) was more Nordic in style. This historical tendency also made itself felt in the building of detached houses, which took off during this period. Among others, Hans J. Holm adopted the Herholdt line with works like *Mineralogisk Museum* (Mineralogical Museum) in Copenhagen (1888-1893).

The other tendency in the architecture of this period was far more international and worked with a broader spectrum of inspirations, mainly from the Italian and French Renaissance, but there was also a place for Gothic and Dutch Renaissance. The adherents of this fashion, who have since been referred to as 'the Europeans', took the lead about 1870 with Ferdinand Meldahl as the principal figure. The aspect of the facade, the choice of style and decoration, were ascribed great importance, as the architect's supreme objective was to create the right mood. The idiosyncrasy of the materials was less important, and in this period of stucco architecture, the facades were often plastered. The freedom in the choice of style is reflected in Meldahl's 1859-1862 rebuilding of the mansion of Pederstrup on Lolland in French Renaissance style. Meldahl's most important work – and probably the most important work of the time – was the completion in 1894 of *Frederikskirken* (The Marble Church) in Copenhagen. The blocks of houses at Bredgade 63-65 (1886-87) and Tordenskjoldsgade 1 (1866), both built by Ferdinand Jensen, are consistent exponents of historical and stucco architecture. Vilhelm Dahlerup also adopted this style with for instance Tivoli's Pantomime Theatre and the Royal Theatre, both from 1874 and both in Copenhagen.

National Romanticism, Jugendstil, etc.

Towards the turn of the century, Martin Nyrop took up position as a kind of successor to Herholdt. The insistence on workmanship was still as great as ever. Nyrop represented the National Romantic tendency, in which the Danish and the Nordic occupied the central place in architecture. However, he chose the City Hall in Siena as the inspiration for the new Copenhagen City Hall, built between 1892 and 1905. He gave it a picturesque appearance, and he was generous in scattering subtle details throughout the building. The Elias Church on Vesterbro in Copenhagen (1905-1908) he gave a mediaeval robustness and twin towers like those of Tveje Merløse Church near Holbæk. Inspired by the Nyrop tendency was, among many others, the city architect Ludvig Fenger, who together with Ludvig Clausen built the Eastern Electricity Station in Copenhagen (1901-1902) in an Italianate brick architectural style. With Nyrop a greater element of individualism had made its appearance in architecture. Hack Kampmann, too, was notable for his personal interpretation of the trends of the day, both in the Regional Archive in Viborg (1889-1991) and the extension to Dahlerup's *Ny Carlsberg Glyptotek* in Copenhagen (1901-1906).

Jugendstil, which was very common elsewhere at the turn of the century, only made a brief appearance in Denmark, with few adherents apart from Anton Rosen. Rosen's Savoy Hotel (1906) and Palace Hotel (1912) and Aage Langeland-Mathiesen's block at Østbanegade 11 (1904), all in Copenhagen, are some of the quite small number of examples.

As early as 1886, H.B. Storck had built the Abel Cathrine Foundation in Copenhagen in a restrained, Ba-roque idiom. In this he anticipated the main quality in the work of Ulrik Plesner, that is to say Neo-Baroque. The compact mass, the bulk, the finished form and the powerful textural effect were essential factors. Perhaps Plesner achieved his major importance through his building of apartment blocks, including *Åhusene* in Copenhagen (1895-1898). The Neo-Baroque also formed the foundation for Thorvald Jørgensen's design for the present Christiansborg Palace in Copenhagen (1907-1928).

With the aim of giving guidance to people so that good, sound small houses could be built throughout the country in accordance with Danish architectural tradition, the first decades of the 20th century saw the establishment first of *Tegnehjælpen* (the Council for Design Assistance) by the Society of Academic Architects in 1907 and then *Bedre Byggeskik* (the Better Architectural Design Association) in 1915. Guidance was to be given through practical instruc-

Martin Nyrop, 1849-1921, is one of the most important representatives of the so-called national romantic tendency in historicist architecture. He found his inspiration both in North Italian architecture and old Scandinavian architectural styles, which were reinterpreted to form a very individualistic idiom with emphasis on good workmanship and the textural qualities of the material. Nyrop was a determined opponent of the stuccoed architecture that was so much in vogue at the time, and instead he fought for the use of 'honest and genuine' materials such as bricks, wood and slates. Among Nyrop's major works are Bispebjerg Hospital (1907-1918) and the church Eliaskirken in Vesterbro (1905-1908), while his greatest achievement is Copenhagen City Hall (1892-1905), in which Nordic and southern European impulses, not least from the City Hall in Siena, have been adapted with great personal vitality to produce a festive, popular and easily grasped building, which both inside and outside reflects Nyrop's lively imagination and vibrant delight in colour.

Elisabeth Buchwald

The block of flats called Hornbækhus was built by Kay Fisker in 1923. The facades are subject to a strict, regular composition with the windows in a fixed rhythmical pattern. The neo-classical idiom is severe, without any superfluous effects. The large, open courtyard in the centre of the square was designed by the landscape gardener N.G. Brandt.

tion, standard designs, courses for craftsmen from country districts, etc. One of the results can be seen in the Finsensvej project in Copenhagen, built 1914-1919 by K.T. Seest and Hans Koch. The movement included several of the leading architects of the day, including P.V. Jensen-Klint, who made an intensive study of the qualities of Danish mediaeval brick architecture, an aesthetics that received its purest expression in the Grundtvig Church in Copenhagen (1921-1940).

Classicism

About 1910, the younger generation of architects felt the need to tighten things up a bit. The Neo-Baroque gave way to a classicist tendency that was helped on its way by Carl Jacobsen's offer to pay for a Baroque spire for C.F. Hansen's Cathedral, a gesture that opened people's eyes to the qualities in Hansen's Neo-Classicism. Carl Petersen led the way with his Faaborg Museum (1912-1913). The ideals were now symmetry, regularity and rhythmical repetition. Neo-Classicism coincided with an upsurge of apartment blocks in Copenhagen,

and it was not least here the new ideals were to be found. The layout of the flats themselves, however, still came second to the aesthetic demands of the facade. Povl Baumann's blocks in Struenseegade and Hans Tavsensgade in Copenhagen (1919-1920) and Kay Fisker's *Hornbækhus* (1923) set the tone. Architects also found a new task in the building of terraced houses. *Bakkehusene* in Copenhagen (1921-1923) by Ivar Bentsen and Thorkild Henningsen were a pioneering work that had several successors.

The Main Police Station (*Politigården*) in Copenhagen (1918-1924) is a special triumph from that time, powerful, simple and inward-looking on the outside and monumental in its open courtyard and its unadorned, commanding detail. The building was started by Hack Kampmann and completed mainly under the direction of Aage Rafn. Holger Jacobsen was one of those taking part in the work, and he was himself to produce a building with a touch of the same mannerist, dangerous bulk, the new stage of The Royal Theatre, known as *Stærekassen* (The

Nesting Box) in Copenhagen (1929-1931).

Modernism

The transition from Neo-Classicism to functionalism took place about 1930. The 1930 Stockholm Exhibition is seen as the event that introduced functionalism into Denmark. The ideal expounded by the foreign pioneers, first and foremost Walter Gropius and the Bauhaus School in Germany and Le Corbusier in France, was a rational and functional architecture that had a social objective, not least in the field of housing. The new materials were concrete, iron and glass, which were joined together in constructively 'honest' structures without the decorative tendencies of earlier ages. The functionalism style found favour in virtually all areas of building. Inspired by Le Corbusier, Mogens Lassen built a number of individual houses in Klampenborg in the 1930s. In the field of apartment blocks, Arne Jacobsen was responsible for the white Bellavista (1934), also in Klampenborg.

Along with this international trend, there also existed in Denmark a more traditional tendency, which certainly allowed itself to be influenced by the ideals of the age, but which made special use of native materials and a more traditional idiom, as is seen for instance in Århus University by Kay Fisker, C.F. Møller and Povl Stegmann, started in 1932. This tendency represented a sober, functional view of architecture. Among the leading architects were Povl Baumann with the apartment block Storgården in Copenhagen (1935) and not least Kay Fisker. Fisker replaced his terse and compact Neo-Classical idiom with the same qualities in a functionalist approach. Together with C.F. Møller he built the apartment blocks at Vodroffsvej 2 (1930) and Vestersøhus (1935-1939) in Copenhagen. In this

Arne Jacobsen, 1902-1971, was one of the architects who helped to introduce functionalism into Denmark in the 1930s. One of his earliest major works was his plan for Bellevue in Klampenborg (1931-1936), a charming combination of theatre, sea swimming pool and houses in which the simple, cubist, whitewashed appearance heralded new architectural ideals. The versatile and productive Jacobsen gained great importance through his work in almost all areas of architecture and generated a renewal both in housing, in public buildings such as town halls and schools, in factory design and applied art. Among many other things, Jacobsen was the architect behind two of the most discussed architectural projects of the time, Århus City Hall (1939-1942) and the new building for the National Bank in Copenhagen (1965-1978). In later years, Jacobsen was able to establish his position as one of the most important European architects with a number of famous buildings in other countries including England and Germany, for example St Catherine's College in Oxford (1966), the Danish Embassy in London (1969-1977) and the City Hall in Mainz (1970-1973).

Elisabeth Buchwald

Vestersøhus near Sankt Jørgens Sø (lake in Copenhagen) was built 1935-1939 by Kay Fisker and C.F. Møller. For many years after this it represented the ideal of the characteristic block with verandas and bay windows, that both provided good, light rooms and gave the otherwise very long facade a regular, rhythmical modulation in which repetition was not reduced to the trivial.

latter they created the ideal of a block with projecting balconies. The buildings were turned to catch the sun, the plans of the flats were unconventional, and the rooms were placed as most appropriate.

The architecture of the 1940s showed signs of the difficult conditions in the wake of the Second World War. The lack of building materials soon made itself felt and forced a return to traditional building methods and financially rational solutions. The sign of the times was the smaller building projects such as terraced or link houses, for instance Viggo Møller-Jensen's Atelierhuse (studio houses) at Utterslev (1943) and Søndergårdsparken at Bagsværd (1950), both near Copenhagen, by Povl Ernst Hoff and Bennet Windinge.

After the Second World War

After the war, there was a considerable interest in foreign architecture among Danish architects, and attention was concentrated particularly on Modernism in the USA, personified by Mies van der Rohe and Frank Lloyd Wright. The trend was reflected not least in individual houses, which were given irregular ground plans, flat roofs, open plan and rooms giving into one another, and large glass facades that broke down the traditional boundaries in buildings and created an intimate link between inside and outside. Characteristics of this kind are found in several of the houses which the architects built for themselves, for instance Jørn Utzon's in Hellebæk, north of Elsinore (1952). The same characteristics, which also showed

In the Bellavista housing complex, built in 1934 in Klampenborg north of Copenhagen, Arne Jacobsen worked in the spirit of international functionalism. The flats, which overlook the Øresund, were provided with balconies and large areas of glass. Like their foreign counterparts, the houses have flat roofs and stand with flat, whitewashed facades, all of which in fact hides the fact that they are made from traditional materials, bricks with iron girders between – not concrete.

CULTURE

Jørn Utzon, b.1918, is probably the most important of 20th-century Danish architects. He derived his earliest inspiration from foreign architects such as Alvar Aalto and Frank Lloyd Wright, whose organic conception of architecture was of great significance for Utzon's own expressive and sculptural nature-inspired architecture. Utzon experienced his international breakthrough in 1957 when he rather surprisingly won the international competition to build an opera house in Sydney in Australia, a visionary building project with a roof consisting of 60-metre-high concrete shells opening out towards the harbour like billowing sails. For various reasons, Utzon resigned as architect to the project in 1966, but the Opera House, which is considered to be one of the most important 20th-century works of architecture, made Utzon world-famous and resulted in his being given commissions far and wide, including the Melli Bank in Teheran (1963) and the parliament building in Kuwait (1978-1985). In Denmark Utzon has only been responsible for a small number of buildings: in addition to some of the country's earliest high density low buildings from around 1960, there is Bagsværd Church (1977) and Paustian's furniture store (1987) in the Nordhavn district of Copenhagen. In April 1998 Utzon received the Sonning Award.

Elisabeth Buchwald

the influence of Japanese architecture, were used by Jørgen Bo and Vilhelm Wohlert for the Louisiana Museum of Modern Art in Humlebæk in 1956-1958. From Mies van der Rohe, the cool classical Modernism also gained a foothold; this was based on pure proportions, simple, strict forms and the new technological potential of steel constructions with curtain wall facades. This was done principally by Arne Jacobsen, who at this time was the leading Modernist of international standing with buildings in Copenhagen such as Jespersen & Son's offices in Nyropsgade (1953), Rødovre Town Hall (1955) and SAS Royal Hotel (1960).

At the beginning of the 1960s a significant change took place in conditions governing Danish building. The State now began to invest in industrialised building, one result of which was the building of huge residential complexes. This kind of prefabricated and precast building actually coincided with the architectural ideals of clear and rational building design. Building in concrete made its appearance in earnest in Denmark in Høje Gladsaxe to the north of Copenhagen, built 1960-1964 by the architects Hoff & Windinge. A start had been made as early as 1950 on building high-rise flats at Bellahøj, also near Copenhagen, but the very tall residential blocks brought with them living problems and social problems, and criticism was not long in coming. An alternative arose in *Fællestegnestuen*'s estate from 1963-1966 in Albertslund Syd, where low buildings spread over the ground like a carpet, and where there were also experiments in separating wheeled

The SAS building encompassing the Royal Hotel was built in 1960 by Arne Jacobsen. The idiom is that of international modernism, and the model the American skyscraper. Arne Jacobsen took charge of everything in the building, not only the actual constructional details, but also the arrangement and the furniture.

Johan Otto von Spreckelsen, 1929-1987, is the architect behind several of Denmark's modern church buildings, including Vangede Church north of Copenhagen (1974) and Stavnsholt Church in Farum (1981). He makes obvious use of the square – but also the sphere, the cylinder and the pyramid, geometrical shapes which Spreckelsen used time and time again in his work. Perhaps most clearly in the main work, which was to be the culmination and end of his relatively short career, *La Grande Arche* in the La Défense district in Paris, inaugurated in 1989, two years after the death of the architect. It is a 110-metre-high construction in concrete, marble and glass, shaped as a combination of a cube and an arch forming a simple, powerful and symbolical end to the six-kilometre-long 'historical' axis run-ning east from the Tuillerie Gardens near the Louvre through the old *Arc de Triomphe* in Place de l'Étoile to the modern business district of La Défense in the west.

Elisabeth Buchwald

The Danish School of Journalism in Århus was built 1971-1973 to the design of the Kjær & Richter firm of architects. Modernism, which at this time was being questioned by many, was still the guiding factor in designing this building. The School has since been extended with other buildings.

and pedestrian traffic. In Galgebakken (1973-1974), prefabricated buildings also in Albertslund, the architects Hanne Marcussen, Jens Peter Storgård and Anne and Jørn Ørum-Nielsen aimed to create a better framework around the social lives of those living there, partly by building houses around small, semi-private roads.

In the late 1960s and early 1970s, Friis & Moltke directed various building projects in which the raw surface of the concrete was exposed. These buildings, for instance Scanticon near Århus (1969) have since become known as 'casemate architecture'

and are to a certain extent related to the brutalism known from abroad, but which never really established itself in Denmark. In 1973-1976, Jørn Utzon built Bagsværd Church near Copenhagen with a modest and rational exterior, while he continued the organic line in his work in the undulating lines of the ceiling in the body of the church.

Post-Modernism and Other Movements

The actual showdown with Modernism was particularly marked in residential building, and the decisive breach came with the Tinggården estate by the firm of architects *Vandkunsten* in Herfølge (1978). Tinggården was not the first criticism of modernism, but it was the first vision of a new and alternative residential environment to be brought to fruition. It paid homage to the ideal of small, intimate residential enclaves which should preferably be in touch with nature. Architecturally speaking, Tinggården was built in a varied and informal mould, in which the elements of concrete were hidden

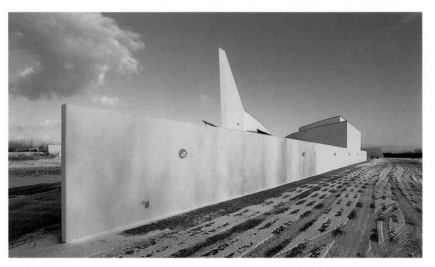

behind unpretentious and familiar native materials such as wooden cladding and facing walls. This low, but dense complex set the tone for residential building throughout the 1970s and 1980s, for instance in Solbjerghave by Fællestegnestuen in Frederiksberg, Copenhagen (1980).

In Denmark, Tinggården's idiom anticipated Post-Modernism, which originally opened up for a culturally relevant style of building, possibly based on regional characteristics. Nor were references to historical architecture and striking contrasts alien to this movement. The spokesmen for the theory were in particular Nielsen, Nielsen & Nielsen, with estates such as Villa Atzen in Horsens (1986).

In addition to Post-Modernism, Danish architecture since about 1970 has been characterised by various architectural trends that have thrived

As a young architect, *Henning Larsen*, b.1925, was an associate of Arne Jacobsen, but in the 1960s – after establishing his own firm – he gained a reputation through his successful participation in international architecture competitions. He won for instance the competition for a new university in the Norwegian city of Trondheim, the first stage of which was completed 1976-1978. Henning Larsen's main work, however, is the Saudi Arabian Foreign Ministry in Riyadh (1982-1984), a monumental, fortress-like building in which Islamic and European building traditions are elegantly combined. The various spaces in the building and the exciting use of light are characteristic of Henning Larsen's architecture, as are the covered 'bazaar streets' and 'squares' on several floors, themes found again in several of his other works, including the Copenhagen Business School in Frederiksberg (1988-1989) and the central library in Gentofte (1984-1985) to the north of Copenhagen.

Elisabeth Buchwald

In the second half of the 20th century several Danish architects have been responsible for a number of major, prestigious buildings abroad. Johan Otto von Spreckelsen's *Cube*, inaugurated in 1989 (top left), Jørn Utzon's Opera House in Sydney, Australia, 1957-1974, (top right), and the Foreign Ministry in Riyadh in Saudi Arabia by Henning Larsen (bottom), completed 1984.

side by side. Late Modernism represents a refinement of the forms of Modernism, as is seen in a number of buildings by Danish architects abroad, for instance Dissing & Weitling's art museum in North Rhine Westphalia (1986), Krohn and Hartvig Rasmussen's National Museum in Bahrain (1988) and J.O. von Spreckelsen's *La Grande Arche* in Paris (1989). Neo-Rationalism, which has its source in Italy, has similarly found its way to Danish architects, first in the town plan for Høje Taastrup and the design of the town centre, undertaken since 1978 by Jacob Blegvad's firm of architects and Claus Bonderup. The classical element is seen in both Poul Ingemann, e.g. in his

residential complex at Blangstedgård near Odense (1988), and in Henning Larsen in *Handelshøjskolen* (Copenhagen Business School) in Frederiksberg (1989). Deconstructivism has a few advocates in Denmark, but only a small number of buildings, for example the dwellings for the elderly in Frederiksberg by the architect firm Box 25 (1992). Most recently the firm of architects, Schmidt, Hammer & Lassen, have in 1999 extended the Royal Library with a building called the Black Diamond, a neo-modernist, monumental monolith with blank, reflecting facades which sits on the Copenhagen harbour front.

Vibeke Andersson Møller

Landscape Gardening

Danish ornamental and landscape gardening has by and large followed the same pattern as in the rest of Europe, where the artistic design of gardens has alternated between two principles: a regular, architectural style derived from residential building, and an irregular, scenic style with the natural landscape as its model.

Before the Reformation in 1536 gardens were cultivated behind the walls of monasteries and convents; it is from these that the cruciform garden, often with a well at the centre, derives. The monastery and convent gardens came under the Crown after the Reformation, and here we see some of the first royal Renaissance gardens, for instance Lundehave near Kronborg in Elsinore. The gardens were still hedged in and consisted of separate sections arranged as a pattern on a surface without any axial relation to the house.

During the reign of Frederik IV at the beginning of the 18th century a number of Baroque gardens were established, inspired by the great French style of André le Nôtre. Building and garden were merged into a single, grandiose experience, symmetrically placed around a central axis. J.C. Krieger was the master of this great style with the gardens of Frederiksberg, Fredensborg and Frederiksborg palaces (1720s) and Ledreborg (1740s).

Partly resulting from a changed view of nature, a number of the magnificent Baroque parks were transformed at the end of the 18th century, inspired by the English garden.

Frederiksborg Castle in Hillerød was built at the beginning of the 17th century for King Christian IV. In front of the castle there is a Baroque garden that was laid out in the 18th century. As is characteristic of this style of garden, the castle and garden share the same central axis.

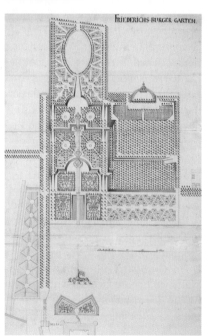

Rosenborg Castle in Copenhagen was originally a summer house in the park called Kongens Have, which Christian IV had laid out in 1606 outside the city ramparts. The building was given its present aspect in the 1630s. Over the years, the park underwent a series of changes and was opened to the public and is today one of the city's most popular green areas. The picture shows the famous bed of crocuses laid out in the lawn in front of the castle like a carpet covered with geometrical patterns. It was designed in 1964 by the landscape gardener Ingwer Ingwersen.

The landscape gardener C.Th. Sørensen's 1948 allotment gardens in Nærum to the north of Copenhagen consist exclusively of small gardens formed by oval hedges and set in grass. From the plan of a single garden it can be seen how the house is conceived as being partly placed in the actual hedge as an element in the strictly architectural line of the hedge. The design of the actual garden, meanwhile, was left to the owner, who could thus put his own stamp on it.

With irregular planting and winding paths, they were broken down into a kind of atmospheric garden. Liselund from the 1790s shows the delight in nature of the time. With industrialisation and technological developments, new 'art garden' interpretations of the style were established with landscape gardeners like H.A. Flindt and Edvard Glæsel as their exponents. The garden became smaller and was more architecturally integrated with the house. From 1900 onwards one of the advocates of this style was the landscape gardener Erik Erstad-Jørgensen.

With G.N. Brandt the whole question of gardens came up in earnest, with parks such as Hellerup Strandpark (1912-1918) and Mariebjerg Cemetery in Gentofte (1925-36) as the expressions of epoch-making new ideas and a new aesthetics. Urban developments brought with them new possibilities for a policy towards nature, and landscape gardening was expanded to include apartment block gardens, housing estates, sports centres, cemeteries, allotments, green areas and paths. Today planning has moved away from small private house gardens towards larger public parks, for instance the university parks in Århus (1931-1947) by C.Th. Sørensen, and Odense (1970-1973) by Jørgen Vesterholt, the *Musikhus* (concert hall) in Århus (1979) by Sven Hansen, the City Park in Vejle (1994) by Preben Skaarup and Herning Square(1996) by Jeppe Aagaard Andersen. The motorway system and bridge building have also been subjected to landscaping, for instance the work of Edith and Ole Nørgaard on the Lyngby motorway in 1965-1974 and Møller og Grønborg's planning of others, including the Jutland motorway (c. 1970). In addition, since the first conservation act (1917) the conservation movement has developed from the ideal merely of conserving nature into an effort to take care of nature, with larger cohesive areas as the basis of its work.

Lulu Salto Stephensen

Visual Arts

Early History

The oldest evidence of visual art and handicrafts in Denmark stems from the Mesolithic Maglemose Culture (c. 9300-6800 BC). A feature of the Mesolithic Age are the geometrical patterns carved in tools of bone and antler and in amber pendants; occasionally stylised animals and human figures are found. In the Mesolithic Ertebølle Culture (c. 5400-3900 BC) we find regional stylistic differences for the first time, in that the hour-glass-shaped patterns made up of a large number of close lines are seen to be a particularly East Jutland phenomenon. Larger pieces of amber were used to make figures of animals such as birds and wild boar; a bear measuring 6.5 cm found on the shore in Fanø is of particularly high quality.

During the early and middle parts of the Neolithic Age, ceramics were the most important materials for art-like forms of expression. About 3000 BC an artistic pinnacle was reached with a complicated, compact ornamentation covering whole surfaces, formed by pressing in small bones, mussels, opercula from fish, etc. The ornamentation appears in strictly composed perpendicular zones, while mainly chevron bands form horizontal patterns. In a few clay vessels there are remains of a chalk paste showing that the patterns have been brought out in white in contrast to the dark surface.

Ceramics lost their importance as an art form in the Late Neolithic Age and the Early Bronze Age. At the beginning of the Early Bronze Age c. 1700 BC, the bronzes were decorated with a strict chevron ornamentation inspired by the southern European Bronze Age cultures, but a character-istic style soon developed in Scandinavia, built up around a spiral design. The discovery of the cult image of the Sun Chariot illustrates this; the gold covered bronze disk, the sun, is being drawn by a horse which is reproduced elegantly and with a sure sense of form, cast by the use of a cire perdue technique. By the middle of the Bronze Age (c. 1000 BC), the spiral ornamentations were replaced by star-like designs. In the Late Bronze Age (c. 1000-500 BC) the spiral is again seen in the bronzes, this time as part of harmonious compositions of rippling bands. From the Bronze Age we also have three-dimensional human and animal figures. Some have presumably been fixed on small models of ships used at cult ceremonies. The most important figural motif of the Bronze Age is the ship, which had a significant role as a religious symbol. A large number of reproductions of ships are known from certain types of bronze objects and in petroglyph art.

In the pre-Roman Iron Age (c. 500 BC to the birth of Christ) we see on the terminal knots of torques whorls indicative of Celtic influence. Towards the end of the period particularly delicate, thin-walled luxury ceramics emerged. In the older Roman Iron Age ceramics reached a peak in which local styles can be identified. The North Jutlandic ceramics are much praised for their

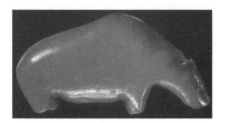

The amber figure of a bear found on a beach in Fanø in 1991; the National Museum. By simple means the Stone Age artist has been able to give both character and life to the small, 6.5 cm-long figure. It must be seen as one of the best mesolithic works of art we know. Some slight signs of wear show that there was once a thread round the neck of the bear; it was presumably worn as some kind of amulet.

This unusually big and beautifully made belt ornament from a bog near Langstrup near Asminderød in North Zealand measures 27 cm in diameter and is decorated with four concentric series of spiral designs. Spiral designs of this kind are characteristic of the middle of the Early Bronze Age, about 1350 BC.

deeply incised chevron patterns, which produce the effect of a delicate relief.

About the time of the birth of Christ, gold became a popular material, and the small pendants, breloques, with delicate patterns in granulation and filigree indicate a highly developed goldsmith's art. From the most opulent later Roman Iron Age graves stem bangles and rings decorated with stylised serpents' heads. The importance of gold continued into the Germanic Iron Age where after 400 AD excellent works are known, for instance the scabbard mountings and bracteates with stylised animal figures in a specific Scandinavian style. Also belonging to this period with its abundance of gold are the heavy golden horns from Gallehus, decorated with a profusion of figures.

The centuries after 400 saw the development of the characteristic Scandinavian animal ornamentation found especially on ornaments of gilt bronze. The oldest stylised animal figures are anatomically more or less correctly reproduced. The individual animal shapes, however, were soon broken down, and plane ornaments were made of limbs and bodies. It is the wavy, interwoven animal figures from the Late Germanic Iron Age that form the background of the various animal styles of the Viking Age. The latest of these, the Urnes style, with its sweeping animal figures in elegant, thin lines, continued to adorn the wooden churches in the early Middle Ages.

Flemming Kaul

Romanesque Art

As the Christian faith and culture took root in Denmark, the visual arts came to reflect the country's posi-

Black burnished, 35-cm-high earthenware jar found in a grave near Hobro in North Jutland; The National Museum. With its elegant shape and the deeply cut, finely proportioned ornamentation, this jar is a splendid example of the high quality of ceramics in the early Roman Iron Age (0-180 AD). In the northern part of Jutland it is usually angled patterns that dominate, in eastern Jutland mostly key patterns, while in southern Jutland broad, soft horizontal patterns were the most common.

tion vis-à-vis Romanesque Europe. Among the few extant Christian pictures from the 10th and 11th centuries can be named the runic inscriptions on the large Jelling Stone (second half of the 10th century) and the serpentine ornamentation on the Hørning plank, a remnant of a stave church from the 11th century. From c. 1100 the international character of Denmark's Romanesque art is quite obvious. This is true of both murals and stone and wooden sculptures and of the fire-gilded ornamentation of the golden altars.

Not least the murals bear witness to the lively contacts with southern and western Europe, indeed as far as the Byzantine Empire in the east. There is a profusion of 12th century paintings in Zealand. The churches in Måløv, Jørlunde, Slaglille, Sæby and Kirke Hyllinge contain murals on a high artistic level with clear links with i.a. Byzantine art. Most of the colours used were extremely costly and in many cases they were imported from far away. The paintings were mainly done as true frescoes on wet plaster in clear, well-arranged geometrical compositions. The figures, represented in calm and dignified postures, are placed in one or two picture friezes on the church walls. The friezes are separated and framed by richly varied ornamental bands, fashioned as key pattern borders, plant ornamentation, etc. The background colour is blue (usually ultramarine) or green.

Stone sculptures are usually done in granite, and the greatest number and best material is found in Jutland. Hundreds of fonts, decorated doorways and reliefs in the church walls show an array of motifs, of which lions and other animals of prey are among the most common. It is often extremely difficult to interpret these motifs as the messages contained in the pictures are by no means always unambiguous. In the best instances the idiom is terse and supple with an exquisite compositional play between the picture and its framework. Among the Romanesque master masons Horder deserves special attention. The name appears on a stone from Løvenholm (now in the National Museum) and has been interpreted as the master's signature; granite sculptures in several churches in Djursland and a large number of fonts are attributed to him.

One of the most important Romanesque sculptures is a relief of the Descent from the Cross above the main so-called *Cat's Head Door*

Gilt pendant of bronze, found in 1994 near Tissø in West Zealand; The National Museum. In an elegant, almost heraldic fashion, the 4-cm-long brooch, which can be dated to the 10th century AD, represents an eagle with large eyes, bent beak and powerfully scored wings and tail. It is a splendid example of the brooches of high quality that were worn by the aristocracy of the Viking Age.

The Åby Crucifix, c. 1100; The National Museum. The 51.5 cm-tall Romanesque sculpture from Åby church in Århus is executed in fire-gilt copper sheets and has originally been fixed to a cross that has been lost. Christ is depicted as King, with a crown on His head, fully conscious and with wide-open eyes. The expression is stylised, and the loin cloth stands as an independent abstract decoration.

in Ribe Cathedral (second half of the 12th century), which in an extremely poignant manner makes the utmost use of the space in the semi-circular tympanon. In the first half of the 13th century a triangular relief was added to it, representing the Heavenly Jerusalem.

A special group of works in Danish Romanesque art consists of the so-called *golden altars*, which have survived in greater numbers in Denmark than in any other country. There are altogether seven altar decorations, of which two can still be seen in the churches of Sahl near Holstebro and Stadil near the Ringkøbing Fjord. The golden altars consist of thin, fire-gilded copper sheets fixed on a wooden core. The sheets are worked up into reliefs from the back, patterned by engraving and decorated with rock crystal. The earliest, for instance the Lisbjerg altar, which is in the National Museum, date from 1135-50, and the latest, such as the one from Stadil, are from c. 1235.

Gothic Art

It is the tradition in histories of Danish art to show Gothic as starting about the middle of the 13th century, but in reality the transition was protracted and smooth. In the work with murals, there came new artistic demands as more churches (most, however, not until the 15th century) had their original flat wooden ceilings replaced by bricked vaulting. It is a quite different compositional task to adorn a curved, triangular severy rather than a flat wall, for which reason the use of models such as paintings from books became rather more complicated.

The figures in the Gothic murals no longer appear against a coloured background, but are painted directly on to the white lime. Throughout the Gothic period there is an increasing tendency to fill in the white areas between the figures with stars, flowers and other ornamentation. From about 1400 the murals were given to a new kind of pattern, the woodcut. In this relationship lies perhaps part of the explanation of why in most cases the pictures are more reminiscent of coloured drawings than of real painting. They often have a far more conventional and local character than the Romanesque murals, and this tendency is reinforced towards the end of the Middle Ages in the 16th century. Gothic murals are found throughout the country, and a large part of the adornments can be grouped in 'workshops' such as the Elmelunde workshop, the Isefjord workshop, etc.

A more internationally oriented form of Danish Gothic is often represented in the carved and painted wooden altarpieces and crucifixes.

The Descent from the Cross; Granite relief above the Cat Door in Ribe Cathedral, executed in the second half of the 11th century. Jesus with the regal crown is being carried by Nicodemus and Joseph of Arimathea, while Mary is kissing His hand and St John is mourning on the right. The composition, which is skilfully fitted in the semi-circular arch, is closely related to similar reliefs in northern Spanish churches near the route taken by pilgrims on their way to Santiago de Compostela.

From about 1400 the altarpieces were made in the form of cupboards with carved decorations and with panels that could be opened or closed in keeping with the events of the church year. One of the earliest examples is the altarpiece from 1398 on the high altar in Lund Cathedral in present-day Sweden. In many cases these cupboard altarpieces achieved quite impressive dimensions as for instance the altarpiece on the high altar in Århus Cathedral by the Lübeck sculptor Bernt Notke from 1479, which reaches a height of 9.25 m. Notke's style is highly influenced by realism, giving the figures a more portrait-like, non-idealised character.

Claus Berg is one of the greatest sculptors in Denmark in the late Middle Ages, his workshop in Odense at the beginning of the 16th century producing altarpieces, crucifixes, pulpits and other furnishings for many Danish churches. Claus Berg came from Lübeck, but the style which he brought to Denmark is southern German. It is sometimes described as Baroque Gothic, as composition and detail often suggest dramatic movement. Claus Berg's greatest work is the altarpiece on the high altar in St Knud's Church in Odense, from c. 1515-1525. Another of the outstanding sculptors of the period was Hans Brüggemann, whose most important work is the totally unpainted altarpiece for the high altar in Schleswig Cathedral, in present-day North Germany, from 1521, originally executed for the monastic church in Bordesholm near Kiel.

The breach with the Catholic Church resulting from the Reformation in 1536 put an almost complete end to 'great' art. Sculptors like Claus Berg were forced to leave the country, for lack of orders if for nothing else. On the other hand murals continued to be painted without interruption for some decades, with largely the same stylistic characteristics as in the final years of Catholicism.

Hans Jørgen Frederiksen

The Renaissance

After the breach with the Catholic Church in 1536, Christian III established himself as head of the national church. The subsequent confiscation of church property came to form a solid economic foundation for the increase of royal power. In succeeding decades the king became the undisputed major consumer of art in the country, and this art became more and more consciously exploited to glorify the kingdom, the true evangelical faith and the monarch's own person and family.

Under Christian III the idiom and ideology of the Renaissance established itself in general. The dissemination of the new concepts was achieved primarily through immigrant artists or printed graphics. The painter and engraver Jacob Binck from Cologne played an essential role as promoter of contemporary forms from the Netherlands and Germany, and with his paintings, medallions and graphics had a decisive influence on

The Last Supper, mural from 1496 in Bellinge Church near Odense. In this portrayal of the Last Supper, the artist has made use of the curved, triangular surface in the severy to create the special shape of the long, draped table.

The sculptor Claus Berg's great crucifix in Vindinge Church in Funen was executed c. 1520 in painted oak. In expressive realism, the suffering Christ with the crown of thorns and wearing a loin cloth that almost seems to be fluttering in the breeze, is depicted in keeping with the late mediaeval conception of the Crucified Christ. The points of the cross are decorated with the symbols of the four Evangelists.

the development of secular portrait painting.

In the years following the Reformation church layouts were altered to take account of Lutheran precepts, although in many cases tolerance was shown to Catholic furnishing and frescoes. New acquisitions were modest, the most important being pulpits and benches. Together with new mural decorations and illustrated editions of the Bible, for instance Christian III's Danish Bible (1550), these show that pictures continued to be acknowledged as a didactic aid by the first reformers. In harmony with the increased cult of the individual in the Renaissance, funeral art at this time experienced a period of growth with countless sculpted tombstones and painted or carved wall monuments.

The age of Frederik II – the second half of the 16th century – is marked by affluence and growth. To an even greater extent than his father, Frederik II competed with both the nobility and other European courts in exploiting art as a means of increasing prestige and denoting status. The normative artistic impulses were received from the Netherlands, whose leading sculptor, Cornelis

Floris from Antwerp, produced more funeral works for Denmark than for any other country; these included the magnificent tombs for Frederik I (1551-1555) in Schleswig Cathedral, Herluf Trolle and Birgitte Gøye (1566-1568) in Herlufsholm Church and for Christian III (1569-1579) in Roskilde Cathedral.

The dominant artistic achievement was the rebuilding and redesigning of Kronborg Castle in Elsinore (1574-1586). The site attracted a large number of Netherlandish artists and artisans, who often remained in Elsinore, which came to be known as 'little Amsterdam'. Their descendants continued to work in Denmark without losing touch with developments in the Netherlands, the van Steenwinckel and Isaacsz families being examples of this. Gert van Groningen was the leading sculptor until 1576, and he was followed by his son Herman Gertsen. The workshop, which was responsible for the main gateway to Kronborg, might perhaps have included the idiosyncratic sculptor known as 'the Copenhagen alabaster master', whose works (the Krognos memorial in Ringsted Church, 1575, and the altarpiece for Lund Cathedral, 1577) betoken the breakthrough of the High Renaissance in Denmark.

In 1577 the king changed his plans for the modernisation of Kronborg and put the Mechelen architect Antonis van Opbergen in charge. The level of ambition was noticeably raised. Sculptors like Gert van Egen from Mechelen, who was later given the commission for the memorial to Frederik II (1594-1598) in Roskilde Cathedral, now put their stamp on the castle with a more classical Floris-like style (the entrance to the castle chapel and the altarpiece in it); the Nuremberg Georg Labenwolff's bronze fountain was erected in the

In 1581, Hans Knieper was commissioned to produce a series of woven tapestries to decorate the Banqueting Hall in Kronborg in Helsingør. The *Kronborg Tapestries*, which were completed in 1586, depict 111 Danish kings. In this one, which is the last in the series and is now in The National Museum, Frederik II is portrayed in armour with crown, orb and sceptre, and to the right of him stands Prince Christian (IV); in the background are the castles of Kronborg and Frederiksborg, which the King had built. In the fields above can be seen the emblem of the Order of the Elephant together with a brief, rhymed account of Frederik's life.

courtyard, while the Banqueting Hall was provided with a richly carved ceiling, doors and marble fireplaces. All this burned down in 1629, but the table canopy and a number of the 40 life-size tapestry portraits of Danish kings, woven between 1581 and 1586 by immigrant Flemish weavers under the leadership of Hans Knieper from Antwerp, still survive.

At the same time, a study for the tapestry of Frederik II is the oldest full-length painted portrait in Denmark (1581). As a model for the king's portrait, Knieper has presumably based himself on a bust executed by J.G. van der Schardt in 1577-1579. This kind of portrait was also engrav-ed by the Flensburg Melchior Lorck, who was working for the Danish king at this time. At the same time as the king's monumental demonstrations of his power, the higher reaches of the nobility, also keen to build, turned to their mansions. Only a few remnants of their interior decorations have survived, but the sculptors' ebullient decorations in gateways, fireplaces, etc. show that the nobility often borrowed artists and artisans working on the great royal projects, as is seen from the most remarkable mansion of the period, the astronomer Tycho Brahe's long lost Uranienborg on the island of Ven. Here Hans van Steenwinckel the elder collaborated with others including Hans Knieper and the portrait painter Tobias Gemperle from Augsburg.

Birgitte Bøggild Johannsen, Hugo Johannsen

Baroque

Christian IV carried out a conscious and active art policy. Like his predecessors, he introduced architects and sculptors from abroad in order to adorn and glorify the kingdom in general and the court in particular. The economic foundation for this artistic activity was in part the funds deriving from the Sound Dues imposed on ships sailing between the Baltic and the Kattegat.

Life at court was consciously staged with a view to fulfilling certain aesthetical and allegorical-political needs. At the great dynastic festivities such as coronations, weddings, etc., splendid processions and tournaments were organised, music and ballet performed, triumphal arches built and firework displays arranged. With their magnificent embellishments, the castles and palaces fitted in beautifully as part of this representative stage decoration.

Painting continued principally to be the domain of foreign artists, mainly from the Netherlands. It was often closely linked with the architecture and functional as adornment in the interiors. Apart from their purely aesthetic role in the overall effect of the different rooms, the narrative content of the pictures clearly also had a didactic purpose. Among the most extensive room decorations of this period is the series of large oil paintings for the ceiling in the Great Hall in Rosenborg Palace in Copenhagen, painted after 1615 by artists including Frantz Clein, Reinhold Timm, Pieter Isaacsz and his son Isaac Isaacsz. An extremely complicated iconographic programme lies behind the altogether 24 canvases, of which only 15 have survived (at Kronborg in Elsinore). They depict the conditions of human life according to the dominant philosophical and cosmological systems of the day (the planets, the ages of Man, the elements, the temperaments, the liberal arts, etc.).

At Kronborg Morten van Steenwinckel was responsible for the painted ceilings of *The Planet Gods* in the Queen's Chamber (1631-1632). For the ceiling in the King's Chamber, the Utrecht artist Gerrit van Honthorst executed scenes from

Melchior Lorck: *The Holy Family*, painted on wood and bearing the artist's monogram, dated 1552; Statens Museum for Kunst. Melchior Lorck was born in Flensborg and spent a large part of his life travelling in Europe and Turkey. This picture of Mary with the Infant Jesus and John the Baptist with the Lamb shows influences from Italian, German and Netherlandish art. Elizabeth and Joseph are seen on the left in this scene, the right half of which seems to be set in the round building standing out in the landscape.

Heliodor of Emessa's novel *Aithiopika*; these can probably be viewed as an allegory of one of the royal marriages. The same model was used by Karel van Mander III for a series of ten pictures, whose original destination and decorative intentions are unknown (nine have survived and are in the Staatliche Kunstsammlungen in Kassel in Germany). Kronborg was the intended recipient of the grandiose, but never completed project, which today goes under the name of The National Historical Paintings (started 1637); 12 have survived in locations such as Skokloster and Drottningholm Castle, both in Sweden. A few others have been returned to Denmark.

Among the royal portrait painters of European standing, mention must be made of Pieter Isaacsz, Jacob van Doordt, Karel van Mander and Abraham Wuchters; the latter two were moreover active in doing portraits of the men and women of the nobility. Prints served to disseminate portraits, including those of the king, and here Albert Haelwegh was the undisputed master.

Adriaen de Vries' *Neptune Fountain* at Frederiksborg Castle in Hillerød (1615-1622) has a place of its own in the sculpture of this period on account of its elegant and imaginatively mannered style; this work became Swedish booty in 1659, and the figures were taken to Drottningholm Castle; the fountain in Frederiksborg was reconstructed in 1888. Under Christian IV, many of the country's churches were adorned with furniture in the ornamented style known as the auricular style.

After the death of Christian IV, several of the artists continued to work under his son, Frederik III. Among the interesting new painters was Wolfgang Heimbach, who produced portraits and genre paintings,

often in the form of night pieces in the spirit of Caravaggio, while Jürgen Ovens mainly worked in a more pompous, allegorical idiom. Abel Schrøder the Younger's altarpiece from 1661-1662 in Holmen's Church in Copenhagen is done in unpainted oak and achieves its effect solely through its vivid figure scenes, surrounded by richly sculpted ornamentation.

Christian V's first court painter and master builder was Lambert van Haven whose designs included the elegant Audience Chamber in Frederiksborg Castle; the chamber was adorned 1683-1686 with paintings by the royal portrait painter Jacob d'Agar. A.C. Lamoureux' equestrian statue of the king (1685-1688) in Kongens Nytorv in Copenhagen stands as one of the principal sculptural monuments of the time. Remarkable, too, are Thomas Quellinus's splendid tombs in many Danish churches, dramatically composed, executed in rare, differently coloured types of marble and framed by monumental architectural components.

Karel van Mander III: *Christian IV*, painted 1643-1644; Frederiksborg Museum. The King was painted by one of the leading portrait artists of the day, the third generation of the Dutch painter family of van Mander. He is portrayed both as King and General, his helmet and crown lying side by side on the table to the right, while the Order of the Elephant hangs on his armour. On the wall at the back, bottom left, there is a glimpse of the King's great pride and joy, the rebuilt Frederiksborg Castle.

Abraham Wuchters' *Jupiter and Juno*, painted ceiling from c. 1660 in Rosenborg. Frederik III had two of the rooms in his father's summer house redone. Christian IV's bedroom, which subsequently became Queen Sophie Amalie's room, was decorated with paintings paying homage to the gods of the heavens, the earth and the sea. The supreme gods – Juno bearing the Queen's features – are here depicted in a sumptuous Baroque style which betrays the painter's Flemish background.

With Frederik IV's court painter Benoît Le Coffre, the portrait style from Louis XIV's court finally reached Denmark at the beginning of the 18th century. With the building of Frederiksberg Castle in Copenhagen (1699-1709) there was again a need for monumental decorations. The painted ceilings were executed by Le Coffre, including the illusionistic *A Masquerade* (c. 1704), and by Hendrik Krock, who also took part in decorating Fredensborg Palace near Copenhagen (built 1719-1721). The most outstanding portrait painter of the age, Balthasar Denner, gives an interesting insight into the customs and fashions of the upper classes, as for instance in *Coffee Party at the Home of the Reventlow Family* (c. 1743-1749, Pederstrup, Lolland).

Johan Salomon Wahl was appointed court painter to Christian VI, but he had already worked for the previous monarch. Wahl's portraits are closely related to those of Andreas Møller, though Møller is less stiff and more attractive. Johan Hörner, who was also a fine still life painter, now became what Denner had formerly been for the aristocracy and rich bourgeoisie. Christiansborg Palace, which was inaugurated in 1740, was decorated exclusively with paintings (139 in all) by the most famous French artists of the day. Art under Christian VI can be described as the last, ornate phase of late Baroque, which most often merely repeated the accepted rules and norms of the previous century.

Wahl's successor in the realm of

portrait art was the Swede C.G. Pilo, who heralded the Rococo in Denmark. In the middle of the 18th century, with his elegant brush strokes and use of colour together with his dramatic compositions, he became an incomparable interpreter of Frederik V and his court. With Louis Tocqué, whom Count A.G. Moltke for a time brought in from France, there emerged for the first time a less pompous, more natural and modern style painting in Denmark.

Several portrait painters tried to rival Pilo, first and foremost Vigilius Erichsen and Peder Als. Erichsen's magnificent full-length portrait of the Dowager Queen Juliane Marie (1776, Statens Museum for Kunst) was his principal Danish work. He subsequently worked in Russia. In his best works Peder Als anticipated the Romantic conception of portraiture as for instance in the portrait of Johannes Wiedewelt (1758, Frederiksborg Museum). The Swedish-born Johan Hörner also established himself as a portrait painter, and in the field of miniatures, the European-trained Cornelius Høyer was a supreme master.

Jens Peter Munk

Neo-Classicism

In 1738 the first Danish academy of fine arts was established under Christian VI, appointing several foreign artists as teachers, including C.G. Pilo, the German painter and architect C.M. Tuscher and the French sculptor L.-A. Le Clerc. The Danish architect Niels Eigtved became supervisor of the academy in 1748, and when the Royal Danish Academy of Fine Arts was founded in 1754, located in Charlottenborg in Copenhagen, Eigtved became its first Director. The first generation of Danish-born artists – the painters Nicolai Abildgaard, Jens Juel and Erik Pauel-

sen – was trained in the Charlottenborg Academy. Until the 1770s the teachers were predominantly foreigners, including the sculptor J.-F.-J. Saly, who was the Director of the Academy until 1771, and who executed the equestrian monument of Frederik V in Amalienborg Square in Copenhagen. Among the Danish professors there was Johannes Wiedewelt, who trained in France and Rome. Here, he was influenced by the German art theorist J.J. Winckelmann and introduced his Neo-Classical theories to Denmark, both in his own sculptures, among which were the sarcophagi of Christian VI and Frederik V in Roskilde Cathedral, and in his book *Thoughts on Taste in the Arts in General* from 1762.

The Academy pupils competed for prizes and medals, and the major

Balthasar Denner: *The Artist and His Family Making Music*, painted c. 1730; Statens Museum for Kunst. Denner had trained in Germany and worked as a portraitist in several northern European courts. A powerful sense of family, a frugal life and simple clothing in discreet colours were the characteristics of the religious Mennonite environment from which Denner came.

As a painter and architect, *Nicolai Abildgaard*, 1743-1809, was a leading figure in Danish neo-classicism and early Romanticism. He trained in the Royal Danish Academy of Fine Arts in Copenhagen, and during a stay in Rome he made a close study of Classical and Renaissance idiom. Here, he also executed the main work of his youth, *Wounded*

Philoctetes (1774-1775, The Danish National Gallery). Abildgaard took the inspiration for his motifs from the world of literature, principally portraying the unbalanced and passionate, and his many extant drawings reflect his vivid imagination. In his idiom he was closely related to J.H. Füssli, whom he met during his stay in Rome. As a Professor (from 1778) and later Director (1788-1791 and from 1801) in The Royal Danish Academy of Fine Arts in Copenhagen Abildgaard exerted a great influence on the young artists of his day. He created a large number of works for the royal family, including ten large-scale paintings representing the deeds of the Oldenborg monarchs for the Great Hall in Christiansborg Palace. Seven of them were lost in the fire of 1794, but the sketches are still in existence in Statens Museum for Kunst, which owns the largest collection of Abildgaard's works. After c. 1800, Abildgaard mainly painted motifs from the Classical world. One of his architectural designs was the Apis Temple in Frederiksberg Garden.

Vibeke Skov

Nicolai Abildgaard: *Wounded Philoctetes*, painted in Rome 1774-1775; Statens Museum for Kunst. Abildgaard has portrayed the legendary Greek hero who on his way to Troy was bitten in the foot by a poisonous snake and, suffering from a malodorous sore, was abandoned by his friends on the island of Lemnos. The powerfully illuminated, crouching body, clearly in great pain, exploits the surface of the picture to the extreme. The painter sent the picture to the Academy in Copenhagen as a demonstration of the skills he had acquired during his study journey to Rome, during which he was inspired by Antique sculptures such as the *Belvedere Torso*.

gold medal was accompanied by the possibility of prolonged study visit to France and Italy. For Nicolai Abildgaard the study years in Rome 1772-1776 were of the greatest significance. Here he could move among the works of art of Antiquity and the Renaissance and make the acquaintance of the European artists of his day, including J.T. Sergel and J.H. Füssli. Abildgaard's literary and historical knowledge was greater than that of any other Danish artist. His painting combined the Neo-Classical ideals of serenity and the sublime with a Pre-Romantic intensity.

His main work, a series of representations of the history of the kings of the Oldenborg dynasty, was destroyed with Christiansborg Palace in the 1794 fire; but he left a large number of smaller paintings, including some with motifs from the works of Shakespeare, Holberg and Classical authors.

Erik Pauelsen was the first to make national landscape painting his speciality, executing dramatic scenes from Norway during a journey there in 1788. Jens Juel, too, was a pioneer in Danish landscape painting, though his principal field was

J.-F.-J. Saly: *Equestrian Statue of Frederik V* in Amalienborg Palace Square. This bronze statue was commissioned in 1752 from the French sculptor Saly, who two years later became Professor and Director in the newly-founded Royal Danish Academy of Fine Arts in Copenhagen. Asiatisk Kompagni funded the expensive sculpture, which was cast in 1768 and unveiled in the palace square in 1771. The equestrian statue of Marcus Aurelius in the Capitol in Rome is one of its models, and it stands as one of the major works of European sculpture, harmonising perfectly with the square and the mansions surrounding it.

Jens Juel: *Picture of the Ryberg Family*, painted 1796-1797; Statens Museum for Kunst. From the middle of the 1780s, Juel painted a number of large-scale representative group portraits. In beautiful rural surroundings, he has here presented the merchant Niels Ryberg, sitting on a bench under an old oak tree together with his son and daughter-in-law.

portraits. Inspired by contemporary English and French art, Juel introduced a more 'natural' presentation of his royal, noble and bourgeois customers, while often presenting a landscape or landscaped garden as a background to his portraits.

Soon after 1800 the next generation of artists trained in Paris, modelling themselves on the leading painters of the Napoleonic era, with J.-L. David at their head. The painter C.G. Kratzenstein Stub, who died young, was Denmark's only Romantic painter, while J.L. Lund went from Paris to Rome, where he came under the influence of the German Nazarenes. However, it fell to C.W. Eckersberg to introduce the French ideas to his pupils at the Academy of Fine Arts in Copenhagen, where he was appointed professor in 1818.

The Golden Age

C.W. Eckersberg's teaching was an important influence on the following generation's study of nature, in which landscape painting based on sketches done *en plein air* came to represent the inner as well as the outer world. Realism, kept in check by an underlying idealism, is characteristic of the period between 1816 and 1848, which

is popularly referred to as the Golden Age. There is no contemporary use of this term, which is formed by analogy with the term as used in Danish literary history.

Like most of his pupils, Eckersberg worked in almost all genres of his art: history painting, portraits and landscapes as well as marine painting. The object of the Academy teaching was principally to train history painters, but the country's economic difficulties after the national bankruptcy in 1813 left no possibility of developing this elevated genre to any great extent. Portrait painting was the most reliable source of income, but Eckersberg and his pupils also received a few commissions for religious paintings. C.F. Hansen's new Christiansborg Palace was adorned with large paintings by Eckersberg and J.L. Lund and sculptural friezes by H.E. Freund (*The Ragnarok Frieze*, started 1825) and H.V. Bissen.

Scandinavian myths and legends made their appearance in visual art as a result of the national awakening in the 1770s, and they were treated by both Abildgaard and Erik Pauelsen. Later J.L. Lund, Kratzenstein Stub and Eckersberg produced paintings on Nordic subjects for the Academy of Fine Arts, while Constantin Hansen and Lorenz Frølich gave intensive treatment to the legends of the Scandinavian gods and to Danish history.

The most famous artist of the period, the sculptor Bertel Thorvaldsen, did not concern himself with Nordic themes, but derived his inspiration from Antiquity. Resident in Rome 1797-1838, Thorvaldsen was the first Danish artist to achieve a place in the history of European art. His unique reputation was an inspiration in his native land, also after his death, not least through the museum that was

built in Copenhagen 1839-1848 to house his works and collections. Thorvaldsen's first great success, *Jason* (1802-1803) was followed by a large number of other works from ancient mythology as well as monuments such as the equestrian statue of Prince Poniatowski in Warsaw and the monument to Pope Pius VII in St Peter's Church in Rome. He also executed busts and portrait statues for a large European clientele; in the years following 1821 in Denmark he worked on statues for the newly-built Cathedral, with figures representing Jesus and the twelve Apostles and the Angel of Baptism.

Young artists from all over Europe, for whom a stay in Rome was the most important element in their artistic education, gathered around Thorvaldsen. The grand style of the Classical works in Italy set the limits of the realism that was just beginning to make its appearance in the works of the painters Constantin Hansen and Jørgen Roed. A contrasting tendency is found in Wilhelm Marstrand and Martinus Rørbye, who in the 1830s introduced an anecdotal kind of genre painting. Jørgen Sonne, Christen Dalsgaard and Frederik Vermehren provided a heroic treatment of the lives of Danish fishermen and farmers, inspired by the art historian N.L.

Bertel Thorvaldsen: *Maria Fjodorovna Barjatinskaja*, marble sculpture from 1818; Thorvaldsen's Museum. Thorvaldsen's studio in Rome produced countless portraits for clients throughout Europe. In a dress inspired by the Classical models in fashion at the time, he has here portrayed a 25-year-old Russian princess with a Classical serenity undisturbed by the momentary contemplative gesture.

C.W. Eckersberg: *A Naked Woman Arranging Her Hair in Front of a Mirror, Seen from Behind*; painting from c. 1841, The Hirschsprung Collection. An essential part of the tuition in the Academy of Fine Arts was drawing and painting from a nude – male – model, but around 1830, as a professor at the Academy, Eckersberg also introduced the study of female models. A harmoniously simple and sophisticated composition distinguishes this picture, painted by the mature Eckersberg. The eye is not content to rest on the well-proportioned anatomy of the back, but is drawn to the mirror, the frame of which, however, only provides the setting for part of the woman's face and body.

Høyen, who like the sculptor H.E. Freund exerted a profound influence on the thinking of the younger artists. Freund's home in Materialgården in Copenhagen, decorated in Pompeiian style and filled with furniture inspired by the models of Antiquity, was a meeting place for them. This decorative art was further developed on a monumental scale in such places as the Entrance Hall in Copenhagen University by Constantin Hansen, H.V. Bissen and Georg Hilker.

The most gifted of Eckersberg's students was Christen Købke, whose short career represents one of the high points in Danish art. Købke's portraits of his family circle and his close friends are honest portrayals of

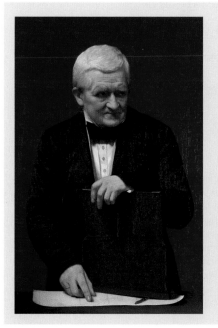

Through his art and his work as professor at The Royal Danish Academy of Fine Arts in Copenhagen, *C.W. Eckersberg*, 1783-1853, who is known as the 'father of Danish painting', was of crucial importance to the generation of Golden Age painters in Denmark. Before being appointed Professor at the Academy in 1818, Eckersberg had been a pupil of J.-L. David in Paris, who taught him the importance of being faithful to nature and the well-balanced composition and simple, light colouring of neo-classicism. Eckersberg went on to Rome in 1813, and there he joined the circle around Thorvaldsen and executed a large number of architectural pictures and views of the city based on a mixture of sober realism and the classical principles of composition. A major work from Rome is the portrait of Thorvaldsen (1814, Charlottenborg). The appointment as Professor in Copenhagen led to numerous commissions for portraits from the King, aristocracy and ordinary citizens, and in addition Eckersberg produced some large scale history paintings, altarpieces and a large number of seascapes. In particular in his later years Eckersberg was preoccupied with the theory of perspective, which together with plein air painting played an important part in his teaching. Among Eckersberg's pupils were Christen Købke, Wilhelm Marstrand and Constantin Hansen.

Vibeke Skov

Christen Købke: *Scene Outside the North Gate of the Citadel*, painted 1834; the Ny Carlsberg Glyptotek. As a pupil of C.W. Eckersberg, Købke made an accurate study of nature and paid meticulous attention to his composition, which often led to his spending long periods working on his paintings. This picture of a summer's day at the entrance to the Citadel in Copenhagen – where Købke had grown up – cost him three months of daily struggle, as he has recalled in a letter to his sister.

everyday life, but he also demonstrates boldness in his compositions and colour schemes, especially in the portraits of his fellow artists. He sought the motifs for his landscapes in the immediate neighbourhood of Copenhagen, and with his pictures of Frederiksborg Castle he created sensitive paintings of one of Denmark's great historical monuments. Købke

Christen Købke, 1810-1848, was only twelve years old when he became a pupil at the Royal Danish Academy of Fine Arts in Copenhagen. C.W. Eckersberg was of the greatest importance for his artistic development, and Købke was taught by him from 1828 to 1832. Købke, who during a short life painted the finest landscapes and portraits of the Danish Golden Age, mainly took his motifs from close to his home; until 1833 this was the fortress known as The Citadel, and then Blegdammen near the Sortedam Lake in Copenhagen. It is from here that some of his best pictures stem, a large number of well-composed and colouristically harmonious paintings, for instance *View of Østerbro in the Light of Morning* from 1836 (Statens Museum for Kunst), and drawings and studies. Most of Købke's portraits were also of those close to him: family members and friends. From the mid-1830s he included Frederiksborg Castle in his narrow range of motifs and experimented with larger formats. Købke was here under the influence of the

national romantic tendencies of the time, not least resulting from personal contacts with the 'ideologue' of the movement, the art historian N.L. Høyen, and with the painter J.Th. Lundbye. In keeping with this influence, impulses from the German national romantic painter C.D. Friedrich are discernible in some of Købke's works.

Vibeke Skov

Constantin Hansen: *A company of Danish Artists in Rome*, painted 1837; Statens Museum for Kunst. In his Roman lodgings, with a tiled floor and doors opened to the balcony overlooking the city, Constantin Hansen has portrayed a group of Golden Age artists. Placed along a delicately sinu-ous line incorporating both surface and space, we see from left to right: Hansen himself, Gottlieb Bindesbøll and Martinus Rørbye, Wilhelm Marstrand, Albert Küchler and Ditlev Blunck together with Jørgen Sonne, and finally Constantin Hansen's dog to round off the composition.

did not occupy a prominent place in his day, and neither did the excellent portrait painter C.A. Jensen, whose career and artistic ambitions were opposed by N.L. Høyen.

National landscape painting dominated in the 1840s, from Zealand in the cases of J. Th. Lundbye and P.C. Skovgaard, and from Jutland with Dankvart Dreyer, Christen Dalsgaard and Martinus Rørbye.

Almost all important Danish artists studied in Italy in the 1830s and 1840s. They frequently paid visits to the Norwegian painter J.C. Dahl in Dresden, whose relationship with Danish art continued to be close and inspirational. Munich was also an artistic centre where Danish artists settled for shorter or longer periods, these including Jørgen Sonne and Wilhelm Bendz. In contrast to the international outlook of the 18th century as seen in Abildgaard and Juel, nationalism for the generation after Eckersberg meant ignorance of the major international trends in France and England. The national character took precedence over an awareness of contemporary European art.

Charlotte Christensen

National Romanticism

By the mid-19th century a turning point had been reached in artistic developments in Denmark. In the 1850s, the Golden Age was replaced by a period of stagnation that over the next two decades actually turned into a period of decline.

In sculpture it was principally Bissen who took up the Classical legacy after Thorvaldsen and added to it certain qualities from the National Romantic tendencies of the time; his famous war memorial to the Danish soldier, *Landsoldaten*, (1850-1858) in Fredericia is the example par excellence of his late fusing of these two – originally separate – main tendencies in the sculptural art of the Golden Age. J.A. Jerichau, too, started out from Thorvaldsen, but Classicism's idealised treatment of form here gave way to some extent to dramatic and psychological forms of expression which conflicted with Thorvaldsen's principles.

In painting, the Golden Age tradition was maintained in the bourgeois classicism of the Eckersberg school, which mingled the French inheritance from J.-L. David with impulses from German Biedermeier and a powerful admixture of Danish National Romanticism. The principal figures in this period include Constantin Hansen, Jørgen Roed, Wilhelm Marstrand, Frederik Vermehren and Julius Exner. The national traditions of the 1840s in landscape painting were in succeeding decades continued in particular by P.C. Skovgaard and Vilhelm Kyhn. For the remainder of the century, this tradition lived on with remarkable tenacity, especially in Kyhn's many younger admirers.

By the 1860s, the bourgeois-national art tradition was already marked by a visibly growing lack of drive: The treatment of form was weakened by an increasingly meticulous tendency to break down the overall effect into an infinite number of details and nuances together with a corresponding predilection for subsuming the colours of the picture into a brownish overall tone known as *galleritone*.

There were isolated attempts to break out of this decadence. Most remarkable was the so-called 'Neo-Baroque' movement, the most important exponent of which was Carl Bloch. In boldly conceived, dramatic figure compositions, with roots in the Italian, Spanish and Northern European Baroque realisms of the 17th century, he sought to recreate a monumental and powerful historical painting; a typical example is *Samson in the Philistine Treadmill* (1863, Statens Museum for Kunst). Other approaches to an invigorating confrontation with the con-

P.C. Skovgaard: *Beech Forest in May*, painted 1857; Statens Museum for Kunst. Near a mansion close to Vordingborg in South Zealand, Skovgaard has painted a beech forest that has just come into full leaf, a piece of cultivated Danish natural scenery with well-dressed children going for a walk with their Broholm dog.

The Skagen Painters is a general designation for a group of Scandinavian painters who worked in Skagen with Brøndums Hotel as their rallying ground from the mid-1870s to the beginning of the present century. Under the influence of French plein air painting they portrayed fisher-folk, other Skagen residents and the sea, and they were also fond of portraying each other. The Danish representatives of this school of artists included Michael and Anna Ancher, P.S. Krøyer and Viggo Johansen. Michael Ancher, (1849-1927), who came to Skagen in 1874, applied a sober realism to his portrayals of the laborious everyday lives of the poor fishermen and their heroic efforts as lifeboatmen at sea. Anna Ancher (1859-1935), who as the daughter of an innkeeper had grown up in Skagen, took her motifs from the everyday indoor lives of the residents there and her own relatives, whom she portrayed tenderly and with a sure sense of light and colour. P.S. Krøyer (1851-1909) is in particular known for his light, atmospheric summer landscapes, bluish beach scenes and cheerful lunch scenes, while Viggo Johansen (1851-1935) painted impressionistic landscapes and interiors. Among the other painters in the Skagen school were Laurits Tuxen, the Norwegian Christian Krohg and the Swede Oscar Björck.

Vibeke Skov

servatism of the national school are seen at the time. Otto Bache went to Paris as early as the 1860s to seek new inspiration in the French naturalism of the day.

This reinvigorating tendency really only took off in earnest in the following decade when a large number of young Danish painters felt the need to free themselves from Danish self-sufficiency and seek new impulses abroad. Laurits Tuxen, Theodor Philipsen, P.S. Krøyer and many others went to Paris in the 1870s,

Anna Ancher: *The Girl in the Kitchen*, painted 1883-1886; The Hirschsprung Collection. The picture is also known under the title of The Red Skirt. A quiet everyday scene is depicted here, so that it is the sunshine and colours that create life and atmosphere in the harmoniously composed interior with the woman standing with her back to us. Anna Ancher, who was born in Skagen, took her inspiration partly from 17th-century Dutch art for her paintings of home, family and the everyday lives of the people of Skagen.

where they attended the private art school of the Realist Léon Bonnat. National conservatism suffered an ignominious defeat in 1878 on account of the severe criticisms which the international press levelled at Danish art in the World Exhibition in Paris. This really gave impetus to the young avant garde. In opposition to the Academy of Fine Arts, the stronghold of national self-sufficiency, the Artists' Free Study Schools were founded at the beginning of the 1880s, with Tuxen and Krøyer among those teaching on the basis of their contacts with contemporary French art.

Realism and Naturalism
The 1880s were to be the decade of Realism and Naturalism. The closely related aims of the two currents mingled with each other and were not clearly distinguishable from each other in most of the young artists of the time. This applied in particular to the Skagen painters, who combined realistic figure painting and depictions of the life of the ordinary people with a naturalistic open-air study of light, colour and atmosphere. In addition to Krøyer, Anna and

Michael Ancher together with Viggo Johansen were the main figures in this colony of Scandinavian artists. Among the other Danish pioneers for new trends in the art of the 1880s mention must be made here of Hans Smidth and L.A. Ring, who both went in the direction of distinct social realism, seeking their motifs among farmers and farm workers. In 1882, Kristian Zahrtmann took over the tuition in the free study schools, and his powerful colourism together with his strong sense of form was of great importance to several generations of pupils, including especially the Funen artists Johannes Larsen, Fritz Syberg and Peter Hansen as well as Poul S. Christiansen and Niels Larsen Stevns. A special position in the pioneering Naturalist art of the 1880s is occupied by the 'cattle painter' Theodor Philipsen, who through personal contact with Paul Gauguin developed into the sole Danish Impressionist of his generation. The picture *Autumn in the Deer Park* from 1886 (Statens Museum for Kunst) is an epoch-making work in this context. Among the younger artists for whom Philipsen was of significance as an inspira-

P.S.Krøyer: *Summer Evening near Skagen. The Artist's Wife with Her Dog on the Beach*, painted 1892; Skagens Museum. In 1889 Krøyer had married the painter Marie Triepche, who unlike Anna Ancher did not have the opportunity of developing her artistic gifts in her marriage with the virtuosos painter. Marie often posed for Krøyer's tender portrayals of his beautiful wife, as here with their dog in the romantic light of the twilight hour.

tion were Albert Gottschalk and several of the Funen artists.

Alongside these tendencies, historical painting underwent a new period of growth. After Frederiksborg Castle had been ravaged by fire in 1859 and rebuilt between 1860 and 1875, it was fitted out to house a collection of national historical paintings, and this provided new tasks for the historical painters. It was the art-loving brewer Carl Jacobsen who financed the establishment of this generous forum for artists wishing to depict the history of their country.

Sculpture did not undergo a rapid development like that seen in painting. Only a single artist, August Saabye, emerges as a memorable naturalistic pioneer in the sculpture of the period.

In 1891, The Free Exhibition was established as a counterblast to the conservative annual exhibition at the Charlottenborg Academy of Fine Arts in Copenhagen. The decade was particularly marked by a new generation's search for style and an urge for intellectual engagement as a reaction to the sensual naturalism of the 1880s. The new driving forces in this kind of painting included Joakim and Niels Skovgaard, Vilhelm Hammershøi, Johan Rohde, Agnes and Harald Slott-Møller, J.F. Willumsen and Ejnar Nielsen. One particular feature of the new search for a style was often a historicising cult of monumental decorative painting; the main achievement of the period was Joakim Skovgaard's gigantic fresco in Viborg Cathedral, executed between 1901 and 1906 with the assistance among others of Larsen Stevns, who later undertook several tasks of a similar kind. Symbolist forms of expression were now seen, and a new stylised treatment of form and surface was introduced, related to the international Art Nouveau movement. In sculpture, the Skovgaard brothers and Willumsen made important contributions to a renewal of a related kind, and in addition Symbolism found its most original representative in Niels Hansen Jacobsen.

Finn Terman Frederiksen

The First Decades of the Twentieth Century

Especially thanks to the Funen artists, Naturalism and Impressionism managed to retain a position of prominence in Danish art for some time into the twentieth century. However, between 1905 and the First World War there were clear signs of a change of direction. At the same time as Aksel Jørgensen and P. Rostrup Bøyesen painted the dark sides and outposts of the city, an idealistic opposition to open-air painting was arising among a number of young artists including Oluf Hartmann and Jens Adolf Jerichau. Their dramatic figure pictures with mythological references drew on the ideas of Vitalism and Symbolism and was given strong encouragement by the art historian Vilhelm Wanscher, who pleaded for a return to the 'grand style' of the Renaissance and Baroque in painting. Related to these painters was the sculptor Kai Nielsen, whose work is shot through with Vitalist ideas and a predilection for the erotic. In particular he specialised in mythological representations of the childhood of mankind.

A broad modernistic breakthrough came late to Denmark, only really asserting itself during the First World War. However, in the decade preceding the war a number artists from the young generation began to look towards Post-Impressionistic French art, first Sigurd Swane, Harald Giersing, Edvard Weie and the Swedish-born Karl Isakson, and later Olaf Rude and William Scharff. In the first instance it was Cézanne who made the greatest impression, except on Sigurd Swane, whose scintillating, light-filled paintings represented a combination of Fauvism and Impressionism. About 1910 Giersing revealed himself as a leading figure in the confrontation with Naturalism's subservience to the optical reality, both in his paintings with gentle stippling deriving from Neo-Impressionism, in cool studio paintings with Expressionist forebears and in his articles arguing in favour of an art that placed work with the medium itself in first

Peter Hansen: *The Ploughman Turns*, painted 1900-1902; Faaborg Museum. A small group of the painter Kristian Zahrtmann's gifted pupils came from Funen and became known under the name of 'The Funen Painters'. They were also disparagingly called 'The Peasant Painters' because they took many of their motifs from life in the country and the small towns, life that was down-to-earth and intimate. However, it was rather the picturesque qualities, colour and light, that concerned Peter Hansen and some of the others in pictures such as this of the man ploughing the rich soil, a keenly sensed portrayal of a momentary situation.

Even by the time he first exhibited at Charlottenborg in 1885 with his *Portrait of a Girl* (The Hirschsprung Collection, Copenhagen), *Vilhelm Hammershøi*, 1864-1916, had already discovered the manner of expression which was to be characteristic of his artistic production in the future: a severe architectural composition and a narrow range of colours entirely dominated by shades of grey. Throughout his life he was preoccupied with a strictly limited circle of motifs encompassing interiors from his home, portraits of his family and friends, and architecture and landscape paintings. Light and air are of central importance in Hammershøi's paintings, often assuming an almost physical consistency. He is best known for his many interiors portraying simple and sparsely furnished rooms. They are often devoid of human figures, but in many there is an isolated female figure, usually stationary and with her face turned away. In the 1890s Hammershøi executed a number of architecture paintings, especially of Amalienborg and Christiansborg Palace, both of which are shrouded in a light mist like that in his Zealand landscapes. Hammershøi's stylish and delicately shaded paintings assumed an isolated position in relation to the predominantly naturalistic Danish art of the day. In 1891 he was one of those helping to establish *Den Frie Udstilling* (The Free Exhibition).

Vibeke Skov

place. At the same time the artists of this generation found a common meeting place and world of motifs on the island of Christiansø near Bornholm. Karl Isakson and Edvard Weie were leading figures in the circle of artists who later became known as the Bornholm School. A characteristic feature of these two was a cultivation of pure colour that took the pure spectral colours as its

starting point, a task which after Isakson's death in 1922 Weie continued in great, romantic compositions.

1915 saw the formation of a new artists' organisation: it took the name of Grønningen and encompassed a large group of the Modernists. However, some Modernists stood aloof from this organisation, for instance, Jais Nielsen, who worked on a surface-accentuating, schematic cubism, and Vilhelm Lundstrøm, who in 1917-1918 introduced collage, montage and the non-figurative picture into Denmark. Together with these pioneers, the artists in Grønningen took part in the Modernistic breakthrough that erupted with explosive force during the First World War, stimulated both by a large number of modernists from the rest of Scandinavia who were living in Copenhagen during the war, and by extraordinary economic circumstances.

Modernism was in retreat in the post-war period. However, the group calling itself The Four, consisting of

Vilhelm Hammershøi: *Dust Motes Dancing in Sunlight*, painted 1900; The Ordrupgaard Collection. The sunbeams filtering through the window panes, are given substance by the particles of dust.

J.F. Willumsen: *Nature Fear. After the Storm No 2*, painted 1916; J.F. Willumsens Museum. Several of Willumsen's pictures from mountainous regions and coasts, executed at the beginning of the 20th century, express an optimistic relationship to light, air and sea. In this picture, which Willumsen painted during the First World War, the life-giving powers of nature have 'got out of control' and become demonic and destructive in a vision in glaring light and strident colours of Man's angst.

Axel Salto, Karl Larsen, Svend Johansen and Vilhelm Lundstrøm represented in the 1920s a continuation of the French connection, often in the form of an art characterised by purism and classicism. A representational art, resting on geometrical construction principles, was at the same time being developed by Georg Jacobsen in Paris in close association with the Mexican painter Diego Rivera.

Sculpture was not central to Danish Modernism, but a few individuals did help to represent the movement: Adam Fischer with stereometrically simplified statuettes, Johannes Bjerg and Einar Utzon-Frank with form-conscious, stylised figures. Gerhard Henning worked on giving sculptural form to the erotic, in particular with a number of female figures. However, as time passed he was influenced by a new classicism which was also to be seen in Johannes Bjerg, Adam Fischer, Astrid Noack and Utzon-Frank. Not least Utzon-Frank's classicism came to be representative of the sculpture of the inter-war years, partly by dint of the many large commissions he received, partly through his work over many years in the School of Sculpture in the Academy of Fine

Edvard Weie: *Mindet. Christiansø*, painted 1912; Statens Museum for Kunst. Weie was one of the artists who worked on Christiansø near Bornholm at the beginning of the 20th century. Here they found sea and cliffs, vegetation and light reminiscent of Italy, and it was cheap to live here. Weie's many pictures of the little grove called Mindet is characterised by broad, rhythmical brush strokes and harmoniously modulated, light-drenched colours.

Kai Nielsen: *The Århus Girl*; bronze sculpture from 1921; the Ny Carlsberg Glyptotek. As in several other figures of girls and women, Kai Nielsen has with a both robust and delicate sensuousness portrayed the way in which the young woman's modesty gives way to an awakening consciousness of sexuality and fertility

Arts, where he was professor 1918-1955. From the second half of the 1930s naturalistic sculpture experienced a renaissance with Mogens Bøggild and Knud Nellemose. Aksel Jørgensen was another professor of influence at the Academy of Fine Arts where he influenced several generations of sculptors by insisting on universal principles of composition, engaging in social matters and experimenting with graphic work.

Expressionism, Surrealism and Abstract Art

Another new direction in the inter-war years was Expressionist landscape painting, with Jens Søndergaard and Oluf Høst as its main representatives. In addition to these movements the period was marked by a younger generation's confrontation with the light French colours and formalism of Modernism. Among the artists representing this tendency were Niels Lergaard, Lauritz Hartz and Karl Bovin. The last two were among the originators in 1932 of the group of artists called Corner. The sombre, earth-coloured, often deliberately rough and unpolished painting which was typical of the group from the end of the 1920s and earned them the nickname of 'the dark painters', was replaced in the 1930s by the brighter tone and more flowing brush that were typical of the period. And that was to be seen, too, among the lyrical painters of nature and everyday life who gradually came to typify Grønningen, for example Erik Hoppe and Knud Agger.

Consistently constructivist art made little general impact on Denmark, but it had one representative in Franciska Clausen, who spent the inter-war years in Germany and France, where she was originally the pupil and close collaborator of Fernand Léger, later a co-founder of the

group called Cercle et Carré, which exhorted the international avant-garde of Constructivism to oppose the progress of Surrealism.

Surrealism came to Denmark at the beginning of the 1930s, introduced by Wilhelm Freddie, Vilhelm Bjerke Petersen, Ejler Bille and Richard Mortensen. In 1934 the last three were the driving force behind the exhibition and periodical Linien, which stood for a Miró-inspired, abstract Surrealism. In 1935 Bjerke Petersen left the group and formed in collaboration with Wilhelm Freddie a figurative Surrealist group with contacts with the international Surrealist movement. Bille, Henry Heerup, Sonja Ferlov Mancoba, Robert Jacobsen and Richard Mortensen have all executed sculptures linked to the ideas and idiom of Surrealism, especially smaller figures which

Vilhelm Lundstrøm: *Composition*, painted 1929; Aarhus Kunstmuseum. In a simplified idiom and strict composition, Lundstrøm painted works that were often dominated by a large, white, enamel jug. The forms are close to the basic solid geometrical forms recommended by Cézanne – the cone, the cube and the sphere.

combine abstraction with organic form. In continuation of this came Erik Thommesen's abstractions deriving from human figures and Sonja Ferlov Mancoba's later figures based on the mask.

Hanne Abildgaard

Post-1945

The isolation of Danish artists during the Second World War intensified the need to become a part of international artistic life. Immediately after the end of the war painters including Mogens Andersen, Gunnar Aagaard Andersen and Richard Mortensen and the sculptor Robert Jacobsen went to Paris. While Mogens Andersen derived his inspiration from the lyrical and abstract French art of the inter-war years, Mortensen and Jacobsen became preoccupied with the new concrete and non-figurative art centred on the

Franciska Clausen: *The Vase and the Pipes*, painted 1929; Aarhus Kunstmuseum. The picture was painted at the time of her break with the French painter Fernand Léger. In clear symbolical language it tells of the distinction between male and female, the pipes and the vase, the broken relationship and the withered flowers.

Galérie Denise René in Paris. With this, Mortensen left the expressionism which had once brought him close to surrealism, while Robert

Erik Hoppe: *Street Scene. The View from Thorvaldsens Museum Looking Towards Frederiksholms Kanal*, painted 1935-1936; Louisiana. The row of houses along Frederiksholms Kanal in Copenhagen is a recurrent motif in Hoppe's pictures from this period.

Jacobsen, who was still influenced by the fantastic painter and sculptor Henry Heerup, purged his sculpture of every figurative association. Robert Jacobsen's position as the most important, internationally known Danish sculptor of the post-war era has perhaps only been disputed by the surrealist Jørgen Haugen Sørensen and the very versatile and considerably younger Per Kirkeby.

Encouraged by related French influences, the group of artists called Linien II was formed in 1947 in Copenhagen, including among its members Richard Mortensen, Robert Jacobsen, Albert Mertz, Ib Geertsen, Søren Georg Jensen, Gunnar Aagaard Andersen, Paul Gadegaard, Preben Hornung and others. For several of them, the new objective art became a collective experience through which they passed on their way to a more personal expression. Irrespective of all differences among themselves, the artists in Linien II formed their own line vis-à-vis the Cobra painting which became Denmark's most important contribution to post-war European art.

Cobra was formed in 1948 in Paris by a number of spontaneously abstract painters from Denmark, Belgium and Holland, with the Belgian poet Christian Dotremont and the Dane Asger Jorn as its anchormen. The name Cobra was formed from Copenhagen, Brussels and Amsterdam. Jorn's almost all-embracing creativity and his many contacts guaranteed the group's international character and outlook. In the three years during which it was possible to keep Cobra together as a movement, the operation was kept going with intense energy, fostering several exhibitions and periodicals. But the typical Cobra style of painting culminated only after the international group had been formally disbanded in 1951. Among the most important Danish artists were Egill Jacobsen, Carl-Henning Pedersen and Else Alfelt. Others such as Ejler Bille and Erik Thommesen were further away in relation to Cobra and distanced themselves from the international aims of the movement. Together with the painter Harald Leth they formed the March Exhibition as early as 1951.

In discreet protest against the abstraction in Linien II and Cobra there arose in the middle of the 1950s a moralistic, humanist art that – in the case of Svend Wiig Hansen and Dan Sterup-Hansen – had as its central feature the concept of mankind under threat, or else chose as its themes the urban community in the shadow of atomic war, as was the case with the Renaissance-influenced graphic artist Palle Nielsen. They were Academy pupils of Aksel Jørgensen, and the exhibitions 'Mennesket' (Mankind) in Clausens Art Gallery, together with individual associations of artists (like for instance Corner and Kammeraterne (The Comrades)), represented more traditional, figurative art. At the same time a group of older painters

Jens Søndergaard: *City Hall Square*, painted 1930; Statens Museum for Kunst. In this painting, in which Copenhagen City Hall can just be distinguished on the left, the snow creates light and life and contrast in the bustling, expressive and colourful pictorial manner characteristic of Søndergaard.

including Jens Søndergaard, Erik Hoppe and Niels Lergaard cultivated the expressive potential of colour in relation to intimate, personally experienced motifs. The 1950s were a time of upheaval, with ever sharper distinctions between on the one hand tradition and renewal and on the other national roots and international influences.

Experimental Art

Meanwhile, the internationalisation of Danish artistic life was being intensified: In 1958 the Louisiana Museum of Modern Art opened in Humlebæk. At the same time major international exhibitions made it ever easier for Danish artists to follow movements abroad. Especially the stir caused by Documenta II in Kassel in 1959 helped to reinforce the influence not least of American art in Denmark. Developments in West Germany were also soon striking enough to challenge the traditionally strong position of French art in Danish artistic life. A German resident in Denmark, Arthur Köpcke, opened a gallery in Copenhagen in 1958, which for the following four years became an ideologically important platform for a number of boundary-breaking experimental happenings, etc. in the as yet somewhat provincial Copenhagen exhibition life. The traditional view of art

Robert Jacobsen, 1912-1993, was self-taught as a sculptor and graphic artist. His earliest sculptures were figures in wood and stone, including a series of *Fabulous Beasts*, the shape of which was inspired by the encounter with Asger Jorn in the 1940s. In 1947, Robert Jacobsen went to Paris, where he settled and became linked to the Galerie Denise René. That same year he began to work in iron, and he left the closed form, moving instead to open iron constructions of rivetted elements. These non-figurative sculptures, which at first were painted black, are a kind of spatial drawing, characterised by simplicity and rhythmical elegance. During the 1950s Robert Jacobsen developed small, imaginative, humanoid figures of scrap, dolls, which were inspired by the African art he himself collected. Later, he incorporated colours into his constructivist sculptures, and about 1965 he started on large-scale reliefs in wood and iron. In addition, he undertook a large number of official adornments in Denmark and abroad. Alongside his sculptural work, Robert Jacobsen went in for coloured graphics. He lived in France until 1969 and was a professor at the Academies of Fine Arts in Munich (1962-1981) and Copenhagen (1976-1985).

Vibeke Skov

was also disputed by others: The first Danish Fluxus festival was held in Nikolaj Church in Copenhagen in 1962, just two years after the movement had been launched in Wiesbaden in Germany, and the Danish section of Fluxus encompassed actions and happenings by, for instance, the composer Henning Christiansen and the sculptor Eric Andersen. In protest at the exhibitions in Charlottenborg and the Artists' Autumn Exhibition, the

Robert Jacobsen: *Untitled*; sculpture in wrought iron from c. 1959; Louisiana. A move Robert Jacobsen had made towards non-representational art at the beginning of the 1940s reached its full flowering during his stay in France, with sculptures in iron based on simple geometrical shapes.

Asger Jorn, 1914-1973, is one of the most important Danish artists of the post-war period. After staying in Paris, where he was a pupil of Fernand Léger from 1936-1937, Jorn joined the group of Danish abstract artists. Together with Belgian and Dutch artists, he founded the Cobra Group in 1948, living abroad, mainly in Paris, from 1953. With his starting point in surrealism, primitive art and Nordic medieval art, and influenced by e.g. Paul Klee and Joan Miró, Asger Jorn developed in the 1940s a spontaneous, imaginative, abstract, expressionistic form of painting. He worked impulsively, but often returned to his work and adapted not only his own work, but that of others. One of Jorn's main works is the huge *Stalingrad* (Silkeborg Kunstmuseum), which he worked on periodically between 1957 and 1972. Other important works are the large ceramic relief and the long tapestry in Århus Statsgymnasium (1959-1960). Asger Jorn worked incessantly, often in series, and moved from one form of artistic expression to another: from painting to drawing, collage, ceramics, lithography and sculpture, and he also wrote many books on art. In 1953 he gave his collection of his own and others' works to Silkeborg Kunstmuseum, and his work – extensive as it is – can also be seen in a large number of museums in Europe and the USA. Jorn has had a great influence on later Danish painters, including Per Kirkeby.

Vibeke Skov

Summer Exhibition was founded in 1961 with the intention of giving young experimental artists a place in which they could exhibit; in 1963 the Summer Exhibition was thus the framework for the Fluxus Festival.

Particularly far-reaching importance could be attached to the foundation in 1961 of The Experimental School of Fine Arts on the initiative of the artist Paul Gernes and the art historian Troels Andersen. The Eks School, as it became known, was a rebellion against the technical and figuratively determined teaching in the Academy of Fine Arts schools of painting and the School of Graphic Arts, which until well into the 1980s were run by pupils of Aksel Jørgensen. Without any fixed programme, the new school disseminated ideas from conceptual art, process art and American pop art. At the same time it defended the depersonalisation of art and its approach to a form of expression that was socially responsible. Common to some of the pupils in the school, for instance Bjørn Nørgaard and Per Kirkeby, is their artistic and technical versatility, but also their critical awareness of the surrounding world. Bjørn Nørgaard's politically coloured *Hesteofring* (Horse Sacrifice) in a field in 1970 was one of the actions that gave rise to the most debate of them all. Popular outrage at the turbulent development of art in the direction of new forms and ideas culminated when a modern sculpture by Peter Bonnén was bought from the Summer Exhibition by the State Fund for the Arts in 1965. The sale gave rise to a storm of protest against this fund which had been established in 1964.

Vis-à-vis the Eks School and the democratic ideals of its artists there was another faction, international and with its roots in America: In 1974 Mogens Møller, Hein Heinsen and Stig Brøgger established the Institute for Skala Art, which experimented with the development of an art whose dimensions and minimalist character allowed the work to appear as strikingly – and logically – as possible in the public arena. In this ideological heyday, art by women artists came more and more to the fore thanks to major exhibitions with artists including Kirsten Justesen, Jytte Rex and Lene Adler Petersen. The examination of the interplay between space and art from Linien II was continued by the group calling itself New Abstraction, which was founded in 1976, and whose most influential members were Merete Barker, Torben Ebbesen, Finn Mickelborg and Niels Nedergaard, and then by Atelieret (the Studio) Leifsgade 22. From this workshop collective, where the study of materials has been a particular focal point, come artists working in sculpture such as Anita Jørgensen, Finn Reinbothe, Frans Kannik and Finn Naur Petersen.

Asger Jorn: *Red Meadows, Green Boys*, painted 1966-1968; Louisiana. As sources for his experimental artistic products, Asger Jorn made use, among other things, of medieval art, children's pictures and primitive art. This painting, like many others of his works, is populated by beings and masks as non-figurative elements in the midst of the abstract.

Painting, Sculpture and Video Art
Painting declined throughout the 1970s, though there were exceptions. A strong position has been adopted by Arne Haugen Sørensen, who in an overwhelmingly dramatic and virtuoso painted world of pictures has combined traits from Cobra with abstract surrealism. A number of expressionistic painters gathered for a time around the *Violet Sol* (Violet

Richard Mortensen: *Lieurey*, painted 1955; Randers Kunstmuseum. After the Second World War, Richard Mortensen together with others including Robert Jacobsen, developed a non-figurative, constructivist form of expression. His sober, stringent and well-considered idiom can be seen in the painting, in which tensions in the picture plane between lines, colours and shapes also bring in the pictorial space.

Jørgen Haugen Sørensen: *The Rough Ones Bear, the Smooth Ones Slip*, executed in granite 1984. The interplay between the rough and the smoothly polished stone surfaces is typical of several of Haugen Sørensen's works. This sculpture, financed by the Municipality of Copenhagen and the Danish Arts Foundation, is placed on the busy Nørrebrogade in Copenhagen against a wall around the cemetery Assistens Kirkegård.

Sun) group. And the by now internationally recognised Per Kirkeby has cultivated painting along with other forms of expression and media like sculpture, graphic art, poetry, fiction and film. Other painters who started in abstract expressionism and came into prominence in the 1980s are Jens Birkemose and Peter Brandes.

One of the most dramatic manifestations of the 1980s, *Kniven på hovedet* (The Knife on the Head) in Trane-

Per Kirkeby: *Green Spring*, painted 1988; Louisiana. In his pictures Per Kirkeby has cultivated an expressive abstract form. Impressions from landscapes, from other works of art or from pictures in the mass media are often seen as spaces of indeterminate character emerging on account of the stratified application of brush strokes and coloured surfaces.

gården 1982 was an exhibition of works by pupils in Stig Brøgger's class at the Academy of Fine Arts, with contributions from artists including Peter Bonde, Claus Carstensen, Kehnet Nielsen and Nina Sten-Knudsen. While this new, wild, impulsive painting at first was interpreted as a reaction against the conceptual art of the 1970s and a return to free expressionism, the considerations behind the painting were not unrelated to strategies from conceptual art. More daring and revolutionary in their use of materials were the artists of a like age who gathered around *Værkstedet Værst* (Workshop Worst) such as Erik A. Frandsen, Christian Lemmerz and Lars Nørgaard. These artists have each separately moved away from their collective, mainly German-influenced starting point. Lars Ravn, Inge Ellegaard and Knud Odde Sørensen have had related attitudes to art and expressed themselves in similar ways at the same time. A more painterly and figurative attitude has been seen in the expressive neo-romantic Lise

On 30 January 1970 Bjørn Nørgaard organised a happening in a field in Horns Herred, when together with Lene Adler Petersen as a priestess carrying a black cross, and the violin-playing Henning Christiansen, he undertook a ritual dissection of a horse that had just been slaughtered. The action was a commentary on what Nørgaard himself called 'the ritual murders in Vietnam', and it attracted a great deal of attention and caused considerable scandal at a time when it was possible to follow the Vietnam war closely on television.

Malinovsky and the macabre neo-surrealist Michael Kvium.

With the variety within the work of the same artist and its combinations of styles and materials, the new sculpture following the new wild painting in the middle of the 1980s seems to be more pluralistic by nature than earlier painting. The group of young sculptors who drew most attention to themselves towards the end of the 1980s included Morten

Bjørn Nørgaard, born 1947, is one of the most prominent Danish visual artists, with an extensive oeuvre, ranging from actions and happenings through film to sculpture and textile art. Like Per Kirkeby he started his artistic career at the School of Experimental Art, where from 1964, inspired by among others Joseph Beuys, he was involved in collaborative works and happenings such as *Den kvindelige Kristus* (1969, The Female Christ) and *Hes-*

teofringen (1970, The Horse Sacrifice), which provoked intense debate in large sections of Danish society. Nørgaard continued his experiments with graphic art, ceramics, film production and other activities, but since the 1970s his main interest has been sculpture. His fertile imagination, partly drawing on the art of former times and other cultures, and his delight in unusual combinations of widely different materials – concrete, marble, glazed ceramics, glass, etc. – have found expression in a series of monumental sculptures such as *Menneskemuren* (1982, The Human Wall) and the 26-metre-high *Tors tårn* (1986, Thor's Tower). These large works are created in partnership with workmen and specialists and installed in public places in several cities in Denmark; others are located in Danish and Nordic art museums. One of Nørgaard's biggest commissions has been 11 large tapestries (1990-2000) with motifs from Danish history for hanging in the banqueting hall at Christiansborg Palace in Copenhagen; they were woven at Les Gobelins in Paris. Nørgaard was a professor at the Royal Danish Academy of Fine Arts 1985-1993.

Peter Kühn-Nielsen

He works in painting, graphic art and sculpture, he has produced films – including one on Asger Jorn – and written a large number of books. As one of the driving forces behind Den Eksperimenterende Kunstskole (The Experimental Art School), Per Kirkeby has from 1962 taken part in several exhibitions and happenings, including *Arctic I-III* (1967-1968), which derived from his participation (as a geologist) in expeditions to Greenland. In his first paintings from the 1960s he experimented with form and material, and the pictures were often collage-like, composed of traced silhouette figures fitted into a formless space of coloured mists. Since the 1970s Kirkeby has worked in a more thoroughgoing colouristic expressionism in which the figurative element has been either partially or entirely absent. His starting point might be motifs from nature – a tree trunk, the fungi of the forest floor – or from the history of art – a torso, architectural ruins. As a sculptor Per Kirkeby has executed simple, but often large-scale, monumental brick sculptures and dark bronze sculptures. In the period 1978-1989 he was Professor at the Academy of Fine Arts in Karlsruhe and in 1989 he was appointed Professor in Frankfurt. He is represented in many museums in Denmark and abroad.

Per Kirkeby, b. 1938, is the contemporary Danish artist to have made the greatest impression abroad, where throughout the 1980s and 1990s he took part in many important exhibitions of contemporary art, including the Documenta in Kassel.

Vibeke Skov

Stræde, Henrik B. Andersen, Øivind Nygaard and Elisabeth Toubro. They work on the basis of influences from older sculptors such as the important Willy Ørskov and Hein Heinsen, both of whom taught at the Academy of Fine Arts on the basis of a reflective, philosophical and critical view of art. This intellectually based view of art, which has reduced the value of art as provocation and its infection by a media society with growing significance, has been challenged by groups such as *Baghuset*.

In the 1990s several Danish artists have made their mark internationally in the field of video art and video installation art. Several of these Danish artists have lived and worked in New York and Berlin for considerable periods of time, thereby establishing the necessary foreign contacts. Among the leading artists are Torben Christensen, who has teached at the School of Media Arts of the Royal Danish Academy of Fine Arts, and the younger artists Peter Land, Gitte Villesen, Pia Rönnicke, Joachim Køster, Ann Lislegaard and Lisa Strömbeck. Traditionally, video art has been based on narrative content, often focused on a personal

Kehnet Nielsen: *The Knife on the Head*, painting, 1982; Statens Museum for Kunst. The inspiration derives i.a. from German neo-expressionism in 'Die Neuen Wilden'. The picture shows the icons of pop art, the Coca-Cola bottles against a rough sketch of J.F. Willumsen on the right – with another bottle under his chin – as he is seen on the famous *Family Vase* from 1891.

story, but some artists have also represented the documentary genre. Generally speaking female artists have dominated this media more than their male counterparts. This situation reflects a long-waited breakthrough of gender equality within the arts.

Peter Michael Hornung

In the Danish West Indies, Jacob A. Weng (1864-1905) worked as a portrait, interior and landscape photographer from the 1890s. With a sense of the picturesque and exotic he has in this photograph from about 1900 portrayed the street called Kongensgade in Frederiksted on St. Croix.

Photography

19 August 1839 is the official birthday of photography. In September that year, the former marine officer Christian Tuxen Falbe was the first Dane to make daguerreotypes in Paris and send them to his patron in Copenhagen, Prince Christian Frederik (later King Christian VIII), who immediately deposited them together with an accompanying camera with the physicist H.C. Ørsted. Thanks to

With his carefully arranged portraits, the Aalborg photographer Heinrich Tønnies anticipated both the style and the approach of some of the 20th century's most prominent photographic artists: the German August Sander and the American Irving Penn. From its establishment in 1856 and until Tønnies' death in 1903, the studio produced some 75,000 portraits, including these two journeymen in their Sunday best.

Ørsted's pupils and helped by a Danish edition of Daguerre's own instructions, the new medium quickly awakened the recognition and interest of the Danes. In 1842 the daguerreotypist Mads Alstrup was the first to open a portrait studio in the capital; ten years later, Copenhagen had over 100 studios, and the provinces quickly followed suit. The rapid spread was due to the cheap carte de visite photography which in the 1870s and 1880s provided an income for, for instance, the Aalborg photographer Heinrich Tønnies. Peter Elfelt became particularly well known and in 1900 was appointed photographer to the Royal Danish Court, but he used his many talents to photograph Denmark from end to end. Dry plates and other simplified methods around the turn of the century gave an impetus to amateur photography, in which pictorial landscape and genre photography was cultivated by the merchant Sigvart Werner, the doctor Julius Møller and others. Photographic societies were formed and pictures were distributed via so-called portfolio clubs and discussed in periodicals. The society called *Danske Kamera Piktorialister* (Danish Camera Pictorialists), founded in the 1930s, embarked on a crusade, led by its chairman H.B.J. Cramer and lasting right up to the 1970s, to have photography accepted as an art form. A counter-movement to pictorialism, the 1920s' Neue Sachlichkeit, only really became known in Denmark when Keld Helmer-Petersen in 1948 published his abstract colour studies, *122 Colour Photographs*.

In the 1890s, press photography was introduced into Danish newspapers, but it was not until the 1950s that photographic reporting was established nationwide. Stimulated by the humanism of the post-war era and with the photographic bureau Magnum as a model, Jesper Høm and Gregers Nielsen and others formed the documentary group Delta Photos, whose dissolution in 1972 led to groupings with a more clearly defined social and political aim such as Ragnarok and 2. Maj, founded

respectively by Morten Bo and Henrik Saxgren. Photographers such as Viggo Rivad and Krass Clement chose the independence of the freelance. In his *American Pictures* (1977), Jacob Holdt was also a loner, reviving his compatriot Jacob A. Riis' campaign for social justice in the USA of the day.

Between 1946 and 1976 the portrait photographer Aage Remfeldt arranged twenty 'International exhibitions of photographic art' in the Copenhagen art gallery at Charlottenborg. In the 1970s this sphere of interest was renewed with the interplay between the galleries GCP in Copenhagen, Image in Århus and a new generation of photographers who 'think' pictures before exposing them: the landscape photographer Kirsten Klein, the pioneers of staged photography Nanna Bisp Büchert and Lis Steincke as well as the magic realist Per Bak Jensen. A number of visual artists including Richard Winther, Stig Brøgger, Jytte Rex, Peter Brandes and Ane Mette Ruge also

Keld Helmer-Petersen's international fame was heralded already with his first book from 1948, *122 Farvefotografier* (122 Colour Photographs), from which this picture of the ends of a couple of sheds is taken. To use colour photography as an independent, non-figurative artistic expression was new at that time and immediately placed Helmer-Petersen in the photographic avant-garde.

With this picture from 1944, the chief photographer of the newspaper Politiken for a generation, Erik Petersen, illustrated this all clear after an air raid warning during the German occupation of Denmark. However, Danish readers could at the same time read a gentle commentary on the well-known concept at that time of 'going underground'.

introduced photography in a quite decisive way. The nascent interest in photography as an art form in the Royal Academy of Fine Arts typifies the picture of the Danish photography around 2000, with new names happily mixing the classic technique of photography with digitalised forms of expression, for instance Lisa Rosenmeier.

Since 1902 the Royal Library has built up the largest picture collection in the country (c. 10 million pictures). In 1984 *Danmarks Fotomuseum* (the Danish Museum of Photography) opened in Herning, in 1987 came *Museet for Fotokunst* (the Museum of Photographic Art) in Odense, and in 1999 *Det Nationale Fotomuseum* (the National Museum of Photography) in Copenhagen.

Finn Thrane

In Lisa Rosenmeier, the seductive power of advertisement photography finds a sophisticated artist who can beat advertisement at its own game. The picture derives from the series *The Perfect Life* (1992), which in large format was displayed in buses and on hoardings in Copenhagen.

Applied Art and Design

Apart from the jewellery, pottery and cultic objects from pre-historic and Viking times, Danish applied art only began to take shape during the Renaissance. The field of art that was only later isolated as applied art had until then been characterised by anonymous objects for everyday use or by imported works of art. From the end of the 16th century tapestries were woven for the royal house and the aristocracy, e.g. Hans Knieper's Kronborg tapestries, and splendid gold and silver works, including Christian IV's crown, were produced for the same circle of customers. Danish furniture design as such is only known from the 18th century; however, the elder and younger Hans Gudewerth's richly carved chests indicate the existence of sophisticated carving. Biblical motifs are incorporated into a detailed, three-dimensional decoration adorned with architectural and plant motifs and grotesque ornamentation.

With absolutism and mercantilism a start was made to the production in Denmark of more sophisticated articles for everyday use, inspired both by imported articles and directly by artists brought in for the pur-

Tureen with lid from the *Flora Danica* service produced by the Royal Copenhagen Porcelain Manufactory 1790-1802.

pose. The first faience factory in Scandinavia was founded in 1722 in Store Kongensgade in Copenhagen with the production of blue-painted decorations inspired by export porcelain and Delft ware. A couple of decades later more faience factories were established, producing polychrome flower decorations inspired by German and French ceramics, and later by English stoneware. In 1775 Denmark acquired its own first porcelain factory, the Royal Copenhagen Porcelain Manufactory, and porcelain gradually supplanted faience. Despite the influence from the South, an individual style was developed, especially in flower-decorated dinner services, of which Flora Danica was the flagship. The damask weaving mill in Køng was founded in 1774, and both in the capital and in the provinces, people deserted the smooth hollow-ware silver first for the vertically fluted and then the spirally fluted.

The softer forms of the Rococo long went hand in hand with Classicism – a feature which in general has been characteristic of Danish applied art. Where interior design was mainly French-inspired on account of the many artists brought in to work at for example Christiansborg Palace and Amalienborg, the furniture of the Baroque and Rococo were influenced rather by German style. With the establishment in 1754 of the Royal Danish Academy of Fine Arts, the teachers accepted responsibility for providing tuition in drawing for artisan apprentices in order to raise standards, but right up to the present day Danish furniture design has particularly been distinguished by the idiom created by the architects. C.F. Harsdorff designed mahogany

Water jug and dish of gold, the work of Frederik Fabritius 1731; Det Kongelige Sølvkammer (The Royal Plate Room), Christiansborg. The jug and the dish belong to the gold toilet set of the Danish queens, produced for Queen Sophie Magdalene by Frederik Fabritius of the famous family of goldsmiths.

furniture in a terse, Doric classicism, whose simple, clear construction and form contain features that were to be characteristic of later Danish furniture. English Neo-Classicism made its mark with delicate, painted furniture decorated with classical motifs by J.C. Lillie and others. The influence from this was later seen in what was known as the bourgeois Empire style.

Nineteenth-century Classicism and Historicism

The first half of the nineteenth century was characterised by various forms of Classicism running in parallel. G.F. Hetsch's key position as professor in the Academy of Fine Arts and artistic director of the Royal Copenhagen Porcelain Manufactory had implications for porcelain, silver, bronze and, to a lesser extent,

Thorvald Bindesbøll, dish of fired and glazed clay with inscribed decoration, made in Copenhagen Pottery Factory in Valby in 1899. In the 1880s, Bindesbøll developed a personal ornamental style, brought to full development in the 1890s. He specialised in imaginative decoration of dishes and large-format vases, and this was a new departure opening to the abstract art of the 20th century's.

furniture. By far the greater part of Danish furniture was made in an English-inspired simple Classicism in mahogany with inlaid citruswood decorations of classical figures and borders. The light horsehair upholstered armchair and bench with latticework back never lost their popularity and reappeared during the classicism of the 1920s. Of importance was the group of neo-antique furniture copied from Greek and Roman wall paintings, vases and reliefs as a reaction to the French-inspired Empire style and absolutism. Nicolai Abildgaard, H.E. Freund, Gottlieb Bindesbøll and other Golden Age artists, with their Pompeiian interiors and furniture in which form and construction were given priority, created the basis for the work of coming generations. Empire silver had the same simplicity, often with undecorated surfaces. Stylistically, historicism after c. 1840 became more of a parenthesis; nevertheless, technique was refined in all areas of applied art in this period of boom. The clientele was still not large enough for industrial production as such, but the workmanship was on a level with that abroad, and the prerequisites for international competition were created. This came when a number of artists took active part in the new directions and engaged in arts and crafts.

Skønvirke

The freely modelled ceramic art was related to the general European Arts and Crafts movement, but did not remain an isolated phenomenon. By 1885 the Bing & Grøndahl Porcelain Manufactory (founded 1853) was moving in a new direction with Pietro Krohn's Japanese-inspired Heron Service. In 1897 Krohn was followed as artistic director by J.F. Willumsen,

whose time was characterised by a sophisticated artistic production which in the World Exhibition in 1900 made the factory known once and for all. With Arnold Krog, the Royal Copenhagen Porcelain Manufactory created new design underglaze painting from 1885. Under Krog's directorship the blue fluted china which he had 'inherited' was supplemented with a number of new forms and patterns which for the next 100 years provided the factory's financial foundation. The plant and animal motifs which became particularly common in the art nouveau period were in Denmark given their own national individuality. By the 19th century Nordic flora and fauna had already replaced the classical Roman. With inspiration from Japanese art, motifs were now devised whose national element can be seen in the landscapes which together with flora and fauna were painted in blue/grey underglazing. Related tendencies, but with a different artistic idiom, are found in Georg Jensen's silverware. In 1908 the painter Johan Rohde became

Sven Brasch, poster for *La Dame aux Camélias* at the Casino Theatre in Copenhagen; lithograph 1922; The Danish Museum of Decorative Art. Sven Brasch's film, music and theatre posters helped to make him internationally known. His approach is the elegant woman, graphically presented in a few colours in which black and the ground colour of the paper are contrasted with one or two powerful colours. The message is clear and quickly read.

Silver jug designed by Henning Koppel and made in Georg Jensen's Workshop 1952; The Danish Museum of Decorative Art. In the 1950s, classical Danish functionalism met opposition partly from American-Japanese minimalism, partly from a painting and sculptural organic style represented by i.a. Henning Koppel's work in silver and porcelain.

associated with the silversmith workshop. His relatively small applied art production, which also includes furniture, betokens a culmination in the collaboration between artist and craftsman, as well as in the style, where a simple, national classicism and Japonism received a new expression.

In the same way Danish classicism became a starting point for the country's greatest designer in the modern sense of the word. Thorvald Bindesbøll's very personal ornamentation found its real expression in ceramics in his meeting with Japanese art, and his non-figurative ornamentation was the predecessor of 20th-century abstraction. His silver, embroidery and book craft were outstanding, while his furniture rather betokens a search for new modes of expression. *Skønvirke* ('Fairwork') was the name given to this new Danish art. The expression underlines the national element and the fact that it is about

*handi*work. A number of architects, not least Martin Nyrop and Anton Rosen, revived national craft and design. In 1907 the Society for the Promotion of Hedebo embroidery and in 1913 the Danish Domestic Crafts Weaving Workshop were founded. Together with the revival of tapestry weaving and lacework, these initiatives had far-reaching significance. Today, a freer form of pictorial weaving is practised by a large number of women artists, while several painters, including Asger Jorn and Bjørn Nørgaard, have created cartoons for major tapestries.

Danish Modernism

An important prerequisite for Functionalism in Denmark was again Classicism, the national characteristic of which once more made itself felt in a number of architects. In 1924 the Academy of Fine Arts established a school for furniture design, and in 1927 the Guild of Cabinet

Georg Jensen, 1866-1935, belonged to the generation of artists from about 1900 who made liberal art their starting point in seeking a renewal of applied arts. After

training as a goldsmith and from 1892 as a sculptor in the Royal Danish Academy of Fine Arts, he opened his own silversmith's workshop in 1904. His production of jewellery in the cheaper silver set with semi-precious stones and amber is characterised by the wealth of his ornamental fantasy. Leaves and flower shapes were treated with hammer blows, and the silver acquired a greyish tone through patination. His hollow ware was decorated with moulded and soldered ornamentation in the quasi-naturalistic style of the time. These characteristics also marked the products designed by associated artists. A range of well-designed hollow ware with classical shapes and subdued leaf ornamentation was created throughout the 1930s by Johan Rohde. Some of them are still in production in Georg Jensen's Workshop, which became part of Royal Copenhagen in 1985, since 1997 Royal Scandinavia.

Mirjam Gelfer-Jørgensen

Makers began annual exhibitions of Danish furniture designed by architects in order to counter the import of furniture and factory production. Kaare Klint's tuition in the Academy of Fine Arts established the norm right up to 1956; proportion studies, traditions of materials and construction were the starting point for a renewal of Danish furniture design. The reaction to the Bauhaus school and industry was expressed partly in the careful attention to every detail. At the end of the 1920s, a group of architects led by the creator of the PH lamp, Poul Henningsen, initiated a campaign against everything that did not serve a useful purpose.

The Fritz Hansen furniture company produced inexpensive furniture made of steel tubing, which was partly a failure, and of rounded beech sticks, which was a great sales success. In the 1940s a succession of well-made and inexpensive furniture was made for Co-op Denmark with Børge Mogensen as one of the designers. The porcelain factories and the Holmegaard Glassworks produced services that lived up to the demand of the day for good form and quality. Textiles, wallpapers and ornaments gradually introduced softer lines to the simple functionalist style. Marie Gudme Leth's printed calico curtains with flowers in many colours, and Gerda Henning's woven materials with figures were parallelled by the flowers in coffee services, and the sale of figurines, vases and ornaments in ceramics, glass and various metals rose noticeably. Only in the 1970s did the sale of porcelain figures stagnate. From the classicism of the 1920s grew a repertoire of forms, characterised by simplicity and precision, which made their mark on applied art. Of particular interest are Just Andersen's metalware products, Jacob Bang's abundant production of glass for everyday use for the Holmegaard Glassworks, and Axel Salto's, Patrick Nordstrøm's and Nathalie Krebs' stoneware, in which the enthusiasm for the shapes and glazing of Chinese Sung ceramics is obvious.

Danish Design

The concept of *Danish Design* was based on the post-war era's more international taste, in which the social and the 'modern' might well be retained, but where tradition still played a part. Simple, well-formed and material-conscious applied art was to oppose the import of mass-produced goods, and with a high ethical standard of craftsmanship it gained international recognition. Ceramics entered a period of strength with a number of individual workshops concentrating on the

In 1924, the architect *Kaare Klint*, 1888-1954, became the first Lecturer in Furniture Design at the Royal Danish Academy of Fine Arts in Copenhagen. Through his teaching and with his own work, he made an impact on several generations of Danish furniture designers; a few of them, for instance Finn Juhl, he inspired to a counter-reaction. At a time when modernism was rejecting former models, Kaare Klint took his starting point in the experience of materials and construction going back to Classicism, combining this with proportion studies. His furniture fitted into a Danish classical tradition that was hereby given new life. He also found models in English furniture from the 18th century, the Shakers in the USA, and anonymous pieces of southern European furniture, and he re-fashioned and simplified them to produce modern furniture. *Rudolf Rasmussen's Snedkerier* (Cabinet Maker's) in Copenhagen provided him with exquisite mahogany, the surface of which was easy to work, but where on the other hand fine contouring emphasises both form and construction. Each detail, brass fittings, hand-woven coverings and perfect leather, stresses the high level of quality which is particularly typical of Kaare Klint's museum furniture, for example that for the Museum of Decorative Art in Copenhagen.

Mirjam Gelfer-Jørgensen

1 Jens Brøtterup: mahogany chair, 1794-1803. **2** Herman Ernst Freund: armchair of mahogany with cane seat and embroidered cushion and back, 1830-1835. **3** Hans J. Wegner: chair of ash with seat of paper yarn PP 66, *Chinese Chair No 4*, 1845. **4** Arne Jacobsen: *The Egg*, easy chair in artificial fibre with black leather, 1957. All these chairs are in the Museum of Decorative Art.

material, the glazing and a subdued, secondary decoration to simple everyday objects, which nevertheless were not primarily intended to be used. In 1949 Sigvard Bernadotte and Acton Bjørn established the first drawing office for industrial design; one of those working there was Jacob Jensen, whose minimalist radio designs for Bang & Olufsen combined Danish and international idiom.

The use of specialist craftsmen and architects in the applied arts was fruitful and made certain furniture very popular, e.g. Arne Jacobsen's tubular steel chairs, which have been produced ever since the 1950s.

Finally, the Bauhaus style, via the USA, reached Denmark with Poul Kjærholm's minimalist furniture. Finn Juhl's expressive, organic furniture was a reaction against this style and the aesthetics of the Kaare Klint school, while Hans J. Wegner took a more relaxed attitude to the concept of style. As a trained cabinet maker he worked his way forward to solutions which partly stemmed from tradition and partly were freely invented. The porcelain factories distinguished themselves after 1945 with new, simple dinner and coffee services alongside the traditional ones. In an attempt to strengthen the production and marketing of applied

Gertrud Vasegaard, b.1913, is a remarkable representative of a widespread tendency in modern Danish ceramics. The shapes from which she started were those of basic utility objects such as bowls, vases and cups. In 1948 she was appointed to the Bing & Grøndahl Porcelain Manufactory, and with the new glazings being produced there she ensured that the stoneware mass can be felt in such a way that the textural effect of the material once more comes into its own. Her decorations consist of simple ornamentation, engraved, pressed or painted in contrasting colours. Gertrud Vasegaard created three porcelain services for Royal Copenhagen in white and blue-white. In her more recent works one senses the 'turning' of the cylinder, the high or low oval, more strongly, often emphasised by a simple, linear decoration which is a variation of the predilection of Danish artist craftsmen for stripes.

Mirjam Gelfer-Jørgensen

Bente Hansen, amoeba-shaped stoneware jar with lid, c. 1977; The Danish Museum of Decorative Art. The strength of Danish ceramics today resides in a number of – especially female – pottery artists for whom new shapes naturally develop from working with the materials. Bente Hansen has established herself with a style characterised by an often powerful sculptural impact, in which textural effects in clay and glazing play a conspicuous part.

Nanna Ditzel, bench for two, made in sycamore and aeroplane veneer with silk screen printing for Fredericia Stolefabrik 1989 (now Fredericia Furniture A/S).

art products, the Royal Copenhagen Group, was formed in 1985 on the basis of a merger of the major Danish manufacturers of applied arts. In 1997 the major Danish and Swedish applied arts Companies merged to form Royal Scandinavia.

As in other parts of the world, the last decade of the 20th century has been marked by a growing number of workshops for the applied arts. Ceramics occupy a strong position with simple practical shapes in which decoration and colour are subordinated to the material. The new jewellery workshops on the other hand are experimenting with shapes and materials, while the studio glass that appeared in the 1970s concentrated mainly on what is safe and saleable, although glass is establishing itself with a broad spectrum of manifestations and effects. Among many furniture

Jacob Jensen, b.1926, was a qualified furniture upholsterer and trained in the College of Arts and Crafts; this was supplemented with an early association with Bernadotte & Bjørn's drawing office, the first industrial design drawing office in Denmark. Jacob Jensen's ability to work with shape was quickly combined with his skill at finding solutions to problems of a technical nature. In 1962 he set up his own drawing office on a hillside sloping down to the Limfjord in North Jutland. It is from here he derives inspiration for his severe, horizontal, minimalist idiom, in which the characteristic qualities of Danish neo-classicism can be discerned in shape and colour. This applies especially to his many works for the electronics firm of Bang & Olufsen (music system), the success of which is to a great extent dependent on the design types developed by Jacob Jensen in the 1960s.

Mirjam Gelfer-Jørgensen

From the left: Margrethe bowl, Rosti, 1950. Coffee maker, Bodum, 1958. Children's tricycle, Rabo, 1972. Necklaces, Dyrberg/Kern, 1999. Sunlounger, Trip Trap, 1990-1991.

Industrial Design

After the Second World War, international design was dominated by two tendencies: on the one hand there was functionalism, which contrary to the original intention developed into a style, a mannerism, and on the other hand there was commonplace architecture and interior design, which even after 30 years of functionalism was non-functional in many ways.

Danish design stressed an organic functionalism that was liberating itself from functionalism's rigid geometrical shapes, but at the same time represented a new and more demanding simplicity and a concept of design based on a genuine interest in the interplay between user, tools and surroundings.

Several factors converged in the course of these developments: a vibrant tradition of craftsmanship and a demand for high quality, a period marked by frugality with its need for economy in construction and for durability, and not least a world that suddenly opened up. The interplay with the user became the essential element, and care for detail and respect for the materials in construction and manufacture were features common to them all.

From the left: IC-3 train, DSB, 1991. The trademark of the supermarket chain Netto, 1991. Stereo set, AV 9000, Bang & Olufsen, 1992.

The foundations for this trend were laid before the war through works by pioneers such as Poul Henningsen (the PH lamp principle, 1926) and K.V. Engelhardt (design in public buildings).

The ideas which were formerly largely limited to Danish designers now constitute an element in the training of designers throughout the world. Danish industrial design continues to occupy a distinguished international position, which is confirmed by Denmark's placing in the competition for international distinctions resulting from works by designers and design undertakings such as Bernadotte & Bjørn, which was the first real industrial design undertaking in Denmark, the designers Henning Moldenhawer, Jacob Jensen and later David Lewis, Jan Trägårdh, Erik Magnussen, Knud Holscher, Dissing+Weitling, Christian Bjørn, Niels Jørgen Haugesen and a new generation of young designers several of whom come from abroad.

Danish design spans a far wider range of production than previously. Among the present-day design-oriented firms there are Bang & Olufsen, the LEGO Group, Kompan, Novo Nordisk, Danfoss, Grundfos, VELUX, Coloplast, Fritz Hansen, Louis Poulsen, etc.

Industrial graphic design is also part of the picture, with modern pioneers like the graphic artists Niels Hartmann, who launched the first major Danish identity programmes, Jørgen Oksen with his work for The Agricultural Marketing Board and Verner Nertoft, who was responsible for Bang & Olufsen's graphic design in the 1960s and 1970s.

Although many of the ideals on which Danish design was based in the 1940s and 1950s remain unchanged, design has undergone a development from a concept based first on content and then on form, to one in which the planning of form and content receive equal weight; design has become an integral part of product development.

The early 2000s has seen a fusion of product design and graphic design and, in a wider sense, of the strategy and design of a given company. The aim is to create total coherence from product design to graphic communication and architecture – intended to be a visible expression of the values and goals of the company.

Jens Bernsen

experiments it is traditional pieces that are being produced, although the increased use of colour in the 1980s also left its traces in Denmark. The industry makes increasing use of industrial designers, and functional, visually satisfying solutions have been created making use of lighter technology. Only the textile industry is characterised by specialist art craftsmen.

At the end of the century there is a clear distinction between handicraft products, which have direct links to free artistic creation, applied art, which seems to have stagnated, and industrial design, which for better or for worse has gained a foothold in the area of applied art production. However, there are some signs that handicraft products are on the point of recapturing some of the lost territory.

Mirjam Gelfer-Jørgensen

Nanna Hertoft: *Reflections in Water*; tapestry from 1990 in wool, flax and strips of cotton rag; The Danish Museum of Decorative Art. Textile art has had a prominent place in the Scandinavian applied art of the 20th century.

Literature

Before Writing

The great stories of creation, of gods and human beings, of ragnarok (the twilight of the gods) and the new earth and the new heaven were composed long before the earliest written accounts. From pictures on small metal plates, bracteates, found in recent years, we know that Scandinavian mythology was fully developed and recited as long ago as the 5th century BC. This is common Nordic material that was only written down in Iceland soon after 1200 AD (in the Edda) and then between 1190 and 1210 (often in quite distorted form) by the Danish historian Saxo Grammaticus. But it is these mythical stories that form the roots of Danish/Nordic culture. It is a metaphorical universe to which later literature – from Pre-Romanticism onwards – returns time after time, retelling and interpreting. And in the Grundtvigian folk high schools the stories of the ancient gods and giants have for over a hundred years played their part in moulding the broad sweep of popular culture. Although the myths had religious subject matter, they must be seen as the oldest collection of stories, a metaphorical universe that helped create a Danish and Scandinavian identity.

The Oldest Written Work

The runic inscriptions, mainly from the Viking Age, are like an open book in the Danish countryside. Several of the great runic stones are still freely accessible, subjected to wind and weather, more or less where they have stood for a thousand years. They are not really literature in a narrow sense, but the runic inscriptions are the oldest written documents in Denmark. Lapidary in form, sometimes containing alliteration and a little rhythm, they usually only contain information about a dead warrior and about the man who wrote the runes, but they can also contain invocations and magic and the names of people and gods. The Jelling Stones are the great national treasure, the larger of the two, with its figure of Christ and heathen ornamentation, containing Harald Bluetooth's declaration that he united Denmark and made the Danes Christian.

The discovery in 1639 and 1734 of the two golden horns, with their ornamentation and the runic inscription on the shorter of the two, had far-reaching literary consequences – not least thanks to Adam Oehlenschläger's Romantic programme poem *Guldhornene* (The Golden Horns), written after the theft of the horns in 1802. The poem attained the status of literary mythology and was later part of the stuff of general culture.

The Middle Ages

Monastery and Church;
Literature in Latin

The Middle Ages were the great age of manuscripts. The Catholic

Jutlandic Law, established in 1241 by Valdemar II The Victorious, is a Danish linguistic monument. With its rich ornamentation this 1479 manuscript from Skovkloster near Næstved is outstanding in the history of writing.

monasteries were the vehicles of literary culture, which by dint of the Latin language and the studies which the learned prelates undertook abroad was an international culture. It was in this framework that the first great work of Danish literature was written, Saxo's history of Denmark, *Gesta Danorum* (The Deeds of the Danes), a description of events under the Danish kings from the earliest legendary history up to the time at which the book was written (immediately after 1200 AD). This is a work of literature of European format, written in late silver age Latin. It is the oldest written foundation for a Danish identity, fashioned by an international culture. As to the most ancient material, this is a goldmine, a free adaptation of legend and myth. Saxo is a main source for the works of later ages, both in Denmark and abroad (e.g. the Hamlet legend).

Alongside Saxo's prose there is another monumental work in Latin, Anders Sunesen's *Hexaëmeron* (The Six Days), written perhaps around 1200 or possibly between 1223 and the death of Anders Sunesen in 1228.

This, too, is a literary achievement of international stature, a didactic hexameter poem about the Creation and a theological-allegorical interpretation of what was created. A subtle and profoundly learned work and a distillation of mediaeval Catholicism's view of the world. Anders Sunesen was Absalon's successor as Archbishop of Lund, and the man to whom Saxo, on completing his own work about 1220, dedicated his foreword. *Hexaëmeron* was first printed as late as 1892 and translated into Danish verse in 1985.

Literature in the Vernacular
Side by side with Latin literature there is also a mediaeval literature in the vernacular. As linguistic monuments the regional laws (Jutlandic Law, Zealand Law, Scanian Law) are of special interest, and they are also important as sources of cultural history.

Ballads are the principal mediaeval literature in the vernacular. There are but few scattered bits of evidence of the ballads from the Middle Ages themselves, but by the time of the

Renaissance they were already being written down in the poetry albums of ladies of the aristocracy. How old the ballads are has been the subject of widely divergent views, but it must be supposed that most of them stem from about the middle of the 14th century and up to the end of the 15th century. The fairy-tale-like ballads of magic and the novel-like ballads of chivalry constituting the major part of the ballads that have been handed down to us, often have a considerable literary value through their sharply defined and genuinely tragic conflicts or their boisterous humour, and through the emotive refrains with which they are all provided. In an international context the Danish ballad tradition is remarkable for its relatively homogeneous character, its very early redactions and finally because Denmark is the country that can boast of the oldest printed editions of the ballads: Anders Sørensen Vedel's *Hundredvisebog* (Book of a Hundred Ballads) 1591, Mette Gjøe's *Tragica* 1657 and Peder Syv's edition of 1695. These printed editions have kept the ballads alive in an oral – and later written – tradition until far into the 19th century. When the ballads were rediscovered by the Romantics they exerted an enormous influence on the poetical language throughout the 19th century and inspired a host of imitations and re-creations. And from that time the ballads were an essential element in the Danish literary identity.

The Renaissance

Both the manuscript literature (which circulated in hand-written copies) and the Latin literature continued throughout the 16th, 17th and 18th centuries. But the Renaissance meant the breakthrough of the printed book (16th century, continuing into the 17th century). It was the age of learned works (the historian Anders Sørensen Vedel, the speculative doctor Petrus Severinus alias Peder Sørensen, famous throughout Europe, the astronomer Tycho Brahe and others). But as the Renaissance and the Lutheran Reformation were contemporary with each other, it was principally the age of Bible translations and hymn writing. The hymns of the new church were given a standard edition in Hans Thomesen's Hymn Book of 1569. Most of the hymns here were adaptations and translations from German, but by the end of the century the Reformation had found its first Danish poet in Hans Christensen Sthen (*En liden Vandrebog* – A Little Book for Wanderers – c. 1590, a prayer book containing a number of original hymns). Several of Sthen's hymns, their simple tone influenced by the ballad, have retained their place right up to the present day. His didactic religious poem *Lyckens Hiul* (The Wheel of Fortune) illustrates the view that took the place of the established mediaeval conviction: the world is now seen as a changeable and unpredictable place from which one has to flee to the security of the superior metaphysical world.

At the crossroads between Renaissance and baroque, Ditlev Ahlefeldt formulated this model of existence in exemplary fashion in the Foreword to his Memoires (c. 1680). Ahlefeldt was an opponent of absolutism. Christian IV's daughter, Leonora Christina, married to the high traitor Corfitz Ulfeldt and imprisoned in the Blue Tower for 22 years, came into direct conflict with the new absolutist monarchy. Her *Jammers Minde* (Memory of Woe) (commenced 1673-1674) is an impressive human document from that time, and filled with keen observations of life. Here we find the undaunted sense of realism to which the philosophy of the age gave rise.

The Baroque

The baroque (c. 1650-1720) was a period of growth in Danish literature. The new absolute monarchy wanted to produce a well-regulated society, and in parallel with this, literature embarked on producing rules for language and poetry. The 17th century produced a succession of grammars and prosodies and a few theories of poetry, of which the most important was Peder Syv's *Nogle Betenkninger over det cimbriske Sprog* (Some Thoughts on the Cimbrian Language) (1663). The baroque was the age when literature as an institution became aware of itself. Writers sought to compete with foreign languages in creating a literary language that was capable of achieving things. The language and forms of baroque literature are characterised by impressive rhetorical inventiveness and power, and they reveal an appetite for life that measures up to its stark celebration of the inconstancy of fortune and the certainty of death. There was both temporal and religious literature at that time. The printed temporal literature encompassed panegyric and funeral poems in the grand style (like those of Thomas Kingo), topographical poems and bucolic poems (like those of Anders Bording). Most of the temporal poetry of the day remained unpublished and was circulated in copies. The religious literature culminated in Thomas Kingo's *Aandelige Siunge-Koor* (Spiritual Song Choir) (1674 and 1681). Contemporary with Kingo were the great Norwegian hymn-writer Dorte Engelbretsdatter (*Sjælens Sang-Offer* – Song-Offering of the Soul, 1678) and her fellow-countryman Petter Dass.

Grandiloquent high baroque is found in the work of Elias Naur, the author of hymns and the verse epic *Golgatha paa Parnasso* (Golgotha on Parnassus) (1689).

The Transition to the Enlightenment – Man at the Centre

At the height of absolutism Ludvig Holberg gave temporal literature an international profile. Holberg brought home with him from his travels abroad the classicism that cultivated simple and pure form and the ideas of the Enlightenment, which put Man and human reason at the centre of things. As the author of legal, geographical and historical works, and works deriving from common-sense reasoning, Holberg sought to 'examine accepted notions' and disseminate the light of reason. As the author of comedies for the first Danish theatre, the theatre in Lille Grønnegade in Copenhagen, he created between 1722 and 1728 the foundation for the Danish theatrical tradition. Both the mock-epic poem *Peder Paars* (1719-1720) and the comedies reveal that Holberg considered the scope of reason to be significantly more limited than did the subsequent Enlightenment proper. His fundamental view was still affected by the turbulent world picture of the Renaissance and the baroque, something which makes of his comedies exuberant and highly realistic pictures of life.

The pietist hymns of H.A. Brorson also put Man at the centre as a counter to the orthodoxy of the previous century. Brorson originated from the baroque and to a great extent shared its view of the turbulent world (as is seen from his poem *The Pitiful End of Lisbon*, 1756). However, in continuation of German pietism he looked to the mystical experience as a countermeasure to the world's inconstancy. In his collection of hymns entitled *Troens rare Klenodie* (The Rare Jewel of Faith, 1739) he sometimes courted stylistic simplicity and intensity of feeling and sometimes complex symbolical pictures of the rebirth of the soul through the wounds of Christ. Amazingly elegant rococo sounds are the hallmark of the posthumously published *Svanesang* (Swansong, 1765), religious songs intended for private devotions.

The world as an (unreliable) voyage was also a prominent theme with Ambrosius Stub, from whose roving life as a poet there flowed rococo scenery, pietist hymns and drinking songs.

The Enlightenment

Not until about 1750 did the Enlightenment establish itself as a broad movement in Danish literature, borne of a new affluent middle-class self-assurance and the progress of the new empirical sciences. Two institutions created the framework for the new literature: The Royal Theatre, which was founded in 1748 and became the central institution of manners and culture in Denmark right up to the second half of the 19th century, and the Society for the Furtherance of the Fine and Useful Sciences (founded 1759). Within the framework of these two the age developed its fundamentally new ideas on the well-ordered world, its conceptions of morals and gentle, humane Christianity, and not least its ideals of linguistic culture. With a foundation in the re-created Sorø Academy, to which Holberg had left his fortune, Jens Schelderup Sneedorff became the literary strategist of the Enlightenment and the champion of the new, French-inspired prose style. The wonderful economy of the well-ordered world were sung by the Norwegian Christian Braun-

mann Tullin, who emerged as the great celebrated poet of the twin kingdom in the 1760s. The age is moreover reflected by the hymn-writer Birgitte Boye, the author of plays and a collection of *Moral Stories*, Charlotte Dorothea Biehl, and the irrepressible humorist Johan Herman Wessel.

In the last decade of the century Enlightenment was reinvigorated with a new sensitivity on the part of, among others, poets like Thomas Thaarup and Knud Lyne Rahbek. The Rahbek home in Copenhagen, Bakkehuset, with Kamma Rahbek as its intellectual focus, became a meeting place for people and literary ideas at the transitional time between Enlightenment, Romanticism and the incipient 'Golden Age'. Around 1800 the ideas of the Enlightenment and enthusiasm for the French Revolution led to the exile of authors such as Malthe Conrad Bruun and Peter Andreas Heiberg.

Pre-Romanticism

Many currents came together in the work of Johannes Ewald, but first and foremost he proclaimed a new poetical self-assurance in which it was art that provided identity, whereas the private personality of the writer – as indeed happened with Ewald, as portrayed in his memoirs *Levnet og Meeninger* (Life and Opinions, c. 1774ff.) – must be lost as the fuel that is spent in the creation of art. As a poet he raised language to the level of the sublime. As a dramatist he touched on the conflict he knew from himself between feeling and the established order in the plays *Adam og Eva* (Adam and Eve, 1769) and *Balders Død* (The Death of Balder, 1773-1775). The greatest acclaim in his own day, however, he won with the celebratory national play *Fiskerne*

(The Fishermen, 1779), which glorifies the moral strength of the people.

Jens Baggesen gave pre-Romanticism an international touch. On the basis of revolutionary moods of the heart and politics he wrote his brilliant travel account and confession *Labyrinten* (The Labyrinth, 1792-1793). About half of his work was written in German, including his European success *Parthenaïs* (1802/03), a hexameter idyll half way between the German writer of idylls, Voss, and the frenetical poetical enthusiasm of pre-Romanticism.

Romanticism and the Golden Age

Romanticism made its appearance in Denmark soon after 1800 and received its particular resonance and form thanks to the national débâcle during the Napoleonic Wars. The ideas and subject range of German Romanticism were seized on with great alacrity by Danish writers. On the one hand the poet Schack Staffeldt brought inspiration home after spending several years in Germany in the 1790s, and on the other the scientist and philosopher Henrik Steffens came to Copenhagen in 1802 and spread the message in a series of lectures in Elers College and in discussions with Adam Oehlenschläger. As a result of these, Oehlenschläger experienced a poetical awakening and emerged as the central figure in early Danish Romanticism, followed by Nicolai Frederik Severin Grundtvig and Carsten Hauch, while Bernhard Severin Ingeman went his own way, closer to Staffeldt and the more radical German Romanticism. At different speeds they all moved in directions that led them away from the original visionary Romanticism and into work that was national, popular and historical in content, and often critical of contemporary manners.

In a way, Romanticism had a long-lasting influence on Denmark, in that its cult of poetry as a life force was mingled with a religious/Christian belief in eternity, providing the basic materials for a common poetical creed throughout the first half of the 19th century. In addition, it established a poetical language (partly influenced by that of the medieval ballad) that typified much Danish poetry until the end of the century. But in its purest form Romanticism as such was a short-lived intermezzo. The bourgeois culture from the late 18th century continued unabated and made its mark on the fundamental view of life, invigorated with ample influence from Goethe. Goethe's brand of humanism, Christianity, morals and watered-down Romanticism make up the principal elements of the period which in view of the unique richness of all the arts at this time has become known as the Golden Age.

Whereas Oehlenschläger was the foremost personality in Romanticism proper, the dramatist and critic Johan Ludvig Heiberg was the leading figure in the new direction which Romanticism took as it turned towards everyday life and subjects demanding a more richly facetted psychology ('the interesting'). The circle around Heiberg and his wife Johanne Luise Heiberg became a major cultural factor in the 1820s and 1830s. Another member of the circle was Heiberg's mother, Thomasine Gyllembourg, who with her poeticised and moderately religious/moral stories of everyday life achieved great popularity at the time and became the main representative of the spirit of the age known as Biedermeier.

A New Reality is Established

In the 1820s and more especially in the 1830s, literature changed its general course under the influence

Even on the basis of his first works, *Adam Oehlenschläger*, 1779-1850 was assured of a position as the leading figure of Danish Romanticism.

His *Digte* (1803, Poems) were the starting signal for the new literature. This volume included the poem *Guldhornene* (The Golden Horns) and the short reading drama summing up the philosophy of universal Romanticism *St. Hansaften-Spil* (Midsummer Eve Play), both of which became part of literary mythology for later writers and were to form part of the Danish cultural tradition until far into the 20th century. The same applies to his verse reading drama *Aladdin* (from *Poetiske Skrifter*, Poetical Writings, 1805), which until about the time of the First World War constituted an essential text for later writers, whether they agreed or disagreed with the ideas in it.

Oehlenschläger created a new, sensuous poetical language and brought new life to poetry; after the publication of *Nordiske Digte* (1807, Nordic Poems) he turned Nordic mythology and legend into a living source of inspiration for literature and cultural life and breathed new life into Danish drama through his great tragedies (e.g. *Hakon Jarl*, 1807) (Earl Hakon the Mighty), and then later through more psychological plays such as *Dina* (1842).

After a prolonged journey abroad 1805-1809 (including visits to Goethe in Weimar and Madame de Staël in Paris) Oehlenschläger became Professor of Aesthetics in 1810. In 1829 he was proclaimed the King of Nordic Poetry by Esaias Tegnér, but after 1813 he encountered a good deal of criticism in Denmark on account of what was seen to be too great a production of plays, and also his determined concentration on Nordic themes, even at a time which demanded a more realistic presentation of the present. At the same time he relinquished Romanticism and replaced it with a humane bourgeois idealism. He wrote some of his works (e.g. the play *Correggio*) in German and won widespread recognition in Germany.

There is a great deal of humour and humanity in Oehlenschläger's work, particularly in his letters and his autobiography.

Johan de Mylius

of European fashions and encouraged by liberal economic and political thinking, all of which late absolutism was unable to suppress. Modernity was intoned in poetry by erotic poets such as Christian Winther and Emil Aarestrup, in the case of the latter also in his political poems.

That this was a transitional period, 'the political period', was demonstrated even by Søren Kierkegaard. Among the principal figures were the outsiders Steen Steensen Blicher, N.F.S. Grundtvig (who, however, had a widespread following from the 1840s onwards), Hans Christian Andersen and Søren Kierkegaard. With them the boundaries of late absolutism were crossed, and styles, problems and views of the public proclaiming something new were adopted. Blicher's realistic, disillusioned stories (sometimes in dialect) from Jutland – a part of Denmark that had not hitherto appeared in literature – heralded the realism of a

Thanks to his fairy tales and stories, *Hans Christian Andersen*, 1805-1875, is probably the most widely read author in the world today, but even in his own time he was read and known from Russia in the east to America in the west. His career from the lowest stratum of society in his native town of Odense in Funen via his problematic adaptation to the official and bourgeois circles in Copenhagen and further still until he became a familiar guest in the country mansions of Denmark, the palaces of kings and princes and the entire cultural stage of Europe provided him with material for many of his works and for no fewer than three autobiographies, the final version being *Mit Livs Eventyr* (1855, The Fairy Tale of My Life (with later supplements)). Modern editions of his correspondence and diaries have produced an unusually comprehensive insight into his life and his complex personality.

Andersen's fairy tales and stories (about 190 in all, written 1835-1872) are addressed to both adults and children and are stylistically and thematically deeply original. In addition he wrote novels, travel accounts (he spent a large part of his life travelling abroad), poems and works for the theatre (including libretti for operas and ballad operas).

Although Andersen's work has its roots in Romanticism he is a modern spirit thanks to his social experience, his psychological insight, his belief in progress and industrial development. The special quality in his fairy tales is also precisely the combination of poetry, fantasy tale and everyday reality.

Johan de Mylius

later age. Grundtvig, with a mixture of didactic zeal, unadorned Christianity and Romantic faith in the Spirit and the living word (of God), reformed Church and congregation through the revivalist movement he gave rise to. Thanks to the folk high school movement that emanated from him, he was a formative influence in establishing the Danes understanding of themselves and a Danish view of education and general culture. And throughout the rest of the century this movement became the basis upon which the rural population formed their sense of identity until they took political power in 1901 – and it continued to be felt well into the 20th century's social democratic culture. In his own career, Hans Christian Andersen broke through the barriers existing in the inflexible, bourgeois late absolutism of the time. In the fairy tale, which he transformed from the traditional popular fairy tale into a capricious, contemporary, realistic genre entirely of its own kind, he expressed the manifold and complex experiences which made him into a great psychologist, a man who was able to understand the interplay between people. At the same time he became an unorthodox religious spirit in a quest to which he never found a final answer. In many ways Andersen stood at the limit of his time, enthusiastic about the new technology in his confidence in progress and more humane conditions. Kierkegaard would have nothing to do with this 'superficial nonsense', but likewise stood at the frontier of the period, intensifying the demand for truth in the individual's way of life. With a mixture of Christian idealism and psychological realism he pointed to reality as the place where the life of the individual must be measured.

About and immediately after the fall of absolutism in 1849, a new kind of society began to emerge. The age called for new initiatives, bringing into the foreground the debate on women's emancipation. With Mathilde Fibiger as a front figure a number of women authors entered the stage to take part in the literary discussion of the problem. Realists like Meïr Aron Goldschmidt and Hans Egede Schack captured the intellectual identity of the age, delving into its innermost recesses.

The Modern Breakthrough
A new literature and a new ideological front, a cultural radicalism, broke through in the course of the 1870s to reach full flower in the 1880s. It was a common Scandinavian movement whose critical standard-bearers were Georg and Edvard Brandes. The Modern Breakthrough, as it came to be called by Georg Brandes (1883) was closely connected to industrialisation, the new sciences and the political conflicts surrounding the phasing out of the last remains of absolutist society. The process culminated in a landowners' dictatorship lasting until 1901 – the age of provisional laws which provided a spur for the work of Henrik Pontoppidan. As the decades up to the turn of the century were a period of dismantling and transformation, it was inevitable that the modern breakthrough in Denmark should largely take the form of a confrontation with the culture of the past.

This confrontation came to occupy a greater space in literature than did the new developments taking place in society, industry and

The book was an important instrument of enlightenment in the attempts of the workers' movement to influence society. The Workers' Reading Society was founded in 1871, as can be seen from the banner carrying as its motto Jens Peter Jacobsen's words 'Light on the land is what we seek'.

Georg Brandes, 1842-1927, critic, writer on culture, literary and cultural historian. With his literary criticism (in book form including *Æsthetiske Studier* (1868, Aesthetic Studies) and *Kritiker og Portraiter* (1870, Criticisms and Portraits), and with the lectures delivered at Copenhagen University from 1871 to 1883 (with some interruptions) on the subject of *Hovedstrømninger i det nittende Aarhundredes Litteratur* (Main Currents in Nineteenth Century Literature) he renewed both the concept of literature and literary criticism in Denmark. He interacted closely with the profound changes in the society and culture of the day and placed himself in a leading position in relation to young literature, as was clear from *Det moderne Gennembruds Mænd* (1883, The Men of the Modern Breakthrough).

His original demand for progressive, realistic literature debating problems gradually to some extent gave way to a cult of the great individual as the 'source of culture'. This occurred partly under the impression of the opposition he encountered in official Denmark, desertions by some of his own literary disciples, and was further developed by his voluntary exile in Berlin 1877-1883. This change in attitudes coincided with his discovery of Nietzsche and led to the great biographies of Goethe, Voltaire, Caesar and others.

Together with his brother, the drama critic, dramatist and politician Edvard Brandes, and the politician Viggo Hørup, Georg Brandes represented the start of the Danish cultural trend which later became known as cultural radicalism, and which is still a noticeable feature of the Danish cultural scene. Throughout his life, Georg Brandes maintained a powerful commitment to individual and political freedom, one effect of which was to persuade him to translate Stuart Mill's *On the Subjection of Women* and to speak out on behalf of oppressed peoples.

Georg Brandes became a leading cultural figure throughout Scandinavia and similarly prominent in the European arena.

Johan de Mylius

technology, to which writers in general closed their eyes. This was the age of the decadent novel: Jens Peter Jacobsen's *Niels Lyhne*, Herman Bang's *Haabløse Slægter* (Generations without Hope) and others. The Church and Christianity and middle-class morality, especially sexual morality, were in the firing line, while Darwinism forced its way into the foreground as a view typical of the time. The modern breakthrough, naturalist in its early stages and realist subsequently, led to a new absorption in the life of the individual, partly inspired by the existential radical philosopher Friedrich Nietzsche, whom Georg Brandes introduced in 1888.

With his translation of John Stuart Mills' *On the Subjection of Women*, Georg Brandes, appearing on a European, not merely a Danish or Scandinavian stage, started a debate on women's emancipation, but women authors of the day (Amalie

Skram, Erna Juel-Hansen and others) established their own modern breakthrough.

In the country at large the ground was being prepared for the assumption of power by the farmers in 1901. This was the result of the folk high school movement's post-Romantic message to a social class in the process of establishing its own cultural self-awareness. Here the foundations were laid for the very extensive literature mirroring rural society that is so much a characteristic of Denmark from around 1900 until 1950.

Since the modern breakthrough, radicalism has remained a typical feature of Danish cultural and political life right up to the present day. At the same time the ideological polarisation led to a situation in which more than one kind of culture and literature existed side by side after the collapse of the unified culture of absolutism. That, too, is a characteristic still found today.

Symbolism and Fin-de-Siècle Literature

Towards the turn of the century the intense preoccupation with natural phenomena which was part and parcel of naturalism and realism developed into a great wave of nature poetry, the greatest concentrated phenomenon of its kind in Denmark (Johannes Jørgensen, Viggo Stuckenberg, Sophus Claussen, Ludvig Holstein). Similarly it was a time when the focus on the individual that distinguished the crisis literature of naturalism and realism was further intensified into a subjective, emotive (often pessimistic) view of the surrounding world, linked to a new tendency to religion (Johannes Jørgensen, Helge Rode). As the editor of the periodical *Taarnet* (The Tower), Jørgensen introduced French symbolism, to which especially Sophus

Claussen dedicated himself in his preoccupation with the compelling experiences of art.

Towards the turn of the century the novel of decadence took on a more desperate sense of doom: Johannes V. Jensen's *Einar Elkær* and *Kongens Fald* (The Fall of the King), Ernesto Dalgas' *Lidelsens Vej* (The Way of Suffering), Martin Andersen Nexø's *Dryss* (Waste). Art nouveau that was characteristic of the architecture and applied arts of the day asserted itself especially in the prose works of Harald Kidde and Sophus Michaëlis, here as elsewhere with its roots in the prose of Jens Peter Jacobsen.

The Popular Breakthrough

At the same time as the political system changed in 1901 there were new signals in painting (the Funen group of painters), music (Carl Nielsen) and literature. What became known as the popular breakthrough in literature – in reality the breakthrough for contemporary realism that was heralded in the 1870s and 1880s – covered a wide area socially and ideologically, but the main effort was literature about rural society.

Johannes V. Jensen became the great linguistic innovator of the period, the man who in general introduced a new kind of literature in the 20th century. Authors as different as Tom Kristensen and Martin A. Hansen as well as Klaus Rifbjerg have declared their indebtedness to this author who shared the ideology of the popular breakthrough but went much further in both subject matter and viewpoint. Martin Andersen Nexø was the first of the great proletarian writers.

Otherwise it was a feature of the period leading up to the First World War that alongside this popular breakthrough, works were still being

written in continuation of the modern breakthrough, not least the new women's literature in which Agnes Henningsen scandalised her contemporaries by writing and living according to the more liberal norms of the day. Johannes V. Jensen's sister, Thit Jensen, the author of both historical and contemporary novels, stood as a leading figure in the debate around the role of women and sexuality.

The Inter-War Period

The international *isms*, some of them deriving from the visual art of the day, made their mark on Danish literature starting at the time of the First World War. The first was expressionism, partly inspired by Johannes V. Jensen – found i.a. in the poetry and novels of Emil Bønnelycke and Tom Kristensen. It was followed by a scattering of surrealism (from Jens August Schade via Bodil Bech and Tove Meyer and on to Gustaf Munch-Petersen). Although these isms were the precursors of the later modernism, they were nevertheless only marginal phenomena in the literature of the day, the main characteristic of which was a miscellaneous flow of broadly descriptive realism: from the bourgeois, naturalistic Jacob Paludan through sociological and social critical literature (collective novels, novels about the class struggle and broad, socially based novels of personal development) to the new, Freud-inspired psychological work of authors such as Hans Christian Branner.

Particularly the 1930s were characterised by a division between a cultural-radical, at times socialist tendency and an otherwise quite inhomogeneous group of authors who continued writing in well-proven modes with a broad (conservative) public appeal. Among the cultural radicals the outstanding figure was the architect, designer of lamps and furniture, review writer and cultural polemicist Poul Henningsen (PH). On the conservative front it was especially the pastor and dramatist Kaj Munk who attracted attention. Karen Blixen (Isak Dinesen), whose books from the middle of the 1930s started to appear first in the USA and then in Denmark, occupied a position of her own. A declared aristocratic conservatism was accompanied by a rebellious femininity in her stories and was in fact the expression of a Nietzsche-inspired criticism of culture that dated back to the 1890s and articulated itself in the cult of the wisdom contained in myth.

The Heretica Period

By the end of the 1930s, Paul la Cour was already taking steps to resurrect symbolism, arguing for it in a mani-

Under the pseudonym of *Isak Dinesen*, *Karen Blixen*, 1885-1962, wrote a number of collections of surprising, often complicated stories in the genre for which she herself invented the name 'Gothic tales' in her American first edition.

Her first book, *Seven Gothic Tales* was published in New York in 1934 in her own English version and was a great success, being published the same year in England and Sweden. On the basis of this position, she conquered the Danish literary world (*Syv fantastiske Fortællinger*, 1935), achieving a great success which she could scarcely have expected with her consciously un-modern stories in a literature that was predominantly the realm of social realism and psychoanalytical fiction.

The background to her launching herself on the international stage was a lengthy period spent in Kenya (1913-1931) as a coffee farmer. She had married a Swedish relative, Baron Bror Blixen-Finecke, and went off with him to try her fortune in the then British East Africa on a farm near the Ngong Hills outside Nairobi. The failure of the marriage, the failure of the farm and the death of her lover, the aristocratic game hunter Denys Finch Hatton, drove her back to Denmark, where she settled in Rungstedlund and started writing as an element in her struggle to establish her existential and financial position.

In 1937 came the poetical memoirs *Den afrikanske Farm* (Out of Africa) and in 1942 *Vinter-Eventyr* (Winter's Tales), in which her narrative art culminates, simpler and more concentrated than in the first collection, but still sublimely fascinating and disturbing.

Aristocratic milieux and norms and an aesthetic, Nietzschean anti-humanism play a consciously provocative role on the surface of her stories, which, however, in the questions they pose about fate, meaning, identity are textually modern and profoundly universal in their humanity.

Johan de Mylius

Villy Sørensen, 1929-2001, helped establish a contemporary norm as both a writer of fiction and an essayist (taking aesthetics, cultural philosophy and cultural criticism as his themes). Together with Klaus Rifbjerg he edited the periodical Vindrosen 1959-1963, an important time in the establishment of modernism and neo-radicalism in Denmark.

Sørensen's fiction is modest in extent, consisting really only of three collections of short stories, *Sære historier* (1953, Strange Stories), *Ufarlige historier* (1955, Harmless Tales) and *Formynderfortællinger* (1964, Tutelary Tales), and then *De mange og De enkelte og andre småhistorier* (1986, Another Metamorphosis and Other Fictions). Particularly the first two of these betokened a completely new way of writing, the so-called 'absurd story', in reality a modern variant of the fairy-tale genre or the fantastic story in the tradition of a Hans Christian Andersen or Karen Blixen.

Typical themes for the two collections are repression (treated in a Freudian manner with a cultural critical perspective), disintegration and art as a means of providing an identity and solving crises. At a later date Villy Sørensen produced a re-telling of the story of Aladdin (1981) and recreations of Scandinavian mythological tales in *Ragnarok – en gudefortælling* (1982, The Downfall of the Gods) and Classical mythology, *Apollons oprør* (1989, The Rebellion of Apollo).

As an essayist Villy Sørensen achieved a position of something approaching a one-man university. Countless critics and students of literature have come under the influence of the critical radicalism, the aesthetic analysis and philosophy of books such as *Digtere og dæmoner* (1959, Poets and Demons, (forming a background to almost all the stories)) and *Hverken-eller* (1961, Neither-Nor). In contrast to the general American-French tendency of the post-war years, Villy Sørensen identified himself closely with the German cultural tradition (Hermann Broch, Thomas Mann, the young Marx, Nietzsche, Kafka and Schopenhauer, – on the last three of whom he wrote books). In addition he wrote studies on *Seneca* (1976) and *Jesus og Kristus* (1992, Jesus and Christ) and translated works by Seneca and Erasmus of Rotterdam.

In 1978, together with the physicist Niels I. Meyer and the politician K. Helveg Petersen, he produced a work analysing society and proposing a utopian social ideal, Oprør fra midten (Revolt from the Centre), which gave rise to great popular debate.

Johan de Mylius

festo entitled *Fragmenter af en Dagbog* (Fragments of a Diary). A group of authors formed itself around the periodical Heretica, led by Martin A. Hansen, Ole Wivel and Thorkild Bjørnvig and marking a break with naturalism and realism and its view of mankind. Instead they took religion, ethics, art, form or universal nature as their basis. Common to many authors and writers at the time during and immediately after the German Occupation was the experience of a profound cultural crisis which on the basis of sympathy with modernist pictorial art was given a visionary expression with religious overtones in the poetry of Ole Sarvig, and, in a more optimistic light, that of the young Frank Jæger.

Post-War Modernism and Traditionalism

International modernism found its Danish expression in the circle around Heretica: Martin A. Hansen's experimental short stories, Branner's experiments with stream of consciousness in short stories, drama and novels, Sarvig's poetry. But it was an ethically concerned modernism. In the 1950s a modernism made its breakthrough that to a far greater extent took modernity for granted and found adequate expression for it. Villy Sørensen founded a new, freely imaginative and apparently 'absurd' narrative style. Both his philosophy and his creative writing started from a sharpened linguistic awareness that was able to portray loss of identity and alienation. For

Klaus Rifbjerg, b.1931, one of the principal figures in Danish post-war literature and cultural criticism, a rejuvenator especially of lyric poetry, in which he was a pioneer of Danish modernism at the beginning of the 1960s. His work is very extensive both in the number of titles and the range of genres and modes of expression, characterised by vigorous productive energy and great linguistic inventiveness.

The collection of poems entitled *Konfrontation* (1960, Confrontation) which tests the ego and the senses against an alienating material reality was a breakthrough for Rifbjerg the poet and at the same time the beginning of the 'incomprehensible' modernism of the 1960s. It was followed up by the great associative poem *Camouflage* (1961), but by 1965 in his *Amagerdigte* (Poems from Amager) Rifbjerg was already moving into a new simplicity. In the late *Kandestedersuite* (1994, Kandesteder Suite), however, Rifbjerg has recaptured some of the tone of his early modernism.

In prose, *Den kroniske uskyld* (1958, Chronic Innocence), a novel about a generation that got off to a bad start in its personal development and its sexuality, Rifbjerg created the image of himself as an author who was both provocative and scandalous. The novel has since become a classic and is the first clear sign in Rifbjerg's work of the theme of puberty which has reappeared in much of the later fiction. The collection of short stories – *og andre historier* (1964, – and other stories) keeps to the same range of themes but is at the same time a decided move into prose modernism. From the later novels, the Freudian inspired *Operaelskeren* (1966, The Opera Lover) and *Anna (jeg) Anna* (1969, Anna (I) Anna) deserve special mention. In many books from the and 1980s, Rifbjerg has eagerly launched into a hybrid form of fiction and offensive portrayals of reality which have kept him and his readers on their toes. As a dramatist, too, and especially in the field of television drama, Rifbjerg has been productive.

As a literary critic and writer on culture, originally in the newspaper Information and subsequently in Politiken, and as the editor of the periodical Vindrosen 1959-63, Rifbjerg achieved a central position in Danish cultural life which was further reinforced by his years as Director of the Gyldendal publishing house (1984-1992).

Johan de Mylius

Klaus Rifbjerg the path led him away from the stance of an angry young man in an increasingly experimental direction, culminating in the volume of poems entitled *Konfrontation* and the suite of poems called *Camouflage*. After the 1970s his substantial production moved in other directions more responsive to public taste, but in his poetry his pioneering qualities and his spirited realism coalesced with a linguistic energy which has made of him an innovator on a level with Johannes V. Jensen and Adam Oehlenschläger.

The greatest public impact was seen in Leif Panduro's television drama revealing the fundamental absurdity of the middle classes. Throughout the 1960s and in the beginning of the 1970s there was a movement away from a preoccupation with 'the absurd' (the young Benny Andersen's poetry and short

Henrik Stangerup, 1937-1998, pursued a versatile career as novelist, journalist, essayist and film director. His first novel, *Slangen i brystet* (1969, Snake in the Heart), influenced by the neo-realistic trend of the time, is about a Danish journalist who goes off the rails in Paris. In the 1970s his novels took a turn towards polemic social comment. *Løgn over løgn* (1971, Lie upon Lie) is a confrontation with the ascetic Puritanism which according to Stangerup characterised the cultural left wing of the day. *Manden der ville være skyldig* (1973, The Man Who Wanted to Be Guilty) is an attack on the welfare state from an existentialist perspective. *Fjenden i forkøbet* (1978, Forestalling the Enemy) is an autobiographical novel which, with great openness, recounts artistic and personal crises in the author's life.

In the following years Stangerup wrote his principal work, a trilogy of historical novels inspired by Søren Kierkegaard's ideas about the aesthetic, ethical and religious man. *Vejen til Lagoa Santa* (1981, The Road to Lagoa Santa) is about the ethicist, the Danish 19th century naturalist P.W. Lund, who turned his back on European civilisation and settled in Brazil. The protagonist of *Det er svært at dø i Dieppe* (1985, The Seducer : It is Hard to Die in Dieppe) is the aesthete and critic P.L. Møller, who lived a dissolute life in Paris in the 1850s. Finally the religious stage is represented by the title character of *Broder Jacob* (1991, Brother Jacob), a Danish Franciscan driven into exile by the Reformation. He ends up as a missionary and fearless spokesman for the Indian population. The trilogy gave expression to Stangerup's criticism of Danish Puritanism in a colourful epic of international perspective and format.

Stangerup's films are inspired by French culture, with which he became thoroughly familiar during several protracted sojourns in the country. The most original is *Jorden er flad* (1977, The Earth is Flat), which transplants the action in Ludvig Holberg's comedy *Erasmus Montanus* (published 1731) to 17th century Brazil. As interpreted by Stangerup, the story of the arrogant peasant student who returns to his destitute childhood environment becomes a universally valid account of the intelligentsia's betrayal of the people from which they spring.

Like his novels and films, Stangerup's extensive essay writing also testifies to his international outlook and uncompromising attitude towards intellectual conformity of every kind. But the essays, which are collected for instance in *I flugtens tegn* (1993, Flight is the Order of the Day), also include penetrating characterisations of countrymen such as Kierkegaard, the man of letters Georg Brandes and film director Carl Th. Dreyer – men who, like the protagonists in Stangerup's novels, were too distinctive and intractable to fit into the cultural pattern of their day.

Søren Schou

stories, Peter Seeberg's then widely discussed prose, Ivan Malinowski's poetry, etc.) towards a constructivist or formalist modernism with Hans-Jørgen Nielsen as one of its spokesmen and culminating in Inger Christensen's linguistic creation, *Det* (It), Svend Åge Madsen's novels (including *Sæt verden er til* – Suppose the World Exists) and Per Højholt's mischievous textual sequences. Henrik Nordbrandt occupies a special position with his melancholy, musical poetry.

Alongside modernism there were also other currents: an existential-historical documentarism in the work of Thorkild Hansen; in the case of Tage Skou-Hansen and Erik Aalbæk Jensen a broad critical and existential realism in the tradition of Henrik Pontoppidan; autobiographically-tinged work with social, psychological perspectives and depictions of women's lives from Tove Ditlevsen; Anders Bodelsen's, Christian Kampmann's and Henrik Stangerup's contemporary realism.

The Public and Privatisation

The student revolution of 1968 led to a vigorous renewal of the ideological debate and a consequent loss of interest in the exclusive literary experiments. During the 1970s a new proletarian literature emerged, and more particularly a new wave of

Ib Michael, b. Rasmussen, 1945, is Denmark's answer to Latin America's magic realism, a cosmopolitan, travelling writer of fairytales. His books, especially novels but also short stories and pictorial poems, are fantastic, dramatic and melodious narratives, full of both exotic travels, miraculous coincidences and sensuous reality. They are characterised by mystical experience which e.g. draws on Indian and Buddhistic philosophy and fantastical literature. Time, space and persons are juxtaposed despite enormous jumps in time and transformations, opposing tendencies are kept together in a dynamic balance of excitement. Having written his first imaginative books, Ib Michael travelled to meet Indian cultures in South and Central America and collected material about nature, myth and politics which he made use of in books such as *Mayalandet* (1973, The Mayaland) and the great, visionary novel *Rejsen tilbage* (1977, The Journey Back). In this book 'the immortal soldier' is an important mythological figure who walks through time and space under different aspects. He is one of Ib Michael's most constant transformation figures and a central figure in *Kejserfortællingen* (1981, Tiger's Tale) dealing with the history of China and *Kilroy Kilroy* (1989) where the tibetan culture and fight for freedom resonate with the characters' search for identity.

In his three 'novels of memory' *Vanillepigen* (1991, The Vanilla Girl), *Den tolvte rytter* (1993, The Midnight Soldier) and *Brev til Månen* (1995, Letter to the Moon), Ib Michael makes use of a surprising mixture of ethnography and mystical-realistic fiction while telling the story of his own childhood and genealogy. He switches brilliantly between now and then, between the local and global, between sensuous description of the situation and the transition to myth and history. In the great novel *Prins* (1997, Prince) Ib Michael also endeavours to combine imagination and reality, and this dream characterises the whole body of his work, including *Kejserens Atlas* (2001, The Emperor's Atlas).

Anders Østergaard

confessions and intimate revelations. The everyday quality of so-called chopped-up prose, poetry texts close to ordinary speech, became a popular and much read poetical form at the same time as the lyrical avant-garde rather more quietly developed in for instance the computer-science-oriented texts of Klaus Høeck.

Mythologies, Post-Modernism and New Inventive Writing

In the 1980s and 1990s readers had become satiated with confessions concerning intimate everyday life and with form without form. At the same time as student marxism was declining under the rise of non-socialist politics, literature turned back to its own roots as literature. The modernism of a new generation with Michael Strunge, Bo Green Jensen, Pia Tafdrup and Søren Ulrik Thomsen is not only inspired by rock music and a modern body consciousness, but has also freely been able to look back to romantic and symbolist forms. The last two names in the above list have formulated their ideas in theories of poetry. A practised realist like Henrik Stangerup moved via ideological and personal confrontations into the realm of cultural history and mythology. A number of lyric poets, inspired by older modernists like Ole Sarvig and Jørgen Gustava Brandt, turned again to the hymn, which has been one of the cornerstones of Danish literature, but which had generally speaking lain untouched since Grundtvig. A new religiosity together with the contemporary preoccupation with the Universe and Nature formed the background of the renewed interest in the hymn. A critical environmental consciousness was given universal and mythological dimensions in the nature motifs of Thorkild Bjørnvig and Vagn Lundbye.

women's writing, including the work of Jette Drewsen, Vita Andersen and Dea Trier Mørch, who stood at the centre of a protracted public debate. The severe ideological criticism of the function and forms of literature, which thrived in the university environment, helped to force authors' interests towards an everyday life free from ideologies, private thoughts,

Peter Høeg, b.1957, had great success at the beginning of the 1990s with *Frøken Smillas fornemmelse for sne* (1992, Miss Smilla's Feeling for Snow), a thriller critical of civilisation and portraying a woman's schismatic relationship to European and Eskimo culture. The novel, the tone of which ranges from cool analysis to compassion and poetry, has been translated into a vast number of languages and filmed by Bille August.

Before this comet-like ascent, Høeg had already established himself as one of the major writers of contemporary Danish fiction, with the novel *Forestilling om det 20. århundrede* (1988, The History of Danish Dreams), a magical realistic presentation of Danish dreams and notions throughout a century, and with *Fortællinger om natten* (1990, Tales of the Night), nine stories written in a style reminiscent of Karen Blixen. Each of these centers on one of the classical forms of art or sciences; a motif common to them all is love and its conditions.

Høeg's critical view of culture and his ability to understand sympathetically lives that go wrong appears in his fourth novel, *De måske egnede* (1993,

Borderliners), at one and the same time an analysis of time as a subjective phenomenon and a moving description of a boy fighting to avoid being crushed by the school system.

The sceptical approach to the world of science in *Frøken Smillas fornemmelse for sne* is echoed in *Kvinden og aben* (1996, The Woman and the Ape). This novel examines the sense of fulfilment felt by an alcoholic upper-class woman who saves a monkey of a hitherto unknown species from the clutches of the scientists.

The main characters in the latest three books written by Peter Høeg all inhabit the shadowy area on the periphery of normality and social structure: Miss Smilla who stems from an ethnic minority and finds it impossible to fit in, the boy at the bottom of the social hierarchy in *De måske egnede*, and the ape in *Kvinden og aben*, more human than the human beings themselves. The woman, the child and the animal are used symbolically by the author to remind us that there is something fundamentally wrong with our modern-day existence. Peter Høeg's imaginative and uncompromising examination of the problems in our culture, and of our unsatisfactory grasp of love, the sexes, money and power, sets him apart as a great Danish and international writer.

May Schack

These decades saw the emergence of a lively narrative art. Kirsten Thorup wrote about women's experiences in prose that balances between a socially-tinged, far-reaching realism and a psychological interior world. To a great extent, prose writers have worked with hybrid forms, somewhere between novel and memoir for instance in the case of Suzanne Brøgger, and between realism and highly conscious style in Peter Seeberg and Jens Smærup Sørensen. Dorrit Willumsen has in a series of frightening portrayals depicted modern people as mechanical models and victims of a distorted social order. Life as an anthology of human fates in common isolation is found in Peer Hultberg's analytical prose. The internationally widespread hybrid form of realism and fantastic narration, magic realism, has also made its special mark in Danish literature in various ways, but with wide international appeal in the work of Ib Michael and Peter Høeg. The fact that Karen Blixen has been one of the most read and discussed of the older generation during this time has also had its effect. However, despite the affinities in the imaginative writing, there is a considerable gap between the divine staging of the world in Karen Blixen's stories and diffuse postmodernism and the pioneering body consciousness that, with varying intensity, asserted itself in Danish literature in the latter half of the 1980s and into the 1990s.

Johan de Mylius

Danish Literature by the Turn of the Millenium

In 1987 the Danish Writer's School was established, headed by the poet and critic Poul Borum. Several of the school's students have asserted themselves as experimental poets or prose writers. Represented by e.g. Solvej Balle, the last decade has, in particular, seen the emergence of a phenomenalistic, often minimalist, prose fiction breaking with more traditional and social causal explanations. However, Jens Christian Grøndahl has seen new possibilities in the psychological search of the realistic tradition. In a number of novels written with a sure sense of style, he has described the identity problems facing today's men and women. Some of the elder, established writers have written their chief works in the 1990s and the beginning of the new millenium, e.g. Peer Hultberg, known for his special stream-of-unconsciousness technique, Vibeke Grønfeldt, making her mark with eccentric novels criticising our civilisation, and within systemic poetry, Klaus Høeck has proved to be the great master with his monumental poet sequences. During that same period, the great travel biographies of culture critic Carsten Jensen have brought new life to the essay genre. This varied picture of Danish literature moving into the new millenium is characterised by variety both in style of expression, genres and choices.

May Schack

Children's Literature

Children's literature emerged in Denmark in the first half of the 19th century and the most important Danish contribution to children's literature remains Hans Christian Andersen's *Eventyr, fortalte for Børn* (1835, Fairy Tales, Told for Children). Today's writers of children's literature such as Bent Haller and Louis Jensen continue to find inspiration in Andersen's fairy tales and stories. Furthermore, Andersen's fairy tales continue to live on in the universe of Danish children through illustrated versions made by the important illustrators Ib Spang Olsen and Svend Otto S. A certain influence from Andersen's own pictures can be seen in works of younger illustrators, e.g. Lilian Brøgger and Cato Thau-Jensen.

Danish literature for children is a varied field publishing over a thousand titles a year, and today it is more characterised by aesthetics than by pedagogy. The character of the picture books and prose stories published varies widely including e.g. realistic, humorous, fantastic and psychological stories. Cecil Bødker's series about the boy Silas (1967-2001) anticipated the present fantasy wave, because it deals with universal human relations within a mythical universe. Stories written by Ole Lund Kirkegaard, Kim Fupz Aakeson and Bjarne Reuter are often characterised by humor, but with linguistic precision they also describe the serious sides of a child's world. With their important works, these writers have reached a large and even international audience.

Nina Christensen

Theatre and Drama

As in the surrounding countries, pre-Christian rituals in Denmark presumably contained elements of acting, but nothing is known with certainty. Nor are there any written sources for mediaeval liturgical drama in the church, although murals and extant props point to the existence of such drama. The most elaborate Scandinavian hagiographic miracle play, on the subject of 'Saint Knud Lavard', (*Ludus de Sancto Kanuto Duce*), was probably performed in the market square in Ringsted. It is known in a version from about 1500, but may well be based on earlier models.

School Drama

There was school drama even in late Catholic times, but it was the Protestant school drama that came to constitute a significant movement of cultural policy in the market towns. The kings, too, were happy to be entertained by school drama with its biblical, moralising and satirical subjects. The texts were often translated from Latin and German, but a native Danish drama established itself with the Viborg clergyman Hieronymus Justesen Ranch as its most original talent. His *Karrig Nidding* (Nithing the Niggard) from about 1600 is a proper character comedy with traces of old carnival farce. However, at the beginning of the 17th century the church's views on the theatre changed in the wake of the Lutheran orthodoxy that was now the order of the day. It was argued that the theatre led people into sin and vice.

Strolling Players

In time, professional troupes of players, who travelled around in Europe in the second half of the 16th century, began to come to Denmark. Thus in 1586 Frederik II had an English troupe in his service, including the comic actor William Kempe, who later acted for Shakespeare. Later the groups of strolling players, who after c. 1600 were mainly German and Dutch speakers, travelled around in Denmark, performing among other things the extravagant so-called Haupt- und Staatsaktionen. The monarchy's wish to give dramatical expression to its own greatness, especially under Christian IV, took on ever more spectacular forms. The wedding of the heir to the throne in 1634 was a gigantic investment; The Grand Bedding of the Couple was a panoply of comedy, music, dance and fireworks lasting for over a fortnight. Here the court ballet was introduced, a kind of allegorical total theatre with the most distinguished members of the court themselves among the actors.

Theatre for Court and City

The model for the absolute monarchy was naturally France. As Crown Prince, Christian V had visited Louis XIV and was inspired both to a grandiose cult of the monarch in opera ballets and to putting on French classical drama. Under Christian V and Frederik IV French court companies came and went, and they also gave public performances. René Magnon de Montaigu, who belonged to the Molière school, came to Denmark in 1686 and in 1700 became the leader of the royal company. From temporary stages in, among other places, Copenhagen Castle, the company moved in 1703 into the newly erected opera house in Bredgade in

For the royal wedding, Det Store Bilager (the Grand Bedding of the Couple), in 1634, the morality *Tragoedia von den Tugenden und Lastern* (The Tragedy of Virtues and Vices) was performed in the outer courtyard of Copenhagen Palace, and it concluded with a gigantic firework display. The structure was that of a medieval simultaneous stage with various symbolical localities: The Castle of Hope, the Dragon's Castle and the Jaws of Hell swallowing the exiled vices. This print is by Crispin de Pas from the illustrated book version of the festivities from 1648.

Copenhagen, which was intended for both the court and the city. Within a few years, however, the project proved not to be viable, and the building was put to other use; it is today the seat of the The High Court of Eastern Denmark (*Østre Landsret*). Inspired by, among other things, the Venetian opera stages, Frederik IV built a castle theatre which was inaugurated in 1712 and contained boxes and stage machinery, just as there had been in the Opera House. Montaigu here presented a repertoire of festive allegorical plays and French drama.

With the renewed demand for entertainment after the Great Northern War (1700-1721) there were performances in German which lavishly mixed drama, acrobatics, mechanics and tableaux. As a new theatre and centre for entertainment a theatre was opened in Copenhagen in 1722 in Lille Grønnegade, the present-day Ny Adelgade. Meanwhile, the king had dismissed his court players, and the thought now arose of opening a Danish-language theatre under the direction of Montaigu in the Lille Grønnegade theatre. Here, Ludvig Holberg created a sati-

Danish intellectual life up to the European level. His comedies represent only a small part of an enormous output comprising many kinds of creative writing plus science and philosophy. Examples are his *Moralske Tanker* (Moral Thoughts) and *Epistler* (Epistles) written in the spirit of Seneca and Montaigne. As a dramatist Holberg was close to Molière and was at the same time fascinated by the robust comedy of Italian commedia dell'arte. However, although his gallery of characters has foreign forebears – the old fathers, the young lovers, the wily servants, etc. – Holberg created a comedy based on the Denmark of his own day, with recognisable types, usually such as were found in Copenhagen; and there was a constant emphasis on the fact that there is a moral purpose behind the fun. This latter aspect was also a pragmatic quality of use to Holberg outside the theatre: Since 1717, he had been a professor at the University, and as such it was not entirely appropriate for him to spend his time on such frivolous things as the theatre.

Bent Holm

Ludvig Holberg, 1684-1754, was the author who created a professional Danish drama. Born in Bergen in Norway, he was a keen traveller especially during his younger years, and France and Italy were of particular significance for his artistic development. He had an international outlook and worked consciously to bring

rical modern drama with a gallery of bourgeois characters, in harmony with the general endeavour of the time to raise people's cultural and moral levels and turn them into efficient members of society. The satire was also directed against what was said to be the old-fashioned Hauptund Staatsaktionen, and thereby at the irrational theatricality of the Baroque. Several of the actors were students, which immediately caused conflict with the university: The old theological antipathy to the theatre re-emerged. In 1722 the theatre opened with Molière's *L'Avare*, and there was the first professional performance of an original Danish drama, Holberg's *Den politiske kandestøber* (The Political Tinker). The main inspiration was Molière, but Holberg also had a liking for the robust comedy of Italian commedia

dell'arte. In the long run, the public deserted the theatre, and it had to close in 1727. The 1728 Fire of Copenhagen put a complete end to theatres: Frederik IV had religious scruples, and his pietist son, Christian VI introduced a de facto ban on the theatre, which was maintained until his death in 1746.

The Royal Theatre

Theatrical life began to flourish again, and in 1748 Danish comedy could move into Eigtved's elegant theatre on Kongens Nytorv in Copenhagen. Formally, it was the king who lent his name to the theatre, but in 1750 he passed it on to the city of Copenhagen – along with a sizeable debt. The idea of a theatre for court and city had now been realised, and it was from the start characterised by Holbergian dramatic techniques. In time, however, the emphasis shifted from ridiculing vice to glorifying virtue, which went hand in hand with a new moral sensibility such as is found in Charlotta Dorothea Biehl's comedies from the 1760s and 1770s.

In 1770 the theatre actually came under royal directorship as The Royal Danish Theatre, and from 1772 it was directly financed by the Privy Purse and formally subject to the Lord Chamberlain's Office. The theatre was given a prominent place in the incipient public debate. Although the elevated and musical genres were parodied in Johan Herman Wessel's *Kærlighed uden strømper* (Love Without Stockings) (1773), a growing interest in national and patriotic themes at the end of the 18th century resulted in a number of original Danish tragedies and music dramas with motifs taken from mythology, history and the life of the ordinary people.

National Romanticism on the German model reached the theatre at the beginning of the 19th century,

not least in the work of Adam Oehlenschläger, who made his début as a dramatist with *Hakon Jarl* (Earl Hakon the Mighty) (1808).

This was an impassioned dramatic form, in contrast to the Holbergian sober-mindedness that had typified the national repertoire from the start. The way had been prepared for Shakespeare, and *Hamlet* had its Danish premiere in 1813. On the other side stood Johan Ludvig Heiberg, who as a critic in the 1820s made strict demands on form and inspired by Parisian theatre created the vaudeville – charming, satirical and musical portrayals of the little world of the bourgeoisie. The theatre was bathed in a radiance of its own at this time. To write for the stage was a matter of some prestige, and The Royal Theatre came to be seen as a leading cultural institution. There were several outstanding talents among those associated with it, and authors competed in writing for them, in particular for Johanne Luise Heiberg, the undisputed prima

A result of the growing consciousness of the middle classes at the end of the 18th century was the formation of private drama associations in the provinces leading to the building of theatres, initially in Odense in 1795. In 1817 the Helsingør Drama Association built its theatre in a neo-classical style. This is now preserved in *Den Gamle By, Danmarks Købstadsmuseum* (The Old Town, The National Open Air Museum of Urban History and Culture) in Århus, where it has for a number of years also been used as a theatre for comedy and opera in the summer season.

donna of Romanticism, whose range stretched from the romantic and erotic to the passionate and demonic, though always observing the boundaries of aesthetics and good taste. After the end of the absolute monarchy The Royal Theatre was in 1849 placed under State control and given a commoner as director – in the first instance Johan Ludvig Heiberg, whose aesthetical ideals soon came into conflict with the realism that was pushing itself forward in the middle of the century.

The present Royal Theatre was opened at the same time (1874) and in the same style as the Paris Opéra. It was well suited to opera and ballet, but scarcely the ideal setting for the sitting-room drama that reached new peaks with the premieres of Henrik Ibsen's dramas (such as *Et dukkehjem*, 1879, A Doll's House). This stage naturalism established a link with the controversial literary and political currents centred on the brothers Georg and Edvard Brandes. The demands for authenticity in setting and psychology were implemented from the 1880s by the director William Bloch. With this, the meticulous director had once and for all made his appearance as a key figure in theatrical performances. Naturalism was also the hallmark of the drama school established in 1886.

Amateur Theatre

Since the latter half of the 18th century the middle classes had gone mad about the theatre – a theatre run by themselves on a non-professional basis. In the long run, the foundations were laid here for a healthy tradition of amateur drama, often related to the folk high school movement (and from 1948 organised under the aegis of the Danish Amateur Theatre Association). At the same time drama clubs were becoming important as a means of extending professional drama to the provinces, where from c. 1820 their stages were used by touring groups of actors. This also created the basis for permanent theatres in the major provincial cities.

New Theatres

While The Royal Theatre was increasingly becoming the place for the educated, the broader public started going to the 'secondary theatres', which were permitted with the introduction of democracy, the Casino from 1848 being the first of them. However, The Royal Theatre retained an absolute monopoly of the more serious repertoire until 1889. On the other hand, Holberg, Oehlenschläger, Heiberg, etc. could well be staged, often by itinerant groups, in the provinces. At the beginning of the 20th century the theatres in Århus and Odense had also established themselves with their own permanent companies performing a repertoire varying from plays reminiscent of The Royal Theatre to others of a lighter kind. Aalborg followed suit in 1937. After the First World War The Royal Theatre's monopoly was further undermined: the Dagmar Theatre and the Betty Nansen Theatre established themselves as artistic competitors to The Royal Theatre in Copenhagen.

For and Against Naturalism

The pioneering formal experiments throughout Europe at the beginning of the century did not generally speaking have any repercussions in Denmark. Gordon Craig's non-naturalistic staging of Ibsen's *Kongsemnerne* (The Pretenders) in The Royal Theatre in 1926 was thus a resounding fiasco. Experiments were largely left to amateur or semi-professional experimental theatres, or to a daring

Johanne Luise Heiberg, née Pätges, 1812-1890, the undisputed prima donna of the Romantic age. She began as a child in the ballet school of the Royal Theatre in 1820, but finally moved into drama when Johan Ludvig Heiberg wrote the vaudeville *Aprilsnarrene* (The April Fools) for her in 1826. They married in 1831, and Johanne Luise thereby found herself at the centre of Copenhagen intellectual life. Dramatists vied with each other to write parts for her: from the dreamily erotic to the passionate and demonic, but also with due respect to Romanticism's ideal of beauty. The philosopher Søren Kierkegaard wrote a detailed description of her art. After leaving the stage, she worked for some years as a producer, not least of a couple of plays by Henrik Ibsen. Mrs Heiberg left one of the greatest works of Danish memoir literature, *Et Liv gjenoplivet i Erindringen* (1891-1892, A Life Re-Lived in Memory). Her career is often compared with that of Hans Christian Andersen, and in 1981 the Swedish dramatist Per Olov Enquist brought the two together in *Fra regnormenes liv* (From the Life of the Earthworms).

Bent Holm

small theatre such as Riddersalen, which in 1935 staged Kjeld Abell's satirical play *Melodien der blev væk* (The Melody That Got Lost), the greatest success of the inter-war years. The 1930s were characterised by important dramatists like Kaj Munk, Carl Erik Soya and Kjeld Abell, who were performed in both the private theatres and The Royal Theatre, where especially Abell helped breach the well-established naturalist tradition. During the German occupation (1940-1945), foreign impulses were naturally limited, and the theatres had to carry on under a state censorship no longer based on moral views, but with a direct political motivation.

Absurdism and Social Realism

Very soon after the war ended, the modern international repertoire made its appearance, for instance French absurdism and English social realism in the 1950s. Absurdism was in particular promoted by the Student Theatre, which acted as an experimental stage for gifted young talents who later came to leave their mark on the professional theatre as directors, actors and playwrights. Radio and television theatre soon also opened up to this repertoire and these figures. The theatres then followed suit. Bertolt Brecht became firmly established in the theatre in the 1960s. And with this, a subject that was to dominate the next ten years had made its appearance: sociological and political (Brecht-inspired) drama as opposed to a more fantastic (Artaud-inspired) view of the theatre. In the small theatres that emerged in the 1960s, the first of which was Fiolteatret from 1962, absurdism was in the forefront.

Radio and Television Theatre

Radio drama was originally seen as a means of enlightening the public and a vehicle for culture. From 1925 broadcasts were made of the Danish School Theatre's performances of classics, and within a few years the repertoire consisted of a mixture of adapted stage drama and original plays for radio. Major stage artists like Poul Reumert thus reached a broader public. From the 1950s radio theatre obtained the technical opportunity of going its own way. The 1960s saw the emergence of plays specifically for radio, and Danish authors could here experiment independently of the financial constraints by which the theatres were bound. From the 1950s television drama underwent a similar development, from being tied to the theatre and the idea of 'the great classics' to independent artistic expressions. The creation of original Danish television drama was in particular a high priority 1970-1985. It had a particularly powerful representative in Leif Panduro's bittersweet portrayal of the traumas behind a bourgeois facade.

The 1960s and 1970s

The establishment of a Ministry for Cultural Affairs in 1961 brought an end to the situation in which The Royal Theatre belonged under the Ministry of Education and other theatres under the Ministry of Justice. The Theatre Act of 1963 determined among other things the framework for support for the

Bodil Ipsen's and Poul Reumert's scintillating acting together throughout the greater part of half a century was legendary. Here in Molière's *Tartuffe* it is the seduction scene between Elmire and Tartuffe, Act 3, Scene 3, in the Dagmar Theatre version. In 1925 Reumert had the unique experience of playing Tartuffe in French in Molière's own theatre, the Comédie-Française in Paris.

provincial theatres in Århus, Aalborg and Odense, and through grants it gave the Theatre Council a significant influence on the areas of theatre life outside the fixed institutional framework. In general, the 1960s and 1970s were a time of important cultural initiatives pointing to democratisation and decentralisation both at a political level and among the many experimental or socially critical theatre groups addressing themselves to a different public from the established theatres, including the younger age groups. Children had so far mainly been provided for by the Danish School Theatre. When the School Theatre was disbanded in 1968, the way was clear for an array of itinerant theatre groups treating the problems of children and young people in their own language. In many respects, Denmark became a pioneer in drama for children and young people. Of great significance for experimental drama, also in an international perspective, was Eugenio Barba's Odin Theatre, established in Holstebro in 1966. In training, changes were also made in relation to the established institutions: The Royal Theatre Drama School was disbanded in 1968, and the National School of Dramatic Art opened, first with an eye to training actors, and then subsequently directors, set designers and technicians.

From 1971 cultural democracy also asserted itself in the form of a scheme run by the theatre-goers' organisation ARTE, making it possible to take out tickets for a number of performances at a reduced price. Legislation later applied the model to the whole country, the Act coming into force in 1975, with state and county support. This has without any doubt had a positive influence on the sale of tickets, but it has also been criticised, among other things for preventing flexibility in the planning of the theatres.

The 1980s and 1990s

Provisions for regional theatres from 1979 brought some group theatres under the aegis of the county and local authorities, with the institutionalisation inevitably resulting from that. Social preoccupations were replaced in the 1980s and 1990s by the exploration of aesthetical and artistic effects. A generation of younger producers found more fragmented ways of expressing themselves. A very dynamic and direct tone, appealing particularly to a young audience, came into its own in 1992 when the Dr. Dante group took over the Aveny Theatre. Concurrently, a new generation of dramatists was emerging, often with a blend of ironic realism and linguistic exuberance bordering upon the absurd. Otherwise, as grants became more and more difficult to come by, the picture was one of a return to a repertoire more certain to appeal to a large audience. Placed outside the institutions, performance theatre was especially characteristic of the early 1990s, when Hotel Pro Forma in particular made an international reputation for itself. Performances derived from avant-garde art and happenings, breaking down the boundaries between the forms of expression and cultivating visual and sound effects. At the end of the 1990s The Royal Theatre was in an unsettled state. A debate flared up about the traditional housing of the different art forms

Klaus Hoffmeyer, b. 1938. Despite an unconventional start in student drama and French absurdism, the stage and television director Klaus Hoffmeyer has made his mark on theatrical life for many years. He has translated Artaud into Danish. His interest in the more irrational and impassioned aspects of drama have revealed themselves in his staging of great, sometimes Romantic, drama by, for instance, Shakespeare, Wagner and Oehlenschläger – in clear contrast to the dominant Danish love of normality and realism. His commitment to contemporary theatre is especially seen in his work with Danish drama, in particular the absurdist Jess Ørnsbo. After starting with the student theatre Hoffmeyer moved to television drama and the experimental theatres, after which, via an association lasting many years with Aarhus Teater he progressed to The Royal Theatre, where in 1986 he became a permanent producer and subsequently acting Head of the Drama Department.

Bent Holm

(opera, ballet and drama) under one roof and the feeling that the architectural setting was outdated gave rise to discussion of the siting of a new playhouse, which is planned to be built at Kvæsthusbroen by the Port of Copenhagen. A new opera house, designed by the architect Henning Larsen and donated by the AP Møller foundation, is planned to be built on Holmen in 2005/2006. From the 1997-1998 season The Royal Theatre began to focus on younger directors and designers, and thus on a younger audience. Inspired from modern German theatre, this period saw a general tendency to focus on the director's often significant concept, not least in rather radical stagings of classical works

Bent Holm

On the 300th anniversary of Ludvig Holbergs birth, 1984, Peter Langdal staged *Erasmus Montanus* on the Betty Nansen Theatre in Copenhagen. The performance broke with naturalist conventions and played on the commedia dell'-arte roots of the play, to which was added clowning and revue comedy.

In 1992 the Cantabile 2 Theatre staged a four-hour performance version of Dante's *Inferno*, directed by the director of the theatre Nullo Facchini and with settings by Bjarne Solberg. Bodies, costumes, landscape and buildings created a progression of evocative images. The procession started at Holmen's Church in Copenhagen and continued via Bagsværd Lake north of the city, where there was an idiosyncratic refreshment scene in the water, seen here with Lisa Brand and Anna Lyons. The show was subsequently taken to Germany and elsewhere.

Revue

On New Year's Eve 1849, Erik Bøgh presented the first Danish revue in the Casino Theatre in Copenhagen. It consisted of a series of independent numbers loosely connected by a character going through them all. This kind of relaxed entertainment appealed in particular to the middle classes. Gradually, the frame story disappeared, leaving only the individual numbers, which needed no connection with each other.

1873 saw the start of the summer revues. The travelling companies saw the potential of this genre, and there was soon a summer revue in any self-respecting city. At the same time the first revue stars made their appearance; in the 1890s Frederik Jensen was the great draw at the Nørrebro Theatre. The revues became ever more sumptuous, culminating in the Scala revues from 1912-1930 under the direction of Frede Skaarup; it was here that Liva Weel made her great breakthrough. However, the contents were drowned by the décor. The tendency was for the revue texts uncritically to base themselves on the established order by ridiculing anything that varied from the norm.

The reaction came in the middle of the 1920s with Ludvig Brandstrup's Co-Optimists, an intimate kind of revue which with little in the way of props once more put the word at the centre of things. However, these revues did not have any great satirical impact; that, on the other hand, was the prerogative of the PH revues which from 1929 to the end of the 1930s, under the leadership of the architect and author Poul Henningsen, used the revue as a weapon in the cultural debate of the day. The revue was to be about real people, so attitudes as well as actions were reintroduced. However, it continued to be the broad, politically neutral revues that dominated. Stars like Osvald Helmuth sang the great song of the performance, and many revue songs have become evergreens over the years.

During the German occupation (1940-1945) the revue showed itself able to play on the unsaid as a subtle contribution to the resistance struggle. In the 1950s Stig Lommer introduced a more crazy approach in his ABC revues, with the two comedians Kellerdirk, i.e. Kjeld Petersen and Dirch Passer, in the lead. From 1961 the critical, satirical revue experienced a revival, first on the student stage with Erik Knudsen and Finn Savery's *Frihed – det bedste guld* (Freedom – the Best Gold), and later also in the Fiolteater and in Dronningmølle with contributions by, among others, Jesper Jensen, Klaus Rifbjerg and Johannes Møllehave.

On 31 May 1940, scarcely two months after the German occupation of Denmark, there was the première of Kjeld Abell's revue comedy *Dyveke*, with lyrics by Poul Henningsen, and with Liva Weel in the title role as Christian II's mistress. The song *Man binder os paa Mund og Haand* (They Bind us Hand and Mouth) enjoyed great popularity for its allusions to the occupying forces. *Dyveke* was performed altogether about 400 times.

In the 1960s, radio and television began putting on revue programmes, which meant that many of the obvious themes had been used up before the summer performances could be staged. Consequently, a large number of revues moved in the direction of a greater musical content and a particularly humorous way of looking at life, e.g. with Jesper Klein and his group, Klyderne in the second half of the 1970s, or as in the Hjørring revues which – during the time Per Pallesen was their director (1979-1997) – went from strength to strength with a great sense of style and a break-neck tempo. In the 1980s and 1990s entertainers such as Linie 3, Pallesen/Pilmark and recently Det Brune Punktum entertained with shows that may be regarded as a continuation of the traditional revues.

Erik Hvidt

With great talent and a sure sense of timing, Per Pallesen, seen here in the 1991 Hjørring Revue, has developed Danish revue into elegant, spirited entertainment with a characteristic baroque humour.

Dance

Dance came into fashion in the European courts in the 17th century, with the French court as the splendid model. With a mixture of able amateurs and budding professionals, the court ballet evolved with beauty and splendour based on harmony and balance. It reflected both the heavenly harmony of the Universe and the monarchs' conception of how their states appeared, or ought to appear. Denmark, too, learned from France. The first Danish court ballet was performed in 1634 at the wedding of Prince Christian and

Magdalena Sibylla, and it culminated under Frederik III, whose queen, Sophie Amalie, was a ballet enthusiast and led the court in dancing as an amazon, a peasant girl, a Spanish lady or the muse of war.

In the 18th century theatre dancing moved further and further away from social dancing, and in the Grønnegade Theatre in Copenhagen – the first Danish-language theatre – dance was an important element both in Ludvig Holberg's and Molière's comedies and as independent entertainment. Among the performers was the French dancer Jean Baptiste Landé, who later founded the Imperial Ballet in St Petersburg. The links between the Danish ballet and the ballet of the major countries was thus present from the start.

Ballet had a lean time under pietist rule, but when The Danish Theatre opened at Kongens Nytorv in Copenhagen in 1748 dance was represented again, although there were only very few Danish ballet artists. Most of them – both ballet masters and dancers – were international artists from Germany, Italy and France.

The foundations were gradually laid for a Danish corps de ballet. 1771 saw the foundation of The Royal Theatre Ballet School that is still the mainstay of the Royal Danish Ballet, and in 1775 the Italian Vincenzo Galeotti came to Copenhagen as a ballet master, dancer and choreographer. He was responsible for the first great period of ballet in Denmark, and he directed the Royal Danish Ballet until his death in 1816.

Galeotti introduced *le ballet d'action*, in which the action was expressed through dance and pantomime. He produced ballet versions of Voltaire and Shakespeare and created the first Scandinavian ballet, *Lagertha*, which in 1801 was one of the works heralding Romanticism in the Danish theatre. Of his 49 works, only *Amors og Balletmesterens Luner* (The Whims of Cupid and the Ballet Master) from 1786 has survived. On the other hand, no other ballet in the world has been danced for so long in unbroken tradition.

The great name in 19th-century Danish ballet was August Bournonville, who was born in Copenhagen and became artistic director at the Royal Theatre in 1830, remaining there with few breaks until 1877. From his training in Europe and his travels he knew the demands and the standards in the world of international ballet, and he raised the level of Danish ballet. He made it at one and the same time international in ability and national in style and repertoire, with the special character which is its mark even to the present day and which makes it interesting from an international viewpoint. Bournonville wrote the choreographies for some 50 ballets, of which just under 10 have survived, and this is a bigger repertoire from the Romantic period than any other company can boast. Among the surviving works are *La Sylphide* (1836), *Napoli* (1842), *Kermessen i Brügge* (The Kermesse in Bruges) (1851) and *Et Folkesagn* (A Folk Tale) (1854).

After August Bournonville the Danish ballet went through a quiet period. His successors sustained the tradition, first and foremost Hans Beck, who in the 1890s collected steps and variations for the so-called Bournonville Schools.

The renewal of Danish ballet came in the 20th century. Guest appearances by Michail Fokin in 1925 and George Balanchine 1930-1931 provid-

ed inspiration. However, it was Harald Lander who led the ballet to a new series of triumphs in which the life blood was the play of contrasts between the demands of a modern repertoire and loyalty to the Bournonville tradition, which Harald Lander cultivated together with Valborg Borchsenius. Lander, who was artistic director 1932-1951, was also a choreographer, and with a repertoire built around the prima ballerina Margot Lander, he achieved unparalleled popularity for the ballet. Working together with the composer Knudåge Riisager and the author Kjeld Abell he used the ballet as a national standard bearer during the German occupation 1940-1945, and after the Second World War he stood at the head of a really impressive

There has been an unbroken tradition of performances of August Bournonville's *The Sylphide* since it was first staged by the Royal Danish Ballet in 1836. Arne Villumsen as the young Scot, James, and Lis Jeppesen in the title role at the 1979 Bournonville Festival marking the cetenary of August Bournonville's death.

Harald Lander's *Etudes* to Knudåge Riisager's music based on Czerny's studies is the great Danish work for ballet of the 20th century. Created in 1948, it depicts the technique and aesthetics of classical ballet. From the training session to the grand stage performance.

company. The peak of his creations was *Etudes* (1948), which later came to form the basis for his own international fame. In the Lander era ballets by Nini Theilade, Niels Bjørn Larsen and Børge Ralov were also important. In 1934, Børge Ralov together with Kjeld Abell and the composer Bernhard Christensen created Denmark's first modern ballet, *Enken i Spejlet* (The Widow in the Mirror).

The Royal Danish Ballet continued its progress towards international status throughout the 1950s. Each year summer festivals were arranged, and there were crucial tours to London in 1953 and Edinburgh in 1955, with the international breakthrough coming as a result of their visit to the USA in 1956. Many of the best choreographers of the day came to Copenhagen to work with the Royal Danish Ballet: George Balanchine, Birgit Cullberg, Roland Petit and Frederick Ashton, who in 1955 created the first Western version of Prokofiev's *Romeo and Juliet* for the Royal Ballet. Niels Bjørn Larsen, the greatest Danish mime artist of the 20th century, was artistic director in the 1950s and the first half of the 1960s, his place being taken for a couple of years (1956-1958) by the principal dancer Frank Schaufuss.

In 1966 Flemming Flindt took over the post of artistic director, and a new age began, primarily marked by the fact that Flindt introduced modern dance into the repertoire. He himself made his début as a choreographer with *La leçon* (The Lesson) (1963), based on a play by Eugène Ionesco, with whom he also co-operated on the great success of the day, *Dødens triumf* (The Triumph of Death) (1971). The Danish dancers danced in bare feet in Paul Taylor's *Aureole* (1968), and a large number of other modern dance choreographers made their way into the repertoire.

Henning Kronstam was artistic director 1978-1985. The international reputation of the Ballet was confirmed through tours and through the 1979 Bournonville Festival. The hundredth anniversary of the death of Bournonville was an occasion that demonstrated that through its legacy from the Romantic age Denmark occupies a special place on the world map. Frank Andersen, artistic director 1985-1994, continued the Bournonville tradition and in 1991 persuaded Queen Margrethe II to design the set for *A Folk Tale*. Peter Schaufuss, who was artistic director 1994-1995, continued this progress towards a Danish repertoire. Danish choreographers, meanwhile, are few and far between, but Anna Lærkesen has created works that are an idiosyncratic continuation of the neo-classical style, and Kim Brandstrup, the English-Danish Tim Rushton and

Scene from Flemming Flindt's *The Triumph of Death* with music by Thomas Koppel. The first performance was on television in 1971. The following year the dance drama was transferred to The Royal Theatre, where it created a sensation with its sensitive expressivity and a few, highly advertised nude scenes. The picture from the television version shows the scene 'The Isolated House', in which the master of the house allows himself to be sprayed all over with disinfectant in order to avoid death.

the Russian-Danish Alexei Ratmansky are also interesting names. From 1997 to 1999 the British Maina Gielgud was the first woman to become artistic director, and she was also the first non-Dane to hold the post since 1823. In 1999 Aage Thordal-Christensen took over the position as artistic director assisted by Dinna Bjørn as Bournonville consultant. In 2002 Frank Andersen is back as artistic director, planning the Bournonville Festival in 2005.

Of international choreographers it was especially John Neumeier and John Cranko in the 1970s and 1980s who gave free rein to the Danish dancers' sense of psychological drama, but generally speaking, the Royal Danish Ballet around 2000 stands as a modern, classical company with a repertoire stretching from Balanchine to the great Russian classics such as Tchaikovsky's *Swan Lake*, *Sleeping Beauty* and *The Nutcracker*.

Dance outside The Royal Theatre was for a long time very modest. Since 1844 the Tivoli Pantomime Theatre has cultivated a pantomime form deriving from the Italian commedia dell'arte, blended with a Danish ballet tradition. And for most

of the 20th century, the Pantomime Theatre also housed the only permanent ballet company outside the Royal Theatre. It was disbanded in 1991, but on the other hand, every year since the mid-1970s Tivoli has invited leading foreign companies to perform there. Other initiatives like Elsa Marianne von Rosen's and Allan Fridericia's Scandinavian Ballet in the 1960s were important at that time, but only survived for a short time.

Modern dance was late in coming to Denmark. Martha Graham visited Copenhagen in 1954, but only in the 1960s did small groups start working with dance inspired by modern American personalities like Martha Graham and Merce Cunningham. Among the most important were the women's group Living Movement, founded 1971-1972, and Eske Holm's group, founded 1975. None of the initiatives from the 1970s lasted for long. On the other hand, *Nyt Dansk Danseteater* (the New Danish Dance Theatre), arising from Randi Patterson's projects around 1980, has survived. With Randi Patterson herself, Warren Spears and Anette Abildgaard as choreographers, Denmark finally acquired a modern company of standing, as has been demonstrated in a number of major performances. From 2001 Tim Rushton is artistic director. Interest in dance has also been fostered by the major summer events like the Festival of Fools and Dancin' City, which have brought the most up-to-date international dance to Copenhagen. The situation in the beginning of the 21st century is an active dance life with a number of smaller groups like Corona, Kreutzmann Dance, Åben Scene in Copenhagen, and Granhøj Dans in Århus, as well as several freelance choreographers like Tim Feldmann, Kitt Johnson and Sara Gebran. The training establishment *Dansens Hus* (House of Dance) was founded in 1985; in 1992, Denmark finally acquired an institutional course in modern dance, and in addition Copenhagen acquired *Dansescenen* (Stage of Modern Dance), which focuses on modern dance.

The *Billedstofteater* (Picture Theatre), later called Hotel Pro Forma, has been active in the borderland between dance and theatre, appearing for the first time in 1977. Here, Kirsten Dehlholm creates performances with a bizarre, surrealist and vibrant visual fantasy. After centuries in which there has only been ballet, theatre dance in Denmark at the end of the 20th century can provide a vast array of styles and manners of expression, extending to new and at times provocative ideas of what dance is all about.

Erik Aschengreen

Music

The Earliest Times

The earliest evidence of musical activity in Denmark are the large, twisting bronze horns dating from the Bronze Age. Soon after the first examples (three pairs) were found in a bog in 1797, the name *lur* was attached to them. 61 lurs have been found (the most recent in 1988) in southern Scandinavia and the Baltic area, most of them in Denmark (38). They tend to be found in pairs, but it is uncertain what they were used for. The same applies to the two golden horns found in Gallehus, which some people have interpreted as musical instruments.

The scant knowledge about musical life in Denmark in the period up to and around the introduction of Christianity derives from the scaldic poetry, sagas and chronicles which the historian Saxo Grammaticus also used as the basis of his history of Denmark, *Gesta Danorum* (c. 1200). Here, we hear of the power that mu-

sic had over King Erik the Kind-Hearted, and of travelling musicians (*leikari*), who are spoken of with scorn, whereas singers and poets enjoy great esteem. In the 13th century and early 14th century German minnesingers like Tannhäuser and Frauenlob appeared at Danish courts. The only written evidence of secular song in Danish from this time is a verse added to the so-called *Codex runicus*, containing the Scanian Law. The text, beginning with the words *Drømdæ mik æn drøm i nat* (I Dreamed Me a Dream Last Night), is written in runes, while the music is written in a non-rhythmic notation on a four-line staff. After the murder of King Knud (Canute) the Holy in 1086, English monks were brought to Denmark by his brother, King Erik the Kind-Hearted, to venerate his memory. The music composed to celebrate this first Danish martyr has been lost; on the other hand the liturgy for his nephew Knud Lavard (1170) has survived.

Drømdæ mik æn drøm i nat (I Dreamed Me a Dream Last Night). The song shown here consists of a text written in runes and a melody. It is presumably the first two lines of a four-lined stanza of a ballad. Apart from a possible refrain, the melody is considered to be complete.

Two pages of the manuscript containing the complete liturgy for the two feasts for Saint Knud Lavard, the feast of his passion, 7 January, and the feast of his translation, 25 June. The liturgy is ascribed to the English Benedictines in Ringsted Monastery. The sections of the Mass for the feast of the translation were in all probability used at the great church festival in Ringsted on 25 June 1170 when Knud Lavard was canonised and his son, Valdemar I The Great, crowned his son Knud as King-elect. The well-preserved manuscript is a copy presumed to date from the end of the 13th century.

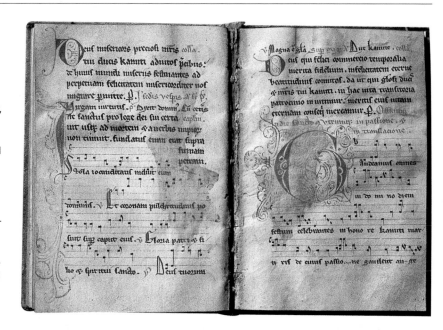

In 1103 the St Laurentius Church in Lund in present-day Sweden was raised to an archiepiscopal seat, and in 1145 the new cathedral was given the first choir statutes in Scandinavia. Some sequences contained in Lund's 'book of gifts' (*Liber daticus Lundensis*, c. 1170) suggest connections with France and the new university in Paris, but very little is known about the music in Danish churches from this time. It is, however, known that before long organs were installed in the larger churches, for instance Ribe Cathedral c. 1290 and Lund Cathedral before 1330.

About 1200 Giraldus Cambrensis described part-singing that he had heard in Northern England; he ascribes this manner of singing to the Danish and Norwegian immigrants who had lived in the area for generations. The earliest polyphonic songs contained in a Danish source (perhaps apart from a hymn in the Knud Lavard liturgy) are in a manuscript from c. 1450.

John Bergsagel

16th and 17th Centuries
Like their foreign counterparts, the Danish kings spent a great deal of money on surrounding themselves with music. Court music had since ancient times been organised in three groups: A permanent *corps of trumpeters* was linked to the court on the occasion of the coronation of Christian I in 1448, while the first list of a *corps of singers* (Kantori) is from 1519, at which time the chapel royal also included an instrumental ensemble. Although little music has survived from this period, it is nevertheless possible from a number of sources to form an impression of some aspects of the music at court. Two sets of hand-written, only partially surviving books for voices dated 1541 and 1556 give an idea of how works by the leading foreign masters of the day had found their way to Copenhagen by the middle of the 16th century. The collections, which were used by the chapel royal under Christian III, contain music by Netherlandish, Italian, French, German and Danish composers. A collec-

tion of music from Flensburg provides a source for the understanding of musical life under Frederik II, including the music sung at the inauguration of the magnificent Kronborg Fountain in 1583. Court music reached a temporary climax under Christian IV, who to a hitherto unknown extent spent money on training local talents and bringing in foreign masters.

The most important of the king's Danish musicians was Mogens Pedersøn, who had a collection of madrigals printed in Venice and later published his main work of church music, *Pratum spirituale* in Copenhagen. Among the many foreign musicians, special mention should be made of the English John Dowland, known for his melancholy songs with lute accompaniment, and the Dresden conductor Heinrich Schütz, who spent several periods in Denmark and directed the court music at the great festivities in 1634 occasioned by the wedding of Prince Christian.

The move towards church reform at this time can be sensed in some early attempts, in 1528, to introduce hymns in Danish. That same year saw the publication of the first Danish liturgy in the vernacular, the so-called *Malmø Mass*, although Lutheranism was not established as the official religion of Denmark until 1536.

After a few desultory attempts, music for the theatre was properly established during the reigns of Frederik III and Christian V, not least under the impact of the music from the court of *le roi soleil* in Versailles; at the Danish court, too, lavish French-inspired allegorical court ballets were performed. From here it was not a great step to operas lasting for the entire evening, and these were introduced with the performance of *Der vereinigte Götterstreit* on the king's birthday in 1689. When the performance was repeated a couple of days later before a wider circle of invited guests, the theatre caught fire, and many people were killed, which put a damper on interest in opera for a time.

Much of the court music was written for use in church. But outside court circles there was naturally also a need for church music. After the Reformation in 1536 Lutheran hymns for the congregation soon established themselves, and in 1569 the first authorised hymn book was published in Denmark, Thomesen's Hymn Book, furnished with beautifully printed melodies for the individual hymns. Thomesen's Hymn Book was the everyday hymn book in the church; Jesperssøn's *Graduale* from 1573 was intended for the parish clerk and the choir and was in particular for use at the morning service. This was replaced in 1699 by Thomas Kingo's *Graduale* reflecting the new organisation of the church under absolutism.

Music naturally also had a place outside the court and the church. Comedies including music were being performed in schools and at the university. In the towns the criers

At *Det Store Bilager* (the Grand Bedding of the Couple), the great celebration in Copenhagen in 1634 on the occasion of the elected Prince Christian's betrothal to Princess Magdalena Sibylla of Saxony, a corps of musicians rode at the head of the procession. This contemporary print shows a drummer followed by four pairs of trumpeters.

blew their trumpets to proclaim the passage of the day and mark important events in the daily life of the town; and in the homes, people sang songs. What we call 'popular ballads' represent a particularly varied repertoire; they were written down by aristocratic ladies in the middle of the 16th century, and were of great importance to the music and poetry of the 19th century.

Niels Krabbe

18th and 19th Centuries

Opera and Concerts

To replace the burned-down Sophie Amalienborg, Frederik IV opened a new opera house in Copenhagen in 1703, the first performance in it being an opera by the Italian Bartolomeo Bernardi. Reinhard Keiser visited the city with his Hamburg opera company 1721-1723, and in 1722 two French actors were given permission to establish a theatre in Copenhagen, where they staged comedies by writers including Molière and Holberg, many with music. However, it soon met with financial difficulties and after the Fire of Copenhagen in 1728 it was forced to close completely. Theatrical performances were forbidden during the reign of the pietist king, Christian VI. The theatre did not reopen until 1747, and the following year under the name of The Danish Theatre it moved into a new building. Music was at first provided by the Town Musician and his men, but from 1770 the king's own orchestra, *Det Kongelige Kapel* (The Royal Orchestra), was permanently linked to the theatre.

Musical gatherings and public concerts took place in Copenhagen from the beginning of the 18th century, partly under the auspices of the Music Society (founded 1744) in which J.E. Iversen, J.A. Scheibe and Holberg were the driving forces. It was forced to close in 1749, prey to its enemy the Italian opera, but soon new societies and clubs arose, in which amateurs could show off their talents, from time to time aided by professional musicians, including those from the Royal Orchestra.

With guest performances in 1747 and the following years by Mingotti's Italian opera company, opera really became established in Copenhagen. Mingotti brought with him in turn the conductors Gluck, Salabrini and Sarti. The last two of these remained in the service of the court for a number of years, and Sarti provided the music for the first *syngespil*, a play with music to a Danish text (1756). More memorable were Johannes Ewald's *Balders Død* (The Death of Balder) (1779) and *Fiskerne* (The Fishermen) (1780), with national themes and with music by the German-born J.E. Hartmann. J.A.P. Schulz' *Høstgildet* (The Harvest Celebration) (1790) and *Peters Bryllup* (Peter's Wedding) (1793) established the Danish syngespil as a highly popular form of entertainment. Some of the songs from them became well known among the population at large, as did Schulz's simple *Lieder im Volkston*. His successor, F.L.Æ. Kunzen followed up his success with a large number of works (including *Holger Danske*). Schulz and Kunzen also introduced the Danes to the music of Haydn and Mozart. Their own music bears the stamp of French comic opera and the Viennese school. Ballet music was composed by Claus Schall.

A particularly Danish flavour in music was in fact provided by immigrant composers from Germany. C.E.F. Weyse came to Copenhagen from Altona in 1789 at the age of 15, becoming a pupil of Schulz. He stayed until his death in 1842 and was the composer who created the

Danish Romantic song, the romance. Friedrich Kuhlau, who came to Copenhagen in 1810, never became quite so Danish, but he wrote music for the festival play *Elverhøi* (The Elfin Mound) (1828), in which one of the melodies was that of the Danish national anthem, King Christian. They were originally pianists and both later became famous as composers for the theatre. Weyse also became known as a church musician, while Kuhlau's name was especially associated with the flute. Some of Weyse's romances come from his syngespil, for instance *Sovedrikken* (The Sleeping Draught) (1809), *Et Eventyr i Rosenborg Have* (An Adventure in Rosenborg Park) (1827) and *Festen paa Kenilworth* (The Festival at Kenilworth) (1836). Of Kuhlau's operas it was especially *Røverborgen* (The Robbers' Castle) (1814) and the Rossini-inspired *Lulu* (1824) that enjoyed success.

Since the end of the 18th century, The Royal Theatre had been the meeting place for cultured academics and the upper ranks of the bourgeoisie. After 1836 it was also possible to forgather in the Music Society, which had been founded with the intention of publishing Danish music, but which developed into an institution for arranging concerts. From 1850 it was under the direction of Niels W. Gade, who became internationally recognised through his concert overture *Efterklange af Ossian* (Echoes of Ossian) (1840) and his *First Symphony* (1842), the first works of Danish National Romanticism. For some years, Gade, together with Mendelssohn had been a conductor in the Leipzig Gewandhaus, but he returned home because of the Schleswig-Holstein war in 1848, and he now became a central figure in musical life together with J.P.E. Hartmann. The two of them helped found the Royal Danish Academy of Music in 1867, and in addition they both worked as organists. Hartmann wrote the opera *Liden Kirsten* (Little Kirsten) (1846) and music for a num-

Friedrich Kuhlau, 1786-1832, was born in Uelzen in Germany and started his career in 1804 as a pianist in Hamburg. In 1810, however, he fled to Copenhagen to avoid Napoleon's occupying troops. His appearance in The Royal Theatre in 1811 with his *Piano Concerto* was a success, and he subsequently settled in the city. However, he often travelled abroad, not least to Vienna, where he met Beethoven, on whom he modelled himself. Kuhlau's many compositions for piano and especially for flute are intended for both the amateur and the virtuoso. Many of them were written for financial or educational reasons and were quickly published both in Denmark and abroad. Kuhlau wrote the music for several ballad operas, including *Lulu* (1824) and his best known work, the music for the national festival drama *Elverhøi* (1828, The Elfin Mound) to a text by J.L. Heiberg, which is the piece most often performed in The Royal Theatre.

Anne Ørbæk Jensen

Among the many lively scenes painted by Wilhelm Marstrand, is this atmospheric picture from the Waage Petersen home in Copenhagen, *Et musikalsk aftenselskab* (A Musical Evening Gathering), from 1834; Frederiksborg Museum. With the picture of Kuhlau hanging on the wall to the right, a group of the leading musical personalities of the time are gathered around Weyse at the piano.

ber of ballets and plays on national subjects. Gade wrote eight symphonies and choral works in all such as *Elverskud* (The Elf King's Daughter) (1854).

Especially older vocal music was performed in the Cæcilie Society, founded 1851 by Henrik Rung.

The romance, the song with piano accompaniment, was in the second half of the 19th century cultivated by Peter Heise, who also wrote the opera *Drot og Marsk* (King and Marshal) (1877), and by Peter Erasmus Lange-Müller.

Church Music

Pietism had come to Denmark through Brorson's poetry and made its mark on church music through Pontoppidan's *Hymn Book* (1742), which was the last containing the music for the hymn melodies. After this, organ accompaniment with the hymn singing became general, and the chorale books suggest slow, formal choral singing towards the end

of the 18th century. N.F.S. Grundtvig's hymns led to a need for livelier hymn tunes, and the romance gradually had an impact on the churches, as is seen in the chorale books by Berggreen (1853), Rung (1857) and Barnekow (1878). Towards the end of the 19th century Thomas Laub reacted against this secular tendency. His restitution of the old melodies found its expression in the chorale book entitled *Dansk Kirkesang* (Danish Church Song) (1918).

Popular Song

National and political movements, including those leading to the 1849 Constitution, and later popular groupings, for instance those centred on the folk high school movement and the workers' movement, created a basis for community singing, which gave the impetus to a large number of melodies and song books throughout the 19th century. This formed the background for a reform of popular song at the beginning of the

the same time composed extensively within almost every kind of music. He was particularly noted for a Danish-Nordic style, including *Guldhornene* (1832, The Golden Horns) and *Vølvens Spaadom* (1872, The Sibyl's Prophecy).

He composed a great deal of stage music, in which the opera *Liden Kirsten* (1846, Little Kirsten) occupies a central position, along with the Nordic ballets *Valkyrien* (1861, The Valkyrie) and *Thrymskviden* (1868, The Lay of Thrym). Hartmann's chamber music, especially his piano music, is remarkable, and in his day he was highly respected for his cantatas and songs. As an administrator in the Music Society and a teacher in the Academy of Music in Copenhagen he exercised a decisive influence on Danish musical life in the second half of the nineteenth century.

Anne Ørbæk Jensen

Johan Peter Emilius Hartmann, 1805-1900, came from a family of musicians and received his musical training at home and by listening to the music played in The Royal Theatre. In his everyday life he worked as a lawyer and organist and at

20th century, with work by composers like Thorvald Aagaard, Carl Nielsen and Oluf Ring.

Carsten E. Hatting

The 20th Century

In the early decades of the 20th century, Danish music was first and foremost marked by Carl Nielsen's six symphonies, his operas, chamber music, songs and piano music. He is considered one of the greatest Danish composers ever. For his part, Rued Langgaard in his very substantial production maintained a style related to late Romanticism.

Composers born in the first half of the century grew up with classical aesthetics as their background, as expressed both in Carl Nielsen and in Finn Høffding, Vagn Holmboe and Herman D. Koppel. Common to them all was a self-understanding created within the sphere of Danish and Nordic music. Younger composers such as Niels Viggo Bentzon, Per

Nørgård, Pelle Gudmundsen-Holmgreen and Bent Lorentzen felt a much greater need to look towards central European Modernism. They reacted critically to the aesthetics of modernism, Per Nørgård in the shape of 'the universe of the Nordic', which was a declaration of love for a Nordic tone with Vagn Holmboe and Jean Sibelius as guiding lights. But his enquiring mind soon found this compositional credo too narrow. His breach with it meant soundings in the new musical environment of Central Europe.

Other composers of the same generation – Gudmundsen-Holmgreen, Ib Nørholm, Henning Christiansen and the younger Ole Buck – reacted to the complexity of modernism by aiming at the opposite: they composed in an extremely simple manner. They represented the new simplicity in Danish music, a quite distinct version of minimalism. They insisted on many forms of expression, collages, ironical play with quotations and stylistic elements from older music. Later, these composers changed direction and each created his personal perspective to his own earlier work.

The composers who voluntarily allowed themselves to be engulfed by modernism found life difficult in a musical environment that was not mature enough to accept their uncompromising attitude to musical material. This applies, for instance, to Gunnar Berg, who was one of the first to adopt a serial technique.

Axel Borup-Jørgensen's music is also founded on modernist aesthetics, but without a dogmatic, consistent attitude to expression and form; Borup-Jørgensen works with lyrical image formations which are sensitive studies in aphoristic form, with chamber music as his preferred genre.

The starting point for Bent Lorentzen was serial music, and he moved in the direction of the international avant-garde. In the 1960s and 1970s he was inspired by electronic music, but like other pioneers of the day, chose to renounce pure electronic music. Mogens Winkel Holm has never belonged to any movement or aesthetic school, so in his compositions he could start in post-war central European modernism, without its dogmatics at any time having been an aesthetic lodestar for him.

In the early days of electronic music Else Marie Pade and Jørgen Plaetner were the pioneers who blazed a trail with electro-acoustic music.

Among Danish composers born in the 1920s we find a number who have distinguished themselves with original works characterised by consistency of form and movement and clarity of expression: Tage Nielsen, Poul Rovsing Olsen, Leif Thybo and Erik Norby. An outsider like Bernhard Lewkovitch also belongs to this group.

The dogmatic philosophy of inno-

Niels W. Gade, 1817-1890, received his first real training as a violin pupil from the violinist Friderich Wexschall. In 1840 he won the Music Society Prize for his *Ossian* Overture, which together with the

First Symphony (1842) filled Mendelssohn in Leipzig with enthusiasm. Gade went to Leipzig and worked there partly as a conductor at the Gewandhaus concerts until returning to Copenhagen in 1848. Here, from 1850, he became the leader of the Music Society chorus and orchestra, which gave him a dominant position in the musical life of the city. He performed a large number of modern German and Danish works at the Society's concerts, including many of his own compositions, both symphonies, chamber music and what was known as concert pieces, e.g. *Elverskud* (1851-54, The Elf King's Daughter). He made use of his many international contacts in planning the concerts. In addition, he worked as an organist and in his everyday life was head of the Academy of Music that was established in Copenhagen in 1867.

Anne Ørbæk Jensen

his production, marked by an interesting treatment of motifs and rhythmical intensity. Nielsen's ability to characterise is seen in his operas, *Saul og David* (1898-1901, Saul and David) and *Maskarade* (1904-1906, Masquerade) and in lesser vocal works such as *Fynsk Foraar* (1921, Springtime in Funen). His simple folksong-like songs became very widely known and still form an important part of Danish singing tradition. In chamber music, Carl Nielsen revealed a sense for the individual instrument, e.g. in his *Quintet for Wind Instruments* (1922), and this is also heard in his *Violin Concerto* (1911) and *Flute Concerto* (1926), and in the monumental organ composition *Commotio* (1930-31). Carl Nielsen described his model, Mozart, in an essay which together with many of his other writings, published in *Levende Musik* (1925, Living Music) and the memoirs *Min fynske Barndom* (1927, My Childhood in Funen) exerted an influence on the musical views of the time, all supplemented by his work as a conductor.

Anne Ørbæk Jensen

Carl Nielsen, 1865-1931, is the most important figure in Danish musical life in the 20th century, exerting a great influence on later generations of Danish and Scandinavian composers. The symphonies, especially nos 3-5, are at the very heart of

vation in the 1950s is no longer of any significance in determining norms, but the experience remains, with a demand for inner cohesion and consistency. This seems to be the key to a composer like Poul Ruders. At first he wrote works filled with irony, distance and pastiche, as did other prominent figures of his generation: Bo Holten, Karl Aage Rasmussen and Hans Abrahamsen. In the course of the 1980s, Poul Ruders, like his colleagues, freed himself from this distancing manner of expressing himself.

The last two decades of the 20th century showed new talents in electro-acoustic and computer music such as Gunnar Møller Pedersen, Ivar Frounberg and Wayne Siegel. Their contemporaries Bent Sørensen, Erik Højsgaard, Anders Norden-toft, Niels Rosing-Schow, Svend Hvidtfelt Nielsen, Karsten Fundal and John Frandsen have shown themselves to be influential in their generation.

Anders Beyer

Jazz

Jazz came to Denmark, first with American gramophone records, and then as the result of visiting musicians and orchestras. The first Danish jazz band was formed by the saxophonist Valdemar Eiberg in 1923, and in the years immediately following pioneers emerged like the saxophonist Kai Ewans, the trombonist Peter Rasmussen and the pianist Leo Mathisen, who were all active as soloists and band leaders throughout the 1930s and 1940s. Musically and professionally, Danish jazz experi-

The American tenor saxophonist Dexter Gordon, seen here during a concert in the Montmartre Jazz House in 1963, was one of the many foreign jazz musicians who spent either a long or a short time in Copenhagen. Through their performances alongside Danish musicians, they helped build up the city's reputation among jazz lovers.

enced a golden age during the German occupation 1940-1945, when younger names such as the violinist Svend Asmussen and the pianist Kjeld Bonfils also came to the fore. A sudden decline followed the liberation, as almost the whole established generation slipped into the background. From 1950 older and newer styles were introduced, on an amateur basis now, and only from about 1960 was there again a basis for professional music making. Since then, Danish jazz has won a more secure foothold in Denmark and has achieved considerable international reputation with orchestras like the Radio Big Band and Pierre Dørge's New Jungle orchestra (Danish state ensemble 1993-1996) and with musicians like the trumpeter Palle Mikkelborg, the double bass player Niels-Henning Ørsted Pedersen, the saxophonist John Tchicai and the percussionist Marilyn Mazur. Two Copenhagen jazz houses, Montmartre (1961-1991) and Copenhagen Jazzhouse (since 1991), have been of great significance for international and Danish jazz life, and so has Copenhagen Jazz Festival (since 1979). In 1986 the Rhythmic Music Conservatory was established in Copenhagen.

Erik Wiedemann

Per Nørgård, b.1932, is a pupil of Vagn Holmboe and Finn Høffding, supplemented with training in the Royal Danish Academy of Music. Until c. 1960 his compositions were endowed with a special Nordic tone, as can be heard for instance in *Konstellationer* (Constellations) (1958). After encountering the Central European style he experimented in his dramatic works with quotations and collage. For instance in works such as *Fragment* I-IV and V (1959-1961), Per Nørgård developed the so-called infinity series with specific combinations of intervals, and he also worked with the golden mean. These principles found expression in *Rejse ind i den gyldne skærm* (Journey into the Golden Screen) (1968) and *Canon* (1970-1972), and he developed them further, partly under the influence of music from the Far East for instance in the opera *Siddharta* (1973-1979). In his recent works Per Nørgård is preoccupied with the concept of time and inspired by the poet Adolph Wölfli, e.g. in the opera *Det guddommelige Tivoli* (1983, The Divine Circus) and this, supplemented by his work as a teacher and writer, places him at the centre of contemporary Danish musical life.In 1996 he was awarded the Léonie Sonning Prize for Music on which occasion his *Piano Concerto in due tempi* was given its first performance.

Anne Ørbæk Jensen

Rock

Post-war Danish youth music was in the 1950s marked by the americanisation of the entertainment industry that took place throughout Western Europe. The dance, films and records of the rock'n'roll culture were exported, and in Denmark it was jazz and dance bands, including Ib Glindemann and Peter Plejl's orchestras and the soloists Ib 'Rock' Jensen and Otto Brandenburg that at first presented the new style. At the end of the 1950s bands were formed that on the model of the English group The Shadows played what became known as barbed-wire music. Among the best known groups were The Cliffters and The Rocking Ghosts. The English rhythm and blues style of the 1960s inspired The Beefeaters and The Defenders, whereas The Hitmakers and Sir Henry and his Butlers were more influenced by beat music. In 1967 the group Steppeulvene issued the LP *Hip*, which signified a break-

Since its start in 1979, the Copenhagen Jazz Festival has been an annual event over 10 days in July. The festival includes a number of free outdoor concerts in the city squares, jazz houses and cafés. Here we see the tenor saxophonist Sonny Rollins at Christiansborg Ridebane in July 1993.

through for a truly Danish beat music. The texts, written in Danish, were imaginative and personal, and the music was clearly influenced by folk rock (including Bob Dylan) and

Niels-Henning Ørsted Pedersen, b. 1946. In 1991 the internationally highly esteemed jazz double bass player Niels-Henning Ørsted Pedersen was awarded the Nordic Council Music Prize. It was the

first time this prize for composition went to a performing musician, which must be ascribed to his international standing. He is presumably the internationally most sought-after Danish instrumentalist, who has travelled and recorded with many of the greatest jazz soloists, and he has also a particular ability to interpret Danish songs and folk melodies, partly in collaboration with the pianist Kenny Drew. His talent was soon seen to be of international quality; as a 16-year-old he received an offer from Count Basie and did a recording with the pianist Bud Powell, and since the 1970s he has for longish periods been the permanent double bass player for Oscar Peterson. In addition, he has often played in trios, partly collectively with the trumpeter Palle Mikkelborg and the keyboard player Kenneth Knudsen, and partly under his own name, usually with guitar and drums.

Erik Wiedeman

Safri Duo consists of Morten Friis (to the left) and Uffe Savery. In 2001 they found enormous international success with their international prize-winning dance-trance album Episode II. Before this breakthrough the duo, formed in 1988, had achieved international recognition for their percussion transcriptions of classical works and for performances of their own music compositions.

American West Coast rock. Influence from the American music scene also inspired groups such as Savage Rose, Alrune Rod and Young Flowers. The music was in general enquiring and experimental at the end of the 1960s, and many jazz musicians began to play beat music, for instance in the groups Maxwells, Burning' Red Ivanhoe and Blue Sun. In the late 1960s, beat music was replaced by the rock music of the 1970s. The texts were argumentative and critical of society, and a political rock scene arose around for instance Røde Mor and Jomfru Ane Band. One of the greatest successes of Danish rock, Gasolin (1969-1978) (with the singer and composer Kim Larsen) created a particular Danish brand of rock music with idiomatic texts and easily sung melodies. Other well-known names creating the profile of Danish rock were Shu-bi-dua, C.V. Jørgensen and the Århus groups Gnags and Shit & Chanel, who demonstrated that rock music was not only a Copenhagen phenomenon.

The rock scene of the 1980s was marked by well-sounding and splendidly produced pop and rock music, created, for instance, by Sneakers (with Sanne Salomonsen) and the soloists Lis Sørensen, Anne Linnet and Sebastian, but groups inspired by punk and new wave such as Kliché, Sods/Sort Sol and Miss B. Haven also marked the musical scene of the day. The group TV-2 enjoyed a success with its commentaries on the life style of the 1980s. The trend of the 1990s and the early 2000s has been for rock to be internationalised due to the globalisation of the music industry. Groups like Aqua, Michael Learns to Rock and Safri Duo have aimed for international careers and many rock musicians use English texts, e.g. Thomas Helmig, Lars H.U.G., Dicte, and D-A-D. Alongside this, hip hop has been finding a Danish idiom with names like Humleridderne, Den Gale Pose and Østkyst Hustlers. But there is still a niche for socially committed troubadours like Johnny Madsen, Lars Lilholt, and Poul Krebs, who carry on singing in Danish. In the 1990s guitar rock groups such as Dizzy Mizz Lizzy, Kashmir and Psyched up Janis gained ground, inspired by the grunge movement, but a thriving electronica

The Roskilde Festival is Denmark's greatest rock festival (90,000 paying participants and 25,000 voluntary helpers in 1998). Since the start in 1970 the festival has grown in size and has become an international annual event in Denmark. About half of those attending and a large proportion of the artists come from abroad. In the jubilee year 1995 the festival site was considerably extended, and the public facilities were also improved, including a railway halt built for the occasion. International artists who have played at the Roskilde Festival include U2, Neil Young, Bob Marley, The Cure, Bob Dylan and Eric Clapton.

scene has also developed, including e.g. Sorten Muld, who records techno arrangements of old Danish folk songs, the ambient Future 3 and the Goa-trance group Koxbox, who have both gained international attention.

Charlotte Rørdam Larsen, Carsten Berthelsen

Folk Music

Folk music in Denmark is affected by the country's openness to cultural influences from abroad and the contact between town and country.

Vocal folk music consists of a main group of songs (medieval ballads, echoes of them from the 16th and 17th centuries and more modern ballads), and then some smaller genres (rhymes, jingles and calls), song games and popular hymns. Instrumental folk music is mainly dance music, but it has also been used in connection with ceremonies and work. There are three main kinds of professional musicians: fiddlers in the country districts, (musicians playing at dances and balls, often with music as a secondary source of income), street singers and public house entertainers in the towns.

Medieval ballads have survived in song tradition until the 21st century. Some 600 songs of this type with more than 2000 melody variants are still known. The ballads were used for the chain dance in the Middle Ages, and later they have been sung as solos. The melodies contain some of the oldest and most idiosyncratic folk music in Denmark, including formulaic structures and pentatonic traits without an unambiguous tonic. In the 16th and 17th centuries new religious, secular and historical types of song were developed with a clearer modal character with cadences and a firmer metrical and architectural structure. In the 18th and 19th centuries various types of song in something resembling major and minor keys emerged, in which something approaching harmony was noticeable in the melodies, and the forms became more symmetrical. About 1800 the major tonality became universal both in ballads and in popular dance music.

Itinerant entertainers and performers provided impulses for folk music in the Middle Ages. Resident town and military musicians were drawn from their ranks in the late Middle Ages, and between c. 1650 and 1800 town musicians had the monopoly of all paid music making for townspeople and peasants. They would often lease rural areas to local musicians. The Polish dance was very popular with the peasantry in the 18th century, and the minuet and 'English' dance (longways and quadrilles) were accepted into the folk tradition. In some dance melodies originating before 1780 we find irregular phrasal structures, modal and minor tonalities and a formulaic quality. After 1800 the melodies almost always consist of repeated passages of eight bars. Only in dance melodies from a few localities – Fanø and Læsø – can we find other tonalities than major today. The characteristic new dances in the 19th century were pair dances such as the waltz, the hopsa, polka, mazurka, gallop and schottische and various figure dances. Regional differences in both repertoire and manner of playing still exist at the end of the 20th century.

In the period from the Middle Ages to 1800 we have a certain amount of scattered information about the use of instruments such as the

fiddle, bagpipes, various types of zither (*langeleg, humle*), hurdy-gurdy, dulcimer, Jew's harp, drums, shawm and various flutes. About 1700, drums and the 'peasant fiddle' were the most important peasant instruments (either together or alone). The old fiddle was replaced in the 18th century by the violin as the main instrument for rural musicians. The shawm/clarinet, flute and cello were in use about 1800. Soldiers introduced military instruments like the oboe, the bassoon and the French horn. At least from the beginning of the 19th century the musicians' instruments were professionally produced, perhaps even factory-made. Outdoors in the 19th century they used trumpets, cornets and trombones, and these were introduced into the dance hall in the second half of the 19th century, when the ensembles were expanded to five or six players. From the 1870s the accordion came into use, and it soon became as important an instrument as the violin. The guitar has been a typical street singer instrument in the towns since the middle of the 19th century. With the advent of new American dance forms after the First World War, the piano and drums were often introduced into the dance orchestra. Of native Danish instruments we can mention the folk clarinet (*skalmeje*), village horn (*byhorn*), town drum (*bytromme*) – a cylindrical drum – and rumbling pot (*rumlepot*) and various kinds of instruments played by shepherd and cowherd boys.

The youth revolt in the 1960s led to an interest in Irish, Scottish and American folk music (folk revival), and since the 1970s there has also been an active interest in Danish, Scandinavian and other kinds of folk music. One result of this is the large, annual folk music festivals in Tønder

The music festival in the town Tønder, South Jutland, has been held every year since 1975 and been the setting for a large number of appearances by danish and foreign folk music groups. Violinist Harald Haugaard and saxophonist Hans Mydtskov from the Danish group Serras are here opening the festival in 2001.

(since 1975) and Skagen (since 1970) as well as many smaller gatherings of musicians.

Jens Henrik Koudal

Institutions and Musical Life

The modern institutionalised Danish musical life arose in the 19th century on the European model and on the basis of private initiative. Conservatoires and orchestras were founded, publishers established, and the performance of music blossomed within the framework of music societies of various kinds. This pattern changed during the 1930s when the gramophone and radio began to establish themselves to the detriment of live performances. Since then it has increasingly been seen as a public duty to train musicians and support and develop musical life at all levels throughout the country. This trend was confirmed in 1976 in the Music Act, which is based on the principle of a decentralised policy of support. The financial support for musical life has been greatly increased over the years, so that jazz, rock and experimental forms of music also benefit.

Denmark has two operas, seven professional symphony orchestras, 7,000 unionised musicians and composers, over 100 music festivals and a nationwide network of music schools for children and young people. On the commercial side there is a large number of recording companies and publishers, several of which passed into foreign ownership in the 1980s and 1990s.

Bendt Viinholt Nielsen

Operas
The Royal Danish Opera, founded in c. 1750
Danish National Opera, founded in 1947

Symphony Orchestras
The Royal Orchestra, founded in 1448
The Tivoli Symphony Orchestra, founded in 1843; since 1965, the orchestra plays during the winter season as a regional orchestra under the name of the Zealand Symphony Orchestra*
The Danish Radio Symphony Orchestra, founded in 1925
Århus Symphony Orchestra*, founded in 1935
The Radio Light Orchestra, founded in 1939
Aalborg Symphony Orchestra*, founded in 1943
Odense Symphony Orchestra*, founded in 1946
The South Jutland Symphony Orchestra*, founded in 1963
Collegium Musicum, founded in 1981

*Regional orchestras

Cinema

Silent Films

The first film show in Denmark took place in June 1896 in the Panorama cinema on the Town Hall Square in Copenhagen, with a selection of films produced abroad. The first Dane to make a film was the photographer Peter Elfelt, who between 1896 and 1912 made some 200 documentary films on life in Denmark; the first was *Kørsel med grønlandske Hunde* (Travel with Greenlandic Dogs). He also made the first feature film, *Henrettelsen* (1903, The Execution).

In 1906 the cinema owner Ole Olsen founded the first Danish film-producing company, Nordisk Films Kompagni, which derived its income particularly from the considerable export market for short films of various kinds. Not until 1909 were other Danish companies established, and

Asta Nielsen, 1881-1972, Danish silent film actress and one of the greatest of all silent film stars. In her first film, Urban Gad's *Afgrunden* (The Abyss or The Woman Always Pays) in 1910, she made her name internationally famous. With the story of the nice girl who falls in love with a faithless circus artist and finally murders him, she laid the foundations for the erotic melodrama, and her playing style showed a body language suited to cinema, less theatrical than had been seen before. In 1911 she was invited to go to Germany and there, partly for her own production company, she played in more than 70 films, finishing with the sound film *Unmögliche Liebe* (1932, Impossible Love).

She was equally adept at playing a flapper, an ageing woman, a harlot and a proletarian, woman and man, Spaniard and Eskimo. Asta Nielsen has become especially famous for her acting in films about powerful and tragic love, in which her women characters suffer and die or kill for unrequited love, for instance *Die arme Jenny* (1912, Poor Jenny).

Anne Jerslev

in 1910 the number had reached ten. From spring 1910 Nordisk Film changed its policy and aimed at contemporary films, partly inspired by the Århus Fotorama company's *Den hvide Slavehandel* (1910, The White Slave Trade), which was the first multi-reel Danish film (lasting more than 30 min.). With the greater length of the films came greater preoccupation with the setting and a growing artistic awareness. This is seen in Urban Gad's *Afgrunden* (1910, The Abyss or The Woman Always Pays) for the Kosmorama company, which turned Asta Nielsen into Europe's first great female film star. The film was an erotic melodrama, and this became the preferred genre throughout the ensuing years' 'golden age' of Danish film. Nordisk Film's first essay in this genre, August Blom's *Ved Fængslets Port* (1911, Temptations of a Great City), was a breakthrough for Valdemar Psilander, who became the greatest male star of the period. In 1911 Nordisk Film was the first of the major European companies to devote itself entirely to full-length feature films which could be sold in several hundred copies abroad. It was in particular the technical and photographic quality that impressed audiences abroad. The financial success of the company, which in 1912 gave shareholders a dividend of 60%, led to the establishment of a number of competing companies. Most, however, only survived for a short time. After 1913 Danish cinema began to lose its leading position. Foreign film companies also began to make full-length feature films, and the competition became intense. Several Danish companies began to produce ambitious literary films, including Holger-

Carl Th. Dreyer, 1889-1968, Danish film director. Dreyer was an uncompromising, perfectionist loner in Danish cinema, and he is counted as one of the most important creative geniuses in cinema. He started as a feature film director in 1919 for Nordisk Film Kompagni with the dramatic family saga *Præsidenten* (The President), which was followed by *Blade af Satans Bog* (1920, Leaves from Satan's Book).

This film was too sombre for Nordisk Film, and Dreyer was forced to produce his next five films in turn in Sweden, Germany and for other Danish film companies. *Du skal ære din Hustru* (The Master of the House) from 1925 ensured him an appointment with a French film company, and for them he made his famous *La passion de Jeanne d'Arc* (1928, The Passion of Joan of Arc), one of the finest artistic achievements from the silent film era. This film confirmed Dreyer's international reputation, but the company fell into financial difficulties, and he was only able to make his next film, *Vampyr* (Vampire) thanks to a wealthy patron. In 1934 Dreyer returned to Denmark to a time marked by adversity and abandoned projects. Only in 1943 did he come to produce his next feature film, *Vredens Dag* (Day of Wrath), a tragic love story played against the background of the persecution of witches in the 17th century. In the years following the Second World War, Dreyer

contributed to the official Danish production of short films with, for instance, *De naaede Færgen* (1948, They Caught the Ferry), but again a long time elapsed before he was able to make his next feature film, *Ordet* (1955, The Word), a brilliant film version of Kaj Munk's play, which assured Dreyer of even greater international recognition. His last film was *Gertrud* (1964), which was seen as very controversial after its première, but which has since been considered as one of the great works of modern cinema.

Martin Drouzy

Madsen's *Elskovsleg* (1913, Love's Devotee) and August Blom's *Atlantis* (1913) based respectively on novels by Arthur Schnitzler and Gerhart Hauptmann. In 1914 the pacifist *Ned med Vaabnene* (Lay Down Your Arms) was made with a script by Carl Th. Dreyer based on Bertha von Suttner's novel. In addition, Nordisk Film produced a large number of shorter comedies, mostly directed by Lau Lauritzen. The independent Benjamin Christensen had great success with the spy film *Det hemmelighedsfulde X* (1914, The Mysterious X or Sealed Orders) and the crime melodrama *Hævnens Nat* (1916, Blind Justice or The Night of Revenge), both of which are major works in the history of the Danish cinema.

During the First World War the USA became the leading film nation in the world, and Danish exports dwindled. After the war there were only a few companies left, Filmfabrikken Danmark, which produced exclusively documentary films, the new Dansk Film Co., which had specialised in films starring the outstanding popular actor Olaf Fønss, and Nordisk Film, which was more and more falling into difficulties. In the years immediately following the war, Dreyer made his appearance as director at Nordisk Film with the melodrama *Præsidenten* (1919, The President), followed by the ambitious *Blade af Satans Bog* (1921, Leaves from Satan's Book), inspired by the American director D.W. Griffiths' *Intolerance* (1916) in both technique (quick, dramatic cutting) and theme, which is that of evil in the world over the ages. After this the company had to confine itself to producing films almost exclusively by the new artistic director A.W. Sandberg. His large-scale literary film adaptations, including the novels of Charles Dickens, did not, however, enjoy the expected successes. In 1929 the company went into liquidation, but was already that same year reconstructed as a sound film company.

In 1920 the first Danish cartoon film appeared, *De tre smaa Mænd* (The Three Little Men) created by Robert Storm Petersen, who after producing a number of small animation films withdrew again.

The greatest successes in Danish cinema in the 1920s were due to the Palladium company, founded in 1921 with Lau Lauritzen as artistic director. He created the comedy couple Fyrtaarnet og Bivognen (Fy og Bi) (Long and Short), played by Carl Schenstrøm and Harald Madsen. Fy og Bi played the principal parts in

Maria Falconetti in Carl Th. Dreyer's masterpiece *The Passion of Joan of Arc* (1928) about the trial and death of the French saint.

many farces that enjoyed international success. Among the most successful were *Vester Vov Vov* (1927, People of the North Sea) and *Don Quixote* (1925), filmed in Spain, which was an imaginative attempt at retelling the old story. Palladium was also behind Dreyer's most important Danish silent film, the intimate family drama *Du skal ære din Hustru* (1925, The Master of the House), which brought the director an invitation to make a film about Joan of Arc in France.

Marguerite Engberg

The First sound Films

At the end of the 1920s Danish film production had reached a crossroads. Silent films were being replaced by sound films, and everywhere in the world experiments were being carried out with the new technique. Danish technology and cinema were soon engaged in this. Two Danish engineers had been working on a sound film system since 1918, and in October 1923 the result of their efforts was shown for the first time under the name of Petersen and Poulsen's Sound Film System.

In 1929 Nordisk Film was re-established as a sound film company on the basis of the new sound system, and already 1930 saw the premiere of the first Scandinavian sound film (though without Danish dialogue) with the title *Eskimo*, which was a French, German and Norwegian co-production directed by George Schneevoigt. It was not a success, but Schneevoigt's next feature film, the first with Danish dialogue, *Præsten i Vejlby* (1931, The Pastor of Vejlby) based on Steen Steensen Blicher's short story, certainly was. With this Nordisk Film's dominance of the Danish market was reinforced, as was the part played in it by Schneevoigt himself. He was responsible for most Danish films between 1930-1933, in particular several great Danish comedy successes of the 1930's, for instance *Odds 777* (1932).

The Recovery of the 1930s

To the Danes, cinema was the great entertainment phenomenon of the 1930s. It was cheap to go to the cinema, and the number of cinemas and tickets sold grew steadily. The most fashionable films came from the USA, but Danish comedies, including those from new companies like ASA (1937), were highly acclaimed, and actors like Marguerite Viby, Liva Weel, Ib Schønberg and Poul Reichhardt achieved great popularity. Meanwhile Danish films were criticised for their poor quality, and in connection with new laws governing the cinema enacted 1933 and 1938 there was a discussion of how the survival and quality of Danish films could be ensured. The Film Act of 1938 established a number of national organs: the Film Council, the Film Fund and the National Film Board were established to regulate the development of Danish cinema.

Documentary films were also characteristic of Danish cinema in the 1930s. The National Film Board together with Dansk Kulturfilm (established in 1932) created the framework for a Danish production of educational films, short films and documentary films. One of the most controversial films of the 1930s was Poul Henningsen's *Danmark* (1935), which had modern jazz as background music and employed an advanced, rhythmical montage style. Dansk Kulturfilm's production *Kongen bød* (1938, The King Commanded) on adscription and its abolition achieved wide distribution. New production companies arose such as Minerva-Film in 1935, in which Theodor Christensen and Karl Roos

KRUDT MED KNALD

Fyrtaarnet and Bivognen (Carl Schenstrøm and Harald Madsen), also known as Fy and Bi (Long and Short), were among Denmark's most popular film stars throughout the silent film era, and they were also known abroad. Their characteristic silhouettes are here pictured on the poster for the comic film *Krudt med Knald* (Gunpowder with a Bang) from 1931.

demonstrated their abilities with new-style documentary films, for instance *C – et Hjørne af Sjælland* (1938, C – A Corner of Zealand) and *Iran – det nye Persien* (1939, Iran – the New Persia).

Danish Cinema During the Occupation

The German occupation of Denmark 1940-1945 provided particularly favourable conditions for the Danish cinema, because the Germans quickly prohibited the import of films from the Allied countries. There was an appreciable rise in the number of film productions, and Danish cinema achieved a special national status. A great number of educational and documentary films were made, portraying everyday life in Denmark and Danish culture seen from many angles. To go to the cinema when a Danish film was being shown became a symbolical expression of resistance to the Occupation.

It was still comedies and farces that dominated, and the film stars from the 1930s who were the biggest draw. But more serious films were also made such as Svend Methling's

Sommerglæder (1940, Summer Joys), based on the story by Herman Bang. Directors like Bodil Ipsen and Lau Lauritzen jr. made names for themselves with the psychological thrillers *Afsporet* (1942, Derailed), *Mordets Melodi* (1944, Melody of Murder) and *Besættelse* (1944, Possession) which showed that they mastered the language of modern cinema and at the same time could provide a credible picture of Danish reality. Johan Jacobsen also impressed audiences with his episode film *Otte Akkorder* (1944, Eight Chords).

The greatest Danish film from the Occupation, however, was Carl Th. Dreyer's masterpiece *Vredens Dag* (1943, The Day of Wrath), a story from the 17th century about the oppression of sensuality and love by an arid system. Among other things, the film could be seen as an allegorical commentary on the Occupation.

The Post-War Years: the Occupation as a Theme, Films for Young People and Popular Comedies

A number of directors succeeded in raising the artistic standard in the first years after the war and thus continued the trend from the Occupation into the 1950s. In the immediate post-war years the theme of the Occupation played an important part. In 1945 Bodil Ipsen and Lau Lauritzen jr. produced *De røde Enge* (The Red Meadows), and Johan Jacobsen *Den usynlige Hær* (The Invisible Army), two films about the Occupation which combined realism, melodrama and pathos. Films of a more sober and profound nature soon appeared, and there were also documentaries, including Theodor Christensen's partly illegally filmed *Det gælder din Frihed* (1946, Your Freedom is at Stake), made for the Danish Freedom Council, and the more official, subdued version celebrating the tenth anniversary of the liberation: *De fem År* (1955, The Five Years).

The realistic line was adopted in several films, e.g. Bjarne Henning-Jensen's *Ditte Menneskebarn* (1946, Ditte, Child of Man) based on Martin Andersen Nexø's novel, Johan Jacobsen's *Soldaten og Jenny* (1947, The Soldier and Jenny) and Bodil Ipsen and Lau Lauritzen jr.'s realistic portrayal of a drinker in *Café Paradis* (1950).

Together with his wife Astrid, Bjarne Henning-Jensen gave a portrayal of children from the slums in *De pokkers Unger* (1947, The Hooligans), which focused on the problems of youth, which became a favourite theme in the films of the day and also the subject of public debate. The first films on the problems of young people kept to a realistic and pessimistic style and stressed the dangers and temptations of youth, for instance *Farlig Ungdom* (1953, Dangerous Youth), *Blændværk* (1955, Delusion) and *Bundfald* (1957, Dregs). A new style heralding the new and more dominant role to be played by youth culture in the welfare society of the 1960s could be seen in the film *De sjove år* (1959, The Fun Years).

The period from 1945 to 1960 was also characterised in Danish cinema

The film *De røde heste* (The Red Horses) (1950), which was directed by Alice O'Fredericks and Jon Iversen after the novel by Morten Korch, was one of the most popular post-war Danish light melodramas. Tove Maës and Poul Reichhardt play the young lovers in the film, which was the first of a long succession of film versions of Korch's novels.

by a renewal of the traditional Danish genres. In 1950 there was the premiere of the ASA film company's first adaptation of one of Morten Korch's novels, *De røde heste* (The Red Horses), which became one of Danish film's greatest financial successes, and by 1976 it had been followed by in all 18 films based on Korch's work. These films established a new standard for Danish popular comedy. They were placed in a familiar rural setting which had a comforting feel at a time of frenzied change and modernisation, and at the same time the films managed to introduce certain elements from the thriller and the melodrama. Other popular comedy films were the *Far til Fire* (Father of Four) films (1953-1961 and 1971), based on a popular strip cartoon series about a single father and his four lively children, and the *Poeten og Lillemor* (The Poet and His Muse) films (1959-1961), similarly based on a popular strip cartoon series about a young artist and the contemporary problems he has to face, and finally the farce-like, humorous *Soldaterkammerater* (Comrades in Arms) films (1959-1962 and 1968). In 1948 Denmark was also given its own film prize, when the Association of Film Reviewers began to award what is known as the Bodil Prize in January each year.

Osvald Helmuth and Ebbe Rode played the unlikely couple of friends who against all expectations find each other in Bent Christensen's film *Harry og kammertjeneren* (1961, Harry and the Valet). A new note was struck with this film, which painted an accurate and humorous picture of the Denmark of the day.

The New Wave and Competition from Television

About 1960 The New Wave in French cinema spread to that of other European countries. At the same time, since 1960 television has become an international mass medium offering many films, as a result of which Danish cinemas and film production have come under increasing pressure. In earlier legislation cinema was viewed as entertainment on which tax was to be levied, and with the help of the licensing system for cinemas, which with numerous adjustments existed until 1972, the State regulated the right of the cinema owners to obtain a licence. The object of this was to prevent the concentration and merging of distribution, production and cinema-owning activities. By means of the system of licensing, an attempt was at the same time made to put into effect a cultural policy which made demands on the composition of the film repertoire. In addition, the cinemas paid certain taxes which could also be exploited in the service of a cultural policy for film.

In the first modern Film Act of 1964, meanwhile, arrangements for subsidies to the cinema were introduced, and the Act gave support to film as a branch of art which nevertheless was still to derive much of its income from the sale of tickets. With the 1972 Act the Danish Film Institute was established, and support for film production was now based on a budgetary grant. At the same time the cinema licensing system was abolished, opening up the potential of a free market. Since 1972 the great majority of Danish films have been made with State support, and since 1981 very few Danish films have been produced on the basis of private finance alone. In 1989 the so-called 50/50 system was introduced (in 1997 changed to a 60/40 system), providing for a greater possibility for both State and private finance; the idea was that film producers who could themselves provide guarantees for 50% (60%) of a film's production costs could, irrespective of the opinions of cinema consultants, seek cover for the remaining 50% (40%) from the directors of the Danish Film Institute. In the beginning of the 21st century state support still plays a major role at the same time as international developments have made international co-financing and -production a European or global basis ever more necessary.

A new generation of film directors emerged between 1960 and 1972, using a new and more modern, realistic film language. Astrid Henning-Jensen continued in the direction she had already taken with *Utro* (1966, Unfaithful) and later with *Vinterbørn* (1978, Winter's Children), while Bent Christensen with the excellent social comedies *Harry og*

kammertjeneren (1961, Harry and the Valet) and *Naboerne* (1966, The Neighbours), for which he wrote the script together with Leif Panduro, effected a renewal of the Danish popular comedy. The two most important directors in the New Wave were Palle Kjærulff-Schmidt, who worked closely together with the author Klaus Rifbjerg, and Henning Carlsen. Kjærulff-Schmidt made his name with the fine realistic psychological studies *Weekend* (1962) and *Der var engang en krig* (1966, Once There Was a War). Henning Carlsen started with the illegally filmed *Dilemma* (1962) about South Africa and achieved an international breakthrough with his film version of Knut Hamsun's novel *Sult* (1966, Hunger). A unique film masterpiece was created by Sven and Lene Grønlykke with *Balladen om Carl-Henning* (1969, The Ballad of Carl-Henning).

Apart from this relatively limited production of quality films in the 1960s, Danish cinema in general continued with the well-tried popular formulae. With the freeing of picture pornography in 1969, the soft porn genre was introduced, and this provided increased export potential. The Danish tradition for farce was continued, not least with the welfare satire *Vi er allesammen tossede* (1959, We're All Daft) with Dirch Passer and Kjeld Petersen in two of their greatest roles.

In 1954 the director Erik Balling was given a leading role in Nordisk Film, on the basis of which he was able to renew the style in the Danish popular film. His most important achievement was the series of films on the Olsen Gang, 13 films made between 1968 and 1981. These well-structured films are about a trio of Danish petty criminals who are admittedly at first cheated by Big

Olsen-banden på sporet (1975, The Olsen Gang on the Trail) was the seventh film with the popular Danish gang of petty criminals doggedly trying one imaginative feat after another. There were altogether 13 films about the Olsen Gang, all directed by Erik Balling, and in addition to being popular at home, they achieved fame in e.g. Norway, Sweden and Germany.

Business and foreign criminal syndicates, but finally through their own inventiveness they win over superior forces. The series was one of Danish cinema's greatest successes and has been exported to many countries. In 1998 the series acquired a post-script with *Olsenbandens sidste stik* (The Olsen Gang – The Final Mission) directed by Tom Hedegaard and Morten Arnfred.

Danish documentaries also turned in new directions during this period. About 1960, Henning Carlsen and Tørk Haxthausen created a modern documentary style. The leading figure in the short film and documentary film genre was, however, Jørgen Roos, who among other things with his films from Greenland, e.g. the prize-winning Knud (1966) on the arctic explorer Knud Rasmussen, took the Danish documentary film tradition in new directions.

International Success and Innovation

The popular genres continued to predominate after the introduction of the new Film Act of 1972. Film versions of novels and cinema realism achieved an international breakthrough with the two Oscar-winning films, Gabriel Axel's adaptation of Karen Blixen's *Babettes gæstebud* (1987, Babette's Feast) and Bille August's *Pelle Erobreren* (1987, Pelle the Conqueror), based on Martin Andersen Nexø's novel. August's next film, *Den gode vilje* (1991, The Best Intentions), based on Ingmar Bergman's memoirs, was also an international success. However, although August's use of literary classics or bestsellers gave him a huge success with the audience in the case of *The House of the Spirits* (1993) and *Smilla's Sense of Snow* (1997) it did not give him the same success with the critics. At the same

Stéphane Audran played the main role in *Babette's Feast* (1987), Gabriel Axel's film version of the story by Karen Blixen. It was not least Stéphane Audran's achievement as Babette that won the film an Oscar in 1988.

time the avant-garde movement in film received its international breakthrough with Lars von Trier's film *Forbrydelsens element* (1984, The Element of Crime), *Europa* (or *Zentropa*, 1991), *Riget* (1994, The Kingdom) and *Riget II* (1997, The Kingdom II). Together with Lars von Trier's very successful melodrama *Breaking the Waves* (1996) this meant a new and larger audience.

However, behind the internationally known foreground figures there is also a broader production that has managed to survive despite the decline in the annual number of films since the 1970s. The realistic film tradition covers a wide field with portrayals of working class life in Morten Arnfred's *Johnny Larsen* (1979) and Søren Kragh-Jacobsen's socially aware portraits of young people and historical realism in *Skyggen af Emma* (1988, Emma's Shadow) and *Drengene fra Sankt Petri* (1991, The Boys from St. Petri). In addition, in a series of often prize-winning films, e.g. *Drenge* (1977, Boys) and *Kundskabens træ* (1981, The Tree of Knowledge) Nils Malmros has explored children growing up and the lives of young people in the provinces with great psychological insight. A change in theme and aesthetics came with the tragic film *Kærlighedens*

Pelle Hvenegaard and Max von Sydow in *Pelle Erobreren* (1987, Pelle the Conqueror), Bille August's film version of the first part of Martin Andersen Nexø's novel. Pelle and his father have just arrived in Bornholm from Sweden to begin a new life, but they continue to find only dire poverty. The film was awarded both the Golden Palms and an Oscar in 1988, and Max von Sydow's acting was nominated for an Oscar for the best male actor in a leading role.

smerte (1992, Pain of Love) and the historical film in international style *Barbara* (1997), based on a novel by Jørgen-Frantz Jacobsen. This was the film that took top place for attendances at Danish cinemas in 1997.

Directors like Bille August and Søren Kragh-Jakobsen have also gained prizes for their films for children, and since the 1980s a number of quality Danish cartoons have been created, e.g. Jannik Hastrup's *Fuglekrigen* (1990, The War of the Birds).

Renewal of Danish Mainstream Genres

There has always been a minor tradition of genres like thriller and crime in danish cinema. During the 1970s it was films such as Esben Høilund Carlsen's *Nitten røde roser* (1974, Nineteen Red Roses) and Anders Refn's *Strømer* (1976, Copper). But starting with Ole Bornedal's *Nattevagten* (1994, remade into the American version *Nightwatch* in 1998), a more internationally influenced thriller, a

Bille August, b. 1948. Since the end of the 1980s the film and television director Bille August has to a large extent been instrumental in gaining an international profile for Danish cinema. In his early film and television production, which includes such films as *Honningmåne* (1978, In My Life) and the television play *Maj* (1982), August showed himself to be a gifted creator of visual poetry, who can depict family life, women's fates and alienation in the welfare society with deep psychological understanding. In *Zappa* (1983), *Tro, håb og kærlighed* (1984, Twist and Shout) and *Busters verden* (1984, Buster's World), all based on novels by Bjarne Reuter, he explores the conflict-filled and magic world of the youth of the 1960s. *Pelle Erobreren* (1987, Pelle the Conqueror), based on Martin Andersen Nexø's novel, won both the Golden Palms in Cannes and an Oscar. Here August created both a social historical epic and a beautiful psychological study of a boy and his father. Augusts's international breakthrough was followed by the film and television series *Den gode vilje* (1991, The Best Intentions) with a script by Ingmar Bergman. This film, too, was awarded the Golden Palms in Cannes. Together with *Jerusalem* (1996) based on a novel by the swedish author Selma Lagerlöf, these two films form a sort of Nordic epic film-triology. A move towards the international mainstream film however began with the ambitious film version of Isabel Allende's bestseller *The House of the Spirits* (1993) with a strong international cast, and the just as ambitious film version of Peter Høeg's bestselling thriller *Smilla's Sense of Snow* (1997) to be followed by a new film version of Victor Hugo's immortal story *Les Misérables* (1998). B. August made his come-back with the Scandinavian closet play *En sang for Martin* (2001, A song for Martin).

Ib Bondebjerg

new generation of directors appeared who were influenced by not least American genre traditions. The most promising names are Thomas Vinterberg, Nicolas Winding Refn, Niels Arden Oplev, Anders Rønnow-Klarlund and Lasse Spang Olsen who made the spectacular action-comedy *I Kina spiser de hunde* (1999, In China They Eat Dogs).

Comedy is another genre that was completely renewed. Erik Clausen stands as one of the period's most important figures in the renewal of popular comedy and farce with its coarse, critical folksiness in films like *Cirkus Casablanca* (1981) and *De frigjorte* (1993, A Fish out of Water). In this genre there are also Helle Ryslinge's modern comedies like *Flamberede hjerter* (1986, Flambéed

Hearts), Michael Wikke and Steen Rasmussen's *Russian Pizza Blues* (1992) and Susanne Bier's romantic comedy *Den eneste ene* (1999, The One and Only), which is directed with a sure touch and became one of the biggest Danish box office successes of the decade. Lotte Svendsen created a socially conscious comedy genre with surrealistic elements in the short fiction film *Royal Blues* (1999) and the feature film *Bornholms stemme* (1999, Gone with the Fish). Jonas Elmer's debut feature film and Bodil Award Winner *Let's Get Lost* (1997) also represented a significant renewal of the comedy genre. The most recent example of a new strong comedy tradition in Danish film is Anette K. Olesen's debut film *Små ulykker* (2002, Minor

Lars von Trier, b. 1956. The Danish film director Lars von Trier with the motto: 'film should be like a stone in your shoe', makes deeply personal and technically brilliant films with an international appeal. In 1995 Trier was among the film directors who took the initiative to form the Dogma 95 manifesto which challenged all the established cinematic 'rules' and drew international attention to Danish film.

Trier clearly demonstrated his talent already when making his controversial graduation film *Befrielsesbilleder* (1982, Images of a Relief) about the last days of the Occupation. His breakthrough came with the English-language *The Element of Crime* (1984), a hypnotic crime story from a Europe in decline. It was the first part of his European trilogy and was followed by the self-reflecting *Epidemic* (1987) about a film that

never came to anything, and the grandiose international production *Europa* or *Zentropa* (1991), set in Germany in 1945. For television, Trier has directed *Euripedes' Medea* (1987), freely adapted from Carl Th. Dreyer's posthumous manuscript, and the television series *Riget* and *Riget II* (The Kingdom and The Kingdom II, 1994 and 1997), a metaphysical thriller made like a soap opera in a hospital environment. With *Riget* Trier for the first time engaged with the public at large, and he continued to do this in his 'Gold Heart' trilogy: beginning with *Breaking the Waves* (1996), a compulsive melodrama whose main elements are sex and religion; followed by the radical Dogme film *Idioterne* (1998, The Idiots) which defies most film conventions in its depiction of a group of young people playing retarded; and finally ending with the modern musical *Dancer in the Dark* (2000) which featured the Islandic singer Björk in the lead role and won the Golden Palms in Cannes that same year. Furthermore, Trier was prime mover in the interactive *D-dag* (2000, D-Day) project inviting television viewers to edit their own version of a story shot in four different versions in the hour preceding the turn of the millennium and broadcast simultanously on 1 January 2000 on six television channels. Trier has also made advertising films and music videos and since 1991 he has been working on a 'filmic monument' called *Dimension*, a work of fiction of which he is filming a little bit every year until the première planned for 2025.

Eva Jørholt

Danish cartoon film produced several international successes in the 1990s. This is a scene from *Hjælp! Jeg er en fisk* (Help! I'm a Fish) from 2000.

Mishaps), which won the award as best European film at the Berlin Film Festival the same year.

Denmark's international fame for films for children also gained a new international dimension, especially with a new animated film production. In 1995 the veteran Jannik Hastrup made *Aberne og det hemmelige våben* (The Monkeys and the Secret Weapon) and the other Danish veteran Flemming Quist Møller created *Jungledyret Hugo* (1993, Amazon Jack), and two of the representatives of a new generation, Stefan Fjeldmark and Michael Hegner made the international co-production *Hjælp! Jeg er en fisk* (2000, Help! I'm a Fish). A new generation of directors also developed more spectacular children's films like Jesper W. Nielsen's historical epic *Den sidste viking* (1997, The Last Viking), Peter Flinth's *Ørnens øje* (1997, Eye of the Eagle) and Lars Hesselholdt's *Falkehjerte* (1999, Katja's Adventure). At the same time a new magic realism about children's everyday life mixing social realism and an imaginary universe can be found in Lone Scherfig's *Når mor kommer hjem* (1998, On Our Own) and Jesper W. Nielsen's *Forbudt for børn* (1998, Little Big Sister).

In the field of documentary films Jon Bang Carlsen and Jørgen Leth are among those to have attracted attention. Bang Carlsen has i.a. made portrait films maintaining a balance between fact and fiction, for instance *En rig mand* (1979, A Rich Man) and *Hotel of the Stars* (1981). Leth has produced both experimental short films like *Livet i Danmark* (1971, Life in Denmark) and epic documentaries like *Stjernerne og vandbærerne* (1973, Stars and Watercarriers). Women directors like Dola Bonfils, Anne Wivel and Jytte Rex also play an important part in modern Danish documentary and avant garde films. Also in documentary films, a younger generation has started both to experiment with the portrayal of reality and to experiment with the aesthetic form, for instance Tómas Gislason in films like *Patrioterne* (1997, The Patriots) or the award winning *Den højeste straf* (2000, Maximum Penalty). In 2002 Sami Saif and Phie Ambo were the first Danes to win the international award at the Amsterdam Film Festival (the documentary equivalent to the Golden Palms) for their very personal story *Family* (2001) about Saifs search for his father and family in Yemen.

Dogme 95 and International Expansion

Around the year 2000 it was still directors like Bille August and Lars

von Trier who, with major international co-productions, epitomised Danish cinema. This new, strong international position was further emphasised when Lars von Trier won the Golden Palms for *Dancer in the Dark* (2000), set to the music of the islandic singer Björk who also plays the lead. Alongside these two major figures there were, however, many new directors of popular comedies, realistic films, thrillers and documentaries that continued the international success of August and Trier. As early as in 1995 Lars von Trier and Thomas Vinterberg jointly formulated the artistic manifesto Dogme 95, which turned low budget film aesthetics into a rich, provocative cinematic principle. In 1998 this led to a major breakthrough for Thomas Vinterberg's *Festen* (The Celebration) which was awarded the Special Jury Prize at Cannes and subsequently sold to more than 25 countries. At the same time, Lars von Trier's own Dogme film *Idioterne* (1998, The Idiots) attracted much attention. In 1999 the third Dogme film, *Mifunes sidste sang* (1999, Mifune) by Søren Kragh-Jacobsen, was awarded a Silver Bear at the Berlin Film Festival, and in 2000 the fourth Dogme film *The King is Alive* directed by Kristian Levring succeeded to be screened in Cannes. The Dogme success continued with

Lone Scherfig's unusual romantic comedy *Italiensk for begyndere* (2000, Italian for Beginners), a film that did not only win the Silver Bear in Berlin (2001) but also became a big box-office success, not only in Denmark, but also in many other European countries and in the USA. To this should be added the above-mentioned success achieved by Anette K. Olesen's Dogme film *Små Ulykker* (Minor Mishaps). A new generation in Danish cinema has made its mark.

In the 1990s the Danish film production environment developed and several new companies were established. Zentropa is the best known company, established by Peter Aalbæk Jensen and Lars von Trier in 1992. However, Nimbus and Balboa have also been important to the new wave, and the illustrious producer Per Holst has, likewise, been influential. In 1997 all Danish film institutions were merged into The Danish Film Institute and with this new strong organisation, the injection of financial resources and subsidy schemes it should be possible to maintain the breadth of Danish film production and its international and national success. In 2001 Danish cinema had its best year since the 1950s with around 30% of the cinema market in Denmark and enjoying considerable success abroad.

Ib Bondebjerg

The posters from four Dogme films: *Festen* (The Celebration), *Idioterne* (The Idiots), *Mifunes sidste sang* (Mifune) and *The King is Alive*. The directors of the Dogme films swear e.g. to use a hand-held camera, to shoot on location and not to produce sound or light apart from the images.

Mass Media

1634-1848: The Breakthrough of the Printed Media

There were fly-sheets in Denmark from 1482, but the first real newspaper did not appear until 1634. It was a weekly paper published under royal licence, and like the majority of newspapers up to 1750 it was primarily a copy of German newspapers. The most striking publication was Anders Bording's versified monthly periodical *Den Danske Mercurius* (1666-1677), which sang the praises of the policy of the absolute monarchy. By means of grants of privileges, censorship, and various prohibitions, the State controlled the publication of printed media right up to 1848, entailing limitation of public debate in periodicals and, especially, newspapers. Of newspapers, it was especially E.H. Berling's Copenhagen newspaper – subsequently the *Berlingske Tidende* – which from 1749 took the lead in circulation, number of advertisements and up-to-date news coverage. A provincial press as such only began to appear from 1767 (*Aalborg Stiftstidende*). Not until 1834 was opposition voiced in the newspapers.

1848-1914: The Four Paper System

With the 1849 Constitution's introduction of press freedom (more precisely defined in the Press Act of 1851) all kinds of newspapers underwent a period of rapid growth until 1914. This growth also had its roots in the improvement in people's reading ability after the introduction of seven years' compulsory teaching in 1814, the general growth in population and the increased buying power and shorter working hours in the majority of the working population.

The general politicisation and the often sharp political differences after 1848 meant that the press came mainly to consist of party-political organs. The four political parties established newspapers throughout the country. Newspapers already in existence were largely associated with the *Højre* (the Conservative People's Party), but during the period 1865-1885 *Venstre* (the Liberal Party) gained the backing of 50 local papers in the provinces. After 1872 the Social Democratic papers followed: the Copenhagen *Social-Demokraten* (1872-1959, when it was renamed *Aktuelt*) with some 20 associated newspapers in the provinces (known as the A-newspapers). From 1905 the Copenhagen newspaper *Politiken* (1884-) was followed by a score of local newspapers as the organ of the party *Det Radikale Venstre* (the Social Liberal Party).

During this time, local conditions gradually found coverage in the provincial newspapers. The press in general went through a period of growth, with dedicated political and social discussion, cultural journalism and a vastly increased news service resulting from telegraphed reports from Ritzau's news agency (1866-), and this was paralleled by a strong growth in both circulation and revenue from advertising, as well as improved and mechanised printing techniques.

Side by side with the daily newspapers there was a large number of periodicals: political weeklies, contemporary debate weeklies, mixed cultural periodicals and satirical periodicals. These stagnated as the daily papers took over their contents. On the other hand almost all other kinds of Danish periodicals continued to grow. Very large circulations were reached by certain illustrated weeklies, first *Illustreret Tidende* (1859-1924), then i.a. Carl Aller's magazine *Familie Journalen* (1877-) and Egmont H. Petersen's *Hjemmet* (1904-).

1850 saw the emergence also of district and advertisement weeklies in and around Copenhagen, then in the major cities and the new towns built around railway stations. By 1914 there were some 50 papers of this kind. However, it was the monthly periodicals from the ever-increasing number of leisure associations, parish associations and trade unions that saw the greatest growth. Including the technical and scientific journals there were now something like 1000 different publications in Denmark, 150 being independent daily newspapers.

1914-45: Press Reform

In 1905, the editor-in-chief of Politiken, Henrik Cavling, effected a change in the newspaper's contents, journalism and layout (known as the 'press reform'). From having its main emphasis on party politics, opinion and cultural debate, the newspaper now, on the American pattern, aimed at a broad spectrum of news about local, general, financial and social events, reports and a readers' service, and the party-political commitment was reduced. During the First World War, almost all the newspapers in Copenhagen underwent a revision along these lines. It was Politiken and later Berlingske Tidende that managed the change best, and it was the tabloid papers belonging to these two publishers, *Ekstra Bladet*

The front cover of the Danish State Railways magazine *Ud & Se*'s 15th anniversary issue from April 1995 was a reproduction of Aage Rasmussen's poster showing the *Little Belt Bridge* from 1951. The magazine is an example of the wide-ranging Danish customers' magazine containing everything from crossword puzzles to short stories by respected Danish authors.

(1904-) and *B.T.* (1916-) respectively that gradually secured the largest circulations. Otherwise, only the Århus morning newspaper *Jyllands-Posten* (1871-) tried and could keep pace on a national basis.

The press reform also spread to the bigger and more viable provincial newspapers during the inter-war years. A significant change took place as a result of the newspaper monopoly of news coverage being broken in 1926 with the introduction of news broadcasts in the radio. After 1920 the rise in total circulation of the daily press from 1 to 1.75 million copies merely reflected the increase in the population. The period of the German occupation 1940-1945 was an exception, even though the press was subject to German censorship and people were also reading the illegal newspapers, one of which has survived until now, i.e. the small independent opinion-forming *Information* (1945-). After 1950 newspaper sales stagnated. In 2001 about 1,45 million copies were sold daily.

1945-2002: Newspaper Closures and the Present Situation

From about 1930, in each of the 30-40 principal areas of provincial newspapers, there was a process of concentration around the most viable newspaper, while the others declined and later faced closure despite various kinds of subventions from parties and organisations. This process continued between 1950 and 1970, so that the strongest newspaper was finally left unopposed. The closure of newspapers meant that the number of daily papers with an independent editorship fell from 123 in 1945 to 29 in 2001. Of these, seven are sold nationwide, while the others are regional papers serving their local areas with news and advertisements. Both the small local papers and the slightly larger regional ones, which flourished until 1980, have been having problems and have lost ground.

Among the factors behind the closure of newspapers, special mention must be made of the increased demands being made on journalistic resources in all areas of coverage, and the fiercer competition from the electronic media: television news programmes began in 1965 (*TV-Avisen*), and Radio Denmark's Program 3 (*P3*) has broadcast news on the hour since 1975. In the 1980s local radio and TV stations entered the scene, and in 1988 came the final breaching of the monopoly which, since 1925, the State had granted to *Danmarks Radio*, financed by licence-fees and with public-service obligations.

Developments in the other printed media have contributed to the weakening of the daily press. For instance, the weekly district and advertising papers have shown an appreciable rise in number and circulation since the start of the 1960s, and in 2001 about 290 of these papers were distributed with a combined circulation of 8 million. One of these, *Søndagsavisen* (1978-), which besides advertising contains a quantity of editorial matter, appears in 14 editions throughout Denmark with a combined circulation of 1.5 million. Most of the other papers of this type are small, and nearly half of them are published by the dailies. The papers that in the short run survived newspaper closures best were the two selling purely by the piece, also called the lunch-time, mid-day or tabloid papers, *B.T.* and *Ekstra Bladet*. Then as now, these were dominated by sensational material, conflicts, many photographs and a great deal of sport, entertainment and strip cartoons. With this the newspapers won the younger people from the whole country, often those less accustomed to reading, doubling their circulation between 1955 and 1980; since then – up to 2001 – they have lost half of their readers, as a large proportion of their target group no longer reads newspapers. However, both B.T. and Ekstra Bladet have circulations of some 125,000 nationwide, since 1988 on Sundays, too.

The growth of the noon tabloids weakened the morning papers, and together with large-scale strikes over the introduction of new printing

A glimpse of the editorial offices of the newspaper *Morgenavisen Jyllands-Posten*.

techniques, this created new crises for both *Politiken* in 1971-1972 and *Berlingske Tidende* 1977-1982. Meanwhile, the morning papers have had some success in overcoming the crisis and adapting to the education and business structure of the 1990s.

Of the seven national morning papers, only *Morgenavisen Jyllands-Posten* has its headquarters outside Copenhagen. From being a rugged bourgeois regional paper for western Denmark, since 1970 it has developed into the equal in news and advertising of what were the two largest morning papers, Politiken and Berlingske Tidende. In 2001 it had Denmark's largest weekday and Sunday circulation, including considerable sales in the Copenhagen area.

Politiken and Berlingske Tidende have dominated the Copenhagen press for 65 years in equal competition and with well-entrenched differences in attitude, choice of subject and journalism. Politiken is the social radical all-round newspaper with its strength in reporting, small news items and liberal cultural material, while Berlingske Tidende is the moderately conservative newspaper based on economic-political and cultural material and a large number of advertisements. In 2001 these two papers had a weekday circulation of about 143,000 and 152,000 respectively and a Sunday circulation of 186,000 and 188,000 respectively. This is clearly smaller than that of Jyllands-Posten (180,000 and 243,000 respectively) but at least three times that of any other of the four smaller nationals, each of which survives in a particular niche.

Life has been easiest for the specialised business paper *Børsen* (1896-), which despite competition from *Erhvervsbladet* (1974-), a freesheet, has considerable advertising income. This is something which the politically independent opinion-forming dailies *Kristeligt Dagblad* (1896-) and *Information* (1945-) lack, as did, until 2001, Aktuelt – the longest surviving Social Democratic party newspaper. The last 50 years of its life, Aktuelt received subventions from its trade-union owners.

Today all nationals still have a particular ideological profile, but they have gradually given up following a party line. This also applied to Aktuelt which sought to find a niche as a political newspaper of high quality as an alternative to

Copies of Dailies

Relative to most western countries, many Danes take a newspaper.

In Denmark the circulation figures were stable between 1983 and 1989, but then fell by about 12%. The mid-day newspapers *B.T.* and *Ekstra Bladet* fell by 31%, provincial newspapers by 15%, while the national newspapers maintained their circulation, which in 1999 was 20% greater than in 1983. Since 1983, the total number of newspapers has fallen from 48 to 31 in 1999. In 1999, about 1.6 million newspapers were sold each day, and these were read by 3 million readers, or 68% of the population of 13 years of age and over. In 1999 74% read a newspaper every day. It is especially the very young, the unemployed and the oldest members of the community who are less inclined to read a newspaper, and in general there are slightly fewer female than male readers. On an ordinary day, the Danes spend about half an hour reading a newspaper.

Ole E. Andersen

Copies of dailies per 1,000 adult inhabitants (2000)

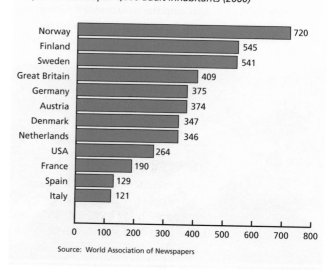

Source: World Association of Newspapers

DENMARK

The printing press of Politiken situated by the Town Hall Square in Copenhagen, where two of the biggest newspapers in the country, the morning *Politiken* and the mid-day *Ekstra Bladet*, are printed.

day-to-day circulation, which between 1913 and 1970 corresponded to over 100% of households, was in 1985 down to 85% and in 1997 64% (on Sundays 58%). As before, c. 30-35% of the population read two newspapers a day, but in 1998 there were 30%, especially the young, who did not read a newspaper at all. Well-educated, active adults mainly derive their knowledge of the world, the country and society from the newspaper, but a solid majority prefer television.

In September 2001 two free dailies started publishing in Copenhagen, both distributed in the streets and railway stations: First *MetroXpress* (published by Swedish based Metro International) and shortly after *Urban* (published by the Berlingske Group).

The circulation of popular weekly magazines has stagnated, but women's and family magazines have continued to enjoy large sales. Two new lowmarket weeklies started publication in 1997: Egmont Publishing's *HER og NU* (169,000) and Aller's *KIG IND* (112,000).

There has been increasing concentration, which is now quite noticeable: The Aller Press has 61% of all magazines, while Egmont has 27%. This dominant position is broken by magazine-like specialist and membership publications such as the Co-operative Wholesale Society's *Samvirke* (1945-) and *Det Bedste* (The Reader's Digest, 1946-). The magazine and specialist press has become more specialised, for instance with monthlies such as *Bo Bedre* (1961-) and the popular science magazine *Illustreret Videnskab* (1984-), and with specialist computer journals. In addition, there are in Denmark a number of customer-orientated magazines such as *Helse* (1955-) and the Danish Railways' *Ud & Se* (1980-),

Information (21,000). Instead, the national newspapers compete on quality and the balance of coverage of politics, foreign affairs, the arts, and business, as well as on many kinds of advertising, both large and small. An ever more common way of emphasising the newspapers' profile has been the publication of various theme supplements on specific days of the week.

In 2001 the local newspapers had a circulation of c. 629,000 copies (352,000 on Sundays), but since 1980 the circulation has gradually fallen by 20%. They have survived economically by merging to form larger regional units, today totalling 21 local newspapers. Furthermore, they have begun a practical and economic co-operation with the three largest newspaper publishers which are economically responsible for 67% of today's newspaper publication (The Berlingske Group alone accounts for 34%). Today the local newspaper cover nearly 40% of households in their area, corresponding to a fall of 50% over the past 30 years.

In the middle of the 1990s, however, people's sense of loyalty to their newspaper had been undermined, and with it the fact that the percentage of population covered by those papers had also been reduced. The as well as magazines distributed for free such as the housing journal *Idé-nyt* (1973-).

The general and independent periodicals have had low circulations and shaky finances since 1945. Even so, some of them have influenced opinion – among literary magazines *Heretica* (1948-1953) and *Vindrosen* (1954-1973), and among political journals *Finanstidende* (1915-1989), *Frit Danmark* (1942-1982), *Politisk Revy* (1963-1987) and *Notat* (1973-). *Børsens Nyhedsmagasin* was started in 1985 as a weekly news magazine, but is currently published twice a month with its main emphasis on economic matters. *Weekendavisen* has the greatest importance today. It originally appeared daily (until 1971 as *Berlingske Aftenavis*), but now appears every Friday and emphasises on coverage of literature and the arts, its circulation being 66,000 copies in 2001. *Ugebrevet Mandag Morgen* (The Mandag Morgen Weekly) is a newsletter focusing on politics and financial news and today it has a great influence on the current debate.

Niels Thomsen

Radio 1922-1980

The first Danish radio broadcasts aimed at a broad public were transmitted in 1922. Radio was controlled by legislation on telegraphy and as such a state monopoly according to an act from 1907, which nevertheless opened the way for experimental broadcasts. Such experiments were undertaken especially by two amateur radio associations with the participation of newspapers. The contents were mainly music and, from 1923, weekly news broadcasts, of which the daily newspaper Politiken's *Radioavis* was the first.

After increased competition – known as the 'ether war' – the associations and other interested parties were experimentally brought together under the aegis of the State in 1925 in *Radioordningen* (The Radio System), which in 1926 was replaced by *Statsradiofonien* (The State Radio). In 1959 this was renamed *Danmarks Radio* (DR). Radio became a special element in the policy governing education and culture, and the programmes were to be of an 'all-round cultural and informative nature' (so-called public service). Finance was to be derived from a licence fee, which ensured that it was only those making use of the radio who paid for it. Broadcasting hours were gradually increased from 2-3 hours a day to 14 hours in 1939, by which time 80% of the population had a radio. News broadcasts were brief and controlled by the print media as

Use of television
The Danes watch television less than the average European. Generally speaking, television is watched most in southern Europe and least in Scandinavia. In the 1980s the numbers of hours during which Danes watched television were very stable, but between 1990 and 1999 the number rose by about 24% as more and more viewers have been able to receive satellite television via the hybrid network or from satellite aerials. An average family can receive 14 television stations. The youngest, aged 4-11, watch least television, those over 55 most, i.e. about 3 1/3 hours daily.

Ole E. Andersen

Minutes per day per adult inhabitant (2000)

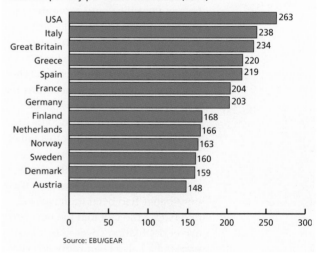

USA	263
Italy	238
Great Britain	234
Greece	220
Spain	219
France	204
Germany	203
Finland	168
Netherlands	166
Norway	163
Sweden	160
Denmark	159
Austria	148

Source: EBU/GEAR

Jørn Hjorting in the studio of Radio 2, located in Valby, just before the last radio broadcast of his career in March 2000. For 40 years, Jørn Hjorting was a well-known and beloved radio personality, especially known for his phone-in request programme *De ringer, vi spiller* (You Call, We Play), broadcast on Danmarks Radio. He hosted this programme for almost 30 years, talking to the listeners and playing their music requests.

The television channel TV2's studios in its headquarters in Kvægtorvet in Odense. The picture is from 1988, the year when the opening of TV2 also meant the end of Danish Radio's hitherto monopoly of national television transmissions. Since its launch, the proportion of viewers for TV2 has steadily grown, so that measured in viewer numbers, the channel is the biggest television transmitter in 2002.

Pressens Radioavis until 1964.

During the German occupation radio was subjected to German censorship, but programmes in Danish were broadcast by the BBC from 1940-1945 and by Swedish Radio from 1944-1945. The introduction of more than one radio channel started in 1951 with *Program 2* (P2), which was given the task of broadcasting classical music, lengthy discussion programmes and background information. *Program 3* (P3), with pop music, arrived in 1963 after competition from the private and advertisement-funded stations *Radio Mercur* (1958-1962) and *Danmarks Commercielle Radio* (1960-1961). Their broadcasts consisted of pop music and light entertainment programmes of a kind only occasionally heard on DR, and they

reached as many listeners as the broadly based *Program 1* (P1), until they ceased broadcasting: Mercur as the result of a change in legislation making its broadcasts illegal. Mercur broadcast programmes in stereo from 1961, and DR from 1969. From the 1950s the medium wave frequencies had gradually been supplemented with FM frequencies, in which P3 had been placed. To this was added in the 1960s a nationwide system of regional radio that was gathered together under a provincial department in 1973.

Television 1932-1980
The first Danish experimental television transmissions were arranged by Politiken in 1932, and it was possible to receive the BBC programmes between 1936 and 1939. Television technology was publicly demonstrated 1947-1948, and Statsradiofonien put out experimental transmissions 1949-1950, regular programmes 1951-1953 and daily transmissions starting in 1954. Since it was regarded as merely 'radio with pictures' television was at first placed within the purview of the Radio Act of 1959 and thereby automatically formed part of the state monopoly. The network was serviced by the Post and Telegraph Authority, which provided country-wide coverage from 1960. The number of hours rose

Danish television programmes come from the two national public service channels, Danmarks Radio (DR1, DR2), which has about a 31% market share of viewers, and TV2 (TV2, TV2 Zulu), which, including its eight regional stations, has 36%. The commercial satellite channel TV3 (TV3, TV3+) has 11% of the market (twice this among the half of the population that can receive TV3). Local television divides the remaining 22% with foreign language channels from neighbouring countries and via satellite.

Radio programmes come from Danmarks Radio's four national programmes, which together cover c. 67% of demand, and over 300 independent local radio stations. DR's radio programmes are structured so that *Program 1 (P1)* broadcasts a wide rage of, especially, informative and cultural programmes, *Program 2 (P2musik)* focuses on classical music, while *Program 3 (P3)* is a music and news channel catering principally for younger listeners. *Program 4 (P4)* mainly broadcasts entertainment and regional news.

steadily from c. 1 hour a day in the 1950s to 10 hours from DR at the beginning of the 1990s.

As in the case of radio, the programmes were originally made by DR itself, but this required a large production apparatus with a large number of employees, and a top-heavy bureaucracy and the inability to make changes became a problem. Since the 1960s, about 50% or the programmes have been of a factual nature, including news transmission, in which *TV-Avisen* replaced the newsreel *TV-Aktuelt* in 1965, and c.

50% have been foreign programmes with the emphasis on films and series. Colour transmissions were started in 1968 and stereo was introduced c. 1990.

Radio and Television Since the 1980s

Concessions for local television and radio were introduced in 1983 as an experiment, in which for instance the Copenhagen channel *Kanal 2* was established as a pay channel in foreign ownership. Local radio was finally permitted in 1985, local televi-

Danmarks Radio's Radio Theatre has a long tradition of performances of a broad spectrum of radio drama. Here, from the left to the right, we see Hardy Rafn, Axel Strøby and Frits Helmuth in a moment of concentration during the performance of George Tabori's play *Den 25. time* (The 25th Hour) in 1981.

Numerous reporters attended the press conference of 27 November 2001 in the Prime Minister's Office. The new Prime Minister Anders Fogh Rasmussen (in front) from the Liberal Party and the Conservative leader Bendt Bendtsen held this press conference after having presented Denmark's new government.

sion in 1988, and financing from advertisements from 1988-1989. A number of television stations with Kanal 2 at their head formed an almost national network in the form of Kanal Danmark under the multinational Scandinavian Broadcasting System (SBS). The Copenhagen music radio *The Voice* (1984-) established a network and was a great success, as were *Radio Viborg* (1984-) and other west Danish local radio stations.

DR's national television monopoly was broken with the opening in 1988 of *TV 2/Danmark* and eight regional TV 2 stations. Both DR and TV 2 were given professional boards of directors, which in the case of DR took the place of the Radio Council (a politically constituted board of management), and TV 2, like DR, has a public service duty. But TV 2, in contrast to DR, is independent, financed by advertisements and primarily running on the basis of commissioned programmes from independent producers, which has been of advantage not least to the film industry. This led to programmes of a popular nature in contrast to DR and in competition with the commercial, especially foreign, channels.

With the Act on the multi-use ca-

ble network from 1985, foreign channels, including satellite channels, could be made available by cable, which was outside the broadcasting monopoly of the Post and Telegraph Authority. This gave the telephone companies an important role in the broadcasting of TV, and in 1999 60% of Danes were able to watch cable TV on hybrid net. In addition, 16% had dish arials. One of the newcomers to the extended range of TV was the advertising – financed, Swedish-owned TV3, which in 1999 had a 11% share of Danish viewers. TV 2 had a 36% share, and DR, which in 1996 started up its second channel, DR2, had a 31% share. The proportion of households with more than one TV set was 44%. In October 2000 TV 2 introduced a second channel, TV 2 Zulu.

Video

In the 1970s video was launched without success, but improved machines employing the VHS system, and the marketing of video films has since the beginning of the 1980s led to a rapid increase in use. In 1997 75% of the population owned a video recorder. Expenditure on video films has been rising, from about 500 million kroner in 1985 to about 690 million kroner in 1999. In the 1980s rentals dominated the field almost exclusively, but from the 1990s purchased cassettes have accounted for an increasing percentage.

Kaare Schmidt

Geography and the Environment

Climate

The Danish climate is determined by the country's position on the edge of the continent of Europe close to large sea areas and in the zone of prevailing westerlies. This position results in cool summers with a mean temperature of around 16° C and winters that are not particularly cold, with mean temperatures of around 0.5° C. Denmark is thus placed in the temperate climate zone. There is a good deal of wind, strongest in the winter and weakest in the summer. Precipitation falls throughout the year, with the greatest rainfall in September, October and November. The smallest amounts of precipitation occur in February and April. The regular distribution of precipitation throughout the year is due to Den-

mark's position in the belt of prevailing westerlies, where the predominant wind directions are west and southwest. Series of low pressure systems (cyclones) moving northeastwards, often forming over Newfoundland, are the basis of the characteristically changeable weather: within a few days the weather changes typically from steady precipitation preceding a warm front to brighter or slightly misty weather, possibly still with a little drizzle in the following warmer mass of air. Finally, the passage of the cold front will produce precipitation in the form of heavy showers followed by clear weather with few clouds.

Within the Danish area there are only slight temperature differences from place to place. In winter, the lowest temperatures are found in areas removed from the sea. In summer, the highest average temperatures are in southern Zealand and Lolland-Falster. The areas near the coast experience smaller differences in temperature between summer and winter on account of the equalising effect of the sea.

The precipitation pattern also shows moderate differences from district to district. The area near Storebælt has the lowest annual rainfall with approximately 500 mm, while the southern parts of Central Jutland have the highest with over 900 mm.

Climatic changes can be observed over various intervals of time. In order to obviate chance variations in temperature and precipitation, the climate figures are worked out for a period of 30 years. The 30-year period starting in 1961 was completed in 1990. Differences can be observed when this is compared with the preceding period, 1931-1960. Thus, it

Yearly precipitation distribution.

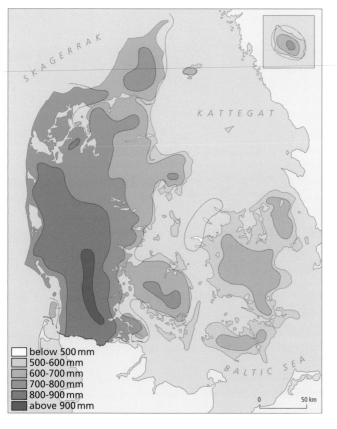

below 500 mm
500-600 mm
600-700 mm
700-800 mm
800-900 mm
above 900 mm

SKAGERRAK

KATTEGAT

BALTIC SEA

0   50 km

has emerged that the mean temperature in Denmark has fallen by 0.2° C, and that it is especially lower temperatures in the period July to September that have led to this.

Precipitation on an annual basis has risen by 46 mm; the summer months have become drier, while in particular the autumn months have become wetter.

The number of hours of sunshine denotes the number of hours with direct sunshine. This number has declined from 1,729 to 1,670 hours per year. This drop of almost 5% can partly be due to an increased number of aerosols (pollution particles) in the air together with a change in the prevailing wind directions, both resulting in an increase in cloud cover. The prevailing directions of the wind have changed little from one 30-year period to the next. The frequency of south and southwest winds has increased in relation to an earlier higher frequency of westerly winds, so that the prevailing direction of the wind has backed approximately 5°.

The Danish climate shows variations in keeping with periodic changes in the global climatic system. Viewed over a longer period of time,

the temperature in Denmark has never been constant. Cold periods have replaced warm periods, and the greatest variations in climate are indicated by glacial and interglacial periods. In particularly warm periods, for instance during the Stone Age, the mean temperature for July was a couple of degrees higher than it is at present.

Mogens Lerbech Jensen

Denmark has an average of 170 wet days a year. In the summer, sudden and powerful showers are common but the downpours rarely last long.

Climate
Average figures for the period 1961-1990

	Whole year	Jan.	Feb.	Mar.	Apr.	May	Jun.	Jul.	Aug.	Sept.	Oct.	Nov.	Dec.
Temperature (C)													
Monthly average	7.7	0	0	2.1	5.7	10.8	14.3	15.6	15.7	12.7	9.1	4.7	1.6
Absolute maximum*	36.4	12.0	15.8	22.2	28.6	32.8	35.5	35.3	36.4	32.3	24.1	18.5	14.5
Absolute minimum*	-31.2	-31.2	-29.0	-27.0	-19.0	-8.0	-3.5	-0.9	-2.0	-5.6	-11.9	-21.3	-25.6
Days with frost	84	19	19	15	6.6	0.7	0	0	0	0.2	1.8	7.3	15
Summer days (max. temp. >25° C)	7.2	0	0	0	0	0.2	1.9	2.6	2.3	0.1	0	0	0
Precipitation (mm)													
Monthly average	712	57	38	46	41	48	55	66	67	73	76	79	66
Highest precipitation in 24 hour period at one station		50	62	54	67	77	153	169	151	133	101	62	46
Number of days with precipitation (>0.1 mm)	168	16	12	14	12	12	11	13	13	15	16	18	16

* Maximum and minimum figures for the period 1874-1994

Source: DMI

Geology

The Danish landscape was formed largely during the last ice age and the time thereafter. Beneath the present landscape, however, are rocks and deposits from much earlier times.

The Deep Structure

Crystalline rocks, which comprise the oldest component of the basement, extend beneath the entire country at varying depths. The crystalline basement reaches the surface on the island of Bornholm that forms part of the Fenno-Scandian Border Zone which runs in a northwesterly direction through Scania and the Kattegat to North Jutland.

The Fenno-Scandian Border Zone divides the Scandinavian basement area (the area known as the Baltic Shield) from the northwest European Basin, where the basement is generally found at greater depths. The basin includes the Norwegian-Danish Basin and the North German Basin, which are separated by the Ringkøbing-Funen Ridge where the basement occurs relatively close to the surface.

The present relief of the basement is the result of movements in the Earth's crust which took place long after the basement itself had been formed.

The Precambrian Era

The crystalline basement dates back to the Precambrian era, and consists of gneiss and granite created by metamorphic and igneous processes deep in the Earth's crust in connection with mountain-building events. In places, black dolerite dykes cut through the gneiss and the granite.

The Bornholm basement was formed at the same time as the basement in southeast Sweden, some 1,750-1,500 million years ago. The basement in the rest of Denmark, which has been studied in a small number of deep borings, is much younger. It is comparable to the basement in the south of Norway and the west of Sweden which was formed some 1,150-800 million years ago.

The formation of the crystalline basement was followed by a period of several hundred million years during

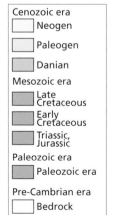

Subsurface map showing the geological layers below the Quarternary ice age deposits.

Cenozoic era
- Neogen
- Paleogen
- Danian

Mesozoic era
- Late Cretaceous
- Early Cretaceous
- Triassic, Jurassic

Paleozoic era
- Paleozoic era

Pre-Cambrian era
- Bedrock

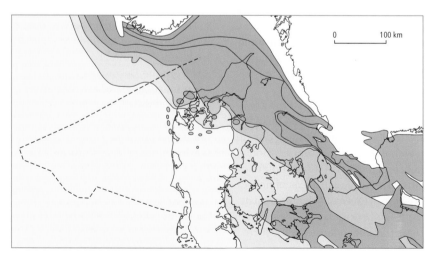

0   100 km

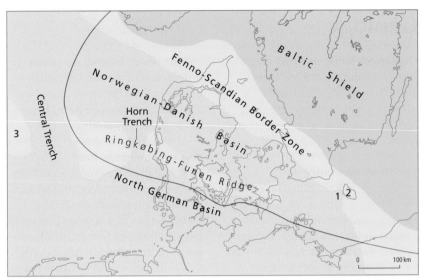

1. Rønne Trench
2. Bornholm Horst
3. Mid-North Sea ridge

————— Caledonian deformation front (north-eastern boundary for Caledonian-influenced older Paleozoic rocks in Denmark

The structure of the Danish subsurface. Denmark is part of the northwest European Basin which borders the Baltic Shield. They are separated by a fault zone known as the Fenno-Scandian Border Zone. The Ringkøbing-Funen Ridge, an area where the basement is located relatively close to the surface (up to 2 km below it) divides the Danish area into the Norwegian-Danish Basin and the North German Basin. The basement in these basins is found at depths of up to 8 km.

which the wind and the weather wore away the mountains, resulting in a relatively flat topography.

The Paleozoic Era (approx. 540-245 million years ago)

At the beginning of the Paleozoic era, sediments covered the flat basement surface; first reddish, continental sandstone and then a series of marine sandstone, limestone and large amounts of dark grey to black shale. These deposits date from the Cambrian, Ordovician and Silurian periods and are known from surface outcrops on Bornholm and a small number of deep borings that have been carried out elsewhere in the country.

The deposits show that the area was covered by a relatively shallow sea for long periods of time, during which the sea floor was occasionally deficient in oxygen. Local uplift occurred, resulting in areas of non-deposition. Traces of volcanic activity from the Ordovician and Silurian periods have been found in the form of volcanic ash and lava flows.

Great thicknesses of sediments dating back to the younger Silurian period indicate that the elevation of the land was greater than previously. This marks the beginnings of the Caledonian mountain-building. The Caledonian mountain range stretched from Norway down through the North Sea area and into northern Germany and Poland. With the exception of the southernmost part of Jutland, Denmark lay outside the area covered by this mountain range.

During the Devonian period, northwest Europe was a highland subject to weathering and erosion. No deposits from the Devonian age have been found in Denmark. At the beginning of the Carboniferous period, a sea covering Central Europe reached the southern part of Denmark leaving limestone deposits known from borings on the island of Falster. The middle of the Carboniferous period saw the Hercynian period of mountain building, which resulted in a mountain range that extended through Central Europe. The land area of northern Europe expanded significantly as a result. Continental sediments were deposited here during the Late Carboniferous period, as indicated by a boring in the Kattegat.

The transition to the Permian period was marked by major volcanic activity and faulting which led to the formation of the northwest European Basin.

The Permian period brought with it a desert-like climate which, at the beginning of the period, led to the deposit of red, continental sediments. Towards the end of the period, the sea transgressed from the north, forming a large inland sea. The dry climate meant that this inland sea was subject to strong evaporation, and a more than 1 km-thick sequence of evaporites was formed which included large amounts of rock salt.

During the following geological periods, the horizontal salt layer underwent transformations which resulted in the formation of salt diapirs. These diapirs created plug-like bodies which may be up to several kilometres in height, cutting across the overlying sequence of sediment.

The Mesozoic Era (approx. 245-65 million years ago)

A desert climate dominated throughout the Triassic period. A stratigraphic sequence several kilometres in thickness was formed, consisting of red, continental sand and clay sediments. Towards the edges of the basin, these deposits were replaced by coarse layers of gravel. The dry climate also resulted in evaporites such as rock salt. In the middle of the Triassic period, the sea advanced from the south and covered parts of the Danish area.

Towards the end of the Triassic period, the climate in the area became more humid. This change was to last throughout the Jurassic period and the first part of the Cretaceous period.

During the Jurassic and early Cretaceous periods, large parts of northwest Europe were covered by the sea. There was a number of both large and small islands, as well as the large Scandinavian land area. Dark clay sediments were deposited on the sea floor forming layers which, in certain places, reached considerable thicknesses. The coastal areas near Scandinavia consisted of flood and delta plains which were covered in vegetation that would later be transformed into the coal seams which can be found, for example, on the island of Bornholm. In the middle of the Jurassic period, tectonic uplift resulted in parts of the basin being elevated above sea level. Later during this period and the early part of the Cretaceous period, the land was once again covered by the sea.

In the middle of the Cretaceous period, a rise in sea level resulted in most of northwest Europe being inundated. The sediments deposited in this sea were mainly carbonates: First reddish marl, followed by up to two kilometres of clean, white chalk known from Møns Klint and the chalk pits near Aalborg. Bornholm, which was nearer the coast, shows signs of sandy deposits and a number of breaks in the sedimentation.

Towards the end of the Cretaceous period, an area stretching along the Fenno-Scandian Border Zone underwent marked deformation and uplift, in all likelihood as a result of the formation of the Alps in southern Europe. Alpine folding continued over a long period of time and culminated in the following Tertiary period.

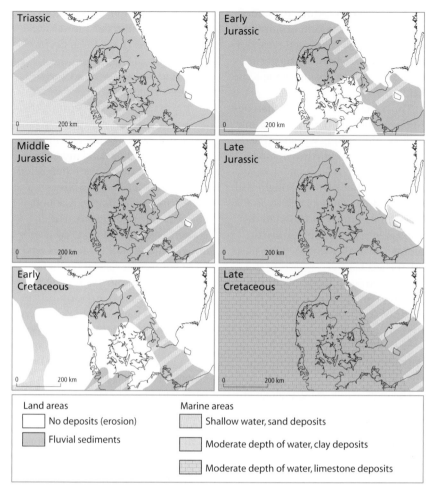

The formation of the Danish landscape during the Mesozoic era. The desert-like climate of the Triassic period was followed by a more humid era during the Jurassic and Early Cretaceous periods. The sea gradually invaded the Danish area leaving dark clay sediments. In the middle of the Jurassic period, tectonic uplift resulted in drainage of parts of the basin. Later during the Jurassic period, and all through the Cretaceous period, the sea level rose substantially leaving only very few areas in northwest Europe above water. During Late Cretaceous, sediments of red marl and limestone were deposited.

Land areas

☐ No deposits (erosion)

▨ Fluvial sediments

Marine areas

▨ Shallow water, sand deposits

▨ Moderate depth of water, clay deposits

▨ Moderate depth of water, limestone deposits

The Tertiary Period (approx. 65-1.6 million years ago)

Whilst the deposits from the previous geological periods are mostly known from deep borings, those from the Tertiary period are often accessible near the Earth's surface.

Deposits from the oldest Tertiary period (Danian) are similar to the youngest deposits from the Cretaceous period; they consist of marine limestone with no obvious influence from nearby land masses. This situation gradually changed with an increasing amount of land-derived clay being added to the deposits. This re-

sulted first in deposits of marl, followed by the formation of a viscous clay known as plastic clay which mainly dates back to the Eocene period. At one stage during this development, powerful volcanic activity resulted in the deposition of numerous layers of ash. This volcanism was related to movements of the continents which resulted in the opening of the North Atlantic.

Towards the end of the Eocene period, tectonic unrest led to disruptions in the sedimentation process in parts of the basin. At around the same time, Scandinavia began to rise and formed a pronounced highland from which rivers transported clay and sand out to the sea.

The Oligocene period brought clayey marine sediments containing fine sand. During the Miocene period the continental deposits increased, creating sandy flood plains and delta plains which began to spread westwards into what was then the North Sea. These events led to the Danish area being above sea level during the Miocene period, forming a low, flat landscape. The climate was mild and wet and the vegetation, which was plentiful, would later form the lignite (brown coal) known from Central and West Jutland.

The Quarternary Period (1.6 million years ago-present day)

During the Quarternary period, the climate fluctuated between cold and warm periods known as ice ages and

Møns Klint consists of chalk composed of calcareous shells from microscopic algae and the remains of other organisms. These lived in the tropical seas of the Cretaceous period which covered Denmark some 100 million years ago. Ice age glaciers have since pushed huge slices of chalk up into impressive heights, locally up to 100 m above sea level. Because of the chalk content, these steep cliffs are only eroded slowly by the sea.

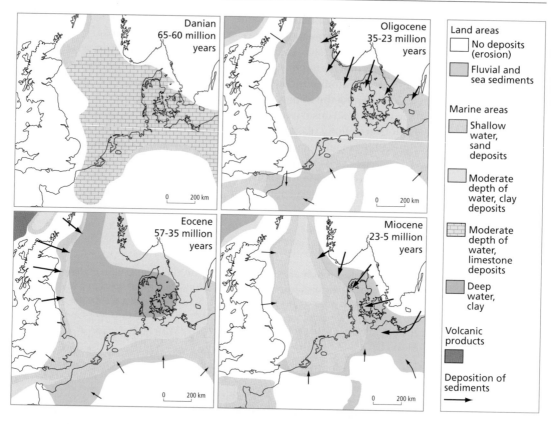

The geological conditions which prevailed in Denmark during the Tertiary period were determined by the country's position in the eastern part of the almost bowl-shaped North Sea Basin. The developments can be divided into three main stages.

The first stage includes the Danian period. The Danish area was totally covered by the sea, and a layer of limestone up to 350 m thick was created by the deposits of calcareous shells from animals and algae. The depth of the water probably varied between 50 and 200 m. The low concentration of sand and clay in the limestone layer indicates that the relief of the surrounding land areas was fairly low.

The second stage began during the Late Paleozoic era in connection with the opening of the northern Atlantic Sea. Scotland and the surrounding land areas rose, whilst the central parts of the North Sea fell. The water was more than 500 m deep. The biogenic limestone production fell, and large amounts of sand and clay from the Scotland area were led into the basin. Only the finest particles reached the Danish area where they make up the so-called plastic clay.

The third stage began at the beginning of the Oligocene period when sediments began to be deposited in the northeast as a result of the rise of the Scandinavian Peninsula and the northern part of Denmark. Throughout the rest of the Tertiary period the area continued to rise, in places up to more than 1 km. The rise in the land led to erosion, and sandy sediments were washed into the northeasterly part of the basin. As the marginal edges of the basin filled up and were drained, the main part of the sediment area was pushed into the central and southern parts of the North Sea Basin which continued to sink. Here, the deposits from the Miocene and Pliocene periods are up to 1,500 m thick.

The present distribution of the Mesozoic and Tertiary sediments in Denmark came about as a result of the uplift and erosion which took place at the end of the Tertiary period in the Scandinavian area.

interglacial stages. During the ice ages the sea level was very low. Glaciers appeared in the Scandinavian highland, later spreading to the surrounding lowlands including Denmark. During the interglacial stages, the ice disappeared and the distribution of land and sea was similar to today. Traces of four ice ages and three interglacial stages have been found in Denmark, along with signs of the period which followed the last ice age. This postglacial period incorporates the present day.

The only thing known about the first ice age, known as the Menapian period, is that Denmark was covered by ice. The only evidence of the Cromerian interglacial stage which followed the Menapian comes from a small number of lake sediments. No marine sediments have been found from this period. The Elsterian ice age, which followed, was an important ice age during which the ice sheet extended as far as Central Europe. Traces of three different glacial advances have been found in Denmark. At the end of the Elsterian period, and during the subsequent Holsteinian interglacial stage, parts of the south of Jutland and the Limfjord area were covered by the sea. Little is known about the land area during the Holsteinian interglacial stage, since the only remnants that have been found are a small number of lake sediments.

The maximum extent of the ice in northern Europe during the last ice ages.

During the subsequent Saalian ice age, the ice sheet again reached Central Europe. Signs of another three glacial advances have been found in Denmark dating back to this period. The Saalian period left its mark on the landscape in West Jutland in the form of the so-called 'hill islands' surrounded by melt water plains from the last ice age, the Weichselian period.

The northernmost part of Jutland was covered by the sea right from the end of the Saalian period, throughout the Eemian interglacial stage and during the first part of the Weichselian ice age. The southern part of Denmark, on the other hand, was only submerged during the Eemian period. A number of lake deposits have been found dating back to this period, one of which contains traces of the people who lived in the area at that time.

During the Weichselian period, the last ice age, Denmark was a tundra plain which was repeatedly invaded by glaciers. The main glacial event was an ice advance towards the *main line of ice stagnation* in Jutland; it was while the ice stood here that the melt water plains around the *hill islands* were formed. The glaciers then advanced to the ice margin in the east of Jutland. Glacial deposits on the Danish islands were left during the following period and bear witness to the presence of a number of terminal moraines. It was these events during the Weichselian period which resulted in the formation of the Danish ice age landscape.

Towards the end of the Weichselian period, the northernmost part of Jutland was covered by the sea. Subsequent uplift then introduced the so-called 'Continental period' which lasted into the first part of the subsequent postglacial period that began some 10,000 years ago. By

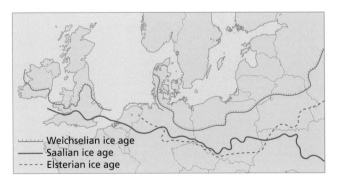

····· Weichselian ice age
—— Saalian ice age
- - - - Elsterian ice age

Deglaciation stages.

1 Approximately 18,000 years ago, the ice stretched as far as the terminal moraine marking the main line of ice stagnation. Meltwater plains were created in front of the ice body, around the moraine deposits from the proceeding Saalian ice age. The West Jutland meltwater plains/hill island landscape was created.

2 The deglaciation stage had begun. A terminal moraine was formed across Mors, Fur and Himmerland. The Gudenå river flowed in front of the ice margin northwards through Skals Ådal to Hjarbæk Fjord.

3 Renewed ice advance of the so-called Young Baltic ice came from the southeast; this glacier was stationary for a while near the East Jutland terminal moraine some 16,000 years ago. The Yoldia Sea covered large parts of Vendsyssel; the hills known as Mols Bjerge and the heath plains of Tirstrup Hedeslette were created. The Gudenå river reached Randers Fjord.

4 The Little Belt and the Great Belt glaciers made renewed advances. On Funen, the stagnant ice had begun to melt. The meltwater plains of Bregninge Hedeslette and the Odsherred-Buerne were created.

5 The Øresund glacier covered North and East Zealand; Møn was squeezed between two glacial lobes.

Legend:
- Ice with ice margin lines
- Stagnant ice
- Older ice age landscapes
- Younger ice age landscapes
- Meltwater landscapes
- Terminal moraine lines
- Sea
- Sea floor, previously land

then, the ice had melted away in the south of Scandinavia and the forests were beginning to move into Denmark. The country was much larger during the Continental period than it is now; the land stretched as far as England. The Continental period was followed by the Flandrian transgression during the Stone Age, when vast areas of land were submerged as a result of a rapid rise in sea level. This was followed by an uplift of the northern part of Denmark, exposing large areas of the sea floor. The present coastline began to take shape.

Gunnar Larsen

The Evolution of the Landscape

The Danish landscape is the result of dramatic climatic changes. Most of the terrain was formed by glacier activity during the arctic conditions which prevailed during the Weichselian ice age some 115,000-11,500 years ago. The only main exceptions to this are the coastal areas and the dunes.

For most of the Weichselian ice age, Denmark was an open tundra landscape with sparse vegetation. Some 18,000 years ago glaciers from the north and the east reached the *main stationary line* which runs from Bovbjerg across Hald to Padborg in Jutland. Here, the ice margin was relatively stable for a time. West of this line are the *hill islands* which constitute the most elevated landscape from the former ice age, the Saalian period. Throughout the Weichselian ice age, these hills were subject to drifting snow, frost erosion, spring floods, solifluction and erosion. The meltwater flowed from the ice sheet margin across low-lying parts of the landscape, burying them in sand and gravel; this resulted in the formation of the large outwash plains known as *heath plains*. North and east of the main stationary line young moraine landscapes of different shapes and forms are found. Mar-

ginal moraines or terminal moraines were created along the edge of the ice sheet. Some were formed as a result of the advancing ice compacting the material in front of it as it moved; others consisted of meltwater deposits which built up along a stationary ice margin. Small outwash plains were locally created in front of the ice. Central depressions are found behind these, consisting of even, low-lying basal tills, shaped by ice lobes. These areas have in many cases later been flooded. The active ice shaped the landscape beneath it in a number of different ways. As the glacier slid across the bed beneath it, it created a smooth basal till landscape with long drumlins running in the direction of the flow. These relatively low hills are found in the north of Funen, Central Zealand and on Lolland. The basal till landscapes comprise some of the best agricultural land in Denmark.

In front of the ice, the meltwater created a number of wide extra-marginal meltwater valleys, some of which ran parallel to the front of the glacier. Long stretches of the Gudenå river, the longest watercourse in Denmark, run along such a former meltwater valley. In summer in particular, the meltwater flowed beneath

A gully from the late glacial period with a recent valley floor and a small trench. The absence of a river and the abundant vegetation seem to indicate that the gully was formed at a time when the climate was very different. Signs are that there was an abundance of meltwater and bare soil. The sides of the gully are stepped, creating sheep paths which have been strengthened by the passing of many generations of animals.

the ice towards the front of the glacier in large subglacial canals. Depending on whether the water eroded the ground beneath it, or whether sediments of sand and gravel were deposited in the fissures, deep steep-sided subglacial tunnel valleys and long eskers were formed. The tunnel valleys have barriers across them and are often partly filled by elongated lakes. The largest tunnel valleys are found in the east of Jutland near Viborg, Vejle and Kolding, whilst the majority of eskers are found on the islands, for example on Central Funen and in the south and east of Zealand. Both tunnel valleys and eskers ran parallel to the direction of the glacier's flow.

In other cases, the ice flow ceased and the surface of the glacier split into a myriad of water-filled basins and rivers. This was accompanied by a gradual deposition of clay, sand and gravel. These deposits have left 'negative' images of the original ice-dammed basins, and are characterised by uneven terrain and un-drained depressions, a so-called stagnant ice landscape. Superb examples of this type of hilly landscape are found in Central Funen and in West Zealand. The hills are steep-sided and flat on top and are known as *ice lake hills* or *kames*. They consist mainly of stratified sand and gravel and represent an important resource of raw material.

The ice was presumably more than two kilometres thick in the east of the country and depressed the Earth's crust by several hundred metres.

When the ice melted, the land rose again, though only after a long delay. This gave the sea time to flood large areas during the deglaciation period, particularly around North Jutland. The North Sea and the Kattegat were then glacial seas, and de-

posits from these are found at heights of 20-60 m near Vendsyssel in North Jutland.

Approximately 6,000 years ago, the *Littorina Sea* (also known as the *Stone Age Sea*) in the northern part of Denmark reached a relatively higher level than today. It flowed into a number of East Jutland valleys, creating a flat valley floor. In Central Jutland, the water reached as far as Viborg. Many overgrown littoral cliffs from this period can today be found above the present coastline. Since then, the land around Vendsyssel has risen 15 m in relation to the sea. South of a line between Nissum Fjord and North Falster, however, the land has sunk a few metres below the present sea level. Eroded littoral cliffs are often seen in these areas. In the tidal areas i Sydvestjylland, marshes created under partly natural conditions keep pace with the relative subsidence of the land.

The most important landscape elements created since the ice age are mostly found near the coasts. The appearance of the coast changes constantly as a result of erosion and shifting sands. Large dune areas are found in particular along the west coast of Jutland, where active coastal

Nellesø lake in the foreground is part of the subglacial stream trench formation west of Farum in North Zealand. The many lakes and hollows in the landscape are kettle holes. Many slopes are used for grazing or have been planted with trees.

DENMARK

The hilly landscape by the coast south of Frederikshavn in North Jutland. The town is visible in the background. In the foreground is the E45 main road, built on a cultivated plain which was formed by deposits from the Littorina Sea. The plain is bordered on the left by a high shrub-covered slope which the Littorina Sea has carved into the 70-80 m moraine hills. The contours have later been softened by landslides and soil creep.

dunes are found closest to the sea, and behind these are inactive, overgrown green dunes and grey dunes. The inland dunes, found on heath plains like the one near Billund, have also been inactive for long periods. The dune areas along the coast were dominated by recurring periods of shifting sands during the Holocene period. The last of these lasted from the 14th to the 20th century. The climate then was comparatively cool and windy. Floods in the 19th century broke through many of the isthmuses on the west coast of Jutland. Efforts to prevent sand drift, combined with fewer storms, meant that the shifting sands gradually receded towards the end of the 19th century, or as early as the 18th century in North Zealand.

The formation of the landscape behind the coastline has been influenced in particular by the presence of Man and his use of the country's natural resources.

Ole Humlum

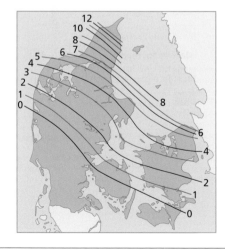

The isostatic uplift since the end of the last ice age. The lines (isobases) indicate the level (in metres above sea level) of sea deposits created since the last ice age.

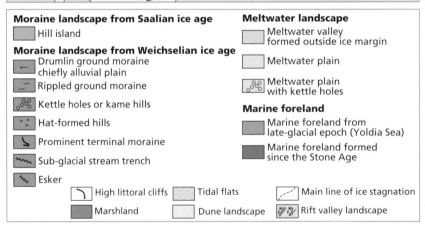

The most important elements in the landscape.

Moraine landscape from Saalian ice age

Hill island

Moraine landscape from Weichselian ice age

Drumlin ground moraine chiefly alluvial plain

Rippled ground moraine

Kettle holes or kame hills

Hat-formed hills

Prominent terminal moraine

Sub-glacial stream trench

Esker

Meltwater landscape

Meltwater valley formed outside ice margin

Meltwater plain

Meltwater plain with kettle holes

Marine foreland

Marine foreland from late-glacial epoch (Yoldia Sea)

Marine foreland formed since the Stone Age

High littoral cliffs

Marshland

Tidal flats

Dune landscape

Main line of ice stagnation

Rift valley landscape

DENMARK

The Cultural Landscape

The present Danish landscape is the result of cultural developments which have lasted several thousand years. During this time, Man, through his activities, has radically transformed the landscape by clearing forests, cultivating land and building settlements.

The Open Countryside

The open countryside comprises the land which lies outside the built-up areas, and where activities are mainly centred around the use of natural resources. The open country in Denmark is totally dominated by farming, since approximately 65% of the total area is used for agriculture and another 12% for forestry. The landscape is characterised by well-cultivated fields, hedges, earth and stone walls, and scattered woods. Large forests are rare. Small towns, farms and houses lie strewn across the scenery, connected by a finely woven communications network. The scattered agricultural habitation is characteristic of Denmark. The lines of field boundaries and other perimeters are sharp, often completely straight; untended areas are very rare. Only near the coast, outside the holiday housing areas, has the landscape been left to develop naturally. The vegetation in certain wetland areas is also natural. Large watercourses are rare, and their tributaries are often controlled by pipes and conduits.

Extensive farming and forest clearing began 6,000 years ago at the end of the Stone Age, and developed further during the Iron Age and the Viking period. At the end of the Iron Age, the heaths and commons crept onto the meagre soil and the forests took over some of the better land as marginal farming was once again dropped. During the Middle Ages, many new settlements appeared in the forest areas that had previously escaped clearing.

The 18th and 19th centuries saw a number of far-reaching changes, not least due to the land reforms introduced in the 1780s, which created a completely new structure of farm land. The village areas in the east of Denmark, where land was divided into small plots, took on a new character with the Enclosures Act, the introduction of freeholds and the spread of habitations, particularly in larger villages. The landscape was drastically transformed, as the scattered strips of land owned by individual holdings in the open field system were exchanged for a smaller number of larger fields. As far as field work was concerned, this new arrangement proved a great deal more efficient; a number of advances in farming techniques were also introduced from the middle of the 19th century, including the transition from the wheel plough to the swing plough, the introduction of clover in the grassland and meadows, and new draining and marling techniques. There was a significant increase in yield.

During the last decades of the 19th century, farming underwent a complete transformation; the emphasis shifted from the production of bread grain to the cultivation of forage crops for the growing livestock production. The shift towards the export of farm products brought new elements into the cultural landscape: the road network was expanded and railways began to be built. A number of co-operatives with links to farming, such as dairies, also began to

The dominant soil types in Denmark are coarse sand, clayey sand and sandy clay, each of which covers about 1/4 of the area. Areas with fine sand account for 1/10, while clay and peat each cover 1/20 of the area. On the basis of soil type and quality, Denmark can be naturally divided into three main regions: the Islands including parts of East Jutland, West Jutland and North Jutland.

The clayey areas dominate in the Islands and in East Jutland. In addition clayey soils dominate around the western part of the Limfjord. These soils are naturally nutritious and have a high water holding capacity. In the spring they might become waterlogged because of low permeability of the subsoil, for which reason most of these areas are drained. The areas on the Islands are often calcareous from a depth of c. 1m and below, while chalk in the soils in Jutland is not common. Clayey areas with calcareous subsoil constitute the most fertile agricultural areas in the country, that is to say land of the highest quality.

In West Jutland coarse sandy areas dominate representing the lowest quality soils. Highly productive agriculture in these areas requires not only fertilisers and lime, but also irrigation, as these poor agricultural areas easily dry out in the summer as a consequence of a poor water holding capacity.

North Jutland, both the undulating moraine landscape and the coastal foreland are dominated by fine sandy soils. These areas occupy a middle position between the fertile eastern Danish and the

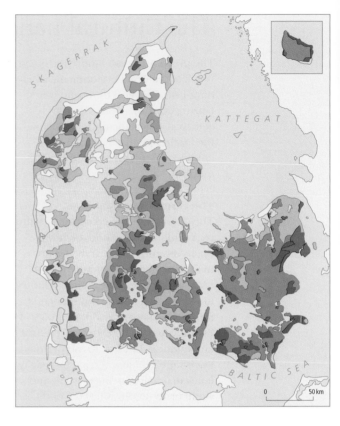

poor West Jutlandic areas, and they are of medium quality. They are not so nutritious as the clayey soils, but they have a high water holding capacity. Large areas of the coastal foreland are waterlogged, and here we find some of the major bogs in Denmark, including the so-called *vildmoser*.

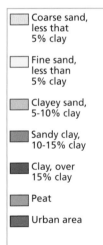

Coarse sand, less that 5% clay

Fine sand, less than 5% clay

Clayey sand, 5-10% clay

Sandy clay, 10-15% clay

Clay, over 15% clay

Peat

Urban area

spring up at the edge of villages. Signs of the new industrial society began to effect the open country. The 19th century saw an intensification in farming across the country. This, along with the reclamation of the heaths in Jutland, led to the number of holdings being doubled over the course of the century. For the next hundred years, the landscape was dominated by almost 200,000 farms using efficient farming methods and crop rotation.

At the beginning of the 19th century, a clear line was drawn between

farming activities and the forests with the Forest Reserve Act of 1805. Lines of demarcation were drawn up and fixed, and the forests have since been a permanent feature of the cultural landscape. They were to be used for the production of timber and fuel, and were no longer to be utilized for grazing.

During the last decades of the 20th century, the open country has once again seen extensive changes. There has been a tendency towards fewer and larger specialised agricultural production units, even though a number of agricultural laws meant to protect the freeholds and the family holdings have tried to limit the amalgamation of smaller holdings and the rise in larger units. Increasing numbers of huge, uniform fields have appeared as a result of mechanisation, resulting in a much less varied landscape.

The Urban and Rural Zones Act of 1969 introduced an administrative division between the rural and urban areas. The act, which since 1991 has been known as the Planning Act, imposed strict restrictions on land usage and the building of plants and installations in the open country. These restrictions have had a limiting effect on developments in the rural districts. Since the 1970s, EC/EU regulations, including the latest Set-aside Scheme, along with the county regional plans, have all left their mark on the landscape. The number of holiday housing areas and conservation areas has also grown.

The extended usage of the Danish landscape, including the intensive farming all over the country, has been encouraged by the prevailing natural conditions, the mild Atlantic climate and the flat terrain. Short distances to the sea have also made it possible to drain wetlands and waterlogged areas. Large parts of eastern Denmark (the islands and East Jutland) have very fertile soil, based on geologically young deposits that date back to the last ice age and are particularly high in nutrients. West Jutland, by contrast, is characterised by sandy soil which is partly derived from former ice age deposits. Here, the heaths and the fields have fought for control of the land over the past five millenniums, and the area has only really been fully exploited during the 20th century as a result of new technology, fertilisation and irrigation. North Jutland, i.e. Himmerland and the North Jutland Island, is dominated by sandy soil and wetlands with huge bogs. The fertile soil by the western Limfjord set this area apart from the rest of North Jutland.

These different regions have been subject to a number of common social influences over the last few centuries; legislation, economic control, better technology and increasing environmental and natural protection have all left their traces. Country-wide regulations have produced very different results in eastern Denmark, West Jutland and North Jutland, depending on the prevailing natural conditions in each area.

East Denmark (East Jutland and the Islands)

The varied terrain in East Denmark is dominated by clay and highly calcareous moraine flats and hills. This so-called young moraine formation has produced highly fertile land. The landscape is dominated by large, closely spaced homogeneous fields given over to the cultivation of crops. Fertilisation, crop spraying and drainage have resulted in huge, weed-free carpets of corn and seed crops which cover the hills and the hollows, blurring the contours of the landscape. Grazing cattle are a relatively rare sight. Small, scattered deciduous forests and hedges, and the large East Jutland valleys with their meadows and coppices, break the monotony of the landscape.

The present settlement structure in the open country is dense and made up of a variety of farms, one-family houses, villages and small service centres. Larger communities, generally former market towns, are predominantly found near the coast and at the bottom of the fjords; these urban areas have begun to encroach onto the open country. The 21st century traffic network is completely dominated by the car: bridges and motorways provide links between the communities in East Denmark. Sailing previously provided a cheap, significant way to reach the various parts of the country, but it is now becoming too expensive and the costs are threatening the inhabitants of many of the smaller islands. Despite the many technological advances of the last century, the landscape in East Denmark still contains traces of former civilisations in the shape of burial mounds, churches and old farms, as well as the area patterns found around the old manors and villages. The manors, most of which are found on Funen, Lolland and the south of Zealand, have huge fertile fields surrounded by quickset hedges, ditches and stone walls and hundreds of acres of woodland. Long tree-lined avenues, grandiose buildings and landscaped grounds have been left over from the Renaissance and the period of absolutism. Many of the large landed estates today find it difficult to finance the upkeep of the listed buildings and parks.

The owners of the manors previously protected the forests against overexploitation, and large areas of deciduous forest could therefore be found in East Denmark around 1800, at a time when the rest of the country was almost completely devoid of woodland. In North Zealand the King had game preserves set up in many of the larger forests, characterised by a network of straight paths arranged in the shape of a star. These old forests have preserved many signs of earlier civilisations, including several high-ridged furlongs and large numbers of burial mounds.

Like the manors, the villages also provide evidence of earlier civilisa-

tions. After the land reforms at the end of the 18th century, the manors had to relinquish many of the tenant farms which slowly reverted to freehold status. The ancient open field system was abolished, and the Enclosures Act meant that each farm was assigned a consolidated piece of land. In many villages, the farms stayed in their original places near the church. Today, such villages reflect small mediaeval centres. Radiating from the heart of such villages were the fences and ditches that marked the new property boundaries typical of the time. Modified examples of such stellate patterns, with roads and fences radiating outwards like the spokes of a wheel, are found around many small towns today. The Enclosures Act and the cultivation of the commons meant that many farms were moved to new locations, forming a block re-allotment pattern. After the Forest Reserve Act of 1805, impoverished wooded areas were given over to farming, and smallholdings were frequently erected on these marginal parcels of land. Such small properties are generally

Store Dyrehave (The Great Deer Park) south of Hillerød. In the middle of the foreground, the straight forest paths meet and create a star-shaped pattern. These paths were created back in the 1670s for the Kings hunts. Large parts of the forest have been planted with conifers which are economically well suited to the sandy, barred soil in the area.

The Ledreborg manor and the grounds southwest of Roskilde. In the foreground is the symmetrical arrangement which incorporates the park, the main buildings, the servants' quarters and the gatehouse. This type of cultural landscape also incorporates vast numbers of farm buildings, large fields, solitary mature trees and large areas of woodland. In the background towards Lejre Vig cove, the terrain is rather broken with limited tree growth and scattered buildings.

advantage of dispensations in the zone regulations and agricultural legislation to build installations in the open country.

The cultivated land has changed character; intensively farmed fields have replaced the old hay meadows and the commons which have now almost disappeared in East Denmark. Fields were first drained via a network of open ditches, but from approximately 1850 onwards these were replaced by underground drainage pipes made of clay, later of plastic. The wet, sour areas found in the fields were either reduced or completely eradicated. The old system of open ditches can still be seen in some forests. The streams which run through the arable land are generally forced into straight canals or led through pipes.

found on the borders of the land belonging to the villages, squeezed onto small plots on the edges of the woods and moors. The characteristic pattern of scattered farms and houses found in East Denmark came about as a result of the rise in the number of smaller holdings which followed the scattering and division of the larger farms. It did not, however, prevent a move from the country to the towns, the growing urbanisation or the increased emigration to the USA and elsewhere. With support from the State, groups of identical smallholdings were set up as a result of laws passed in 1899 and 1919 (the conversion of entailed estates) in order to counteract the migration from the rural districts. These smallholdings are often located on strips of fertile soil from larger farms and represent a particular pattern of development found on North Funen, Lolland and Als. The last smallholding colonies were built in the 1950s. The number of farms has since fallen drastically as a result of amalgamations and leasehold agreements. In many places, companies have taken

The few remaining water holes are either natural or man-made watering holes, or the remains of former gravel or marl pits. Almost every clayey field used to have a water hole in former times. Peat-digging continued far into the 20th century, leaving rectangular ponds and small lakes surrounded by thickets. Many of the smaller water holes and ponds which got in the way of the large agricultural machines have been eliminated; others have been converted into coverts and game shelters. Since 1980 there has been a backlash from groups with interests in recreational activities of various kinds: many reclaimed areas have once again been turned into lakes, and watercourses are once more allowed to meander at will.

The Nature Conservation Act of 1992 protects the commons, meadows, bogs and dikes which were created as a result of earlier agricultural production methods. There has also been an attempt to convert mineral pits into recreational nature reserves

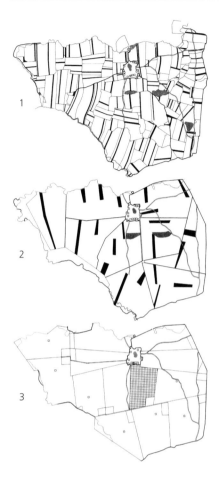

The three maps of Årslev (Sønderup Sogn, Slagelse Herred) have been taken from the original maps (at a scale of 1:4,000) and show the characteristic stages in the development of a Danish village.

1 The town was measured up in 1768 by C.C. Gercken in connection with the planned sale of the Antvorskov yeomanry district. The map shows a village arranged round a common with 14 farms. Each farm had 108 selions distributed across the same number of furlongs, which were in turn divided into 3 fields, separated by fences.

2 In 1786, the open fields were rearranged and a system of crop rotation introduced. The arable land was divided into 9 areas that were fenced by a ditch or a hawthorn-covered bank. One of the farms was closed down, and each of the remaining 13 farms were given 2 or 3 lots in each of the 9 larger areas. Each farm now had just 22 lots of land.

3 When land strips were subsequently exchanged in 1795, 7 farms were moved out into the fields while the remaining 6 stayed in the village. Each farm was then given a compact plot of land with its allotted selions and meadows. A strip of land measuring around 1.5 hectares was taken from every farm's plot of approximately 30 hectares to create a smallholding.

such as those found in North Zealand.

East Denmark consists of several hundred islands of varying sizes, and there are many natural bays and fjords. This accounts for the relatively long coastline, almost 6000 km. In character, the coastline ranges from moraine and lime cliffs to sandy beach ridge plains and lush littoral meadows. The coast no longer has the same significance as of yore; until 1900, it was the centre of the sailing and fishing industries.

Following the loss of South Jutland in 1864, the farming community needed new land and a number of small and large bays around North Funen, North Zealand and Lolland-Falster were reclaimed. Some of these reclamations were hugely successful in economic terms, including the Lammefjord in northwest Zealand. Others were too sandy to yield any profit. The 20th century's welfare state has given new significance to the coasts as the centre for a number of outdoor pursuits and the location for an ever-growing number of holiday homes. Since 1950, the holiday housing areas near the coast have grown significantly in East Denmark, but legislation from 1937 ensures that the beaches cannot be developed or spoiled by destroying the natural environment. In addition,

Landscape by Horns Herred north of Selsø, with Roskilde Fjord and Jyllinge in the background. Also seen in the background is the compact village of Østby showing the fields arranged in the typical star pattern. In the foreground is the row of smallholdings which were built in 1922 on land from the large Selsø farm. Both these features are characteristic of the cultural landscape in the east of Denmark.

the public has been guaranteed access to all beaches. Nature conservationists particularly want to preserve the meadows in the coastal zone and the internationally rare moraine cliff coasts.

The landscape on *Bornholm* is highly unusual because of the bedrock and the mixture of lush and barren areas found within a very small region. Both the 100 m high bedrock horst in the north of the island, and the old sedimentary deposits found in the south, are generally overlaid by moraine which is rich in nutrients. The Almindingen in the centre of the island is dominated by sandy and water-logged soil, with the odd rocks sticking up here and there. Since the beginning of the 19th century, woodlands have been planted in this area known as Højlyngen. The area, which was covered in thicket and heather, was formerly the property of the King but was generally used for communal grazing. Højlyngen now forms part of a belt of more recent municipal plantations which stretches from Neksø in

the east to Hammeren in the northwest. There are also a number of small woods on the commons and in the narrow rift valleys. Pine plantations have been planted north of Rønne and near Dueodde as protection against sand drift.

There is a wide, fertile belt of agricultural land round the Almindingen; freehold farms with some 20-50 hectares have been scattered around the area for many, many years, free of the open-field system and local squires. The production methods and the crops grown here are similar to those on other islands in the east of Denmark. Apart from Åkirkeby, towns are located on the coast alongside a number of small fishing harbours which are slowly being turned into holiday towns.

Raw materials (granite, coal and clay) have been subject to intensive industrial exploitation, which has left countless small quarries and gravel pits. A number of large pits are found between Hammeren and Rønne, partly or completely abandoned and now overrun by fresh vegetation and with colourful lakes and ponds.

Groups of rocks, stone walls, burial mounds and monoliths surrounded by lush fields and deciduous woodland merge to form a fascinating scenery which is rich in contrasts. Large numbers of tourists are drawn to the area, and hotels, boarding houses, camping sites and holiday houses all leave their mark on the cultural landscape.

West Jutland

Despite the meagre soil, this part of the country still looks well-cultivated with fields, plantations and narrow meadows along the watercourses. The arable land is often divided into small parcels which are framed by quickset hedges. This is most often seen on the sandy soils of the flat outwash plains, but can also be found on the surrounding moraine areas where the landscape is divided by mile-long windbreaks set at right angles to the West Wind. In the clayey parts of the moraine areas, the soil is of such quality that the land can be left open without windbreaks. The intensive farming system found in West Jutland combine technology with the correct choice of crops, the construction of windbreaks and the use of irrigation plants. Traces can still be found of former irrigation plants in fixed canals and ditches along the rivers.

The shifting sands which threaten the farmland every spring have been curbed by windbreaks and, since 1987, far more effectively by the compulsory use of more winter crop cover. The well-cultivated land is the result of almost 100 years of hard work spent reclaiming the heaths which dominated the West Jutland landscape well into the 20th century; the last extensive reclamation project was carried out as late as the 1950s. Whilst the heaths were reclaimed and cultivated to produce arable land, other areas with infertile soil were set aside and planted with conifers. The choice of trees has become more varied at the beginning of the 21st century. The plantations now include deciduous trees to ensure that they can provide a more varied range of recreational activities and greater diversity in the animal and plant species found in the area.

Developments in the open country have created a pattern of scattered farms and houses; small and medium-sized industrial towns and service centres have evolved in step with the cultivation of the heaths. Many of the oldest houses and farms lie side by side along rivers or wetland areas, and are connected by roads which run parallel to the

watercourse. These farms were originally tied to the old meadow-field-heath production cycle, in which the nourishment found in the hay in the meadows is used by the animals, whose manure is then spread on the fields where corn is grown; the heath was an outfield which was occasionally cultivated to produce a single grain crop. Older buildings can also be found on the more fertile soil on the moraine, where the farms are even more scattered than elsewhere.

Between the river valley farms and the old groups of holdings in the moraine areas lie more recent dwellings. These were originally small freeholds which grew together with the cultivation of the heaths. Agricultural activities in West Jutland peaked in the 1960s. Employment then fell and some of the farms grew; this is visible today from the large buildings which have been expanded and modernised as a result of tenancy agreements with neighbouring farms. Hedges are removed and open ditches drained to create larger and more productive fields. As a result, the landscape becomes more open.

The reclamation of the heaths and the wetlands created a basis for a huge increase in the population. This, in turn, produced a reserve of manpower. Since the 1930s, people have been migrating to the towns including Herning, Ikast and Billund, meeting the need for workers which has been created by the many new industrial concerns.

West Jutland heath plain with meltwater flats southwest of Viborg. The landscape was created during the deglaciation stage at the end of the last ice age: First the meltwater flowed to the North Sea creating the first flat, then to the Limfjord creating the bottom flat. The dense grass on the lowest flat shows how difficult it is to maintain the heather now that the old methods of burning the heather and removing the heath peat are no longer used.

Locally, West Jutland has been dominated by huge lignite pits which have left a harsh landscape of overgrown mounds and deep lakes. Similar wastelands can be seen on some of the protected heaths and in the richly wooded Midtjyske Søhøjland (Lake Highland of Central Jutland), as well as along the border zone between West and East Jutland.

Apart from Bovbjerg, the west coast between Thyborøn and Blåvands Huk is low and dominated by sandy lagoons protected against the North Sea by tongues of land that are naturally reinforced by the littoral dunes whose white crests can be seen many miles away. The sea has been eating away at the land ever since the Stone Age, and during the last 200 years or so it has managed to advance a couple of metres a year. The State has made increasing efforts to stem the erosion of the coastline. Since 1862, groynes made of stones and reinforced concrete girders have been constructed in the most vulnerable places. Breakwaters of heavy rocks have also been built parallel to the coast, supplemented with sand and gravel pumped up from the seabed:

one could say that the coast is effectively fed. The belt of coastal dunes which are prevented from creeping inland when vegetation is planted on them, instead slides into the sea. This has made it necessary to reinforce existing dikes with concrete boulders. The spits of land near Harboør and Nissum Fjord are sand-covered cement dikes built to protect the fertile meadows and fields around the low-lying lagoons.

Holmsland Klit, a natural great spit on Ringkøbing Fjord, is wide with large dunes that act as a natural fortification against the sea; reinforcements have only had to be constructed in a few places. Old farms with the traditional quadrilateral layout can still be found amidst the rapidly increasing number of holiday homes and cottages. Further south towards Blåvands Huk, the sea and the wind have created dune landscapes which sometimes stretch inland for several miles.

The coastal area in southwest Jutland is a highly regulated and partly man-made landscape, where it has been necessary to build dikes to survive. The area consists of tidal flats

Land use developments between 1847 and 1991 in a typical West Jutland landscape, here Skjernådalen (the Skjernå Valley) by Sønder Felding some 25 km southwest of Herning. Between 1871 and 1911, the farms grew as irrigation canals (such as Skjernå Nørrekanal) were constructed and manmade meadows were introduced onto the arable land. Great technical efforts and the use of artificial fertilizers have turned the heaths into arable land over the course of the 20th century.

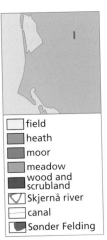

- field
- heath
- moor
- meadow
- wood and scrubland
- Skjernå river
- canal
- Sønder Felding

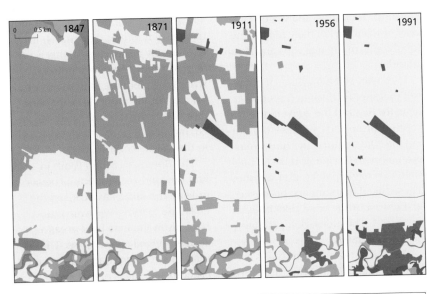

0   0.5 km   1847   1871   1911   1956   1991

and huge, flat salt marshes. The large outwash plains in the hinterland continue westward far as the marshes and the tidal flats; only in few places do the flat moraine areas come down as far as the sea. The whole area is bordered to the west by the Skallingen peninsula and the dune islands of Fanø, Mandø and Rømø.

The salt marshes probably constitute the one area in Denmark where the battle between Man and Nature has been most dramatic. There are daily tides of 1-2 m; floods of up to 5 m above *DNN* (*Dansk Normal Nul* – Danish Ordnance Datum), combined with a strong westerly wind, create a constant risk of flooding which is very much a part of daily life for the inhabitants of the marshes and dune islands.

There are still a number of open salt marshes furthest to the north near Ho Bay, but the coast to the south is protected by dikes built during the 20th century. In Tøndermarsken close to Germany, it is still possible to see one polder after another. These diked marshes are bordered to the west by the great dike built in 1979-1981. The oldest polders date back to the 1500s.

The soil in the salt marshes is good, but the fact that they are situated at only 0-2 m above sea level has meant that they have had to be drained via a close network of ditches which divide the landscape into small rectangular plots. The many corn fields date from more recent times; until the middle of the 20th century, the moist meadows were only used to graze sheep and cattle. This is still true in more exposed locations, such as the foreland west of the dikes and in the protected polders close to the border.

The large marsh farms and houses have been built in rows along the border zone between the salt marshes and the surrounding old moraines and outwash plains – the so-called geestland – away from the danger of flooding. The marsh itself is generally undeveloped; this is not true of Tøndermarsken, however, where the pioneers built their homes on man-made mounds in the meadows. After the dikes were constructed, farms and houses were also built in the lower marshes.

The Rømø road dam (built in 1948) and the land reclamation projects outside the dikes have caused the coastline to move westwards and have given the new land areas a straight-edged appearance. These man-made landscapes help to counteract the effects of storm surge on

The marshes by Højer seen from the south. Outside the projecting dike (built between 1979 and 1981) is the Jutland Wadden Sea. A salt-water lake has been created behind the dike in Margrethe-kog for the bird life. In the middle of the picture are a number of water-filled clay pits. These border the Højerdiget dike (built 1861), which protects Ny Frederikskog which is visible with its farms and cultivated fields. In the background is Højer which is located in front of the hill island landscape (the geestland) which lies just a little higher than the flat marshland.

The outermost tip of Jutland, the Grenen peninsula on the Skagens Odde spit. The Skagerrak and the Kattegat meet here and the waves crash up from both 'sides'. Enormous amounts of sand are brought here by the waves every year from the west coast of Jutland, and the spit is expanding both eastwards and northwards. The recently deposited sands quickly change shape and position depending on the prevailing weather conditions. Thousands of tourists visit this exciting location every year.

the coast and thereby protect both the dikes and the land behind them.

On Rømø and Fanø, the holiday houses and the tourist industry all leave their unmistakable stamp on the landscape. During the summer months, the number of people on the islands increases greatly, putting an enormous strain on the environment.

North Jutland

North Jutland consists of the regions of Thy, Mors and Salling along with Hanherred, Vendsyssel and Himmerland. A third of the total area consists of sandy coasts with big dunes and low, marshy plains left over from the Littorina Sea during the Stone Age. Fertile soil is only found in Thy (not counting the area along the North Sea coast), Mors and Salling, and the

cultural landscape here is highly reminiscent of East Denmark. Elsewhere, shifting sands and wet areas have caused big problems; only the technological advances of the last hundred years have enabled farmers to overcome the inherent obstacles. The sandy Littorina plains have risen between 4 and 10 m since the Stone Age, and the area has a number of littoral cliffs formed during different geological periods by the action of the sea. These are generally found in the west and, to a lesser extent, in the east.

The coast itself mainly consists of sandy beaches with small sandy cliffs behind them. In places, however, promontories formed by ice age sediments and limestone jut out onto the coast as can be seen at Lodbjerg, Hanstholm, Rubjerg, Hirtshals and Frederikshavn. Huge dunes, some stretching up to 7 kilometres inland, have been formed by sand blown up from the coast. The dune belts are dominated by large, dark conifer plantations, intermixed here and there with white dunes, heaths and heather bogs. In the 16th and 17th centuries, shifting sands drove the population back from the coastal areas. It was only in the 19th century that the State managed to bring the sand-drift under control by planting dune grasses and conifers. These dune plantations became a common sight after 1880. The barren dune zone allowed limited sheep farming and some inshore fishing from the beaches; since then, fishing activities have been centred around the new fishing harbours, but there are still signs of the earlier customs in the shape of slipways and old houses. The dune zone is generally sparsely developed, but large holiday housing developments have sprung up since 1930 wherever nature conservation regulations and shifting sands have allowed, particularly in Vendsyssel. The Skagens Odde spit is one of the most remarkable dune regions in the area, not only because of its extent (it stretches 30 kilometres out into the sea), but also because of its huge migrating dunes. A prime example of this type of dune is the sparsely vegetated Råbjerg Mile which is still very active. More fertile cultivated areas are, however, found in the strictly controlled 'dune desert', particularly towards the Kattegat and in the reclaimed lake Gårdbo Sø.

There are other unusual terrains and culture landscapes in North Jutland. The extensive, low-lying marine plains created by the Littorina Sea stretch from the dune belts of the Jammerbugten, along the Limfjord to the Kattegat coast and southwards to Mariager Fjord. A vast number of isolated hill areas with moraines and underlying limestone deposits are found on the plains. In the border zone between these two types of terrain lie rows of old farms, built as ribbon developments between the grass and grain areas. The marine flats between Thy and the Fjerritslev area are only 1-3 m above sea level. Until the middle of the 19th century, the plains were divided by several shallow bays known as Vejlerne. Reclaiming these bays turned out to be a financial failure as the resulting land was both sandy and infertile. Today meadows, reed swamps and lakes regulated by moderate drainage make up the 50 square kilometres area which became a nature reserve in 1960.

Since the Iron Age, several bogs have appeared on the plains north and southeast of Aalborg. The two most important examples are the approximately 100 square kilometres raised bogs known as Store Vildmose and Lille Vildmose. The first is located in Vendsyssel, the second in

The central part of the Råbjerg Mile dune on the Skagens Odde spit. The shifting sands have been given a free rein here on this huge protected migrating dune. The barren, infertile sand has been shaped into 1-2 m high waves which constantly collapse. The wind blows the sand in from the west (to the right in the picture). In the background are the conifer protection forests and the moraine formations by Frederikshavn 30 km to the south.

The Rubjerg Knude lighthouse was built in 1900 at the top of the cliff, 65 m above the sea. Shifting sands meant that the 23 m high lighthouse had to be closed in 1968. Attempts to halt the shifting sands from the heavily eroded cliff have proved unsuccessful, and in 1994 efforts to keep the lighthouse clear were abandoned. The picture was taken in 1991.

Himmerland. The peat layer in these bogs is up to 5 m thick. Store Vildmose, which was drained and marled after peat-cutting at the beginning of the 1900s, was bought up and redeveloped by the State. Grass fields were sown for the rearing of disease-free cattle; the area was later divided into plots and sold off and long rows of farms were built. Other areas of the moor have been set aside as a nature reserve. Lille Vildmose has evidence of two lakes which were drained and farmed in approximately 1760. After 1930, the State cultivated the northeasterly part of the moor before dividing it up into small-holdings in the 1950s. The north-westerly quarter of the moor consists of dark, barren peat bogs where the peat has been partly cut to produce peat-moss litter. The southern half is a raised bog overgrown with heather which, together with Tofte Skov, has been enclosed and turned into a deer park with red deer and wild boar.

Central Vendsyssel is higher than the Littorina plains and is equally divided between high moraine formations and Yoldia flats consisting of sea deposits from the end of the last ice age. The soil is sandy in both areas and farming is hindered by drifting soil, despite the use of winter crop cover and the many windbreaks that have been constructed. Large streams such as Uggerby Å and Voers Å have worn away deep trenches in the terrain during the isostatic uplift which has taken place since the ice age. The old farm buildings are seldom grouped in villages, but are instead scattered round the area on both types of terrain. Ever since the 17th century, single farms have been much more common in Vendsyssel than elsewhere in Denmark. This is reflected in the isolated locations of the churches built during the Middle Ages. Numerous small towns appeared during the 20th century to serve the scattered countryside population. These are generally found by crossroads and near the railway stations which have since been closed down.

Denmark's capital is more than 800 years old. Seen from the air, the old town centre (a little to the left of the middle in the picture) is easily recognisable. The buildings are close together and surrounded by lakes, the harbour fairway and the old ramparts which have been turned into parks, including the Tivoli Gardens. Buildings are seldom more than 5 stories high, with the exception of the verdigris-covered church spires and towers. Just a few minutes' walk south of the centre lies the Amager Fælled common (to the right in the picture), a 30 square km nature reserve. Outside the old town centre are districts where the housing blocks were only built after 1850.

In Himmerland, villages are much more common than in Vendsyssel and the terrain consists of large, 60-100 m tall rounded moraine formations where the underground limestone is found close to the surface. Deep, wide erosion valleys and the fossil coasts created by the Littorina sea have carved out moraine formations which now rise steeply over the valleys and the Littorina plains. After the Second World War the valleys and the marine plains were drained and cultivated.

In East Himmerland, the white calcareous soil is visible on many hillsides and freshly turned fields. Both old and active limestone quarries are a common sight. The close proximity of Aalborg has meant that older settlements have been supplemented with new housing estates. The central and southeastern parts of Himmerland have always been covered by forests; the best known of these is Rold Skov. The wooded areas have grown during the last century as the older forests have been expanded and new trees planted on the heathland and sandy fields. West Himmerland, like Vendsyssel, is plagued by drifting soil. Remains of the heaths which used to cover large parts of the area can still be found on the hillsides; most are subject to conservation laws or have been planted and cultivated. Southeast of Løgstør, however, there is a 10 km stretch of heathland hills which still show traces of Iron Age fields. There are also a few large plantations from around 1890. More recent developments in the countryside are distributed between the old villages and the new service centres. Large farms are few and far between, partly because allotment associations were very active during the first half of the 20th century when many smallholdings were created. There are surprisingly few holiday houses in the Himmerland area.

Kristen Marius Jensen,
Hans Kuhlman

The Built-up Area
The earliest real towns in Denmark (which date back to the 9th and 10th centuries) arose as a result of the need to sell the surplus output pro-

duced by the farming community. The natural conditions imposed on agriculture were thus crucial to the size and number of towns that were established. Prior to industrialisation, the areas with infertile soil, such as the heaths in western and central areas of Jutland, had small towns that were few and far between. Large numbers of small market towns appeared along the coasts during the Middle Ages, closely connected with shipping. The presence of certain raw materials and the availability of water power have also played a role historically, particularly during the time before industrialisation. Many towns were established because of the easy access to water power, including Frederiksværk, Hellebæk, Brede and Silkeborg. Others, such as Nivå and Egernsund, prospered because of the presence of smooth clay used in the tile works.

The rapid expansion of the towns between 1860-1940 was closely linked to industrialisation. During this period, the number of towns and the urban population rose steeply; in 1860 there were approximately 400,000 Danes distributed across 83 towns. In 1940, the number of towns had risen to 628 with a total population of 2.5 million. During the same period, the urban population's share of the total national population rose from 23% to 63%. It was mostly the large and medium-sized towns which grew during the urbanisation phase. Other medium-sized and small towns, particularly those located close to larger cities, have prospered since the Second World War, particularly in North Zealand. Since 1980, however, this growth has stopped.

The commercial and industrial development of the towns has always been closely linked with easy access to the prevalent method of transport. In older times, this was particularly true of shipping. Today, access to the national road network (motorways) and air transport plays an important role. The development of individual towns has also been greatly influenced by their administrative and political importance. Copenhagen, which was a modest harbour in the 11th century, underwent rapid growth after it came under the rule of Bishop Absalon in the 12th century, and later in the 15th and 16th centuries when it became the country's capital. Present-day parallels can be drawn with the small towns that suddenly became administrative centres when the municipalities were amalgamated in 1970. These communities all proceeded to grow drastically in size over the next 30 years.

The Urban Distribution Pattern
The urban distribution pattern, which profiles the size and relative position of the towns, constantly changes. It does so slowly, however, due to the large investments which have been made in the physical structure of the towns and their relatively long useful life. The urban distribution pattern in Denmark was partly shaped during the Middle Ages and partly

Major Danish cities (2001)	
	Number of citizens
Copenhagen*	1,081,673
Århus	218,380
Odense	144,849
Aalborg	119,996
Esbjerg	73,076
Randers	56,008
Kolding	53,687
Horsens	48,837
Vejle	48,402
Roskilde	43,210
* Continous built-up area	
Source: Statistics Denmark.	

during the urbanisation phase when the present relative proportions of the towns were established. Copenhagen enjoys special status as the capital; the political centralisation in the 17th century guaranteed the city a dominant position in the country, and it prospered dramatically during industrialisation. With approximately 30% of Denmark's population living in the capital, Copenhagen assumes the same national position as e.g. Budapest, Vienna, Paris and London. Denmark's urban distribution pattern can thus be described as mono-centric unlike the pattern in the Netherlands, Belgium and Germany which have several equal centres as opposed to a single dominant city.

In 2000, the towns were home to approximately 85% of the population. In addition to Copenhagen, the provincial centres include the towns of Århus, Odense and Aalborg. Together, these four cities are home to 29% of the total urban population out of the country's 1421 towns (1999). They are centrally located within their own regions (unlike Copenhagen after the surrender of Scania, Halland and Blekinge in 1658) and are home to the main services, including the universities, national newspapers, television and radio stations, as well as the headquarters of many national and international companies.

There are 60 towns in Denmark with between 10,000 and 100,000 inhabitants, including Hjørring, Herning, Thisted, Kolding, Randers, Svendborg and Nykøbing Falster. These are all regional centres and often serve as administrative centres in their area. There are 435 smaller market towns and large villages, etc. with between 1,000 and 10,000 inhabitants (and suburbs such as Dragør and Farum near Copenhagen, Hjortshøj and Lisbjerg near Århus). Being local centres, they often serve a smaller surrounding area with retail trade and services. Furthermore, the largest of these towns and villages are home to vocational courses and upper secondary schools. In the smaller towns (under 1,000 inhabitants) there is seldom anything other than local services such as grocers' shops, schools and kindergartens.

Most of the larger towns in Denmark have a wide basis for trade and industry; very few are dominated by a single sector, which is to a larger extent the case in some of the medium-sized and smaller towns, particularly Billund (with the Lego factory), Bjerringbro (with the Grundfos pump factory), Nordborg (with the industrial group Danfoss) and the fishing and ferry towns Hirtshals, Hanstholm and Hvidesande.

Urban Structure

Individual towns consist of a number of districts (residential quarters and industrial areas, a town centre and sometimes a harbour area), where the town's main functions are located. There are also recreational areas and transport networks connecting the different districts.

In larger towns, which are often market towns with a long history, the centre is easily recognisable by the street layout and the age and arrangement of the buildings. The centre is normally dominated by the retail trade as well as certain services and administrative functions. Activities are generally focused around a market square or a quay, illustrating the town's origins as a centre for trade. The centre has generally over the centuries become more densely built-up as new stories, back premises and lateral additions were added to existing buildings. The floor-area ratio, i.e. the ratio of floorspace to the area of the site, has thereby increased. While residential areas estates generally have a floor-area ratio of between 10 and 20, the ratio in town centres and inner city areas is often more than 200. Urban renewal and redevelopment have managed to reduce the ratio in the worst affected areas drastically since the 1960s.

The historical heart of the regional towns is usually dominated by the business quarter, often known as the city, which incorporates large numbers of shops, offices, institutions, theatres, restaurants, etc. Residential premises are found in a variety of districts, all of which reflect the period in which they were built. Examples include the compact residential blocks from the industrial period, the open park developments of the 1940s and the huge, featureless post-war residential areas consisting of either social housing developments or detached one-family houses, clearly separated. The more recent business districts are often placed at the edge of existing towns, near the large access roads.

The medium-sized provincial centres are often very like the regional centres in their structure. The division into distinct areas is often less clear, however, and individual neighbourhoods are often much smaller in size. These towns generally try to cater for their surrounding area by providing pedestrian shopping areas along the former main streets. The courtyards of old blocks are often turned into car parks, and the historical town centre is usually surrounded by a ringroad which conveys the traffic into the available car parks. Outside the ringroad lie the residential neighbourhoods and the business districts. Herning and Roskilde are good examples of towns of this type. The actual residential districts are dominated by open developments, predominantly one-family houses and terraced houses, as well as a number of blocks of flats.

The centres in the smaller market towns generally consist of one- or two-storey buildings along the most important roads such as the highway and the access road to the railway station. Around the centre lies mainly smaller houses. New types of development appeared in most market towns during the industrial period, including industrial districts, railway station districts and perhaps working-class areas. The area between the old districts and these new areas is often marked by city parks, large industrial plants (gas and electricity), station areas or quay areas and cemeteries. At the beginning of the 20th century, developments became more open in character; institutions and large open areas intended for recreational use began to appear.

Many smaller towns are relatively unimportant in size and historical terms, particularly those which are centred around railway stations or ferry ports. Here, developments are seldom differentiated; only local services such as grocers' shops, bakeries, garages and local schools are easily distinguished from residential houses. Many of these small towns lost a large part of their trade and industry in the middle of the 1970s.

Hans Thor Andersen

Inland Waters

The inland waters in Denmark (the Skagerrak, the Kattegat and the Belts) create a shallow transition between the oceanic North Sea and the continental Baltic Sea.

Development

The sea bed of Denmark's inland waters is characterised by an uneven topography created by ice age glaciers and the sea itself. During the last stage of the ice age, a number of ice advances spread from the southeast up through the belts. Each ice advance left moraine deposits, and with the arrival of the sea these created a number of transverse reefs and grounds, stretching from Djursland in the north to Gedser in the south. A narrow, uneven reach with depths of over 20 m connects the Kattegat and the Baltic Sea through the Great Belt. The course of the Little Belt is even more complicated, with a barrier depth of just under 20 m, and the Sound gets 'blocked' already at Drogden where the depth is only 8 m.

Dynamic Conditions

The uneven floor, frequently interrupted by narrow ramifications, hinders an efficient flow and divides the sea bed into a large number of basins in which sediments, including polluted silt from waste water, are deposited. Oxygen deficiency is a recurring problem, particularly during warm summers.

There is a large inflow of fresh water into the Baltic, which causes a tremendous outflow of brackish surface water into the inland waters in Denmark; at the same time, saline deep water is transported from the North Sea to the Baltic. There is a definite boundary between the two bodies of water. Friction causes a certain amount of mixing between the two layers, so the salt content of the surface water increases on the way to the North Sea while the salt content near the sea bed is reduced on the way to the Baltic. This two-layer movement is heavily influenced by wind conditions. Heavy winds can cause large differences in water levels between the Kattegat and the western part of the Baltic (± 0.8 m) due to the pressure exerted on the water body by the wind (wind pressure). This creates a surface inclination which results in a large movement of water to the north or the south depending on the direction of the wind. The current velocity in-

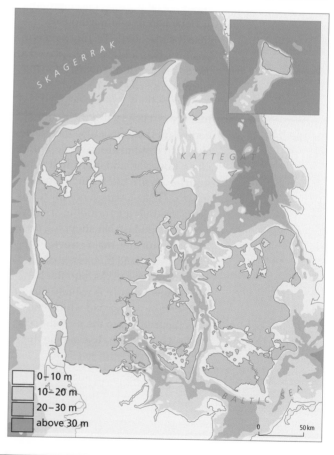

Depth map of the Danish inland waters.

0–10 m
10–20 m
20–30 m
above 30 m

SKAGERRAK

KATTEGAT

BALTIC SEA

0   50 km

creases and can reach speeds of up to approximately 4 m/s in the Belts. Water level differences caused by tides (tidal amplitude) are greatest near the North Sea (1-2 m) and smallest near the Baltic (0.1 m).

The temperature of the water is controlled by the exchange of heat with the atmosphere, and the average surface-water temperature varies between 0-2° C in February and 18° C in August, while the bottom temperature varies only between 4° C and 12° C.

Sailing

The Great Belt's deep trench is used by the majority of the ships with a draught of over 10 m that sail through Danish waters; despite markings from Hatterrev to the Langeland belt, it is recommended to take a pilot. Before the steamers came, the small draught of the sailing ships allowed them to call almost anywhere on the coast of Denmark. When the draught exceeded 5 m, however, almost every market town even had to deepen its harbour channel. The water in the traditional fjord harbours is very shallow, while the harbours on the straits such as Aalborg, Fredericia, Svendborg and Stigsnæs are deep and 'self-cleaning' because of their proximity to deep trenches with strong currents. In the course of the 1960s, as the tonnage and the draught of vessels increased even further, the original quay depths of 10 m became inadequate. Refineries and electricity works in particular had to create new deep-water harbours. One example of these new harbours is Stigsnæs by the Great Belt which, at 18 m, boasts Denmark's greatest depth of quay.

Erik Buch, Horst Meesenburg

Ecosystem and Environmental Protection

Ecological cycles have been undergoing great changes since the 1950s, due primarily to the huge increase in the amount of energy and raw materials consumed. Large amounts of chemicals have entered the cycles as a result. In an attempt to stem these developments, the government has introduced comprehensive legislation governing the development and usage of the Danish landscape. The aim is 'to seek to ensure the quality of the exterior surroundings that have a bearing on our health and recreational activities, and to preserve a varied plant and animal life' as stated in Denmark's first en-

vironmental law (The Environmental Protection Act) of 1974. The term 'the exterior surroundings' has now become 'the environment' in everyday language.

From Nature to Culture
Massive changes had already taken place in the ecological cycles during earlier times. The Danish landscape has undergone constant change since it was formed by the ice over 12,000 years ago. The changes have been caused by both natural and man-made factors. During a long period between 6000-500 BC, the country was almost covered by lime

The development of the forests, the grassland and the heaths from the Stone Age to the present day. Denmark was once covered by forest, but the trees had to give way to the crops and the livestock. The grassland has gradually taken over in most of the country. The differences in soil and climate have played a vital role in the development of the landscape. Most marked is the difference between the clayey moraine soil in the east of the country and the sandy soil in West Jutland where large areas were turned into heathland over several thousand years.

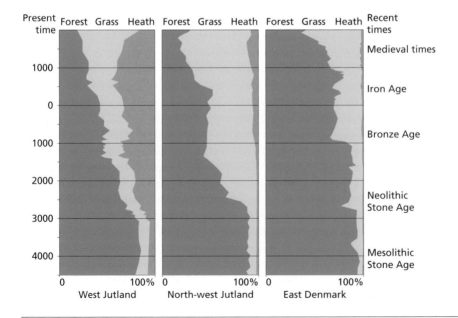

The Disappearance of the Forests

During the Iron Age, Man began to clear large areas of forest. Land was needed for the cultivation of crops. This was the beginnings of the open Danish cultural landscape, a landscape which today is almost entirely given over to farming.

Farming requires a continuous supply of energy because it disturbs the natural development of the ecosystem. Unless arable land is tended constantly, the natural ecological processes would bring the forest back into the areas that have been cleared.

For centuries after the forest clearings of the Iron Age, periods where the forests again gained ground alternated with periods when cultivated areas increased. Up until 1800, wood was the most important source of energy for heating. It was also an important element in the construction of houses and fences and the production of tools. Farm animals also grazed in the forest. In some places, the forest disappeared because it was used as fuel for e.g. the glass industry and the saltworks. In the 16th and 17th centuries the Danish military, including the Navy, laid claim to a huge number of mature oaks.

Around 1600, 20-25% of the country was covered in forests. Over the next 200 years, however, the forests were subjected to such violent felling that the forested area in 1805, the year of the Forest Reserve Act, was less than 4% of the country's total area – the smallest ever. The new regulations concerning, for example, replanting allowed the forests to prosper once again, and in the early 2000s they covered approximately 12% of the country. But the new forests were nothing like those of old: the slow-growing beech and oak trees had been replaced by fast-growing conifers.

It took more than 2,000 mature oaks to build a ship of the line such as Trekroner, Christian IV's flagship on his expedition to England in 1606. The consumption of oak in the European armaments race contributed greatly to the decline of the forests. At the end of the 16th century, the forests covered 20-25% of the total area. This figure had fallen to less than 4% some 200 years later.

forests, interspersed here and there by oaks and elm trees. The climate then turned colder and wetter and beech trees began to appear. Animal and plant life was formed as part of a natural process of development; the energy from the sun was used effectively and substances circulated in almost closed cycles. The forest was a natural ecosystem until Man began to make his mark by felling the forests and creating arable land. Denmark became a cultural landscape.

In the early 2000s, the Danish ecosystem is very different from the early forest landscape. Energy consumption has multiplied as we increasingly use solar energy to supplement other energy sources based on fossil fuels such as oil and coal. The use of this extra energy has also led to an increase in the consumption of chemicals. The former closed chemical cycles have been replaced by more open cycles, and large amounts of chemicals are transported in and out of the country. Even though these developments have taken more than 2,000 years, the chemical cycles have only really changed character during the 20th century, particularly after 1950.

The shifting sands became a pressing problem at the end of the 18th century, and a number of regulations aimed at combating the problem were introduced, the latest in 1792. By public villeinage, farmers were ordered to plant marram grass on the dunes. The roots of this grass bind the sand, making it particularly well-adapted to growing in this environment.

Together with the cooler and wetter climate of 'the little ice age', the huge reduction in the forested area affected the ecological cycles in several ways in the period before 1700. The ground water rose almost across the entire country, in some places by several metres. Lakes, bogs and watercourses flooded the land creating new bogs and water meadows. The high water content of the soil meant that the growing season of the crops was shortened to approximately 100 days, and that the soil became more acidic. Shifting sand had had such an effect that almost 5% of the total arable land in Jutland had to be abandoned. The sand problem was also caused by the felling of the forests which had originally extended as far as the coast. The sand strangled many watercourses, contributing to the rise in the water table. Fewer and fewer plant nutrients were returned to the soil and were instead removed when crops were harvested; the soil became particularly deficient in nitrogen.

The Landscapes of the Golden Age

In the 18th and 19th centuries, the situation was reversed. The appearance of the landscape changed once again, as did the ecological cycles. Projects to prevent sand drift were put into operation after legislation concerning the shifting sands was introduced in 1792. The acidic soils were neutralised with marl, and land reclamation projects created additional arable land. The water table was lowered by regulating the watercourses and by constructing a dense network of canals and ditches in the fields. The nitrogen balance of the soil was improved considerably with the introduction of cultivated clover and other leguminous plants into the crop rotation cycle. The leguminous plants live in symbiosis with micro-organisms that are capable of converting atmospheric nitrogen into a nitrogen compound which is used by the plants.

The result was the landscape that has been immortalised in the paintings and poems of the Golden Age:

Green beech forests, deer by a watering hole, quickset hedges and clover meadows. This was how large parts of eastern Denmark looked around 1830. In West and Central Jutland, the artists were mostly drawn by the huge heaths. The changes were less dramatic in Jutland with its sandy soil than on the moraine flats in East Denmark. Despite being an artistic ideal, the Golden Age image of the Danish landscape has become reality in the minds of many Danes.

New Raw Materials and Fuels – Greater Energy Consumption

Coal and iron became the most important new raw materials during the 16th and 17th centuries as wood became more and more scarce. Both coal and iron had to be imported and therefore came to play a large role in the ecological cycles. Consumption continued to rise well into the 20th century. Coal was later supplemented by other energy sources, principally oil and gas. The Danish landscape was no longer capable of supplying sufficient energy to satisfy the population. Instead, fossil fuels from the energy stocks created by vegetation several million years earlier were taken into use. The growth in energy consumption was far quicker than the increase in the population. Energy consumption can therefore be used as a measure of living standards, as well as an expression of the human impact on the ecological cycles.

At the beginning of the 20th century, the yearly consumption of energy for heating, electricity production, transport and industry was approximately 50 PJ (petajoule = 10^{15} joules). In 1960, this rose to approximately 300 PJ, and 15 years later, it had reached almost 800 PJ. Between 1975 and the early 2000s energy consumption almost re-mained unchanged. The majority of the energy was used in towns and in connection with transport. Energy consumption also rose rapidly within the farming community.

In the years immediately prior to the Second World War, agriculture consumed approximately 8 PJ in addition to the solar energy used. Of this, indirect consumption in the shape of artificial fertilisers accounted for some 2.5 PJ. In 1970, this figure was 6 times higher, and ten years later the indirect energy consumption had risen even further. Thus the consumption of non-solar energy increased tenfold in just 50 years. Yields had of course also risen, but the amount of foodstuffs produced had only grown by approximately 40% over the same period. The rise in yield did not, therefore, correspond to the rise in the amount of energy consumed.

Greater Amounts of Chemicals

The increase in energy consumption affected the country's ecosystem in two ways. Burning coal, oil and gas emitted greater amounts of carbon dioxide, sulphur dioxide and nitrogen oxides to the air along with soot and dust particles containing heavy metals such as cadmium, mercury and lead. It also created slag and ash, most of which ended up in refuse dumps. Leakage from these pits allowed the heavy metals to end up in the environment.

The rise in the production of goods also led to a rise in the cycling of chemicals. Many new compounds, such as PCB and pesticides, began to appear. These chemicals were emitted into the soil, air and water, or collected in refuse dumps. Between 1975 and 1996 the quantity of refuse produced rose from around 5 million tonnes to more than 12 million tonnes – the equivalent of

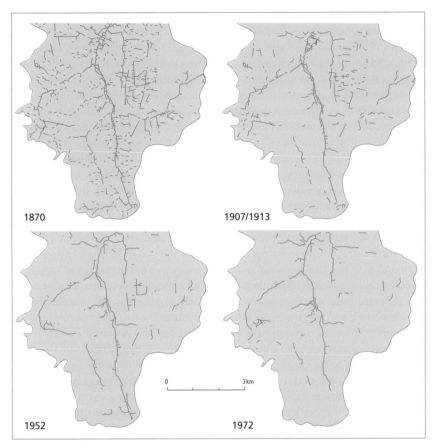

1870

1907/1913

0   3 km

1952

1972

Section of the Lyngbygård river system between Silkeborg and Århus. At the beginning of the 19th century there were more open watercourses than ever before. The drainage projects instigated during the previous century resulted in tens of thousands of new ditches and canals. But the continued extension of the arable land required larger, uniform areas and thousands of kilometres of watercourses were piped and replaced by drains. Plant and animal life was badly affected and the chemicals which entered the water from the cultivated fields were no longer processed as effectively as before.

almost 2 tonnes per person in Denmark.

Changes in Farming

The structure of the farming community and the methods of working employed have changed greatly, particularly since 1950. Gradually fewer, but larger, farms began to appear. Mechanisation and specialisation continued apace. Livestock farmers centred around the south-westerly areas of the country. The mixed herds disappeared and farmers concentrated on either pigs or cattle. Furthermore, the number of pigs rose considerably between 1950 and the early 2000s, from approximately 3 to 12 million, while the number of cattle fell from approximately 3 to c. 2 million during that same period. In East Jutland and in the islands, the cultivation of plants dominated and the corn crop expanded at the expense of grasses and root crops. At the same time, energy consumption rose as did the consumption of fertilisers and pesticides. The uneven distribution of agricultural activities in the different areas of the country meant that some livestock farmers produced more manure than they needed for their crops.

Until 1940, animal manure was the most important source of fertiliser. From 1950 onwards, however, the consumption of imported artificial nitrogen fertiliser rose to approximately 120,000 tonnes in 1960. By 1980, this figure had risen again to almost 400,000 tonnes. The amount of animal manure also rose in step with the growing pig population, from around 50,000 tonnes in 1900 to more than three times as much in the early 2000s.

As more nitrogen was introduced into the cycle in the agricultural areas, it began to spread to other areas of the country. Between 1950 and 1980, the amount of nitrogen introduced into the fields rose from approximately 100 kg per hectare to more than double that amount. The amount of nitrogen which was removed in the shape of agricultural products, however, only multiplied by 1.5. That meant that smaller and smaller amounts of the nitrogen added to the soil actually ended up in the agricultural products, and the amount of nitrogen introduced into the environment rose accordingly. In the middle of the 1980s, this amount was even greater. Around 230,000 tonnes seeped through the soil to the ground water or out into the watercourses, the lakes and the sea. Another 100,000 tonnes were sent out into the atmosphere.

Changes in the Environment
Rising amounts of organic matter from homes and industry led to an oxygen deficiency in the aquatic environment, and occasionally caused large numbers of fish to die. The emission of nitrogen and phosphorus led to increasing growth of algae, the decay of which produced greater oxygen deficiency. The content of nitrates in ground water used by the water works tripled between the 1950s and the 1980s. In some places, the nitrate content rose above 45 mg nitrogen per litre ground water. The emission of sulphur dioxide and nitrogen oxides to the air was damaging to people, animals and plants, as well as to buildings and materials, and led to both land and water becoming acidified. In some places, the amounts of heavy metals, pesticides and other toxins that were emitted were so great that fish and plants died or became unfit for human consumption because they contained too much poison.

Open Cycles
The change towards more open cycles, with greater movement of elements from one area to another, was not limited to Denmark. The country's 'export' and 'import' of chemicals also grew. This was first and foremost true of air-borne chemicals, but applied also to substances in the sea. At the beginning of the 1990s, Denmark emitted approximately 100,000 tonnes of sulphur (sulphur dioxide) a year, most of which drifted away to other countries. In return, we 'imported' approximately 34,000 tonnes of sulphur dioxide, mostly from Germany and England.

Unlike the sulphur dioxide, almost half of the ammonium emitted was deposited in Denmark. Most of it came from the agricultural areas, and only small amounts were introduced from other countries. The sum total of nitrate and ammonium deposits tripled between 1950 and 1980. Nitrogen was thereby spread across the whole landscape and provided additional nutrition for plants.

This, in turn, affected the ecological cycles, particularly in the lakes, moors and heaths which were lacking in nutrients.

Pollution Control and Environmental Protection

In the 1960s, the continued, wide-reaching changes in the ecological cycles increased the need for action. This is reflected in the extent and character of the measures that were instigated by the State in the area of the environment. Between 1945 and 1985, the number of new laws concerning 'the exterior surroundings' by far exceeded similar legislation introduced over the last 200 years. The regulations only really began to affect energy consumption and the

chemical cycles in the years leading up to and following the Environmental Protection Act of 1974.

In the beginning, the legislation was mostly aimed at limiting the emission of chemicals to the air, soil and water. The answer was felt to be purification and, to a lesser extent, an attempt to change production methods and the pattern of consumption. 'Pollution control' preceded 'environmental protection'.

Before 1950, the waste water from homes and industry was mostly sent into the watercourses, lakes and sea without really being treated in any way. This gradually changed. Between 1975 and the middle of the 1980s, the municipal water purifying plants took in an amount of waste

Where the environment is concerned, Denmark excels in the areas of planning and purification technology. This has helped to create a sound basis for the export of Danish environmental technology and expertise in connection with the treatment of dang-

erous waste and the purification of waste water and flue gas. Kommunekemi A/S, which was established in 1971 in Nyborg and is owned by Danish municipalities, has since 1986 treated approximately 100,000 tonnes of oil and chemical waste a year.

Viborg Purification Plant; a biological purification plant with open sedimentation tanks and active sludge tanks for the removal of organic material, phosphorus and nitrogen. The sewage is treated in digesting tanks and in the covered buildings. Public environmental planning and the treatment of wastewater from homes and industry are high on the agenda in Denmark. Environmental planning and the construction of purification plants have become important export commodities since the beginning of the 1980s.

water that corresponded to around 10 million p.e. (person equivalents). In 1970, 20% of this waste water was treated biologically. 15 years later, almost 80% passed through biological and biological-chemical purification plants, and at the beginning of the 2000s, some 90% of the waste water underwent further purification. In the middle of the 1980s, the plants emitted approximately 24,000 tonnes of nitrogen, some 7,000 tonnes of phosphorus and around 72,000 tonnes of organic matter to the aquatic environment. During the same period, the industry contributed some 5,000 tonnes of nitrogen, approximately 3,500 tonnes of phosphorus and almost 50,000 tonnes of organic matter.

Similar actions were introduced to combat the emission of dust particles, sulphur dioxide and nitrogen oxides to the air from industry and power stations. Higher smokestacks were built and longer waste water pipes constructed. This 'diluted the pollution'. These regulations were increasingly combined with actions aimed at the actual source of the pollution. Fuels containing high percentages of sulphur and heavy metals were replaced by others which caused less pollution. The pesticide action plan from 1986 aimed to halve the consumption of pesticides over a ten-year period. In 1985, this con-

sumption was almost 9,000 tonnes. The Chemical Law of 1980 also means that new compounds and products have to be evaluated by the environmental authorities before coming into use.

Regulations reduced Denmark's consumption of freon (CFCs) by 60% between 1986 and 1992 and since 1995 the use of CFC has been prohibited. Measures were also taken to reduce the consumption of heavy metals. Lead emissions from cars fell from around 900 tonnes in 1977 to approximately 30 tonnes in 1993. The reduction was partly due to lower duties being imposed on lead-free petrol compared to leaded petrol, and partly to the car industry's reaction to growing national environmental concerns.

Cleaner Environment, Cleaner Nature

From 1970 onwards, the growing interest in the environment was accompanied by a wish to make better use of the open country for recreational activities. This was particularly true amongst the urban population, who in 1970 accounted for approximately 80% of the total population as against approximately 40% at the beginning of the century. The need was influenced by longer holidays, shorter working hours and a greater surplus of money. From the middle of the 1980s attention also began to focus on providing a clean environment and a varied landscape to ensure that tourism, an important source of national income, would prosper.

Legislation gradually gained the dual objective of improving the environment and creating more 'nature'. Some rules came about as a result of Danish initiatives, others emerged as a result of co-operation with other EU countries. The first in-

An urban regeneration project in Kolding municipality was completed in 1994. The ecological considerations and values inherent in the project has brought it wide acclaim. The wastewater from a block containing 129 homes and 6 businesses is led away to the pyramid-shaped bioplant where it is purified using micro-organisms, plants and fish. The purified water is led into the ground water via a root zone plant. A sun cell plant supplies the bioplant, the footpath lighting, the water pumps and the compost boilers with electricity. Rainwater is collected for use in toilets.

cluded a series of action plans aimed at reducing the emission of chemicals to the aquatic environment. The Aquatic Environment Plan of 1987 aimed to halve the emission of nitrogen and to reduce the emission of phosphorus by 80% over a period of 5 years. This was to be done by further purification of the waste water from homes and industry, and a change in the production methods employed by the farming community.

It did not prove possible to realise all the goals set out by the Aquatic Environment Plan in the allotted time-scale. But just a few years after the plan had been instigated, it had produced a number of changes in the appearance of the landscape and the ecological cycles. In 1993 the emission of phosphorus to the aqua-

tic environment had almost been reduced to planned levels, whilst the emission of nitrogen had hardly changed. The effects on the aquatic

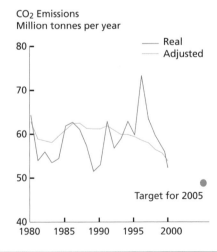

CO₂ Emissions
Million tonnes per year

Real
Adjusted

Target for 2005

In the 1990s several agreements were concluded on the reduction of the emissions of carbon dioxide (CO_2) which increase the greenhouse effect and, thus, change the world's climate. The adjusted figures show the estimated emissions deriving from national energy consumption when deducting the export of electricity produced on coal-fired power plants.
Source: The Ministry of the Environment.

plant and animal life were still few and far between. There were, however, striking signs in the open country that some of the changes intended by the new legislation had indeed taken place. The brown and black fields which had dominated the winter landscape during the past 30-40 years were gradually being replaced by green fields sown with winter cover crops and other types of vegetation. This was linked in particular to the efforts to reduce the emissions of nitrates to the ground water.

For the first time in over 30 years, whole fields covered in red poppies and blue cornflowers appeared in 1993. This setting aside of the land will help to limit the consumption of energy and fertilisers. But the aim, first and foremost, is to reduce the level of agricultural products being produced. This is also the objective of other EU regulations, including the agreement on marginal land such as low-lying meadows and sandy soils. This type of area is no longer to be intensively farmed but instead left to lie fallow, planted with trees or used for livestock grazing.

Lakes, watercourses and wetlands, which had been reclaimed and converted to arable land over the past few centuries, are now being re-created through regeneration and restoration efforts. Watercourses play a fundamental role in the water cycle. At the beginning of the 18th century, thousands of kilometres of ditches were dug as part of the plan to drain the arable land. At the end of the 19th century, a new series of drainage projects were instigated during which even the areas near the watercourses were reclaimed. At the same time, many open ditches and small watercourses were drained, the watering holes in the fields were dried out or filled in, and the watercourses were altered to straight canals. More pipes were laid and the watercourses were systematically managed so the fields could be kept dry. This reduced the distance the water had to travel to reach the sea, but it also destroyed the living conditions for the plants and animals in the watercourses, and reduced the ability of the water to handle household sewage and fertilisers. The development was reversed with the Watercourse Act of 1982, and previous management schemes have gradually been replaced by new methods which respect the animal and plant life and at the same time ensure that water is led off the fields. Buffer zones are also being created along the watercourses, lakes and windbreaks to ensure that fertilisers and pesticides do not spread as easily from the fields to these 'nature' areas. These zones also provide better living conditions for the wild plants and animals.

The conservation of meadows, commons and heaths has become more widespread in an attempt to retain the characteristic traits of the Danish landscape. The Forestry Act of 1989 aims to double the forested

SO₂ Emissions
1,000 tonnes per year

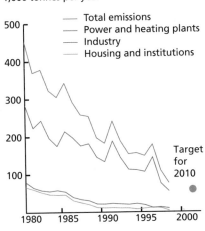

The conversion to fuels with a lower sulphur content and the purification of waste gases have helped reducing the emissions of sulphur dioxide (SO$_2$), especially from power plants and industries to a level below the target for 2010, that is 55,000 tonnes. Source: The Ministry of the Environment.

area over the course of the next 100 years.

Towards Closed Cycles and Sustainable Development

In the 1970s, national regulations increasingly tried to limit the consumption of energy and raw materials. Energy consumption has been reduced by insulating buildings more efficiently, and by using equipment and machinery with lower energy requirements. Higher environmental duties on energy consumption, along with increased use of renewable sources of energy such as solar and wind power, have also had an effect.

The rise in the consumption of raw materials has also been stemmed, in particular by the conversion to production methods using less energy and fewer new raw materials and, thus, creating less waste.

New products are analysed during their entire life cycle – 'from cradle to grave' – to control their effects on the environment. These measures make it possible to intervene in production phases characterised by a particularly high degree of resource consumption and pollution and furthermore, they ensure that as many products as possible can be recycled to manufacture new products. The obligation to produce green accounts and the introduction of environmental management that increases the companies' awareness of the production's environmental impact have had the same effect. Especially since the international environmental conference in Rio in 1992, the concept of sustainable development has become a guideline for environmental policies. In the early 2000s more than 3/4 of the Danish municipalities had begun the Agenda-21 work to support sustainable development through local strategies.

Carsten Hunding

Vegetation

The Danish flora consists of approximately 1,200 species of higher plants, i.e. pteridophytes, conifers and flowering plants. A couple of hundred of these species are imported or adventive species, anthropochores, which have been able to maintain their numbers through reproduction by seeds. Many of the medicinal plants of yore such as calamus and motherwort, and herbs, including lovage and ground elder, belong to this group together with water thyme, rice grass and giant hogweed. There still remain around 1,000 naturally native, indigenous, Danish species. Books on Danish flora may contain over 1,500 species, but more than 300 species of plants have not become naturalised

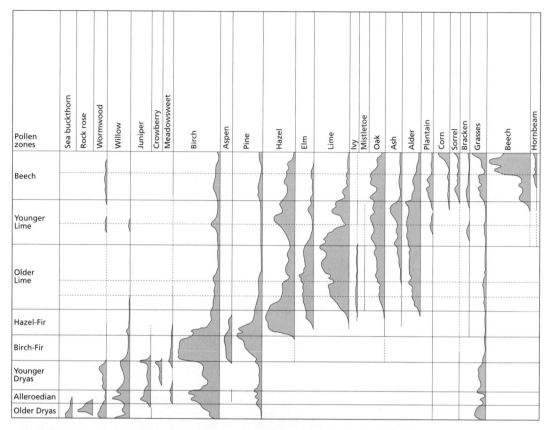

Pollen zones	Sea buckthorn	Rock rose	Wormwood	Willow	Juniper	Crowberry	Meadowsweet	Birch	Aspen	Pine	Hazel	Elm	Lime	Ivy	Mistletoe	Oak	Ash	Alder	Plantain	Corn	Sorrel	Bracken	Grasses	Beech	Hornbeam
Beech																									
Younger Lime																									
Older Lime																									
Hazel-Fir																									
Birch-Fir																									
Younger Dryas																									
Alleroedian																									
Older Dryas																									

Pollen diagram for East Denmark showing the development of the vegetation over the last 12,000 years, i.e. the last part of the last ice age and the present interglacial period. In the Birch-Fir period, the forest spread across Denmark and this period constitutes the beginning of the interglacial period. Pollen diagrams are constructed using borings from lakes and moors, and they provide information on the plant life of the past. A knowledge of the pollen composition from different periods can be used to date e.g. archaeological artefacts from which small amounts of pollen can be removed.

after their arrival, and constitute a very unstable and changeable element. Denmark's flora belongs to the temperate, nemoral deciduous forest zone.

Of the approximately 640 mosses found in Denmark, there are around 150 species of liverwort and some 490 leaf mosses and bog mosses; around 900 species of lichen have been found. The numbers for other groups of plants are more uncertain; there are some 3,000 species of large fungi and several thousand species of microscopic fungi. There are also some 350 species of attached algae, to which can be added a large number of plankton algae. Finally, there is an unknown number of bacterial species.

The Development of the Danish Flora

The present-day flora is the temporary result of a long period of development, which derives its character partly from the shifting glacial and inter-glacial periods. The last ice age continued for about 100,000 years and ended c. 11,500 years ago. During this long period glaciers covered eastern Denmark for only 10% of the time. For the remainder of the glacial period the flora consisted mostly of cold-tolerant plant species, the so-called dryas flora, many of which are today found widely scattered across Europe. There are, then, no extant plant communities of today corresponding to those found during the last ice age.

For the first thousand years after the ice age, the land was covered by forest; first birch and juniper, then birch and pine followed by hazel, which was later replaced by lime as the most common species of tree. On fertile ground there were few openings where light-demanding plants could thrive; instead, these species found suitable habitats in places where erosion prevented dense, permanent tree growth. The shore, in particular, was a refuge. This also apply for species belonging to the dryas flora which today are found on the chalky coastal cliffs near Hanstholm, Løgstør and Høje Møn. The coast of northwest Zealand, where rainfall is particularly low, is similarly a refuge for many of the plant species of the late glacial period. In the infertile parts of western Jutland the forests had a more open structure consisting of lime, hazel, some birch, oak, grasses and patches of heather.

Man's Influence on the Flora

Only with the introduction of agriculture around 4,000 BC did Man begin to exert any decisive influence on the flora. Forest areas were cleared, and a number of new habitats arose. Many plant species that had so far grown on raised coastlines, coastal cliffs and other places open to the light, now found new habitats in

Wild, Danish berries. Top: elder, *Sambucus nigra*. The flowers can be used to make elderflower syrup and the berries can be boiled to produce a drink which is high in vitamin C. Second from top: wood strawberry, *Fragaria vesca*. The 1/2–1 cm fruits have a fine, delicate taste. Third from top: blackberry, *Rubus fructicosus*. Bottom: bog whortleberry, *Vaccinium uliginosum*, which is common in West and North Jutland but rare in the rest of the country. The berries has less taste than their close relative the blueberry.

agricultural areas. Narrow-leafed plantain, sheep's bit, wormwood and many species of grass were characteristic inhabitants of pastures, while species of Chenopodiaceae could be found in cultivated fields. The wealth of species increased, and new habitats emerged. The oldest heathland areas date back to around 2800 BC; their numbers and extent subsequently increased and several stretches of heathland in central Jutland are only 600-700 years old. Cleared meadows became more common during the Iron Age when the scythe came into use. The oldest beech forests date back to around 1500 BC; this type of forest has since been common in eastern Denmark.

The greatest diversity of plant species was presumably reached in the Middle Ages and up to the first part of the 20th century before intensive farming was practiced and before artificial fertilisers and pesticides became widely used.

More than 150 years ago, 20-25% of the country had such a high water table that cultivation was impossible; through draining this has now been reduced to only 1-3%. The change has naturally been of great significance for the flora in the marshes, along lakes and streams, and a number of swamp species which were once widespread throughout the country are now rare and in danger of extinction.

Since the 1950s, the use of artificial fertilisers has increased significantly and nutrients are no longer a limiting factor in agricultural production. Consequently, the extensively used natural types lost their economic significance and were either turned into more productive areas or abandoned. Recent figures indicate that there are around 42,000 hectares of salt meadows, 46,000 hectares of fresh meadows and 7,600 hec-

tares of pasture land. There are approximately 70,000 hectares of heathland if dunes and raised logs are included. This represents a halving of the area in relation to the figures for 1960. The remaining culture-determined habitats have similarly been in decline – a trend which has continued despite legislation.

Agricultural methods have been shown to have far greater impact on the flora than traffic, flower picking or the digging up of flowers. In recent years, airborne nutrients and pesticides have also increasingly affected the composition of the vegetation, and in certain urban and agricultural areas air pollution has become a direct threat to the flora. The significant growth of traffic and urbanisation has resulted in native plants being reduced both in number and extent, while adventive species are spreading. Thus, the compo-

O.D. Ottesens painting *Spring in Charlottenlund Wood* (1860) depicts most of the spring flowers found in the wood under an old beech tree. The white wood anemone dominates the picture, but there are also yellow and blue wood anemones, wood sorrel, cowslips and oxlip, pilewort, hollow corydalis and some unopened early orchis and wood burdocks.

Dandelions by a gravemound. The common dandelion is a collective term for a whole group of different elementary species. All Danish varieties reproduce asexually, and a single plant can therefore produce a large body of flowers. The seeds are spread by the wind, and even small pieces of the tap-root can produce a new plant; the dandelion is almost impossible to get rid off.

sition of the Danish plant communities is changing.

Endangered Species

Denmark has a large number of higher plant species that are rare or becoming rare. Dependent on the underlying causes, such species are designated as acutely threatened or vulnerable. There are around 40 acutely threatened species in danger of disappearing within the near future, and this number is still rising.

Dune eyebright, *Euphrasia dunensis*, is only found in Denmark and is very rare. It grows on lime dunes in North Jutland (e.g. near Bulbjerg) and flowers in July-August.

Some 80 species are classed as vulnerable, meaning that they are expected to become acutely threatened. This number, on the other hand, is falling, something that is ascribed to the protection of various nature types through legislation together with successful care of the countryside and the protection of certain species, for instance all members of the orchid family are now protected.

Some habitats have turned out to be more threatened than others. This is partly reflected in the distribution of extinct, acutely threatened and vulnerable species related to the different areas. Most threatened are heathland, pastures, fringes and slopes open to the light, after which come meadows, marshes, bogs and springs, and finally forest areas. Lakes, streams and rivers are less threatened, and least threatened are the sea and salt-influenced coastal communities and the dunes. The major threats can be defined as overgrowing, planting, cultivation, draining, pollution and urbanisation.

Among the various plant groups, lichen are among the most exposed, with some 70% of species being threatened. Sulphur dioxide, nitrogen pollution and acidification are the most important reasons. As for fungi and the higher plants, 20-30% of the species are under threat, for reasons generally stemming from human activities.

Bent Aaby

Animal Life

The temperate northern coastal climate and the mostly fertile soil in a gently undulating landscape divided by fjords and sounds, together with the late arrival of flora and fauna in Denmark (after the last ice age) provide the most important conditions determining the animal life on which, today more than ever, Man has made his mark. On land, Danish animal life is clearly affected by intensive agriculture, urban development and the consequent pollution. At sea, human influence is seen especially in fishing, the discharge of sewage and the addition of nutrients, principally nitrates stemming from agriculture.

The Development of the Fauna

Along with the soil, damp, mild winters and cool summers have determined the natural types of vegetation. Originally, 80-90% of the country was covered by a mixed deciduous forest. Danish animal life was therefore predominantly a forest fauna, as it still is when reckoned in the number of animal species.

The undisturbed forest contains many species which, in a complicated food chain, make use of the

It is not surprising that the mute swan has been chosen as Denmark's national bird. A huge number of these birds overwinter in the country: whilst just 3-4 pairs were left when the mute swan was declared a protected species in 1926, the breeding population now consists of approximately 4,000 pairs. The shallow Danish waters provide ample food year round for moulting and overwintering mute swans and for non-breeding young birds. Up to 75,000 birds can be found here, or some 40% of the total northwest European population.

high and stable production of the forest so that scarcely anything is wasted. The forest is characterised by many specialised and often rare species. This is not true of the modern, rationally run and often planted forest. The lack of large, dead or dying trees and branches, together with a reduction in the number of wet areas, has led to a reduction in the number of animal species in these new forests.

It is impossible to determine accurately the total number of animal species in Denmark. In 1995 the National Forest and Nature Agency estimated the number of free, naturally occurring and breeding species of vertebrates in Denmark at 424, including 49 mammals, 209 birds, 5 reptiles, 14 amphibians, 37 freshwater fish and 110 saltwater fish. Far more uncertain is the estimated number of invertebrates, put at 21,000, of which insects alone account for 18,000. In 1997 the Danish catalogue ('Red List') of plants and animals most in need of protection showed that 54% of these had their habitat in the forest. This includes, for instance, the pine marten and 14 other species of mammal, 74 species of bird, 2 species of reptile, 5 species of amphibian, 15 species of freshwater fish and 964 species of beetle. These latter make up 26% of the beetles in need of protection.

Forests were formerly the dominant type of landscape; today it is agricultural land which covers almost 2/3 of the land area. Taking area into account, it is the fauna found on agricultural land which is most significant in Denmark. This may well be true in terms of the number of individuals, but is far from true in terms of the number of

Few know that Denmark has an indigenous population of bird spiders, but there is one species which is native to the country. The 15-17 mm *Atypus affinis* lives a hidden life inside a funnel of silk on warm, south-facing slopes. *Atypus* is often overlooked because of its secretive lifestyle, and was for a time believed to be extinct in Denmark until the species was rediscovered in East Jutland in 1994.

different species. The fauna found on agricultural land consists of a limited selection of species from the original fauna, supplemented by several other species introduced or advented by Man.

Whereas stability used to be a characteristic of the undisturbed forest, allowing many specialist species to settle and adapt, the conditions on agricultural land are, in contrast, very unstable. Fields are treated mechanically and chemically several times a year, and the vegetation cover is removed and changed, often annually. As a result, only a limited number of species can survive solely in cultivated areas. A large proportion of the animal life on agricultural land is consequently dependent on the availability of small biotopes in the form of live hedges, field margins, ponds, spinneys and other not cultivated areas.

Perennial crops, a minimal use of fertiliser and pesticides, and a closely interrelated and varied pattern of small biotopes are what produce the most abundant animal and plant life. But until recently, the trend has been in the exactly opposite direction. In future years some improvement is expected as a result of changed agricultural support systems and more active nature protection.

The hare, the partridge and the skylark presumably spread throughout the country in the wake of cultivation. The steep decline in these species in our days is probably due to the decreasing variation in crops, the decline in the number of biotopes and a reduction in the food available as a result of pesticides.

The drainage of wetlands as a result of agricultural methods has had a drastic effect on the fauna. In agricultural land, between 95% and 98% of the original wetlands have disappeared during the course of the 19th and 20th centuries. This is significant when we seek to explain why 5 out of 14 Danish amphibian species are today considered to be in need of protection.

The urban landscape becomes increasingly impoverished in fauna the nearer we come to the city centres, where the rock dove, the house sparrow and the brown rat are the only vertebrates certain to be found. But in a country with no mountains, buildings in the cities can provide homes for species such as rock doves, black redstarts and swifts that would otherwise be rare or no longer exist.

In the residential areas on the outskirts of towns, there is a far greater variety of animal life. Although the number of species is still limited, the number of individuals per unit of

The fox is becoming much more common in and around the towns. It lives on the small birds and rodents found in gardens and open spaces. It will also take leftovers which have been put out onto the terrace or the bird table for the birds, or even scraps which have been thrown in the bin.

area is very high. Here we find foxes, hedgehogs and house martens in addition to an array of birds species of which the most common are the house sparrow, tree sparrow, blackbird, great titmouse and starling.

Denmark has a sea area of 104,000 square kilometres and a land area of 43,000 square kilometres, meaning that around two thirds of Denmark consists of sea. What animals can thrive there depends, among other things, on the depth of the water, the current and the salinity. The almost ocean water of the North Sea, with a salt content of 3.5%, has a far greater number of species (approximately 1,500) than the brackish waters to the east of Bornholm, where the salt content is under 1% (around 200 species).

Danish waters are generally shallow; only in the Skagerrak does the depth exceed 100 metres. The bottom is usually soft and consists of sand or mud. This leads to a relative paucity of marine species, something that has not been improved over the last few decades by the arrival of large quantities of fertiliser from land. Large parts of the sea bed are now affected by an annual reduction in oxygen, and are no longer able to provide a habitat for perennial fauna. The fauna is richer in shallow waters, where the oxygen conditions are better, especially on reefs and mussel beds.

Marine animal life is rich and varied: Plankton, such as jellyfish and copepods float in the water; nekton such as porpoise, cod, herring and plaice swim around freely; sea-bed fauna can be divided into in-fauna in the seabed such as cockles and lug worms, and epi-fauna on top of the seabed such as common mussels, crabs and starfish.

Finally, there are seals and sea birds. Due to the combination of low coasts, shallow water, currents, salinity and nutrition, the Danish waters are unique in international significance as resting grounds or wintering grounds for sea birds. Over 20% of the total number of individuals of some 28 bird species appear in Danish waters every year. Many other species of migrant water birds are dependent on the Danish waters and coasts, making the regulation of hunting and other activity in these areas an important international responsibility for Denmark.

Lakes, rivers, marshes, dunes, moorland and salt meadows are all homes to specific animal and plant life. The first three are by nature highly nutritious and therefore both productive and home to many species. However, the injection of large amounts of fertiliser via water and

Pink-footed geese in West Jutland. The breeding population in Svalbard consists of approximately 30,000 geese which migrate at the end of September to the west coast of Jutland. They are found in particular around Vest Stadil Fjord and Filsø lake. In the middle of October, the birds fly on towards the Netherlands and Belgium but return at the end of December and in January to Tøndermarsken and Ballum Enge. They graze here for some time, and birds which came to the area weighing around 2.2 kilo generally put on between 700-800 gram; a useful energy reserve for their imminent migration. Between March and May, the geese move on to Svalbard. In many places they are given corn to lure them away from the freshly-sown fields.

air has generally had a negative effect on the number of species in all habitats. In the rivers, establishment of obstructions in the form of dams and water mills over the centuries has meant that most of the Danish migrant fish today need special attention. Thus sturgeon, alice shad, twaite shad and white-finned miller's thumb have disappeared from Denmark within the last hundred years.

Preservation and Nature Conservancy

Danish animal life is typical of a densely populated industrialised society. However, an ever more efficient management regime for the natural environment is under development, and consideration for the environment is being incorporated into the individual social sectors. The growing efforts being made to improve conditions for animal life are desperately needed. Conservation is needed for certain species such as the cormorant, the numbers of which, after it was protected in 1980, grew from 2,000 to 40,000 pairs in 2001. In the case of other species, such as the fire-bellied toad, the need is for the re-establishment of its habitats.

For other species the primary

An approximately 2.5 cm long tooth from the *Pholidosaurus* crocodile, found in 1987 at the base of the Jydegård formation in Robbedale, some 5 km southeast of Rønne. The formation dates back to the Early Cretaceous period. The deposits also contain traces of hybodontids, a number of different types of bony fishes such as pycnodontiforms, large ganoids and small primitive teleosts. The environment seems to have been a brackish or fresh lagune protected by a sand bank.

need is a more general change towards being 'nature friendly' in terms of production and the organisation of society. This applies especially to the animal life in the forests and on agricultural land. More untouched areas of forest, perennial crops, permanent pastures and other extensively exploited areas will have significance for the fauna, both the forest fauna of which there are many species, and the agricultural fauna so rich in individuals.

For all species of animal, as for nature as a whole, it is true that their continued presence and distribution in Denmark is in the hands of man more than anything else. In an intensively exploited land (and sea) such as ours, it is thus a social and political question as to how much and what kind of wildlife we want.

Peder Agger

History

History

Prehistory

The Palaeolithic Period (until c. 9300 BC)

Denmark was probably inhabited as far back as the last interglacial period some 120,000 years ago, and possibly also in the warmer phases during the last ice age. The oldest existing evidence of human habitation which has been found are the settlement sites of the reindeer hunters from the Bølling period, 12500-12000 BC; this was the first warm phase at the end of the last ice age. During the next warm phase, the Allerød period, 11800-11000 BC, the first open woodland appeared and reindeer, elk and giant deer became the staple diet for a growing population of hunters. The last cold phase, Younger Dryas, 11000-9300 BC, brought the tundra back and again left the stage open for a small population of reindeer hunters.

Grave from the Ertebølle culture, approximately 5000 BC, found on the Bøgebakken near Vedbæk in North Zealand. The young woman was buried along with her jewellery made of animal teeth. By her side lies a new-born baby placed on the wing of a swan. The discovery is on display at Gammel Holtegård.

The Mesolithic Period (c. 9300-3900 BC)

During the period after the end of the ice age, hunters spread across the extensive area which connected Denmark to England during the Continental period. The forest was relatively light in the beginning with bison, wild horses, elk and aurochs. In time, the forest became more dense and red deer and roe-deer became the commonest game. Settlements were often situated near the edges of lakes which have since become bogs. In the east of Denmark, the peat in these bogs has preserved a rich variety of weapons and tools, bones from slaughtered animals and the remains of dwellings, including hut floors made of wood and bark. During the Atlantic period, 6400-3900 BC, the sea level rose so much that the northern parts of Denmark were divided into islands, and deep fjords cut into the landscape. A dense forest dominated by limetrees spread

The rib of a red deer with a flint arrowhead, found near Maglelyng in Store Åmose Bog in Zealand. The animal survived its confrontation with the Stone Age hunters around 4500-3700 BC.

The passage grave known as King Svend's Mound on Lolland is an example of the megalithic tombs of the early peasant culture; it was built around 3200 BC. Approximately 2,500 dolmens and gallery graves have been preserved in Denmark, but they represent only a fraction of the many thousands which were originally erected.

across the land. The population was found mostly near the coasts and lived on fish and shellfish, supplemented by hunting and sealing. Food scraps were piled up in kitchen middens which contained huge numbers of oyster shells. Grave finds bear witness to care and respect for the dead.

The Neolithic Period (3900-1700 BC)
Agriculture and animal husbandry were introduced in Denmark c. 3900 BC. Wheat and barley were grown and oxen, sheep, goats and pigs domesticated. Large parts of the land were cultivated during the oldest peasant culture, 3900- 2800 BC, and the earliest farmers were energetic builders. They constructed large assembly areas surrounded by moats and palisades like the one found near Sarup on Funen. They also built the oldest stone burial monuments, the dolmens and the passage graves, many thousands of which have been preserved in Denmark. Flint mines were opened and a whole new industry emerged which specialised in the production of elegant, polished flint axes. Large numbers of offerings have been

found, including clay pots, flint tools and amber ornaments, and there is evidence of human and animal sacrifices. The first metal was brought into the country from Central Europe in the shape of simple ornaments and flat axe heads made of copper.

A picture of a changing lifestyle emerges with the finds from the Single Grave Culture (the period 2800-2400 BC). The ritualistic existence of earlier communities seems to have disappeared. Our knowledge

A collection of flint axes from Hagel-bjerggård near Ringsted, approximately 3500 BC. The flint from the white chalk in East Denmark is ideal for the production of this type of tool. Axes and other implements were often thrown into lakes or rivers as offerings to higher powers.

Historical Overview

12000-9300 BC	Late Ice Age. Immigration of the first hunters.
9300-3900 BC	Mesolithic Period. Hunting and fishing.
3900-1700 BC	Neolithic Period. Farming and animal husbandry. Dolmens and passage graves are built.
1700-500 BC	Bronze Age.
500 BC-750AD	Iron Age. Rudimentary conurbations in the 8th century.
866-867	The Vikings capture York.
C. 965	Harald I Bluetooth introduces Christianity in Denmark.
1157-1241	The Age of the Valdemars. Denmark gains supremacy over large parts of the southern Baltic areas.
1241	*Jyske Lov* (Jutlandic Law).
1282	Erik V (Klipping) is the first Danish king to seal a coronation charter.
1286	Erik V (Klipping) is murdered in Finderup Barn.
C. 1350-1400	Plague, the Black Death; many farms are deserted.
1397-1523	The Kalmar Union with Norway and Sweden. However, Sweden breaks away for long periods.
1479	The foundation of the University of Copenhagen.
1520	The Massacre of Stockholm; Christian II executes more than 80 Swedish opponents.
1534-1536	The Count's Feud, civil war in Denmark.
1536	The Reformation. Norway is formally incorporated into Denmark.
1563-1570	The Nordic Seven Years' War.
1611-1613	The Kalmar War between Denmark and Sweden.
1625-1629	Denmark's participation in the Thirty Years' War (the Kaiser War).
1643-1645	The Torstensson Feud. Parts of Denmark and Norway are ceded to Sweden.
1657-1660	The Karl Gustav Wars. Denmark cedes all provinces east of Øresund, with the exception of Bornholm, to Sweden.
1660-1661	Absolutism is introduced.
1675-1679	The Scania War between Denmark and Sweden.
1683	Christian V's Danish Law.
1709-1720	The Great Nordic War.
1733	The introduction of adscription.
1755-1807	The Palmy Days, Danish shipping and trade flourish.
1788	The abolition of adscription.
1801	The Battle of Copenhagen.
1807-1814	At war with England. Denmark cedes Norway to Sweden at the Peace of Kiel in 1814.
1844	The first folk high school is established in Rødding.
1848	The abolition of absolutism.
1848-1851	The First Schleswig War. The Three Years' War.
1849	The June Constitution, Denmark's first free constitution.
1864	The Second Schleswig War; Denmark has to cede Schleswig, Holstein and Lauenburg.
1870-1901	Constitutional struggle between conservatives and liberals.
1871	A socialist movement is founded.
1901	Change of political system; introduction of Cabinet responsibility.
1914-1918	Denmark is neutral during the First World War.
1915	Constitutional reform, women and servants are enfranchised.
1920	Reunion with South Jutland after a plebiscite.
1940-1945	Denmark occupied by Germany.
1943	The August Uprising. Government by Civil Service Heads; The Danish Freedom Council is formed.
1944	Iceland becomes an independent republic.
1945	Denmark is a founder member of the UN.
1949	Denmark joins NATO.
1953	A new Constitution and a new Act of Succession, the Landsting (second chamber) is abolished and female succession is rendered possible.
1973	Denmark is admitted to the EC and after a landslide election three new parties enter the Danish Parliament the Folketing.
1979	Greenland obtains Home Rule.
1993	Denmark joins the EU.
1998	Denmark adopts the Amsterdam Treaty.
2000	Danish participation in the Single European Currency, the euro, is rejected by referendum.

of this period is almost exclusively based on discoveries from grave mounds, where single graves indicate equal respect for both men and women. From this time onwards, carts were used for transport and large areas were cultivated. Settlements were also found near the coasts where people lived mainly by fishing, hunting and sealing.

The last period of the Stone Age, 2400-1700 BC, known as the Dagger period, coincided with the early Bronze Age in the British Isles and Central Europe. Weapons and tools made of copper and bronze were introduced and provided a challenge for those who made flint tools. The result can be seen in the excellent examples of imitations in flint of foreign bronze daggers. At the end of the period, the production of metal implements finally gained a foothold, and there is evidence of an emerging new social stratification. This is reflected in finds from settlements with both small and much larger long houses. Burial customs varied from simple interments below ground or in passage graves, to burials in stone cists or log coffins covered with large mounds.

The Bronze Age (c. 1700-500 BC)
The domed grave mounds from the early Bronze Age still characterise the Danish landscape. The mounds contain burials which often give an accurate picture of the people from that period. The National Museum's collection of oak-coffin graves shows people dressed in their costumes such as the famous find from Egtved with a young lady wearing a string skirt. Women have been buried with their hair piled up in elaborate styles and wearing their bronze and gold jewellery, men with their weapons. Huge mounds and the remains of monumental long houses point to

class differences within the farming community. During the early Bronze Age, until c. 1100 BC, these farmers reclaimed more and more land for cultivation and especially grazing. The fields were ploughed with the primitive plough of the period, the ard, and covered an area of between 300 square metres and 1,000 square metres. Dwellings were situated by themselves or in small groups, and the same site was often inhabited for several centuries. From the late Bronze Age, c. 1100-500 BC, evidence has been found of princely burials. One example is the Lusehøj mound near Voldtofte on Funen. This was a centre of affluence, as evidenced by the concentration of gold finds there. Another such centre has been found near Boeslunde on Zealand.

Rock carvings and bronze sculptures, such as the Sun Chariot from Trundholm, provide an insight into the religious beliefs of the Bronze Age. Pictures of ships are very common. Finds of lures, bronze helmets, ceremonial axes, weapons and women's ornaments also point to various forms of worship. Imported items such as weapons, shields and bronze vessels show that there was a lively exchange with southern parts of Central Europe, particularly the Alpine region.

The Iron Age (c. 500 BC-750 AD)
Our knowledge of the earliest Iron Age is very limited. The graves were simple cremation graves and farm dwellings were small and surrounded by fences. These were the first signs of organised villages. In time, the dwellings changed in design and farms became larger. Just before the beginning of our era, there are signs of an increasingly stratified society. The few miraculously well-preserved bog bodies bring us very close to the people of that time. The Tollund

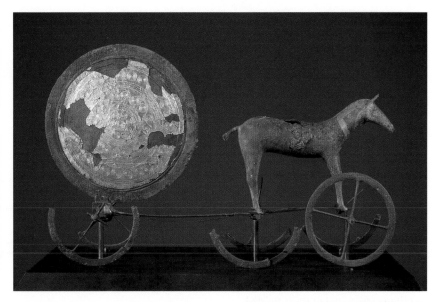

Lure from the younger Bronze Age, approximately 900-700 BC, found in 1808 in a bog near Tellerup on Funen. It is still possible to produce a tune on the lures which were originally played in pairs. During the Bronze Age their deep, resounding tones would have been heard at ceremonies and formal events.

The Sun Chariot from Trundholm Bog in the northwest of Zealand, found in 1902. The sun, drawn by a horse, is placed on a six-wheeled chariot. The sun disc is approximately 26 cm across; it is made of two bronze plates which have been soldered together using an outer ring. One side has been gold plated. Details of the horse are rendering eyes, mane and harness. The image of the horse-drawn sun is known from other finds and can be linked with the religious beliefs of the Bronze Age. The Sun Chariot was offered as a sacrifice around 1400 BC. Today, it is one of the most important exhibits at The National Museum in Copenhagen.

Man and the Grauballe Man date from the early Iron Age and were probably killed and thrown into the water as punishment or as an offering to the gods. The most remarkable finds from the pre-Roman Iron Age (500-1 BC) have also been discovered in bogs. The oldest war booty offering, known as the Hjortspring find, contains the remains of the oldest prehistoric Danish vessel. It is of the same type as the craft known from Bronze Age rock carvings. The weapons found with it, however, are of Celtic origin. Other finds from the end of the period include the Dejbjerg wagons and the large cauldrons from Brå and Gundestrup which bear witness to connections with the Celts. These precious vessels were brought back during the turbulent period when the Germanic Cimbrians and Teutons were roaming Europe and attacking the northern boundary of the Roman Empire.

Well-preserved finds, dating back to the beginning of our era, from settlements and village mounds in Jutland shed light on agriculture in the early Iron Age. Small fields, bounded by low earthen banks, represent a farming method which began during the Bronze Age and was used until around 200-300 AD. Many of these prehistoric fields were abandoned during the early Iron Age and have therefore been preserved. The fields may have been abandoned because the soil was exhausted, or because of the social and economic changes which took place during the course of the Iron Age. These changes led to larger farms, new farming methods with the main emphasis on cattle, as well as changes in the structure of ownership. The history of agricultural developments throughout the first millennium AD is illustrated by large settlement excavations like the one near Vorbasse in South Jutland where it is possible to follow the development from the small scattered farmhouses of the early Iron Age to villages with large farms from the late Iron Age.

There are numerous finds of Roman objects such as weapons, elaborate household utensils and precious metals from the Roman Iron Age (c. 0-400 AD). During the early Roman Iron Age (c. 0-200 AD) imported items consisted of high-quality handicrafts. The silver cups from the Hoby find come from Capua in the south of Italy, and may have been a gift from an important Roman. During the late Roman Iron Age (c. 200-400 AD), imports were mostly mass-produced provincial Roman goods. The many imported items in the Danish finds point to close trade links with the Roman Empire, mainly via the sea routes. A clear shift seems to have taken place in several ways at the transition from the early to the late Roman Iron Age. The main body of the war booty finds from Thorsbjerg, Vimose, Illerup and Nydam date back to the late Roman period. They bear witness to conflicts be-

tween regional communities immediately prior to the Migration period. Many of the oldest ramparts date back to the Roman Iron Age. Advanced maritime defences included barriers consisting of connected rows of piles. The clinker-built boats from Nydam Mose were not equipped with sails but were rowed, and represent a stage in ship-building which led to the Viking ships. The oldest coastal trading centres date from c. 300 AD, and there are also signs of a governing elite who may have exercised control over large areas. Graves rich in treasure have been found, amongst other places, at

In 1950, the well-preserved body of a man from the older Iron Age was found in Tollund Bog near Silkeborg. The body has been carbon-14 dated to 400 BC. The Tollund man was hanged, probably for breaking the law. Apart from a pointed skin bonnet and a belt, he had been buried naked in the bog. His head and a replica of his body are on display at the Silkeborg Museum; it was not possible to preserve the rest of the corpse.

Small figure (6.7 cm high) made of sheet gold found near Slipshavn by Nyborg. The naked man with a neck ring is probably a deity from around 500 AD.

Himlingøje in East Zealand. In Gudme on Funen, a chiefly residence with huge halls controlled a centre for trade, craft and worship. The earliest runic inscriptions in Old Norse have been found on the weapons and tools from the war booty offerings.

The Golden Horns from Gallehus in South Jutland, the most important prehistoric Danish gold find with the longest of the ancient runic inscriptions, were stolen in 1802. The horns came from the early Germanic Iron Age (c. 400-550 AD), a period which is well represented by a number of hoards with late Roman gold coins, neck and arm rings and gold bracteates. From the beginning of the late Germanic Iron Age, c. 550-750 AD, there are remarkable finds of small plaquettes, *guldgubber*, with tiny pictures of men and women. These seem to be concentrated around

particular sites which once had a central function, such as Sorte Muld on Bornholm. The traditional Nordic artistic style was developed on these gold plaquettes, as well as on ornaments and metal mounts produced during the Germanic Iron Age. The semi-abstract animal ornamentation, which was used well into the Viking period, was dominant. The oldest royal hall at Lejre in Zealand and the oldest Dannevirke ramparts, both from the second half of the 7th century, may be evidence that the country was governed by a royal power during the late Iron Age.

Poul Otto Nielsen

The Viking Age

Throughout its early history, Denmark had many contacts with the outside world, but with the beginning of the Viking Age, c. 750 AD, the country really became part of European history. The Danes became most notorious as the Vikings who plundered churches and monasteries, but behind this rather one-sided picture there lies a far more complex interplay of political and cultural factors.

The large Jelling Stone is sometimes referred to as Denmark's birth certificate. Harald Bluetooth had a runic inscription carved into this side of the stone in memory of the fact that he 'made the Danes Christians'. A relief carving represents Christ on the cross, depicted here as the conquering ruler; the stone was probably painted. The king also had a wooden church built in Jelling to which he moved the body of his father, Gorm the Old, who had previously been buried in the northernmost of the two Jelling mounds. The stone can today be found outside the present church in Jelling, on the very spot where it was first erected.

The Viking fort at Trelleborg lies near Slagelse on a promontory between two rivers. The fort was built according to a strict geometrical plan: there are openings in the circular ramparts at all four points of the compass; these were connected by wood-block paved tracks. This divided the open space (156 m diameter) into four sections where wooden buildings constructed around a quadrangle were built. The 19 m wide ramparts were surrounded by a moat, and outside the ramparts were another 15 houses which were equally protected by a moat which also encompassed the fort's burial site. Similar complexes have been found in the northeast of Jutland (Fyrkat), in North Jutland (Aggersborg) and in Odense (Nonnebakken). The Trelleborg and Fyrkat forts have been dated using dendrochronology to around 980; the two other forts are thought to date from the same period.

The Unification of the Country and Royal Power

As early as 700, Denmark was ruled by a stronger royal power than had existed before; a king named Angantyr (Ongendus) can probably be linked to Ribe where a regulated seasonal trading centre was established just after 700.

Around 700, the Merovingian domination crumbled and the outlying provinces of the Frankish empire gained their independence. This paved the way for a Danish display of power in the southern parts of the North Sea area with Saxony and Friesland, and Ribe became Denmark's first international trading centre. When Charlemagne and the Carolingians attempted to re-establish the power of the Franks around 800, it resulted in clashes with the Danes under Godfred; he would neither relinquish his power in Friesland and amongst the Abodrites, nor renounce the tributary income which he had obtained during the weakness of the Merovingians. In order to safeguard this income, he moved the traders from the Abodrite area to Hedeby, a town he had recently established in what is now North Germany, and fortified Denmark's southern border with a new rampart. Godfred's battles with Charlemagne were not just simple poaching on his preserves, but clashes between two empire builders.

Godfred was murdered in 810 and after his death, several branches of the royal family fought for power. The power struggle often forced those involved into exile, and Denmark's rulers were constantly under threat from rivals who returned home with booty from Viking raids or, like Harald Klak, with reinforcements from abroad. After 827, Horik I, son of Godfred, emerged as sole ruler until a bloody civil war in the middle of the 9th century killed both him and many others.

Domestic affairs are obscure until some time around 900, when a dynasty which is thought to have returned from Sweden seized power. Then followed the Jelling dynasty who had also returned from abroad and came to power at the beginning of the 10th century. Harald Bluetooth (Harald I) claims on his runic stone in Jelling to have conquered all of Denmark. Possibly the word Denmark – which first appears at the end of the 9th century but is probably much older – only covered the Danish territory east of the Great Belt, and Harald must therefore have added these to the Jutland kingdom he inherited from his father, Gorm the Old.

There was a great deal of building activity throughout the Viking Age around Denmark, pointing to a royal power capable of organising the resources of the country for a common purpose. Many examples are from Harald Bluetooth's time: New additions to the Dannevirke ramparts, the fortresses of the Trelleborg type, the Ravning Enge bridge and the Jelling complex, and it is possible that Hedeby, Ribe and Århus were all fortified during his reign. In order to complete these projects, the population must have been put under an obligation to work, but there is very little evidence concerning the organisation of society. There is not likely to have been any strict military organisation of the type which emerged during the subsequent wars. The most important basis for the royal power has probably been its control over the chieftains who held the real power on a local level. The royal housecarls would have been the real instrument of power. Knud (Canute) the Holy (Knud IV) attempted to extend the royal powers considerably by instituting new royal rights, and by suggesting that public administration of justice should replace the private one. His demands for fixed contributions towards the military seem to have cost him his life.

At a very early stage, the king received an income from trade and probably also from mintage. Sceattas may have been coined at Ribe in the 720s, and Danish coins were also minted during the reigns of Horik I and Harald Bluetooth. During the reign of Knud the Great (Knud II), there were mints in several places around the country.

The area acquired by Denmark during the Viking Age lasted more or less during the Middle Ages. Of all the Scandinavian countries, Denmark had the largest population living in the smallest area. Southern Norway was considered part of the Danish kingdom, and the Danish influence in Norway was so strong that Norwegian chieftains only managed to gain control of larger parts of Norway during Danish periods of weakness. Sweden was united even later than that, and the Danes exerted a strong influence both during the Viking Age and the following centuries.

Danish monarchs

before 714 mentioned 777, 782, 798	Angantyr (Ongendus)	1157-1182	Valdemar I den Store (Valdemar I the Great)
	Sigfred	1182-1202	Knud VI (Canute VI)
before 812	Harald	1202-1241	Valdemar II Sejr (Valdemar II the Victorious)
mentioned			
804 d. 810	Godfred (Godfrey)	1241-1250	Erik IV Plovpenning (Erik IV Ploughpenny)
810-812	Hemming	1250-1252	Abel
812-813	Harald Klak and Reginfred	1252-1259	Christoffer I
		1259-1286	Erik V Klipping
813-827	several sons of God-fred together	1286-1320	Erik VI Menved
		1320-1326	Christoffer II
827-854	Horik I	1326-1329	Valdemar III
854-864/873	Horik II Child	1329-1332	Christoffer II
mentioned 873	Sigfred and Halvdan	1332-1340	(interregnum)
after 891	Helge	1340-1375	Valdemar IV Atterdag
	Olaf 'from Sweden'	1375-1387	Oluf II Håkonsson
	Gnupa	1387-1412	Margrete I
	Sigtryk	1412-1439	Erik VII af Pommern (Erik VII of Pomerania)
mentioned 909/916	Knud I Hardegon (Hardeknud Svend-sen)	1440-1448	Christoffer III af Bayern (Christoffer III of Bavaria)
mentioned 936, d. 958	Gorm the Old		
d. 987 at the latest	Harald I Bluetooth	**The House of Oldenborg**	
mentioned 1014	Svend I Tveskæg (Svend Forkbeard)	1448-1481	Christian I
		1481-1513	Hans
1014-1018	Harald II	1513-1523	Christian II
1018-1035	Knud II den Store (Canute II the Great)	1523-1533	Frederik I
		1533-1534	(interregnum)
1035-1042	Knud III Hardeknud (Canute III Harde-canute)	1534-1559	Christian III
		1559-1588	Frederik II
		1588-1648	Christian IV
1042-1047	Magnus (I) den Gode (Magnus the Good)	1648-1670	Frederik III
		1670-1699	Christian V
1047-1076	Svend II Estridsen	1699-1730	Frederik IV
1076-1080	Harald III Hen	1730-1746	Christian VI
1080-1086	Knud IV den Hellige (St Canute IV)	1746-1766	Frederik V
		1766-1808	Christian VII
1086-1095	Oluf I Hunger	1808-1839	Frederik VI
1095-1103	Erik I Ejegod (Erik I the Evergood)	1839-1848	Christian VIII
		1848-1863	Frederik VII
1104-1134	Niels		
1134-1137	Erik II Emune	**The House of Glücksborg**	
1137-1146	Erik III Lam	1863-1906	Christian IX
1146-1157	Svend III Grathe, Knud V (Canute V) and Valdemar I den Store (Valdemar I the Great)	1906-1912	Frederik VIII
		1912-1947	Christian X
		1947-1972	Frederik IX
		1972-	Margrethe II

The Viking treasure from Lymose Forest, a silver cache found in 1942 on the northern tip of Falster. Eleven pieces of silver and 393 coins were found, all foreign: 1 Arabian dirham, 1 Byzantine coin, 9 English and 382 German coins. The treasure was hidden in the ground around 1000. The majority of the coins come from the area near Harzen where coins were minted and where silver was found at the end of the 10th century in Rammelsberg. The find shows the importance these mines had for all of northern Europe.

The Viking Expeditions

The Viking expeditions which, from c. 800, made the Scandinavians known and feared in large parts of Europe, varied from war between states to interference in each other's affairs and coastal raids. The expeditions were previously thought to have been connected with mass emigration from Scandinavia, but it is now believed that the armies numbered in the hundreds rather than in the thousands and that they were primarily interested in pillage, even though a number of them ended up settling in England and Normandy.

From around 830, internal strife in the Frankish empire allowed Danish chieftains, who were often exiled members of the Danish royal family, to demand tributes from the Franks; others chose to fight alongside the Franks against other Vikings, or to take part in their internal battles. The Viking raids culminated in the 880s with a prolonged siege of Paris. A number of chieftains were granted fiefs near the mouths of rivers in exchange for preventing other Vikings from gaining access to the waterways. Only a single fief, Normandy, was to last.

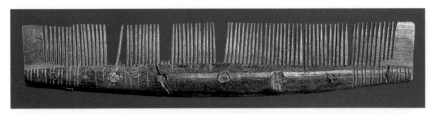

This comb from the late Viking Age was found in a burned-down pit house in Århus. The inscription, in Danish runes, reads *HIKUIN*, which is probably the English name *Hægwin*. Combs, which were some of the most common personal effects, were often made by professional craftsmen.

England and Ireland were regularly visited by Vikings from around 800. To begin with, they simply pillaged the area and disappeared again, but in time they stayed through the winter and took part in local conflicts as political parties, not least in Ireland. In England, a Viking army managed to conquer three of the four Anglo-Saxon kingdoms 865-80, and the Danes settled here for good. Place names point to a strong Danish influence in North and East England, even though the Danes in large parts of the area came under English kings before 920. Renewed Viking raids on England towards the end of the 10th century finally allowed the Danish kings to conquer the country. Svend Forkbeard (Svend I) began to demand tributes shortly after he became king of Denmark. He was quickly joined by other Viking chieftains from both Denmark, Norway and Sweden. He died in 1014 shortly after having conquered England, but Knud the Great reconquered the country in 1016. He became king of England, Denmark and Norway and even managed to gain some control in Sweden, but never managed to establish a lasting empire.

Trade and Towns
Denmark traded extensively with the rest of Europe during the time of the Viking expeditions. Ribe became a seasonal trading place as early as 700, and both Ribe and Hedeby, which is believed to have had a stable population of around 1,000 during the Viking Age and probably more during the peak season, developed into important towns. More towns appeared during the 11th century: Viborg and Odense which, like Ringsted, were old thingsteads and religious centres where many people often gathered, Århus, Aalborg, Slagel-

Our knowledge about Viking ships was considerably increased when five different vessels were found in Roskilde Fjord near Skuldelev. The find was excavated in 1957-1962. Copies have subsequently been made of four of these ships, and practical experiments have given us greater insight into the navigation methods of the time. Seen here is *Helge Ask*, a copy of wreck number 5, a small warship from around 1040.

Harald Bluetooth is said to have been converted to Christianity by a missionary named Poppo. Poppo (with the halo) is here seen baptising the king. The embossed gilded copper plate is one of seven found in Tamdrup Church near Horsens which depict the king's conversion. They were originally made for a reliquary for Poppo. The plates, which are believed to date from the 13th century, are on display at the National Museum.

se, Roskilde, Lund in what is now Sweden, and many others. Roskilde and Lund both emerged as centres of the royal power and the Church. Coins were minted in all these towns; money economy was developed during the Viking Age. Many different goods were imported from near and far; imports from Norway such as iron and soapstone, and other goods from Sweden and western Europe,

all found their way to the Danish villages. Less is known about the goods exported from Denmark, but these may have included perishable goods such as cattle and timber. When Arab traders made the long journey to Hedeby, however, they came to buy slaves, which the Vikings also sold in markets around Europe and the Orient.

Transport was generally via sea routes; the Vikings had many different types of ship, including large and small warships and merchant ships which sailed the domestic waters and the oceans. It was previously believed that the Vikings were pirates one day and traders the next, but a large, heavy merchant ship was hardly the ideal tool on a Viking expedition. Road traffic by wagon or by sledge during the winter also played an important role, and many bridges were built during the Viking Age, including the one over Ravning Enge.

The Introduction of Christianity
These contacts with the outside world brought strong cultural influ-

In 1998, in Nybro north of Varde in West Jutland, archaeologists found a great bridge and road construction dating from 761, the early Viking Age. The construction is 50-60 metres long and is well-preserved. It might have formed part of the road from Ribe where an important trading post was founded in the beginning of the 8th century.

ences into the country, not least as regards religion. As early as 700, a missionary named Willibrord sought to bring Christianity to the Danes. Missionary work was closely connected to politics from the very beginning. As well as wanting to spread Christianity, the Franks wanted to gain a foothold in Denmark, and some of those involved in the fight for the Danish throne proved willing to help. Harald Klak sought the help of Louis the Pious (Louis I) and prompted a Frankish invasion of Jutland in 815; in 826 he was baptised, but when he was banished from Denmark the following year, his missionary Ansgar failed to make much progress; only 25 years later did he manage to establish churches at Hedeby and Ribe, and these only survived for a very short period of time. Denmark's conversion to Christianity more than 100 years later followed strong political pressure from Germany. In 948, Otto the Great nominated bishops for the dioceses of Schleswig, Ribe and Århus under the archdiocese of Hamburg-Bremen. Put under such pressure, Harald Bluetooth himself embraced Christianity around 965, but chose to be baptised by a missionary known as Poppo, who did not hail from Hamburg-Bremen, and it is not known whether the bishops who were nominated in 948 ever came to work in Denmark – Harald's hostile relations with Germany would seem to have made it very unlikely. Svend Forkbeard and Knud the Great fetched clergymen to Denmark from England, and Knud probably contemplated connecting the Danish Church to the English, possibly with Roskilde as the archiepiscopal see subordinated to Canterbury just like York. Around 1060, Svend Estridsen (Svend II) introduced a proper church organisation with eight dioceses:

Schleswig, Ribe, Århus, Viborg, Vendsyssel, Odense, Roskilde and Lund. He also sought to establish an independent Danish archiepiscopal see, but this was not achieved until 1103 when Erik Ejegod (Erik I) made Lund the archiepiscopal see for the whole of Scandinavia.

Peasant society in the Viking Age
It was previously thought that society was made up of farmers who were all free and equal, who owned smallholdings and who sat on district and national things and had their say in the affairs of their society. It has become clear, however, that the distribution of wealth was very uneven and that only a small percentage of the population enjoyed full civic rights. Great landowners owned huge properties and the land was to a large extent divided up into large farms which were far bigger than smallholdings, and were often

Denmark during the Viking Age, showing the towns and the most important forts.

Farming during the Viking Age was predominantly based on animal husbandry, and the villages moved within their surrounding area at intervals of some hundreds of years. These moves ceased in the centuries after the Viking Age, and it was only then, in connection with a transition to grain cultivation which entailed extensive land clearing, that the division of the large farms into smaller plots began. This led to the creation of many new settlements with names ending in -*torp* (now -*rup*, -*drup*, -*trup* and -*strup*), -*rød*, etc., names which are still found on the map of Denmark today.

Niels Lund

Frescoes often provide a glimpse of the hard conditions people lived under during the early Middle Age. The example seen here comes from around 1125-1150 and is found in Todbjerg Church north of Århus. It shows how hard man had to work to cultivate the soil. The painting depicts the banishment of Adam and Eve from the Garden of Eden, and their subsequent toil. Adam is shown using a hoe like the farmers of his time; Eve is seen spinning yarn.

grouped in villages. We often meet the leading men of the local communities in the runic inscriptions. *Alle* on the Glavendrup stone was a *gode*, a chieftain with both religious and secular duties, like *Roulv* on the Helnæs stone. These chieftains would have had their own *lith*, their own troop of warriors, as did the chieftains long after the Viking Age. The ordinary men and women appear only rarely in the historical sources. Prisoners of war often became thralls, and thralls have been found at burial sites, but nothing is known about the thralls themselves or the effect which this practice of bondage had on society. Some craftsmen were thralls, others were clearly free and travelled round between the towns and markets, working also on the farms.

It used to be commonly believed that the Viking Age brought about a wave of emigration and domestic colonisation within Denmark. It was therefore thought that the population increased at a rapid rate, and that the country was overpopulated. The internal expansion of settlements which had been thought to have occurred during the Viking Age did not, however, take place until later.

The Middle Ages

The murder in 1086 of Knud the Holy (Knud IV) by the Danish nobles put a temporary stop to the radical expansion of the Danish royal power. After this, the kings were forced to accept that they had to rule in accordance with the interests of the great nobles and the clergy. The position of the Church was strengthened after the creation of an independent Danish archiepiscopal see at Lund in 1103 and up to the middle of the 12th century, the royal power was further weakened by internal strife between the descendants of Svend Estridsen. The fight for the throne led to a number of murders within the royal family. In 1131, Prince Magnus killed his rival Knud Lavard in Haraldsted Skov near Ringsted. This period of violence only ended in 1157 when Knud Lavard's son, Valdemar the Great (Valdemar I), defeated his opponents and seized the throne.

The Great Period of the Valdemars 1157-1241
That is how Danish historians describe the period which followed.

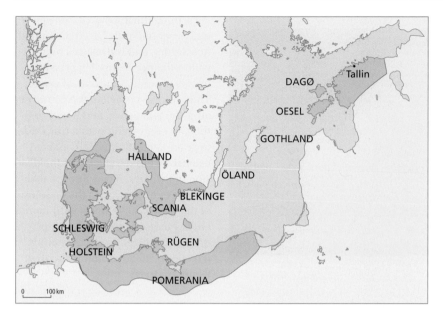

DAGØ

Tallin

OESEL

GOTHLAND

HALLAND

ÖLAND

BLEKINGE

SCANIA

SCHLESWIG

HOLSTEIN

RÜGEN

POMERANIA

0   100 km

Danish expansion policies in the first two decades of the 13th century created a short-lived Baltic empire which extended as far as Estonia

Under Valdemar the Great (Valdemar I), and his two sons Knud VI and Valdemar the Victorious (Valdemar II), the power of the Crown was decisively strengthened. The Wendic tribes which had terrorised the land were also defeated at this time, and the Danish territory expanded considerably. In 1169 the Danes took over Arkona, a Slavic place of worship on the island of Rügen, and put it under the Episcopal seat of Roskilde. In 1219 they gained control of Estonia during the crusades. Holstein was also incorporated into the extensive kingdom of the Valdemars and the town of Lübeck paid homage to the Danish king as their overlord. Danish power culminated around 1200, and Valdemar II rightly bore the by-name Valdemar the Victorious. But soon the kingdom crumbled. Valdemar and his son were taken prisoner on the island of Lyø, and the king was only released on payment of a large ransom. The control of the Baltic was lost and attempts to regain it led to the defeat at Bornhöved in Holstein in 1227. The great period had come to an end.

Economic growth, which corresponded to European developments in general, went hand in hand with the extension of the Crown's powers. The administration increased its income by taxes and fines and by mintage, and people were increasingly able to pay their way with money. One source in particular, *King Valdemar's Cadaster* (survey), gives an insight into the many resources available to the throne around 1200. The old military duty to serve, the *leding*, was partially replaced by monetary charges. At the same time, the king introduced privileges which meant that the clergy and the lords of the manor serving in the military were exempt from paying taxes.

With the help of the Church, the Crown gradually gained more control over the judiciary powers of the local things, and *Jyske Lov* (Jutlandic Law) from 1241 marks the king's wish to be seen as the nation's law-giver. The clergy, however, led by the Archbishop of Lund, quickly created a separate clerical legal system and gained extensive independence underpinned by the acquisition of

The cathedral in Lund became the centre for the Danish Church. Work on the long, vaulted crypt in the church did not begin until the beginning of the 12th century, under the direction of a Lombard master builder named Donatus who had been summoned by Archbishop Asser.

land and the introduction of tithes. It was the affluent Church which created links with the European centres of learning, including Paris. Archbishop Anders Sunesen's Latin poem *Hexaëmeron*, written around 1200, perfectly summed up international theological ideas, and Saxo Grammaticus' official history, *Gesta Danorum*, written at the beginning of the 13th century, gave the country a clearer conception of its national identity. For the first time ever, the Danes were able to read the history of the heroic deeds of their forefathers.

The population of Denmark grew to more than 3/4 million people. Space was made for all these new mouths by new forest clearings and new rural settlements, but a growing number of towns were also able to accommodate the growing popula-

tion. A network of market towns appeared as the economy of the country developed, allowing every farmer access to a market where he could sell his product within the distance of a day's journey. The society which gradually developed in the urban areas differed from the rural aristocratic one. Whereas the villages were characterised by the small landowners who were tied to the larger farms, the 13th century saw the rise of a municipal system of government by a council located in cathedral cities and market towns. The character of international trade also changed, and instead of trading luxury goods such as skins, furs and slaves, people began to buy and sell everyday products. The old Nordic-Slav trade which was centred around Schleswig and Gothland gradually diminished and was replaced by new trade tied to the expanding town of Lübeck and the other new cities in the north of Germany.

Conflict and the Disintegration of the Kingdom

After the death of Valdemar II, the years between 1241 and 1340 were characterised by conflict and disintegration. 'When he died, the crown tumbled from the head of the Danes' states one historical record.

Rivalry within the royal family resulted in the murder of two kings. In 1250, Count Abel of South Jutland had his brother Erik Plovpenning (Erik IV) murdered. Yet another regicide took place in 1286, when Erik Klipping (Erik V) was killed by his own men. The internal strife within the royal family became linked to its bitter struggle with the two archbishops, Jakob Erlandsen and Jens Grand. It seems as if the royal power was consolidated around 1300 under Erik Menved (Erik VI), but it turned out that it was instead heading for total ruin. The Crown was forced to borrow huge sums, not only to cover

the cost of the attempts to expand the kingdom into North Germany, but also to pay for the Court and the new castles that were being built. It tried to raise the necessary funds by imposing new extraordinary taxes, but the nobility was reluctant to approve them. The only thing the Crown could really do to raise funds was to pawn its land and *len*. In administrative terms, the 200 or so districts in

Monasticism reached Denmark at the end of the 11th century. In 1135, the great noble Peder Bodilsen allowed a monastic community of Benedictine monks the right to settle in Næstved. He guaranteed the future of the monastery with several large donations. An illustration from the Næstved monastery's necrology, which dates from the second half of the 13th century, depicts the nobleman handing St Peter his church.

Hammershus, built around the middle of the 13th century on the northwest coast of Bornholm. The fortress served as the administrative centre of the island for several centuries. At the end of the 17th century, all administrative functions were moved to Rønne; Hammershus lost its importance and was allowed to fall into disrepair until it was listed in 1822. At the bottom is the bridge which provides the only link between the rock on which the fortress stands and the rest of the island.

In 1361 Valdemar Atterdag (Valdemar IV) conquered Gothland. On 27 July a battle took place between the king and the people of the island outside the gates of Visby. Archaeologist have today found a number of mass graves which hold the bodies of those who fell during the fighting. Here is a soldier from one of the graves, wearing a chain mail hood.

the country had gradually been grouped into larger units known as *len*. Each len had a royal castle as its centre and was headed by a bailiff or a lord lieutenant as he was increasingly known. Individual len and entire regions were now pawned to princes and wealthy members of the nobility in capitalisation of power. By 1325, half the len had been leased and between 1332-1340, when the country had no ruler, the entire kingdom was under the control of Holstein or Sweden. The Crown was a hollow shell devoid of power.

Denmark underwent radical social changes during these years and emerged as a divided nation made up of a number of estates of the realm. The lords of the manor became a separate military and landowning class exempt from paying taxes, gradually absorbing Europe's culture of chivalry. The clergy were also different in that they extended separate legal powers, and the same was true of the towns where separate city laws were introduced. When it came to running the country, it was still only the great nobles and the church leaders that had any say. Decisions were generally taken at the national assemblies which became known as *hof* (*danehof*). Here, taxes were granted and new kings were forced to agree to coronation charters which guaranteed the privileged position of the nobility and the Church.

Everyone in this new society needed a master, and many peasants sought the protection of a lord or a member of the clergy against payment. The higher classes strengthened their power by building a large number of castles, and by 1330 almost every parish in the country had a fortified castle. It was only in 1396 that the Crown was able to take on these private castles.

The Restoration of the Kingdom and the Black Death

These two were to shape the reign of Valdemar Atterdag (Valdemar IV) in the years between 1340-1375. 'The Black Death' reached Denmark in 1350 and wiped out a large part of the population. It returned in 1360 and 1368-1369 and led to a crisis and a number of social changes; in the countryside, many fields and farms were deserted. At the same time Valdemar Atterdag tried, with both cunning and violence, to regain the parts of the kingdom that had been pawned. In 1360 he succeeded and a new, stronger royal power emerged. The nature of the relationship between the king and the people was set out in the King's Peace of 1360, a national contract between the two parties which confirmed the existing division into estates of the realm. In 1361, a successful attempt was made to enlarge the kingdom by conquering Gothland, which resulted in a war with the North German Hanseatic towns that felt their privileges were under threat. Even though the Hanseatics won the war, the episode indicated that their political leadership was no longer unchallenged.

Valdemar Atterdag's greatest triumph in foreign policy proved to be the marriage between his daughter

Margrete and King Håkon VI of Norway. After Valdemar's death in 1375, Margrete's son Oluf was elected king of Denmark and she ruled in his name. After the deaths of Håkon and Oluf, Margrete was elected Queen of Denmark in 1387; the following year she became the queen of Norway and soon after, the Swedish nobles made her the ruler of Sweden.

The Kalmar Union

In 1397, the Kalmar Union created a constitutional basis for the union of the three states when Erik of Pomerania (Erik VII), one of Margrete's relatives, was made king of all Scandinavia. Norway remained under Danish rule until 1814, but the alliance with Sweden never gained the same permanence since the Swedes made repeated attempts to break away from the Danish predominance. The first Swedish fight for independence was the uprising of 1434-1436; after that, the Swedish *rådsstyre* (ruling council) alternated between self rule and subservience to the Danish Crown throughout the 15th century. Christian II's brutal attempt to pacify Swedish resistance at the Massacre of Stockholm in 1520, where more than 80 union opponents were executed, had the exactly opposite effect. Under the leadership of Gustav Vasa (Gustav I), a new Swedish uprising finally led to the dissolution of the Union, and Sweden became a new north European kingdom in keen competition with Denmark-Norway.

South Jutland

South Jutland, or Schleswig as it came to be called, had been lost to Holstein during the troubled years of the 14th century, and repeated attempts by Valdemar Atterdag, Queen Margrete and Erik of Pomerania to regain the duchy ended in defeat at the Peace of Vordingborg in 1435.

Ships provided a link between the various parts of the kingdom of Denmark and the outside world. A fresco in Bregninge Church in West Zealand from around 1375 depicts a ship being attacked by devils, whilst the sailors call to St Nicholas for help.

Events took a surprising turn in 1459, when the childless Prince Adolf VIII of Schleswig-Holstein died. In 1460, the Schleswig-Holstein nobility and the Danish King Christian I came to an agreement which made him Duke of Schleswig and Count of Holstein. In return, he had to promise that the countries would never be divided, which proved to be vital during the 19th century's national struggle. An attempt to expand the kingdom even further by taking over the peasant freestate of the Ditmarshes in 1500 failed pitifully.

Society in the Late Middle Ages

After the crises of the 14th century, the country recovered its strength and experienced renewed economic growth during the late Middle Ages. The deserted farms were rebuilt during the course of the 15th century, and approximately 80,000 farmers were able to make a living on the larger farms in a more independent position. With the help of the Crown, the towns began to free themselves from Hanseatic dominance. The revenue which the Danish king had previously received from the Hanseatic-dominated Scania markets, was now instead collected as customs duties from the many Dutch and English ships which sailed through the Sound. The basis of the Crown's revenue was further improved by

The golden age of the nobility 1536-1660 is distinguished, amongst other things, by the skilful and imaginative work of the goldsmiths; even everyday toiletries could be transformed into veritable works of art. This 68 mm long piece of gold jewellery from the end of the 16th century was found near Viborg. It is formed like a toothpick with cut diamonds and enamel and was worn on a chain around the neck.

the Crown lands which Valdemar Atterdag and Margrete had acquired, and which were put under the management of the len. The central administration also became more established and Copenhagen was increasingly acknowledged as the country's capital after Erik of Pomerania took over the city from the Bishop of Roskilde. The central position of the town was strengthened when a university was founded there in 1479.

Whilst the lesser nobility were troubled by declining incomes from the peasants, the wealthiest part of the nobility gained more land and built up huge estates. The clergy and these prominent estate owners sat in the *Rigsråd* (national assembly) and ran the country together with the king. The other estates, citizens and peasants, had little say in the affairs of the kingdom. They were only rarely given their say at the assemblies of the Estates of the Realm which were convened very infrequently, usually for the purpose of sanctioning royal taxes. A number of popular uprisings, which culminated in the civil war known as *Grevens Fejde* (The Count's Feud) in 1534-1536, only made the ruling classes stick closer together.

Bjørn Poulsen

Reformation and Absolutism
The Denmark of today was only a small part of the huge kingdom which Christian III took over in 1536 after victory in the civil war. At that time, Denmark included Scania, Halland, Blekinge, Gothland and Oesel. Furthermore, Norway and its extensive North Atlantic possessions (the Faeroe Islands, Iceland and Greenland) had formed a personal union with Denmark since the Kalmar Union was established in 1397. The section concerning Norway in Christian III's coronation charter of 1536 emphasised that Norway was as much part of Denmark as Jutland. Furthermore, the Oldenburg monarch was Duke of Holstein and also Duke of Schleswig, which was under an oath of fealty to the Danish Crown.

The period between 1536 and 1720 saw many changes. Economically and socially, the period can be divided into two halves. The 16th century was a period of boom, but around 1600 a trade crisis set in. The crisis deepened during the following decades and became a long-term slump which only began to abate around 1740. A turnaround in domestic policy occurred in 1660. Christian III's coronation charter had given the *Rigsråd* a final say in the affairs of the kingdom. The dominance of the aristocracy lasted until 1660-1661, when absolute monarchy was established in line with other European kingdoms. Great changes took place in the structure of society, and the schism within the clergy in 1536 which resulted in the Lutheran State Church also affected the nation deeply. Both in church and in school, Danes were instructed in the new creed and turned into loyal subjects. Foreign policy was dominated by the rivalry with Sweden and problems concerning access to the Baltic caused by Denmark's geographical location. Sweden had left the Kalmar Union in 1523 and was intent on challenging Denmark's leading position in the North.

Danish society was made up of a highly privileged nobility, the clergy, a middle class and an underprivileged peasant class. Little is known about the size of the population during the 16th century. We do know, however, that the number of people in the country was rising. Around 1650, the total population

Wilhelm Marstrand's *Christian IV on the Trefoldigheden*; oil painting, approximately 1864, Frederiksborg Museum; preliminary study for the mural in Christian IV's Chapel in Roskilde Cathedral. During the naval battle of Kolberger Heide on 1 July 1644, the 67-year-old king lost his right eye. The picture seeks to recreate the heroic moment when the wounded king gets back up to join in the fighting. Marstrand's interpretation has become part of Danish folklore and the picture, along with the king's blood-spattered clothes which are kept at Rosenborg Castle, have kept the legend alive in the minds of the people. Marstrand did not work from the clothes the king actually wore during the battle, but based his representation of Christian IV on Karel van Mander's portraits which were painted at the beginning of the 1640s. The picture of the elderly king with long hair is the most popular image of the monarch. It has been reiterated time after time in various versions of J.L. Heiberg's play *Elverhøi* (The Elfin Mound) (1828) and by the statues in Nyboder in Copenhagen (1900) and on the Stortorvet square in Oslo (1880).

was approximately 800,000 if we include Scania. When Scania was lost in 1660, this total fell to approximately 600,000, but by 1720 it had again reached almost 700,000.

The peasants who managed the 60,000 farms in the country accounted for approximately 75% of the total population, the clergy for around 5% – the same percentage as those without any means. There were ap-proximately 100,000 people living in towns (approximately 15%), of which approximately 30,000 lived in Copenhagen. The nobility counted only around 2000; nevertheless, they owned almost half the land in the country spread across some 700 manors and a large number of copy-hold farms.

Denmark was very much a farm-ing community. Corn and cattle, which constituted the only export articles, were mainly sold to the densely populated Netherlands. There was no industry to speak of, even though Christian IV attempted to set up some industry in the capital and also tried to establish a mining industry in Norway. All his attempts were unsuccessful, however, and it was only at the end of the 17th century that wartime conditions gave a boost to international trade. Non-agrarian production and international shipping were still a thing of the future.

Aristocratic Government

The system of government which was obtained between 1536-1660 is generally known as aristocratic government. It was a constitutional form of government in that the king was formally elected by the estates of the realm, in practice by the nobles in the *Rigsråd*, which, however, always elected the king's oldest son. The king, in turn, had to sign a constitutional charter which divided the power between the Crown and the Rigsråd. The latter was a council made up of a dozen members of the high nobility who also took the most important government posts. Policies were written by the king and the Rigsråd; the rest of the population had no say in government matters. The population could only be deprived of all political control because government finances were based on Crown revenue, which meant that the government did not generally impose any direct taxes on the people. In principle, the government was self-financing through the Crown lands, which made up approximately half of the cultivated land in the country, the Sound Tolls and a number of other, minor, sources of income.

This system worked adequately until the beginning of the 17th century. Under normal circumstances,

the activities of the state were not very costly, being generally limited to maintaining law and order and to ensuring the privileges of the estates. In addition, the administration had to ensure that the necessary funding existed to finance its foreign policy, which included the army and the navy. These were only activated in times of war and crisis, however. The many wars that were fought during the 17th century therefore put the system under great pressure. The traditional sources of revenue proved unable to finance the many military campaigns, and the usual revenue increasingly had to be supplemented by direct taxation. This put the Rigsråd into a very awkward position indeed. The members of the nobility were, according to the privileges they had been accorded, exempt from taxation. This meant that the burden of taxation fell solely on those groups who were least able to meet the demands. After the unsuccessful German War (the Kaiser War) 1625-1629 the frustration felt by the lower classes became obvious. Their anger was directed at the Rigsråd which was accused of looking after their own interests rather than those of the State. The growing financial crisis cast doubt on the credibility of the Rigsråd, and it finally collapsed in 1660-1661 when the country's political system changed.

Absolutism

Absolutism was a result of the lengthy political crisis and the acute state of emergency which resulted from the last of the Karl Gustav wars against Sweden in 1657-1660. Despite his weak position when elected king in 1648, Frederik III's political skill allowed him to succeed in ousting two of his main adversaries in the Rigsråd as early as the 1650s. The two were the seneschal Corfitz Ulfeldt

Paying homage to the despot – Copenhagen, 18 October 1660; Frederik III is seated on the canopied stage on the left of the picture. Rays of light from the sky strike the stage, bathing the scene in celestial light. The huge crowds paying homage to the autocratic monarch have been strongly emphasised by the Danish painter Michael van Haven (1625-1679). This painting, along with others depicting the anointment and crowning of Frederik III, were commissioned for Rosenborg Castle.

and the governor of Norway Hannibal Sehested, who were both Frederik's brothers-in-law. The king's heroic conduct during the siege of Copenhagen in the winter of 1659 had, in addition, made him widely popular at a time when the nobility and the Rigsråd were increasingly being discredited. In October 1660, these events led the estates – the nobility only reluctantly – to create a hereditary monarchy. The new system meant that the king was no longer dependent on the Rigsråd, and he immediately used his new power to introduce absolutism, which was temporarily established on 10 January 1661 in the Hereditary Monarchy Act before being fully set out in *Kongeloven* (the Royal Law) of 1665, the basic law of Danish absolutism.

The change of system in 1660-1661 introduced a hectic period of reforms which culminated during the reign of Christian V (1670-1699), and lasted until the reign of his successor, Frederik IV. The aim was to consolidate the new system of government and to ensure that Denmark became a well-organised, hierarchical society with the absolute monarch as its focal point.

The aristocratic departmental government now became a collegiate administration divided into different government departments. The old division into estates was replaced by a new hierarchy in which the officials of the Crown took the leading positions. The old hereditary nobility were deprived of most of its privileges and were suddenly joined by a large number of 'new men'. In the course of a lifetime, Denmark was transformed from a self-managing mediaeval society divided into estates to a modern bureaucracy. Legislation was standardised as all laws were collected in a systematically organised Statute Book, *Christian V's Danske Lov 1683* (Danish Law), which applied to the whole country and thereby replaced the old provin-

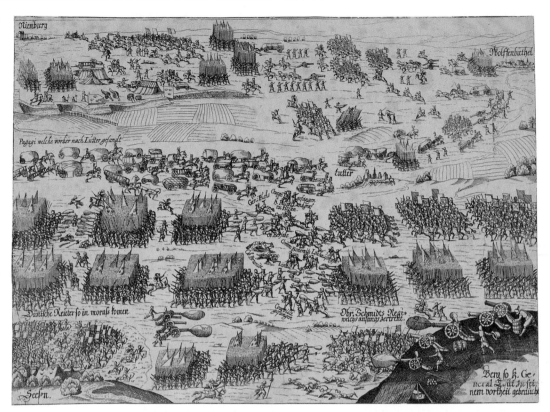

During the Thirty Years' War, Christian IV's army met the soldiers of the German Kaiser under the leadership of General Tilly outside the Lutter am Barenberge fortress on the edge of Harzen in 1626. This contemporary engraving depicts the battle scene; at the bottom to the right are the canons of the Kaiser which have been set up on a hillside. From here, they can fire on the Danes (seen to the left at the bottom of the picture) who have already been forced into the marsh. The battle ended in total defeat for the Danes; Christian IV held his position for as long as possible but finally had to beat a hasty retreat.

cial laws. With the help of the astronomer Ole Rømer, new uniform systems of weights and measures were introduced; the greatest administrative feat, however, was a full survey and registration of all agricultural land in the country. The land register was intended to enable the administration to create a uniform basis for taxation, and proved that the State had discarded the old system of relying on revenue from crown lands and gone over to direct taxation of land owners and land users. Although the big landowners continued to play an important role in the administration of taxes and the conscription of soldiers, and although the first absolute monarchs found it difficult to find their political position in relation to the new large bureaucracy, there is little doubt that the reforms which were introduced at the end of the 17th century created a solid foundation for the stable bureaucratic absolutism of the 18th century.

The spiritual life of the population was strongly influenced by the Reformation throughout the whole of this period. The Danish Church was subservient to the State, which purposely used the widely ramified organisation and its school system as a useful means of indoctrinating the population with the Lutheran dogma of the divinity of authority. At the end of the 16th century, the reformation rebellion had settled into Lutheran orthodoxy. There was no real reaction against this indoctrination until 1700, when Evangelical movements from Germany brought a call for a devotional life of a more intense personal nature. The national Church allowed the mother tongue to become better established, although Latin continued to play an important role as a language of learning. The most noteworthy contributions in Danish during this period include Chancellor Arild Huitfeldt's *Danmarks Riges Krønike* (The Chronicle of the Kingdom of Denmark) from the 1590s, in which he describes the history of the Danes from Saxo Grammaticus up to his own time in a very pithy style. Also worthy of note are the hymns written at the end of the 17th century by Thomas Kingo, the Bishop of Odense, who admirably demonstrated how expressive the Danish language could be in the hands of an expert. These examples also highlight another contemporary issue: A feeling of Danish national identity was slowly beginning to emerge amongst the leading strata of society.

Foreign Policy

With a few exceptions, foreign policy was the responsibility of the king. During the reign of Christian III, relations with Sweden were peaceful. Following the religious upheavals, the main goal was to secure Denmark's position amongst the Protestants, and attention therefore turned towards the German territory. Denmark was the leading power in the North, and the Baltic was still more or less a closed Danish-dominated sea, guarded by the strong Danish navy. Danish sovereignty was best demonstrated when foreign merchant vessels dutifully cast anchor at Elsinore to pay their Sound Tolls to the Danish Crown.

Around 1560, both Denmark and

This painting by the Dutch artist Daniel Vertangen depicts the Storming of Copenhagen on the night between 10 and 11 February 1659. In the middle is Copenhagen Castle, to the right is the battle for Christianshavn. Karl X Gustav of Sweden planned to let the main body of his army advance across the ice to the beach at Kalvebod Strand and attack Slotsholmen from there. The Danes, however, defended themselves with a violent cannonade and the attack was averted. The victory increased support for Frederik III, and it is said that he was in the thick of the action throughout the duration of the battle.

Sweden changed rulers, and the period of peaceful coexistence came to an end. Under the leadership of Erik XIV, Sweden was intent on destroying the supremacy of the Danes, and Frederik II dreamt of resurrecting the Kalmar Union under Danish leadership. These differences finally resulted in *Den Nordiske Syvårskrig* (the Scandinavian Seven Years' War) (1563-1570), which eventually ended in mutual exhaustion without any frontiers having been moved. The next confrontation was the Kalmar War (1611-1613) which was initiated by the Danes. Once again the aim

was to force Sweden back under Danish supremacy, and once again the attempt failed. This war was to be Denmark's last attempt to resurrect the old union. The balance of power in the North now shifted in favour of a dynamic Sweden under the leadership of Gustav II Adolf.

The decisive turning point in Denmark's foreign policy came in 1625-1629 with Christian IV's involvement in the Thirty Years' War. His catastrophic defeat at Lutter am Barenberge in 1626 broke Denmark in military terms. The humiliating peace agreement in 1629 and Gustav II

Denmark after 1660. With the conclusion of peace after the Torstensson War 1643-1645, and the Karl Gustav Wars 1657-1660, all former Danish areas east of the Sound came under Swedish rule. The only exception was Bornholm which fought its way back to Denmark in 1658-1659. Norway had to concede Bohuslän, Härjedalen and Jämtland, but were given back Trondheim Provinde at the Peace of Copenhagen in 1660. The area had previously been conceded to the Swedes at the Peace of Roskilde in 1658.

Adolf's military triumphs in Germany from 1630 onwards clearly showed that Sweden had become the leading power in the Baltic region while Denmark, though its territory was intact, had been beaten and isolated. For the next 30 years, Denmark's survival as an independent state was at risk. During the subsequent three Dano-Swedish wars, the Torstensson Feud of 1643-1645 and the two Karl Gustav wars between 1657-1660, it was Sweden who tried to force Denmark into its Baltic Empire, and when Karl X Gustav led the Swedish army across the ice-covered Danish belts in February 1659, the plan almost succeeded. The catastrophe was only avoided because foreign powers, led by the Netherlands, forced the Swedes to agree to peace. A price had to be paid, however, and Denmark ceded all provinces east of the Sound to Sweden with the exception of Bornholm. The country was thus reduced to around a third of its former size and the main artery of Baltic trade, the Sound, became international waters, which was very much in the interest of the Western naval powers.

The last two Dano-Swedish wars, the *Skånske Krig* (Scania War) 1675-1679, and *Store Nordiske Krig* (Great Nordic War) 1709-1720, were both started by the Danes in an attempt to win back Scania from the ailing Swedish superpower, and break the troubling alliance between Sweden and the Dukes of Gottorp. Even though the Danes more or less won both wars, they did not succeed in reclaiming Scania since the big European powers opposed it. In acknowledgement of this, and because Sweden had again been reduced to the same level as Denmark, the government dropped the Dano-Swedish issue from the foreign policy agenda. The border through the Sound was there to stay. The Gottorp issue was satisfactorily resolved at the same time, and the lengthy Danish-Swedish rivalry was soon replaced by a new partnership in the shadow of the emerging Russian power. The peace of 1720 introduced a long period of peaceful coexistence between the two Nordic kingdoms.

Knud J.V. Jespersen

The Long Peace and the Short War, 1720-1814

The peace in 1720 marked the end of the last Dano-Swedish war, and the time up to the war with Britain 1807-

1814 was the longest period of peace that Denmark has ever enjoyed. The first years of peace were dominated by the struggle to repay the debts of war, combined with a serious agricultural crisis. The population of the kingdom, however, rose slowly from around 700,000 in 1720 to 978,000 in 1807 and reached approximately 1 million in 1814, when peace reigned once again. Around 1750 the general European boom reached Denmark in the shape of increasing demands for agricultural products and tonnage. The boom created the basis for the flourishing overseas trade and shipping under Danish neutrality during the wars between the great powers. But Denmark's exploitation of its neutral position brought the country into open conflict with Britain in 1801. The boom also affected the mentality and attitude of the people. A Danish national identity began to emerge amongst the bourgeoisie, and the tension between Danish and German took hold. The notions of freedom and equality which were discussed during the Age of Enlightenment made educated Danes question the divine right of kings even before news of the French Revolution in 1789 reached Denmark.

Foreign Policy

The foreign policy which safeguarded the State and the peace was not without its problems. Even though Sweden had been reduced to a power on a level with Denmark-Norway in 1720, Denmark dropped any further plans to regain the provinces east of the Sound by military means. With the Oath of Fealty from 1721, Frederik IV brought the Gottorp parts of Schleswig under Danish rule, but it required a long, intensive diplomatic and political effort to solve the Gottorp issue to Denmark's satisfaction. It did not happen until 1773 with the treaty on the exchange of land, in which the Duke of Gottorp renounced his Schleswig holdings and exchanged his parts of Holstein with Oldenburg, the native land of the Danish dynasty. In 1772, however, Gustav III's coup d'état in Sweden created far more serious problems for the united Danish-Norwegian state. The Swedish royal powers were now much stronger and the country began a concentrated campaign to acquire Norway. In 1773, Denmark reacted by entering into The Eternal Alliance with Russia. The alliance, which bound both countries to guard the territory of the other, put Denmark in a subservient position and forced it to conduct a foreign policy which did not interfere with vital Russian interests. The alliance did, however, provide Denmark with the protection it needed right up to the closing phase of the Napoleonic Wars in 1812; and until 1807, the Danish government was able to concentrate its efforts and its resources on a policy of neutrality which greatly benefited Danish trade and shipping.

Absolutism

Absolutism had a solid constitutional foundation in the Hereditary Monarchy Act of 1661 and *Kongeloven* (the Royal Law or Lex Regia) of 1665, and its principles were incorporated in *Danske Lov* (Danish Law) in 1683. As a political system, the Danish absolutism changed in line with society. Frederik IV could still run his kingdom like a thrifty landowner; under Christian VI, however, the actual political leadership began to shift from the king to the ministers in the council. In practical terms, Frederik V handed over the political power to his Lord High Steward, A.G. Moltke, who ruled the country in agreement

Count *C.D.F. Reventlow* (1748-1827) and his brother *Johan Ludvig* (1751-1801) were some of the main protagonists behind the coup in 1784. He served as Chief of the Exchequer between 1784 and 1813, and turned the department into the central office of administration and legislation for internal economic affairs. In 1797 he was made a minister. C.D.F. Reventlow had a strong influence on Danish society in the 19th and 20th centuries through the laws and administrative practices he introduced. He was behind the Great Land Commission in 1786 which introduced the laws on tenure in 1787, and the laws on the abolition of adscription in 1788. He was the driving force behind the agricultural legislation at the end of the 18th century. He also wrote the revolutionary Road Act of 1793, as well as the Forest Reserve Act of 1805 which still forms the basis for all Danish legislation on forests and wood- land. He was also involved with the Education Act of 1814.

Claus Bjørn

with the ministers. Crisis struck the monarchy when those closest to the King realised that the young Christian VII was mad. His physician J.F. Struensee, who was also the Queen's lover, seized all power in 1770 and ruled the country through cabinet orders which were signed by the King or issued with his consent. Struensee was overthrown and executed in 1772, and the King was made to set up a new political institution, the State Council, where the monarch was to hear the advice of his ministers on all matters before reaching any decision. This system remained in force until the fall of absolutism in 1848. Behind the scenes, however, the real power shifted between the Court, the Cabinet and the Council of State. The young crown prince Frederik (VI) seized power after a coup in 1784 with the express intention of weakening the Court and the Cabinet and strengthening the Council of State. At the end of the 1790s, however, Frederik changed to a Cabinet government which lasted until 1814 when the Council of State was re-established, this time permanently.

The officials working within the central administration slowly began to acquire real political influence, but it was characteristic of Danish absolutism that the large rural population never saw the king's officials locally. In order to function, the monarchy had delegated responsibility for the collection of taxes and for conscription and, to a large extent, law enforcement to the Danish landowners. It was only towards the end of the 18th century when the agricultural reforms were introduced that the absolute monarch ceased delegating responsibility and began to establish a system of local administration with participation by the people.

Economy

The country's economy underwent steady growth during the first 50 years of the long period of peace. The economic institutions were gradually

Denmark as a Colonial Power

The Danish-Norwegian colonial history forms part of the European expansion. The purpose was to establish trading stations in the parts of the world which provided Europe with silk, porcelain, spices and other exotic goods.

In 1616 Christian IV granted privileges to the Danish East India Company and in 1620 the Company entered into agreement with the local prince to take over the town of Tranquebar on the south-east coast of India. Later in the 17th century several other companies were established, building fortified trading stations on the African Gold Coast and settling the island of St Thomas in the Caribbean Sea.

The forts in Africa were also established in agreement with local sovereigns; however, regional wars changed the power structures several times. Until 1803 the economy was based on slave trade.

The Danish West Indies consisted of St Thomas (settled 1672), St John (settled 1718) and St Croix (purchased 1733). With these possessions in hand, Denmark aimed at establishing a Danish production of tobacco, cotton and sugar. The islands were almost uninhabited but immigration from neighbouring islands created a propertied class which brought their African slaves with them. On Danish initiative, the slave population increased, already accounting for 80% of the population in 1720.

In 1755, the Indian possessions were expanded to include the town of Serampore (Frederiksnagore), trading offices were established in several places and, furthermore, Denmark made repeated attempts to colonise the Nicobar Islands, located north-west of Sumatra.

In the second half of the 18th century the companies' trade monopoly with the colonies was abolished and Danish world trade reached its peak. In this, the colonies played an important role serving both as bases for trade and suppliers of goods. The Danish-Norwegian neutrality during the wars of this period formed the basis of the economic prosperity, enabling Copenhagen to be the centre of supply of West Indian sugar to northern Europe.

After the Napoleonic Wars, Denmark was unable to regain its prior position within world trade and, thus the tropical colonies lost their importance. In 1845 the Danish possessions in India were sold and in 1850 the African forts were surrendered to Great Britain.

The sugar from St Croix continued to cover a large part of the Danish market through the 19th century, but it proved difficult to make a profit on the sugar cultivation, i.a. due to the abolition of slavery and the progress of other sugar-producing colonies. Already in 1852 it was proposed that Denmark should sell the islands. They were considered to be a burden, and many Danes did not hold the mainly English speaking Danish West Indians of African origin to be 'real' Danes.

The Danish government and the majority of votes cast in a Danish referendum in 1916 favoured the sale of the islands to the USA, accomplished in 1917.

To sum up, Denmark, despite its many attempts, did not, in the long run, have the necessary economic background to manifest itself as a colonial power in the tropic regions. It was played out when larger European powers, through large conquests, developed their trading stations into true colonial empires during the 19th century. What remained to be done was for Denmark to adjust its relations to the former Norwegian dependencies: Iceland, the Faeroe Islands and Greenland. In fact, these countries exerted a certain influence on Danish history in what remained of the 20th century, but in contrast to the West Indies, the population in these countries were considered to have familial ties to Denmark.

Per Nielsen

modernised and a sound basis was created for the boom and the agricultural reforms which were to follow. Agricultural production rose in line with the slow increase in the population. During the agricultural crisis of the 1730s, however, the absolute monarch supported the landowners to the detriment of the tenant farmers. Adscription was introduced in 1733, tying the farm workers to the place where they were born and preventing men from leaving the estates without the permission of the landowners. The official reason for the introduction of adscription was that manpower was required for the militia, but the system also provided landowners with cheap labour. The government turned a blind eye as the practice of villeinage became increasingly common, not only during the agricultural crisis but also during the ensuing boom. A number of institutions were set up by the government around this time: *Kommercekollegiet* (the Board of Trade) in 1735, *Kurantbanken* (the first note-issuing bank) in 1736 and the Merchant's Guild in 1742. These were all intended as instruments for the economic control of the urban society in line with the mercantilist philosophy of the time. This economic control by means of subsidies, privileges and monopolies was gradually abolished at the end of the 18th century as new enterprises were able to function independently and a liberalist policy proved more appropriate.

Agriculture
The extensive agricultural reforms introduced during the last 35 years of the long period of peace revolutionised the farming system. The mediaeval open-field system was abolished in all the 5,000 or so villages, and the fields cultivated by the individual farms were now collected into a single parcel of land. Around 15,000 farms out of a total of almost 60,000 were torn down and rebuilt on the new holdings, and almost half of all tenant farmers bought their holdings and became freeholders. The restructuring was mostly initiated by the landowners and tenant farmers themselves who felt that this change was vital if the agricultural output was to be increased. The government took a back seat in the whole process, partly out of respect for the landowners' right of ownership and disposal, and partly because the government was unable to provide a great deal of loan capital for the tenant farmers wishing to buy their own properties. The government's most important contribution was the legal protection it provided for those who stayed on as tenant farmers. At the time, there is little doubt that the nation considered the abolition of adscription in 1788 the most important of all the agricultural reforms. The freedom-loving, landowner-hating bourgeoisie of Copenhagen, made up of merchants and officials, marked the event by erecting *Frihedsstøtten* (the Liberty Memorial) in the capital. The restructuring had many important long-term effects: It broke the old feudal ties between the landowners and the land users, and it created the new independent, selfsufficient farming class and thus the sharp distinction between the rural middle classes and the lower class made up of smallholders and farm workers.

Overseas trade
The flourishing years of Danish overseas trade brought prosperity to many, particularly in Copenhagen, and thereby created a new political self-awareness. This wealth was the product of a number of factors: The

In 1780 the Royal Copenhagen Porcelain Manufactory sold a group of figures in memory of the Law of Indigenous Rights of 1776. In keeping with the autocracy ideology of the autocratic state, the united native land is represented by a mother with her three equally loved children: Denmark, Norway and Holstein. Even at this time, however, the outward appearance of harmony hid internal national tensions which resulted from the unequal treatment given to the different parts of the state.

international boom in trade and shipping; the nation's policy of neutrality which meant that Danish ships were in great demand on the oceans; the huge quantities of overseas goods which were channelled through Copenhagen to the European markets; the income from shipping under the neutral Danish flag. One particular branch of overseas trade concerned the transport of slaves from Africa to the West Indies. The Danish king created an international sensation when he banned the Danes from taking part in this traffic in human beings in 1792. In actual fact, however, the king had merely taken a conscious economic decision to halt a trade which the great powers would have forced Denmark to stop anyway.

Freedom of Expression
In the 18th century, the nation's freedom of expression was limited by official censorship and the self-censorship which most authors exercised so as not to fall out of favour with the country's leaders and the patrons of the arts. Censorship went against the free exchange of ideas advocated by the Age of Enlightenment, however, and was very leniently enforced under Frederik V. Nevertheless, Struensee caused a stir in Europe when he had Christian VII abolish censorship

completely at the stroke of a pen in 1770. Legislation introduced during the ensuing years stated clearly that authors were responsible for what they wrote, and that the printers would be held responsible if they printed anything that had been written anonymously. Denmark nevertheless enjoyed near total freedom of expression during the last 15 years of the 18th century, and controversial topics such as religion, the Church, absolutism and the structure of society were relatively openly discussed. The debate was conducted in the newspapers and periodicals and in the clubs; it was during these years that terms such as the King were replaced by the State and subject by citizen. This phenomenon has been described as opinion-led absolutism. In 1799, those in power lost their patience and imposed strict limits on the freedom of expression, and during the war with Britain in 1807-1814 censorship was reintroduced.

National Identity
A national identity began to develop already in the middle of the 18th century, which is fairly early compared to the rest of Europe. It had previously only been those in power who identified themselves with their native country and its history, whereas ordinary citizens thought no further than the town, the parish and the region. As early as the 1740s, however, the young well-educated sons of the middle class had begun to identify themselves with their nation, its language and its history, both in intellectual and emotional terms. This was partly a reaction against the foreign aristocracy at the Court and in government, and against the Danish aristocracy who adopted the language and culture of the foreigners and openly regarded Denmark as a culturally underdeveloped country.

The revolt against Struensee was partly provoked by his German language and his foreign birth. The group which overthrew him in 1772 consciously sought to stabilise their own power through a Danish and conservative policy. This nationalism culminated in 1776 with the Law of Indigenous Rights which made it illegal for anyone but Danish citizens to hold a government post. The law was also an attempt to stem the conflicts which had begun to emerge between the Danish, Norwegian and German members of the population by deliberately instilling a sense of patriotism towards the conglomerate state. It proved impossible to put an end to the hostility between Danes and Germans, however, and in the autumn of 1789 the situation came to a head with the so-called German Feud which definitely made anti-German sentiments a regrettable, but very real, part of the Danish early identity.

War

The war came in 1807 when Britain attacked Denmark, bombarded Copenhagen and sailed away with the entire Danish fleet. Denmark had already provoked Britain in 1798 by letting her warships act as escort vessels providing protection for the many, not always strictly neutral, activities which were conducted under the Danish flag. In July 1800, the convoy conflict gave rise to the Freya affair, in which Britain forced Denmark to put an end to the convoys. When Denmark then sought the help of Russia and entered into the League of Armed Neutrality in December 1800, Britain responded with war. On 2 April 1801, Admiral Nelson defeated the Danish line of defence in the Sound off the capital during the Battle of Copenhagen. Under threat of bombardment from the British ships in the Sound, Britain forced Denmark to suspend its membership of the League of Armed Neutrality and relinquish its policy of offensive neutrality.

The British attack in 1807 was designed to prevent Napoleon from gaining control of the Danish navy and thus putting him in a position to cut off Britain's vital Baltic trade. Denmark then allied herself with Na-

C.A. Lorentzen's painting of the final stage of the Battle of Copenhagen was completed already in 1801. It shows Crown Prince Frederik surrounded by his staff on Kastelspynten point at three o'clock in the afternoon, when the boat with Nelson's messenger arrives with a letter regarding the ceasefire. A bright ray of light falls on the white flag in the centre of the picture. The national myth had been born: it was the English who, after more than four hours of fighting, had to beg for peace. The painting is on display at the Frederiksborg Museum.

poleon and joined the Continental System. In 1808 a French-Spanish auxiliary corps came to Denmark, and, trying to keep themselves warm, Spanish soldiers accidentally burnt Koldinghus (Castle of Kolding) to the ground. However, the situation in Spain changed and on 2 May 1808 Spain rose in rebellion against Napoleon. Thus, in the summer of 1808, 9,000 of the 13,000 soldiers of the Spanish corps under General la Romana were brought back to Spain with the help of the English navy in order to fight against Napoleon. Despite the efforts of the Danish gunboats and privateers, Denmark did not succeed in blocking the passage of the strong British convoys through Danish straits. The result of the war was the State Bankruptcy in 1813, and at the Peace of Kiel the following year Frederik VI had to cede Norway to the king of Sweden.

Ole Feldbæk

Consultative Assemblies and Constitution, 1814-1849

Following the Peace of Kiel, the Danish monarchy comprised just four parts: The kingdom of Denmark (in-cluding the Faeroe Isands, Iceland and Greenland) and the duchies of Schleswig, Holstein and (later) Lauenburg. Denmark was reduced to a small state and was forced to fall into line with the wishes of the great powers. The colonies in India and Africa were sold in 1845 and 1850. The Faeroe Islands and Greenland were governed from Copenhagen, while a consultative *Alting* was reintroduced in Iceland in 1843. In 1874, the Alting assumed responsibility for all legislative matters.

The period which followed the Napoleonic Wars was marked by stagnation. The war had badly affected the economy; trade and shipping showed a pronounced decline and after the State Bankruptcy in 1813 inflation rose sharply. The latter problem was solved to a certain extent when the National Bank in Copenhagen became the sole note-issuing bank in 1818. Agriculture was hit by British import duties on corn and, from 1818 onwards, by a marked fall in prices. The situation was eventually stabilised at the end of the 1820s, and by the 1830s agriculture began to prosper once again. The success

The Stænderhuset in Viborg. The building originally housed the High Court which replaced the Landsting in Jutland's former capital. Between 1836 and 1848, this was also the home of Jutland's own assembly. It is the first, and so far only, time in Denmark's recent history that Jutland has had its own separate assembly. The building was torn down in 1871.

of the farming community slowly began to affect business in the towns.

In 1815, Holstein had been promised a consultative assembly, and following the July Revolution in France in 1830, the duchies finally began to demand the introduction of a Schleswig-Holstein assembly. In order to keep its promise to Holstein, while still maintaining the unity of the kingdom, the government of Frederik VI decided in 1831 to introduce the Consultative Provincial Assemblies in Holstein, Schleswig, Jutland and the islands. Only those in possession of property were eligible to vote or sit on the assemblies, leaving only three groups: Landowners, landlords in the towns and property-owners in the country, i.e. those who owned the larger farms. Regardless of censorship, a public political debate, which was partly conducted through the newspapers, began to take shape. The consultative assemblies first met in 1835-1836 and to-gether with the government, they introduced a system of local self-government in Copenhagen (1837), as well as in the market towns (1840) and the rural municipalities (1841) and a revised Customs Act in 1838. Generally speaking, the assemblies wanted control over state finances and urged the government to practice strict economy; the peasants wanted the agricultural reforms to continue and the liberals, with the help of the academics and the businessmen, wanted a more liberal economy, greater freedom of the press and more influence for the constitutional assemblies.

The 1840s were a period of great upheaval in Denmark. Both the urban and the rural population became more involved in the affairs of society. The national conflict in the duchies worsened, and in the 1840s the liberal opposition became The National Liberals. During the same period, the economic boom took

Frederik VII, the giver of the Constitution, was a well-loved king who was nicknamed Frederik the Popular. His popularity grew in the years after his death in 1863, and statues were erected around the country showing him as a placid, down-to-earth ruler. An equestrian statue of the king was erected in 1873 on the open space in front of Christiansborg Castle in Copenhagen. It was started by H.V. Bissen and completed by his son Vilhelm Bissen. The citizen king in his everyday clothes towers in front of the building in which the Constitution is now administered.

hold for good. Agriculture was still the country's principal industry but industrialisation slowly began to appear, particularly in Copenhagen. Great Britain became the main market for agricultural products from Denmark, and the terms of trade between the two countries developed positively for many years, particularly as far as agriculture was concerned.

Around the same time, a peasant movement began to stir in Zealand and on the islands of Lolland and Falster. The peasants wanted something done about the existing ties between the landowners and the tenants. These demands overshadowed all other business at the consultative assembly held in Roskilde in 1844, and in November 1845, the government felt compelled to issue *Bonde-cirkulæret* (the Peasants' Bill) in order to restrict the political activities of the peasants. The bill brought the peasants, who had until then been loyal to the king, closer to the National Liberals. *Bondevennernes Selskab* (the Society of Friends of the Peasants) was set up in 1846 to promote the cause of the peasants.

When Christian VIII ascended the throne in 1839, the country had great expectations; as king of Norway he had introduced the constitutional monarchy in 1814 through the Eidsvoll constitution. As king of Denmark, however, he refused to acknowledge any limitations to his absolute power. He did, however, introduce administrative reforms and appointed the moderate liberal A.S. Ørsted as prime minister in 1842. But political developments slowly brought a realisation that absolutism would not survive the accession of a new king. Christian VIII therefore prepared a number of constitutional changes before his death, and the National Constitutional Assembly was formed after an election on 5

October 1848. The ensuing debates on a free constitution lasted many months, but on 5 June 1849 Frederik VII was finally able to sign Denmark's first constitution, commonly known as the June Constitution. In democratic terms, the document was well ahead of its time in guaranteeing the civic rights of the people and introducing a bicameral system (the *Folketing* and the *Landsting*) which gave all men the right to vote, though with certain restrictions in the case of the Landsting. It was already possible to discern the main political divide between those who were sympathetic to the political claims of the peasants on the one side, and the National Liberals and other moderates on the other.

Claus Bjørn

The June Constitution, 1849-1864
From the very first meetings of the *Rigsdag* (parliament), the peasants' representatives appeared to be forming a united party. This was not the case for the other representatives: At the centre was a large group of liberals who appeared to have no real party structure, but had gathered round a number of prominent figures, including D.G. Monrad. The group was very heterogeneous but did include a large number of academics. To the right of them was a smaller group of older civil servants and landowners who were against the constitution.

The economy was liberalised around the middle of the 19th century. The Trade Act of 1857 eliminated the old division between town and country. The Sound Tolls were abolished the same year, and the Customs Act of 1863 was introduced as a moderately liberal reform. Work on the railways and the telegraph plants took off during the 1850s, gasworks were built in the larger towns and in 1857 C.F. Tietgen founded *Privatbanken*, the first modern-day Danish bank of commerce.

The main political issue of the peasants' party was the abolition of the old system of tenure. In 1861, however, this merely led to a number of modifications in the law relating to tenants and landowners. On the other hand, the standard of living of both small and big farmers improved considerably.

The Schleswig Issue

The position of the duchies within the monarchy was a central issue from the beginning of the century until 1864. In 1815, almost a third of the total population of Denmark and the duchies was German, and Holstein was by then better developed in economic terms than the kingdom. Holstein and Lauenburg were both part of the German Confederation and were both German in linguistic and cultural terms. Schleswig was more divided; the majority of the landowners, town-dwellers and peasants in South Schleswig were German-speaking, whilst the North Schleswig peasants mostly spoke Danish. In 1830, the liberals in the duchies called for a liberal constitution for a united Schleswig-Holstein. Their demands were ignored by Frederik VI and his autocratic government, and the most prominent of the Schleswig-Holstein supporters, Uwe Jens Lornsen, was imprisoned. The consultative agreement of 1831 sought to preserve the unity of the kingdom; the question of a consultative assembly for Holstein was resolved and the two duchies remained separate. The differences between Danish and German persisted, however, and the idea of a Schleswig-Holstein found support in Duke Christian August of Augustenborg's hereditary claim to the two duchies,

should the male Oldenburg line as expected die out. In November 1842, the national issue gave rise to open conflict when the right to speak Danish at the consultative assembly in Schleswig was insisted on. Separate Danish and Schleswig-Holstein movements quickly formed. In Denmark, the National Liberals took on the Danish cause in Schleswig. In 1842, Orla Lehmann demanded that Schleswig be incorporated into Denmark; Lehmann wanted the southern border of Denmark to coincide with the River Ejder between Schleswig and Holstein. Faced with increasing demands for German unification, Danish nationalism found further support in a new Scandinavian movement which furthered Nordic unity. The government tried to mediate between Danish and German, but had to reject the hereditary claim of the Duke of Augustenborg. In The Open Letter of 1846, Christian VIII upheld the hereditary claim of the Oldenburg line and the continued existence of the united monarchy, but rejected the National Liberals' demands for a closer alliance with Schleswig, known as the Eider Policy.

Following Christian VIII's death

Reserves from 1848 on the march, painted in 1851 by Nicolai Habbe. It is a romanticised nationalistic image complete with barrow, a beautiful girl, sweet country children and a wagon driven by a brave peasant. The soldiers' red tunic and white bandoleer later made a perfect target for the enemy, but here all is pure idyll.

The catastrophic events of 1864 with the hardships endured during the winter campaign, the unavoidable defeat and the determined endurance of the privates, have all been brought together in this definitive grey and black painting by Niels Simonsen from 1864. The work is entitled *Infantrymen save a canon during the retreat from the Dannevirke*. The painting hangs in the Frederiksborg Museum.

in January 1848, the government promised a change of constitution which would maintain the division between the kingdom and the duchies.

The February Revolution in Paris that same year triggered a revolutionary movement across Europe, and nationalists on both sides became more radical. At a meeting in Rendsborg, demands were put forward for a free Schleswig-Holstein constitution and for Schleswig's incorporation into the German Confederation. Accounts of the meeting led the National Liberals to demand the resignation of the government, and on 22 March a new cabinet with National-Liberal members came to power under the leadership of A.W. Moltke; the Schleswig-Holstein demands were rejected and Schleswig's connection with Denmark was upheld. A provisional German Schleswig-Holstein government was set up in Kiel the night between 23 and 24 March and on 24 March the Rendsborg fortress was captured and the civil war had broken out.

The Three Years' War 1848-1851
Two weeks after a victory over the Schleswig-Holstein army at Bov on 9 April, the Danes were defeated near Schleswig by a united Schleswig-Holstein-Prussian army, and the troops were subsequently recalled to Als and Jutland. After pressure especially from the Russians, Prussia then withdrew and agreed to a cease-fire with Denmark in July. The cease-fire did not extend to Schleswig-Holstein, and in September the duchies introduced a democratic constitution. With the exception of Dybbøl and Als, the Schleswig-Holstein government had control of Schleswig.

In April 1849, war broke out once again; the Danish navy suffered losses in an attack on Eckernförde, and after intense fighting at Kolding the Danish troops had to withdraw northwards. On 6 July, however, Denmark won a decisive battle at Fredericia, and Prussia signed a new cease-fire agreement. In July 1850, Prussia agreed to peace both on her own behalf and on behalf of the German Confederation. But Schleswig-Holstein continued to fight and the Battle at Isted that same month was a dearly bought victory for the Danes. It was only at the very beginning of

1851 that the Schleswig-Holsteiners finally put down their weapons. Despite Schleswig-Holstein's defeat, the Three Years' War was not a victory for Denmark. The united monarchy survived but was plagued by a bitter national conflict, and the pro-German population increasingly saw the Danes as an occupying force. The Language Edicts, which introduced Danish as the language of the Church and the schools in Central Schleswig in 1851, were seen by the pro-German population as a infringement of their rights. The peace agreement was dictated by the big powers, in particular Russia, and in 1851-1852 Denmark had to agree that Schleswig would not be more closely tied to the kingdom than Holstein; at the same time prince Christian (IX) of Glücksborg was acknowledged as the hereditary heir to the entire monarchy. A common constitution for the whole kingdom never proved successful, and it was formally annulled for Holstein and Lauenburg in 1858.

The War of 1864

As a result of the agreements which had been reached with the great powers in 1851-1852, Denmark was forced to accept German intervention in matters relating to the duchies. In 1857, however, Denmark tried once again to get Schleswig tied to the kingdom. In 1863, the Danish government finally took decisive action: Holstein was separated from the kingdom and a common constitution for Denmark and Schleswig, known as the November Constitution, was passed on 13 November. Frederik VII died two days later, but Christian IX signed the new constitution. It was an open challenge to the German powers, and on 1 February 1864 Prussia and Austria declared war on Denmark. The Danish army

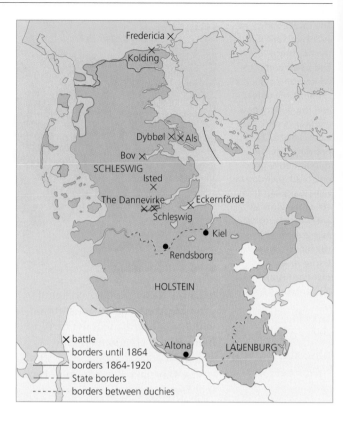

The Schleswig Wars 1848-1851 and 1864.

evacuated the old Dannevirke defences in the south and took up a position near Dybbøl, which was captured on 18 April by the Prussians. A cease-fire, during which the German troops occupied Jutland, was broken by Denmark, and at the end of July the German troops took Als. The war had been irretrievably lost. At the Peace of Vienna in October, Denmark had to cede Schleswig, Holstein and Lauenburg.

The Danish-German conflict had dominated Danish politics for a generation. The great powers had imposed serious limits on Denmark's freedom of action, and after 1864 the country's foreign policy was determined by the relationship with Germany, which was far superior in military terms, a relationship which was further complicated by the remaining Danish population in Schleswig. After 1864, successive Da-

This red Danish milch cow was born in 1880 and belonged to a farmer named Christian Bjerregaard from Elkenøre on Falster. It was a so-called 'flanker' at the great exhibition in Copenhagen in 1888, where a working dairy was one of the main attractions. At the time, the agricultural community was in the midst of the shift to dairy farming, and the red Danish dairy breed was created as a result of intensive breeding between the old country breed and the angler cattle from Schleswig.

nish governments maintained a policy of strict neutrality in their dealings with the outside world. The defeat emphasised the powerlessness of Danish foreign policy, but it also stimulated a national regeneration.

The Modern Breakthrough, 1864-1901

The farming community experienced great changes during the second half of the 19th century; more land was cultivated and production was reorganised. The change from the cultivation of plants to livestock farming had already begun, but it accelerated in 1875 when the farming community was hit by falling corn prices. From having been an exporter of corn, Denmark suddenly had to import it, and exports to Great Britain changed to processed goods such as butter and, from around 1890, bacon

and eggs. Agricultural products accounted for 85-90% of the country's exports, and production rose sharply. The manors had previously maintained a leading position, but in the 1880s the farmers set up co-operatives such as dairies and bacon factories. The co-operative movement is the most obvious sign of the restructuring which took place within the farming community during the last part of the 19th century; the medium-sized and smaller farms suddenly gained a prominent position in agricultural production. With the farmers at the centre, a characteristic culture began to develop during the 1860s. In addition to the co-operatives, this included technical skills, the Church and the education system. Around the turn of the century, this new culture had replaced the old peasant culture with a modern, self-sufficient culture with the farm and the family firmly at the centre.

Religious Movements
Religious movements were an important part of these developments. In the 1820s, many of those who lived in the countryside, particularly in Funen and Zealand, became involved in the religious revival which through wide-spread lay preaching

The use of violence as a political weapon is very rare in recent Danish history. On 21 October 1885, however, a printer named Julius Rasmussen fired a gun at Prime Minister Estrup outside his home. The shot was deflected by a thick coat button and Estrup escaped unscathed. The event was exploited politically; the government gained a welcome argument for further action and the opposition had to distance itself from the attempted murder.

urged followers to personal acceptance of the Christian principles. Having originally been established as a layman's association in 1853, the *Home Mission* became a strong revival movement within the Danish National Church during the 1860s. The Home Mission had its roots in Evangelicalism, and was characterised by the demand for personal conversion. It became particularly popular during the 1890s. *Grundtvigianism*, based on N.F.S. Grundtvig's belief that baptism, Holy Communion and Profession of Faith were the most important elements of the concept of Christianity, also developed during the last half of the 19th century into a comprehensive popular movement. As Grundtvigianism spread, free schools and folk high schools were established and a number of elective congregations (which chose their own minister), as well as independent congregations began to appear. All these had a lasting effect on the culture of the rural population.

The Development of the Towns
The towns developed rapidly during this period, and the rural population's share of the total population fell from just below 80% to a little over 60%. There was also a growth in urban trades, particularly in skilled trades, the service trades and minor industries working for the home market. Industrialisation, which had previously been centred around Copenhagen and the other large towns, spread to the smaller market towns in the 1890s. Copenhagen grew rapidly during this period, numbering 400,000 inhabitants by the turn of the century.

Politics
The political life of the nation changed character after 1864. First and foremost, the National Liberals lost their leading position, and in 1866 an amendment to the Danish-Schleswig constitution resulted in a Landsting which gave the big landowners greater power. The National

The workers at L. Andersen's bell foundry in Århus after the labour dispute of 1899. The conflict began in Jutland, and employers responded with a nation-wide lockout which lasted from May to September and affected almost 40,000 workers. The dispute came close to breaking the unions, and employers saw the result as a victory. The September Agreement of 1899 did, however, establish a framework for the structure of the two main unions which has endured until the present day.

Liberals were gradually swallowed up by the party *Højre* (the Right), which brought together the conservative forces, while in 1870, a number of opposition groups amalgamated to form *Det Forenede Venstre* (the United Left) which won a majority in the Folketing in 1872 and demanded the reintroduction of the June Constitution, Cabinet responsibility and further reforms. Højre upheld the equality of status for the Landsting and the Folketing and maintained that the king still had the right to choose his ministers. The battle lines were drawn for a conflict between the Conservative government and the liberal majority in the Folketing which came to mark the years between 1872 and 1894.

The conflict was primarily caused by the division between the farmers and those who had so far held the power, namely the civil servants and the landowners. The Conservative governments between 1875-1894 under the leadership of Prime Minister J.B.S. Estrup stuck firmly to their guns and the conflict quickly became a bitter struggle. The first provisional Finance Act was introduced in 1877. During the Period of the Provisional Laws between 1885-1894, the Right continued to govern through these provisional finance acts, forcing through a measure for the building of the fortifications around Copenhagen in 1886-1894. The Left tried to obstruct Estrup's policy through a policy of obstruction, but was weakened by internal division between the moderates led by Frede Bojsen, and the radicals led by Christen Berg and Viggo Hørup. In the 1880s, the radicals furthermore split into Berg's Danish Left and Hørup's European Left.

In spite of gains in the elections prior to 1884 and continued attacks on Estrup's government, the Left did not succeed in bringing about a change of system. At the end of the 1880s, the moderate members within the Left began a policy of negotiation with the Right. In 1891, a number of social Acts were passed by a majority in the Rigsdag, and in March 1894 the moderates on both sides reached an agreement. Although Estrup stepped down, the Right stayed in power until 1901, becoming increasingly dependent on the Left majority. In 1895, the members of the Left who were against conciliation formed *Venstrereformpartiet* (the Left Reform Party) under the leadership of J.C. Christensen. In the spring of 1901, it became clear that the Right could not stay in power, and in July the Left Reform Party formed a new government.

The Labour Movement
The labour movement in Denmark began to evolve in line with the rapid expansion of the towns, the abolition of the guild system in 1857 and the incipient industrialisation. A socialist labour movement was founded in 1871 on the initiative of Louis Pio as a unified organisation made up of the different trades and a political party which later became the Social Democratic Party. The movement met with strong opposition from the authorities. In May 1872 the conflict led to a direct confrontation between the workers and the authorities and the leaders were arrested. After a short period of growth, the movement went through another crisis in 1877 when the leaders were paid off by the police to emigrate to the USA. From c. 1880, however, the labour movement managed to rebuild itself, and in 1884 the first Social Democrats were voted into the Folketing where they aligned themselves with the Left. During the 1890s a trade union movement began to emerge and quickly gained strong support. After an extensive labour dispute, a compromise was reached between the employers' organisations and the trade unions in September 1899. The so-called September Agreement established the right of the trade unions to represent the workers,

The Education Act of 1814 introduced compulsory schooling for everyone, and around 1850 illiteracy had been completely eradicated. A better diet, improved hygiene and medical advances had raised the average life expectancy.

A huge number of people moved from the countryside into the towns and many, though not quite as many as in Norway and Sweden, emigrated, especially to the USA. Old ideas and lifestyles went by the board along with many traditional cultural notions. Change became a way of life. The society based on rank was abolished in 1849 and the old distinctions between the estates were transformed into a new social stratification based on property and income. The peasant society gradually became divided into farmers, smallholders and day labourers; in the towns, employer/employee relations were introduced, and society's growing need for services led to the appearance of a stratum of salaried workers and new groups of independent businessmen.

Women still had no part in the political rights granted to men, but new legislation granted them more rights than before, and by the end of the 19th century they began to enter the labour market where many of them found employment in the service sector.

Claus Bjørn

Constitutional Amendments and Reforms, 1901-1913

When the political system was changed in 1901, a new constitutional practice was introduced, prohibiting any government from staying in power when faced with a vote of no confidence from a majority in the Folketing. The Left Reform Party came to power in 1901 and had an absolute majority in the Folketing until 1906. The Right and the Inde-

On 1 September 1901, the Change of System was celebrated in Copenhagen. A procession of around 10,000 people marched from Kongens Have (The King's Garden) to Amalienborg Castle, despite the rain and the bitter wind. On the square in front of the castle, Christian IX was praised for finally giving in to the call for a government that was based on a majority in the Folketing.

and the right of the employers to direct and distribute the work. At the turn of the century the labour movement was still making progress, and in 1901 the Social Democratic Party won 14 of the 114 seats in the Folketing. The Social Democrats continued to follow the Left until 1901, but the tension between the two parties already began to show towards the end of the 1890s.

The Great Transformation

Danish society underwent a complete transformation between 1864 and 1901; signs of what was to come had already been seen prior to this period but now the changes began to affect everyone. Life in 1901 differed in almost every way from life back in 1814; the population had grown dramatically and their standard of living had greatly improved.

pendent Conservatives kept their majority in the Landsting, however, forcing the government to consult one or the other when passing laws. The Left Reform Party lost its majority in 1906 following a split in 1905, resulting in the creation of *Det Radikale Venstre* (the Social Liberal Party) which soon gained a central position in Danish politics. The four large parties which were to dominate Danish politics in the years to come had now emerged. None of them have ever held an absolute majority; successive governments have only been able to carry through their own policies by co-operating with one or more of the other parties. Compromise had become a key element in Danish politics.

The time leading up to the First World War saw a number of reforms. Under the leadership of the eminent tactician J.C. Christensen, the Left Reform Party carried through some of the most important parts of the party's programme: A tax reform in 1903 replaced land and property taxes with income tax and capital tax and introduced a land tax assessment. The three-year upper

secondary school was introduced in the same year and was linked to the elementary school by a middle school. A law was passed introducing elected parish councils. Women were initially given the right to vote in these parish council elections, and in 1908 the Rigsdag also gave them the right to vote in municipal council elections. A number of new laws concerning the labour market were brought in to supplement the existing collective bargaining system. Government authorisation and state subsidies for unemployment benefit schemes were introduced in 1907. Conciliation procedures were introduced in 1910 along with the Permanent Court of Arbitration (now known as *Arbejdsretten*, the Industrial Court).

The Left Reform Party, from 1910 *Venstre* (The Liberals), and J.C. Christensen were weakened when it was discovered in 1908 that the Minister of Justice, P.A. Alberti, had been involved in large-scale embezzlement and fraud, though J.C. Christensen was acquitted following impeachments for having been responsible. A lengthy debate concerning an

Soldiers on watch by the Øresund coast in August 1914. Denmark managed to hold on to its neutrality during First World War, but 60,000 men were still called up at the beginning of the war for the so-called defence force. The majority of them were to man the Copenhagen fortifications, but a small number were stationed in Jutland.

Poster designed by Thor Bøgelund in connection with the 1920 referendum on the future nationality of Schleswig. The classic Mother Denmark figure is a replica of a picture from 1850-1851 by Elisabeth Jerichau Baumann. The original painting depicted the Danish victory at Isted during the Three Years' War (1848-1851). The woman wore a coat of mail and carried a sword aimed at the German eagle. In the poster, the coat of mail has been replaced by a large robe, and a leafy branch symbolising peace has taken the place of the sword.

amendment to the constitution began shortly after and only ended during the First World War with the passing of the 1915 constitution as the coping stone in the large programme of reforms; it abolished the limited franchise associated with the Landsting and enfranchised women and servants. It also brought in proportional representation for Folketing elections, resulting in a fairer distribution of the seats.

The time was favourable for reforms in economic terms. Both agriculture and industry were seeing strong growth, and the number of people employed in industry, trade and transport rose dramatically. Danish industry was the world leader in many areas, e.g. the development of diesel engines for ships. Agriculture benefited from the change to livestock farming, and in 1914, agricultural products still accounted for almost 90% of the Danish export market with butter and bacon for the British market as the most important items.

In matters relating to foreign policy, Denmark was in an ambiguous

position. The country was economically dependent on exports to Great Britain, but as regards security policy it was dependent on the relationship with its ever more powerful German neighbour. This latter connection was made even more complicated by the existence of the pro-Danish people in Schleswig. They were at times subjected to harsh repression which imbued contemporary patriotic sentiments with a strong anti-German flavour. Successive Danish governments chose to keep a low profile in the international arena. There was a general agreement to continue the policy of neutrality, and an unspoken acknowledgement that it had to be carried out in a way which did not offend Germany.

Despite this understanding, there was no agreement between the parties on defence policy. The Right wanted to build up a strong military defence; the Social Liberals and the Social Democrats demanded total or partial disarmament. In 1909, the Right and the Liberals entered into an agreement which strengthened the armed forces and Copenhagen's coast defences. Both the Social Liberal Party and the Social-Democratic Party made gains at the Folketing elections in 1913 and with support from the Social Democrats, a Social Liberal government was set up under the leadership of C.Th. Zahle. The new government stayed in power until 1920.

Neutrality, Regulation and Political Conflicts, 1914-1920

Although Denmark managed to retain its neutral status during World War I, it largely had to adhere to Germany's wishes. The Great Belt, for example, was blocked by mines despite an international obligation to keep the strait open. A large defence force was called up and posted largely around Copenhagen. The Danes were not entirely unaffected by the war: 275 of the merchant navy's ships were sunk, some 700 seamen lost their lives and almost 6,000 people from South Jutland were killed on active service in the German army. Economically, the country kept a balance between the warring parties by entering into separate trade agreements which involved export bans so that the blockades could not be avoided by re-exporting goods from Denmark.

Internally, the political parties entered into a truce which, by and large, lasted until the end of the war. Based on the August Laws of 1914, the government and the Rigsdag constructed an elaborate system of regulations which affected every economic and social area, included price policy, supply policy and rationing systems, and to a certain extent also income distribution policy which meant a widening of state powers.

The territory around the Danish West Indies gained increased strategic importance during the First World War. The United States were concerned by the interest shown in the Danish islands by a number of German companies, and in 1915 they sought to buy the islands from the Danish government. A selling price of 25 million dollars was agreed the following year and the sale went through after a referendum in December. The islands were officially handed over on 1 April 1917.

The political truce broke down immediately after the end of the First World War and the Opposition, which then consisted of the Liberals and the Conservative People's Party (until 1915 *Højre* 'Right'), demanded that the regulations be abolished. The government hesitated, however,

because of the delicate social balance and the fear of a post-war crisis. Despite these divisions, a number of land laws were passed in 1919 which changed the system of ownership for the large estates and took over land which was used to set up approximately 6,000 smallholdings.

The Social Democratic Party began to come under strong fire for its moderate policies by those on the left of the political spectrum. The conflict, which was partly inspired by the revolutions in the central and eastern parts of Europe, was intensified by growing social hardships. In 1918-1919, the militant workers succeeded in pushing through the labour market's demand from 1889 for an eight-hour working day. The 1919 agreement between the Danish Employers' Federation and the Federation of Trade Unions incorporated both this demand and an improved cost-of-living adjustment system.

Germany's collapse made it possible to solve the Schleswig issue. It was stipulated in the Treaty of Versailles that the future of the area should be decided by plebiscite, and the first vote was held in North Schleswig on 10 February 1920 when three quarters of the population voted in favour of a union with Denmark. A second vote was held on 14 March the same year in Central Schleswig (which included Flensburg) and produced the opposite result. The plebiscite gave rise to strong feelings of patriotism on both sides. In 1919, the Dannevirke Movement had called for a border along the Dannevirke; after the second vote the nationalists became determined that Flensburg should be returned despite the result of the referendum.

The nationalists' anger over the border north of Flensburg exploded at the end of March 1920. The border issue, combined with continuing

The Bridge across Lillebælt (Little Belt) under construction. The link between Jutland and Funen was inaugurated in 1935, and the complex technical structure provides a fitting testimony to Danish engineering excellence. The labour-intensive bridge work also provided a means of lowering the rate of unemployment at the beginning of the 1930s.

objections towards the system of regulations, finally resulted in a violent attack on the government and pressure on Christian X to dismiss it. On 29 March the King dismissed Zahle's government, thereby giving rise to the Easter Crisis. The Folketing was in recess for Easter so no majority was shown to be against the government. The following day, the King appointed a caretaker government which was given the task of calling an election. Christian X's actions were interpreted by the Social Liberals and the Social Democrats as a coup, and they immediately called for the restoration of parliamentary democracy. Their demand was strongly backed by the labour movement which threatened to declare a general strike. Large demonstrations were held by the workers who demanded a republic to replace the monarchy. The situation was exacerbated by the threat of a large-scale labour conflict. After intense negotiations, the party leaders finally arrived at an agreement on the morning of Easter Day. A new caretaker government was to be appointed and

given the sole task of calling an election. Even though the crisis was one of the most serious in the recent political history of Denmark, its conclusion helped to consolidate the principle of Cabinet responsibility.

From Liberalism to State Intervention, 1920-1929

The election in April 1920 brought in a Liberal government supported by the Conservative People's Party. The new government faced difficulties as a result of the post-war crisis which affected both agriculture and industry and created almost chaotic conditions within the banking sector; several banks collapsed, including Scandinavia's largest bank, the *Landmandsbank*, which had to be bailed out by the government in 1922. The crisis was aggravated by a premature revaluation of the krone. The 1920s were plagued by high unemployment which peaked between 1922-1923 and 1925-1928, and by large-scale labour disputes. In 1924, the Liberal government was succeeded by the country's first Social Democratic government with the strong and gifted tactician Th. Stauning as Prime Minister. Stauning's government also ran into problems, especially as regards the currency. During the big industrial conflict in 1925, the government prepared state intervention; in the event, however, no action was taken. A comprehensive crisis programme regrettably failed the following year and the government, which lost its majority at the next election, was succeeded by the Liberals. The new Prime Minister was the very liberalistic Th. Madsen-Mygdal, who planned to tackle the crisis by cutting down on public expenditure, introducing tax reductions and intervening in the labour market.

Both agriculture and industry were greatly modernised despite the economic problems; amongst other things, the Ford Motor Company set up Europe's first assembly plant for cars in Denmark.

The 1920s were also characterised by ideological differences. The farmers and the Liberals were in favour of liberalism, whilst the workers and the Social Democrats called for greater power to the State, a wish which was to some extent shared by the Conservative People's Party. At times, these differences seemed to turn into a confrontation between town and country.

In matters of foreign policy, the 1920s were a quiet decade. The country was not threatened by any of the big powers. Denmark participated in the sanctions by the West against the Soviet Union until 1924 when it recognised the Communist government. In 1920, Denmark became a member of the League of Nations. Like the other Nordic countries, Denmark's policy of neutrality did not accord with the League of Nations' collective security system which would involve the country in a conflict with an aggressor. The League's disarmament plans, however, were welcomed by a majority of the Danish population. Even so, it was still a defence issue which toppled the government in 1929, when the Conservatives, led by John Christmas Møller, abstained from voting on the Budget because of their objections to the defence appropriations. The Conservatives were joined by the Social Liberals who equally abstained from voting, whilst the Social Democrats actually voted against.

Economic Crisis and Political Stability, 1929-1940

The Social Democrats and the Social Liberals won the majority at the election in April 1929, and formed a coalition government led by Th. Stauning and P. Munch as Prime Minister and Foreign Minister respectively. This was to become the longest-ruling government of the century. Its extensive reform programme was seriously hampered by the world-wide Depression which hit Denmark in the middle of 1930. Initially, the agricultural sector encountered problems with sales and prices. In the first half of the 1930s, many farmers were affected by debt crisis and resultant foreclosure. In 1931, the towns also began to feel the crisis as businesses went under and jobs were lost. By 1932, unemployment had risen to over 40%. Externally, the government attempted to ease the situation by trade agreements with Great Britain and Germany. At home, it made a number of emergency agreements with one or both opposition parties. In 1932, the Exchange Control Office was set up to control the external sector of the economy, and all parties gradually acknowledged the need for state intervention in the country's economy.

Political extremism flourished in the atmosphere created by the Depression and the Fascist/Nazi movements that had begun to stir in Europe. Denmark's Communist Party (DKP) prospered and succeeded in getting two members elected to the Folketing in 1932, one being the party's chairman for many years, Aksel Larsen. In 1931, right-wing extremists formed the very active *Landbrugernes Sammenslutning* (Agrarian Revival Movement, LS), which organised a huge march to Copenhagen by the country's farmers in order to exert pressure on the Rigsdag and the King. Certain factions within LS were members of the extreme right-wing Fascist or Nazi groups which came and went throughout the 1930s. Their membership was small and they did not get into the Folketing until 1939. Faced with right-wing accusations that democracy was inefficient, the larger parties set out to demonstrate its efficiency by a number of cross-party agreements. The most important of these was known as the *Kanslergade Agreement*, named after the street where Stauning's residence was located. It was entered into by the government and the Left, and completed on 30 January 1933, the day that Hitler became Chancellor of Germany. It provided for a number of measures, including the first of many extensions by law to the collective labour agreement between employers and employees, a devaluation of the krone and state subsidies to the farming community. Finally, the agreement also required the Liberals to withdraw its objections to the Social Reforms which K.K. Steincke, the minister of social affairs, had been striving to introduce for a number of years. The Social Reform of 1933 simplified legislation and laid down the principle of

law. It also introduced fixed charges for social services. When the government succeeded in winning a majority in the Landsting in 1936, it became simpler to pass the reforms. The parties in power, aided by the Conservatives, put forward a proposal for a new constitution but the bill was rejected by a referendum held in 1939.

The emergency agreements blurred the ideological divisions between the parties. On the one hand, purely liberalistic objectives were in decline and on the other hand, the Social Democratic Party abandoned its original socialist goals and became a party for the workers and the people with greater appeal to a wider sector of the population. Their new position was underlined in 1934 by the introduction of Stauning's programme entitled 'Denmark for the People'. The crisis also led to closer co-operation between the State, the administration, the trade organisations and the two sides of industry.

Foreign policy in the 1930s was dominated by the relationship with Germany. Hitler's take-over in 1933, Germany's withdrawal from the League of Nations later that same year and the country's overt rearmament in 1935 meant that Denmark's policy on security and neutrality again had to accommodate its powerful neighbour. The British government furthermore made it clear that Denmark could not expect any military support in the event of a conflict with Germany. The Nordic countries attempted to coordinate their policies of neutrality, but their interests differed to such an extent that they were unable to co-operate on security policy. The question of whether the armed forces should be strengthened had still not been resolved by the parties. An agreement

A German quick-firing gun crew in position in Haderslev on 9 April 1940 at approximately 7.45. Two infantry divisions and a motorised brigade attacked Denmark at 4.15. At the same time, the German emissary handed over the German demands to P. Munch, the Foreign Minister. After several hours of negotiations at Amalienborg Palace with the king, the government finally decided to surrender at approximately 6 o'clock. It took some time, however, before the order to cease fighting reached all units. The battles cost the Danes 16 dead and 23 wounded.

in 1937 did produce more personnel and additional equipment, but only enough to emphasise the country's neutrality. Under no circumstances would Denmark be able to defend itself if the worst came to the worst. In 1939, Germany approached the Nordic countries with a proposed non-aggression treaty. The other countries rejected it, but a few months before the beginning of the war Denmark agreed to sign the non-aggression pact although it was generally felt to be worth less than the paper it was written on.

When war broke out in September 1939, Denmark declared itself neutral. But Denmark's relations with Germany and Great Britain became increasingly precarious as the country tried to remain politically and economically balanced between the two nations.

Lorenz Rerup

The Occupation 1940-1945
German troops occupied Denmark within a few hours on the morning of 9 April 1940. The attack was accompanied by an ultimatum that no resistance was to be offered. Germany would, in exchange, respect the country's political independence; the King and the government gave in. Thus began a 'peaceful occupation' during which Denmark

tried to maintain the illusion of independence. With a few exceptions, the Foreign Ministries handled all communication between the two countries.

England reacted by occupying the Faeroe Islands on 12 April, and attempted to seize Denmark's merchant navy; 2/3 of the ships ended up in allied service. E. Reventlow, the Danish envoy in London, maintained his diplomatic status. H. Kauffmann in Washington, however, reserved his position and in April 1941, he signed an agreement with the USA which gave the States the right to set up military bases in Greenland, which had been under the protection of the States since the outbreak of war.

Political and Economic Co-operation
On principle, the German military required all cases in which it was involved to be tried by its own military courts. The Danes, however, claimed that Danish citizens in the sovereign state of Denmark should always be tried by the Danish courts. As the sabotage activities increased in 1942, a solution had to be found. The resulting system of dual jurisdiction became a millstone for the policy of collaboration.

The policy of collaboration with Germany was matched internally by

Sugar and coffee were already rationed before the occupation; bread, oats and butter were also soon affected. Of the 3,000 calories required by a 'normal' consumer, approximately 1,600 calories were covered by the rations. The rest came from non-rationed goods such as meat, potatoes, fruit and vegetables. The stamps were not supposed to be traded, but black market dealing was rife.

Maj 1941
200 g
Bl. Sæbe el. Vaskepulv.
eller 75 g Sæbespaaner
eller 100 g Sæbe i Stang-
eller Blokform

☑ Gyldig fra 27. Maj 1941
☑ **250 g SMØR**
☑ eller – i Forbindelse med
særligt Mærke – Margarine

Dette Mærke giver i
MAJ 1941
Ret til Køb af
½ kg SUKKER

Christian X on horseback in Amaliegade during the first year of the occupation – a king who became the focal point for a bewildered people who had no-one else to turn to. His popularity was evident from the *Royal Badge* worn by all 'good Danes' during the years of the occupation, and from the jubilant crowds who gathered to commemorate his 70th birthday in the autumn of 1940.

co-operation between the parties. Representatives from the Conservative People's Party and the Liberals joined the Social Democratic government as ministers without portfolios. In July 1940, a new coalition government was formed, with a few ministers who were not affiliated to any particular party, including Erik Scavenius who became Foreign Minister. The close co-operation at Christiansborg had the support of the whole population and a wave of Danish national feeling and patriotism swept across the country. The King became the nation's father figure and a symbol of unity.

The Danish government feared that the Germans would let the Danish Nazi Party come to power. Their fear was unfounded, however, as the Danish Nazis were merely used as a bugbear by the occupying forces. This was not known, however, by the government or the 'revival' circles which were attempting to set up an alternative government consisting of professionals and experts.

Exports had to be diverted to Germany, who was prepared to pay high prices for agricultural products in return for goods such as coal. The price increases which were experienced at the outbreak of war were countered by an automatic index-linked regulation of wages and salaries, but a pay freeze was soon introduced in line with German policy. The Germans did not want labourers in the occupied countries to have a better standard of living than their own workers. As a result, the farmers prospered whilst the real income in towns fell by around 20% in 1940, and the unemployment rate increased. By the end of the occupation, the trade with Germany had produced an export surplus of approximately 3 billion kroner, boosting purchasing power in the Danish society. The German military's construction projects, such as landing strips and the fortifications built on the west coast of Jutland, cost approximately 5 billion kroner and were financed by outlays from *Nationalbanken*, Denmark's central bank.

The main drawback of the policy of collaboration was the dependence on Germany. The government had to limit the freedom of the press and other demands had to be complied

The August Uprising in 1943 centred on Esbjerg (9-11 August), Odense (18-23 August), Aalborg (23-29 August) and Århus (26-29 August). The authorities tried in vain to calm the situation by sending in the police, but in Odense the officers simply ended up on the receiving end of the demonstrators' anger; the irate crowd upended one of the Black Marias.

with, and 'agitators' like the Conservative Christmas Møller and the Social Democrat Hans Hedtoft had to be removed from the political arena. The actions of the Danish Nazis had to be tolerated despite the restrictions on public gatherings. The policy of collaboration did have certain advantages, however, in that unlike the other occupied countries, Danish society escaped Nazification. The army, the navy and the police were still in the hands of the Danish State. Democracy still functioned at a central and local level, and there was no interference in the education sector. The trade organisations went unchallenged, as did all other associations.

When Germany invaded the Soviet Union on 22 June 1941, it demanded that the leading members of the Danish Communist Party be interned. The German orders were complied with much more thoroughly than was demanded and the Danish Communist Party (DKP) was banned, despite the fact that both these actions went against the constitution. All Communists were ousted from the unions. The party went underground and continued its activities, which was the start of the Resistance movement in Denmark.

The government also accepted German demands to create a military corps, known as *Frikorps Danmark*, which was to fight with the Germans against Bolshevism and to sign the Anti-Comintern Pact. When Prime Minister Stauning died in May 1942, he was succeeded by his party colleague Vilhelm Buhl. The economic situation gradually settled down, prices stabilised, unemployment fell (partly because of the need for labour in connection with the German construction work), and the krone was revalued by approximately 8% in relation to the German Reichsmark.

The Policy of Collaboration under Pressure

The illegal activities which began in 1942 put a great deal of pressure on the policy of collaboration. Following Germany's breach of the German-Soviet non-aggression pact, the Communists steadily developed their illegal activities. Together with members of the Conservative People's Party, they published the underground paper known as *Frit Danmark* (Free Denmark), and in April 1942, they launched an active campaign of sabotage. Christmas Møller's escape to England at the beginning of May 1942, and his subsequent radio broadcasts to Denmark, created a great sensation. From the turn of the year 1941-1942, the British Special Operations Executive began to drop parachutists in Denmark with help from the party *Dansk Samling* (the Danish Unity Party). At this time, there was still very little public support for the Resistance movement.

By the autumn of 1942, the Germans were becoming increasingly dissatisfied with the situation in Denmark, partly because of riots when Frikorps Danmark was home on leave, but also because the German army needed to strengthen its anti-invasion defence. A diplomatic crisis erupted following a rather curt telegram from the King thanking Hitler for his birthday greetings. The Telegram Crisis resulted in direct intervention from Hitler in the affairs of the country. The plenipotentiary Renthe-Fink was replaced by Werner Best and a new commander-in-chief, General von Hanneken, was sent to Denmark in November. The occupiers also demanded that the Foreign Minister, Scavenius, be made Prime Minister and that strong action be taken against the Resistance movement; moreover, von Hanneken ordered all Danish military personnel out of Jutland.

Werner Best continued the German policy in close co-operation with Scavenius, realising that co-operation had several advantages. On the one hand, the Germans could take advantage of Denmark's production – agricultural exports corresponded to around one month's consumption in Germany – and on the other they could maintain law and order with the minimum use of German resources. Best managed to bring about that the German authorities allowed a general election to be held on 23 March 1943. The election turned into a trial of strength between the coalition parties and the activists. A record 89.5% turnout gave the coalition parties 93.4% of the

On 29 August 1943, Vice-Admiral A.H. Vedel gave orders that the entire fleet should be sunk to avoid any operative ships falling into German hands. A total of 29 ships were sunk in Holmen in Copenhagen, including the armoured vessel *Peder Skram*. Thirteen vessels managed to escape to Sweden where they were interned.

A Short Stirling dropping weapons and explosives on 4 August 1944 near Højris on Mors. The first weapon drops took place in March 1943, but the number of drops was very limited until August 1944. A total of around 700 tonnes were brought in from England; this included approximately 30% during the last months of 1944, and 67% during 1945. Four crossings with fishing boats were made across the North Sea. The country was divided into three zones with separate reception groups; approximately 60% went to Jutland, around 10% to Funen and the rest to Zealand.

votes; 2.1% voted in favour of the Danish Unity Party and 3.3% voted for the Nazis, etc. The Danish Communist Party (DKP) had been banned, but took part indirectly alongside Free Denmark with a campaign urging voters to return a blank ballot paper, as indeed 1.2% of them did.

The mood gradually began to change during the spring and summer of 1943, partly because of general 'occupation fatigue', partly because of the German defeats at the fronts from the end of 1942. The number of strikes began to rise, as did the number of sabotage actions. In spring 1943, the Resistance movement began to acquire explosives from England.

Despite all this, the 'August Uprising' still came as a surprise. Strikes were organised by the communists in 17 towns across the country, factories, offices and shops closed down and huge riots broke out; Copenhagen had no strikes but there were wide-spread disturbances. The political and union authorities did their best to stop the unrest and the German troops showed moderation in the strike-bound towns, but the Germans wanted the Danish military to be disarmed.

Even though Werner Best played down the scale of the disturbances in his reports to Berlin, Hitler demanded that the Danish government declare a state of emergency and introduce the death penalty for sabotage. The Danes refused. On 29 August, the government presented the King with its resignation. The Germans immediately began to disarm and intern the Danish army and navy, though the latter sank itself, and von Hanneken declared the whole country under martial law.

Government by Civil Service Heads and Continued Resistance
Then, and later, 29 August was seen as the decisive turning point in the relationship between Denmark and Germany. The policy of collaboration was ended and, in the words of Best: 'The political parade horse, Denmark, is dead'.

In the months that followed until the Liberation, the country was governed by the civil service heads of department through orders approved by the supreme court. Collaboration continued on an administrative level, and Danish society escaped Nazification.

Anti-German sentiments were sharpened when the Germans took action against the Danish Jews on

When the liberation announcement was heard over the radio in the evening of 4 May 1945, thousands of Danes tore down their blackout curtains and put candles in the windows. This has since become a firm tradition. Twenty-five years after the liberation, the Post Office issued this stamp, designed by the graphic artist Povl Christensen. The symbolism was evident to all Danes.

Danish Jews fleeing to Sweden. After the Gestapo action against the Danish Jews on the night between 1 and 2 October 1943, more than 7,000 people fled to Sweden while 481 were deported to Theresienstadt. Many ordinary people helped with the illegal rescue action. There are very few authentic pictures from those few days; this one was taken on a cutter on the way from Falster to Ystad. The crossing lasted ten hours and brought ten adults and five children to safety.

the night of 2 October 1943. The operation failed, due partly to Best's duplicity. Fewer than 500 Jews were seized and taken to Theresienstadt, where the vast majority of them survived. Around 7,000 Jews fled to Sweden.

The Danish Freedom Council was established in the middle of September to lead the fight for the country's liberation. The Council included representatives from the most important resistance groups: The Communists, Free Denmark, the Danish Unity Party and the Ring, with Børge Houmann, Mogens Fog, Arne Sørensen and Frode Jakobsen as the most important members. Directives from SOE (Special Operations Executive) helped to unite the different groups; in December orders came that military groups were to be organised, ready to attack the German troops in the rear in case of invasion. A single organisation was now set up to head operations. The military groups were first organised by the Communists and the Danish Unity Party, and then increasingly by members of the Ring, especially because many of the pioneers disappeared: Some went into German prisons and concentration camps, others were interned in Denmark in

the Frøslevlejr camp (about 10,000), and about 10,000 escaped to Sweden.

The Resistance movement grew as more and more military groups were set up. There were around 20,000 members by the end of 1944, and this number had risen to around 50,000 by the time of the Liberation. The groups were armed with handguns from England or Sweden. On the other hand, the sabotage groups (in Copenhagen BOPA and Holger Danske, in the provinces e.g. Valthergruppen in Odense) accounted for a very small percentage of the total. Their actions were mainly directed at the railways (approximately 1,500 attacks) and the industries that worked for the Germans (another 2,800 attacks). Ships and shipyards constituted another important target and created a strong threat which was taken extremely seriously by the Germans.

After the military personnel had been freed in October 1943, the army began to operate alongside the Freedom Council. Officers gathered in special groups in Copenhagen and formed a separate brigade in Sweden known as Danforce. Officers were given leading positions around the country, and from June 1944 the Resistance Movement was secretly financed by the State.

The Danish Freedom Council and the 'old' politicians were drawn together following the general strike in Copenhagen on 1 July 1944. Together they appealed to the Allies to recognise Denmark as an allied power, but were met by resistance from the Soviets. Negotiations were also held concerning the creation of the first post-war government, and an agreement was finally reached that each side would take half the ministerial posts.

After the events of 29 August 1943,

An English soldier photographed the Liberation celebrations on the Town Hall Square in Copenhagen, 8 May 1945. On the day of the Liberation, 5 May, Major-General Dewing arrived in the capital by air with his staff and a unit of parachutists. The first regular units of *The Royal Dragoons* crossed the Danish-German border on 7 May and reached Copenhagen the following day. The English troops were greeted by jubilant crowds along the whole route through Jutland, Funen and Zealand.

the Gestapo had taken over all investigations concerning the Resistance Movement. At the beginning of 1944, the Germans began their campaign of 'counter terror': Counter-sabotage and reprisal murders were carried out in retaliation for sabotage actions and attacks against the German army (*Wehrmacht*). German attempts to persuade the Danish police to take part in the prevention of sabotage and maintaining law and order during strikes failed, so the police force was disbanded on 19 September 1944 and policemen subsequently sent to concentration camps. The war and the occupation cost around 7,000 Danes their lives.

The last months of the occupation were characterised by increased shortages, poor quality goods, clashes between members of the Resistance and Danes working for the Germans, and a rising crime rate. From February 1945, some 200,000 German refugees from East Prussia

The UN was created in June 1945 at a conference in San Francisco; here the Danish parliamentary envoy, Hartvig Frisch, signs the UN pact. Doubts remained until the very last minute as to whether Denmark would be accepted as an allied power and as a founder of the UN. Following energetic Norwegian diplomatic efforts, however, Denmark was accepted as a full member. The other members of the Danish delegation were, from the left: Counsellor Povl Bang Jensen, Professor Erik Husfeldt and the leader of the delegation, Ambassador Henrik Kauffmann.

In 1960, the Campaign against Atomic Weapons led the first of a number of marches from Holbæk to Copenhagen. This picture from 1962 shows the last and the biggest of these atomic marches. The inspiration came from England; the Atomic Campaign was aimed at atomic weapons and nuclear testing around the world, but was also in favour of maintaining the Danish stand against nuclear armament. The Atomic Campaign was the start of many grassroots movements in the 1960s and 1970s.

arrived in Denmark. Meanwhile, the end of the war was in sight. All German troops in Denmark surrendered to the English on 5 May 1945, except for those stationed on Bornholm which lay within the Soviet theatre of operations. The island was not liberated until 8 May 1945, and Rønne and Nexø were subjected to Soviet air raids prior to the liberation.

Aage Trommer

Denmark in the International Community, 1945-1972

Despite its unclear position during the Second World War, Denmark was recognised as an allied power and founding member of the United Nations in 1945. Many initially assumed that the newa organisation would guarantee peace, but their belief was shattered with the outbreak of the Cold War in 1946-1947. Denmark's security policy had to be adapted in line with the division of Europe. A new superpower, the Soviet Union, lay close to Denmark's borders and its traditional isolated neutrality was no longer adequate. At first, attempts were made to establish a Nordic defensive alliance, but negotiations broke down at the beginning of 1949. Instead, Denmark and Norway became founding members of The North Atlantic Pact in April 1949. For the first few years, Denmark was an 'allied with reservations' because both the public and the politicians had doubts, primarily regarding the stationing of atomic weapons on Danish soil, but also with respect to the rearmament of West Germany and the country's subsequent membership of NATO.

When the liberation government

led by Vilhelm Buhl presented its programme on 9 May 1945, it stated clearly that Denmark's border was unalterable. A heated internal conflict nevertheless erupted over the question of the German border, but by 1947 it was obvious that the border would not be changed. Relations with West Germany improved over the years, and in 1955 the good relations were sealed with the Copenhagen-Bonn declaration concerning the minorities living in the border area. In 1961, a Danish-German Unitary Command was established for NATO's northern sector.

In January 1968, the Danish government asked for renewed assurance from the USA that the ban on atomic weapons on Danish soil would not be violated. The request followed the crash of an nuclear-armed B-52 bomber near Thule in Greenland. It was at first thought that this was an isolated incident in an emergency, but the issue flared up again in 1995 when the Danish government released hitherto unseen information revealing that H.C. Hansen, former Prime Minister and foreign minister, gave the USA permission in 1958 to overfly and land nuclear-armed planes in Greenland, despite the official Danish policy. The information was of great help to the Danes who had taken part in the clean-up operation following the Thule incident in 1968. Their fight for compensation for physical and psychological damage has finally been resolved and their demands met.

Alongside its membership of NATO from 1949, Denmark and the other Nordic countries have contributed greatly to the UN's peace-keeping operations. Danish troops went to Suez in 1956-1957, to the Congo in 1960-1964 and to Cyprus in 1964. Denmark has provided de-

DANMARKS KOMMUNISTISKE PARTI

velopment aid since 1961 and is, in relative terms, one of the largest providers of aid to the developing world. Since 1992, Denmark has complied with UN requirements for a minimum contribution of 1% of the GDP towards development aid.

The financial assistance which Denmark received in 1948 from the Marshall Plan helped to ease the country's currency difficulties. It also provided funds for the import of raw materials and machinery and thereby helped to modernise and rationalise agriculture and industry. Membership of the OEEC (now the OECD) involved Denmark in the internationalisation of the economy through the dismantling of trade and currency restrictions. Denmark did not take part in the creation of the European institutions which led to the Treaty of Rome's European Economic Community (EEC) in 1957-1959. The country did take part, however, in negotiations concerning the European Free Trade Association (EFTA) which was set up in 1960. Denmark's exports were almost equally divided between the two areas, and when

Those who were against EC membership did their best to spread a sense of doom before the referendum on 2 October 1972, when the nation went to the polls to decide whether Denmark should join. Membership of the EC would mean an end to Denmark's life as an independent nation. 'The six', as the then EC countries were known, are seen here as a six-armed squid about to swallow a blissfully unaware little fish the colour of the Danish flag. The poster was distributed by the Danish Communist Party which was amongst the leading EC opponents in 1972. The party later became one of the leading voices of the Popular Movement against the EC after the Danes had voted in favour of membership.

Danish cyclists eager to enter Europe. Hans Bendix's drawing captures the untroubled optimism demonstrated by the EC supporters during the campaign leading up to the referendum on 2 October 1972. The national symbol, the Dannebrog, was used both by those who were for, and those who were against EC membership. The Committee for EC membership included representatives from all spheres of trade and industry, as well as larger organisations and the political parties who were in favour of joining.

DANMARK i EF

KOMITEEN FOR TILSLUTNING TIL EF

Great Britain applied for membership of the EEC in 1961, Denmark immediately followed suit but gave up when the British application was rejected. After yet another failed attempt in 1967, negotiations got under way for a Nordic Economic Union (NORDEK). This idea was later abandoned when countries were once again invited to apply for membership of the EC in 1969. After an intense debate in 1972, the government held a binding referendum in which a majority voted to join the EC, and Denmark's membership took effect at the beginning of 1973. The European co-operation issue had, however, split the nation in two almost equal halves.

Lorenz Rerup,
Niels Finn Christiansen

The Developing Welfare State

A liberation government consisting of an equal number of representatives from the Danish Freedom Council and the political parties had already been prepared during the occupation. When it came to power in May 1945, it instigated a judicial purge of collaborators. Those who were convicted were chiefly Nazis, their henchmen and minor collaborators.

The government's second task was to normalise political life by calling a Folketing election for October 1945. The Danish Communist Party (DKP) won a large following at the expense of the Social Democratic Party. The Liberals prospered and formed a minority government led by Knud Kristensen with support from the Conservatives and the Social Liberals. It was brought down by a vote of no confidence in the Prime Minister due to his agitation for the Schleswig border to be moved. At the election in 1947, the Social Democratic Party regained some of its strength, and led by Hans Hedtoft it formed a minority government which, like the one before it, ran into problems due to the country's economic difficulties. It was followed by a government under the leadership of Erik Eriksen consisting of Liberals and Conservatives. Its chief contribution was the introduction of a major constitutional reform in 1953. The reform brought sweeping changes: The Landsting was abolished, Cabinet responsibility was written into the constitution, sovereignty could be partly surrendered, it was made easier to hold referenda and the post of ombudsman was created. Together with the constitution, the government also introduced a Law of Succession which made it possible for women to succeed to the Danish throne; the Law of Succession does not involve full equality, however, as a younger son will still take precedence over an older daughter.

After the constitutional changes, the government was succeeded by a Social Democratic minority government with support from the Social Liberals. It was first led by Hans

Hedtoft and, following his death in 1955, by H.C. Hansen. After the election in 1957, H.C. Hansen formed a majority coalition of Social Democrats, Social Liberals and the Single Tax Party. It was the first government to profit by the international boom and the domestic economic growth. Denmark had a succession of Social Democratic governments until 1968. Between 1960 and 1962 Viggo Kampmann was Prime Minister, and he was followed by J.O. Krag. These governments generally relied on the support of the Social Liberals, though between 1966-1968 they were supported by the Socialist People's Party (SF) which had been formed in 1959 by Aksel Larsen after the DKP had split. In 1968, a non-socialist party government was formed by the Social Liberals, the Conservative People's Party and the Liberals, led by Hilmar Baunsgaard of the Social Liberal Party. In 1971, J.O. Krag again became the leader of a Social Democratic government; after the 1972 referendum in which a majority voted in favour of Danish membership of the EC, he stepped down in favour of Anker Jørgensen.

Comprehensive programmes had been produced by almost all political parties by the end of the Second World War; the most comprehensive was that of the Social Democratic Party with a welfare strategy covering all aspects of society. The economic problems of the first decade after 1945 prevented reform policy, but from the middle of the 1950s varying parliamentary coalitions implemented a welfare policy which included the national pension scheme (1956), the sickness compensation scheme (1960), disablement insurance (1965)

Car show at the Forum in Copenhagen, 1962. Car sales increased dramatically from the middle of the 1950s; the bright, shining windscreens became a symbol for wealth and success and provided a much-needed source of income for a succession of ministers of Finance. The rising numbers of cars meant that extensive investments had to be made in new roads, including the first motorways, as well as in bridges and ferries. The many new petrol stations which also sprang up were a less welcome addition in towns.

Distribution of seats and vote percentages in elections to the Folketing 1953-2001

	A	B	C	D	E	F	K	LC	O	P	Q	SP	U	V	Y	Z	Ø	others
1953	74	14	30	–	6	–	8	–	–	–	–	1	0	42	–	–	–	–
	41.3	7.8	16.8	–	3.5	–	4.3	–	–	–	–	0.5	2.7	23.1	–	–	–	–
1957	70	14	30	–	9	–	6	–	–	–	–	1	0	45	–	–	–	–
	39.4	7.8	16.6	–	5.3	–	3.1	–	–	–	–	0.4	2.3	25.1	–	–	–	–
1960	76	11	32	–	0	11	0	–	–	–	–	1	6	38	–	–	–	–
	42.1	5.8	17.9	–	2.2	6.1	1.1	–	–	–	–	0.4	3.3	21.1	–	–	–	–
1964	76	10	36	–	0	10	0	–	–	–	–	0	5	38	–	–	–	0
	41.9	5.3	20.1	–	1.3	5.8	1.2	–	–	–	–	0.4	2.5	20.8	–	–	–	0.8
1966	69	13	34	–	0	20	0	4	–	–	–	–	0	35	–	–	–	–
	38.2	7.3	18.7	–	0.7	10.9	0.8	2.5	–	–	–	–	1.6	19.3	–	–	–	–
1968	62	27	37	–	0	11	0	0	–	–	–	0	0	34	4	–	–	–
	34.2	15.0	20.4	–	0.7	6.1	1.0	1.3	–	–	–	0.2	0.5	18.6	2	–	–	–
1971	70	27	31	–	0	17	0	–	–	–	0	0	–	30	0	–	–	–
	37.3	14.4	16.7	–	1.7	9.1	1.4	–	–	–	1.9	0.2	–	15.6	1.6	–	–	–
1973	46	20	16	14	5	11	6	–	–	–	7	–	–	22	0	28	–	–
	25.6	11.2	9.2	7.8	2.9	6	3.6	–	–	–	4	–	–	12.3	1.5	15.9	–	–
1975	53	13	10	4	0	9	7	–	–	–	9	–	–	42	4	24	–	–
	29.9	7.1	5.5	2.2	1.8	5	4.2	–	–	–	5.3	–	–	23.3	2.1	13.6	–	–
1977	65	6	15	11	6	7	7	–	–	–	6	–	–	21	5	26	–	0
	37.0	3.6	8.5	6.4	3.3	3.9	3.7	–	–	–	3.4	–	–	12	2.7	14.6	–	0.9
1979	68	10	22	6	5	11	0	–	–	–	5	–	–	22	6	20	–	0
	38.3	5.4	12.5	3.2	2.6	5.9	1.9	–	–	–	2.6	–	–	12.5	3.7	11	–	0.4
1981	59	9	26	15	0	21	0	–	–	–	4	–	–	20	5	16	–	0
	32.9	5.1	14.5	8.3	1.4	11.3	1.1	–	–	–	2.3	–	–	11.3	2.7	8.9	–	0.2
1984	56	10	42	8	0	21	0	–	–	–	5	–	–	22	5	6	–	0
	31.6	5.5	23.4	4.6	1.5	11.5	0.7	–	–	–	2.7	–	–	12.1	2.7	3.6	–	0.1
1987	54	11	38	9	0	27	0	–	–	4	4	–	–	19	0	9	–	0
	29.3	6.2	20.8	4.8	0.5	14.6	0.9	–	–	2.2	2.4	–	–	10.5	1.4	4.8	–	1.5
1988	55	10	35	9	–	24	0	–	–	0	4	–	–	22	0	16	–	0
	29.8	5.6	19.3	4.7	–	13	0.8	–	–	1.9	2	–	–	11.8	0.6	9	–	1.4
1990	69	7	30	9	0	15	–	–	–	0	4	–	–	29	–	12	0	0
	37.4	3.5	16.0	5.1	0.5	8.3	–	–	–	1.8	2.3	–	–	15.8	–	6.4	1.7	0.9
1994	62	8	27	5	–	13	–	–	–	–	0	–	–	42	–	11	6	1
	34.6	4.6	15.0	2.8	–	7.3	–	–	–	–	1.9	–	–	23.3	–	6.4	3.1	1
1998	63	7	16	8	–	13	–	–	13	–	4	–	0	42	–	4	5	–
	36	3.9	8.9	4.3	–	4.3	–	–	7.4	–	2.5	–	0.3	24	–	2.4	2.7	0
2001	52	9	16	0	–	12	–	–	22	–	4	–	–	56	–	0	4	–
	29.1	5.2	9.1	1.8	–	6.4	–	–	12.0	–	2.3	–	–	31.2	–	0.6	2.4	–

Parties: A: Social Democratic Party. B: Social Liberal Party. C: Conservative People's Party. D: Centre Democratic Party. E: Single Tax Party. F: Socialist People's Party. K: Danish Communist Party. LC: Liberal Centre Party. O: Danish People's Party P: Common Course. Q: Christian People's Party. SP: Schleswig Party. U: The Independents. V: The Liberal Party. Y: Left Socialists. Z: Progress Party. Ø: Unity List. Faeroese and Greenlandic seats not included.

and a sharp rise in unemployment benefits along with a new social statute (1970). This was introduced in connection with the local govern-ment reform which reduced the number of municipalities from 1386 to 275. Between 1971 and 1973, sick pay arrangements were reformed and a health insurance act introduced, abolishing the contributory sickness funds and introducing tax-funded national health insurance. The social and health reforms were rounded off in 1974 by the Social Assistance Act.

The education sector underwent great expansion. Primary and lower secondary education was fundamentally changed in 1958, and the upper secondary schools, vocational training and higher education grew explosively. There was increased government activity in the areas of culture and leisure, especially after the creation of the Ministry of Cultural Affairs in 1961. During the first half of the 1960s, laws were introduced in support of the theatre and the libraries, along with a film foundation and The Danish Art Foundation (*Statens Kunstfond*).

Welfare legislation was based on the principle of universalism, i.e. not only the right of the poor and needy, but the right of all citizens, to benefits in all areas. This principle is characteristic of the Nordic welfare states and is one of the reasons behind the high degree of consensus between political parties and social classes, as reflected in the legislation. Another reason is the absence of an absolute majority by any one political party. Welfare legislation has also consciously been financed through taxes; until the 1980s, this caused an explosive rise in public expenditure and taxation.

From around 1958, the reforms were based on strong economic growth and significant structural changes within the labour market and Danish industry. Productivity grew significantly within both agriculture and industry, which in the agricultural sector led to a reduction in the number of farms and the labour force, while industry expanded.

From the early 1960s, the value of industrial exports surpassed that of agriculture. The strongest growth, however, was in the number of white-collar workers in the service sector, in the private sector and especially in the public sector. Many of the new jobs both here, and in industry, were filled by women.

This second industrial revolution is characterised by a move westward of industry, i.e. away from the old centres and into the countryside and the smaller provincial towns, soaking up the work force no longer needed in agriculture. This led to new social patterns as compared to the old urban working classes, an urbanisation of the countryside. Groups of detached family houses appeared all over the country; many people bought family cars and went on package holidays.

Consumer patterns changed dramatically, and new lifestyles were created which led to cultural clashes and, eventually, to the significant changes in the political patterns experienced in the first half of the 1970s.

The most notable political and cultural clashes of the 1960s and the beginning of the 1970s were between the new generation of youngsters who had grown up with the welfare system, and the older generation

Towards the end of 1973, the OPEC countries threatened to cut oil supplies. In the face of a crippling oil boycott, the government banned all private car journeys on Sundays during the winter of 1973-1974. Some were delighted, including children and cyclists who took full advantage of the empty roads. Others, however, were less impressed. When the oil reserves had been replenished at the beginning of 1974, the ban was finally lifted. The artist Bo Bojesen captured the frustration of some car-drivers in the Politiken newspaper on 25 November 1973.

We have to be nice to dad during his drying out period. It is called withdrawal symptoms...

with their memories of the time before and during the war. The youth revolution had many themes: Anti-nuclear protests, demonstrations against USA involvement in Vietnam and, more generally, against stereotypic democratic processes. The key-words were democratisation and participation at all levels of society. Initially, the changes were felt most strongly within higher education where the Statute that was introduced in 1970 gave students and junior staff a say in the running of the institutions. The political and cultural debate underwent renewed ideologisation during the same period, strongly influenced by Marxism and other radical ideologies. The new activism was expressed in untraditional extra-parliamentarian actions: Protest marches, sit-ins in houses, factories and universities, the so-called 'wildcat' strikes, street theatre and happenings.

Lorenz Rerup,
Niels Finn Christiansen

Political Upheaval, Economic Crisis and Renewed Growth Since 1973

Since 1973, Denmark's economy and foreign policy have been steadily internationalised. Foreign aid has until recently gradually increased, both bilaterally and via the UN, and Denmark continues to contribute peacekeeping troops, e.g. those that were sent to Bosnia, Kosovo and Eritrea/Ethiopia in 2001. Despite widespread support for the country's membership of NATO there was, for a number of years, strong disagreement concerning the actual implementation of the strategy of the alliance. A majority supported the 1977-1978 idea of a nuclear-free Nordic zone. Nato's 'two-track decision' of 1979 meant that new missile systems would be deployed in Europe unless the Warsaw Pact and NATO agreed to limit this type of weapon. The results of this decision were sceptically received by the Danish public and caused a controversy which raged between 1982 and 1988. In what has become known as the policy of footnotes, a so-called alternative majority, supported by a strong popular peace movement, repeatedly instructed the government to put forward reservations against NATO decisions. During the second half of the 1980s, the gap was narrowed. This was partly due to the fact that the Social Liberals, who had been part of the footnote majority, were co-opted into the government in 1988, and partly due to the détente and the collapse of the Communist regimes in eastern and central Europe.

The relationship with the EC, from 1993 the EU, has been a bone of contention ever since 1972. Despite a solid majority in the Folketing for continuous membership and further integration, the public has been split into two almost equal halves in all five referenda held on this subject. The referendum on the single European market in 1986 produced a majority of just over 56%, but the Maastricht Treaty was rejected on 2 June 1992 by 50.7% no votes. The parties for and against thereafter agreed on a 'national compromise', which allowed Denmark certain opt-out clauses in the Edinburgh Agreement. As a result, the Treaty was accepted by a new referendum on 18 May 1993 by 56.8% of the votes. In 1998 the Amsterdam Treaty was accepted by referendum, but in a referendum held in 2000, a majority voted against Denmark's participation in the third phase of the Economic and Monetary Union (EMU) adopting the Single European Currency, the euro.

The Danes had four reservations regarding the Edinburgh Agreement, but at the EU Treaty referendum held on 18 May 1993, a majority of 56.8% voted in favour and 43.2% voted against. The result led youth groups, e.g. the left-wing extremists known as the 'autonomous' group, to declare the Nørrebro area in Copenhagen an 'EU-free zone'. Here, the situation turned into a grim battle between stone-throwing protesters and sharp-shooting police officers. Several official interpretations of the event have been put forward, but it is doubtful whether the episode will ever be fully accounted for.

The 1970s were a turbulent decade in domestic politics. The landslide election of 1973 completely changed the party-political structure. The support for the four old parties fell from around 90% to approximately 58%, and many new parties entered parliament, the most important being the Progress Party and the Centre Democrats, who with around 16% and 8% of the votes respectively attracted a quarter of the voters. The Progress Party, led by Mogens Glistrup, represented a revolt against the welfare state, particularly the increases in taxation and the growth of the public sector. Politics were now characterised by frequent elections, complex coalitions and narrow parliamentary bases for the governments. The Liberals, led by Poul Hartling, governed between 1973 and 1975 with only 22 seats in the Folketing. Until 1982, the Social Democrats formed minority governments led by Anker Jørgensen, 1978-1979 in coalition with the Liberals. Politics during the 1970s were also coloured by a wide range of social movements which sought to influence political decisions in areas such as the environment, nuclear energy and 'green' politics. The women's movement was, without doubt, the most influential of these.

The international economic crisis took hold in Denmark in 1974 and created huge problems for successive governments throughout the next decade. Stagnant economic growth and unemployment were accompanied by high inflation, which the government sought to counter by pursuing an income policy and a number of other measures. By 1982, the Social Democrats had exhausted all possibilities for further deals with the Opposition to combat the crisis, and a right-wing coalition consisting of the Conservative People's Party, the Liberals, the Centre Democrats and the Christian People's Party seized the power under the leadership of the Conservative Poul Schlüter.

The Danish parliamentary election on 20 November 2001 brought a landslide victory to the Liberal-Conservative opposition parties. Liberal leader Anders Fogh Rasmussen became Prime Minister and his Liberal Party became the largest Party in the Folketing. In this photo Anders Fogh Rasmussen arrives at the victory celebration of the Liberal Party, surrounded by reporters and Liberal Party members.

Schlüter led a number of successive non-Socialist governments until 1993 and became the longest-reigning Prime Minister since Stauning. In 1988, the four-party government was replaced by a 'trio' consisting of the Conservative People's Party, the Liberals and the Social Liberals, and in 1990 the coalition was reduced to just the Conservatives and the Liberals. Even though the non-Socialist coalition governments suffered losses at every single election, they achieved significant results in a number of areas, not least through co-operation with the Social Democrats. A vigorous anti-inflationary economic policy was introduced which abolished automatic indexation, reduced public spending and raised the cost of consumer credit. Competitiveness was enhanced, the currency was strengthened and more than 200,000 new jobs were created. Even so, unemployment continued to rise, as did foreign debt and the tax burden. Inflation was brought under control, however, and from the end of the 1980s a number of factors contributed to an improvement of the Danish economy. The international economic situation changed for the better, the balance of trade was improved and the Danish foreign debt was gradually reduced, partly because the country had become almost completely self-sufficient with respect to energy as a result of North Sea oil and gas.

In the middle of this period of economic growth, the right-wing government unexpectedly had to resign in January 1993. Their downfall was caused by the Minister of Justice Erik Ninn-Hansen's violation of the Aliens Act (known as the Tamil Affair), a case which was subsequently tried and became the first Danish impeachment in 80 years. Poul

Schlüter's successor was the Social Democrat Poul Nyrup Rasmussen. He first led a four-party coalition of Social Democrats, Social Liberals, Centre Democrats and representatives of the Christian People's Party; the Christian People's Party lost their seats at the election in September 1994, but Nyrup Rasmussen continued as Prime Minister in a three-party coalition of Social Democrats, Social Liberals and Centre Democrats. In 1996 the Centre Democrats withdrew from the government. The improved trading climate strengthened the Danish economy and made possible a fall in unemployment. But at the same time international competition and European integration restricted the options open to the government and parliament. In the general election of March 1998 the Conservatives suffered a serious setback, partly due to a leadership battle in the party. The Danish People's Party and the Centre Democrats emerged stronger. The Christian People's Party was again represented in the Folketing. Just after the election the Liberal leader, Uffe Ellemann Jensen, and the Conservative leader, Per Stig Møller, resigned. They were replaced by Anders Fogh Rasmussen and Pia Christmas-Møller, but in 1999 Pia Christmas-Møller was replaced by Bendt Bendtsen. Poul Nyrup Rasmussen was able to carry on a recontructed coalition government consisting of the Social Democrats and the Social Liberal Party.

For a number of years attitudes and policies towards immigrants and refugees have been in the forefront of public debate and in 1998 the Aliens Act was tightened considerably. A more salient theme for the politically aware has been the principles and forms by which the welfare society is to be maintained and developed in changing international conditions.

In the light of the terrorist attacks on the World Trade Center and the Pentagon on 11 September 2001, Denmark's international obligations and role featured prominently in the public debate. However, when Poul Nyrup Rasmussen called a general election for 20 November 2001, these problems were overshadowed by Denmark's policies on immigration, and the election campaign centred on refugees and Danes with another ethnic background than Danish. The government was subject to immense pressure from not only The Danish People's Party but also The Liberal Party and The Conservative People's Party. All parties declared their unreserved support for the protection and expansion of the welfare state, but despite this agreement on the goal, large differences remained as to the measures to be taken to reach this goal. The election resulted in the most spectacular change in the political balance of power since 1973. All left-wing parties, and the Social Democratic Party in particular, experienced a violent decline. The Centre Democrats lost all their seats in the Folketing, while the Liberal Party and The Danish People's Party noted a solid increase in the number of seats. The Liberal Party became Denmark's largest political party, and with parliamentary support from the Danish People's Party, Liberal leader Anders Fogh Rasmussen formed a government consisting of the Liberal Party and the Conservative People's Party. The Conservatives Bendt Bendtsen and Per Stig Møller became, respectively, Minister for Economic and Business Affairs and Minister for Foreign Affairs. Liberal Bertel Haarder became Minister for European Affairs and Minister for Refugee, Immigration and Integration Affairs, thus assuming the responsibility of continuing to strengthen the immigration and asylum policy and intensifying integration measures. In order to keep its election promises of tax stop and of strengthening the main areas of concern of the welfare state, the government reduced public expenses in other areas, such as development assistance and environmental protection.

Niels Finn Christiansen

Greenland and the Faeroe Islands

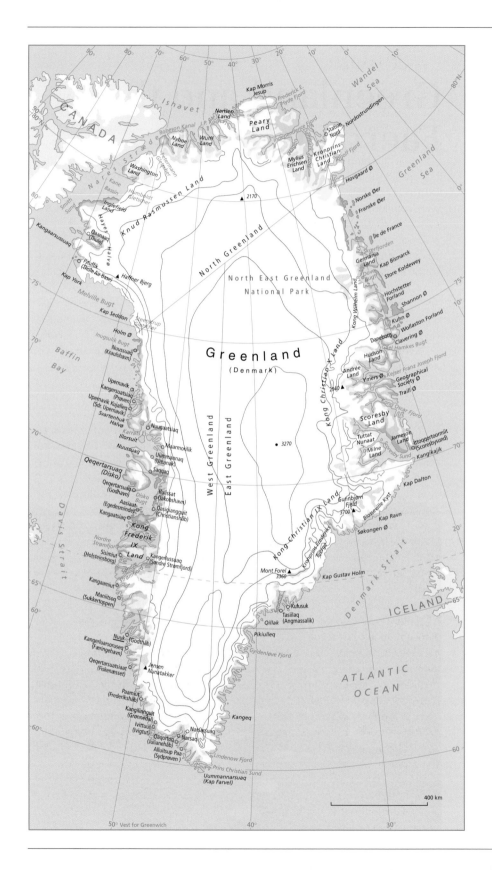

Greenland

Introduction

Greenland has an area of around 2.2 million square kilometres, making it the largest island in the world. The inland ice, which covers approximately 1.8 million square kilometres, is the second largest ice cap in the world. In some places, the ice is up to 3.5 km thick. The northernmost point of the island, Cape Morris Jesup, is the northernmost land area in the world and is situated c. 730 km from the North Pole. The southern point, Cape Farewell, is located at the same latitude as the Nordic capitals Oslo and Helsinki.

Greenland and the Faeroe Islands are part of the kingdom of Denmark, but are largely self-governing. Legislation formally comes under the Danish Folketing which includes two representatives from Greenland, but in practical terms the Greenland Landsting administers almost all legislative matters. This does not apply to the country's foreign policy, Greenland's mineral rights, the police and judicial system, or to the Greenland Command in Grønnedal. The most senior Danish representative in the area is a Commissioner appointed under the Royal Seal.

The majority of the population in Greenland were born on the island. Those who are not local mostly come from Denmark, but the Danish share of the population has been reduced since the end of the 1980s.

In 1960, approximately 42% of the population lived in settlements. Many have since moved to the towns, however, leaving only 19% in the settlements in 1999. More than 2/3 of the population live on the west coast in the Disco Bay area and the central region; with over 13,000 inhabitants, the capital Nuuk is by far the largest town in Greenland.

Fishing plays a huge role in the economy of Greenland, and more than 5000 people are employed in fishing and other associated industries. The public administration sector, however, provides over 8000 jobs, making it the biggest employer.

Climate and Topography

Greenland's large land area means that climate is very varied. Apart from a few protected valleys in southern Greenland, however, the inland ice affects the whole country resulting in a polar climate in which the average temperature never exceeds 10° C, even in the warmest month of the year.

The climate along the east coast is greatly affected by the East Greenland polar current which causes the creation of metre-thick ice cover to form during the winter half. During the summer half, huge ice masses from the Polar Basin drift down along the coast and south of Cape Farewell. These ice masses, known as the field ice, create huge problems for shipping. The problems are not confined to the east coast, but also affect the area around southern Greenland during the spring and summer months. The ice does not reach further north than Paamiut (Frederikshåb); from there and northwards to Sisimiut (Holsteinsborg), the relatively warm current keeps the coast clear of ice all year round.

The waters around the Disco Bay and further northwards along the coast are covered by ice during the winter, but are navigable for the coastal trade during the summer. The navigable period is reduced the further north along the coast one goes.

Greenland
Kalaallit Nunaat
Form of government:
Autonomous home rule, part of the kingdom of Denmark
Area: 2.18 million sp. km of which 341,700 sq. km is not covered by ice
Population: 56,542 inhabitants
Capital: Nuuk (Godthåb) 13,169 inhabitants
Currency: Danish Krone (DKK)

The whole Greenland landscape is affected by the presence of the ice which has left sharp cliffs and carved out long, rounded glacier valleys. Countless islands, both large and small, abound in the Greenland archipelago. There are also large numbers of fjords, many of which cut deep into the landscape. The variations in the climate are clearly mirrored in the vegetation. Southwest Greenland is characterised by dense vegetation which can develop into thicket and woodland in sheltered areas. Generally, however, the island is devoid of trees and covered by sparse vegetation. The number of plant species dwindles as one moves further north and east, and the lack of rain means that large areas of northern Greenland are covered by naked rock.

Geology

The Greenland landscape incorporates three main elements. The first is the core in Central and West Greenland which is approximately 2-3 billion years old. North and south of the core are areas of younger bedrock which is more than 1 billion years old. Finally, there is an area of younger fold mountains in the north east which is less than 250 million years old. The many different factors which have influenced the formation of the landscape have resulted in an abundance of mineral deposits, but harsh conditions and restricted access have so far limited wide-scale commercial exploitation.

Harvesting the Seas

As the snow and ice melts during the summer months, large amounts of nutrient salts are transported into the waters around Greenland, and the long, bright summer encourages an abundant plankton growth which feeds the animal life in the sea. The waters around Greenland are therefore some of the most productive seas in the world, with more than 200 different species of fish, crustaceans and mussels. The population is almost entirely dependent on the bountiful harvest it gathers from the sea.

Shrimps (*Pandalus borealis*) constitute the most important commercial export. The yearly haul of around 70,000 tonnes contributes more than 1 billion kroner to the Greenland economy.

Cod previously played a central role in the development of the economy, but the cod haul has fallen to about 5,000 tonnes (1998) and it is proving increasingly difficult to ensure that cod fishing remains an economically viable industry.

Greenland halibut, on the other hand, has slowly become more important to the economy of the country. The yearly catch of more than 20,000 tonnes comes first and foremost from the northwesterly districts.

Norway haddock, catfish, Atlantic halibut, salmon and char are also important to the local economy.

The animal life of the oceans also includes a number of marine mammals which were essential for the survival of the traditional hunting communities. The most important of these are the five species of seal which are found in the waters around Greenland. The most common is the ringed seal, and the Greenlanders still cull around 80,000 of these every year whereas they also cull 80,000 of all the other species put together. A number of walruses and a very small number of whales are also caught. Considerable sums are involved in the lively trade in meat which is only used locally. The only commercial use of the seals comes from the sale of skins to the Great Greenland tannery in Qa-

Shrimp trawler in Disco Bay. Shrimps constitute Greenland's most important export, and Greenland shrimps have a dominant position on the world market for cold-water prawns (*Pandalus borealis*).

qortoq (Julianehåb). The Home Government provides generous subsidies to the sealers because of the difficulty in selling the skins on the world market.

The rich bird life around the coasts has also played a role in the life of the Greenlanders. In addition to a number of different types of gulls and ducks, of which the most important is the common eider (*Somateria mollisima*), uses have also been found for a number of colony birds, not least Brünnich's guillemot (*Uria lomvie*), known commonly as the polar guillemot.

Hunting and Farming

The reindeer which inhabit the area north of Paamiut (Frederikshåb) in West Greenland have provided local hunters with their most important prey. The reindeer population has varied through the years, and those which were previously found in northeast Greenland have died out as a result of changes in the climate. Reindeer are generally killed by professional hunters in the western regions of Greenland, but large numbers are also culled by non-professional hunters. There are also a number of reindeer ranches in South and West Greenland.

Musk oxen are found in the northeast of Greenland. A small number were moved to the area around Kangerlussuaq (Søndre Strømfjord) in West Greenland in 1960. Their numbers have since increased to such an extent that today they can be hunted.

The polar bear could almost be said to be a marine mammal, since it takes to the sea ice in search of the seals which are its most common prey. Less than 100 bears are shot every year, but they are an important source of income for the hunters in East Greenland because of the high prices fetched by the skins.

Greenland's only gallinacean, the ptarmigan (*Lagopus mutus*), is also hunted as is the snow hare (*Lepus timidus*) and the polar fox (*Alopex lagopus*).

In the southern municipalities, the land is primarily used for sheep farming. There are a total of around 60 farms, and some 300 people are directly dependent on this industry. Some 20,000 lambs are slaughtered every year at the abattoir Neqi A/S in Narsaq. Large numbers are also slaughtered locally on the farms. The products from the sheep-farming industry are almost exclusively sold in Greenland, and although Greenland is not generally thought of as an agricultural country, sheep

The winter frost is severe and the summers short on the tundra, and only very few larger animals can survive the harsh conditions here; one of them is the musk ox. The animals have to move from one grazing ground to another throughout the year to find enough food. In Jameson Land in the east of Greenland, herds of musk oxen move up to the higher plateaux and the cliffs as soon as the snow melts in the spring. Snow drifts remain on the cliffs throughout the dry summer, providing meltwater for a fertile vegetation which is eaten by the musk oxen. When the winter approaches, the animals return to the valleys where the wind keeps the snow off the grass and the shrubs.

farming has proved to be a very viable industry. One of the main reasons for its success is that the locals have made a conscious effort to ensure that they are not dependent on imported feeds. Large areas have been cultivated, and the necessary winter fodder is harvested during the summer. There is no private right of ownership to land in Greenland, so the Home Government is responsible for approving the conditions for the sheep farmers' right to use the land.

Mineral Deposits

Relatively few of the mineral deposits found in Greenland have so far been exploited. The sources that have been exploited, however, include the only known occurrence in the world of cryolite which was mined in Ivittuut (Ivigtut) between 1865 and 1987. Coal was once mined near Qullissat (1924-1970), marble, zinc, lead and silver near Marmorilik (1965-1990) and zinc near Mesters Vig (1956-1963).

Certain mineral deposits may be of future economic interest, including the oil finds on the west coast of Greenland and near Jameson Land

in East Greenland and the diamond, gold, niobium, tantalite, uranium and iron deposits on the island.

Greenland's first hydraulic power plant was built near the Bukse fjord south of Nuuk in 1993. The plant has an output of 30 MW, and power is led from the plant to Nuuk via a high-voltage line which crosses two fjords. The free span of the line across the Ameralik fjord is 5,376 m, making it the longest in the world.

Controlling Local Resources

Greenland's fishing industry, along with other fishing industries around the world, has found it difficult to balance the possibilities presented by modern fishing technology with the need to sustain the natural resources. The rights of exploitation in Greenland are distributed according to two quota systems.

Deep-sea fishing rights are awarded in the form of individually marketable quotas for shrimp, cod and Greenland halibut.

Near-shore fishing rights are not restricted to specific quantities of fish, but are instead awarded to fishermen as a share of the total catch which can be sold amongst the fishermen.

Conservation laws and preservation measures have been introduced for all endangered plant and animal species to safeguard their survival. In addition, the government has turned the entire northeastern area of the country into the world's largest national park in order to ensure the continued existence of the unique nature of Greenland.

The Distribution of the Population

Of the 56,000 people currently living in Greenland, more than 49,000 were born there. The rest mainly come from Denmark (around 7,000). The population has been stable since the end of the 1980s, solely because many of the Danes have been returning to Denmark. With a rate of natural increase of 12 per thousand, the Greenland population is steadily increasing.

Some 45,000 people, or the majority of the population, are resident in the towns. Nuuk is by far the largest with a population of more than 13,000, but there are a number of towns with over 3,000 residents including Qaqortoq, Maniitsoq, Sisimiut, Aasiaat and Ilulissat. Altogether, these 6 towns are home to over 31,000 people.

The rest of the population live in the more than 130 settlements, trading posts and sheep stations around the country. Prior to the end of the 1970s, many people left the remote areas and moved to the towns, but the total number of people living in the settlements has not changed much since this time.

In the last few years, the yearly migration to and from Greenland has numbered 2,000-3,000. More than 90% of this figure represents people moving to and from Denmark, particularly young Greenlanders who are studying there. Education is also one of the main reasons for the approximately 16,000 yearly domestic relocations.

Central West Greenland is the most closely populated area of the island, due largely to the fact that the coast is navigable all the year round which, in turn, has allowed the fishing industry to prosper here. Life in the towns differs markedly from life in the settlements. The limited choice of goods available in the settlements' small shops bears little comparison to the huge array of products on sale in many of the larger towns. Similarly, the settlements are unable to offer the same educational facilities and employment prospects as the towns and in many of the settlements, there is little or no paid work available.

Infrastructure and Communication

Shipping is still the most important infrastuctural element in Greenland

Spring rain in Sisimiut, the second-largest town in Greenland. The motor boats are ready for when the ice breaks. Only a small percentage of the population are full-time hunters and fishermen, but most people own a boat, some fishing tackle and a rifle and hunt and fish in their spare time.

The Illorsuit settlement is located on an island north of Uummannaq, 71E15' northern latitude. The 123 inhabitants survive solely by fishing (Greenland halibut) and sealing. The midnight sun appears for two months at this latitude.

in terms of both volume and value. The well-developed freight system handles transport between Greenland and Denmark, and increasingly also between Greenland and countries such as Iceland and Canada. Although much of Greenland's inland passenger transport is by ship, the majority is now handled by air. Local traffic is by helicopter, whilst transport between the different districts and the largest towns is by plane. The most important air traffic junction is Kangerlussuaq (Sdr. Strømfjord).

KNR, or Kalaallit Nunaata Radioa (the national broadcasting service) is responsible for Greenland's radio and television services. In addition to a large number of locally-produced radio programmes which fill both daytime and evening slots, Greenland also produces a relatively large number of television programmes. However, the majority of the television programmes shown are produced in Denmark.

Despite the huge distances and the character of the landscape, communications in Greenland are extremely well developed. A radio link along

the coast provides a telecommunications link for the entire country based almost entirely on digital technology. External communications, primarily to Denmark, are also well developed. The cable connections with Denmark, which were established in 1961, formerly provided the most important telecommunications link but have now been superseded by satellite communications.

Motor boats are used for fishing and hunting in the summer, but in the winter the dog sledges are the only viable means of transport. The Greenland sledge dog is the result of several centuries of expert breeding which has produced a strong, hardy animal. In order to maintain the breed, it is strictly forbidden to bring dogs to areas where breeding takes place, i.e. from Sisimiut and north.

Seal blubber on sale at the 'Brædtet' market in Aasiat. In most towns in Greenland, part of the local catch is sold through the hunters' own market, commonly known as 'Brædtet'.

The Industrial Structure

Greenland's industrial structure is built around a few relatively large publicly owned companies within the fishing industry, a number of tanneries, wholesalers and retail businesses and the traffic and distribution sectors. Private business accounts for approximately 2,000 small and medium-sized enterprises: Around 600 within the fishing industry, some 350 involved in building and construction work, 300 within trade and 300 within the service industry including hotels, restaurants and banks. The size of the public sector has been a subject of heated debate in both Denmark and Greenland since 1950 when the first privately owned businesses were allowed to start up. The desire for stability and security has so far led the public sector to retain control over the strategically important businesses, mainly because the size of the population is so small that it often proves impossible in some areas to establish a competitive situation.

Sealing

Sealing still plays an important role in the life of the people living in North and East Greenland, although it is no longer the dominant industry in economic terms. In many settlements, the declining cod fishing industry has furthermore made sealing a significant sideline for the inhabitants. The most important aspect of sealing, however, is perhaps its place in the lives of the people and the identity of the nation.

Fishing

The fishing fleet numbers around 300 cutters and 30 shrimp trawlers. The smaller vessels are generally found in the settlements, whilst the trawlers are based in the towns with the largest harbours. The number of people employed in the industry is decreasing due to more effective fishing methods and the falling cod population.

The Fish Processing Industry

Royal Greenland, a limited company which is wholly owned by the Home Government, controls the majority of the fishing industry in Greenland. The company manages 11 factories and 16 smaller plants located in the settlements, as well as two large factories and a few smaller plants in Denmark, a sizeable finished-product plant in Germany. It also runs 6 fishing vessels, the majority of which are shrimp trawlers. The largest factories in Greenland are located near the shrimp fields in the towns of Sisimiut (Holsteinsborg), Maniitsoq (Sukkertoppen), Qasigiannguit (Christianshåb) and Ilullissat (Jakobshavn), and their most important product are the peeled prawns that are sold to the north European market. The company's trawlers produce unpeeled sea-cooked and raw frozen shrimps. The largest prawns are sold to the Japanese market. The company is the world's biggest retailer of cold-water prawns.

The company NUKA A/S is also owned by the Home Government and it runs 26 plants located in the settlements and 2 factories. Finally, the private company Polar Seafood A/S runs one large factory and two small plants.

Services, Trade and Sales

Greenland has a large number of solicitors, accountants and other firms which specialise in consultancy work. These services are all in demand by the shipping companies and the larger private businesses. A few of the largest service providers are subsidiaries of large Danish consultancy firms.

The Greenlandic wholesale and retail business is managed by KNI (Kalaallit Niuerfiat, or 'Greenland Trade'), a publicly owned company. The company is divided into two separate units, Pisiffik A/S, which operates in the 10 largest towns, and Pilersuisoq A/S, which supplies settlements and smaller towns. KNI takes approximately half the total sales, whilst the rest is distributed between FDB's Brugsen and private businesses. Trade and sales together employ around 3,500 people (1996).

The local market, known in every town and settlement as *brædtet* (the board), is an essential component of Greenland's trade. This is the place where fishermen and sealers sell their products directly to the public. Larger towns often have purpose-built facilities with electricity and water, but in the smaller towns and settlements the markets are still held in the open without any facilities.

Public Sector Employment

More than 8,000 civil servants are employed in the public service and administration sector. The Home Rule and the Landsstyre are the big-

gest providers of jobs, mainly within social services, education, telecommunications, KNI and the Landsstyre administration. Many of these jobs are based in the capital Nuuk.

The 18 municipalities employ around 2,600 people within local administration, the education sector and social services including old people's homes, kindergartens, nurseries and youth recreation centres.

The central authorities employ another 300 people, principally within the judicial system and the police.

Social Services

Greenland has a well-developed but cost-consuming social safety net. The state contributed around 1.4 billion kroner to the social system in 1997. The most important services include old-age pension, early retirement pensions, educational grants and social security payments such as family allowance and unemployment benefit. In many settlements, the pension payments represent a large share of the total income.

The first day of school for the pre-school class in Illulisat School. The pearl-embroidered costume worn by the girls is handmade, but their school bags are just like the ones used by children all around the world.

Hvalsey Church. The ruins are one of the best preserved memorials to Middle Age settlements in Greenland. At the end of the 10th century, Nordic farmers and fishermen colonised the fjords in the southwesterly area of the country under the leadership of the Icelander Erik the Red. The settlements remained until the middle of the 15th century. The last written record of the Greenlandic villages describe a wedding between two Icelanders in Hvalsey Church in 1408.

Education

The Home Government is striving to ensure that Greenlanders do not have to leave the island for their education. A number of vocational training programmes have lately been introduced at regional level. 14 local vocational colleges have been set up to provide training in building and construction work, the metal and iron industries, commerce and office work, the food industry and the fishing industry. There are *gymnasier* (upper secondary schools) in the towns Nuuk, Qaqortoq, Aasiaat and Sisimiut.

Higher education establishments include a college of education, a socio-educational college, a number of business colleges and a small university.

International Trade

The import and export trade prospered for a long period of time until stagnation set in during the 1990s, leading to a fall in revenues in both sectors. Export earnings fell due to falling prices for fish and shrimps and the end of ore sales. Imports have also dwindled following a strict economic policy which limits the amount of money available for consumer spending. Greenland's international trade is characterised by a wide range of imports and a very restricted range of exports. The country imports all necessities along with the goods required for production activities. The trade is also heavily dependent on Denmark, and total imports in 1999 amounted to 2.7 billion kroner.

An insignificant home market strongly limits the range of goods which can successfully be produced in Greenland. A small number of production plants have, however, been set up during the last few years: In 1988 a bottling plant for beer and soft drinks was built in Nuuk, and a new hydraulic power plant has also been constructed to reduce oil imports.

Shrimps account for 67% of Greenland's exports, whilst Greenland halibut and cod products, broadly speaking, make up the remaining 33%. The export revenue in 1999 amounted to around 1.9 billion kroner. In 1985, Greenland entered into a fishing agreement with the EU (then the EC), which allows the country to sell its fish products as non-dutiable goods on the European market, and provides Greenland with a yearly income of around 300 million kroner in exchange for the EU fishing rights. The most important trade partners in 1999 were Denmark, Japan, Norway, France, USA and Germany. The trade deficit is met by the block grant from Denmark of over 2,000 million kroner per annum.

Despite Greenland's proximity to Canada, trade is limited to the import of fresh fruit and vegetables. Canada already produces the products which Greenland exports and therefore has little interest in further trade.

Peter A. Friis,
Rasmus Ole Rasmussen

Art and Culture

Eskimo art continues to show signs of the close relationship between form and function. Artefacts were an integral part of everyday life and also of religious life, and art as understood in western Europe did not appear until late. The Greenlandic word for art, *erqumitsuliaq*, literally means 'something odd, which has been constructed' and was only coined after the first meeting with the Europeans. The interpretation of Nature, Man, animals, legends and myth reflected the Eskimo world, in which everything had an *inua* and was considered to be alive. The old adage that animals will only let themselves be killed by a beautiful weapon clearly illustrates this belief.

Decorations are widely used; as reinforcements for the seams of garments, as skeletal decoration on figures and masks, and as women's facial tattoos. Today they are only used decoratively, particularly by artists from East Greenland. The sealers, who carved their own tools, found it just as natural to carve small figures. Sculpture was therefore the dominant art form, also because of the raw materials available (bone and soapstone). The artistic expression was generally realistic, grotesque or more stylised.

As a result of growing interest in the Eskimo culture from expatriate Danes in Greenland, drawing, painting and graphic art started to appear in the middle of the 19th century, and legends, myths, Nature and everyday life were depicted in a narrative naïve-expressionist style. Despite the increased influence of Christianity, biblical images were few and far between. The artists, often catechists (teachers and assistant priests), now emerged from the shadow of anonymity, among them Israil Gormansen and Aron of Kangeq,

who amongst other things painted a large series of water-colours. In 1905, the shaman Mitsuarnianga was persuaded to create two assemblage-like sculptures representing the secret and evil magic being known as a tupilak, who was an important part of the shaman's magic. The connection between art, magic and daily life changed, and a rich variety of tupilak figures, amulets and masks have since been produced, no longer as part of the cult, but purely artistic or commercial commodities. There are now a large number of popular artists working in this area.

At the turn of the century, a dawning nationalism inspired a new school of landscape artists (Lars Møller, later Otto and Peter Rosing), a genre which continues to play an important role today. The production of paints based on Greenlandic rocks over the last few years can also be seen as a search for the country's inherent values.

A number of Greenlanders were educated at art colleges during the 20th century, but even after the foundation of the School of Art in Nuuk in 1972 very few have been able to make

Copies of tupilak figures have been produced in huge numbers since 1905. Three examples of such tupilaks are shown here. Top left: black wood with skeleton design and bone teeth. Bottom left: black wood with eyes. Right: walrus tooth with pupils marked in black. They were collected in East Greenland between 1930 and 1960. Real tupilaks have never been found in Greenland. They were only made under special circumstances using many different materials; parts taken from the bodies of dead children were sometimes included.

Stamps depict all aspects of a country's culture. The artist Jens Rosing's stamps have helped to increase people's knowledge of the Arctic and the culture of Greenland in particular. This stamp shows a scene from the Uummannaq mountain, a typical sealing district.

a living from their art alone. Home Rule brought a wave of decorative commissions for schools and town halls, etc., breaking the small-scale mould. The world of mythology has been a recurring motive in recent times, but abstract and conceptual art can be seen, and land art interprets nature in a new way (Pia Arke). Sculpture still abounds (the Kristoffersen family, Aron Kleist), as does graphic art (Anne-Birthe Hove, Aka Høegh, Arnannguaq Høegh). Thue Christiansen won the competition to design Greenland's flag.

Music and dance were also originally a more integral part of society; the idea of simply listening to music, for example, is a recent phenomenon which only appeared with the emergence of singers such as Rasmus Lyberth. The original drum song and drum dance were used as

part of the shaman's magic activities and also formed part of the so-called song battles, during which conflicts were legally settled by the use of libellous songs. The drum dance is the only truly indigenous form of music, and it is beginning to make a comeback in Greenland as an element in the creation of a national identity. This can be seen at the summer festivals (known as *aasivik*), which are themselves a revival of an old tradition. All other Greenlandic music has been influenced by the outside world, right from hymn singing to the expert use of accordions at the so-called *dansemik* (kalattuut, or folk dancing). New musical genres include *vaigat* which are Greenlandic versions of evergreens and country and western songs, along with the 1970s' politically influenced versions of beat and rock (including the group known as SUME, who sang in their native language and used the old drum song). The 1980s saw the introduction of funk and reggae with groups such as Zidaza and Aalut.

Mathias Storch's futuristic novel *Singnagtugaq* (A Greenlander's Dream) (1915) was the first of many literary works to focus on the Eskimo/Greenlandic identity. The literature contains repeated reflections on the existentialist questions and the relationship between Man and Nature. Recently, poetry in particular has dealt with current problems (Kristian Olsen aaju, Moses Olsen, Dorthe Nathanielsen). The Church influenced literature for many years,

The artist Aka Høegh in front of her contribution to the huge art project near Qaqortoq (Julianehåb). The work is called *Stone and Man*, and the project was set up by Aka Høegh. So far, 10 Nordic artists have carved images into the cliffs around the town. The work is an imposing example of the Greenlandic tradition of drawing, sculpting and carving faces.

and love and sexuality have only slowly regained thematic significance. The painter, sculptor and author Hans Lynge was yet again an exception in this area.

In 1975 the Tuukkaq theatre was set up for local students; in 1985 it became the fourth world's theatre school for Inuits, Samis and native Americans, and the Silamiut experimental theatre in Nuuk took over the original role of the old theatre.

There is still a close relationship between art, culture and everyday life in Greenland today. This is expressed not only in the works of art, but also emphasised by the Cultural Board which was set up by the Landsting in 1988. The dual notion *naturi/kulturilu* (nature/culture) is frequently used in the original White Paper.

Now, as before, the women of Greenland are strongly represented in most art forms and cultural activities.

Inge Mørch Jensen

History

Until around 4500 BC, the remains of the mighty ice cap which had been left over from the last ice age covered parts of Arctic Canada and blocked the way to Greenland. The first people arrived in the northernmost part of Greenland in around 2500 BC, and in the course of a few hundred years the ice-free part of the island became home to an Arctic tribe of hunters known as the palaeo-Eskimos. The warmer climate which appeared once the ice had gone allowed the population to increase rapidly. The Arctic hunters followed the roaming herds of musk oxen and reindeer, and tools made of bone and stones found in the area from Alaska to Greenland show clear signs of cultural homogeneity.

In Arctic Canada, this early culture is known as Pre-Dorset. In Greenland, the period is divided between the Independence I culture, which incorporates the musk ox hunters in the northern part of the country, and the Saqqaq culture, which includes the seal and caribou hunters in the southern part of Greenland. A new wave of migrants from Canada who arrived shortly before 1000 BC are known as the Independence II culture. Signs of this period have only been found in the northern part of the country, and it was followed 500 years later by the Canadian Dorset culture. This is the youngest of the palaeo-Eskimo cultures, and signs of it have only been found in the eastern parts of Canada, right down to sub-Arctic Newfoundland and along the coasts of Greenland. The Dorset culture developed independently from around 500 BC until c. 1200, and the people became especially adapted to sealing and caribou hunting. An abundance of artefacts and carvings have been found from this period.

Towards the end of the 10th century the climate became warmer, and the change affected all those living in the northern hemisphere. Much of the ice in the seas around the Canadian archipelago disappeared, and baleen whales moved into the area to search for food. Eskimo whalers from northern Alaska sailed east in their large, skin-covered boats and reached Greenland in the 12th century. These conditions prevailed during the subsequent neo-Eskimo period which also includes the Thule culture. The Dorset culture disappeared from these areas at around the same time, and later signs of it have only been found in southern Canada and in Greenland.

During the Viking Age, people from Northern Europe began to move west

The expedition cabin known as the Bellows in Foxe Basin in arctic Canada. The hut was built in 1921 to serve as base camp for the Fifth Thule Expedition which, until 1924, carried out ethnographic, archaeological and geographical research amongst the Canadian Eskimos. In the middle of the picture is the expedition leader Knud Rasmussen, and to the right is the ethnographer Kaj Birket-Smith. From here, Knud Rasmussen and two Polar Eskimos set out on the long sled journey which led him westwards through Canada and Alaska and ended with a short visit to the Siberian Eskimos at the East Cape. Knud Rasmussen (1879-1933), who had a number of Eskimo ancestors, was actually born in Greenland and learned as a child to master the Eskimo language. In 1910 he founded a trading post in Thule. The income from the sale of skins at the post was used to fund his seven Thule expeditions, which took him to all areas of Greenland. Knud Rasmussen's extensive literary and scientific legacy was a result of these travels. His insight into Eskimo philosophy, poetry and story-telling art make his books some of the best that have ever been written about the Eskimo culture.

in the North Atlantic, and in 985 the Icelander Erik the Red began to colonise Greenland. The Norse community was based on agriculture and sealing and was economically dependent on contact with Europe. The society was organised as a free state controlled by the big farmers. There are signs of formal trade with the Eskimo population, and it is known that the ivory from walrus and narwhal tusks was highly valued, particularly when paying tithes to the church. The Catholic church appointed the first bishop of Greenland in 1124. In 1261, the Norse community became part of the kingdom of Norway.

During the following centuries, conditions gradually deteriorated for the population of Greenland because of the island's limited economic importance for Norway, the over-exploitation of the limited resources and the notable change in climate. When Denmark, Norway and Sweden were united in 1397, the former Norwegian possessions in the North Atlantic, including Greenland, came under Danish rule. In the 15th century, Europe received the last signs of life from the Norse community which then ceased to exist, some 500 years after it was founded. By then, the Thule culture had spread across the whole of Greenland, but in the preceding centuries the two cultures had existed side by side and there had been extensive trading and commerce.

European interest in the rich fishing grounds around Iceland and Newfoundland led to an increase in shipping in the seas around these areas. The English were dominant, and the growing rivalry in the trade with Asia led them to wonder whether it would be possible to reach the distant markets by sailing north round America. The two Englishmen Martin Frobisher and John Davis sailed the seas between Canada and Greenland in the 1570s and 1580s, and in their attempts to find the Northwest Passage they became the first Europeans for centuries to make contact with the Eskimo population.

At around the same time, the Dutch discovered large numbers of Greenland whales around the Spitzbergen area and began a commercial exploitation of whale oil and baleen. Their actions led to an international conflict concerning the rights to the open seas. The Danish king asserted his historical sovereignty over the northernmost area of the Atlantic, known as the Norwegian Sea, and increased activity in the area eventually led to the rediscovery of Greenland in 1605. The Dutch, however, continued to control the whaling industry, and at the end of the 17th century they began whaling off the coast of West Greenland.

In 1721, Greenland was once again colonised by the Europeans. The Danish-Norwegian priest Hans Egede went to the island to convert the Norse population who, he believed, would by then have lost their Christian faith. A trading station was set up to support the missionary work and to take the trade with the Eski-

mos away from the Dutch. The station was also intended to act as a base for the founding of colonies along the coast.

Trading stations were established along the west coast of Greenland throughout the 18th century. In 1774, all responsibility for the business was handed over to the Royal Greenland Trade Department. Inspectors were appointed in 1782 to control the trade, and standardised product prices were introduced to ensure that the population was not exploited.

The cultural and political life of the country was enhanced during the 19th century by the creation of colleges of education, the publication of the world's first newspaper written in the language of a colonial population, and a form of local administration was introduced, run by officials and a respected sealer from each district, the so-called Managers. The Greenlandic language was kept alive through education, missionary work and the creation of new literature.

In the 19th century, European expeditions met new Eskimo groups outside the colonised parts of West Greenland. The Polar Eskimos were visited in 1818, and in 1823 English whalers met the people of North East Greenland for the first and last

The *Sirius* sled patrol is responsible for maintaining and protecting the sovereignty of the Danish state in the unpopulated areas in the northeast of Greenland, which today are part of one of the largest national parks in the world. The Greenlandic sled patrols were established during The Second World War as part of the defence agreement with the USA, which had taken responsibility for guarding the east cost of Greenland. Today the Danish Ministry of Defence is responsible for these activities, and the Sirius patrol uses the Daneborg weather station as their daily base.

time. In 1884 the people of East Greenland near Ammassalik were also visited for the first time. In 1878, a commission was set up to conduct research into the geography and geology of Greenland. Knud Rasmussen (1879-1933) later became one of the most distinguished Danish-Greenland researchers, and the first person to document the cultural connections between the various Eskimo cultures. His Fifth Thule Expedition, which ended with the long sledge journey from Greenland to the Pacific in 1921-1924, is well known internationally.

The Greenland identity was restored by the cultural awakening which took place just after the turn of the century. The mission was replaced by the Greenland Church, and provincial councils were set up to replace the earlier political institutions. The Greenland Trade organisation took over from the Royal Greenland Trade Department.

The milder climate led to a decrease in sealing and the introduction of the new industries of fishing and sheep farming. In 1917, the USA acknowledged Denmark's sovereignty over the Thule area in northern Greenland. In 1931, Norway occupied parts of East Greenland having declared that Danish sovereignty did not apply to the uninhabited areas. In 1933, the International Court at The Hague finally awarded Denmark sovereignty over the whole of Greenland.

When the Germans occupied Denmark in 1940, the link with Greenland was broken. Henrik Kauffmann, the Danish ambassador to the USA, signed an agreement in which the USA acknowledged Danish sovereignty over the island and agreed to provide both supplies and protection for the duration of the war. In 1941, bases were set up in both West and East Greenland to provide air cover for the Atlantic convoys. The revenues from the increased production of cryolite and the products that were sold covered the costs associated with the USA presence on the island. After the end of the Second World War, Denmark continued the foreign policy which arose from the co-operation with the USA and the kingdom's membership of NATO. The Base Treaty of 1941 was replaced by the Treaty on the Protection of Greenland in 1951. The USA was given permission to build the large Thule Air Base and maintained its bases near Søndre Strømfjord in West Greenland and Kulusuk in East Greenland. Today only the Thule Air Base is under American control, while the country's other airports are maintained by Greenland's Home Rule administration.

Following the war, the politicians of Greenland demanded economic investments and declared that they wanted the country to be opened up to the world. A White Paper was subsequently published in 1950. It suggested that Greenland's administration be replaced by a national council known as the *Landsråd*, and that the Royal Greenland Trade Department's monopoly be lifted. In 1952, the Landsråd approved the proposal

Construction of the Thule Air Base was begun by the Americans in 1951. During the Cold War, it was to serve as an advanced operational base to ensure that USA strategic bombers could reach Moscow and industrial centres in the USSR. The base could also serve as advanced anti-aircraft defence for the American continent. The local Eskimo population had to move north to a new settlement in 1953. In 1999 they were awarded a minor compensation for the loss of their hunting ground.

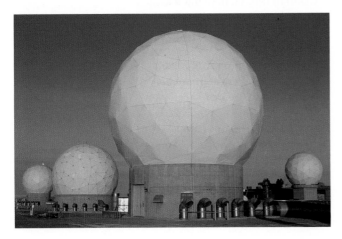

for the new constitution which made Greenland an integral part of Denmark. The proposal was approved in Denmark in 1953 in the constitutional referendum, and two representatives from Greenland were given seats in the Danish Folketing. The country was opened up to private investment, and a thorough overhaul of the infrastructure, the health service and the social services was begun.

In 1964 a select committee issued a White Paper containing a ten-year plan for the social and industrial development of the country. This was followed by a series of new laws passed by the Danish Folketing. A new Civil Servants Act decreed that pay for equal work would depend on whether the recipient was born in Denmark or in Greenland. The act hereby established a difference between Danish and Greenlandic salaries which benefited the Danish minority in Greenland and caused wide-spread opposition. The so-called Birth Place Criterion was seen as discriminatory, and a new political party known as the Inuit Party was created in 1966 to introduce economic equality for all groups. The party did not, however, last very long.

Two factors characterise the first decades of decolonisation: The rising numbers of ethnic Danes – up to a fifth of the total population – and the increased interest of the local population in the political affairs of the country. Since 1967, the democratically elected Landsråd council has chosen its own Greenlandic chairman. In 1975, the local government reform meant that municipal councils acquired power in local matters and control of their own tax revenues. The ten-year plan gave priority to the development of the urban communities; in 1950, 25% of the population lived in the towns, but 25 years after the reform this had risen to 75%. The Greenland economy was not able to finance this policy of concentration, partly because the revenues from the fishing industry dwindled as a result of declining supplies. Once again, the island felt the effects of a climatic change. In the 1970s, new sources of income had to be found through increased mineral and oil exploration.

The wish for added political influence on the domestic economy was one of the reasons behind the new political movements of the 1970s, following the referendum in 1972 on Danish membership of the EC. Despite a majority decision to remain outside the European common market, the country was obliged to adhere to the result of the Danish referendum. The political awakening in Greenland led to the creation of three political parties. *Siumut* emphasised a strong Greenland economic control along Social Democratic principles, *Atassut* advocated the continued co-operation with Denmark and economic freedom for the individual, and *Inuit Ataqatigiit* promoted the ethnic bonds with the populations of northern Canada and Alaska and decreased dependence on Denmark.

In 1973, the political demand for a revision of the relationship between Greenland and Denmark was examined by a committee, which in 1975 advised that a commission be set up to draft a blueprint for Greenland home rule. Three years later, this resulted in the Home Rule Act which was passed by the Danish Folketing and came into power in 1979. Siumut have since held a majority in the Greenlandic parliament, the *Landsting*, and formed the government known as the *Landsstyre*; occasionally, this has been a coalition with one of the two other parties.

The economy is based on a block grant from Denmark and local revenues from industry and taxation, all of which is administered in Greenland. The country left the EC following a referendum in 1982. All political fields of responsibility, with the exception of foreign policy, defence matters and monetary policy were transferred from Denmark to Greenland during the first 15 years of home rule. The government is trying to reduce the need for Danish expertise by creating local educational and cultural institutions. The risk of overdeveloping the administration of the Greenland welfare state which, in the 1990s, received more than 50% of public spending in block grants from Denmark, is obvious. Falling supplies within the fishing industry, the dramatic fall in world market prices for sealskins and the lack of income from the country's few domestic raw materials have all led to increased privatisation of the public sector and a growing need for alternative industries, such as tourism. This development is characteristic of other countries in the North Atlantic region.

The concentration of the population in towns along the west coast of the country and the limited earnings potential have created a proletariat of low-paid workers and unemployed. The consequent effects have been alcohol abuse, violence and one of the highest suicide rates amongst the young in the world. In northern and eastern Greenland, where sealing is still the main industry, employment in administration and the service sector has led many to view sealing as less prestigious than previously in the traditionally male-dominated society. Homicide and suicide amongst the young here seem to be an expression of cultural dissolution. Alleviating this social and cultural dilemma is the greatest economic burden on the young Greenlandic welfare state.

From the outside, the home-ruled Greenland has made its mark in the world and now plays an active role in the Inuit Circumpolar Conference (ICC), founded in 1977 as an umbrella organisation for all Inuit groups in Greenland, Canada, Alaska and Siberia. Coordinating common strategies which aim to strengthen the cultural and linguistic identity is an important part of the work of the ICC. The Arctic populations have here created a platform from which their viewpoints are set out for the large majority societies in the south.

The Greenlandic Home Rule is an inspiration for other indigenous populations in their attempts to achieve similar arrangements. Even though international affairs are outside the realm of Greenlandic politics, the Greenlanders and the Danes partake equally in international negotiations with full respect to the Greenlandic position. Today, Greenland has a little over 50,000 inhabitants, and it is left to these to try to solve the problems which characterise the Arctic minorities and which, as so often in history, have been introduced from the outside world.

H.C. Gulløv

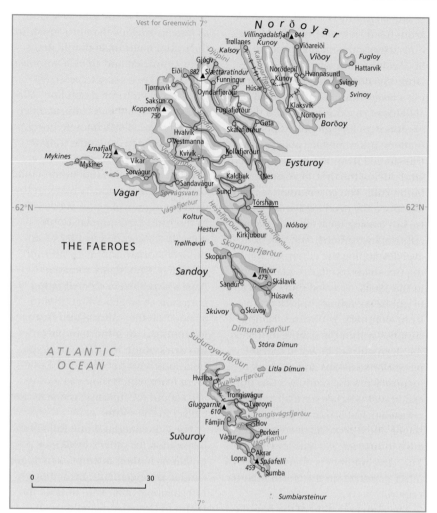

The Faeroes
Føroyar
Form of government:
  Autonomous home
  rule, part of the
  kingdom of Den-
  mark
Area: 1,399 sq. km
Population: 47,000
  inhabitants
Capital: Tórshavn
  (Thorshavn) 18,000
  inhabitants
Currency: Danish
  Krone (DKK)

The Faeroe Islands

Geography

The Faeroe Islands are located in the Atlantic Ocean, almost midway between Norway, Iceland and Scotland and consist of 18 islands separated by narrow sounds and fjords. The nearest land is the Shetland Isles to the southeast at a distance of 162 nautical miles (300 km).

The Faeroe Islands are part of the kingdom of Denmark. The islands were a Danish county until 1948, but have since then been self-governing as laid down in the Home Rule Act.

Defence matters and foreign policy do not come under the Home Rule, but the Faeroese authorities do conduct negotiations regarding fishing rights with other countries, both with and without the participation of the Danish Foreign Office.

The population of the Faeroe Islands tripled during the course of the 19th century, and again during the 20th century. At the end of 1989, the population had reached a high of 47,838. In the following 6 years, this figure fell by 4000 but since 1996 it has been increasing, reaching 47,000 inhabitants at the beginning of the 21st century. The limited information available from previous centuries indicates that the population previously stood at around 4000. The strong growth in the population over the last two centuries is mainly due to the fact that society has ceased to rely on one natural resource, the land, and begun to rely on another, namely the sea. This switch in resources led to new production methods, changes in the infrastructure, new patterns of settlement and new cultural features.

Fisheries and the fishing industry are the main trades, and almost all other industries stem directly from these activities. Shipyards and the production of fishing tackle are the main secondary trades, although attempts have been made to establish other small industries. The limited home market, the distance to the mainland and the relationship with the EU all hinder development. The agricultural sector, in which lamb and milk are the chief products, today has only a marginal economic position.

At the beginning of the 1990s, many significant changes began to affect Faeroese society. Falling fish supplies, severe economic problems, a huge foreign debt and a disastrous emigration dogged the islands in the first part of the 1990s. However, in the second part of the 1990s the situation changed in a positive direction.

Nature

The islands are formed by volcanic rock from the Tertiary period. Long, horizontal beds of basaltic rock are divided by thin layers of pyroclastic rock (volcanic ash). On the northern part of the island of Suðuroy are coal seams which are no longer commercially viable but were exploited previously, particularly during the two World Wars. The ice ages have made the islands what they are today, characterised by a landscape with u-shaped valleys and cirques, separated by peaks and ridges. The highest point on the island is Slættaratindur, 882 m, on the northern part of Eysturoy.

Villingadalsfjall (844 m) on Viðoy hidden in cloud. The village of Viðareiði is surrounded by cultivated grass fields (known as *bø*), whilst most of the island is covered by mountain pastures for summer grazing (called *hauge*). The scenery, including the changeable weather, is very typical of the Faeroe Islands.

Two ocean currents dominate the waters around the Faeroe Islands. The Gulf Stream is a surface current which brings warm bodies of water northwards, keeping the waters around the islands ice-free even in winter. Cold water from the Norwegian Sea moves southwards along the bottom of the ocean. These two separate bodies of water mix to a certain extent, yielding good concentrations of nutrient salts.

The climate is distinctly Oceanic, with predominantly mild winters and rather cool summers. The mean temperature in January is 3.2° C. August is the warmest month with a mean temperature of 10.5° C. There is plenty of rain with 1,334 mm around Tórshavn, but this varies considerably depending on the local topography. The precipitation is greatest during the autumn and winter. The islands lie in the path of the depressions which cross the Atlantic on the way to the European continent, producing frequent strong winds. The Faeroe Islands experienced several hurricanes during the 1990s, with wind speeds above 30 m/second, sometimes even reaching double hurricane force.

Natural Resources

The islands' position in the northern Atlantic dictates the natural resources available to the population for the production of vital necessities and export products. The land was the basis for the old peasant culture, and the accessibility and quality of the agricultural land limited production. The 1870s saw a transition to fishing with the two-masted fishing smacks built in Britain. The modern fishing industry meant that production possibilities and limitations were now dictated by the sea.

Until 1955, the Faeroe Islands had a three-mile fishing limit. Successive expansions to this limit were introduced until the present 200-mile limit was reached in 1977. This created new conditions for the fishing industry which now had sovereign rights to all fishing resources around the islands. Other countries had also expanded their fishing limits, however, depriving the Faeroese of their traditional fishing at Newfoundland, around Greenland and Iceland, and in the Barents Sea and the North Sea. Since 1977, bilateral agreements between countries have been introduced with exchanges of quotas allowing fishing to continue, although to a lesser extent than previously. The exchange of quotas is helped by the fact that certain pelagic species, such as blue whiting and capelin, travel long distances making it difficult for a single country to claim sole rights.

Some 20-25 different species of fish are landed every year on the Faeroe Islands, but cod, haddock and coalfish are the most important in the group of edible fish. The group entitled 'other' comprises species such as greaten silver smelt, Norway pout, Greenland halibut and Atlantic halibut, which are all demersal fish. The most important pelagic species include blue whiting, capelin and salmon, as well as herring which previously had great economic importance. The majority of the fish caught in Faeroese waters are landed by local fishermen. Only whiting are predominantly caught by other countries, particularly Russia and Norway.

Despite the ability to regulate fishing in Faeroese waters, it is evident that the period between 1975 and 1990 saw an over-investment in fishing capacity, leading to an over-exploitation of all species within the 200-mile limit. During the first half of the 1990s, all significant species

The harbour in Thorshavn. The small clinker-built fishing vessels are the modern-day equivalent of the traditional Faeroese *áttamannafar,* an eight-man rowing boat used for coastal fishing.

had been depleted, and this was one of the main reasons behind the economic crisis in the Faeroe Islands in the 1990s. As the prices on the world market were also very low during this period, profitability was low or negative. The public subsidies that were poured into the fishing industry are very much to blame for bad investments and overfishing, but the majority of these subsidy schemes have now been abolished and the Faeroe Islands aims to reduce the fishing capacity.

The Faeroese have tried out various schemes for regulating fishing. From 1975 up to the crisis in the 1990s there was a centralised pricing system, which entailed very high public subsidies. Increases in catch attracted increased support, which was a powerful incentive to employ overcapacity at the catching stage. Certain technical regulative measures, such as mesh sizes of trawls and periodic protection of fishing areas, had very limited effect. For a short period in the 1990s a system was tried out based on individual transferable quotas, but this did not work out as intended, mainly because the transferability was very restrict-

ed. In the 2000s there is a scheme whereby vessels are allocated a certain number of fishing days. However, the number of restrictions on the transferability is ever increasing.

Demography

Migration to and from the Faeroe Islands has varied a great deal. Until the beginning of this century, there was a constant but relatively limited emigration from the islands. Around the time of the First World War, emigration numbers increased considerably and the variation in migration increased. At the beginning of the 1950s, Faeroese industry was in a deep crisis and net emigration during the 1950s sometimes reached hitherto unseen numbers of 500 to 600, and during the five-year period 1951-1955, there was a net emigration of 1.3% of the population. The situation stabilised somewhat over the following decade, but towards the end of the 1960s emigration had increased once again.

Migration to and from the Faeroe Islands evened out around the time of the oil crisis and the resulting economic depression and increased unemployment in Denmark and

Shearing sheep on the island of Eysturoy 1988. Despite strong competition, traditional Faeroese sheep farming continues to this day. Some of the wool is still used to produce handmade Faeroese jumpers.

most of western Europe. The Faeroe Islands did not experience crisis or unemployment during this period. On the contrary, there was great economic activity, many new construction projects were started and other large investments were made. There was great demand for labour, resulting in a considerable influx of Danish and foreign workers.

1989-1990 saw a dramatic change with a severe economic crisis, rising unemployment and a significant emigration. During the five years since this period, there was a net emigration of 4,700 people, or 10% of the population. As most emigrants are young and fit, this has had serious consequences for the population structure. However, it does look as if the situation has stabilised since 1996. The outflow of population halted, being turned into a net inflow.

The Infrastructure
In times gone by, all transport was by open rowing boat across fjords and sounds, or on foot or horseback along the marked paths that linked the settlements.

During the first half of the 20th century, most transport routes were run by private companies. Private enterprise entailed the need for profits, which in turn meant that investments in ships were very modest. The vessels were mostly discarded fishing smacks which were slightly modified, since these were cheap to acquire although not particularly comfortable for the passengers. After the Second World War, the standard of these vessels was gradually raised. A number of jetties were improved or constructed, allowing the ships to moor almost everywhere. As the road network was expanded during the 1960s, a need arose to cross the sounds and fjords by ferries, dams or bridges. The first car ferry arrived in the Faeroe Islands in 1965. By the middle of the 1970s, the government-owned ferry company Strandfaraskip Landsins had taken over all existing routes and improved their standards. Purpose-built car ferries now service all routes between the major islands.

The first road connection between two settlements was completed in

1916 between Sandur and Skopun. In the 1920s and 1930s, more than 200 km of roads were built, covering the larger islands in 14 different segments. These roads were narrow and without any permanent surfacing. Most of these individual segments were extensions of existing sea routes and could, in effect, be seen as access roads. The road network began to be modernised and extended around the middle of the 1950s, and by the early 1990s all settlements in the larger islands had been connected to the road network, with the exception of Gásadalur on Vágar. A bridge connects the two largest islands, Streymoy and Eysturoy, and Borðoy is connected to Viðoy and Kunoy by dams across the narrow sounds. Tunnels enable traffic to move through the high ridges and shorten the distance between settlements.

The first cars arrived on the islands in the 1920s, and by the outbreak of war the number had reached 100. It was only the expansion of the road network in the middle of the 1950s which brought large numbers of cars to the Faeroe Islands. Traffic is heaviest in and around the urban areas of Tórshavn and Nes-Runavík, and along the road which connects these two areas.

During the 1980s, helicopter routes were established to connect the smaller islands and the settlements that were not connected to the road network. Passenger road transport is run by private companies, but is coordinated by a public body known as Bygdaleiðir, which together with the public ferry company has established a coherent and well-developed public transport system which takes in all settlements on the islands. The investments in the infrastructure, particularly in areas such as roads, bridges, tunnels and harbours, have

been considerable and have often been criticised as extravagant and unnecessary, but no modern society can exist without a well-functioning infrastructure. Certain projects have, perhaps, been somewhat lavish, but the real problem was rather that everything had to be done at once, and that these investments thus contributed to the overheating of the economy in the mid-1980s.

Until the beginning of the 1960s, both passenger and goods transport to and from the outside world was all by sea. Today, most passenger traffic is by air, and there are several daily connections all year round. Copenhagen is the main destination, but there are also connections between the Faeroe Islands and Billund, Århus, Aberdeen, Glasgow, Stavanger, Reykjavík and Narsarsuaq. During the summer months there are also sea connections between the Faeroe Islands and Denmark, Norway, Scotland and Iceland.

Production and Industry
The most significant factor in the development of industry over the last many years is the decline of agriculture. In 1845, 68% of the population were employed in farming, whereas today the number is only 1%. The fishing industry took the dominant role, encompassing the largest proportion of the labour force with 54% in 1911, at the height of the fishing smack period. Since then, employment in fishing has fallen and today only 10% of the work force make their living this way. In spite of this, the industry still has fundamental significance for Faeroese society, whose export by and large all derives from it. The most expansive sectors over the last 25 years have been the service industry and trade. This shift from agriculture through fishing to the tertiary industries has signifi-

cantly effected regional developments.

Fishing today and 150 years ago are two very different things. Originally, small open rowing boats were used near the shores. This type of fishing is called *útróður*, meaning 'rowing out' for fishing, which was essentially what people did then. The term *útróður* still refers to fishing in inshore waters, even though larger motorised vessels are now used. This type of fishing was formerly conducted by smallholders, possibly supplementing their income by occasional work as day labourers. For some farmers, fishing supplemented their agricultural activities. This method of combining different activities was significant and lasted well into the 20th century.

Faeroese business life is today based around fishing, the fishing industry and the export of fish products. A wide range of fish products are produced, but the main export is still semi-finished products. Efforts to produce more processed goods, such as ready-prepared fish dishes, are hampered by the trade agreements that the Faeroe Islands have made with the EU, limiting the export of non-dutiable goods to EU countries. The Faeroe Islands did not follow Denmark into the EC/EU, and exceeding these limits attracts high duties.

The land-based fishing industry, which comprises filleting stations in all larger settlements, received its biggest boost in 1964 when the British introduced a ban on the landing of all fresh fish from the Faeroe Islands in British ports in protest against the expansion of the fishing limit to 12 miles. The Faeroese were then forced to process all fish themselves. Most filleting stations were set up by the settlements and their inhabitants. It was therefore not uncommon for investors to include the mu-nicipal treasurer's department, the unions, individual ship-owners and traders, and a wide section of the households in the settlement. The filleting stations were often the biggest or only employer in the settlement. When filleting production was at its highest, there were 22 stations spread across the whole country.

Over-capacity, falling fish supplies and debts made the running of the filleting stations almost impossible at the beginning of the 1990s. Debt rescheduling meant that all except two of the stations were brought under a single mother company named Føroya Fiskavirking, which then ran the industry. Falling fish supplies has

Birds are still hunted here, in this case puffins (*Fratercula arctica*) on the island of Mykínes.

market or are import-substituting, but the relationship with the EU and the tax system, as well as the severely limited domestic market, have resulted in difficult times for this type of production.

Since the 1980s, marine aquaculture specialising in the production of salmon and trout in salt water has expanded dramatically. The first legislation in this area sought to promote small, locally-owned fish farms. During the first 'gold rush' period, the industry grew significantly and prices were relatively high. At the same time, however, production in competing countries increased and prices fell. Other serious problems have also hampered the Faeroese fish farms. The number of fish farms peaked around 1990 (60 farms), but in the latter half of the 1990s the number operating was down to 20.

Foreign Trade

Faeroese exports consist almost exclusively of fish and fish products, though new and second-hand ships occasionally enter the equation. Behind these groups come postage stamps to a value of 30 million Danish kroner a year. This is followed by assorted fishing tackle, woollen goods, skins and 'other' products.

Fish exports comprise the species mentioned above which are exported as salted fish, iced or frozen filets and as processed products. This is supplemented by shrimps, scallops, lobster, salmon and trout, fishmeal and fish oil, and fish waste which is used as mink feed in other countries. Products are generally sold on the European market: Denmark 30%, Great Britain 25% and Germany 9% (1998).

The trade balance was negative throughout the 1980s, but the effect of the economic crisis in 1989 made it positive for several consecutive years

The church in Viðareiði and the Ónargerði rectory serve the 300 inhabitants of the parish. The church was built in 1892; its location so close to the sea is characteristic of many Faeroese churches.

now reduced the industry to 6-8 production sites. Since then, some unused production sites have been sold off to independent private operators.

In addition to the fishing industry itself, there are a number of fishery-related trades and industries including the production of trawls, nets, lines, ropes and wire ropes. The most advanced product is the automatic fishing jig which has been exported to Greenland, Scotland and Russia.

The shipyards in Tórshavn and in Skáli have, since 1962, built steel-hull ships. Most of these are fishing boats but some cargo vessels and other ships have also been constructed, and a number of ships have been commissioned by foreign ship owners. The yards are the only significant heavy industry in the Faeroe Islands. There have been several attempts to develop other types of production which cater for the home

Boat race in Thorshavn harbour during the national festival of Ólavsøkuaftan (St Olav's Eve) on 28 July. Rowing is the national sport of the Faeroe Islands, and this is the yearly championship. St Olav's Day is cele-brated in memory of King Olav's fall at Stiklestad in 1030. The Faeroese Lagting, Europe's oldest parliament, has met at Tinganes (in the centre of the picture) since the end of the 9th century.

due to financial austerity measures and falling purchasing power.

Regional Developments

The agricultural land was the basis for the existence of the old peasant society. The settlements were agricultural production units, and the population reflected the agricultural area and the quality of the land, as expressed in the Faeroese *marketal*, which is not a unit of area but rather an indication of yield which also gives an indication of the owner's rights and responsibilities within the settlement. The largest settlements also had the largest *marketal*. They were almost of equal size, apart from the capital Tórshavn which was not an agricultural settlement but a trading and garrison town which was also home to the islands' administration.

The arrival of the fishing smacks gave rise to a new pattern of settlement as a result of a new factor determining localisation: Natural harbours, where vessels could land their catch and where the fishing smacks could be anchored during the winter half. Combining fishing and agriculture was the norm, and the settlements where new areas were available for cultivation saw a considerable increase in population.

Developments up to the post-war period continued with increased differentiation of the fishing industry, and the growth in trade and service contributed to the establishment of new patterns of settlement. Klaksvík witnessed a dramatic expansion and became the islands' second largest town during the 1950s. Urban trades such as commerce, service, the liberal professions and administration gathered in the largest municipalities, generally in those with the largest catchment areas. In 2001, Tórshavn was the largest municipality with 18,000 inhabitants. The second largest, Klaksvík, had 5,000 inhabitants. The forces of centralisation are also shown by the fact that 38% of the Faeroese population now live in Tórshavn and its suburbs, against only 19% in 1950.

The settlements on the smaller islands have been worst hit by this development. Mykines, which lies furthest to the west, for example, has been reduced from 141 inhabitants in 1950 to under 20 permanent residents in the beginning of the 2000s.

The prosperity of the settlements, and the survival of the smallest villages, has been a political problem for the last 20 years, commonly referred to as *bygdamenning* or 'settlement development'. No real settlement development programmes were ever drawn up, however, but in various ways smaller and outlying settlements were accorded a kind of positive discrimination. But this settlement development policy seems to have been abandoned after the crisis years of the early 1990s.

Rolf Guttesen

Art and Culture

Far into the 19th century, the Faeroese culture was mainly kept alive through oral traditions. Following the Reformation, the spiritual culture was dominated by the Danish language: The hymns of the Church and the home had Danish lyrics but were sung to Faeroese music. This music has now been committed to paper and has inspired a number of present-day composers, singers and choirs. Secular culture has always been dominated by the Faeroese language. The oral tradition has conserved ballads, legends and fairy tales, riddles and proverbs. The best known is *Sjúrðar kvæðini*, a ballad

cycle about Sigurd Fafnersbane and his kin. This is also the title of the first book to be published in Faeroese in 1822. The ballads were recorded during the course of the 19th century and published in *Føroya kvæði, Corpus Carminum Faeroensis* (1951-1972). V.U. Hammershaimb created the first version of written Faeroese in 1846. Faeroese poetry was born in 1876 when students in Copenhagen wrote the first patriotic songs. J.H.O. Djurhuus's visionary poems in *Yrkingar* (Poems) (1914) demonstrated that Faeroese was sufficiently flexible for aesthetic use.

The first nature poets appeared in the 1920s. The most important of these were Christian Matras who wrote in Faeroese, and William Heinesen who wrote in Danish. Nature is also the main theme of the visual arts which emerged around 1900. The first significant painter was Samuel Joensen-Mikines. Of all the artists, Ingálvur av Reyni has moved the furthest away from the landscape theme; his paintings shine a lyrical light on everyday subjects. The landscape forms a background for studies in light, colour and structure by Zacharias Heinesen. Bárður Jákupsson and other painters are rediscovering the figurative. Janus Kamban and Hans Pauli Olsen are the leading figures in sculpture. Since the 1990s the heirs of the earlier women artists, the painter Ruth Smith and the lithographic artist Elinborg Lützen stand out: Sigrun Gunnarsdóttir Niclasen (painting), Astrid Andreasen (textile), Tita Vinther (weaving) and Guðrið Poulsen (ceramics). *Listasavn Føroya*, the Museum of Art in Tórshavn, opened in 1993, provides a fitting setting for the Faeroese visual arts.

The first novel in Faeroese appeared in 1909 and the genre prospered during the 1930s and 1940s with a number of works by William Heinesen, Heðin Brú and Martin Joensen. They describe the transition from the old agricultural society to the modern fishing community. Lyrical modernism reached the Faeroe Islands around 1960 with Guðrið Helmsdal Poulsen's collection of poems entitled *lýtt lot* (Warm Breeze) (1963). Modern poetry is divided into two main groups along language lines. One group is retrospect and introvert in linguistic terms. These poets seek to express themselves in a Faeroese language which is as pure and genuine as possible, they seek out old and forgotten expressions and give them new life. Some, such as Carl Jóhan Jensen, even return to Old Norse. The other group of poets uses colloquial language, loan words and borrowed phrases from both Danish and English. This group includes Rói Patursson who won the 1986 Nordic Council Literary Prize for his collection of poems entitled *Líkasum* (As if) (1986). Common to both groups is a critical attitude to contemporary life and a willingness to experiment with the language. Autobiographies, life histories and stylistic experiments characterise the modern novel, including Gunnar Hoydal's *Undir suðurstjørnum* (The Stars above Andes) (1991). The most prominent figure is Jens Pauli Heinesen, who is the first full-time author writing in Faeroese. One of his main works is an autobiographical künstlerroman in seven volumes known as *Á ferð inn í eina óendaliga søgu* (On Journeying into a Never-ending Story) (1980-1993). Faeroese prose has received a much needed renewal in a post-modern direction with the experimenting novel *Rúm* (Space) (1995) by Carl Jóhan Jensen and Tóroddur Poulsen's prose work *Reglur* (Rule) (1994).

Faeroese music, like the visual arts, is rich and varied despite its short history. Classical music was introduced during the second half of the 19th century. A school of music was set up in 1940 and the first popular songs were recorded during the 1950s.

Janus Kamban's *Bátadráttur* (Boat being dragged out of the sea) from 1968. Janus Kamban's sculptures lend an air of dignity and power to everyday subjects. We get a bird's-eye view of an everyday Faeroese tool which once held an even more important position than it does today. The perspective underlines the well-balanced harmony in the action: 'eitt áttamannafar', a boat rowed by eight men, here being dragged ashore with its thwarts, sails and oars.

Zacharias Heinesen's painting *Sól og tám* (Sun and Haze) from 1986 represents the landscape around the village of Vík.

Practising musicians within folk music, light and classical music are organised in separate associations. There is also an association of composers with over 100 members. Sunleif Rasmussen and Kristian Blak are two of the most notable Faeroese composers. There are a number of societies for traditional Faeroese chain dancing, and the Faeroese are fond of singing, so the islands have more than 600 active choristers.

Malan Marnersdóttir

History

According to written sources, the islands were settled in the early 9th century by Vikings who may have driven away an earlier colony of Irish monks. The free state is not thought to have survived past the beginning of the 11th century when the Faeroe Islands became a Norwegian fief and Christianity was introduced.

When Denmark and Norway were united in 1380, the Faeroe Islands came under Danish rule and when Denmark and Norway again parted company in 1814, the Faeroe Islands remained part of the kingdom of Denmark. Two years later, the Faeroe Islands became a Danish county, and in 1821 the first prefect was appointed to the islands. The Danish constitution of 1849 was also applied to the Faeroe Islands, which thereby became an integral part of the new democratic government with representatives in both chambers of parliament.

In 1856, free trade was introduced in the Faeroe Islands to replace the royal monopoly of 1709. This was an important step in the turbulent development which, over a remarkably short period, transformed the Faeroese agricultural society into a modern fishing nation and opened up the Faeroe Islands to the outside world. The cultural upheavals which were brought about by this development also gave birth to a nationalist movement on the islands. This was started in 1889 with the foundation of the association known as *Føringa-felag*, which was modelled on the association formed by Faeroese students in Copenhagen eight years earlier. The main objective of Føringafelag was to uphold the Faeroese language which was under threat from outside influences, and to make the Faeroese self-reliant. The leading personalities in the nationalist movement were Rasmus Effersøe (1857-1916) and Jóannes Paturson (1866-1946).

In 1906, as a member of the Folketing, Patursson gained the support of the Danish government for a higher degree of home rule in the Faeroe Islands. The offer was not well received in the Faeroe Islands, however, since it was feared that increased home rule would lead to higher taxes. This conflict led to a division over the national issue which resulted in the formation of the *Sambands* party in 1906 and the *Selvstyre* party in 1909. The first party wished to retain ties with Denmark, whilst the latter advocated increased home rule for the islands. The political spectrum only widened in 1925 when the Social Democratic Party was formed, followed in 1935 by the Commerce Party. The left/right split had thus been introduced into Faeroese politics.

The idea of home rule prospered during the Second World War, when the British occupation of the Faeroe Islands meant that all contact with Denmark was suspended, effectively making the islands autonomous. The islands' close neighbour Iceland was declared a republic during the war, and in the Faeroe Islands the time had come to change the old county status after the war. The Danish government put forward a proposal for greater independence, which was the subject of a referendum on the islands on 14 September 1946. The only alternative was secession from Denmark. The result of the vote was very close indeed: 48.7% were in favour of secession, whilst 47.2% were in favour of the government proposal. As many as 4.1% of the ballot papers turned out to be void. Only 66.4% of voters took part, leaving the destiny of the islands in the hands of just a third of the population.

The interpretation of the result of the referendum caused a hectic debate over the following days and the situation was rather chaotic until the Faeroese *Lagting* (parliament) was dissolved by the Danish king on 25 September. When a general election was held, those in favour of continued co-operation with Denmark won, and subsequent negotiations led to the current Home Rule Act of 1948. This act recognises the Faeroe Islands as a self-governing community within the kingdom of Denmark with its own flag and Faeroese as the main language. The Danish language is, however, still significant and Danish is taught to a greater extent than any other foreign language. The Home Rule is managed by the *Lagting*, a democratically elected legislative assembly, and the *Landsstyre*, which is the government of the islands. The Faeroe Islands are also represented in the Danish Folketing by two democratically elected members. Even though foreign policy is a matter of joint concern, the Faeroe Islands did not follow Denmark into the EC in 1972.

In the late 1990s a tense relationship developed between the Faeroe Islands and Denmark. Due e.g. to pronounced decline in fisheries, the Faeroeses had been going through a deep economic crisis since the mid 1980s, and this crisis had to be remedied through aid from the Danish government. The Danish government aid was e.g. intended to prevent a large bank failure, but the whole situation developed into a fraught relationship. The Faeroeses claimed that the Danish government and the bank Den Danske Bank had inflicted a loss of several million on the Faeroese society, because Den Danske Bank had left the responsibility of its subsidiary bank, Føroya Banki, to the Faeroese Landstyre. A subsequent investigation report criticised both Den Danske Bank and the Danish government.

Since then the Faeroese independence movement has gained considerable strength and in the general election to the Lagting of April 1998, the parties favouring autonomy or severance from Denmark gained the majority, mainly due to the considerable progress of the secession party *Tjódveldisflokurrin*. In the early 2000s the Faeroese and Danish governments entered into negotiations concerning a reform of the relationship between the two realms. At the crux of the negotiations are the clearing up of the financial relations and the duration of an interim arrangement in the event of increased home rule or full sovereignty. In this connection the possibilities of exploring and extracting oil in Faeroese waters play a considerable but unclarified role. The investigations of these possibilities will no doubt have great impact on the result of a referendum on full sovereignty, favoured by many Faeroeses. In the early 2002s the negotiations between the Danish government and the Faeroese Landsstyre had not been concluded.

Tom Nauerby,
Niels Finn Christiansen

Oh! to be Danish

An essay by Klaus Rifbjerg

Oh! to be Danish

It is difficult to be a Dane. Seen from the outside, most would say that the opposite was true: That being Danish is the easiest thing in the world. The country is well run, well organised, there is very little difference between high and low, rich and poor, the social safety net is securely in place, etc., etc. Even so, we still feel that something isn't quite right. We don't, for example, travel abroad with the same air of nonchalance as a German or Swede or an American. We are a little more unassuming, we don't raise our voice in restaurants or other public places. Mentally, I suppose you could say we stand there with our hat in our hand, apologetic, a little self-effacing. Except when we do find a role we're comfortable with – and there is little doubt that the football 'roligan' phenomenon could only have come from Denmark! As roligans we feel safe, and the rather dull-witted image doesn't seem to bother us. A roligan is a nice guy with a bottle of lager in one hand and a bit of a beer-belly. He might be wearing a cap, and he'll certainly be wearing a big smile (or a grin) which signals to all and sundry that here comes a guy who likes having a good time and doesn't want any trouble. No-one seems to mind that the term roligan is influenced by Swedish. When it comes down to it, however, it's the Swedes we'd really like to give a good hiding.

Some may therefore say that it is sheer nonsense to claim that it's difficult to be Danish. But if we turn once again to the world outside Denmark, we notice that many people immediately focus on the one subject we don't like to bring up: The high incidence of suicide. We shudder a little and refer to the strict accuracy employed when compiling the statistics. 'In a Catholic country, they'd never allow all suicides to be registered!'. Foreigners haven't just got eyes for the Little Mermaid; the most popular quotes when it comes to describing Denmark and the Danes come from Shakespeare, and the oldest clichés refer to Hamlet's melancholy and fickleness. And we all know, of course, that there is 'something rotten in the state of Denmark'.

If we look at the country's history and geography, then two things have been decisive in making us what we are: We are surrounded by water, and we've lost all the wars we've fought since the year dot. If we look at a map of the Great Roman Empire, there are a few white areas in the north where the Cimbrians, the Lombards and other barbarians lived and shivered with cold. There was once talk of shivering Vikings whose impatience drove them to seek other shores in search of the sun and all the wonderful things they had heard of. Rumours of these foreign shores had managed to reach even the Vikings, who spent most of the year knee-deep in water or seeking shelters from winds which tore across the country from the west.

Since the time of the Vikings, however, this deep-seated need to conquer has almost disappeared or mostly had tragic consequences as witnessed by the record books. Most Danish kings have consistently managed to support the losing side. Every time the country threw itself headlong into battle, defeat was guaranteed. It cost us our Swedish possessions, the loss of Norway and the duchies in the south, and when the

Napoleonic Wars arrived, we not only had to hand over our navy to the English, but our allies were so kind as to come to our assistance, giving the Spanish mercenaries the chance to burn Koldinghus to the ground. In 1864, the Prussians and the Austrians captured a large part of South Jutland, and if anybody thinks that the Three Years' War was a 'real' victory, they need only look at the records which tell a very different story. During the German occupation between 1940 and 1945, there were twice as many people engaged in active service on the German side than there were members of the resistance. Attempts have since been made to convince the population that the resistance movement won the war, but deep down we know that isn't true. The thing that brought us almost unscathed through the Second World War was a policy based on compromise and compliance, common sense and a well-developed ability to recoup outward losses by inward gains.

This is one area where our unease becomes a little more bearable, even though many would deny it. We have learned by our defeats, and the lesson has not been 100% negative, quite the contrary in fact. One of the best traits in our national character is our unsentimental conviction that it is unnecessary to take recourse to violence in order to stake your claim in the world. Instead of resorting to greed, we have learned to use our expertise to get ahead. It might sound a little dull, but it's highly recommendable and our special ability to use our head instead of our fists did not simply fall down from the sky (as the Dannebrog flag is said to have done), but has been mastered over the centuries. It has been a long, hard struggle, and it has hurt, and it hurts so much even today that some

people are actually ashamed of being Danish – which is not very constructive in the long run when trying to build up a national spirit. Many would rightly say that Denmark is a consensus society. But is that really true? A country or a nation or a people are not always the same in all contexts. If that was the case, then any attempt to create a definition would always have to resort to clichés. The Danes were not the same people in the 13th century or in the 19th century, just as the Danes who live on the west coast of Jutland are not like the ones who live on Stevns, and we can safely say that the people living in Copenhagen are quite unlike any others. Seen from the outside, however, there is still a common feature which many people in history have tried to identify without any real success. Well, almost without any success.

In a letter to a friend, the English author George Orwell described his complete lack of interest in ever visiting Denmark. His reluctance was based on a feeling that Denmark is a boring place. In an article on the yearly Nobel prize, The New Yorker wondered who the unknown (Danish) nominees Johannes Vilhelm Jensen and Henrik Pontoppidan might possibly be. A French diplomat described the Danish climate as 'eight months of winter and four months of bad weather'. A German newspaper described the country as a place where every town has a Co-op, two restaurants with the same (expensive and very bad) menu and a Social Security office where everyone can go to get money. It is hardly a cheerful picture, but there is a grain of truth in it. Denmark and the Danes are not 'exciting'. The question is, what are we? If we are unequivocally boring, we might as well get out a rope or a bottle of sleeping tablets now.

But the truth is, of course, somewhat less cut-and-dried. If we examine the way we 'see' ourselves and the country in which we live, 'as we see it', we might just come up with something.

During the Romantic period last century, the certainty that our grand and noble past had come to an end finally began to sink in. This realisation saw the birth of our national spirit, and the Danish landscape was suddenly brought to our notice as never before. Poets and artists were suddenly busy depicting the scenery in various parts of the country. Hans Christian Andersen is a good example: He travelled all the way to the very top of the country, describing all the wonders of nature which are perhaps only visible to those who love them. For the past 200 years we have, in other words, been told to view our native country as something valuable and beautiful and deserving of our care. Although the no-

tion has admittedly been drummed into our heads, it must be true in many ways for us to have heeded it. Denmark is a beautiful country, but you have to look at the details to find the beauty. There are not many natural phenomena here which inspire breathtaking awe, since almost all the available land has been cultivated. But that may just make it seem even more of a miracle: Nature is still here, and it may even be more beautiful because of the way it interacts with the cultural landscape which we are part of and, of course, responsible for.

It may be worth considering this for a moment: In countries which are much larger, the common culture is a far more fleeting notion than it is in Denmark. Our closeness has enabled us to nurture a real sense of community and, when push comes to shove, genuine solidarity. As has been said before, history was a hard but helpful master. We know

we have no call to join in when the loud and boastful nations start gloating. We have no atomic bombs to drop on anyone, no dream of conquest or imperialism. The problems we have with the 'colonies' we still 'possess' (Greenland and the Faeroe Islands) are so great that we would gladly leave them to their own devices were it not for the obligations that 'ownership' brings.

'Too much pomp and striving will bring us no rest / keeping our feet firmly on the ground is the best', wrote one of our great bards, N.F.S. Grundtvig, some time during the last century – no doubt to the annoyance of many an ambitious soul. Even though he was a romantic, he was very down-to-earth in his view of Denmark and the Danes. He was in no way against spiritual advancement. In time, Grundtvig became one of the pioneers of the spiritual movement which created the Denmark of today and shaped the spirit of the Danes. Another figure who was instrumental in shaping the soul of the nation was the Jewish literary historian Georg Brandes, who was the exact opposite of Grundtvig in terms of temperament.

Two important paths merge at this point: The first concerns popular education and national revival, the other deals with internationalism and a new, more open approach. They both lead to a more radical way of thinking, which opens the door to a wide spectrum of new ideas: The co-operative movement, the liberation of women, social equality, sexual emancipation. In other words, the creation of a democratic society 'where few have too much and even fewer too little'.

Getting a radical experiment to succeed in a modern welfare state such as Denmark requires a great deal of talent. There is every chance that you will end up in a grey area between general boredom and stark depression. But perhaps the price we pay for success is that 'normality' spreads, and that the unusual and the extraordinary must take a back seat. Or we could turn the whole thing on its head and say that it is in this normality that genius lies buried, inasmuch as the majority of us would prefer to wake up every morning to a normal life rather than to bombs and grenades and bellowing dictators, or to repeated performances of Wagner's operas or tales of great destinies that ended in flames.

One thing is certain: We haven't produced any of the great dramatists. On the other hand, Denmark has fostered excellent prose writers and poets, philosophers and scientists and a handful of composers who, on closer inspection, also turn out to be poets. Which is also true of our painters.

So what kind of national self-image does all this produce? Is it even possible to delimit and define a national self-image? The answer is a cautious *yes*, and the image must be a little blurred round the edges. All the same, we can discern a faint outline: A Dane is a creature with a big heart and an equally big inferiority complex. The latter is for external use only and shows, paradoxically, that we are finally becoming more successful outside Denmark and have made it to the front pages of the international press. To the amazement of absolutely everyone. To think that it was possible! To think that we little insignificant Danes, with our successful well-organised social structure, our sound economy, our high level of education, our women's lib and our sexual tolerance have come all that way!

There is an inherent contradiction here which borders on the comical, or is at least mildly amusing: A Dane, confronted by a satirical view of himself, will laugh even if it hurts. It is a disarming trait which often turns out to be a good weapon in a tricky situation. Humour always wins in the face of conceit and arrogance, and those who push Denmark and

the Danes too far, or have the audacity to actually invade us, will find that humour is just as harmful a weapon as sugar in a petrol tank. It creates a sense of unease because of its very complexity. It is particularly useful when you want to say a lot or to get a particularly important point across without having to resort to big words or raised voices.

If it is possible to talk about such a thing as national intelligence, then the Danish national intelligence is remarkable because of its willingness to doubt itself. When others become cocksure, the Danes tend to allow themselves a moment of doubt. This doubt is often highly productive, inasmuch as the definition of intelligence is the ability to solve problems and act effectively in unfamiliar and difficult situations – there have, as we have seen, been quite a few of those in Denmark's history and if we look closely, the problems have almost always been solved in a sensible way. If that brings us admiration from the outside world, then we should accept the compliment without further ado. Let us not worry when some silly American journalist mocks Johannes Vilhelm Jensen and his Nobel Prize, or when a foolish German who has spent a week here declares that all Danes are a bunch of boring peasants. Because we know better – even when it comes to the weather!

Sure, it can be grim, and now and then we might want to turn our collar up and jump in the river. But then the light suddenly changes and there's a melody in the air, a whiff of spring to come, the smell of the sea and a blackbird singing on a rooftop. And then you walk on holding your head up, feeling just a little proud.

Even of being a Dane.

Klaus Rifbjerg

Index

Authors

Sources of illustrations

Index

Authors

Hanne Abildgaard, Senior Lecturer, mag.art.

Peder Agger, Professor, cand.scient.

Karin Albrechtsen, Specialist Editor, cand.polit.

Hans Thor Andersen, Senior Lecturer

Jens Sejer Andersen, General Editor

Lars Andersen, cand.mag.

Aage Søgaard Andersen, Senior Lecturer, PhD

Ole E. Andersen, Vice-Chancellor,
    cand.scient.soc.

Otto Andersen, Head of Department

Erik Aschengreen, Reader, dr.phil.

Nils G. Bartholdy, Senior Researcher

John Bergsagel, Professor, dr.phil.

Jens Bernsen, Managing Director, civ.ing.

Carsten Berthelsen, Publisher, mag.art.

Anders Beyer, General Editor, cand.phil.

Peter Bistrup, Librarian

Hans Christian Bjerg, Head Archivist

Claus Bjørn, Senior Lecturer

Peter Bogason, Professor, PhD

Niels Bonde, Senior Lecturer

Ib Bondebjerg, Research Professor, PhD

Else-Marie Boyhus, mag.art.

Ulrik Brandt, Specialist Editor, cand.mag.

Johannes Brix, Medical Specialist, dr.med.

Torben Brostrøm, Professor, Specialist Editor

Erik Buch, Service Chief

Elisabeth Buchwald, mag.art.

Inge Bundsgaard, Provincial Archivist

Niels Jørgen Cappelørn, Director, cand.theol.

Bent Christensen (now departed), Professor,
    dr.jur.

Charlotte Christensen, mag.art.

Me Christensen, Specialist Editor, cand.mag.

Nina Christensen, cand.mag., Assistant Lec-
    turer

Niels Finn Christiansen, Senior Lecturer,
    dr.phil.

Michael H. Clemmesen, Brigadier General

Nina Damsgaard, Museum Manager, mag.art.

Thomas Danielsen, stud.mag.

Henning Dehn-Nielsen, General Editor

Ove W. Dietrich, Specialist Editor

Martin Drouzy (now departed), lic.theol.

Lotte Endsleff, Specialist Editor, cand.scient.

Marguerite Engberg, fil.dr.

Nils Engelbrecht, Specialist Editor, Medical
    Specialist

Preben Etwil, Head of Department, cand.polit.

Ole Feldbæk, Professor, dr.phil.

Finn Terman Frederiksen, Museum Director,
    mag.art.

Hans Jørgen Frederiksen, Senior Lecturer,
    mag.art.

Jørgen Fakstorp, civ.ing.

Hans Folke, Specialist Editor, cand.scient.

Karl-Erik Frandsen, Reader, dr.phil.

Peter A. Friis (now departed), Senior Lecturer

Mirjam Gelfer-Jørgensen, Chief Librarian,
    dr.phil.

Niels Jørgen Gimsing, Professor, civ.ing.

Søren Grauslund, Specialist Editor, cand.polyt.

H.C. Gulløv, Research Professor, dr.phil.

Rolf Guttesen, Senior Lecturer

Niels Hald, Senior Lecturer

Cliff Thaudal Hansen, Picture Editor,
    cand.mag.

Jens Morten Hansen, Director, lic.scient.

Merete Harding, Specialist Editor, Sub-editor,
    PhD

Carsten E. Hatting, Senior Lecturer, mag.art.

Jørgen Hein, Museum Curator, cand.mag.

Mogens Henze, Professor, civ.ing.

Kristian Hjulsager, Head of Department,
    cand.polit.

Erik Hoffmann, Biologist

Bent Holm, Senior Lecturer, dr.phil.

Hans-Henrik Holm, Jean Monnet Professor

Niels Holmquist, Senior Lecturer, cand.scient.

Kristian Hvidt, Editor of the records of parlia-
    mentary debates, dr.phil.

Peter Michael Hornung, mag.art.

Ole Humlum, Senior Lecturer

Carsten Hunding, cand.scient.

Erik Hvidt, mag.art.

Lotte Jacobsen, Specialist Editor, cand.jur.

Per Jacobsen, former Senior Lecturer

Anne Ørbæk Jensen, Research Librarian,
    cand.mag.

Inge Mørch Jensen, cand.mag.

Jørgen Steen Jensen, Chief Curator, cand.art.

Torben Jensen, former Judge of the Supreme
    Court

Kristen Marius Jensen, Senior Lecturer

Mogens Lerbech Jensen, cand.pæd.

Anne Jerslev, Senior Lecturer, PhD

Knud J.V. Jespersen, Professor, dr.phil.

Birgitte Bøggild Johannsen, General Editor,
    mag.art.

Hugo Johannsen, General Editor, mag.art.

Hans Chr. Johansen, Professor, dr.oecon.

Flemming Just, Senior Lecturer, dr.phil.

Eva Jørholt, cand.mag.

Kaj Kampp, Senior Lecturer, cand.scient.

Allan Karker, Senior Lecturer

Flemming Kaul, Museum Curator, mag.art.

Steffen Kjeldgaard-Pedersen, Professor, dr.the-
    ol.

Birgitte Kjær, Museum Curator
Niels Elers Koch, Director, Professor, dr.agro.
Jens Henrik Koudal, Archivist
Niels Krabbe, Senior Lecturer, cand.mag.
Hans Kuhlman, Senior Lecturer
Peter Kühn-Nielsen, Specialist Editor, Art Historian
Charlotte Rørdam Larsen, Senior Lecturer, cand.phil.
Gunnar Larsen, Professor, dr.phil.
Knud Larsen, Permanent Secretary, dr.phil.
Tom Latrup-Pedersen, Senior Lecturer
Eva Lous, Research Librarian, cand.mag.
Jørn Lund, Professor
Niels Lund, Professor, dr.phil.
Flemming Lundgreen-Nielsen, Reader, dr.phil.
John Lundum, High Court Judge
Henrik Breuning Madsen, Professor, dr.scient.
Jørn Madsen, Specialist Editor, cand.scient.
Malan Marnersdóttir, Senior Lecturer, PhD
Peter Maskell, Professor, dr.merc.
Horst Meesenburg, cand.mag.
Olaf Michelsen, Professor, dr.phil.
Jens Peter Munk, Museum Curator, mag.art.
Johan de Mylius, Reader, dr.phil.
John Møller, Director
Vibeke Andersson Møller, Museum Curator, mag.art.
Tom Nauerby, PhD
Bendt Viinholt Nielsen, Librarian
Bue Nielsen, cand.scient.
Poul Otto Nielsen, Museum Chief Curator, mag.art.
Rolf Nielsen, Head of Department
Torben Nielsen, fhv. Chief Librarian, cand.mag.
Vøgg Løwe Nielsen, Head of Division, cand.polit.
Jørn Busch Olsen, Specialist Editor, cand.mag.
Abraham Pais, Professor
Helge Pedersen, Vice-Chancellor
Kim Blanksø Pedersen, cand.scient.
Kjeld Møller Pedersen, Research Professor, cand.oecon.
Olaf Pedersen (now departed), Professor
Kay W. Petersen, Senior Lecturer , dr.scient.
Niels Ploug, Research Director, cand.polit.
Gert Posselt, Specialist Editor, cand.mag.
Bjørn Poulsen, Senior Lecturer, dr.phil.
Anders Holm Rasmussen, Postdoctoral Research Fellow, PhD
Rasmus Ole Rasmussen, Senior Lecturer
Lorenz Rerup (now departed), Consul General, Professor
Klaus Rifbjerg, Author
Mogens Ritsholm, Civ.ing.

Nils Rosdahl, Medical Officer of Health
Mogens Rüdiger, Senior Lecturer, lic.phil.
Jørgen Rygaard, Professor, dr.med.
Peter Ryom, Specialist Editor, dr.phil.
Lulu Salto Stephensen, fil.dr.
May Schack, Specialist Editor, cand.mag.
Kaare Schmidt, Programme Editor
Søren Schou, Senior Lecturer, mag.art.
Thomas Sehested, Specialist Editor, cand.mag.
Vibeke Skov, cand.mag.
Vagn Skovgaard-Petersen, Professor, dr.pæd.
Kai Skriver, Chief Consultant
Jørgen Stenbæk, Senior Lecturer
Karsten Stetkær, Head of Department, cand.oecon.
Ditlev Tamm, Professor, dr.jur. et phil.
Erik Thomsen, Senior Lecturer, cand.scient.
Niels Thomsen, Professor, dr.phil.
Finn Thrane, Museum Director, cand.mag.
Elisabeth Thuesen, Reader, cand.jur., docteur en droit
Jens Tolstrup, Prison Governor, cand.scient.pol.
Carsten Torpe, Head of Department, cand.polit.
Aage Trommer, Senior Lecturer, dr.phil.
Signild Vallgårda, Senior Lecturer, dr.med.
Ole Ventegodt, Specialist Editor, cand.phil.
Åge Myrhøj Vestergård, Specialist Editor, cand.scient.
Poul Villaume, Senior Lecturer, dr.phil.
Suzanne Wang, Course Secretary
Erik Wiedemann, Senior Lecturer, dr.phil.
Torben Wolff, Reader, dr.phil.
Eiler Worsøe, Nature Guide
Hans H. Worsøe, former Provincial Archivist, cand.mag.
Carsten Wulff, Specialist Editor, cand.scient.
Henrik Zahle, Judge of the Supreme Court, dr.jur.
Anders Østergaard, Senior Lecturer
Bent Aaby, Professor

Sources of illustrations

DENMARK